Politics
in Transitional Societies

The Challenge of Change
in Asia, Africa, and Latin America

second edition

Politics
in Transitional Societies

The Challenge of Change
in Asia, Africa, and Latin America

second edition

edited by

harvey g. kebschull

North Carolina State University at Raleigh

NEW YORK
Appleton-Century-Crofts
EDUCATIONAL DIVISION/MEREDITH CORPORATION

To
SUSAN KIM and SHARON LYNN

Copyright © 1973 by
MEREDITH CORPORATION

Copyright © 1968 by Meredith Corporation

73 74 75 76 77 / 10 9 8 7 6 5 4 3 2 1

Library of Congress Card Number: 72-92753

PRINTED IN THE UNITED STATES OF AMERICA

390-49759-2

Maps on pp. xi–xiii: From *World Tensions: Conflict and Accommodation,* 2nd ed.,
Elton Atwater, Kent Forster, and Jan S. Prybyla. Copyright © 1972 by Meredith
Corporation. Reprinted by permission of Appleton-Century-Crofts, Educational
Division, Meredith Corporation.

contents

preface

Since 1968, when the first edition of this book appeared, many events in Asia, Africa, and Latin America claimed for a day or two the big headlines of the world's newspapers. A few more states, such as Fiji, Mauritius, and Nauru, were added to the international community, while some others, such as Nigeria and Pakistan, struggled to prevent the centrifugal forces of secessionist movements from pushing them as presently constituted states into political oblivion. More military coups occurred, as in Uganda and Argentina, while death toppled more leaders from power, most notably Presidents Nasser and Ho Chi Minh. An avowed communist, Salvador Allende, was elected president of Chile, while the Congress Party in India scored another of its major victories in free elections. Fidel Castro continued to have troubles making his socialist economy flourish, while the Middle Eastern states enjoyed greater successes in exacting higher returns from the Western companies pumping oil from their soil. The long and dreary war in Vietnam formally ended in an uncertain peace, but fighting continued there and in Laos and Cambodia.

But behind the headlines, much of life and many of the problems changed little if at all. Millions of persons were still looking for an adequate meal or a job, more millions were added to the world's population with little indication of major successes in reversing the trend, and developmental plans continued to flounder in the face of multiple pressures. On the other hand, bits and pieces of progress were recorded: the Aswan Dam was completed, production of natural rubber increased in Malaysia, and here and there children attended school for the first time, to explore through books and laboratories the exotic world around them.

It is this complex kaleidoscope of change and stagnation, progress and retrogression, success and failure that simultaneously excites attention but also makes analysis so difficult. The vast regions of Asia, Africa, and Latin America cannot be ignored by students of politics, who need to examine a diversity of political systems for a better understanding of political fundamentals for the development of political theories; however, the diversity exacts a high price in time and effort. The audacity of including in one study nations as disparate as those in these three large areas is only partially countered by the recognition that if the dangers of overgeneralization are obvious, the dangers of regarding each nation as essentially unique, with little or nothing in common with others, must also be avoided if progress in understanding and theory-building is to take place.

The problem, consequently, is to identify the similarities and differences and the rates and types of change in institutions, roles, processes, and the like, in what are still, for most Westerners, the dimly perceived areas of the world. Fortunately there is an increasing wealth of information on the characteristics and problems of the transitional states and their societies. Observers and scholars from many countries and disciplines have been busy studying and writing, and they have produced if not a mountain, at least a good-sized anthill of case studies, monographs, and full-length volumes. Since the first edition of this book was published, several new journals have appeared, such as *Comparative Politics* and *Comparative Political Studies,* to provide additional outlets for investigations of continuity and change, and new books regularly appear to chronicle and analyze the trends and problems of development.

The purpose of this edition remains the same as that of its predecessor, namely, to make available in convenient and systematic form some useful information on the nature of transitional societies and their problems as a foundation for more advanced study, and to encourage the development of skills necessary for sophisticated comparative studies that encompass the whole universe of contemporary political systems. For this edition I have sought to record some of the recent events and changes in the mosaic of life in the transitional societies, and to select from the proliferating studies a few that would stimulate an understanding of the problems confronting these societies. For this task I have benefited from a number of suggestions from students and teachers on useful changes and additional sources to consider. I am, of course, most appreciative to the authors and publishers who have consented to have their works included. Less obvious is my debt to scholars whose studies had to be excluded, but from whom I have learned much. As always, I am grateful to my wife, Georgia, for her extensive assistance, but she, like all others, must be held blameless for the errors that remain.

H. G. K.

EUROPE

S O V I E T U N I O N

U. S. S. R.

TURKEY

LEBANON
ISRAEL   SYRIA
JORDAN   IRAQ

IRAN

KUWAIT

BAHRAIN
QATAR
SAUDI ARABIA   UNITED ARAB
EMIRATES

OMAN

YEMEN

PEOPLE'S
DEMOCRATIC REPUBLIC
OF YEMEN

AFGHANISTAN

JAMMU &
KASHMIR

PAKISTAN

NEPAL   SIKKIM
BHUTAN

BANGLADESH

I N D I A

BURMA

MONGOLIA

PEOPLE'S REPUBLIC OF CHINA

NORTH KOREA

SOUTH KOREA

JAPAN

TAIWAN

PHILIPPINES

NORTH
VIETNAM
LAOS
THAILAND
SOUTH
VIETNAM
CAMBODIA

CEYLON

MALDIVE ISLANDS

MALAYSIA   BRUNEI (Br.)

SINGAPORE

I N D O N E S I A

TIMOR
(Port.)

Independent in 1935

Independent since 1945

Protected States

ASIA

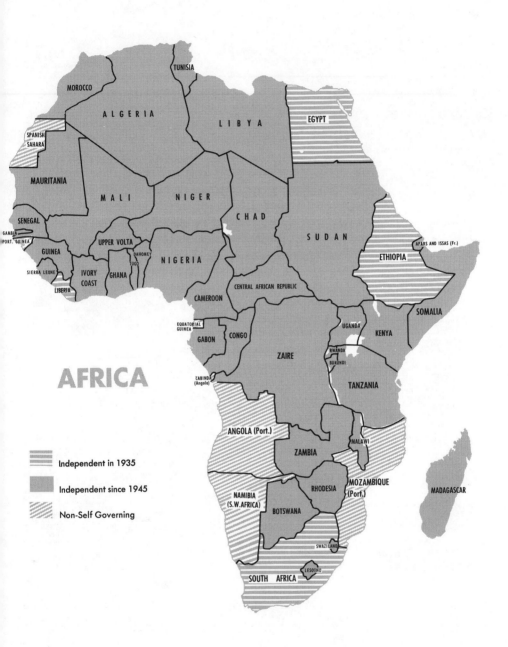

AFRICA

- Independent in 1935
- Independent since 1945
- Non-Self Governing

UNITED STATES

MEXICO

Mexico

BAHAMAS IS. (Br.)

Havana

CUBA

JAMAICA

HAITI

DOMINICAN
REP.

PUERTO RICO
(U.S.A.)

BR.
HONDURAS

GUATEMALA   HONDURAS

EL SALVADOR

NICARAGUA

BARBADOS

TRINIDAD & TOBAGO

COSTA RICA   CANAL ZONE (U.S.A.)

Panamá

PANAMA

Caracas

VENEZUELA

Georgetown

GUYANA

SURINAM
(Hol.)

FR.
GUIANA

Bogota

COLOMBIA

Quito

ECUADOR

GALAPAGOS IS. (Ecuador)

Belém

PERU

B R A Z I L

Lima

Salvador

La Paz

BOLIVIA

Brasilia

Sucre

PARAGUAY

Rio de Janeiro

São Paulo

LATIN AMERICA

C
H
I
L
E

A
R
G
E
N
T
I
N
A

Santiago

Asunción

URUGUAY

Buenos Aires   Montevideo

FALKLAND IS. (Br.)

i. introduction

During the past quarter century, one of the most complex and profound revolutions of modern history has been underway. This revolution, sometimes referred to as the "revolution of rising expectations" or the "revolution of rising resentments," has already drastically altered the structures and dynamics of individual societies and the world community. New states have come into existence throughout most of Asia and Africa as the colonial empires of the European powers have collapsed in the face of the revolutionary demands for independence. In these vast areas, as well as in Latin America, demands for change and progress now vigorously challenge traditional values, institutions, and conditions.

With the struggle for political independence now substantially over, the attention of leaders and scholars has turned to the difficult problems of building strong, prosperous nations and states. At present, the picture presented by the diverse areas of Asia, Africa, and Latin America is mixed and often confusing as few completely adequate answers to these problems have been found. Many hopes and expectations of rapid change have already been frustrated and abandoned in the face of overwhelming difficulties. Deep divisions within the social fabric of society, shortages of critical skills and materials, and the presence of apathy and violence are but a few of the barriers to progress. Nevertheless, dreams persist and plans are formulated, and few of the societies in these areas have remained immune from important changes. It is not an easy task to measure and understand the scope and direction of this revolution; yet, if it is difficult it is also vital, since the peace and prosperity of the world are at stake.

Until the outbreak of World War II, the dominant position of the European colonial powers in Asia and Africa seemed secure. Even then, however, the long-term effects of colonial policy were creating aspira-

1

tions for independence, self-determination, and economic development. The education of a small number of natives, the injection of Western values and beliefs, the construction of transportation and communication systems, and the development of bureaucracies and armed forces all helped to fuel the demands for fundamental political and economic changes. After the war, when their power was shattered and they were under intense pressure from the new world powers—the Soviet Union and the United States—to grant independence to their colonies, the European powers began to yield to the demands of leaders of the independence movements. The United States itself set the example when, in 1946, it granted full independence to the Philippines in fulfillment of its promise made before the war. The following year, India and Pakistan achieved their independence from the British, establishing a trend that could not be reversed. At an unprecedented rate in world history, colonies attained their political independence, only to confront the problems of survival and growth largely through their own initiatives and resources. In Latin America as well, demands for change began to be expressed more persistently and vigorously. Though long independent, many of the Latin American societies, despite their European orientation, had not participated extensively in the social and economic movements that transformed the societies in the northern hemisphere during the nineteenth and twentieth centuries. Thus, while the Latin American states confront particular obstacles to development that are often quite different from those in Asia and Africa, they share the restlessness of a revolutionary age.

Since attaining independence and undertaking to modernize their social, economic, and political systems, the transitional societies in Asia and Africa have attracted considerable scholarly interest from political scientists, economists, sociologists, and others. Similar interest in Latin American societies—long in the hinterland of social science studies—has been stimulated by the concern to understand development on a universal basis. Attention has been focused on the complex processes of social change, economic growth, and political development in an effort to identify and describe the patterns of change now occurring in these societies, and to compare them with those that have taken place in "modern" societies. Are the processes of development similar among the presently developing states? Must they pursue the same courses of change as have taken place in Western states? What, indeed, constitutes development and modernization? What are the relationships between different types of development? To questions such as these, few definitive answers are as yet available, but careful analysis of the changes now occurring in transitional societies will aid in the search for more adequate answers.

The first problem, of course, is to define and describe "transitional societies." Unfortunately, this is not easy to do and no single list can be compiled which commands complete agreement on the part of scholars and political leaders. The difficulty stems from the fact that a multiplicity of important characteristics of a state and its society must be taken into account, and no single summary index is available to determine how states are to be categorized or the relative ranking of the various states in the world with respect to development and modernization. Consequently, it is impossible to establish clearly defined and distinct categories into which the various states of the world can be placed. However, for our purposes, the category "transitional states" will include all the states in Asia, the Middle East, Africa, and Latin America except those few that have already achieved most of the characteristics of contemporary "modern" states: complex, specialized institutions, a highly productive economic system, modern transportation and communication systems, widespread educational opportunities and a high level of literacy, social integration, and political institutions and processes that are capable of making and enforcing public policies.[1]

Since the scope of our study encompasses such a large number of states, it may be useful to survey briefly some of the important differences that exist among them as well as some general characteristics and problems that set them apart, as a group, from the more "modern" states of the present era. It must be emphasized, however, that great diversity exists among the transitional states in their cultures, religions, languages, colonial experiences, economic conditions, and political systems, and that assumptions about a unity of purpose or approaches to their many problems are usually unwarranted. In particular, distinctions need to be drawn between the Latin American and the Afro-Asian states; in many ways, Latin America constitutes the "Fourth World," being more developed (or less underdeveloped) than the other regions with respect to economic indices such as income and production, and to political and social indices such as the number of political parties, interest groups, literacy rates, and regional integration.[2]

---

[1] Many terms have been used to describe the "underdeveloped" states in Asia, Africa, and Latin America, but none of them are fully appropriate or adequate. While the term "backward" has fallen into disfavor, those of "emerging," "the Third World," "transitional," and "developing" are all in common usage. To restrict the term "transitional" only to the states in Asia, the Middle East, Africa, and Latin America is unrealistic, of course, since all states are undergoing some type of transition and change. Nevertheless, in discussing the states in these four areas, the term "transitional" seems preferable to the others in most cases. It indicates a group of states that are less highly developed than some others, it is less value laden, and it implies the possibility of both regression and development occurring with respect to different aspects of a society or to one variable over time within a society.

[2] Edward J. Williams, "Comparative Political Development: Latin America and Afro-Asia," *Comparative Studies in Society and History*, Vol. XI, No. 3 (April, 1969), pp. 342–354.

First we may note some of the striking differences among these states. These variations partially account for the different specific problems confronting the individual developing states, the range of alternative courses of action that can be pursued in attempting to resolve them, and the political institutions and processes that have been established. Some of the developing states are, of course, very large; indeed, several of them are among the largest in the world.[3] Others, however, are among the smallest. In contrast to such giants as mainland China and Brazil—both of which are larger than continental United States—are such diminutive states as Malta and Singapore, each of which is less than 250 square miles. In between these extremes, sizes range widely. Several states—India, Argentina, Saudi Arabia, Zaïre, Algeria, and the Sudan—are approximately one third the size of the continental United States. Many others are considerably smaller: Laos, Ghana, and Ecuador, for example, are about the size of Arizona or Western Germany, while Guatemala, Honduras, Jordan, and Mali are approximately the size of Ohio or New York.

Similar variations are found in the size of the populations of these states. China's estimated 750 million or India's 537 million contrast sharply with the 110,000 in the Maldive Islands. A few states, such as Brazil, Nigeria, Pakistan, and Indonesia, have populations in the 50 to 125 million range, but most states have considerably smaller populations, a number of which are under 5 million, e.g., Burundi, Costa Rica, Paraguay, Jordan, and Singapore.

Although a few states—Bolivia and Laos, for example—are landlocked, and a few others such as Cuba and the Philippines are composed wholly of islands, most states have both land and sea boundaries. Many of them are reasonably compact, but others are confronted with the many social, economic, and political problems that arise from their peculiar shapes. Indonesia, for example, is faced with difficult problems of communication and transportation, since its 3,000 islands extend over 3,000 miles. In Latin America, Chile stretches like a narrow ribbon for over 2,600 miles along the western coast of the continent, averaging only 110 miles in width. The original state of Pakistan was divided into two parts almost 1,000 miles apart; in 1971, East Pakistan broke away to form the independent state of Bangladesh.

The topography of these states is similarly diverse, ranging from the generally level terrain in a few states such as Uruguay to the largely mountainous states like Peru. Within many of these states, the terrain varies considerably, from broad coastal areas to high, rugged mountains. Deserts, swamps, rich valleys, and barren plateaus are features sometimes found within a single state. In Chile, for example, from the long

---

[3] See Appendix for selected data on the transitional states.

seacoast the land rises rapidly to the mountains towering over 19,000 feet in the east. A harsh desert region in the north, in parts of which rain almost never falls, is juxtaposed with a fertile valley in the central part of the state. Similarly in Algeria, a fertile coastal region gives way to a high plateau and mountainous area beyond which the Sahara imposes its barriers to commerce, communications, and transportation. Most developing states lie in the tropics, but temperatures and rainfall vary greatly, depending upon the prevailing winds, mountain ranges, and other topographical features. In some areas, as in northern Brazil, the temperatures and rainfall combine to create an environment basically inhospitable to man, while in other areas in similar latitudes, such as the highlands of Kenya, they create an environment conducive to settlement and the exploitation of natural resources.

These natural resources, in turn, differ markedly among the states. In some the land is rich and fertile, as in much of Indonesia, while in others it is poor and unproductive, either because of natural conditions as in desert regions or because of the poor farming methods employed in so many areas. Mineral resources are similarly variable. Some states, such as Nigeria and Brazil, are known to possess large mineral deposits, while others, such as the Chad, have few apparent resources to exploit. While few states have, as yet, completed surveys of their mineral and other resources, it appears that many of them have some valuable resources that are not currently being exploited.

The diversity in size, topography, and resources among these states is matched by that of their peoples and cultures. There are, of course, many different "kinds" of Asians, Africans, and Latin Americans; they differ in such obvious ways as race, color, language, and culture. Included among the Asians are Chinese, Indians, Indonesians, Burmese, and other groups. In the Middle East reside Turks, Arabs, Jews, and some Negroes. The population of sub-Saharan Africa is composed of several indigenous African races, e.g., the Bushmen, Bantu, and Hottentots, along with nonnative groups including Asians, Arabs, and Europeans. In Latin America Indians, Negroes, *mestizos*, and "whites" constitute the principal groups. Within each of the major racial and ethnic groups there are, in addition, numerous divisions along cultural, linguistic, and tribal lines. Few states are racially or ethnically homogeneous; in most of them are found several major groups and a number of linguistic and cultural minorities.

Politically, these states also differ widely in their formal institutions and processes. A very few, such as Saudi Arabia and Yemen, are still traditional oligarchies in which the hereditary ruler and a small group of princes govern with few restraints. In some others, e.g., Thailand, the powers of the traditional national elite have been circumscribed either by constitutional provisions that provide for popularly elected leaders, or by the emergence of strong modernizing groups such as the armed forces that can effectively restrain the traditional leadership group. Modern political institutions take several forms. States such as India have adopted a modified form of the British parliamentary system, replacing the hereditary monarchy with an elected president. Other states, particularly those in Latin America, have established a presidential form of government, more or less on the American model. Communist China's "parliamentary" form is an important innovation that follows the Soviet Union's format only in the most general terms. Government by the armed forces is found in many states. In some instances, constitutions have been formally suspended while the military leaders hold power "temporarily"; in others, the constitutions have been abrogated and plans are nominally being made for the writing of new ones.

Wide variations are also found in the duration of political independence enjoyed by these states. A few, like Thailand and Afghanistan, have never been completely dominated politically by Western states; though, in most cases, their full independence has been circumscribed from time to time by agreements into which they were coerced. Other states, however, have just recently achieved independence. Some of the most recent additions to the list of independent states include Guyana, Botswana, Lesotho, and Barbados, all former British colonies which attained their independence during 1966. Prior to independence, the new states were subjected to Western control as colonies, mandates, or protectorates, or through other formal arrangements. The early 1960's were particularly vibrant times for achieving independence in sub-Saharan Africa; rapidly—and sometimes without much preparation—the former colonies of France, Britain, and Belgium were released. This subcontinent that a decade ago was almost completely controlled by a few European states is now, with the principal exception of the Portuguese possessions of Angola and Mozambique, divided into over twenty-five independent states. Similarly, all major former colonies in Asia have achieved political independence since the end of World War II. In contrast, most states in Latin America attained their independence during the early decades of the nineteenth century.

Despite the many diverse elements, the developing states nevertheless possess some common characteristics and are confronted by some similar social, economic, and political problems. Compared with those in Western Europe and North America, these nations as a group are economically underdeveloped, far less literate, less socially integrated, and less politically stable. Nevertheless, wide variations exist among the developing states with respect to these characteristics.

Undoubtedly the best known characteristic of the developing states is their low level of economic development. Rarely does the gross national product provide an average per capita income (at market prices) in Asian or African societies exceeding $200 a year; frequently it is less than half that amount.[4] In India, the figure is $88; in Afghanistan, $60; in Kenya, $117; and in Nigeria, $102. Although this figure tends to be significantly higher in most Middle Eastern and Latin American states, it seldom exceeds $500. These low figures reflect the fact that neither agricultural nor industrial production is high on a per capita basis. The large majority of persons in most developing states are engaged in agriculture, fishing, or animal husbandry. The traditional methods employed in these occupations produce few surpluses; in some cases, production does not even provide subsistence for the population. Irrigation projects are primitive and wasteful, and the poor quality and inadequate use of fertilizers fail to replenish the depleted fertility of the soil. Few insecticides are used, and crop destruction by insect invasions or floods and droughts frequently makes the position of the peasant precarious. Herds are of poor quality, and grazing lands are often unable to sustain the animals in a satisfactory condition. Fishing equipment and techniques are primitive and are incapable of supporting large-scale commercial operations.

Dissatisfaction with current methods and levels of production and the resulting low standard of living is one of the principal characteristics of the "revolution of rising expectations."[5] A widespread desire for economic development is evident throughout the underdeveloped world, and progress through industrialization and diversification has become virtually an article of faith. But although many states have devised plans that call for the development of heavy and medium industries, in only a few is there a significant industrial capacity as yet. Several large steel mills, cement plants, and textile mills have been constructed in a few states such as China and India, but in most Asian and African states the largest plants are usually those for the processing of raw materials in preparation for their export. Latin American states have, in general, achieved a higher level of industrialization. In Brazil, for example, automobile assembly and shipbuilding are undertaken, and in Mexico and Chile, among others, a number of medium-size industries have been established. Light

[4] Per capita income figures are, of course, of limited utility since they do not take into account the relative purchasing power of the monetary unit, nor do they indicates the range and distribution of incomes within a state.

[5] The extent and importance of "expectations" is controversial, but as Anthony R. Oberschall notes, "the social scientist should not assume that exposure to modern consumer goods or even politicians' promises automatically generate expectations, as opposed to hopes and aspirations. To what extent hopes and desires, or even aspirations, represent an effective, short term, demand upon the economy and the government in underdeveloped countries is again something about which very little is known." Anthony R. Oberschall, "Rising Expectations and Political Turmoil," *The Journal of Development Studies*, Vol. VI, No. 1 (October, 1969), p. 8. The evidence, he asserts, does not support the conclusion that the revolution of rising expectations has been "a significant causal force to the recent political upheavals" in Uganda or Nigeria. (p. 18.)

industries—manufacturing a variety of small consumer goods such as tools, utensils, and bicycles—are found in many developing states. For all of them, however, a substantial industrial complex represents an aspiration rather than a current reality. In many cases, the development of an industrial complex is dependent not only on the utilization of resources but also on the expansion of markets through trade (and schemes such as common markets) since the internal demand is too limited to sustain large-scale production. For many years to come, most states will have to rely on the major industrial powers to provide their heavy machinery requirements.

One factor that accounts for the intense drive to industrialize and diversify these economies is the present extraordinarily heavy reliance on the export of one crop or product. Oil, for example, accounts for 99 per cent of Chad's exports and 92 per cent of Venezuela's; cotton, for 83 per cent of Rwanda's; and peanuts and peanut products, for 93 per cent of Gambia's. Frequently the primary export is that of a product for which world demand is fairly inflexible, a fact that causes drastic movements in market prices because of short-term fluctuations in supply, thus making a stable income from these exports difficult to maintain.

There are, however, many obstacles to economic development. In some cases, natural resources are inadequate, of poor quality, or not readily accessible. Adequate transportation and communication systems are lacking to handle the demands of a complex industrial society. Investment capital is usually in critically short supply. Even when resources and capital are available, the limited internal markets and the strong competition offered by the major industrial powers for world markets inhibit industrial development. In addition, there are severe shortages of trained and skilled personnel in the developing states to plan and operate an industrial complex. Further, the traditional organizational structures and cultural values in the society often impede economic development. Only gradually are the values, attitudes, and techniques that underlie and are associated with Western industrial societies beginning to emerge. Finally, the political instability of many governments disrupts planning and discourages private investment.

A further characteristic of the economic conditions in the developing states is the striking inequality in incomes and standards of living between the masses and the economic elite. While the masses are poor and in some cases acutely destitute, the elite, in contrast, are often remarkably wealthy. In Colombia, for example, over 40 per cent of the national wealth is controlled by 5 per cent of the population; in Brazil, over 60 per cent is held by less than 20 per cent of the population. The enormous wealth of some Asian families and Middle Eastern aristocrats contrasts sharply with the poverty of the masses in their societies. Those who possess such wealth have little in common with the masses; the two groups live in different worlds, each with its own distinctive manners, dress, values, and often language. In few of these societies is there a substantial economic middle class of businessmen, engineers, technicians, and skilled manual workers.

In most developing states, the masses, besides being poor, are also illiterate. In Senegal, for example, about 95 per cent of the population is illiterate, while in India the figure is 72 per cent and in Iran, 87 per cent. In some Asian and African states, considerable progress has been made in reducing the high level of illiteracy; in Burma, for example, the illiteracy rate is below 43 per cent. The illiteracy rate in most Latin American states has been substantially reduced, though in Bolivia the figure is still 69 per cent and in Haiti, 90 per cent. Contrasts within individual states are again marked. In many rural areas, schools are few or nonexistent. Even when available, the levels of instruction and attendance are poor. In the larger towns and cities, however, instruction is usually much better, and a far higher percentage of school-age children attend classes, often for a period of several years. The number of students who receive more than a primary education is still very small, and only a very few persons are able to attend colleges and universities. Those who do receive an advanced education, sometimes in European and American schools, frequently become the principal voices in society advocating modernization and reform.

Particularly in the new African and Asian states, this "Westernized" intellectual elite is frequently in a position to attempt to carry out its objectives since it constitutes the political elite as well. Whether civilian or military in composition, it is this small group that champions rapid social and economic changes. In some cases, this new intellectual elite, created largely through colonial policies of developing an indigenous civil service and military force, has been joined by the traditional political elite in its efforts to modernize society; in other cases, the traditional elite has sought to retain its privileges and prerogatives in time-honored ways, thus creating a major barrier to the policies and programs of the new political elite. Many of the intellectual elite were instrumental in the drive for political independence. Their positions of authority are based primarily on their ability to motivate and organize their followers in the pursuit of developmental goals, rather than on the traditional bases of authority, birth, and wealth. In most Latin American states, in contrast, the political elite is still drawn from the conservative socio-economic "white" elite, reflecting the fundamentally different pattern of history in Latin American states in comparison with that of most Asian and African states.

Few organized groups exist to bridge the wide gap between the masses and the elite, whether traditional or "modernizing." Rarely are the peasant masses organized to promote their interests and, in many cases, neither are the limited commercial and laboring sectors of the society. Where industrialization is growing, trade unions and business organizations are emerging, but with few exceptions, these organizations are not yet large and politically powerful. Political parties, bureaucracies, and the armed forces provide the principal channels of communication and contact between the elite and the masses. Often the political parties are little more than personal followings of individual leaders, or else broad, comprehensive, nationalistic parties that represent "the general will." Increasingly, the armed forces have assumed a broad range of social, economic, and political functions in addition to their military duties. In Asia and Africa, the military, along with the bureaucracy, is often the principal institutionalized force supporting the "modernizing" elite.

A pronounced characteristic of many developing states—and one that frequently causes the progressive political elite some of its most difficult problems—is the lack of integration among the several cultural and ethnic groups comprising society. In some cases, these relatively autonomous, self-contained, self-sufficient groups have traditionally been hostile toward each other. Each group has its own deeply rooted traditions, values, organizations, lands, and occupations, and often its own language and religion. Frequently these groups are stratified within the state along social, economic, and political lines, further complicating the problem of nation-building.

A few examples illustrate the complex social pattern that exists in many developing states. In Indonesia, the population is divided into sixteen major ethnic groups, each of which occupies a fairly distinct region, speaks its own language or dialect, possesses its own traditional forms of social and political organization, and pursues somewhat different economic activities. Deep-seated differences exist between the Javanese and non-Javanese over social and political issues, with the latter continuing to press their demands for regional autonomy. Similarly, India's social structure is highly complex. Within its enormous population at least twelve major languages are spoken. Although 85 per cent of the population is Hindu, this religion includes a wide variety of sects and beliefs. It forms the basis for the rigid caste system which divides society into thousands of relatively small kinship groups, each with its own rather specific occupation and habits of speech, manners, and dress. Within the half million villages where 80 per cent of the people reside, these caste and kinship ties are particularly strong. The Muslim minority, about 10 per cent of the population, with its distinctively different religious beliefs and social structure, is largely unintegrated into Indian society. In many Asian states, Chinese and Indians form important, unintegrated minority groups. They are found primarily in the urban areas, where they maintain strong, cohesive communities. Engaging in business enterprises and the professions, they constitute alien economic and social groups, frequently disliked and distrusted, but often performing essential roles that would otherwise remain unfilled.

Intricate social patterns are also found in Africa. While in few states other than in Rhodesia and the Union of South Africa are there significant white minorities, the African population is nevertheless divided into many ethnic and cultural groups. In Ghana, three major groups, subdivided into over sixty tribal and lineage groups, can be identified. Five major languages and many dialects are spoken by these groups. Deep-seated animosities divide the various groups in some African states, as in Nigeria, the most populous state, where these divisions threaten to destroy the Nigerian federation. In addition to numerous tribal groups, Asians, Arabs, and Europeans form small but important ethnic groups in a few states, where they are particularly prominent in commercial enterprises and in the professions. These various groups are further divided by religious beliefs, as several native religions are practiced by the Africans, while the Asians and Arabs are primarily Muslims and the Europeans, Christian.

A complex social structure based upon race is also found in many Latin American states. Three distinct groups comprise the three separate classes: Indians, *mestizos,* and "whites." While these groups share a common religion, Roman Catholicism, they are divided in every other respect. Each class has its distinctive customs, language, and occupations. The Indians—and, where they exist in large numbers, the Negroes—occupy the lowest positions. They live apart from the other classes, occupying in particular the more inhospitable areas of the state. There they have established close-knit communities that preserve the traditional Indian customs and practices. Relegated to the most menial occupations and politically without power, they are only rarely able to obtain the education and cultural characteristics that permit them to move upward in the social order. The *mestizos*—those of mixed European and Indian ancestry—form a middle social and cultural group. The "whites" —the descendants of many European groups, Spanish, Portuguese, Irish, German, and others—form the social, economic, and political elite. Their European-based languages and culture, higher rate of literacy, wealth, and occupations form the basis of their dominant position in the social order. In several states they form a minority of the total population, but they own most of the land and control the economic and political sectors of society as well as the social.

The problem of integrating the several ethnic and cultural groups typically found in a developing state is compounded by the solidarity and cohesion of each individual group. Particularly in the rural areas, the basic social and political patterns of the group establish a stable, comprehensive set of personal relationships for its members, determining status, occupation, and values that together provide a sense of personal security. The primary identification and loyalty of the individual to his own immediate group rather than to the larger society has quite often been strengthened in the newly independent states as the different groups, no longer either protected or obstructed by the former colonial power, compete for positions of control. Most leaders confronted with the problem of integrating their societies have relied upon nationalistic appeals and the effects of education, a more complex, interdependent economy, and a higher standard of living. The process of integration is slow, delicate, and uncertain, however, and traditional loyalties and rivalries are not easily surmounted.

As this brief survey suggests, the study of transitional societies, their political systems, and the process of modernization must account for the great diversity of characteristics found in the African, Asian, and Latin American states. In addition to these widely varying characteristics, the different rates and nature of change occurring within the individual states must also be considered. In some cases, the indices of progress show little movement; in others, significant advances have been made, while in still others, regression has occurred. Since no single index of development is available, states may be making certain advances while simultaneously be moving backward along other dimensions of change. Thus, the search for patterns of change and the relationship of different types of change confronts the student of transitional societies with a challenging task. In the chapter that follows, the initial problem of devising a framework for analysis is considered.

SUGGESTED READINGS

Almond, Gabriel A., and James S. Coleman, eds. *The Politics of the Developing Areas*. Princeton, N. J.: Princeton University Press, 1960.

Anderson, Charles W., Fred R. von der Mehden, and Crawford Young. *Issues of Political Development*. Englewood Cliffs, N. J.: Prentice-Hall, Inc., 1967.

Apter, David E. *The Politics of Modernization*. Chicago: University of Chicago Press, 1965.

Eisenstadt, S. N. *Modernization: Protest and Change*. Englewood Cliffs, N. J.: Prentice-Hall, Inc., 1966.

Horowitz, Irving Louis. *Three Worlds of Development*, 2d ed. New York: Oxford University Press, 1972.

Leys, Colin, ed. *Politics and Change in Developing Countries*. Cambridge: Cambridge University Press, 1969.

McCord, William. *The Springtime of Freedom*. New York: Oxford University Press, 1965.

Rustow, Dankwart A. *A World of Nations: Problems of Political Modernization*. Washington, D. C.: Brookings Institution, 1967.

Silvert, Kalman H., ed. *Expectant Peoples: Nationalism and Development*. New York: Random House, 1963.

von der Mehden, Fred R. *Politics of the Developing Nations*. 2d ed. Englewood Cliffs, N. J.: Prentice-Hall, Inc., 1969.

Worsley, Peter. *The Third World*. 2d ed. Chicago: University of Chicago Press, 1970.

ii. comparative politics and political development

In attempting to understand the political systems of the transitional states, the student of comparative politics confronts a variety of problems. For one thing, the emergence of so many new states during the past two decades and the renewed interest in Latin American states have led to problems common to situations of abundance, such as the problem of handling vast amounts of data, organizing and classifying the data, and selecting representative cases for detailed study from which broader generalizations can be made. More difficult than mere numbers are the problems posed by the diversity of cultures, ideologies, institutions, and processes that are found in the enlarged laboratory of comparative studies. Unlike an earlier generation of political scientists who dealt with a fairly homogeneous set of states in Europe and North America, the present-day student of politics must attempt to understand objectively exotic cultures and societies in all parts of the world. To approach that ideal, careful attention must be paid to the development and use of research methods that are comprehensive in scope (i.e., capable of encompassing all relevant factors in societies), precise, and culturally neutral.

Another problem confronting students of politics, especially of the transitional societies, is that of understanding the dynamics of social, economic, and political change in relationship to development and modernization. The inclusion of many new and underdeveloped societies in the political scientist's laboratory has contributed greatly to attempts to conceptualize political development and the developmental processes. What does "political development" mean? What are the relationships of economic development and social change to political development? Can the "stage" theories of economic development be adapted to the study of political development? Do military governments contribute to or inhibit political development? Under what conditions does political violence occur? What factors contribute to the breakdown of the developmental processes?

In attempting to answer questions such as these, political scientists and other scholars have sought to develop more sophisticated research tools and methods than have previously been available. If the "traditional" approaches were characterized by their lack of rigor, their parochialism in considering only Western societies, and their narrow focus on the formal and legal political institutions of society, the new approaches are characterized by their scientific rigor, their universal applicability, and their far broader identification of politically relevant characteristics of society.[1] Unfortunately, none of the new approaches has emerged as clearly superior to all others, and the serious student of politics must weigh the advantages and disadvantages of the different paradigms or approaches to the study of politics that are available for him to use.

It is hardly surprising that political scientists, confronted with the task of analyzing the widely varying political systems in Asia, Africa, and Latin America, in addition to those in Europe and North America, have been forced to reconsider the fundamental question, What *is* politics? What is a political act, and what is the arena in which political acts take place? What phenomena constitute politics in, for example, Ghana, Burma, Brazil, and the United States that can be compared in useful theoretical and practical ways? Although different specific answers have been proposed to these questions, political scientists generally agree that politics involves the organization and exercise of authority within a society for the purposes of establishing and maintaining order, resolving differences between groups and individuals, and promoting common goals. These ends give rise to institutions and processes through which authority is exercised and decisions made on how to achieve the basic goals. The study of politics, then, is the study of the organization and base of authority and the means by which authoritative decisions for a society are made and enforced. However, considerable differences of opinion exist on the question of the proper boundaries delimiting political studies—for example, on the extent to which political scientists should incorporate social, economic, and other data into their analyses in order to encompass all factors that affect, even marginally, the political system. On the one hand, a narrow focus facilitates concentrated attention on a few aspects of politics. However, the tendency is then to focus on the

---

[1] The development of comparative political studies is traced in an interesting essay by Harry Eckstein, "A Perspective on Comparative Politics, Past and Present," in Harry Eckstein and David Apter, eds., *Comparative Politics* (New York: The Free Press, 1963), pp. 3–32.

most obvious "political" elements, the formal, legal structures and processes of government. Such a focus can, of course, be quite misleading, especially when applied to developing political systems. On the other hand, while a broader, more inclusive approach may relate important ancillary social, economic, and other phenomena to politics—and thereby inject a dynamic element into the analysis of politics and change—difficult problems arise in attempting to collect and organize such diverse data and relate it to the political processes.

The various paradigms or approaches that have been proposed are all designed to make the study of politics more systematic and more truly comparative than it has been in the past. They differ, however, with respect to the concepts that are used, the types of hypotheses that are postulated and tested, and the levels of generalization toward which they aim. Only a brief survey of some of the major approaches is possible here, but even this survey will indicate the diversity of the attempts to give order and meaning to the wealth of data becoming available on the various societies of the world.[2]

Can important characteristics of a political system be explained in terms of the personal characteristics of individual actors in that system? Some political scientists think so.[3] They believe that detailed studies of individual personality traits and characteristics will reveal fundamental societal patterns that are, in turn, reflected in the style and performance of the political system. Individual needs are shaped by certain personality characteristics, and the shared needs of large numbers of individuals in a society result in the behavioral patterns that characterize that society. These patterns of behavior can then be analyzed in terms of their impact on formal institutions and processes. Certainly a much greater awareness of the psychological dimensions of politics in the transitional societies has resulted from studies employing a psychological approach, such as Lucian Pye's *Politics, Personality and Nation-Building: Burma's Search for Identity*.[4] However, those who use the psychological ap-

---

[2] Useful discussions of methodological problems and principles may be found in works such as Robert T. Holt and John E. Turner, eds., *The Methodology of Comparative Research* (New York: The Free Press, 1970), James C. Charlesworth, ed., *Contemporary Political Analysis* (New York: The Free Press, 1967), Henry Teune and Adam Przeworski, *The Logic of Comparative Social Inquiry* (New York: John Wiley and Sons, Inc., 1969), Robert T. Golembiewski, William A. Welsh, and William J. Crotty, *A Methodological Primer for Political Scientists* (Chicago: Rand McNally and Company, 1969), Gunnar Heckscher, *Comparative Government and Politics* (London: George Allen and Unwin Ltd., 1957), and Roy C. Macridis, *The Comparative Study of Politics* (New York: Random House, 1955).

[3] The discussion in the next several paragraphs draws heavily from Robert T. Holt and John M. Richardson, Jr., "Competing Paradigms in Comparative Politics," in Holt and Turner, eds., *The Methodology of Comparative Research*, pp. 21–71. The bibliography and notes in Turner and Holt are a useful starting point for those interested in a more detailed examination of methodologies and approaches.

[4] (New Haven: Yale University Press, 1963).

proaches remain vulnerable to the charge that they have yet to specify clearly how their analysis can shift from the micro (individual) level to the macro (societal) level without considerable loss of reliability in explaining either the psychological characteristics of the whole political system or the general functioning of the political system in all its complexity.

A second type of approach widely used in the study of comparative politics is that of systems analysis. The basic assumption underlying this approach is that in politics, as in economics or physics, a set of elements interact in patterns that can be defined and analyzed. The problems of defining the various politically relevant elements, the patterns of their interaction, and the boundaries of the system in which the elements interact have all proved to be difficult, however, in political studies. Nevertheless, this approach has a strong appeal to those who wish to emphasize the interaction of specifically political elements with broader environmental ones. The web of relationships that is discovered to exist thus makes it possible to trace how changes in one element affect the other elements of the system. Despite the problems of defining the terms and concepts with the rigor and precision necessary for sophisticated analyses, the demonstrated power and utility of this approach in other fields of scientific study are certain to continue to attract political scientists to attempt its usage in political studies.

A third approach, and perhaps the most generally influential of all, is that of structural functionalism, of which an example is provided in the second reading of this chapter. Building on the influential works of sociologists such as Max Weber, Talcott Parsons, and others, the structural functionalists in political science, led by Gabriel Almond, have sought to analyze politics through a two-stage process. First, they have tried to identify and conceptualize the essential political functions that must be performed in any viable political system regardless of its size or type, and second, to identify and compare the structures that perform these functions in different societies. The assumption, of course, is that there are basic political functions common to all political systems which, if not adequately performed over time, will result in the deterioration and the eventual collapse of the system. Again, the problem of finding functional concepts that are individually precise and together sufficiently comprehensive to encompass all political phenomena is difficult. If these functions can be stated, an imaginative search can then be initiated to identify the structures performing these functions.

Many political scientists have found the structural functional approach valuable in suggesting relationships between political variables —people, institutions, roles, and processes, for example—that are not readily apparent on the surface. Others, however, find serious weaknesses in this approach. For some, it is too vague and fluid, lacking in precision, and incorporating too many aspects of a society that are not sufficiently political in nature. Others believe the approach tends to emphasize societal and political equilibrium and stability too much, as a consequence of which rapid or radical change is regarded as pathological in nature. Still others feel that the functional categories commonly used are too loose and flexible to have much analytical utility since many kinds of political actions may be placed under several functional headings. Nevertheless, there is widespread agreement that the structural functional approach, by insisting on the commonalities of political systems, has advanced the possibilities of developing truly comparative categories for political study.

Some political scientists believe that the next major advance in comparative studies will come through the use of a quite different type of approach, one that makes extensive use of computers to handle large amounts of data. The assumption is that there are many interesting and important correlations among the political variables of societies which will be discovered only through the examination of aggregate data. Once the problem of securing accurate, comparable data has been solved, not an insignificant problem in itself, computers can be used to search for and test correlations of two or more variables and, using multiple regression analysis, to explain the variation in one variable in terms of several others. But while no one disputes the ability of computers to handle large amounts of data, many doubt the possibility of making inferential use of correlation coefficients, or of moving beyond the level of description to the level of explanation. And until explanations are available, theory-building in its more sophisticated forms is inhibited.

In addition to the methodological problems that arise in the study of transitional societies there are also the problems of analyzing the developmental processes. Just as the structuring of adequate approaches has proved difficult, so too has the conceptualization of political development. In one survey of the usages of the term political development, ten quite distinctive interpretations were identified. They ranged from equating political development with democracy to viewing it as one aspect of a complicated process of social change.[5]

The difficulty is twofold. First, the concept of political development itself must be developed, and second, the processes by which development takes place must be identified. Despite the variety of conceptualizations, most political scientists would probably agree that, as a minimum, political development involves the increasing capacity of a government to govern through increasingly specialized institutions in an increasingly

[5] Lucian W. Pye, *Aspects of Political Development* (Boston: Little, Brown and Company, 1966), pp. 33–45. See also Robert A. Packenham, "Approaches to the Study of Political Development," *World Politics*, Vol. XVII, No. 1 (October, 1964), pp. 108–120.

complex social and economic setting. In some states, even this minimal test of development is difficult to meet, and many governments and political institutions have fallen because the political forces within the state were unable to agree on the course political development was to take. As the evidence of the past two decades strongly indicates, no short straight path leads to the development and modernization of a society. Political decay as well as political development can and does occur, as Samuel Huntington argues in the selection below, and political scientists must attempt to understand the movements in both directions. Throughout this book, references will be made to the strategies of development as well as to the barriers to the developmental processes.

The problems just discussed are, of course, extremely complex, and a brief survey of them cannot do more than highlight some of the principal aspects of the problems and the ways in which they have been attacked. But in addition to the theoretical and methodological problems there are some other difficulties confronting the student of transitional societies that need to be mentioned.

One problem is that of securing the necessary data for analysis. In attempting to compile this data, it will soon become apparent that much of it is unavailable or unreliable. In contrast to the wealth of government statistics and reports available in most European, the North American, and a few other states on social and economic conditions and trends, this type of information on developing states is often sparse, unsystematically compiled, outdated, or inaccurate. Reports of administrative agencies and government corporations are difficult to obtain and, even when available, are often incomplete or distorted. Official records of legislative debates and committee meetings may be available only in summary form, if at all, and court decisions are often unpublished or even unrecorded.

Similarly, relatively little non-official information is available in many states. Few professional groups or civic, social, or economic organizations exist that undertake their own studies of specific problems within their societies. The extensive social science research executed by European and American university faculty members is also rarely duplicated in the developing societies, both because higher education in these latter states has traditionally stressed the humanities, and because their universities and colleges lack the financial resources to underwrite many comprehensive, and often expensive, social studies. Furthermore, political science as a discipline is almost unknown in the educational systems of the developing states. Only a very limited number of trained native political scientists are available to undertake specialized political analyses of their own or other political institutions and processes. Neither are there large numbers of skilled political journalists to contribute their insights into policies and personalities in their political systems.

The many languages and dialects found in the developing areas create additional difficulties. Even though many leaders speak English or French, and many documents are issued in English translations, much important data is not readily available to those without proficiency in non-European languages. The English translations, moreover, often fail to convey the subtleties and nuances that are essential for precise meanings and measurements.

More basic than the language barrier is the psychological obstacle that confronts the student attempting to analyze the social and political systems in Asia and Africa, and to a lesser degree, in Latin America. The problem of defining and understanding unfamiliar cultures, values, and institutions is further complicated by the highly personal, informal, and undifferentiated nature of some political systems. For students accustomed to the pragmatic, rational approach to problems in European and American societies, the irrational and unscientific search for answers to social, economic, and political problems carried on in some societies is disconcerting and incomprehensible. Further complicating the problem of analysis is the social and cultural fragmentation found in some states. While the psychological barrier can probably never be fully overcome, it can, nevertheless, be lessened by thorough preparation and careful attention to details.[6]

Despite all these barriers, the study of transitional societies and their political systems has moved forward vigorously in the last few years. A wealth of literature is available, of which the selections in this book constitute but a very small sample. Much work remains to be done, of course, but the "state of the art" has already advanced far toward achieving a more sophisticated set of concepts and approaches that will enable more comprehensive studies to be undertaken in the fields of comparative politics and political development.

SUGGESTED READINGS

Almond, Gabriel A. Political Development. Boston: Little, Brown and Company, 1970.
———, and G. Bingham Powell, Jr. Comparative Politics: A Developmental Approach. Boston: Little, Brown and Company, 1966.
Apter, David E. Some Conceptual Approaches to the Study of Modernization. Englewood Cliffs, N. J.: Prentice-Hall, Inc., 1968.
Charlesworth, James C., ed. Contemporary Political Analysis. New York: The Free Press, 1967.

[6] The difficulties, as well as the rewards, of conducting research in the developing areas are considered in more detail in Robert E. Ward et al., Studying Politics Abroad (Boston: Little, Brown and Company, 1964).

COMPARATIVE POLITICS AND POLITICAL DEVELOPMENT

Comparative Politics, Vol. I, No. 1 (October, 1968).

Easton, David. *A Framework for Political Analysis*. Englewood Cliffs, N. J.: Prentice-Hall, Inc., 1965.

———. *A Systems Analysis of Political Life*. New York: John Wiley & Sons, 1965.

———. *The Political System*. 2d ed. New York: Alfred A. Knopf, 1971.

Field, George L. *Comparative Political Development*. Ithaca, N. Y.: Cornell University Press, 1967.

Golembiewski, Robert T., William A. Welsh, and William J. Crotty. *A Methodological Primer for Political Scientists*. Chicago: Rand McNally & Company, 1969.

Groth, Alexander J. *Comparative Politics: A Distributive Approach*. New York: The Macmillan Company, 1971.

Holt, Robert T., and John E. Turner, eds. *The Methodology of Comparative Research*. New York: The Free Press, 1970.

Kuhn, Alfred. *The Study of Society: A Unified Approach*. Homewood, Ill.: The Dorsey Press, Inc., 1963.

Macridis, Roy C. *The Study of Comparative Government*. Garden City, New York: Doubleday & Company, 1955.

Merritt, Richard L. *Systematic Approaches to Comparative Politics*. Chicago: Rand McNally & Company, 1970.

———, and Stein Rokkan, eds. *Comparing Nations: The Use of Quantitative Data in Cross-National Research*. New Haven: Yale University Press, 1966.

Organski, A. F. K. *The Stages of Political Development*. New York: Alfred A. Knopf, 1967.

Pye, Lucian W. *Aspects of Political Development*. Boston: Little, Brown and Company, 1966.

Taylor, Charles L., and Michael C. Hudson. *World Handbook of Political and Social Indicators*. 2d ed. New Haven: Yale University Press, 1972.

In the following selection, Lucian Pye highlights some of the most important characteristics of governments and politics in transitional states. This general orientation provides a useful base for the consideration of the methodological problems confronting students of politics, who must find ways of handling a diversity of political systems, as well as for the more detailed discussion of transitional political systems to be undertaken in later chapters.

1. THE NON-WESTERN POLITICAL PROCESS*†

l u c i a n   w.   p y e

The purpose of this article is to outline some of the dominant and distinctive characteristics of the non-Western political process. In recent years, both the student of comparative politics and the field worker in the newly emergent and economically underdeveloped countries have found it helpful to think in terms of a general category of non-Western politics.[1]

There are, of course, great differences among the non-Western societies. Indeed, in the past, comparative analysis was impeded by an appreciation of the rich diversity in the cultural traditions and the historical circumstances of the Western impact; students and researchers found it necessary to concentrate on particular cultures, and as a consequence attention was generally directed to the unique features of each society. Recently, however, attempts to set forth some of the characteristics common to the political life of countries experiencing profound social change have stimulated fruitful discussions among specialists on the different non-Western regions as well as among general students of comparative politics.

For this discussion to continue, it is necessary for specialists on the different areas to advance, in the form of rather bold and unqualified statements, generalized models of the political process common in non-Western societies.[2] Then, by examining the ways in which particular

---

* From "The Non-Western Political Process" by Lucian W. Pye, *The Journal of Politics*, Vol. XX, No. 3 (August, 1958), pp. 468–486. By permission of the publisher and the author.

† This is a revised version of a paper presented at the annual meeting of the American Political Science Association on September 5–7, 1957.

[1] For two excellent discussions of the implications for comparative politics of the current interest in non-Western political systems, see: Sigmund Neumann, "Comparative Politics: A Half-Century Appraisal," *Journal of Politics*, XIX (August, 1957), 269–290; and Dankwart A. Rustow, "New Horizons for Comparative Politics," *World Politics*, IX (July, 1957), 530–549.

[2] The picture of the non-Western political process contained in the following pages was strongly influenced by: George McT. Kahin, Guy J. Pauker, and Lucian W. Pye, "Comparative Politics in Non-Western Countries," *American Political Science Review*, XLIX (December, 1955), 1022–41; Gabriel A. Almond, "Comparative Politi-

COMPARATIVE POLITICS AND POLITICAL DEVELOPMENT

non-Western countries differ from the generalized models, it becomes possible to engage in significant comparative analysis.

1. *In non-Western societies the political sphere is not sharply differentiated from the spheres of social and personal relations.* Among the most powerful influences of the traditional order in any society in transition are those forces which impede the development of a distinct sphere of politics. In most non-Western societies, just as in traditional societies, the pattern of political relationships is largely determined by the pattern of social and personal relations. Power, prestige, and influence are based largely on social status. The political struggle tends to revolve around issues of prestige, influence, and even of personalities, and not primarily around questions of alternative courses of policy action.

The elite who dominate the national politics of most non-Western countries generally represent a remarkably homogeneous group in terms of educational experience and social background. Indeed, the path by which individuals are recruited into their political roles, where not dependent upon ascriptive considerations, is essentially an acculturation process. It is those who have become urbanized, have received the appropriate forms of education, and have demonstrated skill in establishing the necessary personal relations who are admitted to the ranks of the elite. . . .

At the village level it is even more difficult to distinguish a distinct political sphere. The social status of the individual and his personal ties largely determine his political behavior and the range of his influence. The lack of a clear political sphere in such communities places severe limits on the effectiveness of those who come from the outside to perform a political role. . . .

The fundamental framework of non-Western politics is a communal one, and all political behavior is strongly colored by considerations of communal identification. In the more conspicuous cases the larger communal groupings follow ethnic or religious lines. . . .

This essentially communal framework of politics makes it extremely difficult for ideas to command influence in themselves. The response to any advocate of a particular point of view tends to be attuned more to his social position than to the content of his views. Under these conditions it is inappropriate to conceive of an open market place where political ideas can freely compete on their own merits for support. Political discussion tends rather to assume the form of either intracommunal debate or one group justifying its position toward another.

The communal framework also sharply limits freedom in altering

cal Systems," *Journal of Politics,* XVIII (August, 1956), 391–409; Rustow, *op. cit.,* and also his *Politics and Westernization in the Near East,* Center of International Studies (Princeton, 1956).

political allegiances. Any change in political identification generally requires a change in one's social and personal relationships; conversely, any change in social relations tends to result in a change in political identification. . . .

2. *Political parties in non-Western societies tend to take on a world view and represent a way of life.* The lack of a clearly differentiated political sphere means that political associations or groups cannot be clearly oriented to a distinct political arena but tend to be oriented to some aspect of the communal framework of politics. In reflecting the communal base of politics, political parties tend to represent total ways of life. . . . Usually political parties represent some sub-society or simply the personality of a particularly influential individual.

Even secular parties devoted to achieving national sovereignty have tended to develop their own unique world views. Indeed, successful parties tend to become social movements. The indigenous basis for political parties is usually regional, ethnic, or religious groupings, all of which stress considerations not usually emphasized in Western secular politics. . . .

    ✿   ✿   ✿   ✿   ✿

3. *The political process in non-Western societies is characterized by a prevalence of cliques.* The lack of a distinct political sphere and the tendency for political parties to have a world view together provide a framework within which the most structured units of decision-making tend to be personal cliques. Although general considerations of social status determine the broad outlines of power and influence, the particular pattern of political relationships at any time is largely determined by decisions made at the personal level. This is the case because the social structure in non-Western societies is characterized by functionally diffuse relationships; individuals and groups do not have sharply defined and highly specific functions and thus do not represent specific interests that distinguish them from other groupings. . . . The pattern of personal associations provides one of the firmest guides for understanding and action within the political process. Personal cliques are likely to become the key units of decision-making in the political process of most non-Western societies.

    ✿   ✿   ✿   ✿   ✿

4. *The character of political loyalty in non-Western societies gives to the leadership of political groups a high degree of freedom in deter-*

mining matters of strategy and tactics. The communal framework of politics and the tendency for political parties to have world views means that political loyalty is governed more by a sense of identification with the concrete group than by identification with the professed policy goals of the group. The expectation is that the leaders will seek to maximize all the interests of all the members of the group and not just seek to advance particular policies or values.

✧ ✧ ✧ ✧ ✧

5. *Opposition parties and aspiring elites tend to appear as revolutionary movements in non-Western politics.* Since the current leadership in non-Western countries generally conceives of itself as seeking to effect changes in all aspects of life, and since all the political associations tend to have world views, any prospective change in national leadership is likely to seem to have revolutionary implications. . . .

In addition, the broad and diffuse interests of the ruling elites make it easy for them to maintain that they represent the interest of the entire nation. Those seeking power are thus often placed in the position of appearing to be, at best, obstructionists of progress and, at worst, enemies of the country. Competition is not between parties that represent different functional specific interests or between groups that claim greater administrative skills; rather, the struggle takes on some of the qualities of a conflict between differing ways of life.

This situation is important in explaining the failure of responsible opposition parties to develop in most non-Western countries. . . .

6. *The non-Western political process is characterized by a lack of integration among the participants, and this situation is a function of the lack of a unified communications system in the society.* In most non-Western societies there is not a single general political process that is the focus of most political activities throughout the population; rather, there are several distinct and nearly unrelated political processes. The most conspicuous division is that between the dominant national politics of the more urban elements and the more traditional village level of politics. The conflicts that are central to the one may hardly appear in the other.

Those who participate, for example, in the political life of the village are not an integral part of the national politics, since they can act without regard to developments at the central level. Possibly even more significant is the fact that at the village level all the various village groups have their separate and autonomous political processes.

This situation is a reflection of, and is reinforced by, the communication system common to non-Western societies, where the media of mass communication generally reach only to elements of the urban population and to those who participate in the national political process. The vast majority of the people participate only in the traditional word-of-mouth communication system. Even when the media of mass communications do reach the village, through readers of newspapers or owners of radios, there is almost no "feedback" from the village level. The radio talks *to* the villagers but does not talk *with* them. The views of the vast majority of the population are not reflected in the mass media. . . .

The lack of a unified communication system and the fact that the participants are not integrated into a common political process limit the types of political issues that can arise in non-Western societies. For example, although these are essentially agrarian societies in which industrial development is just beginning to take place, there has not yet appeared (in their politics) one of the issues basic to the history of Western politics: the clash between industry and agriculture, between town and countryside. . . .

7. *The non-Western political process is characterized by a high rate of recruitment of new elements to political roles.*[3] The spread of popular politics in traditional societies has meant a constant increase in the number of participants and the types of organizations involved in the political process. This development has been stimulated by the extraordinary rise in the urban population, which has greatly increased the number of people who have some understanding about, and feeling for, politics at the national level. A basic feature of the acculturation process which creates the sub-society of the elite is the development of attitudes common to urban life. It is generally out of the rapid urban growth that there emerge the aspiring elites who demand to be heard. In almost all non-Western societies, there is a distinct strata of urban dwellers who are excluded from direct participation in national politics but whose existence affects the behavior of the current elite.

✿　✿　✿　✿　✿

8. *The non-Western political process is characterized by sharp differences in the political orientation of the generations.* The process of social change in most non-Western societies results in a lack of continuity in the circumstances under which people are recruited to politics. Those who took part in the revolutionary movement against a colonial ruler are not necessarily regarded as indispensable leaders by the new generations; but their revolutionary role is still put forward as sufficient reason for their continued elite status. . . .

[3] Kahin, Pauker, and Pye, *loc. cit.*, p. 1024.

This problem in non-Western societies is further complicated by demographic factors, for such societies are composed of rapidly growing populations that have a high birth rate. In Singapore, Malaya, and Burma, over half the population is under voting age, and the median age in most non-Western countries is in the low twenties. There is thus a constant pressure from the younger generation, whose demands for political influence conflict with the claims of current leaders who conceive of themselves as being still young and with many more years of active life ahead. In most of the newly independent countries, the initial tendency was for cabinet ministers and high officials to be in their thirties and forties, a condition which has colored the career expectations of the youth of succeeding generations, who now face frustration if they cannot achieve comparable status at the same age.

This telescoping of the generations has sharpened the clash of views so that intellectually there is an abnormal gap in political orientations, creating a potential for extreme reversal in policy, should the aspiring elites gain power. Ideas and symbols which are deeply felt by the current leaders, including those relating to the West, may have little meaning for a generation which has not experienced colonial rule.

9. *In non-Western societies there is little consensus as to the legitimate ends and means of political action.* The fundamental fact that non-Western societies are engrossed in a process of discontinuous social change precludes the possibility of a widely shared agreement as to the appropriate ends and means of political activities. In all the important non-Western countries, there are people who have assimilated Western culture to the point that their attitudes and concepts about politics differ little from those common in the West. At the other extreme there is the village peasant who has been little touched by Western influences. Living in different worlds, these individuals can hardly be expected to display a common approach toward political action.

The national leadership, recruited from people who have generally become highly urbanized, is in a position to set the standards for what may appear to be a widely shared consensus about politics. However, more often than not, this apparent national agreement is a reflection only of the distinct qualities of the elite sub-society. . . .

The lack of a distinct political sphere increases the difficulties in achieving agreement about the legitimate scope and forms of political activities. The setting is not one in which political issues are relatively isolated and thus easily communicated and discussed. Instead, a knowledge of national politics requires an intimate acquaintance with the total social life of the elite. The fact that loyalty to the particular group rather than support of general principles is the key to most political behavior strengthens the tendency toward a distinct and individual rather than a shared orientation towards politics.

The situation is further complicated by the fact that, since most of the groupings within the political process represent total ways of life, few are concerned with limited and specific interests. The functionally diffuse character of most groups means that each tends to have its own approaches to political action in terms of both ends and means. . . .

✿   ✿   ✿   ✿   ✿

10. *In non-Western societies the intensity and breadth of political discussion has little relationship to political decision-making.* Western observers are impressed with what they feel is a paradoxical situation in most non-Western countries: the masses seem to be apathetic toward political action and yet, considering the crude systems of communications, they are remarkably well informed about political events. Peasants and villagers often engage in lengthy discussions on matters related to the political world that lies outside their immediate lives, but they rarely seem prepared to translate the information they receive into action that might influence the course of national politics.

The villagers are often responding in the traditional manner to national politics. In most traditional societies, an important function of the elite was to provide entertainment and material for discussion for the common people; but discussions in villages and teashops could center on the activities of an official without creating the expectation that discussion should lead to action. . . .

A second explanation for this pattern of behavior is that one of the important factors in determining social status and prestige within the village or local community is often a command of information about the wider world; knowledge of developments in the sphere of national and even international politics has a value in itself. But skill in discussing political matters again does not raise any expectations of actual participation in the world of politics.

Finally, many of the common people in non-Western societies find it desirable to keep informed about political developments in order to be able to adapt their lives to any major changes. . . .

11. *In the non-Western political process there is a high degree of substitutability of roles.*[4] It seems that in non-Western societies most politically relevant roles are not clearly differentiated but have a functionally diffuse rather than a functionally specific character. For example, the civil bureaucracy is not usually limited to the role of a politically neutral instrument of public administration but may assume some of the functions of a political party or act as an interest group. Sometimes armies act as governments. Even within bureaucracies and governments, individuals may be formally called upon to perform several roles.

[4] See Almond, *loc. cit.*, p. 30.

A shortage of competent personnel encourages such behavior either because one group may feel that the other is not performing its role in an effective manner or because the few skilled administrators are forced to take on concurrent assignments. However, the more fundamental reason for this phenomenon is that in societies just emerging from traditional status, it is not generally expected that any particular group or organization will limit itself to performing a clearly specified function. . . .

12. *In the non-Western political process there are relatively few explicitly organized interest groups with functionally specific roles.* Although there are often large numbers of informal associations in non-Western countries, such groups tend to adopt diffuse orientations that cover all phases of life in much the same manner as the political parties and cliques. It is the rare association that represents a limited and functionally specific interest. Organizations which in name and formal structure are modeled after Western interest groups, such as trade unions and chambers of commerce, generally do not have a clearly defined focus.

In many cases groups, such as trade unions and peasant associations that in form would appear to represent a specific interest, are in fact agents of the government or of a dominant party or movement. . . .

In situations where the associations are autonomous, the tendency is for them to act as protective associations and not as pressure groups. That is, their activities are concentrated on protecting their members from the consequences of governmental decisions and the political power of others. They do not seek to apply pressure openly on the government in order to influence positively the formation of public policy.

✿　✿　✿　✿　✿

13. *In the non-Western political process the national leadership must appeal to an undifferentiated public.* The lack of explicitly organized interest groups and the fact that not all participants are continuously represented in the political process deprive the national leadership of any readily available means for calculating the relative distribution of attitudes and values throughout the society. The national politician cannot easily determine the relative power of those in favor of a particular measure and those opposed; he cannot readily estimate the amount of effort needed to gain the support of the doubtful elements.

It is usually only within the circle of the elite or within the administrative structure that the national leaders can distinguish specific points of view and the relative backing that each commands. In turning to the population as a whole, the leaders find that they have few guides as to how the public may be divided over particular issues. . . .

The inability to speak to a differentiated public encourages a strong propensity toward skillful and highly emotional forms of political articulation on the part of non-Western leaders. Forced to reach for the broadest possible appeals, the political leader tends at times to concentrate heavily on nationalistic sentiments and to present himself as a representative of the nation as a whole rather than of particular interests within the society. This is one of the reasons why some leaders of non-Western countries are often seen paradoxically both as extreme nationalists and as men out of touch with the masses.

14. *The unstructured character of the non-Western political process encourages leaders to adopt more clearly defined positions on international issues than on domestic issues.* Confronted with an undifferentiated public, leaders of non-Western countries often find the international political process more clearly structured than the domestic political scene. Consequently, they can make more refined calculations as to the advantages in taking a definite position in world politics than they can in domestic politics. This situation not only encourages the leaders of some non-Western countries to seek a role in world politics that is out of proportion to their nation's power, but it also allows such leaders to concentrate more on international than on domestic affairs. It should also be noted that in adopting a supra-national role, the current leaders of non-Western countries can heighten the impression that their domestic opposition is an enemy of the national interest.

15. *In non-Western societies the affective or expressive aspect of politics tends to override the problem-solving or public-policy aspect of politics.* Traditional societies have generally developed to a very high order the affective and expressive aspects of politics. Pomp and ceremony are usually basic features of traditional politics, and those who are members of the ruling elite in such societies are generally expected to lead more interesting and exciting lives than those not involved in politics. In contrast, traditional societies have not usually emphasized politics as a means for solving social problems. Questions of policy in such societies are largely limited to providing certain minimum social and economic functions and maintaining the way of life of the elite.

✧ ✧ ✧ ✧ ✧

In part the stress on the affective or expressive aspect of politics is related to the fact that, in most non-Western countries, questions of personal loyalties and identification are recognized as providing the basic issues of politics and the bond between leader and follower is generally an emotional one. In fact, in many non-Western societies, it is considered highly improper and even immoral for people to make loyalty contingent upon their leaders' ability to solve problems of public policy.

In the many non-Western societies in which the problem of national integration is of central importance, the national leaders often feel they must emphasize the symbols and sentiments of national unity since substantive problems of policy may divide the people. . . .

16. *Charismatic leaders tend to prevail in non-Western politics.*[5] Max Weber, in highlighting the characteristics of charismatic authority, specifically related the emergence of charismatic personalities to situations in which the hold of tradition has been weakened. By implication, he suggested that societies experiencing cultural change provide an ideal setting for such leaders since a society in which there is confusion over values is more susceptible to a leader who conveys a sense of mission and appears to be God-sent.

The problem of political communication further reinforces the position of the charismatic leader. Since the population does not share the leadership's modes of reason or standards of judgment, it is difficult to communicate subtle points of view. Communication of emotions is not confronted with such barriers, especially if it is related to considerations of human character and personality. All groups within the population can feel confident of their abilities to judge the worth of a man for what he is, even though they cannot understand his mode of reasoning.

So long as a society has difficulties in communication, the charismatic leader possesses great advantage over his opponents, even though they may have greater ability in rational planning. However, the very lack of precision in the image that a charismatic leader casts, especially in relation to operational policy, does make it possible for opposition to develop as long as it does not directly challenge the leader's charisma. . . .

Charisma is likely to wear thin. A critical question in most non-Western societies that now have charismatic leaders is whether such leadership will in the meantime become institutionalized in the form of rational-legal practices. . . . The critical factor seems to be whether or not the leader encourages the development of functionally specific groups within the society that can genuinely represent particular interests.

17. *The non-Western political process operates largely without benefit of political "brokers."* In most non-Western societies there seems to be no institutionalized role for carrying out the tasks of, first, clarifying and delimiting the distribution of demands and interests within the population, and, next, engaging in the bargaining operation necessary to

5 Kahin, Pauker, and Pye, *loc. cit.*, p. 1025.

accommodate and maximize the satisfaction of those demands and interests in a fashion consistent with the requirements of public policy and administration. In other words, there are no political "brokers."

☼   ☼   ☼   ☼   ☼

In most non-Western societies, the role of the political "broker" has been partially filled by those who perform a "mediator's" role, which consists largely of transmitting the views of the elite to the masses. Such "mediators" are people sufficiently acculturated to the elite society to understand its views but who still have contacts with the more traditional masses. In performing their role, they engage essentially in a public relations operation for the elite, and only to a marginal degree do they communicate to the elite the views of the public. They do not find it essential to identify and articulate the values of their public. Generally, since their influence depends upon their relations with the national leadership, they have not sought to develop an autonomous basis of power or to identify themselves with particular segments of the population as must the political "broker." As a consequence, they have not acted in a fashion that would stimulate the emergence of functionally specific interest groups.

The following selection is drawn from one of the most influential chapters written in the field of comparative politics during the past two decades. In it, Gabriel Almond, a leading exponent of structural functionalism, develops an analytical scheme using seven functional categories. He also notes the variety of structures that may be involved in the performance of these functions. The serious student of comparative methodology will also wish to consider the criticisms of structural functionalism in general and Almond's approach in particular as well as some of the other possible approaches.

2. A FUNCTIONAL APPROACH TO COMPARATIVE POLITICS*

g a b r i e l a. a l m o n d

To find concepts and categories appropriate for the comparison of political systems differing radically in scale, structure, and culture—to say nothing of dealing adequately with the familiar phenomena of Western Europe—we have had to turn to sociological and anthropological theory. Some of the concepts we use . . . , such as *political system, political role, political culture, political structure,* and *political socialization,* have acquired a certain currency among scholars in the field. Perhaps their utility may be said to have been tested. The additional categories which we introduce here have had only a preliminary trial. . . .

It ought also to be pointed out that the search for new concepts reflected in these terms is not an *ad hoc* matter. It reflects an underlying drift toward a new and coherent way of thinking about and studying politics that is implied in such slogans as the "behavioral approach." This urge toward a new conceptual unity is suggested when we compare the new terms with the old. Thus, instead of the concept of the "state," limited as it is by legal and institutional meanings, we prefer "political system"; instead of "powers," which again is a legal concept in connotation, we are beginning to prefer "functions"; instead of "offices" (legal again), we prefer "roles"; instead of "institutions," which again directs us toward formal norms, "structures"; instead of "public opinion" and "citizenship training," formal and rational in meaning, we prefer "political culture" and "political socialization." We are not setting aside public law and philosophy as disciplines, but simply telling them to move over to make room for a growth in political theory that has been long overdue.

❄   ❄   ❄   ❄   ❄

I. THE POLITICAL SYSTEM

If the concept of political system is to serve the purpose to which we wish to put it—that is, separate out analytically the structures which

* From Gabriel A. Almond, "Introduction: A Functional Approach to Comparative Politics," in *The Politics of the Developing Areas,* eds. Gabriel A. Almond and James S. Coleman (copyright © 1960 by Princeton University Press; Princeton Paperback, 1970), pp. 3–55. Reprinted by permission.

perform political functions in all societies regardless of scale, degree of differentiation, and culture—we shall have to specify what we mean by politics and the political system. . . .

✿   ✿   ✿   ✿   ✿

. . . What we propose is that the political system is that system of interactions to be found in all independent societies which performs the functions of integration and adaptation (both internally and vis-à-vis other societies) by means of the employment, or threat of employment, of more or less legitimate physical compulsion. The political system is the legitimate, order-maintaining or transforming system in the society. We use the term "more or less" to modify legitimacy because we do not want to exclude from our definition political systems, like the totalitarian ones, where the degree of legitimacy may be very much in doubt; revolutionary systems, where the basis of legitimacy may be in process of change; or non-Western systems, in which there may be more than one legitimate system in operation. We use the term "physical compulsion" since we believe that we can distinguish political systems from other social systems only by such a specific definition, but this is by no means the same thing as reducing politics to force. Legitimate force is the thread that runs through the inputs and outputs of the political system, giving it its special quality and salience and its coherence as a system. . . .

With the conceptions of input and output we have moved from the definition of "political" to that of "system," for if by the "political" we mean to separate out a certain set of interactions in a society in order to relate it to other sets, by "system" we mean to attribute a particular set of properties to these interactions. Among these properties are (1) comprehensiveness, (2) interdependence, and (3) existence of boundaries. The criterion of comprehensiveness means that when we speak of the political system we include all the interactions—inputs as well as outputs —which affect the use or the threat of use of physical coercion. We mean to include not just the structures based on law, like parliaments, executives, bureaucracies, and courts, or just the associational or formally organized units, like parties, interest groups, and media of communication, but *all of the structures in their political aspects,* including undifferentiated structures like kinship and lineage, status and caste groups, as well as anomic phenomena like riots, street demonstrations, and the like.

By "interdependence" we mean that a change in one subset of interactions (e.g., the electoral reforms of 1832 in England) produces changes in all the other subsets (e.g., the characteristics of the party system, the functions of parliament and cabinet, and so forth). . . .

By the existence of a boundary in the political system, we mean that there are points where other systems end and the political system begins. . . .

*   *   *   *   *

II. THE COMMON PROPERTIES
OF POLITICAL SYSTEMS

The Universe of Political Systems

*   *   *   *   *

. . . What are the common properties of all political systems? What makes the Bergdama band and the United Kingdom members of the same universe? We would suggest that there are four characteristics which all political systems have in common, and in terms of which they may be compared.

1. First, all political systems, including the simplest ones, have political structure. In a sense it is correct to say that even the simplest societies have all of the types of political structure which are to be found in the most complex ones. They may be compared with one another according to the degree and form of structural specialization.

2. Second, the same functions are performed in all political systems, even though these functions may be performed with different frequencies, and by different kinds of structures. Comparisons may be made according to the frequency of the performance of the functions, the kinds of structures performing them, and the style of their performance.

3. Third, all political structure, no matter how specialized, whether it is found in primitive or in modern societies, is multifunctional. Political systems may be compared according to the degree of specificity of function in the structure; but the limiting case, while specialized, still involves substantial multifunctionality.

4. Fourth, all political systems are "mixed" systems in the cultural sense. There are no "all-modern" cultures and structures, in the sense of rationality, and no all-primitive ones, in the sense of traditionality. They differ in the relative dominance of the one as against the other, and in the pattern of mixture of the two components.

The Universality of Political Structure

There is no such thing as a society which maintains internal and external order, which has no "political structure"—i.e., legitimate patterns of interaction by means of which this order is maintained. Furthermore, all the types of political structures which are to be found in the modern systems are to be found in the non-Western and primitive ones. The interactions, or the structures, may be occasional or intermittent. They may not be clearly visible, but to say that there are no structures would be to argue that the performance of the political function is random. . . .

. . . An adequate analysis of a political system must locate and characterize all of these functions, and not simply those performed by the specialized political structure. . . . The rule to follow which we suggest here is: If the functions are there, then the structures must be, even though we may find them tucked away, so to speak, in nooks and crannies of other social systems.

The Universality of the Political Functions

But if all the structures which are to be found in specialized Western systems are also to be found in the non-Western, we are able to locate them only if we ask the correct functional questions. . . .

✿ ✿ ✿ ✿ ✿

. . . The particular functional categories which we employ . . . were developed for the purpose of comparing political systems as whole systems; and particularly for comparing the modern Western ones with the transitional and traditional.

They were derived in a very simple way. The problem essentially was to ask a series of questions based on the distinctive political activities existing in Western complex systems. In other words, we derived our functional categories from the political systems in which structural specialization and functional differentiation have taken place to the greatest extent. Thus the functions performed by associational interest groups in Western systems led us to the question, "How are interests articulated in different political systems?" or the *interest articulation* function. The functions performed by political parties in Western political systems led us to the question, "How are articulated demands or interests aggregated or combined in different political systems?" or the *aggregative function.* The functions performed by specialized media of communication in Western political systems led us to the question, "How is political information communicated in different political systems?" or the *political communication function.* The existence in all political systems of methods of political recruitment and training led us to the question, "How are people recruited to and socialized into political roles and orientations in different political systems?" or the *recruit-*

ment and *socialization function.* Finally, the three authoritative governmental functions, *rule-making, rule application,* and *rule adjudication,* are the old functions of "separation of powers," except that an effort has been made to free them of their structural overtones—rule-making rather than "legislation," rule application rather than "administration." Indeed, this taking over intact of the three functions of "separation of powers" reflects the political bias of this undertaking. It was the conviction of the collaborators in this study that the political functions rather than the governmental ones, the input functions rather than the output, would be most important in characterizing non-Western political systems, and in discriminating types and stages of political development among them.

Our functional categories therefore are as follows:

    A. Input functions
        1. Political socialization and recruitment
        2. Interest articulation
        3. Interest aggregation
        4. Political communication
    B. Output functions
        5. Rule-making
        6. Rule application
        7. Rule adjudication

✻ ✻ ✻ ✻ ✻

III. THE FUNCTIONS OF THE POLITICAL SYSTEM

Political Socialization and Recruitment

✻ ✻ ✻ ✻ ✻

What do we mean by the function of political socialization? We mean that all political systems tend to perpetuate their cultures and structures through time, and that they do this mainly by means of the socializing influences of the primary and secondary structures through which the young of the society pass in the process of maturation. We use the qualifier "mainly" deliberately, since political socialization, like learning in general, does not terminate at the point of maturation, however this is defined in different societies. It is continuous throughout life. . . .

✻ ✻ ✻ ✻ ✻

Political socialization is the process of induction into the political culture. Its end product is a set of attitudes—cognitions, value standards, and feelings—toward the political system, its various roles, and role incumbents. It also includes knowledge of, values affecting, and feelings toward the inputs of demands and claims into the system, and its authoritative outputs.

In comparing the political socialization function in different political systems, it becomes necessary to examine the structures which are involved in the function and the style of the socialization. . . .

❂   ❂   ❂   ❂   ❂

The analysis of the political socialization function in a particular society is basic to the whole field of political analysis, since it not only gives us insight into the pattern of political culture and subcultures in that society, but also locates for us in the socialization processes of the society the points where particular qualities and elements of the political culture are introduced, and the points in the society where these components are being sustained or modified. Furthermore, the study of political socialization and political culture is essential to the understanding of the other political functions. . . .

The relationship between the political socialization function and the *political recruitment function* is comparable to the relationship between Linton's "basic personality" and "status" or "role" personality.[1] All members of societies go through common socialization experiences. Differences in the political cultures of societies are introduced by differences in the political socialization processes in the subcultures of that society, and by differences in socialization into different status groups and roles.

The political recruitment function takes up where the general political socialization function leaves off. It recruits members of the society out of particular subcultures—religious communities, statuses, classes, ethnic communities, and the like—and inducts them into the specialized roles of the political system, trains them in the appropriate skills, provides them with political cognitive maps, values, expectations, and affects.

In comparing the political recruitment function in different political systems, we have again to consider—as we did in the analysis of the political socialization function—the social and political structures which perform the function and the style of the performance. We have to examine in each political system the role of family, kinship, and lineage in recruitment to specialized political roles, status and caste, religious community, ethnic and linguistic origins, social class, schooling and

---

[1] Ralph Linton, *The Cultural Background of Personality*. New York, 1945, pp. 125 ff.

training institutions. We have to examine the structures affecting specific induction patterns—political parties, election systems, bureaucratic examining systems, "in-role political socialization," and channels of recruitment and advancement within the political and authoritative governmental structures. . . .

Styles of political recruitment may be compared according to the way in which ascriptive and particularistic criteria combine with performance and universalistic criteria. Thus, in a modern Western political system, recruitment is affected both by ascriptive and by performance criteria. Kinship, friendship, "school ties," religious affiliation, and status qualities affect recruitment in various important ways, but the more thorough-going the political modernization, the more these ascriptive criteria are contained within or limited by achievement criteria—educational levels, performance levels on examinations, formal records of achievement in political roles, and the like. But the recruitment pattern is both structurally and culturally dualistic. Similarly, in the primitive or traditional political system the recruitment function is dualistic, but the achievement or performance criterion is less explicitly and generally applied. A chief or headman is selected because of his place in a lineage. He may be removed for poor performance according to either sacred or secular norms. He is replaced again by ascriptive criteria.

*   *   *   *   *

Interest Articulation

Every political system has some way of articulating interests, claims, demands for political action. The function of interest articulation . . . is closely related to the political socialization function and the patterns of political culture produced by it. Among the input functions, interest articulation is of crucial importance since it occurs at the boundary of the political system. The particular structures which perform the articulation function and the style of their performance determine the character of the boundary between polity and society.

In characterizing the interest articulation function in a political system and in comparing it with that of other political systems, we have to discover first what kinds of structures perform the function and, second, the style of their performance. Four main types of structures may be involved in interest articulation: (1) institutional interest groups, (2) non-associational interest groups, (3) anomic interest groups, and (4) associational interest groups.

By institutional interest groups we have in mind phenomena occurring within such organizations as legislatures, political executives, armies, bureaucracies, churches, and the like. These are organizations which perform other social or political functions but which, as corporate bodies or through groups within them (such as legislative blocs, officer cliques, higher or lower clergy or religious orders, departments, skill groups, and ideological cliques in bureaucracies), may articulate their own interests or represent the interests of groups in the society.

By non-associational interests we have in mind kinship and lineage groups, ethnic, regional, religious, status and class groups which articulate interests informally, and intermittently, through individuals, cliques, family and religious heads, and the like. Examples might be the complaint of a tribal chief to a paramount chief about tributes or law enforcement affecting his lineage group; a request made by a landowner to a bureaucrat in a social club regarding the tariff on grains; or the complaint of an informal delegation from a linguistic group regarding language instruction in the schools.

The distinguishing characteristic of the institutional interest group is the fact that a formally organized body made up of professionally employed officials or employees, with another function, performs an interest articulation function, or constitutes a base of operations for a clique or subgroup which does. The distinguishing characteristic of the non-associational interest is that the structure of interest articulation is intermittent and often informal.

By anomic interest groups we mean more or less spontaneous breakthroughs into the political system from the society, such as riots and demonstrations. Their distinguishing characteristic is their relative structural and functional lability. We use the term "relative" advisedly, since riots and demonstrations may be deliberately organized and controlled. But even when organized and controlled they have the potentiality of exceeding limits and norms and disturbing or even changing the political system. Though they may begin as interest articulation structures, they may end up performing a recruitment function (i.e., transferring power from one group to another), a rule-making function (i.e., changing the constitution, enacting, revising, or rescinding statutes), a rule application function (i.e., freeing prisoners, rescinding a bureaucratic decision), a rule adjudication function (i.e., "trying" and lynching), an aggregative or a communication function (drawing other interest groups to it, or publicizing a protest).

Associational interest groups are the specialized structures of interest articulation—trade unions, organizations of businessmen or industrialists, ethnic associations, associations organized by religious denominations, civic groups, and the like. Their particular characteristics are explicit representation of the interests of a particular group, orderly procedures for the formulation of interests and demands, and transmission of these demands to other political structures such as political parties, legislatures, bureaucracies.

✿   ✿   ✿   ✿   ✿

The structure and style of interest articulation define the pattern of boundary maintenance between the polity and the society, and within the political system affect the boundaries between the various parts of the political system—parties, legislatures, bureaucracies, and courts. For example, a high incidence of anomic interest articulation will mean poor boundary maintenance between the society and the polity, frequent eruptions of unprocessed claims without controlled direction into the political system. It will affect boundary maintenance within the political system by performing aggregative, rule-making, rule application, and rule adjudication functions outside of appropriate channels and without benefit of appropriate process.

A high incidence of institutional interest articulation is also an indication of poor boundary maintenance between the polity and the society and within the political system. Thus the direct impingement of a church (or parts of a church) or of business corporations on the political system introduces raw or diffuse claims and demands difficult to process or aggregate with other inputs into the political system. Within the political system a high incidence of interest articulation by bureaucratic or military groups creates boundary difficulties among rule application, rule-making, articulative, and aggregative structures, and may indeed result in their atrophy. A high incidence of non-associational interest articulation—in other words, the performance of the interest articulation function intermittently by individuals, informal groups, or representatives of kinship or status groups, and so forth—similarly may represent poor boundary maintenance between the polity and the society. . . . Finally, a high incidence of associational interest articulation may indicate good boundary maintenance between society and polity and may contribute to such maintenance within the subsystems of the political system. Good boundary maintenance is attained by virtue of the regulatory role of associational interest groups in processing raw claims or interest articulations occurring elsewhere in the society and the political system, and directing them in an orderly way and in aggregable form through the party system, legislature, and bureaucracy.

✿   ✿   ✿   ✿   ✿

The Function of Aggregation

Every political system has some way of aggregating the interests, claims, and demands which have been articulated by the interest groups of the polity. Aggregation may be accomplished by means of the formulation of general policies in which interests are combined, accommodated, or otherwise taken account of, or by means of the recruitment of political personnel, more or less committed to a particular pattern of policy. The functions of articulation and aggregation overlap, just as do those of aggregation, recruitment, and rule-making. In certain political systems, such as the authoritarian and the primitive ones, the three functions of articulation, aggregation, and rule-making may be hardly differentiated from one another. In what appears to be a single act, a headman of a primitive society may read cues in his people, aggregate different cues and complaints, and issue an authoritative rule. We might say that he is intermittently interest articulator, aggregator, and rule-maker in the course of this process. . . .

The distinction between interest articulation and aggregation is a fluid one. The narrowest event of interest articulation initiated by a lineage head in a primitive political system, or the smallest constituent unit of a trade association, involves the aggregation of the claims of even smaller groups or of individuals or firms. Modern interest groups—particularly the "peak" associations—carry aggregation quite far, sometimes to the point of "speaking for" whole classes of the society—"labor," "agriculture," "business."

In our definition we reserve the term "aggregation" for the more inclusive levels of the combinatory processes, reserving the term "articulation" for the narrower expressions of interest. This is not the same thing as identifying interest articulation with "pressure groups" and aggregation with "political parties," though again in the developed modern systems these agencies have a distinctive and regulatory relation to these functions.

Actually the aggregative function may be performed within all of the subsystems of the political system—legislative bodies, political executives (cabinets, presidencies, kingships, chieftainships), bureaucracies, media of communication, party systems, interest groups of the various types. Parties, factions, blocs in legislatures; cliques or factions in political executives and bureaucracies; individual parties or party coalitions outside the legislature; and individual interest groups (in particular the civic or "general interest" groups) or *ad hoc* coalitions of interest groups —all perform an aggregative function, either by formulating alternative public policies or by supporting or advocating changes in political personnel.

But again it is the party system which is the distinctively modern structure of political aggregation and which in the modern, developed, democratic political system "regulates" or gives order to the performance of the aggregative function by the other structures. Without a party system the aggregative function may be performed covertly, diffusely, and particularistically, as in a political system such as Spain. . . .

. . . [P]arty systems are classified under four headings (1) authori-

tarian, (2) dominant non-authoritarian, (3) competitive two-party systems, and (4) competitive multiparty systems. Authoritarian party systems may in turn be classified into the totalitarian and authoritarian
varieties. Totalitarian parties aggregate interests by means of the penetration of the social structure of the society and by the transmission and
aggregation of demands and claims through the party structure. Overt
interest articulation is permissible only at the lowest level of individual
complaints against the lower-echelon authorities. Above this level, interest articulation and aggregation are latent or covert. . . .

Authoritarian parties . . . have some of the properties of totalitarian parties, except that the penetration of the party into the social
structure is less complete and some interest groups are permitted to
articulate demands overtly. . . .

Dominant non-authoritarian party systems are usually to be found
in political systems where nationalist movements have been instrumental in attaining emancipation. Most of the significant interest groups,
associational and non-associational, have joined in the nationalist movement around a common program of national independence. In the period following emancipation the nationalist party continues as the greatly dominant party, opposed in elections by relatively small left-wing or
traditionalist and particularist movements. This type of party system is a
formally free one, but the possibility of a coherent loyal opposition is
lacking. Hence the dominant party is confronted by a complex problem
of interest aggregation. . . .

The third type of party system is the competitive two-party system
exemplified by the United Kingdom, the members of the old Commonwealth, and the United States. . . .

Multiparty systems may be divided into two classes—the so-called
"working" multiparty systems of the Scandinavian area and the Low
Countries, and the "immobilist" multiparty systems of France and Italy.
In the Scandinavian version of the multiparty system, some of the parties
are broadly aggregative. . . . Secondly, the political culture is more
homogeneous and fusional of secular and traditional elements. . . .

The characteristics of the "immobilist" type of multiparty system
have been referred to in the discussion of the articulation function
above. In comparison to the working multiparty system, with its relatively homogeneous political culture, the political socialization processes
in countries such as France and Italy tend to produce a fragmented,
isolative political culture, and as a consequence the relations between
interest groups and parties are not of an instrumental bargaining kind.
The boundaries between the articulative and aggregative functions are
poorly maintained. . . .

We may also compare the performance of the aggregative function
in different political systems in terms of its style. We may distinguish
three different kinds of parties from this point of view: (1) secular,

"pragmatic," bargaining parties; (2) absolute value-oriented, *Weltan-schauung* or ideological parties; and (3) particularistic or traditional parties. The secular, pragmatic, bargaining type of party is instrumental and multivalue-oriented and its aggregative potential is relatively high. It is capable of generalized and adaptive programs intended to attract the maximum of interest support. . . .

The *Weltanschauung* or ideological party is absolute value-oriented and is usually revolutionary, reactionary, or oriented toward national independence or power. . . . [T]hey penetrate deeply into the society, almost replace all other social structures and, once securely rooted, are most difficult to dislodge by means short of violence.

The "particularistic" party is limited in its aggregative potential by being identified completely with the interests of a particular ethnic or religious group. . . .

❃   ❃   ❃   ❃   ❃

The Political Communication Function

All of the functions performed in the political system—political socialization and recruitment, interest articulation, interest aggregation, rule-making, rule application, and rule adjudication—are performed *by means of* communication. Parents, teachers, and priests, for example, impart political socialization through communication. Interest group leaders and representatives and party leaders perform their articulation and aggregation functions by communicating demands and policy recommendations. Legislators enact laws on the basis of information communicated to them and by communicating with one another and with other elements of the political system. In performing their functions, bureaucrats receive and analyze information from the society and from various parts of the polity. Similarly, the judicial process is carried on by means of communication.

At first thought, it might appear that there is no political communication function as such, that communication is an aspect of all of the other political functions. But a view such as this comes into conflict with the fact that in the modern political system differentiated media of communication have arisen which have developed a vocational ethics of "neutral" or objective communication. This ethics requires that the dissemination of information ought to be separated from the other political functions such as interest articulation, aggregation, and recruitment.

The separating-out of the communication function is not unique to modern political systems. . . . Primitive political systems have their drummers and runners, medieval towns had their criers, noblemen and kings their heralds. Even when there is no specialized political communicator, we can distinguish in the combined performance of, for example, the interest articulation and communication function the articulative event from the event of communicating the act of articulation. Thus a labor news medium may both advocate a trade union policy and communicate the content of that policy.

Failure to separate out the political communication function from the other political functions would deprive us of an essential tool necessary for distinguishing among political systems and characterizing their performance. It is not accidental that those political systems which have homogeneous political cultures and autonomous and differentiated structures of interest articulation and aggregation—the United Kingdom, the old Commonwealth, and the United States—also have to the greatest extent autonomous and differentiated media of communication. Nor is it accidental that the political systems with fragmented political cultures and relatively undifferentiated structures of interest articulation and aggregation—France and Italy, for example—also have a "press" which tends to be dominated by interest groups and political parties. The whole pattern of function in these political systems is affected by and tends to sustain a fragmented political culture. The control over the media of communication by parties and interest groups means that the audience for political communications is fragmented.

Thus it is essential in characterizing a political system to analyze the performance of the communication function. . . .

✿   ✿   ✿   ✿   ✿

But here, as in the treatment of the other functions, we have to avoid polarizations. The political communication networks of modern political systems are full of latent, diffuse, particularistic, and affective messages. . . .

In order to illustrate this mode of analysis of the political communication function, it may be useful to compare its performance in a modern Western system such as the United States with its performance in a transitional political system such as India. The comparison may be made in four respects: (1) the homogeneity of political information; (2) the mobility of information; (3) the volume of information; (4) the direction of the flow of information.

With respect to the homogeneity of political information, the point has already been made that the existence of autonomous and specialized media of communication and their penetration of the polity as a whole in modern Western political systems do not eliminate latent, diffuse, particularistic, and affective messages but only tend to afford opportunities throughout the political system for such messages to be couched in a manifest, specific, general, and instrumental language of politics. There is, in other words, a system whereby these messages are made manifest and homogeneous. . . . In contrast, in a transitional political system the messages in the communication network are heterogeneous. In the urban, relatively modern areas, specialized media of communication are to be found, but they tend to be organs of interest groups or political parties. Even in the cities, among the illiterate and uneducated elements of the urban population, the impact of the specialized media of communication is relatively limited. The illiterate and certainly the newly urbanized elements of the population tend to persist in a traditional, rural-type network of communication, with kinship, lineage, caste, and language groupings performing the political communication function intermittently, diffusely, and particularistically.

Although here too there are interpreters standing between the modernized and the non-modernized sectors of the urban populations, the problem of interpretation is much more difficult than in the modern Western system. The opinion leader in the United States receives information from the mass media and interprets it for his "opinion followers." These opinion followers tend to speak the same language, share the same values, and have cognitive maps similar to the ones conveyed in the mass media. The politician or interest group leader in an Indian urban area faces a far greater gap between the communication content of the literate modern sector of the Indian city and the illiterate and traditional sector. The gap is one of culture; it may include language in the specific sense, values, and cognitive maps differing radically in amount and specificity of information and in the range of political objects which they include. What has been said of the communication gap in the urban areas of a country like India is true to an even greater extent of connections between the urban and rural and village areas. Here, the problem of interpretation is a massive one. The interpreter, whether he be a bureaucrat, interest group leader, or party leader, cannot readily find equivalents in language, values, and cognitive material to make an accurate translation. There is a genuine block in communication between the urban central and the rural and village periphery. No real penetration by communication is possible, and the audience of the polity consists of a loosely articulated congeries of subaudiences.

This takes us to the second major point of contrast between a modern Western and a transitional system of political communication—the mobility of information. In a modern Western system, neutral information flows freely throughout the polity, from the initiators of information into the neutral secondary media of communication, and into the capillaries of primary communication. In a transitional system, information circulates relatively freely in the urban areas, but never penetrates fully the diffuse and undifferentiated networks of the traditional and rural areas. Obstacles to mobility exist in both the input and the output process.

Third, in the modern Western system, the volume of political information passing through the communication network is far greater than in a transitional system. . . . The volume of flow in a transitional system is uneven. Much information remains covert and latent, and it is consequently difficult to make political estimates accurately and quickly.

Finally, there are important differences in the direction of the flow of information. The output of messages from the authoritative governmental structures in a transitional system tends to be far larger than the input of messages from the society. The government employs the mass media and operates through its own media as well. To be sure, governmental messages cannot be accurately transmitted to "tribesmen," "kinsmen," and "villagers." They may hear the messages over the radio, but they cannot register their meaning precisely. Nevertheless the messages get there physically. On the input side, much important information regarding the needs of the base and periphery of the society never gets explicated, and cannot therefore be fully taken account of by other elements in the political system.

✿ ✿ ✿ ✿ ✿

The Governmental Functions: Rule-Making, Rule Application, Rule Adjudication

. . . [In the analysis of developing areas], far greater stress . . . [must be] placed on the political functions than on the governmental. The primary reasons for this are the indeterminacy of the formal governmental structures in most of the non-Western areas, and the gross deviations in the performance of the governmental functions from the constitutional and legal norms. Most of these political systems either have had, have now, or aspire to constitutions which provide for legislatures, executives, and judiciaries. In the distribution of legal powers they follow either the British, the American, or the French model. But it is the exceptional case in which these institutions perform in any way corresponding to these norms. A careful examination of governmental structures and their formal powers would have yielded little of predictive value.

On the other hand, a careful examination of the political culture of these political systems, the factors making for change, the political socialization processes, patterns of recruitment into politics, and the characteristics of the infrastructure—interest groups, political parties, and media of communication—yield some insight into the directions and tempo of political change. . . .

In a recent paper Shils[2] classifies the "new states" of the non-

[2] Edward Shils, *"Political Development in the New States"* (mimeographed paper prepared for the Committee on Comparative Politics, Social Science Research Council, 1959).

Western world into five groups: (1) political democracies, (2) "tutelary" democracies, (3) modernizing oligarchies, (4) totalitarian oligarchies, and (5) traditional oligarchies. Although these are classes of *political systems*, they each imply a particular state of governmental structure.

The political democracies are those systems with functioning and relatively autonomous legislatures, executives, courts, and with differentiated and autonomous interest groups, political parties, and media of communication. In the non-Western areas, Japan, Turkey, Israel, and Chile are examples which approximate this type.

Tutelary democracies are political systems which have adopted both the formal norms of the democratic polity—universal suffrage, freedom of association, and of speech and publication—and the structural forms of democracy. In addition, the elites of these systems have the goal of democratizing their polities even though they may be unclear as to the requirements—in particular, the requirements in political infrastructure and function. In reality, as Shils points out, these systems are characterized by a concentration of power in the executive and the bureaucracy. The legislature tends to be relatively powerless, and the independence of the judiciary has not been fully attained. A country such as Ghana comes close to this model.

Modernizing oligarchies are political systems controlled by bureaucratic and/or army officer cliques in which democratic constitutions have been suspended or in which they do not exist. The goals of the elites may or may not include democratization. The modernizing impulse usually takes the form of a concern for efficiency and rationality, and an effort to eliminate corruption and traditionality. Modernizing oligarchies are usually strongly motivated toward economic development. The governmental structure of modernizing oligarchies concentrates powers in the hands of a clique of military officers or bureaucrats who are usually placed in control of the chief ministries. Turkey under Atatürk and contemporary Pakistan and the Sudan are examples of modernizing oligarchies.

Totalitarian oligarchy such as exists in North Korea and Viet Minh differs from modernizing oligarchy by the degree of penetration of the society by the polity, the degree of concentration of power in the ruling elite, and the tempo of social mobilization. There have been two types of totalitarianism—the Bolshevist and the traditionalist, such as Nazi Germany and Fascist Italy. Two criteria distinguish the Bolshevist version from the traditional version. National Socialism and Fascism left some autonomy to other institutions, such as the Church, economic interest groups, and kinship and status groups. In addition, its goals took the form of an extremely militant and charismatic nationalism. The Bolshevist version is more thoroughly penetrative of the society, and its goals are revolutionary and global.

Traditional oligarchy is usually monarchic and dynastic in form, based on custom rather than constitution or statute. The ruling elite and the bureaucracy are recruited on the basis of kinship or status. The central governmental institutions control local kinship, lineage, or territorial units only to a limited extent. The goals of the elite are primarily maintenance goals; the capacity and mechanisms for adaptation and change are present only to a limited extent. Nepal, Saudi Arabia, and Yemen are examples of traditional oligarchy.

✿ ✿ ✿ ✿ ✿

The most frequent types of political systems to be found in the non-Western areas are tutelary democracies and modernizing and traditionalistic oligarchies. From a functional point of view, the tutelary democracy tends to concentrate—to a far greater extent than is true of developed democracies—the rule-making function and the rule application function in the executive and the bureaucracy. Because of the rudimentary character of the party system, the interest group system, and the modern media of communication, the executive and the bureaucracy are far more dominant in the performance of the political functions than they are in developed democracies. Furthermore, the cultural dualism of the tutelary democracy is either "isolative" or "incorporative," rather than "fusional," in character. Nevertheless the elites of the tutelary democracies have in their goal system, more or less clearly spelled out, the functional properties of the modern differentiated, fusional political system, with its autonomies and its boundary maintenance pattern.

The modernizing oligarchies are characterized to an even greater extent by the concentration of functions in a ruling clique and in the bureaucracy, and by the absence of a competitive party system. The activities of associational interest groups, to the extent that they exist, are greatly limited, and the media of communication are controlled. But though the activities of interest groups are limited, there is an overt, pluralistic system of interest articulation in which local communities, informal status and lineage groups, and institutional groups take part. Like the tutelary democracy, the modernizing oligarchy is characterized by an incorporative or isolative dualism. Particularistic, diffuse, and ascriptive groups perform the political functions, along with groups that are characterized by "modern" styles although not necessarily penetrated by them.

The development of modern structure in traditionalistic oligarchies is defensive. Thus only the army, the police, and parts of the civil bureaucracy are rationalized in order to control or prevent modernizing tendencies in the society. Thus, while a modernizing oligarchy may use an authoritarian party as an instrument of mobilization and aggregation, this is less likely in a traditionalistic oligarchy where the aggregative, articulative, and communication functions are usually performed by the bureaucracy and/or the army, as well as by kinship or tribal units, status groups, and local units such as villages.

While there is justification for having underplayed the governmental structures in this study, their neglect in the development of the theory of the functions of the polity represents a serious shortcoming in the present analysis. The threefold classification of governmental or output functions into rule-making, rule application, and rule adjudication will not carry us very far in our efforts at precise comparison of the performance of political systems. . . .

What constitutes political development? Despite the attention given to this important subject ever since the former colonies began to achieve their independence after World War II, the concept and the measures of political development have remained quite elusive. One of the more widely accepted formulations of political development is provided below; in it, political development is conceptualized as the increasing ability of a society to deal successfully with six major problems confronting all societies. As yet, no simple measure has been devised which can distinguish easily and precisely the successes and failures of a society in coping with these problems. Consequently, only rather general categories of development are available for purposes of comparing the political development of the various states of the world.

3. THE CONCEPT OF POLITICAL DEVELOPMENT*

l u c i a n   w.   p y e

Some members of the Committee on Comparative Politics of the Social Science Research Council have suggested that it may be useful to conceptualize the processes of political development as involving essentially

*   From *Aspects of Political Development* by Lucian W. Pye. Copyright (c) 1966, Little, Brown and Company (Inc.). Reprinted by permission of the publisher, Little, Brown and Company (Inc.). Selections from pp. 63–67.

six crises that may be met in different sequences but all of which must be successfully dealt with for a society to become a modern nation-state.[1]

The Identity Crisis. The first and most fundamental crisis is that of achieving a common sense of identity. The people in a new state must come to recognize their national territory as being their true homeland, and they must feel as individuals that their own personal identities are in part defined by their identification with their territorially delimited country. In most of the new states traditional forms of identity ranging from tribe or caste to ethnic and linguistic groups compete with the sense of larger national identity.

The identity crisis also involves the resolution of the problem of traditional heritage and modern practices, the dilemma of parochial sentiments and cosmopolitan practices. . . . As long as people feel pulled between two worlds and without roots in any society they cannot have the firm sense of identity necessary for building a stable, modern nation-state.

The Legitimacy Crisis. Closely related to the identity crisis is the problem of achieving agreement about the legitimate nature of authority and the proper responsibilities of government. In many new states the crisis of legitimacy is a straightforward constitutional problem: What should be the relationship between central and local authorities? What are the proper limits of the bureaucracy, or of the army, in the nation's political life? Or possibly the conflict is over how much of the colonial structure of government should be preserved in an independent state.

In other new states the question of legitimacy is more diffuse, and it involves sentiments about what should be the underlying spirit of government and the primary goals of national effort. For example, in some Moslem lands there is a deep desire that the state should in some fashion reflect the spirit of Islam. In other societies the issue of legitimacy involves questions about how far the governmental authorities should directly push economic development as compared with other possible goals. Above all, in transitional societies there can be a deep crisis of authority because all attempts at ruling are challenged by different people for different reasons, and no leaders are able to gain a full command of legitimate authority.

The Penetration Crisis. The critical problems of administration in the new states give rise to the penetration crisis, which involves the problems of government in reaching down into the society and effecting basic policies. . . . [I]n traditional societies government had limited

---

[1] The following analysis of the "crises of development" is based on the forthcoming study by Leonard Binder, James S. Coleman, Joseph LaPalombara, Myron Weiner, and Lucian W. Pye, which will be published by the Princeton University Press as the seventh volume of the Series in Political Development sponsored by the Committee on Comparative Politics of the Social Science Research Council.

demands to make on the society, and in most transitional systems the governments are far more ambitious. This is particularly true if the rulers seek to accelerate the pace of economic development and social change. To carry out significant developmental policies a government must be able to reach down to the village level and touch the daily lives of people.

Yet, . . . a dominant characteristic of transitional societies is the gap between the world of the ruling elite and that of the masses of the people who are still oriented toward their parochial ways. The penetration problem is that of building up the effectiveness of the formal institutions by government and of establishing confidence and rapport between rulers and subjects. Initially governments often find it difficult to motivate the population or to change its values and habits in order to bring support to programs of national development. On the other hand, at times the effectiveness of the government in breaking down old patterns of control can unleash widespread demands for a greater influence on governmental policies. When this occurs the result is another crisis, that of participation.

The Participation Crisis. . . . The participation crisis occurs when there is uncertainty over the appropriate rate of expansion [of popular participation] and when the influx of new participants creates serious strains on the existing institutions. As new segments of the population are brought into the political process, new interests and new issues begin to arise so that the continuity of the old polity is broken and there is the need to reestablish the entire structure of political relations.

In a sense the participation crisis arises out of the emergence of interest groups and the formation of a party system. The question in many new states is whether the expansion in participation is likely to be effectively organized into specific interest groups or whether the pressures will lead only to mass demands and widespread feelings of anomie. It should also be noted that the appearance of a participation crisis does not necessarily signal pressures for democratic processes. The participation crisis can be organized as in totalitarian states to provide the basis for manipulated mass organizations and demonstrational politics.

Integration Crisis. This crisis covers the problems of relating popular politics to governmental performance, and thus it represents the effective and compatible solution of both the penetration and the participation crises. The problem of integration therefore deals with the extent to which the entire polity is organized as a system of interacting relationships, first among the offices and agencies of government, and then among the various groups and interests seeking to make demands upon the system, and finally in the relationships between officials and articulating citizens.

In many of the transitional systems there may be many different groupings of interests, but they hardly interact with each other, and at best each seeks to make its separate demands upon the government. The government must seek to cope with all these demands simultaneously. Yet at the same time the government itself may not be well integrated. The result is a low level of general performance throughout the political system.

The Distribution Crisis. The final crisis in the development process involves questions about how governmental powers are to be used to influence the distribution of goods, services, and values throughout the society. Who is to benefit from government, and what should the government be doing to bring greater benefits to different segments of the society?

Much of the stress on economic development and the popularity of socialist slogans in the new states is a reflection of the basic crisis. In some cases governments seek to meet the problem by directly intervening in the distribution of wealth; in other cases the approach is to strengthen the opportunities and potentialities of the disadvantaged groups.

The Sequences of Development. The particular pattern of development in any country depends largely upon the sequence in which these crises arise and the ways in which they are resolved. It is noteworthy that in the history of England, the model of modern democracies, development tended to follow a path in which the crises arose somewhat separately and largely according to the order in which we have just outlined them. The English developed a sense of national identity early, the issue of the legitimacy of the monarchy and government was well established before the problem of expanding participation appeared and, finally, serious issues of distribution did not arise until after the political system was relatively well integrated.

In contrast, development of the continental European system followed more chaotic patterns. In Italy and Germany the prelude of nation-building did not involve a resolution of the issue of national identity. In France questions of legitimacy and the realities of inadequate integration have persistently frustrated national performance and intensified the crisis of distribution. It was, indeed, the cumulativeness and simultaneity of the crises on the continent that produced the striking differences between the European and the British systems.

The story in modern Asia and Africa seems to be closer to the continental experience than either the British or American. In most of the new states the crises are all appearing simultaneously, and governments are, for example, striving to use the distribution crisis to resolve the identity problem. The efforts to raise the standards of living in these cases are in large part related to creating feelings of basic loyalty to the nation, and this procedure raises the question of how stable such states can become if their citizens' sense of identity is tied too closely to the effectiveness of particular policies.

Although it was apparent to many observers that most of the new states being created after World War II were ill-prepared to assume the full burdens of statehood, a troubled optimism nevertheless prevailed for a time that somehow progress and development would occur. However, it became increasingly clear that even if social and economic development did take place, political development was not assured. The common assumptions about the relationship between economic progress and political progress were not proving to be true. In the excerpt below, Samuel Huntington examines some of the interactions that exist among different types of development, some of which are inimical to the growth of political institutions.

4. POLITICAL DEVELOPMENT AND POLITICAL DECAY [*][†]

s a m u e l   p.   h u n t i n g t o n

"Among the laws that rule human societies," de Tocqueville said, "there is one which seems to be more precise and clear than all others. If men are to remain civilized or to become so, the art of associating together must grow and improve in the same ratio in which the equality of conditions is increased."[1] In much of the world today, equality of political participation is growing much more rapidly than is the "art of associating together." The rates of mobilization and participation are high; the rates of organization and institutionalization are low. De Tocqueville's precondition for civilized society is in danger, if it is not already undermined. In these societies, the conflict between mobilization and institutionalization is the crux of politics. Yet in the fast-growing literature on the politics of the developing areas, political institutionalization usually receives scant treatment. Writers on political development emphasize the processes of modernization and the closely

[*] Excerpts from "Political Development and Political Decay" by Samuel P. Huntington, *World Politics*, Vol. XVII, No. 3 (April, 1965), pp. 386–411. By permission.
[†] I am grateful to the Center for International Affairs, Harvard University, for the support which made this article possible and to Edward C. Banfield, Mather Eliot, Milton J. Esman, H. Field Haviland, Jr., and John D. Montgomery, for their helpful written comments on an earlier draft.
[1] *Democracy in America* (Phillips Bradley edn., New York 1955), II, 118.

related phenomena of social mobilization and increasing political participation. A balanced view of the politics of contemporary Asia, Africa, and Latin America requires more attention to the "art of associating together" and the growth of political institutions. For this purpose, it is useful to distinguish political development from modernization and to identify political development with the institutionalization of political organizations and procedures. Rapid increases in mobilization and participation, the principal political aspects of modernization, undermine political institutions. Rapid modernization, in brief, produces not political development, but political decay.

° ° ° ° °

There is thus much to be gained (as well as something to be lost) by conceiving of political development as a process independent of, although obviously affected by, the process of modernization. In view of the crucial importance of the relationship between mobilization and participation, on the one hand, and the growth of political organizations, on the other, it is useful for many purposes to define political development as the institutionalization of political organizations and procedures. This concept liberates development from modernization. It can be applied to the analysis of political systems of any sort, not just modern ones. It can be defined in reasonably precise ways which are at least theoretically capable of measurement. As a concept, it does not suggest that movement is likely to be in only one direction: institutions, we know, decay and dissolve as well as grow and mature. Most significantly, it focuses attention on the reciprocal interaction between the ongoing social processes of modernization, on the one hand, and the strength, stability, or weakness of political structures, traditional, transitional, or modern, on the other.[2]

The strength of political organizations and procedures varies with their *scope of support* and their *level of institutionalization*. Scope refers simply to the extent to which the political organizations and procedures encompass activity in the society. If only a small upper-class group belongs to political organizations and behaves in terms of a set of procedures, the scope is limited. If, on the other hand, a large segment of the population is politically organized and follows the political procedures, the scope is broad. Institutions are stable, valued, recurring

---

[2] The concept of institutionalization has, of course, been used by other writers concerned with political development—most notably, S. N. Eisenstadt. His definition, however, differs significantly from my approach here. See, in particular, his "Initial Institutional Patterns of Political Modernisation," *Civilisations*, XII (No. 4, 1962), 461–72, and XIII (No. 1, 1963), 15–26; "Institutionalization and Change," *American Sociological Review*, XXIX (April 1964), 235–47; "Social Change, Differentiation and Evolution," *ibid.*, XXIX (June 1964), 375–86.

patterns of behavior. Organizations and procedures vary in their degree of institutionalization. Harvard University and the newly opened suburban high school are both organizations, but Harvard is much more of an institution than is the high school. The seniority system in Congress and President Johnson's select press conferences are both procedures, but seniority is much more institutionalized than are Mr. Johnson's methods of dealing with the press. Institutionalization is the process by which organizations and procedures acquire value and stability. The level of institutionalization of any political system can be defined by the adaptability, complexity, autonomy, and coherence of its organizations and procedures. So also, the level of institutionalization of any particular organization or procedure can be measured by its adaptability, complexity, autonomy, and coherence. If these criteria can be identified and measured, political systems can be compared in terms of their levels of institutionalization. Furthermore, it will be possible to measure increases and decreases in the institutionalization of particular organizations and procedures within a political system.

        ✿   ✿   ✿   ✿   ✿

Social mobilization and political participation are rapidly increasing in Asia, Africa, and Latin America. These processes, in turn, are directly responsible for the deterioration of political institutions in these areas. As Kornhauser has conclusively demonstrated for the Western world, rapid industrialization and urbanization create discontinuities which give rise to mass society. "The *rapid* influx of large numbers of people into *newly* developing urban areas invites mass movements." [3] In areas and industries with very rapid industrial growth, the creation and institutionalization of unions lag, and mass movements are likely among the workers. As unions are organized, they are highly vulnerable to outside influences in their early stages. "The rapid influx of large numbers of people into a new organization (as well as a new area) provides opportunities for mass-oriented elites to penetrate the organization. This is particularly true during the formative periods of organizations, for at such times external constraints must carry the burden of social control until the new participants have come to internalize the values of the organization." [4]

So also in politics. Rapid economic growth breeds political instability [5] Political mobilization, moreover, does not necessarily require the

[3]   William Kornhauser, *The Politics of Mass Society* (Glencoe 1959), 145.
[4]   *Ibid.*, 146.
[5]   See Mancur Olson, Jr., "Rapid Growth as a Destabilizing Force," *Journal of Economic History*, XXVII (December 1963), 529–52; and Bert F. Hoselitz and Myron Weiner, "Economic Development and Political Stability in India," *Dissent*, VIII (Spring 1961), 172–79.

building of factories or even movement to the cities. It may result simply from increases in communications, which can stimulate major increases in aspirations that may be only partially, if at all, satisfied. The result is a "revolution of rising frustrations."[6] Increases in literacy and education may bring more political instability. By Asian standards, Burma, Ceylon, and the Republic of Korea are all highly literate, but no one of them is a model of political stability. Nor does literacy necessarily stimulate democracy: with roughly 75 per cent literacy, Cuba was the fifth most literate country in Latin America (ranking behind Argentina, Uruguay, Chile, and Costa Rica), but the first to go Communist; so also Kerala, with one of the highest literacy rates in India, was the first Indian state to elect a Communist government.[7] Literacy, as Daniel Lerner has suggested, "may be dysfunctional—indeed a serious impediment—to modernization in the societies now seeking (all too rapidly) to transform their institutions."[8]

Increased communication may thus generate demands for more "modernity" than can be delivered. It may also stimulate a reaction against modernity and activate traditional forces. Since the political arena is normally dominated by the more modern groups, it can bring into the arena new, anti-modern groups and break whatever consensus exists among the leading political participants. It may also mobilize minority ethnic groups who had been indifferent to politics but who now acquire a self-consciousness and divide the political system along ethnic lines. Nationalism, it has often been assumed, makes for national integration. But in actuality, nationalism and other forms of ethnic consciousness often stimulate political disintegration, tearing apart the body politic.

Sharp increases in voting and other forms of political participation can also have deleterious effects on political institutions. In Latin America since the 1930's, increases in voting and increases in political instability have gone hand in hand. "Age requirements were lowered, property and literacy requirements were reduced or discarded, and the unscrubbed, unschooled millions on the farms were enfranchised in the name of democracy. They were swept into the political life of the republics so rapidly that existing parties could not absorb many of them, and they learned little about working within the existing political system."[9] The personal identity crises of the elites, caught between tradi-

---

[6] See Daniel Lerner, "Toward a Communication Theory of Modernization," in Lucian W. Pye, ed., *Communications and Political Development* (Princeton 1963), 330 ff.

[7] Cf. Karl W. Deutsch, "Social Mobilization and Political Development," *American Political Science Review*, LV (September 1961), 496.

[8] Daniel Lerner, "The Transformation of Institutions" (mimeo.), 19.

[9] John J. Johnson, *The Military and Society in Latin America* (Stanford 1964), 98–99.

tional and modern cultures, may create additional problems: "In transitional countries the political process often has to bear to an inordinate degree the stresses and strains of people responding to personal needs and seeking solutions to intensely personal problems." [10] Rapid social and economic change calls into question existing values and behavior patterns. It thus often breeds personal corruption. In some circumstances this corruption may play a positive role in the modernizing process, enabling dynamic new groups to get things done which would have been blocked by the existing value system and social structure. At the same time, however, corruption undermines the autonomy and coherence of political institutions. It is hardly accidental that in the 1870's and 1880's a high rate of American economic development coincided with a low point in American governmental integrity.[11]

Institutional decay has become a common phenomenon of the modernizing countries. *Coups d'état* and military interventions in politics are one index of low levels of political institutionalization: they occur where political institutions lack autonomy and coherence. According to one calculation, eleven of twelve modernizing states outside Latin America which were independent before World War II experienced *coups d'état* or attempted coups after World War II. Of twenty states which became independent between World War II and 1959, fourteen had coups or coup attempts by 1963. Of twenty-four states which became independent between 1960 and 1963, seven experienced coups or attempted coups before the end of 1963.[12] Instability in Latin America was less frequent early in the twentieth century than it was in the middle of the century. In the decade from 1917 to 1927, military men occupied the presidencies of the twenty Latin American republics 28.7 per cent of the time; in the decade from 1947 to 1957, military men were presidents 45.5 per cent of the time.[13] In the 1930's and 1940's in countries like Argentina and Colombia, military intervention in politics occurred for the first time in this century. Seventeen of the twenty Latin American states experienced coups or coup attempts between 1945 and 1964, only Chile, Mexico, and Uruguay having clean records of political stability.

In many states the decline of party organizations is reflected in the rise of charismatic leaders who personalize power and weaken institutions which might limit that power. The increasing despotism of

---

[10] Lucian W. Pye, *Politics, Personality and Nation Building* (New Haven 1962), 4–5.
[11] See, in general, Ronald E. Wraith and Edgar Simpkins, *Corruption in Developing Countries* (London 1963).
[12] These figures are calculated from the data in the Appendix of Fred R. von der Mehden, *Politics of the Developing Nations* (Englewood Cliffs, N. J., 1964).
[13] Computed from figures in R. W. Fitzgibbon, "Armies and Politics in Latin America," paper, 7th Round Table, International Political Science Association, Opatija, Yugoslavia, September 1959, 8–9.

Nkrumah, for instance, was accompanied by a marked decline in the institutional strength of the Convention People's Party. In Turkey, Pakistan, and Burma, the Republican People's Party, Muslim League, and AFPFL deteriorated and military intervention eventually ensued. In party organizations and bureaucracies, marked increases in corruption often accompanied significant declines in the effectiveness of governmental services. Particularistic groups—tribal, ethnic, religious—frequently reasserted themselves and further undermined the authority and coherence of political institutions. The legitimacy of post-colonial regimes among their own people was often less than that of the colonial regimes of the Europeans. Economists have argued that the gap between the level of economic well-being of the underdeveloped countries and that of highly developed countries is widening as the absolute increases and even percentage increases of the latter exceed those of the former. Something comparable and perhaps even more marked is occurring in the political field. The level of political institutionalization of the advanced countries has, with a few exceptions such as France, remained relatively stable. The level of political institutionalization of most other countries has declined. As a result, the political gap between them has broadened. In terms of institutional strength, many if not most of the new states reached their peak of political development at the moment of independence.

The differences which may exist in mobilization and institutionalization suggest four ideal-types of politics (see Table 1). Modern, developed, civic polities (the United States, the Soviet Union) have high levels of both mobilization and institutionalization. Primitive polities (such as Banfield's backward society) have low levels of both. Contained polities are highly institutionalized but have low levels of mobilization and participation. The dominant political institutions of contained polities may be either traditional (e.g., monarchies) or modern (e.g., political parties). If they are the former, such polities may well confront great difficulties in adjusting to rising levels of social mobilization. The traditional institutions may wither or collapse, and the result would be a corrupt polity with a high rate of participation but a low level of institutionalization. In the corrupt society, politics is, in Macaulay's phrase, "all sail and no anchor." [14] This type of polity characterizes much, if not most, of the modernizing world. Many of the more advanced Latin American countries, for instance, have achieved comparatively high indices of literacy, per capita national income, and urbanization. But their politics remains notably underdeveloped. Distrust and hatred have produced a continuing low level of political institutionalization. "There is no good faith in America, either among men or among

[14] Thomas B. Macaulay, letter to Henry S. Randall, Courtlandt Village, New York, May 23, 1857, printed in "What Did Macaulay Say About America?" *Bulletin of the New York Public Library*, XXIX (July 1925), 477–79.

POLITICAL DEVELOPMENT AND POLITICAL DECAY

TABLE 1. TYPES OF POLITICAL SYSTEMS

Social Mobilization	Political Institutionalization	
	High	Low
High	Civic	Corrupt
Low	Contained	Primitive

nations," Bolivar once lamented. "Treaties are paper, constitutions books, elections battles, liberty anarchy, and life a torment. The only thing one can do in America is emigrate." [15] Over a century later, the same complaint was heard: "We are not, or do not represent a respectable nation . . . not because we are poor, but because we are disorganized," argued an Ecuadorian newspaper. "With a politics of ambush and of permanent mistrust, one for the other, we . . . cannot properly organize a republic . . . and without organization we cannot merit or attain respect from other nations." [16] So long as a country like Argentina retains a politics of coup and countercoup and a feeble state surrounded by massive social forces, it cannot be considered politically developed, no matter how urbane and prosperous and educated are its citizens.

In reverse fashion, a country may be politically highly developed, with modern political institutions, while still very backward in terms of modernization. India, for instance, is typically held to be the epitome of the underdeveloped society. Judged by the usual criteria of modernization, it was at the bottom of the ladder during the 1950's: per capita GNP of $72, 80 per cent illiterate, over 80 per cent of the population in rural areas, 70 per cent of the work force in agriculture, a dozen major languages, deep caste and religious differences. Yet in terms of political institutionalization, India was far from backward. Indeed, it ranked high not only in comparison with other modernizing countries in Asia, Africa, and Latin America, but also in comparison with many much more modern European countries. A well-developed political system has strong and distinct institutions to perform both the "input" and the "output" functions of politics. India entered independence with not only two organizations, but two highly developed—adaptable, complex, autonomous, and coherent—institutions ready to assume primary responsibility for these functions. The Congress Party, founded in 1885, was one of the oldest and best-organized political parties in the world; the Indian Civil Service, dating from the early nineteenth century, has been appropriately hailed as "one of the greatest administrative systems of all time." [17] The stable, effective, and democratic government of India

[15] Simon Bolivar, quoted in K. H. Silvert, ed., *Expectant Peoples: Nationalism and Development* (New York 1963), 347.
[16] *El Dia*, Quito, November 27, 1943, quoted in Bryce Wood, *The Making of the Good Neighbor Policy* (New York 1961), 318.
[17] Ralph Braibanti, "Public Bureaucracy and Judiciary in Pakistan," in Joseph LaPalombara, ed., *Bureaucracy and Political Development* (Princeton 1963), 373.

COMPARATIVE POLITICS AND POLITICAL DEVELOPMENT

during the first fifteen years of independence rested far more on this institutional inheritance than it did on the charisma of Nehru. In addition, the relatively slow pace of modernization and social mobilization in India did not create demands and strains which the Party and the bureaucracy were unable to handle. So long as these two organizations maintain their institutional strength, it is ridiculous to think of India as politically underdeveloped, no matter how low her per capita income or how high her illiteracy rate.

Almost no other country which became independent after World War II was institutionally as well prepared as India for self-government. In countries like Pakistan and the Sudan, institutional evolution was unbalanced; the civil and military bureaucracies were more highly developed than the political parties, and the military had strong incentives to move into the institutional vacuum on the input side of the political system and to attempt to perform interest aggregation functions. This pattern, of course, has also been common in Latin America. In countries like Guatemala, El Salvador, Peru, and Argentina, John J. Johnson has pointed out, the military is "the country's best organized institution and is thus in a better position to give objective expression to the national will" than are parties or interest groups.[18] In a very different category is a country like North Vietnam, which fought its way into independence with a highly disciplined political organization but which was distinctly weak on the administrative side. The Latin American parallel here would be Mexico, where, as Johnson puts it, "not the armed forces but the PRI is the best organized institution, and the party rather than the armed forces has been the unifying force at the national level." In yet a fourth category are those unfortunate states, such as the Congo, which were born with neither political nor administrative institutions. Many of these new states deficient at independence in one or both types of institutions have also been confronted by high rates of social mobilization and rapidly increasing demands on the political system. . . .

[18]   Johnson, *Military and Society*, 143.

iii. transitional societies

The transition from traditional societies to modern nation-states involves many complex, interrelated changes in cultural values and attitudes, and in social, economic, and political institutions and processes. Some of these changes as they have been occurring in the developing states have been dramatic, obvious, and easily measured. Political independence has been secured by many African and Asian societies that a few years ago were generally regarded as unlikely to be ready for self-government for many decades. Constitutions have been written and modern political institutions formally established. In some states, urban areas have been growing rapidly, and new industries, including some heavy industries, are being established. Strenuous efforts have been made to expand educational facilities as rapidly as possible. Increasing numbers of students are being enrolled, and the high rates of illiteracy have been gradually, and in some cases rapidly, reduced. Per capita income has increased or decreased in response to economic and population growth rates. Death rates, particularly among infants and children, have sharply declined as improvements have been made in medical facilities, public health programs, and diets.

Many of the other changes that are occurring, however, are far more subtle and less readily measured. Changes in values, beliefs, and attitudes within societies are particularly difficult to measure with precision. Nevertheless, it is clear that alterations are occurring within the value and attitude patterns of transitional societies, accompanying changing conditions in the physical environment. In this interplay between values and objective conditions, either may reflect or stimulate changes in the other. More specifically, political values, attitudes, and expectations have also been undergoing various modifications. The national revolutions for political independence, for example, and the trying problems of creating nation-states have had their impact on political values as well as on political institutions. In addition, expectations of further changes in the social, economic, and political systems have injected a dynamic and often unstabilizing element into the political process of many societies.

As these changes take place, tensions and strains of varying intensity result within the fabric of traditional society. The traditional family structure, for example, with its values based upon a closely interwoven network of personal relationships is challenged when members of the family leave the rural village and move to the cities to work.[1] Similarly, mass education has a disruptive effect on the traditional patterns of beliefs and authority. The increasing secularization of society also exacts its toll on traditional religious beliefs, even though ritualized practices may continue long after they have lost their primary meanings. Defenders of the traditional religions are confronted not only by the apathy of many who find little satisfaction in the ancient beliefs and practices, but also by a minority who view the traditional religions as definite obstacles to modernization. Further, the gradually changing economic structure of many societies causes shifts in the distribution of wealth and the realignment and strength of individuals and groups supporting or opposing various economic policies. And, in the political realm, changing social and economic conditions affect the bases of political power and the groups that compete for positions of influence and authority. The authority of conservative traditional leaders is challenged by those who have achieved popular acclaim for their radical programs and by those who have attained control over new instruments of power, such as modern military forces, bureaucracies, or economic institutions.

Of course, the contemporary bases from which development is proceeding vary greatly from society to society in Asia, Africa, and Latin America. The different problems these societies confront and the different policies they pursue reflect the variety of traditional bases from which they have evolved. In some states in general, and in most states in some particulars, this evolution has been exceedingly limited, and the contemporary society is much like the traditional. In a few cases, the pace and scope of changes have been rapidly transforming the traditional bases. Although significant differences may be identified between individual traditional societies, some commonly shared characteristics may also be noted. In general, a traditional society is characterized by its relatively limited economic base (primarily agricultural), a low level of technology, a lack of functionally specific institutions (such as separate religious and political authorities and institutions), a largely illiterate population, a low life expectancy, and a non-scientific, even mystical approach to the problems confronting it. The cultures of tradi-

[1] Henry Rosenfeld, "Change, Barriers to Change, and Contradictions in the Arab Village Family," *American Anthropologist,* Vol. LXX, No. 4 (August, 1970), pp. 732–752.

tional societies reflect these characteristics. The family, tribe, or communal group, providing close personal relationships for its members, establishes the base from which values are derived, rather than the more abstract nation or state. A sense of fatalism often pervades these values, mirroring the inability to overcome natural forces that impede progress. Though some traditional societies have, in the past, attained a fairly high level of development of technology, and skills in art and literature, long periods of stagnation and decline interrupted continuous development.

The changes that have, historically, taken place in traditional societies were stimulated by many forces, both internal and external. The discovery of raw materials and the means to utilize them, changing patterns of economic production, and the development of an alphabet and a written language have provided the base for many changes. Contacts with other societies and cultures, whether through war, trade, travel, or communications have also been important prods for change. In particular, contacts with Western cultures have promoted many changes. In the process of "discovering" and then conquering much of the world through the exercise of their military, economic, technological, and organizational superiority, the European powers implanted in the traditional societies in Asia, Africa, and Latin America many Western ideas, values, skills, and institutions.

The pattern of contact with the West took different forms and had different consequences. In Latin America, the military victories by the Spanish and Portuguese forces over the indigenous Indian societies in the fifteenth and sixteenth centuries provided the base from which the colonial policies of the mother countries were executed. In the Caribbean islands, the native populations were completely exterminated: large numbers were killed in the course of military actions, and the rest succumbed to the diseases and harsh treatment of their European conquerors. Negro slaves were then imported to provide the working force for the Spanish landlords. Elsewhere in Latin America, the defeated Indians, saved from complete extermination through the intervention of the Catholic Church, were nevertheless reduced to a state of abject servility, forced to work on the land and in the mines whose ownership was claimed by the victors. The Spanish and, in Brazil, the Portuguese, having taken possession of the land and its resources, established themselves as the permanent social, political, and economic elite. They created large urban centers from which they administered the policies of exploitation as directed by the mother states. Gradually, a middle cultural group, the *mestizos*, emerged from the intermarriages of the Europeans and Indians. Sharp contrasts developed between each of the three classes with the Indians, *mestizos*, and "whites" each forming a distinct group in terms of social, political, and economic rights and opportunities. In the Caribbean islands, the Negroes and mulattos held positions corresponding to those of the Indians and *mestizos*, respectively. In the process of establishing their permanent settlements, the Spanish and Portuguese brought with them the entire paraphernalia of their cultures. Thus, after political independence was achieved by the settlers early in the nineteenth century, the patterns that had developed over three centuries of colonial rule were continued largely unchanged. For the indigenous Indian populations, the achievement of independence by the white settlers had little meaning, unlike the consequences of this act in almost all African and Asian societies, where the indigenous groups attained control of their governments; it merely involved a change from foreign to domestic "white" rule.

After a long period of political instability, economic stagnation, and little social change, most Latin American states are now in a phase of more rapid change. Increasing industrialization during the past quarter century has been accompanied by increasing urbanization, a higher standard of education to meet the needs of industrial development, a gradual weakening of the rigid class divisions as employment opportunities have grown, and the emergence of political groups capable of challenging the dominant positions of those whose power is based on land ownership. The traditionally conservative social and political attitudes of the Catholic Church and the support given to conservative leaders are also in a state of transition. While the values and institutions that characterized nineteenth century Latin American societies have not been destroyed, they are nevertheless being subjected to intensifying pressures from groups demanding more rapid modernization.

The manner in which the European powers—and much later the United States—penetrated and came to dominate the Asian and African societies was generally quite different from that in Latin America. In Asia, after the initial discoveries by European explorers in the fourteenth and fifteenth centuries, adventurers, missionaries, and traders arrived to provide the first sustained, though limited, contact. In the Philippines, Spanish rule (until 1898, when the islands were surrendered to the United States) produced a social and political pattern resembling that found in the Spanish colonies in Latin America. Elsewhere, however, the Spanish and Portuguese military forces were defeated by other European powers, and British and Dutch traders, whose activities initially had little impact on the native populations, became the principal agents of Western influence. With the establishment of the English East India Company in 1600 and the Dutch East India Company in 1602, the traditional societies were increasingly disrupted as these Companies, eager to protect and promote their economic functions, began to assume governmental functions as well. Various forms of indirect rule, in which the traditional elites were retained but forced to make concessions to the Companies, were employed to maintain order and control.

The activities of these Companies, along with those of the missionaries sent out to convert the native populations, increasingly involved the European governments more directly in Asian affairs. The Companies themselves were replaced by the Dutch and British governments in the late eighteenth and nineteenth centuries, respectively. Together with the French, who had gradually established control over Indochina in the second half of the nineteenth century, the British and Dutch exercised rule over most Asian societies. Both the dominant philosophies of the colonial powers and the nature of the societies over which they ruled differed significantly, however. The Dutch in Indonesia chose to rule indirectly through traditional native rulers. Subscribing to theories of cultural relativism, the Dutch encouraged the development of local cultures while retaining ultimate authority. The effect of this policy was to create two quite distinct spheres of authority and styles of life, the European and the native, with few persons or groups capable of bridging the two worlds. While the authority of the native rulers was gradually undermined as the Dutch increased the authority of the centralized administration, no clear patterns of authority integrating European and native values and institutions emerged from which development could proceed upon the achievement of independence.

The British, on the other hand, were much less inclined toward the paternalistic attitudes and policies of the Dutch. Their objective of establishing law and order, through which policies of economic liberalism could be pursued, led the British to employ both direct and indirect means of control. Where native rulers were strong, indirect rule was exercised; where weak, the British imposed their authority directly over the native societies. In either case, a centralized administration was created and the British legal system introduced. While both the economic policies and British law produced profound changes in the traditional order, British rule imparted a relatively unambiguous concept of government based upon representative political institutions, unlike Dutch rule which attempted to preserve traditional native political institutions.

In contrast to both the Dutch and the British, the French sought to assimilate the societies they ruled into French culture. Although a small group of Vietnamese were successfully assimilated, the bulk of the population retained its strong ties to the native cultures. The result was a fragmented social and political structure, with the Westernized Vietnamese attempting to exert authority over the unassimilated, tradition-oriented masses. The instability of this structure became apparent immediately upon the attainment of independence and the withdrawal of French military and administrative forces. A much different pattern resulted from American rule in the Philippines. By emphasizing the development of democratic parties, institutions, and processes in preparation for eventual independence, a much closer relationship between

TRANSITIONAL SOCIETIES

native political leaders and the people was encouraged. In addition, since independence was the goal, American policy deliberately promoted the development of the social and economic systems (as, for example, through mass education and local industry) considered necessary for a democratic state. These policies were only partially successful, however, in altering the social and economic structures created under Spanish rule, which resembled, in many respects, those found in Latin America. Thus, under the successive impact of Spanish and American rule, traditional Filipino societies were altered in ways significantly different from those ruled by other European powers.

The major Western impact on sub-Saharan Africa came much later than in Asia. Prior to 1885, contact had been limited and sporadic, resulting primarily from the slave trade. Only a few small areas had come under control of the European states, principally at the southern tip of the continent. In 1885, however, the European powers at the Congress of Berlin laid the ground rules governing the division of the continent, and soon Britain, France, Belgium, Portugal, Spain, and, later, Germany established their control over all African societies except Ethiopia, though frequently it was more nominal than truly effective. In the scramble for colonies, boundary lines were drawn and agreed upon that bore little relationship to the cultural and ethnic patterns of the native populations. In a few areas, as in Kenya and Rhodesia, large numbers of Europeans arrived to found permanent white settlements, establishing within these areas a privileged social, economic, and political class.

Imposed upon the radically different traditional African systems were the equally varied colonial policies of the European powers. As in Asia, both direct and indirect forms of rule were utilized. While the British employed several forms of indirect rule in their colonies, the French favored direct rule with the objective of assimilating and incorporating their colonies into a French Union. Belgium, while a colonial power, also ruled directly, as do Spain and Portugal today, but only Portugal shares the French objective of assimilation, though its policies to attain that goal are much different from the French ones. These several forms of rule were, of course, modified at different times by the colonial powers, as was also true in Asia. In general, the British policy of indirect rule produced only gradual changes initially in the traditional African societies. Limited, but slowly expanding educational, employment, and political opportunities were afforded before World War II. After the war, with the sharply increasing demands for independence, the British expanded these opportunities while also establishing political institutions in which the Africans increasingly participated. In the process, the position of the traditional political elites on whom the British had earlier relied was undermined. On the other hand, indirect rule had the effect of encouraging the individual tribal groupings to retain their sense of identity. The preservation of tribal identity led, in turn, to the demands for federal forms of government and in some cases to separatist movements within the newly independent states. In those colonies where large European settlements were established, difficult problems were encountered in creating independent states in which Africans would have a substantial or controlling voice.

The French policy of assimilation had the potentiality for the greatest disruption of the traditional order, since if it were to succeed, substantial changes in traditional values and patterns of authority would be required. As in French Indochina, a small group of Africans successfully made the transition; for the masses, however, the transition was only partial because of both deep-seated resentment toward or disinterest in the assimilation policy and the unwillingness or inability of the French to provide adequate educational, economic, and political opportunities to make the policy successful. Belgium's paternalistic policies, in contrast, were not designed to effectuate a full and rapid Europeanization of their colony. Slow, controlled changes in preparation for independence in the distant future were considered desirable. For example, while a primary education was gradually made available to large numbers of natives, no higher educational institutions were established or education in foreign universities permitted until the 1950's. Similarly, only the lowest levels of the civil service were open until shortly before independence was granted. Plantations and small industries were established to promote economic development, but in all fields of activity, the higher positions were retained almost exclusively for Europeans, which left the Congolese critically short of managerial and political skills at the time independence was attained. Little of this gradual preparation for future independence is found in the contemporary Spanish and Portuguese paternalistic policies, however. Few educational, economic, or political opportunities are made available under the harsh and repressive policies of these colonial powers. Even though the Portuguese assert that individual assimilation of the Africans is the goal, equal status and opportunities with their European counterparts are not available to the assimilated Portuguese Africans, unlike the assimilated French Africans. The repressive policies of Spain and Portugal, augmented by the widespread use of various forms of coercion, have so far enabled them to maintain control of their colonies in spite of growing demands for independence.

In both Asia and sub-Saharan Africa, colonial rule resulted in many basic changes in the traditional societies. Although the colonial policies of the several European powers varied in many important details, in general they (1) brought together within a single colony cultural and ethnic groups that had previously not been politically united, (2) established rationalized bureaucratic structures, staffed at least in the lower ranks by native personnel, (3) created legal systems based on European values and codes, (4) established armed forces and police units partially manned by natives and equipped with some modern weapons, (5) introduced a monetary system patterned after those in Europe and provided for standardized taxes, and (6) created a Western-style, secular educational system.

The impact of many colonial policies was, however, usually felt directly by only a relatively small number of persons. At the rural village level and among groups in the isolated interior regions, the changes introduced by the colonial powers were much less immediately and intensively realized. Yet even at the local level, the forces set in motion by the colonial powers were sufficient over time to disrupt traditional patterns of authority, economic production, and cultural values. In general, the small group of native leaders who were trained within the framework of colonial rule have been determined to carry the modernizing process down to the local level. These Western-trained elites, often coming from the ranks of the bureaucracies and the armed forces, were usually the principal groups in the nationalist movements leading to independence. They demanded for themselves and their peoples those very rights that the colonial powers themselves claim to prize: political independence and its attendant freedom to make their own choices in all areas of social and economic policy. Having achieved independence, these leaders have been attempting to speed and shape the processes of modernization throughout their societies.

In contrast to the relatively recent contact between the European powers and the sub-Saharan African societies, resulting almost immediately in the subjugation of the latter to the former, a long period of contact between the European and Middle Eastern societies preceded the establishment of formal European control. The contributions of ancient societies in the Middle East to Western civilization are, of course, well known. During the past several centuries, however, the economic and political development of the Middle Eastern societies has lagged far behind that in Europe. The once powerful Middle Eastern empires had disintegrated under the impact of domestic strife, foreign attack, and economic stagnation (the latter complicated by the lack of resources, especially arable land). Although a common faith, the Islamic, bound the societies together, political authority was highly fragmented. In an effort to reverse their fortunes in order to compete more successfully in the modern world, some rulers of the Middle Eastern societies have, since the eighteenth century, attempted to incorporate and utilize selected features of European technology and organizational forms. Bureaucracies and military forces were organized along the lines of their European counterparts. Inevitably, other European ideas and values, particularly those concerning nationalism, were injected into the traditional societies by those Western-trained army officers and civil servants charged with constructing modern military machines and administrative institutions. Thus, the goals and some of the processes of modernization were well established in some Middle Eastern societies before European control was directly imposed.

Prior to the late nineteenth century, few European colonies were established in the Middle East. Not until after World War I, when a number of territories such as Syria, Iraq, and Lebanon were designated as mandates of Britain and France, was European control asserted over most of the Middle East except Turkey, Iran, and Saudi Arabia. Yet in neither the colonies, such as Tunisia or Morocco, nor in the mandated territories was European power exercised to the same degree as in the Asian or sub-Saharan colonies. While the control was sufficient to disrupt native political authority, it rarely brought significant benefits of colonialism in the form of stable governments or auxiliary services, such as improved standards of health, education, or transportation and communications networks. Consequently, the legacy of this short period of imperial rule, with its uneven pattern of penetration and control, has been one of bitterness and disillusionment on both sides. The bitterness existing between the Arab states on the one hand, and Britain, France, and the United States on the other, was sharply intensified by the establishment, under auspices of a British mandate, of the state of Israel in 1948, and the struggle over the Suez Canal that culminated in a short war in 1956. Although the Arab-Israeli war in 1967 did not involve the American or European states directly, the crisis led to the rupturing of diplomatic relations by several Arab states with the United States on grounds of the latter's support for Israel.

While many of the changes occurring within the transitional states thus stem quite clearly from the impact of colonial rule, other forces only partially related to colonialism are also helping to reshape traditional societies. As in the case of Latin America, the rapid urbanization taking place in many Asian and some African states is a manifestation of several forces, in addition to that of the colonial policy of establishing cities as administrative and trading centers. Under the pressure of population growth and the surplus of labor in the rural areas, many people are moving to the cities in search of industrial employment and a standard of living unobtainable in the countryside. This search is frequently frustrated, given the limited industrialization that has yet occurred. Nevertheless, the process of urbanization has been a major factor promoting changes in the traditional societies. The movement to the cities tends to undermine the traditional values and personal relationships characteristic of rural societies. Since this movement is often proceeding without an industrial base to supply work for all those seeking it, most cities contain a substantial group of persons who are unemployed or underemployed.[2] Their frustrations in not being able to obtain employ-

[2] Gavin W. Jones, "Underutilisation of Manpower and Demographic Trends in Latin America," *International Labour Review,* Vol. XCVIII, No. 5 (November, 1968), pp. 451–469.

ment and a satisfactory standard of living have on numerous occasions been translated into political action in the form of demonstrations and riots. To a degree unparalleled in Europe and North America, political activity in the developing states centers in the urban areas where the modernizing elite and the restless urban masses dominate the national political processes.

The rapid population growth in both the urban centers and the rural areas, with all its implications for economic and political development, is caused primarily by a sharp decline in infant mortality rates and increasing longevity rather than by an increase in the birth rate. In addition, better medical, sanitary, and public health facilities and practices have reduced the incidence of disease and have contributed to better care for the sick and injured, further reducing the death rate.

Accelerating the changes in traditional societies is the spread of education. As larger numbers of persons become educated, particularly to more advanced levels, traditional values come under increasingly critical examination. Education has become a principal determinant of the modernizing elite, and the requirements of a modern, industrialized state force emphasis to be placed upon the development of a modern, secular educational system. Contributing to the spread of ideas are the mass communications media. Motion pictures, radio, and printed materials bring new ideas and methods to people in the remotest areas as well as to those already involved in the modernization process.

External pressures similarly promote the evolution of traditional societies. To compete in the modern world requires the substantial revision of traditional values and methods of production. Surplus goods must be produced for sale abroad to obtain the necessary exchange for the payment of imported goods. Since the defense of the state no longer rests directly in the hands of the former colonial power, modern military forces must be established and adequately equipped. In many of these societies, the military has become a principal agency for modernization. Strong feelings of nationalism and an uncertain relationship with other states have led to heavy appropriations for defense, including modern, complex weaponry. Supporting skills, industries, and communication and transportation networks are required to make the military forces effective. In addition, the military serves as a modernizing agency through its programs of basic education and advanced technical training.

Under the impact of these various forces, some societies are undergoing a period of rapid transformation. A sense of urgency is apparent among the modernizing elite as they seek to move their societies to a position that will enable them to compete successfully in the modern world. Even where this sense of urgency is much less obvious, as in some Latin American states, demands for modernization are increasingly voiced by segments of society who are unwilling to accept present conditions and who believe that their own positions can be improved. The "revolution of rising expectations" thus inevitably involves substantial changes in the traditional order. Whether the ways and means to realize these expectations can be discovered remains, at present, the unanswerable question.

SUGGESTED READINGS

Alba, Victor. *The Latin Americans.* New York: Frederick A. Praeger, 1969.

Barnett, H. G. *Innovation: The Basis of Cultural Change.* New York: McGraw-Hill Book Company, Inc., 1953.

Barringer, Herbert, George I. Blanksten, and Raymond W. Mack, eds. *Social Change in Developing Areas.* Cambridge: Schenkman Publishing Company, 1965.

Black, Cyril E. *Dynamics of Modernization: A Study in Comparative History.* New York: Harper and Row, Inc., 1966.

Easton, Stewart C. *The Rise and Fall of Western Colonialism.* New York: Frederick A. Praeger, 1964.

Emerson, Rupert. *From Empire to Nation.* Cambridge: Harvard University Press, 1960.

————, and Martin Kilson, eds. *The Political Awakening of Africa.* Englewood Cliffs, N. J.: Prentice-Hall, Inc., 1965.

Foster, George M. *Traditional Cultures: And the Impact of Technological Change.* New York: Harper & Bros., 1962.

Geertz, Clifford, ed. *Old Societies and New States.* New York: The Free Press of Glencoe, 1963.

Gulliver, P. H., ed. *Tradition and Transition in East Africa: Studies of the Tribal Element in the Modern Era.* London: Routledge & Kegan Paul, 1969.

Hagen, Everett E. *On the Theory of Social Change.* Homewood, Ill.: The Dorsey Press, Inc., 1962.

Hunter, Guy. *Modernizing Peasant Societies: A Comparative Study in Asia and Africa.* New York: Oxford University Press, 1969.

Ishwaran, K., ed. *Change and Continuity in India's Villages.* New York: Columbia University Press, 1970.

Lerner, Daniel. *The Passing of Traditional Society.* New York: The Free Press of Glencoe, 1958.

Millikan, Max F., and Donald L. M. Blackmer, eds. *The Emerging Nations: Their Growth and United States Policy.* Boston: Little, Brown and Company, 1961.

Morse, Chandler, Douglas E. Ashford, Frederick T. Bent, William H. Friedland, John W. Lewis, and David Macklin. *Modernization by Design: Social Change in the Twentieth Century.* Ithaca, N. Y.: Cornell University Press, 1969.

Pye, Lucian W., and Sidney Verba, eds. *Political Culture and Political Development.* Princeton, N. J.: Princeton University Press, 1965.

Tuden, Arthur, and Leonard Plotnicov, eds. *Social Stratification in Africa.* New York: The Free Press, 1970.

Wagley, Charles. *The Latin American Tradition: Essays on the Unity and Diversity of Latin American Culture.* New York: Columbia University Press, 1968.

What forces have stimulated changes in traditional societies? The authors of the selection below identify several that have been important historically but, as they indicate, the different characteristics of the various traditional societies have resulted in different response patterns to internal and external pressures for change, as some societies have been more susceptible than others to certain kinds of pressures. Among the forces stimulating change, however, Western colonialism was particularly potent, and the authors analyze some of the principal consequences of that stimulant.

5. THE EMERGING NATIONS*

edited by max f. millikan and donald l. m. blackmer

The nature of the transitional process which we are considering here—and which American policy confronts in many parts of the world—takes its start from the character of the traditional societies that are in the process of being superseded. We begin, therefore, by sketching briefly the major features of traditional societies.

These were societies with hereditary hierarchical rule, living under the sway of customs rather than of law. Their economies were static and remained at the same level of limited technology and low income from one generation to the next. Even though some ancient societies exhibited high proficiency in certain directions, they should be termed traditional since they were incapable of generating a regular flow of inventions and innovations and of moving into a phase of sustained economic growth. Before the appearance of the modern scientific attitude and of

* From *The Emerging Nations: Their Growth and United States Policy,* edited by Max F. Millikan and Donald L. M. Blackmer. Copyright © 1961, Massachusetts Institute of Technology. Reprinted by permission of the publishers, Little, Brown and Company (Inc.). Selections from pp. 3–17.

advances in basic scientific knowledge, no society could produce a continuing flow of new technology. It followed from this limitation that the bulk of men's economic activity was taken up in acquiring food. Typically, at least 75 per cent and often more of the working force in traditional societies was in agriculture. History offers us a wide range of such societies. Some were relatively primitive tribes living within a narrow region, on a self-sufficient base, with tribal rather than territorial political and economic organization, and tenuously connected if at all with other tribes and regions. In parts of Africa and in some areas elsewhere we can still find such isolated and primitive forms of social, political, and economic organization.

Other traditional societies have been made up of loosely organized regions, with fairly elaborate structures of political and social organization and quite sophisticated agricultural techniques, but weak or nonexistent central governments. Medieval Europe, for example, could be described in some such terms, as well as India before the arrival of the European colonial powers.

But some traditional societies were very substantial empires with quite powerful centralized governments, manipulating a corps of civil servants and a military establishment, capable of collecting taxes and maintaining public works over large areas, capable of conquering and administering other regions and of generating a framework for elaborate patterns of trade and even significant industrial development. The Roman and Mayan Empires were such elaborate traditional organizations, as were certain of the Chinese dynasties at the peak of their effectiveness and some of the Middle Eastern empires at various stages of history.

Nor were these societies all primitive intellectually. Some of them, such as the Greek and Chinese, developed philosophy and the arts to levels hardly since surpassed. Societies of the Near East developed the modern alphabet and the number tools on which modern achievements in mathematics are built. In traditional societies of the West there evolved the concept of monotheism, and then Christianity; in India, Buddhism.

The history of traditional societies, and notably of those that had reasonably strong centralized governments, was not static. In times of peace, more acreage was cultivated, trade expanded, the population increased; the government collected taxes efficiently, maintained the irrigation works, and enlarged the opportunities for commerce. The nation extended its boundaries and learned how to administer a large empire. Colonization of distant areas occurred. But then change would come to a halt, and governmental administration would begin to disintegrate; the society would break down. The immediate causes of collapse were various—population pressure, war, disintegration of central rule, and so on. But behind these varied events lay one common circumstance: the society had encountered a new condition to which it could not adapt. Old patterns of behavior persisted even though new circumstances required changed behavior, and the society ceased to function well enough to prevent disaster.

It followed from the preponderant role of agriculture that the ownership and control of land was a decisive factor in social prestige and, usually, in political influence. In some places the bulk of the land was owned by a relatively small number of nobles and the king, and worked by peasants who stood in a feudal, hierarchical relationship to the owners. This condition still exists, for example, in parts of the Middle East. In other countries landownership was quite widely spread, as it was in China, resulting in an endless struggle by the peasants to acquire more land, to establish an economic position relatively independent of the luck of the harvests, and thus to rise in the society. In many of the African tribes, land was owned communally, with no concept of individual tenure and thus little incentive for systematic investment in improvements.

In traditional societies, face-to-face relationships were extremely important, as were the ties to family and clan. Men tended to be bound together and to be valued by one another in terms of such intimate connections rather than because of their ability to perform specific functional tasks. It was very rarely that the average person had dealings with anyone he did not know quite well. Social, political, and even economic relations with strangers were seen as neither necessary nor desirable. Hence human intercourse, which in modern societies would be guided by functional considerations of economic benefit, political advantage, technical exchange, and the like, were in traditional societies much more influenced by codes of friendship, family and tribal loyalty, and hierarchical status.

Although traditional societies sometimes provided a channel for able men of the lower economic classes to rise in power and prestige (often through the civil service and the military establishment), there was a tendency for people to assume that the status of their children and grandchildren would be similar to that of their parents and grandparents. A kind of long-run fatalism pervaded traditional societies despite the ebb and flow of family fortunes and despite the slow evolution of the society as a whole.

The cultural and religious life of traditional societies, and the values they elevated, varied widely. Generally, however, they formed a coherent pattern, giving men a reasonably orderly rationale for the relatively stable round of life they faced, at whatever level in the society they found themselves. They provided a set of relationships of men to one another and to the world about them which gave them a degree of security in facing their appointed destiny within the traditional structure.

○   ○   ○   ○   ○

DISEQUILIBRIUM WITHIN TRADITIONAL SOCIETIES

That change in traditional societies is not determined solely by the impact of the West is clear from the comparative history of India, Indonesia, China, and Japan. The English were well established in India and the Dutch in Indonesia by the middle of the sixteenth century, and channels for the introduction of Western skills and ideas were far more readily available than in China or Japan. Next in degree of contact with the West was China, where the powers established trading beachheads at the important ports and carried on trade with the interior of the country. Japan had the least contact of all, for it ejected Westerners during the first half of the seventeenth century, except for a tiny colony of Dutch traders who were suffered to remain at Deshima Bay at the far tip of the main island. What little contact there was with the West was deliberately permitted to flow through the tiny Deshima Bay funnel. Yet of the four countries mentioned, Japan gave increasing evidence of modernization between 1800 and 1850 and was undergoing rapid change by the last quarter of the nineteenth century, almost three quarters of a century before any of the others.

Clearly factors other than contact with the West were at work within some traditional societies to produce men, institutions, and attitudes conducive to change. . . .

In some societies, for example, the requirements of conducting war led the central government to enlarge the military caste. . . . War also increased the requirements for credit and trade, tending to elevate somewhat the status of moneylenders and of those who managed domestic and foreign commerce—men whose formal place in the traditional hierarchy was usually low. In those traditional societies which assumed imperial responsibility, the management of empire itself strengthened the role and status of the civil servant and the technician.

It appears that a traditional society turned the more readily to modernization if there was any articulate group of men in it with reason to be unhappy about their position. Feeling aggrieved, already questioning the values and attitudes of the traditional society, they were psychologically prepared to accept new ways of life as a means of proving their worth and gaining self-satisfaction, status, and prestige. . . .

○   ○   ○   ○   ○

In Colombia the Spanish conquerors inhabited three high valleys which are the sites of the four main present cities of Colombia. In two of these valleys they developed landed estates and became landed gentry or cattlemen. In the third, Antioquia, because the land was less suitable and because other activities were more attractive, they did not. During the eighteenth and nineteenth centuries, as the historical literature of the time shows, the gentry of the other two valleys looked down on the Antioqueños because they too had not become gentry, and the Antioqueños resented this attitude. Today it is the Antioqueños who are spearheading economic and political modernization throughout Colombia.

In India successive waves of migration over several millennia have resulted in the existence of a number of social groups who even today are very conscious of their historical differences from each other. It is probably significant that much of the effective modern business activity to date in India has been initiated by several of the minority social groups—the Parsis, the Marwari, and others.

Thus social tensions may lead to the rejection of traditional attitudes by certain groups, who turn to new activities which may restore their prestige and sense of achievement. Indeed, it is virtually never the social group in control of a traditional society that leads the way to modernization. That group, which finds the traditional social order satisfactory, virtually always resists change, even if the society is threatened from without and change is necessary to resist that threat.

But this social and psychological dynamic need not, by itself, lead disaffected groups to engage in new sorts of economic activities. Modernization must first become a realistic alternative. Only when new ideas and ways of doing things are introduced from more advanced societies will the possibilities of economic change be perceived as real.

THE IMPACT OF MORE ADVANCED SOCIETIES

The initial impact of a comparatively modernized society on a traditional society most commonly took the form of, or was followed by, occupation and the setting up of colonial administrations, actions that had revolutionary effects on the traditional society in two ways.

First, in pursuit of its own interests (and often, too, in response to an impulse to spread the values and advantages of modern civilization) the colonial power executed specific policies which directly affected the economic, social, political, and cultural life of the traditional society. Ports, docks, roads, and, in some places, railroads were built. These were usually designed primarily for the economic or military advantage of the colonial power; but they had wider effects in creating national markets, commercializing agriculture, helping cities to grow, and bringing backward areas into contact with elements of modern life. Forms of central administration and centralized tax systems were usually set up. Some colonials were drawn into the economic and administrative activities necessary to execute the purposes of the colonial power. Some modern goods and services were diffused, altering the conception of the level of life that men could regard as attainable. To at least a few colonials the opportunity for a Western education was opened. Perhaps most important, the colonial power often introduced the traditional society to the Western tradition of law, to some version of those rules and procedures for the dispensation of justice which transcend and limit the powers of the individuals who exercise political authority.

In short, it was of the nature of the colonial experience that at every level of life it brought the traditional society into contact with some degree of modernization.

The character and extent of the contact with modernization varied with the concept of colonial rule that each power brought to its various colonies. In India, for example, the British made special efforts to train men for both the civil service and the army: the Moslems on the whole opted for military training, the Hindus for the civil service, reflecting in that choice underlying differences in the culture of the two groups in the Indian peninsula. In Burma, on the other hand, the British did relatively little to train either soldiers or civil servants. The French, in their empire, made great efforts to bring a thin top layer of the indigenous leaders as fully as possible into French cultural, intellectual, and political life. The Belgians in the Congo concentrated, for economic reasons, on literacy and vocational training for the lower levels of the labor force and did nothing to prepare an elite for leadership. The Dutch in Indonesia and the Portuguese in East Africa by and large adopted policies designed to limit the extent and the pace of modernization.

But however colonial policy might vary, colonialism nevertheless had one universal direct effect: it disrupted the static traditional societies. In establishing their own control the colonial administrators destroyed the existing power structure. In varying degrees they cast aside the traditional political and administrative system, substituting their own. They often treated the traditional religion with scorn and profaned what had been held holy. They violated many customary and revered human and property rights by introducing Western ideas of law and contract which in the light of traditional morals often must have seemed as wrong to the indigenous people as the Soviet doctrine of the supremacy of the state over the individual seems to the West. In these and other ways the cohesion and integrity of the traditional social and political system were violated.

The second effect of colonialism was indirect but perhaps even more profound than the direct infusion of modern elements. As an increasing number of men in the colonial society became acquainted with the methods and ideas of the West, they reacted against the human and collective humiliation that inevitably accompanied colonial rule; and they sought independence. . . .

Colonial rule was not, however, the only form of intrusion that helped unhinge traditional societies. The defeat of the traditional society in war against a more advanced power often played an important role. This was so, for example, in Germany after the Napoleonic occupation; in Russia after the Crimean War; in Japan after its imposed opening to trade by the West in the shadow of modern naval cannon; in Turkey after the First World War; in China after the defeats by the British in the 1840's and by the Japanese in the 1890's. The demonstration that the traditional form of organization was incapable of maintaining the physical integrity of the nation tended to lower the prestige of the traditional rulers, their values, and their institutions, and it tended to strengthen the hand of those groups in the traditional society— soldiers, intellectuals, men of commerce, civil servants, lesser nobility— who for various, often differing reasons were already interested in making the social changes necessary to increase their own power and the strength and prestige of their society.

＊　＊　＊　＊　＊

The Western example can cause other inner conflicts. After independence, the desire for power and dignity, combined with the recognition of industrialization as a symbol of the power of the West, often provides a powerful emotional stimulus to the desire for industrialization; but it does not inculcate a corresponding desire to live the kinds of lives, perform the kinds of functions, and maintain the kinds of relationships with other individuals that are necessary for industrialization. The fruits of industrialization are urgently desired; the social and psychological changes which go with it may still be unwelcome.

In the countryside, the influence of the West has in several ways stimulated an intense desire by the peasant for land reform. . . .

. . . The point to be made here is that, wherever for any reason landlessness or land scarcity has existed, the spread of egalitarian ideas from the West has given the peasant an increased feeling that something could be done about it and has intensified the demand for land reform. From the French Revolution, through the Taiping Rebellion in China and the Russian Revolution, down to the pressure for land reform in contemporary Egypt and Iran, this has been true.

＊　＊　＊　＊　＊

The introduction of Western ideas has also had profound effects on traditional societies. Among the new ideas were the Western notions that all men stood equal before the law, that they should have equal opportunity to develop their talents, and that policies should be determined and political leadership selected on a universal suffrage basis. In addition to encountering democratic concepts, many of the new intellectuals from the old societies have been exposed during their formative years in the West to Marxist and other socialist theories. These have often had a great appeal because they purport to explain the forces at work in societies in the process of modernization. The theory of the class struggle, Lenin's theory of imperialism, and Communist doctrine on the organization of revolutionary movements have gained considerable currency and influence, and have helped generate dissatisfaction with traditional attitudes and values. Although the traditional societies or those early in the modernization process did not necessarily desire to install modern democratic processes, the infusion of new ideas sometimes led to strong movements toward increased popular participation in the political process—a revolutionary violation of the customs of traditional rule.

In the selection above, powerful forces such as war and colonialism were examined as stimulants to modernization. A different focus is employed by Daniel Lerner in the excerpt below, drawn from one of the better-known attempts to conceptualize the modernizing process. In this excerpt, the author develops his idea of the importance of empathy, that is, "the capacity to see oneself in the other fellow's situation," and the role of mass communications in the expansion of the number of empathic individuals in transitional societies.

6. MODERNIZING STYLES OF LIFE: A THEORY°

daniel lerner

1. THE MOBILE PERSONALITY: EMPATHY

People in the Western culture have become habituated to the sense of change and attuned to its various rhythms. Many generations ago, in the

° Reprinted with permission of The Macmillan Company from *The Passing of Traditional Society* by Daniel Lerner. Copyright 1958 by The Free Press, a Corporation. Selections from pp. 47–60.

TRANSITIONAL SOCIETIES

West, ordinary men found themselves unbound from their native soil and relatively free to move. Once they actually moved in large numbers, from farms to flats and from fields to factories, they became intimate with the idea of change by direct experience.[1] This bore little resemblance to the migrant or crusading hordes of yore, driven by war or famine. This was movement by individuals, each having made a personal choice to seek elsewhere his own version of a better life.

Physical mobility so experienced naturally entrained social mobility, and gradually there grew institutions appropriate to the process. Those who gained heavily by changing their address soon wanted a convenient bank in the neighborhood to secure their treasure; also a law-and-police force to guard the neighborhood against disorder and devaluation; also a voice in prescribing standards of behavior for others.[2] So came into operation a "system" of bourgeois values that embraced social change as normal. Rules of the game had to be worked out for adjudicating conflicts over the direction and rate of change. Who was to gain, how, and how much? As the profits to be gained from mobility became evident to all, conflicts over access to the channels of opportunity became sharper. The process can be traced through the evolution of Western property and tax laws, whose major tendency is to protect the "haves" without disqualifying the "have-nots." [3] It was by protecting every man's *opportunity* to gain that the modern West turned decisively in the direction of social mobility.

Social institutions founded on voluntary participation by mobile individuals required a new array of skills and a new test of merit. Every person, according to the new democratic theory, was equally entitled to acquire the skills needed for shaping his own "future" in the Great Society. The vigorous controversy over public education that agitated the eighteenth century produced a net affirmation of equal opportunity. In every Western country the verdict was pronounced that education should be freely available to all who wanted it, and in some countries whether they wanted it or not. Thus the idea spread that personal mobility is itself a first-order value; the sense grew that social morality is essentially the ethics of social change. A man is what he may become; a society is its potential. These notions passed out of the realm of debate into the Western law and mores.

A mobile society has to encourage rationality, for the calculus of choice shapes individual behavior and conditions its rewards. People come to see the social future as manipulable rather than ordained and their personal prospects in terms of achievement rather than heritage.

[1] See autobiographical literature of human migration, especially W. I. Thomas and F. Znaniecki, *The Polish Peasant in Europe and America*, v. 5 (1927).
[2] Robert Park, *Human Communities* (1952).
[3] S. Ratner, *American Taxation, Its History As A Social Force in Democracy* (1942).

Rationality is purposive: ways of thinking and acting are instruments of intention (not articles of faith); men succeed or fail by the test of what they accomplish (not what they worship). So, whereas traditional man tended to reject innovation by saying "It has never been thus," the contemporary Westerner is more likely to ask "Does it work?" and try the new way without further ado.

The psychic gap between these two postures is vast. It took much interweaving through time, between ways of doing and ways of thinking, before men could work out a style of daily living with change that felt consistent and seamless. The experience of mobility through successive generations gradually evolved participant lifeways which feel "normal" today. Indeed, while past centuries established the public practices of the mobile society, it has been the work of the twentieth century to diffuse widely a *mobile sensibility* so adaptive to change that rearrangement of the self-system is its distinctive mode.

The mobile personality can be described in objective and technical fashion. . . . The mobile person is distinguished by a high capacity for identification with new aspects of his environment; he comes equipped with the mechanisms needed to incorporate new demands upon himself that arise outside of his habitual experience. These mechanisms for enlarging a man's identity operate in two ways. *Projection* facilitates identification by assigning to the object certain preferred attributes of the self—others are "incorporated" because they are like me. (Distantiation or negative identification, in the Freudian sense, results when one projects onto others certain disliked attributes of the self.) *Introjection* enlarges identity by attributing to the self certain desirable attributes of the object—others are "incorporated" because I am like them or want to be like them. We shall use the word *empathy* as shorthand for both these mechanisms. . . .

We are interested in empathy as the inner mechanism which enables newly mobile persons to *operate efficiently* in a changing world. Empathy, to simplify the matter, is the capacity to see oneself in the other fellow's situation. This is an indispensable skill for people moving out of traditional settings. Ability to empathize may make all the difference, for example, when the newly mobile persons are villagers who grew up knowing all the extant individuals, roles and relationships in their environment. Outside his village or tribe, each must meet new individuals, recognize new roles, and learn new relationships involving himself. . . . Our interest is to clarify the process whereby the high empathizer tends to become also the cash customer, the radio listener, the voter.[4]

---

[4] This formulation approaches the typology on American society developed by David Riesman in *The Lonely Crowd* (1950). Cf. my article "Comfort and Fun: Morality in a Nice Society," *The American Scholar* (Spring 1958).

modern society has individual with empathic capacity

It is a major hypothesis of this study that high empathic capacity is the predominant personal style only in modern society, which is distinctively industrial, urban, literate and *participant*. Traditional society is nonparticipant—it deploys people by kinship into communities isolated from each other and from a center; without an urban-rural division of labor, it develops few needs requiring economic interdependence; lacking the bonds of interdependence, people's horizons are limited by locale and their decisions involve only other *known* people in *known* situations. Hence, there is no need for a transpersonal common doctrine formulated in terms of shared secondary symbols—a national "ideology" which enables persons unknown to each other to engage in political controversy or achieve "consensus" by comparing their opinions. Modern society is participant in that it functions by "consensus"—individuals making personal decisions on public issues must concur often enough with other individuals they do not know to make possible a stable common governance. Among the marks of this historic achievement in social organization, which we call Participant Society, are that most people go through school, read newspapers, receive cash payments in jobs they are legally free to change, buy goods for cash in an open market, vote in elections which actually decide among competing candidates, and express opinions on many matters which are not their personal business.

Especially important, for the Participant Style, is the enormous proportion of people who are expected to "have opinions" on public matters—and the corollary expectation of these people that their opinions will matter. It is this subtly complicated structure of reciprocal expectation which sustains widespread empathy. . . .

Physic mobility

. . . The model of behavior developed by modern society is characterized by empathy, a high capacity for rearranging the self-system on short notice. Whereas the isolate communities of traditional society functioned well on the basis of a highly constrictive personality, the interdependent sectors of modern society require widespread participation. This in turn requires an expansive and adaptive self-system, ready to incorporate new roles and to identify personal values with public issues. This is why modernization of any society has involved the great characterological transformation we call psychic mobility. The latent statistical assertion involved here is this: In modern society *more* individuals exhibit *higher* empathic capacity than in any previous society.

As history has not been written in these terms, we were obliged to organize our own forays into historical data to establish a traceline on the evolution of the participant society and the mobile personality. We restrain our account of these forays to some main lines which lead directly to the problem in hand.

2. THE MOBILITY MULTIPLIER: MASS MEDIA

The historic increase of psychic mobility begins with the expansion of physical travel. Historians conventionally date the modern era from the Age of Exploration. . . . This was an initial phase in the modern expansion of human communication. Gradually the technical means of transporting live bodies improved and physical displacement became an experience lived through by millions of plain folk earlier bounden to some ancestral spot. Geographical mobility became, in this phase, the usual vehicle of social mobility. It remained for a later time to make vivid that each mobile soma of the earlier epoch housed a psyche, and to reconstruct transatlantic history in terms of psychic mobility. . . .

The expansion of psychic mobility means that more people now command greater skill in imagining themselves as strange persons in strange situations, places and times than did people in any previous historical epoch. In our time, indeed, the spread of empathy around the world is accelerating. The earlier increase of physical experience through transportation has been multiplied by the spread of *mediated* experience through mass communication. A generation before Columbus sailed to the New World, Gutenberg activated his printing press. . . .

Radio, film and television climax the evolution set into motion by Gutenberg. The mass media opened to the large masses of mankind the infinite *vicarious* universe. Many more millions of persons in the word were to be affected directly, and perhaps more profoundly, by the communication media than by the transportation agencies. By obviating the physical displacement of travel, the media accented the psychic displacement of vicarious experience. For the imaginary universe not only involves more people, but it involves them in a different order of experience. There is a world of difference, we know, between "armchair travel" and actually "being there." What is the difference?

Physical experience of a new environment affronts the sensibility with new perceptions in their complex "natural" setting. The traveler in a strange land perceives simultaneously climate and clothing, body builds and skin textures, gait and speech, feeding and hygiene, work and play—in short, the ensemble of manners and morals that make a "way of life." A usual consequence for the traveler is that the "pattern of culture" among the strangers becomes confused, diverging from his prior stereotype of it and from his preferred model of reality.

Vicarious experience occurs in quite different conditions. Instead of the complexities that attend a "natural" environment, mediated experience exhibits the simplicity of "artificial" settings contrived by the creative communicator. Thus, while the traveler is apt to become bewildered by the profusion of strange sights and sounds, the receiver of communications is likely to be enjoying a composed and orchestrated version of

TRANSITIONAL SOCIETIES

the new reality. He has the benefit of more facile perception of the new experience as a "whole," with the concomitant advantage (which is sometimes illusory) of facile-comprehension. The stimuli of perception, which shape understanding, have been simplified.

✻   ✻   ✻   ✻   ✻

Thus the mass media, by simplifying *perception* (what we "see") while greatly complicating *response* (what we "do"), have been great teachers of interior manipulation. They disciplined Western man in those empathic skills which spell modernity. They also portrayed for him the roles he might confront and elucidated the opinions he might need. Their continuing spread, in our century is performing a similar function on a world scale. The Middle East already shows the marks of this historic encounter. As a young bureaucrat in Iran put it: "The movies are like a teacher to us, who tells us what to do and what not." . . .

3. THE "SYSTEM" OF MODERNITY[5]

A second proposition of this large historical order derives from the observation that modern media systems have flourished only in societies that are modern by other tests. That is, the media spread psychic mobility most efficiently among peoples who have achieved in some measure the antecedent conditions of geographic and social mobility. The converse of this proposition is also true: no modern society functions efficiently without a developed system of mass media. Our historical forays indicate that the conditions which define modernity form an interlocking "system." They grow conjointly, in the normal situation, or they become stunted severally.

It seems clear that people who live together in a common polity will develop patterned ways of distributing *information* along with other commodities. It is less obvious that these information flows will interact with the distribution of power, wealth, status at so many points as to form a system—and, moreover, a system so tightly interwoven that institutional variation in one sector will be accompanied by regular and determinate variation in the other sectors. Yet, just this degree of interaction between communication and social systems is what our historical exploration suggests.

We differentiated two historical systems of public communication, Oral and Media, according to the paradigm: Who says what to whom

[5] For a fuller discussion of the material in this section, see my paper "Communication Systems and Social Systems: A Statistical Exploration in History and Policy," *Behavioral Science* II (October 1957), pp. 266–275.

and how? On these four variables of source, content, audience, channel the ideal types differ as follows:

	Media Systems	Oral Systems
Channel	Broadcast (mediated)	Personal (face-to-face)
Audience	Heterogeneous (mass)	Primary (groups)
Content	Descriptive (news)	Prescriptive (rules)
Source	Professional (skill)	Hierarchical (status)

In media systems, the main flow of public information is operated by a corps of professional communicators, selected according to skill criteria, whose job it is to transmit mainly descriptive messages ("news") through impersonal media (print, radio, film) to relatively undifferentiated mass audiences. In oral systems, public information usually emanates from sources authorized to speak by their place in the social hierarchy, i.e., by status rather than skill criteria. Its contents are typically prescriptive rather than descriptive; news is less salient than "rules" which specify correct behavior toward imminent events directly involving the larger population, such as tax collections and labor drafts. . . . Even these prescriptive messages are normally transmitted via face-to-face oral channels (or via such point-to-point equivalents as letters) to the primary groups of kinship, worship, work and play.

Naturally, few societies in the world today give a perfect fit to either of these idealized sets of paired comparisons. . . . As we move around the world, subjecting our ideal types to empirical data, various elements in the patterns begin to shift. Most countries are in some phase of transition from one system to the other.

But two observations appear to hold for all countries, regardless of continent, culture, or creed. First the *direction* of change is always from oral to media system (no known case exhibiting change in the reverse direction). Secondly, the *degree* of change toward media system appears to correlate significantly with changes in other key sectors of the social system. If these observations are correct, then we are dealing with a "secular trend" of social change that is global in scope. What we have been calling the Western model of modernization is operating on a global scale. Moreover, since this means that other important changes must regularly accompany the development of a media system, there is some point in the frequent references to a "world communication revolution." We here consider the more moderate proposition that a communication system is both index and agent of change in a total social system. This avoids the genetic problem of causality, about which we can only speculate, in order to stress correlational hypotheses which can be tested. On this view, once the modernizing process is started, chicken and egg in fact "cause" each other to develop.

❖   ❖   ❖   ❖   ❖

Having . . . established high pairwise correlations between urbanization-literacy and literacy-media participation, with critical optima for joint growth in each pair, we are in a position to suggest an interpretation in terms of historical phasing. The secular evolution of a participant society appears to involve a regular sequence of three phases. Urbanization comes first, for cities alone have developed the complex of skills and resources which characterize the modern industrial economy. Within this urban matrix develop both of the attributes which distinguish the next two phases—literacy and media growth. There is a close reciprocal relationship between these, for the literate develop the media which in turn spread literacy. But, historically, literacy performs the key function in the second phase. The capacity to read, at first acquired by relatively few people, equips them to perform the varied tasks required in the modernizing society. Not until the third phase, when the elaborate technology of industrial development is fairly well advanced, does a society begin to produce newspapers, radio networks, and motion pictures on a massive scale. This, in turn, accelerates the spread of literacy. Out of this interaction develop those institutions of participation (e.g., voting) which we find in all advanced modern societies. For countries in transition today, these high correlations suggest that literacy and media participation may be considered as a supply-and-demand reciprocal in a communication market whose locus, at least in its historical inception, can only be urban.

The modernization of society involves complex changes at all levels of society, from the individual through various groups to society as a whole. These changes, while often beneficial in many ways, nevertheless impose severe strains upon the fabric of traditional relationships, and the tensions that result can be deeply injurious to the individuals and groups affected by the changes. In the selection below, David Apter examines some of the sources and consequences of the cultural strains most transitional societies are experiencing in quite acute forms.

7. SOURCES OF CULTURAL STRAIN*

d a v i d e. a p t e r

Cultural strain may derive from family division, religious division, anti-traditionalism, urban migration, ethnic competitiveness, racial compartmentalization, economic discrimination, reliance on political solutions, or any combination of these factors. They are all potential sources of cleavage and social tension, for they mirror fundamental differences in outlook and belief from which most new nations suffer in an extreme form. Indeed, the most distinguishing characteristic of new nations is the great range of divergencies incorporated by the casual lines drawn by the colonial political cartographers in another day.

FAMILY DIVISION

Divisions within the family result in wider impacts upon personality than is the case with other, more ordinary, primary and secondary social groupings. The family is endowed with high solidary and affectual qualities. These qualities make the family a key agency of socialization. Basic divisions in the family, which arise from widespread lack of consensus in society at large, reflect themselves in a failing of the family to create stable roles and images of propriety, right conduct, and social responsibility.

Where the family can no longer perform the role of a basic orienting device, those molecules of stability which the family normally represents are themselves diminished. . . . Socialization is weakened when its function is shifted to other primary and secondary organizations. Political groups, clubs, schools and universities, and work associations can absorb only some of the socialization burden. The chief reason, however, that the family can do the socialization job so well is that the internal-

* From "Introduction" to Chapter IX, "Non-Western Government and Politics," pp. 650–654, by David E. Apter. Reprinted with permission of The Macmillan Company from Comparative Politics edited by Harry Eckstein and David E. Apter. Copyright © 1963 by The Free Press of Glencoe, a division of The Macmillan Company.

ization of certain fundamental norms of right and propriety depends upon natural affection and the need for familial approval and makes the socialization process ultimately possible.

In contrast, secondary groupings cannot provide the emotional gratifications that lie behind socialization, unless they take on familial qualities. A political party, having personalized leadership, may be one alternative to the family in the socialization process, if the family becomes a scene of conflict and malintegration. Another alternative is a separatist religious movement. Either way, challenges to the scope of authority in the family make the task of social control by external means, political and social, much more difficult.

Family conflicts are not simply limited to socialization. They appear in conflicts over division of sexual roles—a common difficulty in Moslem countries, for example, and even worse where part of a country follows Moslem practice while another part does not.

Conflicts in the family are, of course, for the most part between generations. The younger elements are often in spiritual rebellion, not simply against their parents, but against what their parents represent in lost opportunity, acceptance of the past, and lack of vision. Indeed, there is much in common between the younger generations in new nations and second-generation Americans. Embarrassment over a way of life that is increasingly regarded as socially marginal is common in both cases.

Of course, the family continues to play a mediating role in all new nations. . . . Typically, however, as the family consists of traditionally oriented members, it will contain conflicts over tradition, ancestral religious factors, land, and the allocation of responsibilities. Where the family is pitched between traditionalism and modernity, it may involve other strains such as that between husband and wife, particularly if the former is better educated than the latter (a common occurrence because of the colonial practice of giving greater educational and occupational opportunities to men).

Whatever their source, conflicts in the family arouse and promote fundamental emotional disequilibrium, which has the effect of increasing hostility between members of a society, adding to the psychological intensity of all other cleavages and conflicts in a society. Most new nations have been traditionally "family centered." When the importance of the family diminishes, all other aspects of social life are profoundly affected.

RELIGIOUS DIVISION

In most new nations there was a close and intimate connection between traditional religious practices and beliefs and the pre-colonial political systems. The colonial period was not only a point of entry for new and alien religious forms, but also involved the secularization of authority. Systems in which the legitimacy of government had in the past relied upon religious myths and beliefs were thus governed by colonial regimes whose claims to rule were based, first, on superior power, second, upon superior institutions, and third, upon efficiency and welfare. Independent governments coming into office may find that the withdrawal of the Europeans involves a sudden resurgence of traditional religious practice that may result in open religious conflicts, some of which had always smouldered under the surface, although others might be quite new. Meanwhile, the new governments try to incorporate a new system of political legitimacy that itself is not entirely dissimilar to religion. New gods are substituted for old ones, to be worshiped in the name of reason and modernity.

This religious aspect of nationhood is extremely important. The very symbol of nationhood and independence is birth, the supreme act of creativity. Such creative acts are endowed with a special mystical appeal. Inevitably the establishment of political legitimacy and the more usual conflicts over religion are intimately connected, especially as in many new nations we find a rebirth of religion through political ideals, often indeed in the name of modernity, secularism, and socialism.

Thus, the problem of religious division extends far beyond the competition between major religious groupings—Moslem, Hindu, Christian—and far beyond ordinary variations in values. The classic conflicts in the West, between the spiritual and secular spheres of life, is not what is at stake here, but rather competing spiritualities; the values of government and leadership, moral proprieties of state action—all these are involved in the religious sphere, no less than what we generally think of as religious matters. It is no accident that the language of nationalism is often the language of religious usage, and the "political kingdom" is both a claim to secular authority, and an ecclesiastical allusion, the one reinforcing the other.

ANTITRADITIONALISM

Closely related to the problem of religious division, the problem of traditionalism lies athwart religious change. We can distinguish several different factors here. First, a good many old issues that were of political origin tend to renew themselves when seen as a fight over custom. These in turn may give meaning to a parochial society that itself has not yet accepted the idea of a larger polity or citizenship. Clan conflicts, arguments over custom, and the like all help to make the continuation of traditional life appear as the fundamental reality, with some modern forms and institutions regarded as more extraneous. Hostages to fortune, traditionalists have been badly used by contemporary political leaders. In Ghana or Eastern Nigeria, for example, traditionalists are viewed with dislike. The Accra Conference of December, 1958, branded "tribalism" as feudal and reactionary. The traditionalists, on the other hand, seek to preserve their power by absorbing "modernity" where possible. Sometimes they are extremely successful in this attempt, as has been shown by the political achievements of the Northern Nigerians or the Kabaka's government in Buganda.

Occasionally a new form of traditionalism appears. This is the traditionalism of the "establishment" versus the politicians. The more usual case of this occurs where the army or the civil service reflects the emphasis on a rational and efficient polity reminiscent of the colonial period. Often fed up with what becomes viewed as political vagrancy, the establishment sees the nation dissipating its energies and resources on inane political battles and steps in, just as, in a previous day, colonial officers would have done to insure "normalcy." This has happened in Burma, where, after restoring order and cleaning up the towns, the army turned the responsibilities for running the state back to the politicians. In Pakistan and the Sudan, where similar situations have occurred, there are few signs that the army is about to restore the politicians. In contrast, in Ghana the clash has resulted in threats by the politicians to "politicize" the civil service, that is, to introduce a spoils system.

*   *   *   *   *

URBAN MIGRATION

The migration of rural people to towns always creates uncertainty. Consider the rural person who decides to leave the intimacy of his surroundings, the warmth of the hearth, and the security of ascertainable career prospects. He knows that the town is exciting, that his kinsmen will help him, and that the rhythm of life will be very different from that which he has known. His is the classic problem of the rural person becoming a townsman—a subject of a very large literature, both scientific and literary. But in new nations this is a particularly complex process. For one thing, there is rarely a sharp division between the rural and the urban area. Many cities in new nations have tightly enclosed rural centers, almost self-contained villages, existing within the town itself, organized around occupational and ethnic clusters. Stubborn differences in outlook and attitude may continue to prevail within the city, without its usual effects of atomization and homogenization. Indeed, many cities in new nations are dormitories for migrant populations rather than urban settlements in a real sense.

At the same time, this is a generational problem. Kinship and religious ties do tend to loosen in cities. Heterogeneous relationships between social groups are inevitable as children are thrown together in schools and as industry and commercial penetration make the town a center of economic and social dynamism. Where loyalties are being robbed of their particularism, the tendency is towards the opposite extreme, particularly among the young—toward atomism, separatism, and personal independence. This is the milieu which produces the political "street urchin," the broker, and the political entrepreneur. They find ready-made political groups in those protective associations, churches, trade unions, and tribal societies, which are characteristic of cities in new nations. Local urban followings propel them into national politics. The effect of town politics is a corrupting one, primarily because towns provide so many opportunities to politicians, with few requirements of accountability. Rarely are the dormitory towns bearers of culture, although they may give rise to senior social elites who are profoundly aware of their self-importance (as well as objects of envy and often fear).

Characteristically the towns in new nations have not experienced a sharp break between rural and urban life, but rather a blending of one into the other. . . .

¤   ¤   ¤   ¤   ¤

ETHNIC COMPETITIVENESS

Too often the ethnic factor is regarded as a somewhat romantic figment of the past, its passing viewed with regret, but what is termed "ethnicity" is not simply of residual interest—a quaint and historical antecedent in a new nation. Quite the contrary: ethnic formation is another form of nationhood. The still remaining primary attachment of many in new nations is not to the polity of the modern state, but to the polity of the ethnic group. Such ethnic attachments do not wither away with the formation of a national state. As a result many new countries experience bitter conflict between ethnic groups that challenges the new politics in demands for federal political arrangements and other claims to autonomy.

Where ethnicity is strong, few institutions can be immune to its effects. In the case of Indonesia, for example, it has proved most difficult to create a civil service free from ethnic conflict. Such conflict has manifested itself in political party affiliations of administrators, and brought competitive party politics inside the administration. A similar situation prevails in parts of former French Africa.

RACIAL COMPARTMENTALIZATION

The problem of racial compartmentalization is most acute in those societies which have a substantial proportion of *white* settlers. Where there are other minority groups in important economic or social positions, such as the Chinese in Thailand, Sarawak, or Malaya, the problems have usually not been acute unless activated from "outside," as, for example, the recent effort of the Chinese government to exhort the Chinese community in Indonesia to resist relocation schemes favored by the Indonesian government.

Racial compartmentalization exists in any society where racial groups have a very high number of transactions within the racial group and very few outside the group. Thus, in South Africa, Kenya, or Southern Rhodesia, a European can live a full life without coming into contact with Africans or Asians except under highly regularized and, in a sense, "ritualized" ways. . . .

How to build a plural society is one problem posed by racial compartmentalization. How to prevent racial conflict from becoming class conflict is another. Where race, culture, and class combine in racial compartmentalization, the outlook for violence and turbulence becomes pronounced. We have only to regard South Africa to see this.[1]

The greatest difficulty with racial compartmentalization is that, once created, the nature of the relationship between the races becomes hardened and fixed so that any alteration of it is tantamount to a social revolution. Under such circumstances any increase in the transactions between racial communities only helps to confirm each in its prejudices.

Commonplace in Western studies of race relations is the idea that as members come to know one another their prejudices slowly begin to give way. Unfortunately this is not the case in plural societies. There is a difference between a racial *group* and a racial *community*. Once a community is built on grounds of race, it repels or tries to render impotent any threats to the stereotyped basis of its conceptions. For a racial *community* cannot dismiss race as trivial or irrelevant if it wishes to maintain its exclusiveness. Under such circumstances, increased contact between *communities* simply means greater prejudice. . . .

ECONOMIC DISCRIMINATION

Economic discrimination tends to carry over its effects long after it is removed. It becomes part of the heritage of nationalists who, explain-

[1] Europeans amount to 21 per cent of the population in South Africa. See *State of the Union, Economic, Financial and Statistical Year Book for South Africa,* Capetown, Culemborg, 1957, p. 37.

ing backwardness as a consequence of Western exploitation, see in their country's inability to "catch up" with the West an extension of an earlier process. We have always tended, however, to regard economic discrimination as something practiced by Europeans against Africans or Asians, whether in the form of large expatriate firms or in the practices of colonialism, including debarment of native peoples from participation in the economy in all but the most subservient positions. This still goes on to some degree in many areas, but by and large both "social welfare colonialism" of the postwar period and effective organization by nationalists have made these forms of discrimination less significant, except in plural societies.

There is some danger that the nationalism of the 1940's, mainly Marxian in its overtones, should result in a reverse kind of economic discrimination. For example, it is quite possible that attitudes toward private investment, resulting from a previous period of aggressive capitalism, should lead politicians to deny any useful role to private investors. By so doing, they can easily make the burden for planning and state enterprise too great. . . .

Another reason that private enterprise is denigrated in new nations is related to the informal and unplanned manner of doing business that is the historical way of the West. When they were protected and controlled by strong colonial oligarchs with a commitment to service and efficiency under the later periods of social welfare colonialism, the colonial territories were in some measure safeguarded against the inroads of uncontrolled commerce. After independence the situation is radically different. . . .

☼   ☼   ☼   ☼   ☼

EMPHASIS ON POLITICAL SOLUTIONS

It is characteristic of new nations that, having won their freedom through political action and having taken over from civil service oligarchies responsible for the major activities of social life and welfare, they should continue to view progress in purely political terms. Politics is at once a major means of social mobility and a source of power and prestige. Thus, government tends to become omnivorous. Indeed, in most new nations government depletes the intellectual resources of regions, towns, and villages, drawing men of ability towards the center and then pushing a few reluctant administrators outward again to handle administrative tasks.

Politics becomes itself society rather than only a part of it. This trend is a most important source of strain in new states, for it causes all social matters to become political. Education, development, and religion

TRANSITIONAL SOCIETIES

all become evaluated in political terms. Planners, politicians, and administrators begin to live by the competitive practices of power rather than an image of public well-being. There is great danger of the public itself being viewed as the greatest of all obstacles, and tension between rulers and ruled becomes acute. Most new nations are democracies and believe in majority rule; but, as Panikkar points out, the right of the majority to exact obedience runs into grave difficulties. The difficulties of new nations stem from the very factors we have been discussing and, if fundamental enough, lead politicians to prefer forms of government other than majority rule.[2]

[2] See K. M. Panikkar, *The Afro-Asian States and Their Problems* (London, Allen & Unwin, 1959), p. 19.

While it is clear that important changes have been taking place in traditional societies over the years, it still remains difficult to obtain an accurate picture of transitional societies. The speed and comprehensiveness with which traditional values and patterns of organization and authority are obliterated or modified varies from society to society and within societies. Old forms often survive long after they have lost their original meaning and importance, while new forms may be adopted only superficially and without possessing deep significance. In the following selection, L. P. Mair explores some of the dimensions of change in Africa and their consequences.

8. SOCIAL CHANGE IN AFRICA*

l. p. m a i r

[handwritten: no society has a single pol. culture / there exists a) mass pol. culture b) elite " / is elite totally distinct from mass or is elite a result of process of acculturation of mass]

Whatever judgments may be passed on the aims and methods of colonial rule in Africa, the historical fact is that it set in motion processes of change which African leaders themselves now wish to carry farther. The techniques of production evolved in the industrial revolution were ex-

* From "Social Change in Africa" by L. P. Mair, *International Affairs*, Vol. XXXVI, No. 4 (October, 1960), pp. 447–456. By permission of the publisher and the author.

[handwritten: range of / pol. culture reaction — 50% in Can. produce a commission / of another prov. fed — conference / — 50% in developing country might / result in revolution, coups. etc. / 100% / 50 / 0]

tended to Africa by what has been through the greater part of history
the principal method of disseminating superior techniques, the extension
of political control. Of course most of the people who were concerned in
the process were not primarily interested in the benefits which would
accrue to Africans, though a few were. One could argue for ever, and for
ever inconclusively, such questions as who got undue advantage out of
it, whether economic development 'really makes people happier', and so
forth. The wider the field over which such questions are asked, the more
impossible it becomes to strike a balance. The fact which is relevant to
the situation today is that Africans, in rejecting their European rulers,
have not sought to reject the techniques of production and of government which those rulers brought to Africa, but, on the contrary, to assert
African control over them. *Négritude* emphatically does not mean a
return to the mode of life of a century ago.

To a superficial observer changes in mode of life are measured by
what can immediately be seen. . . . But it is the kind of change in social
relationships of which these are the signs that interests the student of
society. The process through which Africa is passing can be summarized
as a process of change from small-scale to large-scale organization, economic and political.

* * * * *

What I want to consider is the effect on African society of this
widening of the scale of social relationships. It has resulted in an immense redistribution of population, which is most conspicuous in the
great industrial and commercial centres, but can also be seen in immigration to the limited areas of land that are suitable for growing profitable export crops, such as the coffee lands of East Africa or the cocoa
forest area along the Gulf of Guinea. This physical movement is obvious.
Along with it goes the movement from status to contract, to use Maine's
classic phrase: from reliance on the co-operation of kin and neighbours
to the impersonal cash nexus. The change has not gone nearly as far in
the rural as it has in the urban areas, but it is in progress there too. It is
seen both in a new attitude towards rights over land and in the employment of wage-labour by Africans. Old and new values mix uneasily in
both these fields.

Land, once the cherished, inalienable patrimony of a kin group, is
becoming a negotiable good. Cocoa farms and cotton land are sold for
cash or sometimes rack-rented. But few, if any, Africans will deliberately
divest themselves of all claim to land. It is not yet just one among many
possible sources of income, but has an almost mystical significance, as
well as the social significance carried over from the days of subsistence
agriculture, when those who had no rights over land had to become

though pol. reaction is partially a result of pol. culture.

dependants, or clients, of those with land to spare. This intense desire to have rights in some land, no matter how little, may disappoint the hopes of those who see the key to economic development in making all land freely negotiable.

The interesting fact about the employees of African farmers is that they are invariably immigrants to the areas where they are working. In Ghana they come from the Northern Territories, in Uganda from Ruanda or Tanganyika, or else from the less fertile parts of the Protectorate itself. The explanation that some peoples 'think they are above work' is superficial. Everyone, everywhere, who can buy a machine or pay another person to do his hard manual labour for him, does so. But in a small closed society in which the relationship of employer and labourer has never previously existed, people do not spontaneously enter into it. Such contracts can only be made with outsiders. This fact, however, gives rise to delicate political situations. The immigrants may seek to obtain full membership of the new community, in particular the right to settle on the land, and this is usually opposed by the sons of the soil, as it is for example on the cotton land around Lake Victoria.

o　o　o　o　o

In the last twenty years urban populations in Africa have increased at an enormous rate. Housing has not kept pace with the influx, and all the social problems of the slum have appeared. In those towns which owe their existence to the European 'presence', attempts have been made to control immigration, though only the Union still tries to maintain that Africans ought not to be more than temporary sojourners in its cities. In town the African is dependent for subsistence on a contract with an employer, and for physical security not on tribal authorities but on national laws, enforced by State police. He is plunged right into the world of impersonal cash transactions. He may be able to have wife and children with him—this depends on municipal housing policies—but he can no longer live as a member of a community of a hundred or more all bound by the ties of kinship and recognizing obligations of mutual assistance. . . .

Nevertheless, it is clearly in the towns that modern African society must come into being. It is there that members of the many traditional small-scale societies are brought into constant contact, and do organize themselves in wider associations, as we see in the development of political parties, trade unions, new religions, and even pan-African movements.

To a student of society one of the most interesting aspects of the new urban populations is the interplay of the old ties, based on locality, language, and the recognition, in the chief, of a common political head and symbol of unity, and the new ones based on common interests in the new situation. Both in Nigeria and in Ghana the urban associations of which we hear most are locally based—bodies such as the Ibo improvement unions which assist newcomers from their own home area, raise money for the education of bright boys from home, and at elections, local and general, may be more interested in the home town than in their place of work.

Inevitably the immigrants to urban areas cluster in groups which have language and customs in common and in which the immigrants have kin and personal friends. Little conscious effort is made by anyone in authority to create wider communities; some municipal housing authorities have supposed that all that was needed would be to refuse to delineate 'tribal' areas in new estates. Yet the new common interests of urban dwellers do lead them to submerge tribal divisions in other forms of association.

Trade unions flourish in Nigeria, where under 5 per cent of the population is employed in wage-labour, and indeed throughout West Africa, as well as in the really industrial environment of the copper-belt. A recent study made there shows how, although tribal divisions have by no means lost their meaning, they do not prevent combination on a wider scale where there is a clear community of interest.[1] Competitors for leadership may appeal to tribal sentiment; dissatisfied sections may explain the failure of the union to achieve the results hoped for by the argument that the officials care only for their own tribesmen. But the detached observer can see the development of an urban society as this is generally understood, in which solidarity and opposition are expressions of economic interest and class structure, and no longer primarily of ethnic origin.

The new religions do not seem in practice to have a widely unifying effect, although their doctrines sometimes proclaim the appearance of a prophet sent by God expressly to be the saviour of all Africans. Typically they have expressed disillusionment with Christianity as it has been presented by missionaries—a religion which makes promises to all the children of God, but in practice appears to be no more than the supernatural source of Western domination. African churches have appeared in many places, each with its own Messiah, a man who has lived quite recently. . . .

Unfortunately it is only in the urban areas that the unifying forces of the modern economic and political system have their full effect; and it is characteristic of those African territories which have already attained independence, or are closest to it, that they are still very largely rural. An exception should be made perhaps for the ex-Belgian Congo with its great mining industries; but these industries do not weld together the populations of all its enormous area, but rather form points around which divisions crystallize.

Of course it is above all in the political field that the contradictions

---

[1] A. L. Epstein, *Politics in an Urban African Community* (Manchester University Press, 1958).

TRANSITIONAL SOCIETIES

between the wide and the narrow outlook are most apparent. These contradictions result in a condition which could be called political immaturity in a very different sense from that normally implied by the term. It is not a question of understanding techniques of administration or of accepting constitutional conventions. It is rather that in the African territories the major political issues are questions which the older nations are presumed to have either settled or learned to put up with. Reporters who deplore the absence of programmes and policies in pre-independence elections are wrong in supposing that the only alternative is competition between personalities. Every personality has a following, and the characteristic of this following is that it is a local one. To some extent this results inevitably from the language barriers that divide the African peoples. A leader should be able to speak directly to his followers; where he cannot do this he can only rely on emotive slogans, and such slogans are provided more readily by opposition to colonial rule than by the issues which arise after independence. . . .

'Freedom' in Africa does not mean primarily civil liberties; it means not having to obey somebody you think of as an outsider, and once the most conspicuous outsiders, the expatriates, withdraw, small political units with common traditions begin to look uneasily at their neighbours (with whom they may share a tradition of mutual hostility). These attitudes are identical in essence with the territorial or pan-African nationalisms which command the sympathy of the liberal-minded. They are the nationalisms of the people who still belong to the small-scale society. Their existence presents serious problems for the new States. But they will never be eliminated by homilies about the pettiness of parochialism. People's ideas are necessarily limited to the world of their experience.

The fears of minorities and their demands for greater autonomy are by no means peculiar to Africa or to the newly emerging States. They have appeared in one form or another in every nation, but the older nations have settled by now into moulds which they are not likely to crack. In West Africa, as things stand at present, Ghana and Nigeria illustrate the alternative ways of dealing with minorities—by suppressing them and by seeking to allay their fears. The contrast may merely reflect the fact that Ghana became independent earlier; the Colonial Office wrote a Constitution for Ghana which provided some degree of regional autonomy, but this did not last long. Dr Nkrumah's centralizing policy has culminated in his republic, which gives no recognition to minority groups. Moreover, the recent referendum showed a surprisingly large favourable vote in the minority areas, though of course the Opposition have accused the Government party of intimidation.

☼　☼　☼　☼　☼

In Africa local solidarity is the stronger because so many of the small local groups of which we are speaking have been until recently autonomous political units, each headed and symbolized by its own chief. British administrators are now being taken to task for having recognized these chiefs, a policy which was indubitably in line with popular sentiment at the time of its inception. Critics of this policy have never made it quite clear what alternative they would have preferred. It is true, and is well known, that French administration did not give much administrative responsibility to traditional rulers, but it is less well known that traditional rulers in the French-speaking territories retained considerable political influence, and in some were only formally 'abolished' by the newly created representative assemblies. It is fair, however, to admit that the most conspicuous divisions in these territories comprise wider areas than those associated with individual chiefs.

Except in such cases as Northern Nigeria, Western Uganda, and Basutoland, where rulers do still rule, chiefs are rapidly losing all governmental and administrative functions. This is inevitable in the modern large-scale world; the sphere of authority of the great majority of African chiefs is too small to be any longer meaningful, and the Belgian policy of grouping chiefdoms together and promoting one chief to be paramount had the same disadvantages as the creation of elected councils embracing several traditional units, and no obvious advantages. The same might be said of the Tanganyika federations of native authorities. The present position of most African chiefs is unhappy. In terms of the needs of modern government they are an anachronism. In the eyes of nationalist politicians they have sided with the enemy by accepting responsibility under colonial rule. They are 'reactionary' not in the sense that they themselves are obstructing the modernization of their countries (though they may be), but in the sense that they incarnate the old order in the eyes of the many people who are still more at home in the old order than in the new. Ghanaian fishermen still think, if the catch is not good, that this is because the chief can no longer afford to perform the necessary rituals.

The changes which African societies are going through are not in essence different from those which European societies have experienced as the mass of their populations ceased to be peasants and craftsmen and became agricultural labourers and machine-minders. What makes the changes in Africa so striking is their speed. As one reads the history of the eighteenth century, the seventeenth, the sixteenth, and even farther back, one can find parallels with contemporary events on that continent. The existence, right up to the time of industrialization, of such tiny political units makes a contrast with other parts of the world that have only recently been industrialized. But the most striking contrast between the experience of Africa and the history of Europe lies in the fact that from mediaeval times the rulers of Europe have been able to command the services of literate persons in sufficient numbers to meet the needs of administration as these have been conceived at any given time; and there has been a gradation rather than a gulf in outlook and mode of life between literate and illiterate.

In Africa the gulf is real and deep. The top people are those who have been educated in schools giving instruction in the language of the metropolitan Power. Not all of them have had secondary education; only a few have had more. From them come the politicians, the professional men, the civil servants and technicians. As the colonial governments saw independence approaching, they have done what they could to increase opportunities for professional, particularly technical, training, and some of the large firms have introduced training schemes for their employees. But the difficulty of adequately staffing the public services and industry without recourse to 'expatriates' is everywhere considerable. The new élite are the people whose mode of life is thoroughly Westernized as far as externals are concerned, who live in brick or cement houses and own cars and refrigerators, and they are the source of nationalist leadership and political ideas.

* * * * *

In effect, the political system, although now it is manned by Africans, has been superimposed from outside on the smaller-scale polities that existed before it, and many of the values which it is supposed to represent have not emerged from any local searching of hearts. It is indeed recognized that democracy involves elections, but delicate considerations such as the genuine freedom of the vote, not to mention the tolerance of the majority for the minority, are not apt to be taken very seriously. It is worth recalling that during the greater part of the period of colonial rule government was neither subject to democratic checks nor required to guarantee civil liberties. Nevertheless, it is not my impression that when African politicians take a cavalier line towards democratic procedures they are deliberately imitating their colonial predecessors. Rather, they look on party politics as a battle in the literal sense, and they fight it both in invoking and by breaking the law.

Since the unity of the new States is so precarious, it may well be that their rulers cannot at present afford that tolerance of opposition which is the ideal of representative democracy. It is even possible that a more ruthless programme of technical re-organization than colonial governments have attempted is the only way to save the agricultural resources of Africa from destruction. The crucial problem for the new governments seems likely to be how to be authoritarian enough to maintain stability and carry through their modernizing policies, and yet not so obviously oppressive as to provoke active or passive resistance.

iv. political ideas and ideologies

One of the more striking characteristics of politics in the developing world is the attempt by some leaders to construct and articulate a comprehensive political ideology. The works of a few leaders, such as Léopold Senghor, Mao Tse-tung, and Fidel Castro, have achieved much attention throughout the world, inspiring their friends and causing their opponents concern. Confronted by extraordinarily complex social, political, and economic problems, many leaders have sought to rally and mobilize the intellectual and emotional forces of their followers through an appeal to a blueprint for modernization. This blueprint is often emotionally and forcefully presented by the leaders in an attempt to induce the commitment of the necessary human and material resources for development.

As in other matters, considerable variation is found among the developing societies and their leaders in the extent to which a more or less integrated doctrine of social change has been formulated as well as in the importance of ideological considerations in policy-making. Among the more conservative elites in many Latin American and some Asian and African states, the fundamental beliefs and values upon which policies are predicated remain oriented toward the maintenance of traditional privileges and institutions. Few dramatic social, economic, or political changes are proposed or supported by these elites, though in some cases they are being increasingly challenged by counter elites who demand more rapid and far-reaching changes in the traditional order. On the other hand, some radical revolutionary leaders, impatient with gradual, pragmatic changes, have formulated elaborate ideologies to *due to social fragmentation & disintegration of old order: ① ideology — psychological & emotional basis from which ind. can derive meaning ② legitimize authority ③ bridge social ethnic divisions*

guide and justify their actions designed to reconstruct their societies as rapidly as possible. These leaders seek to generate such enthusiasm for and dedication to their goals that suffering and hardship, if required, will willingly be borne and tolerated during the transitional period. Between these extreme positions of the conservative (or reactionary) and the radical leaders are many others whose approaches to the problems of modernization are, while vigorous, more pragmatic and less encumbered with rigid ideological considerations.

It is easy to overestimate the importance and representativeness of a few vocal and articulate spokesmen; already some of the best known, such as former Presidents Sukarno of Indonesia and Kwame Nkrumah of Ghana, have been replaced by more pragmatic, less spectacular leaders. Further, many "ideologies" are little more than popular revolutionary words and phrases strung together with little coherence or consistency. That being so, it is often difficult to establish a very strong relationship between the "ideology" and political actions. Nevertheless, even though the study of political ideas and ideologies may reveal little about the policies that are, in fact, pursued, the dominant political ideas, no matter how poorly or how well organized and expressed, need to be taken into account in any equation of politics in the transitional societies.[1]

Ideologies can perform several important functions in states that seek and are undergoing rapid change. As we have seen, many of the developing states are confronted by the difficult problems that arise from their social fragmentation and the disintegration of the old order. As the traditional bases of personal identification are being eroded, an ideology may provide an important psychological and emotional base from which individuals can derive meaning and significance for their own participation in a changing society. Thus an ideology provides a framework within which the individual may orient himself to others in an emotionally satisfying manner. In sharing with others in the pursuit of common goals, individuals develop relationships and loyalties with each other which help to fill the voids created by the disruption of the traditional order. The establishment of broad, common goals may also serve to bridge the deep social and ethnic divisions within the society, thereby promoting national unity. In addition, by encouraging a common perspective on societal goals and problems, an ideology helps to legitimize authority. In many cases, the legitimacy of governments in the developing states is weak and in doubt, resulting from the serious divisions of opinion within society concerning the proper bases and structures of political authority. To the extent that leaders can obtain general

---

[1] Christopher Clapham, "The Context of African Political Thought," *The Journal of Modern African Studies*, Vol. VIII, No. 1 (April, 1970), pp. 1–13, and J. D. B. Miller, "Political and Ideological Trends of Underdeveloped Nations," *The Atlantic Community Quarterly*, Vol. VII, No. 3 (Fall, 1969), pp. 421–431.

themes of ideologies.
a) rationalization
b) socialism — efficient means
c) democracy
usually rejection of capitalism

103

POLITICAL IDEAS AND IDEOLOGIES

acceptance of the goals postulated in their ideologies, the legitimacy of their own personal authority and that of the political institutions within the state is enhanced. In short, an ideology that is increasingly accepted performs the vital function of building common beliefs and attitudes among the political elite and masses, uniting the different groups within society in the pursuit of shared goals. The utility of a comprehensive, explicit ideology is, then, greater in most transitional societies than in either more traditional or more modern ones where, in both cases, a higher level of consensus on existing values, institutions, and processes is likely to be found. A major problem confronting leaders of transitional societies is to develop and maintain, in a period of rapid change, consensus on both objectives and the means to achieve them, and an ideology can help to perform this essential function.

Despite important variations in the specific doctrines and the emphases given them, the ideologies articulated by the leaders of the developing nations are all founded on a general idea which, while commonplace to persons in American or European societies, is often revolutionary in the context of the history and present level of development of the transitional states. That basic idea asserts that a better life *is* possible for individuals and groups than the one provided by the traditional order. This better life is conceived in terms of a higher standard of living, the dignity and equality of the nation and state, and the full self-determination by the state of its internal and international affairs. To achieve these goals, fundamental changes are assumed to be required throughout the social, political, and economic systems within the state. On the question of how to achieve these goals, different leaders provide different specific answers. Nevertheless, certain general themes are commonly stressed.

Of the several principal themes comprising the "ideology of modernization and development," that of nationalism is the most pervasive and perhaps persuasive. In addition, there is usually a commitment to the doctrines and values of socialism and democracy, though both of these doctrines are interpreted in several ways. These three themes are woven together into different patterns by the leaders of the developing states.[2] The individual patterns vary, in part, because of different historical experiences, perceptions of the present conditions and problems of society, and aspirations for the future. Particular variations also arise from the cultural, religious, and social characteristics of the individual societies as well as from the personalities of the individual leaders.

The emotional and intellectual commitment to development and modernization exhibited by many leaders of the developing states cannot be understood apart from their perception of the nature and conse-

[2] See the useful compilation of statements in Paul E. Sigmund, Jr., ed., *The Ideologies of the Developing Nations,* 2nd rev. ed. (New York, Frederick A. Praeger, Inc., Publishers, 1972).

quences of political domination and economic exploitation by the major powers over the past several hundred years. Even in the Latin American states, which have been politically independent for over a century, a strong reaction arises from the fear that their economic independence is or can be easily impaired. For most African and Asian leaders, of course, the impact of colonialization and economic imperialism has been much more recent and encompassing. As these leaders perceive the recent history of their societies, the colonial powers drained enormous wealth from their areas while giving little in return. While the major powers improved their own standards of living and enjoyed the benefits of mass education, high standards of health, and political freedom, the exploited areas languished in poverty, disease, and ignorance. In seeking raw materials and markets for their expanding industries and economies, the major powers established political and economic controls from which there seemed no escape. The economies of the underdeveloped areas were frequently made dependent on one or a very few exports, subject to the vicissitudes of world market prices for these raw materials. Through their controls, the colonial powers forced the underdeveloped areas to purchase their finished products with little opportunity to bargain for lower prices. Even the United States, which never possessed extensive colonial holdings, does not escape this harsh criticism. Its gunboat diplomacy and its sanction and support of the exploitative policies pursued by private American firms in Latin America are seen as only a variation—perhaps more subtle, and for that reason more dangerous—of the basic principles of colonial domination and exploitation which were more openly employed by European powers. As a major industrial power, the United States, like its European counterparts, could exercise great influence over the prices paid for the exports of the developing states as well as affect their economies directly through its investments.

This interpretation of colonial relationships obviously has much in common with the classical Marxist-Leninist analysis of imperialism. Indeed, many of these leaders acknowledge the influence of Marx and Lenin on their thinking, though few call themselves Marxists. The importance of the present leaders' interpretation of history is that it produces ambiguous, complex, and sometimes contradictory attitudes toward the present conditions of their societies, the manner in which change should take place, and relationships among sovereign states. On the one hand, these leaders admire the scientific achievements of the technologically advanced societies, even if they are former colonial powers. On the other hand, their interpretation of history stirs feelings of deep resentment and distrust of the advanced societies which, they believe, achieved their superiority largely as a consequence of their exploitative policies, and which today and in the future may employ their superiority in devious ways to perpetuate their dominant power.

Further, this interpretation of history may distort the perception of the nature and causes of present-day problems. By emphasizing the evils arising from colonial policies, fundamental causes indigenous to the society tend to be overlooked or blurred.

To prevent the policies of exploitation and subjugation from continuing, much more than political independence is required, these leaders assert. What is further required is the development of a strong, unified, stable, respected, and prosperous society. This position can be attained through the development of a diversified economy, a broad industrial base, a mass educational system, modern transportation and communication facilities—in short, all the accoutrements of a modern, industrialized society. Only in this way can the full political and economic independence of the state be assured. The problem confronting these leaders is how this desired state of affairs can be achieved.

The first requirement on the road to modernization, according to these leaders, is the achievement of political power. Whether this takes the form of an independence movement against a colonial power or the overthrow of an existing conservative or reactionary government (such as accomplished by Castro's overthrow of Batista in Cuba), the fundamental need is to obtain control of the authoritative instruments of the state. In many areas in Asia and Africa, the present leaders have been faced with two tasks: first, securing political independence from a major European power, and second, establishing the political framework for the nation-state through which the instruments of power could be exercised. In some cases, protracted conflict preceded the attainment of independence; in others, the colonial power seemed almost eager to shed its control. Particularly in the former cases, leaders of the independence movement vigorously espoused the doctrine of nationalism as a rallying call. National self-determination was asserted as a fundamental right, and appeals for support were directed to leaders of those states, such as the United States, that historically have supported this concept. This nationalism, however, as John Kautsky indicates below, differs from the classical European type in that it seeks to erect independent states where none existed before and is not usually founded upon a common language or nationality. In many areas of Asia and Africa, it is not clear just what constitutes the nation that is to be independent or how far the principle of self-determination is to be carried out. In general, the boundaries established by the colonial powers have been retained as the geographic bases of the new states. Yet the several attempts to create larger political unions, such as the unsuccessful Mali Federation in Africa, are indicative of the problem of deciding what groups are to comprise the nation-state. In other cases, leaders of some newly independent states find themselves confronted by groups demanding the same rights to national self-determination that have just been successfully employed against the former colonial power. In Burma, for example, the Karens, a large ethnic minority, have repeatedly sought to establish their own autonomous state.

The development of a common feeling of identification with and loyalty to the geographically defined state remains a major problem in many areas. National leaders are attempting to replace the present primary loyalties of the masses to their individual ethnic and cultural groups with new primary loyalties toward the state.[3] A variety of approaches are used in these attempts to create a feeling of nationalism centering upon the state. Leaders try, for example, to resurrect, preserve, and reinvigorate those traditional loyalties that are compatible with the new loyalty to the state. Local and regional heroes become national heroes, the songs of individual ethnic groups are nationalized, and new symbols that utilize traditional elements are created, such as flags and mottoes. More importantly, programs of national development from which all groups may derive benefits are designed and executed. "Enemies" of the state and its developmental schemes—frequently the former colonial powers—are sometimes created or identified; to overcome these enemies, whether internal or external, leaders may attempt to rally their followers through emotionally charged campaigns to protect the state and its progress. Nationalism is also encouraged through education and the mass communications media when those unique features of national society—its history, symbols, geography, religion, and so on—are stressed.

The creation of nationalistic feelings is considered fundamental to the implementation of developmental policies. *National* development is impeded if local groups cannot cooperate; their disputes and attempts to promote their own interests at the expense of the larger community disrupt national progress. A strong feeling of nationalism inspires a commitment to the larger community and a willingness to work for the promotion of the welfare of the nation and state. Nationalism thus provides an essential psychological base on which the successful execution of national developmental programs must in large part rest. Since nationalism also helps to legitimize the authority of those who plan and enforce these policies, great stress is placed upon developing positive attitudes toward the state and its leaders. Intensive propaganda campaigns are undertaken to promote and intensify feelings of national unity. Many speeches are devoted to a discussion of the state and its achievements and the need to maintain national solidarity, both for purposes of internal development and in order to play a significant role in international affairs. The result is that in most states some progress has been made in creating a sense of nationhood among the various

[3] Frederick W. Frey, "Socialization to National Identification Among Turkish Peasants," *The Journal of Politics,* Vol. XXX, No. 4 (November, 1968), pp. 934–965.

groups within the individual states. Yet the traditional primary identifi-cations with the ethnic, tribal, or other more limited group have by no means disappeared among wide segments of many populations, nor are they likely to be obliterated for many years to come.

A second widely shared doctrine in the ideology of development and modernization is that of socialism. With few exceptions, primarily in some of the Latin American states, the Philippines, and Malaysia, the present leaders of the developing states maintain that the goal of social justice is most readily and properly attained through the active inter-vention of the state in a broad range of social and economic affairs of the society. The specific economic and social principles to which they sub-scribe, however, vary considerably, ranging from those expounded in Communist China and Cuba to those in Chile and India. Typically, the doctrine of socialism has little rigidity; it is commonly developed on the basis of broad principles and shaped and modified as practical problems of development are confronted. Social justice is to be achieved through policies that, while diminishing the traditionally great gap separating the economic and social elite from the poor and illiterate masses, will raise the general standard of living and thus provide greater social and economic equality and opportunity for all persons. Much importance is usually attached to comprehensive central planning by the governments as the means to achieve the most efficient utilization of the often limited resources available for development. While the developmental plans differ in their specific provisions for state ownership or control of land, industry, transportation and communication facilities, and other busi-nesses, extensive public ownership is commonly provided for and justi-fied in terms of the social as well as the economic benefits to be derived by the society as a whole. In addition to developing the economy of the state directly, the plans also provide for the establishment and extension of educational, medical, and other facilities necessary to raise the stan-dard of living.

Laissez-faire capitalism is rejected by many leaders on both intel-lectual and moral grounds. They believe that the competitive aspects of capitalism are wasteful of human and natural resources, that develop-ment through capitalism is slow and inefficient, and that capitalism promotes undesirable social and economic divisions within a society. If the gaps between the rich and the poor within their societies, and between the rich and the poor nations, are to be narrowed quickly, the more leisurely pace of capitalism must be replaced by planned, orderly development. These leaders argue that to attempt to develop a complex industrial economy from their agrarian base through capitalism would result in widening the division between their states and the industrial giants. Here the Soviet example of economic development is suggestive of the speed with which a backward society can achieve a high level of economic development through careful, comprehensive planning. Such planning can utilize and exploit the scientific discoveries and the technology created by capitalism for the rapid transformation of the economy.

At the same time that socialism is regarded as more efficient, it is also viewed as being morally superior to capitalism. By eliminating or substantially restraining the profit motive, leaders seek to avoid the harsh, divisive, and exploitative aspects of capitalism, and the creation of an economic and social elite at the expense of the masses. Socialism is also regarded as conducive to national unity in that the economic policies to be pursued ignore ethnic and cultural differences within the state. Through central planning and control of the economy, all groups within the society can be afforded greater opportunities for their social development.

While often highly critical of capitalism, most leaders also reject the economic and social policies advocated by the communists. Though the rapid industrialization of the Soviet Union elicits admiration, criticisms are leveled against the ruthless regimentation of workers and the agricultural collectivization that accompanied it. The leaders of the developing states regard their humanistic socialism as morally superior to materialistic communism, which, they assert, has so little concern for other than material values. These leaders believe that they can fashion a program of rapid economic development without the more extreme social consequences of human suffering and loss of dignity and freedom that occurred in the Soviet Union. Yet the fact that the Soviet Union possessed no colonies and did not pursue economic policies that openly exploited the developing areas makes the criticisms of Soviet policies less emotional and intense than those directed against capitalism and capitalist states.

For many leaders, the doctrines of socialism and democracy are inseparably interwoven. The social and economic equality promoted by socialism is equated with the political equality inherent in democracy. Nevertheless, just as the concept of socialism is variously interpreted, so is the concept of democracy. Of course, few leaders today, no matter how conservative or liberal, claim to be other than democratic. Similarly, most states are designated as democracies, at least by their own leaders. Political systems as widely divergent as Communist China, Uruguay, and Ethiopia proclaim that democracy is practiced in their societies. Obviously, the term itself has achieved almost universal acceptance. But the component principles within the concept range over a wide spectrum of fundamental rights and privileges, responsibilities and duties, and organizational structures and political processes.

As with the social and economic doctrines to which these leaders generally subscribe, political doctrines are designed to perform two related roles: they are to contribute to the unification of society and to its overall development and modernization. A principal theme in all the various interpretations of democracy is that national unity is promoted by mass political participation. By involving the masses in national politics, the leaders hope to foster a feeling of identification and participation, and thus to override social and economic cleavages within the society. As political solidarity is achieved, the legitimacy of the state, and the government and its policies, is strengthened. Strong governments are considered essential if the goals of modernization and development are to be achieved. To formulate and execute the broad social and economic plans that will transform society, vigorous leadership and strong institutional structures are required; these, in turn, are to be supported by an increasing consensus on the direction society is to take.

Two major interpretations of democracy may be identified in the developing states. Stemming from these different interpretations, different political frameworks in these states have been constructed in terms of institutions, processes, and rights and liberties.

Some leaders assert that national unity and strong, progressive, and responsible governments are best promoted by an interpretation of democracy that emphasizes individual rather than collective rights and duties. Democracy, from this point of view, is based upon the right of every individual freely to express himself and to organize with others for the promotion of particular interests and policies. Democracy is the framework within which these competing views contend for acceptance. Through free debate and discussion, compromises emerge, forming the foundation upon which national unity is built. National unity, in turn, supports stable governments that are endowed with a high degree of legitimacy and capable of exercising direction and control of the society. Consequently, the institutions of government should be constructed to promote the achievement of compromise. The role of the opposition must be respected. Free elections should be held periodically to enable the people to express themselves, selecting their choices from competing programs and candidates. Political parties are necessary to provide the organizational structure through which candidates and programs compete for popular acceptance. An independent judiciary is essential for the protection of political freedoms and rights as well as for the impartial administration of justice. Some leaders advocate additional checks upon the concentration of powers, such as a federal structure for the state, a separation of executive and legislative powers, and a politically neutral civil service.

A fundamentally different interpretation of democracy is presented by some other leaders. In its more extreme form, this interpretation asserts that national unity and development are attainable only through the disciplined subordination of individual interests, the absolute supremacy of a single political party, and a strong, highly centralized government. Only one general will exists, not a multiplicity of competing interests, and those who do not support the general will either lack an adequate understanding of it or purposely deviate from it in order to promote their own selfish interests. The former can be educated into an awareness of the popular will, while the latter must be suppressed. Since only one general interest exists, only one political party is required and permitted to express it. This party encompasses all specific interests within society, from which the general interest arises. Decisions within the party are reached by defining the general will and subordinating specific interests to it. Once decisions are reached, there can be no further dispute since the general will must always be obeyed. Further, since the party represents the general will, it is superior to the state and government. The state is but an important institutional framework for the execution of the general will as determined by the party. Consequently, governmental institutions are to be organized to provide efficient expression of the general will; they are not intended to promote compromise or restrain authority. Thus, no loyal opposition is conceivable, nor is an independent judiciary or a neutral civil service. Efficiency in the implementation of the general will is the standard by which the organization of the government is judged.

Many variations of these two conflicting interpretations of democracy may be found in the developing states, both in theory and in practice. The authoritarian interpretation is often modified by several practices, such as the creation of a mass, rather than an elite, political party, in which large numbers of individuals participate in a meaningful way in determining the general will. On the other hand, the liberal interpretation is sometimes modified by a denial of voting rights to substantial segments of the population, or the legislature, as representative of diverse interests, is effectively subordinated by a strong executive. Yet, whatever the interpretation, the idea of mass political participation is today almost everywhere accepted. Leaders have found that this aspect of democracy can be a potent instrument in mobilizing national unity and in promoting those attitudes necessary for the further development of the social and economic revolutions occurring in their societies.

Only a few years ago, during the height and decline of the Cold War, the doctrine of nonalignment in international affairs was a prominent component of the ideologies of many African and Asian leaders. That doctrine, of decreasing relevance in an increasingly multipolar world, asserted that too close an alignment with either of the major power blocs would be detrimental to political and economic independence and self-determination. Consequently, relations would be promoted with all states, regardless of political beliefs, and aid would be obtained wherever available. Greater prestige—an important consideration for many leaders—was and still is assumed to accrue to those who successfully pursue an independent foreign policy rather than to those who follow too closely the leadership of a great power. Some leaders have argued that the developing states are devising important and morally superior alternatives to those foreign and domestic policies pursued by the great powers and their blocs, and too close an alignment with any power will corrupt the development of these policies. Nonalignment was rarely meant to imply noninvolvement in international affairs, however, and many of the developing states have attempted to play a prominent role in world affairs. But they seek to play this role outside the orbit of the great power blocs, mobilizing among themselves a level of power and moral influence the great powers must heed. This philosophy has been particularly in evidence in the United Nations and its various organs.

The spokesmen for the "revolution of rising expectations" have thus sought to construct and justify a program for revolutionary change. They are simultaneously appalled by conditions within their own societies and stimulated by the possibilities of rapid change. But the changes that they regard as essential will not, they claim, come about through the slow, evolutionary processes that have enabled the present noncommunist industrial powers to attain their positions. Only through the careful planning and execution of comprehensive developmental schemes can significant advances now be made, they assert. Even among the more conservative national leaders there is generally a commitment to industrialization and modernization, though many of them hope that this can be accomplished with relatively little disturbance of the present social order. Their position is challenged, however, by those counter-elites who propose to undertake a far more inclusive revolution which, in the name of justice and equality, will reshape the entire social order.

SUGGESTED READINGS

Abraham, W. E. The Mind of Africa. Chicago: University of Chicago Press, 1962.
Apter, David E., ed. Ideology and Discontent. New York: The Free Press of Glencoe, 1964.
Binder, Leonard. The Ideological Revolution in the Middle East. New York: John Wiley & Sons, Inc., 1964.
Castro, Fidel. History Will Absolve Me. New York: Lyle Stuart, 1961.
Davis, Harold E. Latin American Social Thought Since Independence. Washington, D. C.: University Press of Washington, 1961.
Duffy, James, and Robert A. Manners, eds. Africa Speaks. Princeton, N. J.: D. Van Nostrand Company, Inc., 1961.
Feith, Herbert, and Lance Castles. Indonesian Political Thinking, 1945–1965. Ithaca, N. Y.: Cornell University Press, 1970.

POLITICAL IDEAS AND IDEOLOGIES

Friedland, William H., and Carl G. Rosberg, Jr., eds. *African Socialism*. Stanford, Calif.: Published for the Hoover Institution on War, Revolution, and Peace by Stanford University Press, 1964.

Jack, Homer A., ed. *The Gandhi Reader*. Bloomington, Ind.: Indiana University Press, 1956.

Jorrín, Miguel, and John D. Martz. *Latin-American Political Thought and Ideology*. Chapel Hill, N. C.: The University of North Carolina Press, 1970.

July, Robert W. *The Origins of Modern African Thought*. New York: Frederick A. Praeger, 1968.

Karpat, Kemal H., ed. *Political and Social Thought in the Contemporary Middle East*. New York: Frederick A. Praeger, 1968.

Nkrumah, Kwame. *I Speak of Freedom: A Statement of African Ideology*. New York: Frederick A. Praeger, 1964.

Nyerere, Julius K. *Ujamaa—Essays on Socialism*. New York: Oxford University Press, 1969.

Scott, James C. *Political Ideology in Malaysia: Reality and the Beliefs of an Elite*. New Haven: Yale University Press, 1968.

Senghor, Léopold Sédar. *On African Socialism*. Translated by Mercer Cook. New York: Frederick A. Praeger, 1964.

Sigmund, Paul, Jr., ed. *The Ideologies of the Developing Nations*. 2d rev. ed. New York: Frederick A. Praeger, 1972.

Sithole, Ndabaningi. *African Nationalism*. 2d ed. New York: Oxford University Press, 1968.

Snyder, Louis L. *The New Nationalism*. Ithaca, N. Y.: Cornell University Press, 1968.

Of all the powerful ideas that give rise to potent political emotions and actions, nationalism is clearly dominant in the world today. But, as John Kautsky indicates below, there are several types of nationalism and the types being expressed in Asia, Africa, and Latin America are different from those in Europe. The anti-colonial nationalism of the developing areas faces some unique problems of providing the strong bond of unity, however, for reasons Kautsky discusses. Nevertheless, this type of nationalism may provide a sense of unity for a sufficiently long time for other integrating forces to develop.

9. NATIONALISM*

j o h n   h.   k a u t s k y

—is anti-colonialism

NATIONALISM APART FROM NATIONALITY

The concept of nationalism has taken its meaning from the "national" consciousness which began to grow in France with the Revolution, and from the movements that completely changed the map of Central and Eastern Europe during the following century and a half. Nationalism may be defined from this European experience as an ideology and a movement striving to unite all people who speak a single language, and who share the various cultural characteristics transmitted by that language, in a single independent state and in loyalty to a single government conducted in the people's language. A looser and less meaningful connotation of the word nationalism has also been widespread, which would seem to define it merely as the loyalty and emotional attachment of a population, regardless of its language, to an existing government and state. In this sense, one can refer to Soviet, Swiss, Belgian, and American nationalism, though all of these countries include inhabitants of different language and cultural backgrounds and the languages spoken by at least some of them are also the languages of other countries.

When we now turn to a consideration of what is generally referred to as nationalism in the underdeveloped areas, it becomes clear immediately that we are confronted with a phenomenon quite different from European nationalism. While it might therefore have been preferable to avoid the use of the term with reference to underdeveloped countries altogether, this would be futile in view of its adoption on all sides. We can only hope that the use of a single term to designate the two phenomena will not obscure the differences between them, that an easy assumption that the "nationalism" of underdeveloped countries must be like the "nationalism" of Europe will not obstruct recognition of the quite different forces producing it.

Neither of the two definitions of nationalism we derived from Euro-

* From "Nationalism" by John H. Kautsky, in *Political Change in Underdeveloped Countries* (New York, John Wiley & Sons, Inc., 1962), pp. 32–39. By permission.

pean experience can account for the nationalism of underdeveloped areas. It seeks to create new independent states and governments where there were none before. This is clearly a nationalism different from one that may be defined as loyalty to an already existing state and government (although, once independent states do exist, this kind of nationalism may well emerge in underdeveloped countries, too). However, the nationalism that did create new states in Europe also proves to be irrelevant for the explanation of nationalism in underdeveloped countries, for in Europe the language or nationality factor was, as we saw, a key elèment in its growth. . . .

Being economically backward, the underdeveloped countries have not yet been subject (or were not until very recently) to the economic and political integration that created the pressure for the adoption of a single language in large areas of Europe. Nor, as we have seen, can there be in non-industrialized societies sufficiently widespread participation in politics to provide any large proportion of the population with the loyalty to "their" government that was essential to the growth of European nationalism. Typically, the more backward a country is economically, the more languages or dialects are spoken in a given area or by a given number of people. . . .

In most underdeveloped countries, the existence of numerous languages inhibits communication among the population. Thus, the Chinese do not, in effect, speak a single Chinese language, but several mutually incomprehensible dialects.[1] Even more clearly, there is no such thing as a single Indian or Indonesian language. Some ten or twelve major languages and hundreds of minor tongues and local dialects are spoken in India. Some thirty languages are spoken in the Republic of Indonesia, many of them totally unrelated to each other. In territories in which commerce and communications are not even so highly developed as in these three major Asian countries and which have not, like these countries, been united under a single government for centuries, many more languages may be in use. Thus, in Nigeria a population of approximately 34,000,000 speaks roughly 250 different languages, a situation that is not unusual in much of Africa and among the tribes in the interior of Southeast Asia and Latin America. In Australian-ruled Papua and New Guinea, perhaps the most backward area in the world, 1,750,000 natives speak 500 different languages and dialects, no one language being used by more than 50,000 and some by only 300.

In spite of the fact that most underdeveloped countries are inhabited by numerous "nationalities," i.e., language and culture groups, their

---

[1] The Chinese merely share a single system of writing which, being ideographic, is not bound to any particular language, and is, at any rate, not available to the great bulk of the population. Their intellectuals can communicate in a single language, the Peking dialect of Mandarin Chinese, which serves roughly the same function as Latin in medieval Europe.

nationalists have virtually nowhere sought to change the boundaries of their new states to conform to language lines. . . . [I]t is striking that existing boundaries have remained intact as colony after colony has become independent in recent years and already independent countries, too, have undergone nationalist revolutions. Countries including many language and culture groups, like most African and Asian ones, have not split up and those taking in only part of a single language group, like the Arab ones in the Near East and North Africa, have . . . not united. The colonial boundaries which have thus persisted beyond the attainment of political independence, like the boundaries of older independent under-developed countries, were in virtually all cases drawn without any regard to language or cultural divisions among the natives. They chiefly reflected the political and economic requirements of the colonial powers, or of earlier conquerors, as in China, Turkey, and Latin America. What-ever it may be, then, nationalism in underdeveloped countries—if it does not aim at changing these boundaries—cannot be a movement seeking to unite all people speaking a particular language under a single indepen-dent government.[2]

Only after nationalism has been produced chiefly by other factors, is an attempt sometimes made by Western-trained intellectuals to intro-duce the language and cultural element into it. The artificial resurrec-tion of the Irish language may be a case in point. So is the pan-Arab movement insofar as it is not a mere tool of the nationalist movements of individual Arab states. The continuing failure of Arab unification would seem to indicate that these nationalist movements are in any case a good deal more powerful than pan-Arabism. More significant is the attempt of the Chinese Communist regime, itself a continuation of earlier Kuomin-tang policy, to impose a single language (that of the Peking region) and a simplified system of writing on all of China, a policy required, and facilitated, by the rapid economic and political integration of that area. Similar in nature, though not in the methods used to attain it, is the goal of the Indian government to spread the use of Hindi to all of India.

¤ ¤ ¤ ¤ ¤

Even in India and China, as well as in Ireland and the Arab countries, the desire to make all people under one government speak

[2] On the relationship of nationalism to existing colonial boundaries, see Rupert Emerson, "Nationalism and Political Development," *The Journal of Politics*, XXII, No. 1 (February 1960), 3–28, an article offering many insights into the nature of nationalism in underdeveloped countries. See also William Bascom, "Obstacles to Self-Government," *The Annals of the American Academy of Political and Social Science*, vol. 306 (July 1956), 62–70; C. E. Carrington, "Frontiers in Africa," *Interna-tional Affairs*, XXXVI, No. 4 (October 1960), 424–439; and E. R. Leach, "The Frontiers of 'Burma'," *Comparative Studies in Society and History*, III, No. 1 (Octo-ber 1960), 49–67.

one language (or to give a new autonomous government to those speaking one language) was not among the original motivations underlying the nationalist movement. In most underdeveloped countries no such desire has to this day appeared at all. If the origins of nationalism have nothing to do with nationality, i.e., with a common language and culture, nor with loyalty to an existing independent government, for there is none, then what is nationalism?

Nationalism in underdeveloped countries appears to have in common with European nationalism the desire of people to be rid of alien rulers and to have their own government, and it is probably for this reason that it has been labeled nationalism. In fact, the matter is not so simple, even if we leave aside the point, made at greater length earlier, that in underdeveloped countries, until modernization progresses, most people have no desires with reference to the central government at all, and they do not play any active role in politics. Apart from that, the words "alien" and "own" as just used, however, assume what is yet to be proved, that there is a collectivity of people, somehow defined by a common element other than a language, who share "their" nationalism. Why does a community in the South of India regard a prime minister from the North more as their "own" ruler than a viceroy from Britain? Why does one tribe in the Congo think of a government dominated by another tribe as less "alien" than a government of Belgians? In terms of language differences, these questions cannot be answered.

In some underdeveloped countries, notably Moslem ones, a religion and other cultural characteristics shared by all the natives regardless of their language, but different from those of their colonial rulers, may have been a common element around which their nationalism could have grown. But in many underdeveloped countries there are vast religious and cultural differences among the natives who nevertheless produced a single nationalist movement. And not infrequently, such movements are led by Christian natives who share their religion with their colonial rulers, whom they oppose, rather than with the great majority of the natives whom they claim to represent.

A more important element of unity setting the nationalists apart from their colonial rulers may be race, i.e., physical (as distinguished from cultural) characteristics. Some underdeveloped countries are inhabited by people of more than one race, however, and yet, in the Sudan, a European remains more "alien" to an Arab than a Negro, in Bolivia a "North-American" is more alien to a white nationalist than an Indian, in Cuba the "Yanqui" is regarded by nationalists as the enemy of both whites and Negroes. Sometimes certain unity among the natives has been created by Europeans or Americans who set themselves apart by discriminatory practices directed against all natives or "colored" people regardless of their particular race. The racial factor, then, is undoubtedly an important element in an explanation of nationalist unity in some underdeveloped countries, particularly where all natives are of a single nonwhite race and where it appears as a reaction to racial discrimination by whites. But not everywhere is this the case. There is no clear racial distinction between the European and the native inhabitants of North Africa nor is there between the English and the Irish or between some Americans and some Mexicans or Cubans.

NATIONALISM AS ANTI-COLONIALISM

In the absence of a common language, culture, religion, or race, what is it, then, that provides the focus for the unity among politically conscious elements from all strata of the population that is as characteristic of nationalist movements in underdeveloped countries as of European nationalist movements? Speaking of underdeveloped countries in general, there would seem to be no positive factor at all, but rather the dislike of a common enemy, the colonial power. Since nationalism is based on opposition to the colonial government, it is quite understandable that each colony's nationalist movement should operate within the existing boundaries and should not aim at a change in these boundaries. Thus, Indonesian nationalism is directed at the acquisition of Western New Guinea, because it is ruled by the Netherlands, the former colonial power in Indonesia, but makes no active claims to British-ruled Northern Borneo and Sarawak or Portuguese Timor, even though these are geographically, ethnically, and culturally much closer to Indonesia than Western New Guinea is. That the boundaries of a colony may cut across language and cultural lines is irrelevant; what matters is that they define the very purpose of the movement, anti-colonialism, and a change in them would therefore undermine the power of the movement and its leaders. Hence the general ineffectiveness of unification movements among former colonies, and the opposition by nationalists to movements of secession (as in Indonesia and the Congo), which are regarded as anti-nationalist, i.e., inspired by the colonial power.

However, nationalist movements are not confined to territories that are or were until recently administered by foreign powers as colonies, like India and most of Africa. Quite similar movements have appeared in independent underdeveloped countries like Turkey, China, and Mexico and, more recently, Egypt, Iraq, and Cuba. Unless they are virtually inaccessible, underdeveloped countries almost by necessity stand economically in a colonial relationship to industrial countries, in which the former serve as suppliers of raw materials (often made available by cheap native labor) and sometimes as markets for the industries of the latter. Anti-colonialism, then, must here be understood as opposition not merely to colonialism narrowly defined but also to a colonial economic status.

It is opposition to colonialism so defined and to those natives who benefit from the colonial relationship that constitutes nationalism in underdeveloped countries.[3] As such, nationalism can unite not only people of quite different language and cultural background, but also, interestingly, people of all the major economic and social classes, even though it is directed against certain economic policies. To be sure, in underdeveloped countries, as in Europe, many have been opposed and many indifferent to nationalism. Remarkable unity across social class lines has nevertheless been attained by nationalism. This is probably even more marked in underdeveloped countries than it was in Europe, where first the aristocracy and later important strata among the intellectuals and industrial labor proved to be anti-nationalist. The social tensions which modernization and industrialization produce everywhere and which in Europe were necessarily turned inward, resulting in conflicts dividing societies, are, in underdeveloped countries, largely turned outward. Instead of blaming each other for the difficulties growing out of modernization, the various social strata all blame the colonial power, the result being, not internal conflict, but that internal unity of anti-colonialism which is the basis of nationalism in underdeveloped countries.

[3] An impressive attempt to generalize about the nature of nationalism in Asia and Africa, providing both a wealth of data and much thoughtful interpretation, is Rupert Emerson, *From Empire to Nation* (Cambridge, Mass.: Harvard University Press, 1960). For excellent detailed studies of the bases of nationalism in two underdeveloped areas, see James S. Coleman, *Nigeria: Background to Nationalism* (Los Angeles and Berkeley: University of California Press, 1958) and some of the articles in Walter Z. Laqueur, ed., *The Middle East in Transition* (New York: Frederick A. Praeger, 1958).

Despite a much longer history of active concern and involvement in the affairs of Latin American states as opposed to those of the European colonies in Asia and Africa, North Americans are still often baffled by the peoples and politics of Latin America. Despite their European heritage, the Latin Americans seem to share few of the traditions of their North American neighbors and, indeed, they often take a vigorous anti-American stance. In the selection that follows, Claudio Véliz explores some of the reasons for the uniqueness of Latin American political ideas and practices and the sources of Latin American nationalism.

10. CENTRALISM AND NATIONALISM
IN LATIN AMERICA *

c l a u d i o v é l i z

. . . I would like to suggest three fundamental differences which may account for the apparent inability of Latin America at present to provide a fertile soil for European ideological models and which indicate the type of development likely to dominate its domestic and international political life in the near future. The three differences are the absence in Latin America's historical experience of feudalism, of religious nonconformity and of industrial development which is individually initiated as opposed to that which is centrally encouraged. Conversely, I would suggest that it is precisely in the vertebral centralism of the Latin American tradition that an explanation of recent developments and perhaps even the key to the political future of the region will most probably be discovered.

II

The feudal experience is not part of the cultural tradition of Latin America. Of course the word has often been used pejoratively to describe the relationship between landlord and peasant in Latin America as elsewhere, but in fact feudalism as a political structure never existed in this part of the world. It is important to realize this, because the balance of power between a weak center and a strong periphery, which was characteristic of feudalism, was evidently a major ingredient of European liberalism and all its social-democratic variants.

In spite of the quaint efforts by Mexican revolutionaries, the founders of APRA and others to establish direct lines of descent from the centuries before the coming of the Spaniards, the fact is that Latin America was born into the modern world during the sixteenth century, at least three hundred years after feudalism had disappeared from Western Europe; its institutional structure was fashioned wholesale in Madrid by

* From "Centralism and Nationalism in Latin America" by Claudio Véliz, *Foreign Affairs*, Vol. 47, No. 1 (October, 1968), pp. 69–83. Excerpted by permission from "Foreign Affairs," October 1968, and by permission of the author. Copyright by the Council on Foreign Relations, Inc., New York.

POLITICAL IDEAS AND IDEOLOGIES

the strongest monarchy in Christendom and on the Renaissance model of a centrally controlled polity. . . .

The institutional structure devised for the Indies naturally reflected this unqualified centralism, and no effort was spared to ensure that distance would not facilitate the development of peripheral sites of political power; even to fill a minor post at the Viceroyalty of Peru, consultation with Spain was required, and whoever attempted to depart from the strictest reading of the colonial legislation was punished with severity. Even the most exalted colonial rulers had at the end of their mandate to make the lengthy voyage to Spain to sit at the dreaded *juicio de residencia*. Madrid's power gave muscle to the longest administrative arms in Christendom.

This system survived for three centuries and when it finally collapsed, its legalistic, centralist and authoritarian tradition passed on undiminished to the republican régimes, which had the advantage of shorter lines of communication. It must be remembered that the revolutions of 1810 were not popular uprisings but rather independence movements after the fashion of the one led by Mr. Ian Smith in Rhodesia.

The institutional habit of compromise between alternative centers of political power is not, then, part of the Latin American tradition. The feudal experience of northern Europe, where the central monarchy had to negotiate with a number of lesser centers of power, is simply not known in this part of the world. Here the center has never been decisively challenged and even its major revolutionary experience—that of 1810—was initiated in the name of legitimacy and against the French, who by then represented egalitarianism.

Political centralism remained virtually unassailed during the nineteenth century. . . .

The centralism of the past four centuries has survived well into our times. The three major modern revolutions in Latin America—perhaps the only real ones—have reconstructed society according to strikingly different ideas, yet they have all resulted in single-party systems: the Mexican PRI is unique in the ramifications of its centralist control; the Cuban government party, I would suggest, rules from an authoritarian center because it is Cuban rather than because it is communist; and the Bolivian MNR, although eventually unsuccessful, made a determined attempt to monopolize political power and was later replaced by another régime at least as centralist. The trend that can be perceived in other countries—without considering the outright tyrannies—is clearly toward the establishment of a dominant political party identified with the government. This is seen even in the most sophisticated and democratic states in the region.

The weight of this historical tradition has lately been reinforced by the well-nigh universal trend toward increased participation or intervention by the central government in all aspects of national life. While in, say, Britain, the United States or Sweden, this trend clashes with the prevailing pluralistic and generally liberal concept of political responsibility, in Latin America it reinforces the existing drive for greater central control.

If political centralism has worn well over the last few centuries, the same can also be said of the Catholic Church. . . .

There is, of course, ample evidence of dissent within the Catholic Church in Latin America today, but this stems from anxiety over social and political issues, not over the fundamental religious tenets of official Catholicism. The inroads of Protestantism are also not to be minimized, but so far, even in Chile, where they have been most noticeable, less than 10 percent of the population is registered as belonging to the numerous Protestant sects.

In Europe and North America it was but a short step from religious dissent to political dissent; it does not take exceptional scholarship to trace the nonconformist ancestry of many of the most active reformist parties.

III

As might be expected, political and religious centralism was accompanied by economic centralism, which is not only the product of a long Hispanic tradition but also the result of the way in which industry came to this part of the world. In Europe, industrial activity arose out of a complex cultural situation which resulted in the conscious accumulation of industrial capital over a long period of time. This process owed little or nothing to the intervention of the central government and it led to a dispersion of power. That the central state later came to represent these industrial interests is beside the point; for it to happen, the new industrialists had to challenge the traditional ruling groups and wrest power from them.

Further, the growth of industry ran almost parallel with the growth of cities, and urbanization was a consequence of industrial activity. Industry then was labor intensive and for it to function efficiently a sizeable labor force had to be organized in urban centers. As a result the workers acquired a new political consciousness. Thus it can be said that the impact of industry on traditional European society was revolutionary at least in that it was spearheaded by a newly formed industrial bourgeoisie and it resulted in the formation of a new industrial proletariat.

None of these considerations would seem to apply to the industrialization of Latin America. Here industry has been stimulated largely by external factors such as the great crisis of 1929 (principally affecting Brazil) and the Second World War, which began the process of import substitution. It owed relatively little to domestic determinants. And urbanization in Latin America did not wait for industrialization, which was instead grafted onto a sophisticated, self-conscious, relatively urbanized society. A remarkably large proportion of the population was already living in cities for reasons other than the development of industry. More important perhaps, industrialization owed a very great deal to the direct intervention of the central state—through tariff protection, subsidies, credit policies or straightforward programs of industrial development carried out directly under the aegis of public development corporations. Lastly, the social changes generally associated with industrialization have not occurred in Latin America; there have been many changes but not the ones that scholars and politicians were prepared for.

Latin America has industrialized rapidly, but this has not been the result of the exertions of an industrial bourgeoisie; nor has it produced an industrial proletariat. . . . The industrial labor force in Latin America is not the modern equivalent of the traditional proletariat. Working with an advanced industrial technology, it is smaller, better trained and better paid. It is in fact an aristocracy of labor with incomes which all too often rise above those of vast numbers of white collar workers in the tertiary sector.

As the capacity of industry to absorb large numbers of workers is limited, the massive transformation of peasants into industrial workers has not come to pass. . . .

❋   ❋   ❋   ❋   ❋

As for the Latin American equivalent of the traditional industrial bourgeoisie—forward-looking, adventurous, willing to take risks, ready to innovate, anti-aristocratic and reformist—it simply does not exist. The force for dynamic change has been the central government. Domestic private enterprise has seldom performed with distinction except when instigated and assisted by the government. If all state subsidies and financial commitments were to be withdrawn from private industry, precious little would remain in operation. This has come about partly by default; the so-called industrial bourgeoisie and their clientele have been agile opportunists and mediocre imitators rather than adventurous challengers or originators of new ideas. . . .

❋   ❋   ❋   ❋   ❋

In Europe and the United States it was the dynamic industrial groups that for various reasons became the mainstay—both political and economic—of a development policy aimed at the satisfaction of national aspirations; in Latin America, however, the owners of industry are largely responsible for increasing our external dependence. They have not been innovators, nor have they challenged the established social order or provided political alternatives. Instead they have fallen with remarkable ease into the patterns of imitation and emulation characteristic of social climbing. In fact, it would not be surprising if their major contribution to the contemporary life of Latin America turns out to be the efficient institutionalization of this process; far from weakening the traditional structure, they have become its most loyal and enthusiastic upholders.

To sum up, then, there appears to be no substantial evidence indicating that the tradition of centralism characteristic of Latin American culture is in any significant way being challenged from within. Furthermore, the pressure groups which in Europe and the United States played such an important role in forcing through the changes demanded by the incorporation of industrial technology are either not fitted or not prepared to play a comparable role in Latin America. What sector of society, then, is likely to fulfill this function in the future?

I V

Marx and Lenin have not been the only ones to accept the notion that the state is an instrument, a tool to be used by one group or another to defend its own interests. This concept of the state has figured prominently in the historical tradition of Western Europe (though perhaps more significantly in Britain and the United States). From it derives the conceptual framework which informs much of contemporary sociological and historical analysis—including the study of Latin America. Learned northern observers of the Latin American situation have thus spent much time identifying the pressure groups which are expected to be vying with each other for the control of that supposedly inert instrument, the central state. In their writings, various groups are favored as most likely to assume the leadership of the process that is vaguely described as "modernization." Some place their bets on the rising urban bourgeoisie; others hope or fear that the peasantry will march on the cities and transform everything; others are impressed by the vociferous political activity of the students; while others still stress the reformist aspirations of the "Nasserist" groups in the armed forces.

This type of analysis does not seem to me helpful, largely because it starts from the mistaken premise that the central government in Latin America is at least as "instrumental" as that typical of the European tradition and as likely to respond to the pressures, civilized or not, coming from more or less powerful groups. In Latin America the central government itself is the most powerful pressure group. It extends its power and influence through a highly centralized civil service and through complex and all-embracing systems of social security and patronage which have transformed most of the vast urban service sector into an institutionalized clientele; it controls the major centers of learning and is capable of exercising almost unrestricted control over economic life. The only institutions which could perhaps be regarded as likely rivals, because of their relatively self-contained nature, are the Church and the armed forces, but in either case the rivalry would not be counterbalancing or pluralistic; rather it would tend to emphasize the central and national responsibilities of the government. Whenever pressures from these two sectors are exerted, they encourage the state to exercise still more all-embracing power from the center.

If this powerful and self-conscious pressure group did not earlier exert its potential force to the fullest, it was because the domestic and international conditions prevailing during the hundred years which preceded 1929 were such as to discourage or at least make unnecessary an activist role for the state. . . .

❀   ❀   ❀   ❀   ❀

Apart from other important considerations, the Second World War introduced a virtual moratorium on political development in Latin America. With the world divided into warring factions and the countries of the region more or less in the Allied camp, traditional alignments were redrawn to fit external demands. Even the communist parties and their close associates of the time postponed their struggles against capitalism and loyally collaborated in the efforts to keep the Allies well supplied with raw materials. The hope was also widely entertained that the end of the conflict would bring, as a well-earned reward, a veritable flood of assistance, which would in some undefined way bring back the plentiful days of the past.

Although the nationalistic movements in Latin America had little or nothing in common with Germany save a shared suspicion of the United States or Britain, they were often sympathetic to the Axis, and it required considerable coaxing before they declared for the Allies. It would be facile and mistaken to think that Villarroel in Bolivia, Ibañez in Chile, Vargas in Brazil, Péron in Argentina, Arnulfo Arias in Panama and so many others were simply stooges of an international Nazi conspiracy. It would be closer to the truth to say that these various nationalist movements were essentially domestic and reflected the basic aspirations or dissatisfactions of important urban sectors. The issue of the Canal Zone was foremost in the minds of those who supported Arnulfo Arias at that time; economic imperialism and the Falkland Islands were ever present in Péron's oratory; Villarroel came to power as a result of the frustrations of the Chaco War but also on the assurance that Bolivia would not remain forever a colonial appendage of the tin industry; Vargas represented the drive toward industrialization and economic autonomy. These movements, under whatever name, represented a nationalist alternative to the traditional programs presented by the established parties of Right and Left. At their most successful, they provided the basis for what in the postwar period has generally been described as Latin American populism—perhaps the most revealing portent of the political future of the region.

The widespread feeling that rampant nationalism was the ultimate cause of World War II tended to make the domestic nationalist movements in Latin America appear like the villains of a new black legend. Internationalism became the new religion and international coöperation the accepted morality. But with the slaughter and destruction of the war still fresh in mind, a weary world plunged into yet another total struggle. Mr. Truman's doctrinal declaration dividing the world into two oddly defined camps presented Latin America with a formidable false dilemma. It was clear that Mr. Truman had not really meant each country to choose between democracy and tyranny; there were enough despotic régimes on the side of the angels to make this a doubtful proposition. On the other hand it was apparent even then—and it has since become obvious—that the communist parties in the Latin American countries had no intention of leading revolutionary movements to overthrow their respective governments. In this respect they reflected the pragmatic attitude of the Soviet Union, which accepted Latin America's being within the sphere of influence of the United States. Yet the urgencies of the international situation forced a decision, and anti-communism was raised to the status of dogma by able politicians; although these men were well aware that the local communists did not constitute a serious threat, they kept their eyes fixed on the flow of aid which was invariably directed toward those countries whose loyalty to the Western world was beyond dispute.[1]

[1] "In other parts of the world it may be merely ridiculous to claim that the communists are not revolutionaries, but in Latin America it is a fact that the communist movement has no vigorous revolutionary tradition. There is probably no conservative or liberal party in all of Latin America that has not staged more insurrections and incited more civil wars than the communists. In a continent racked by civil strife the communists' record has been one of remarkable quiescence. Their one major attempt to seize power by force was the 1935 insurrection led by Luiz Carlos Prestes in Brazil, apart from which there have been only some instances of communist participation in risings by noncommunist groups." Ernst Halperin, "Nationalism and Communism in Chile." Cambridge: Massachusetts Institute of Technology, 1965, p. 13.

In the anxiey of the Soviet Union and the United States to marshal their allies into supranational political and military arrangements, the Organization of American States was created. The OAS, which became the Latin American branch of the cold-war policy of the United States, can validly claim to be one of the least impressive of the many postwar pacts. . . .

✿ ✿ ✿ ✿ ✿

V

The feeling of utter dependence has grown deep roots during the years of the cold war. But as the confrontation becomes attenuated by the challenge of France and China to the leadership of the United States and the Soviet Union, by the growth of polycentrism on both sides of the Iron Curtain, and by a measure of détente between the two great powers, a resurgence of nationalism is apparent in Latin America. "A plague on both your houses" is becoming a common attitude; as the tide of cold-war loyalties recedes, Latin Americans are becoming increasingly conscious of national aspirations submerged for too long.

The time may now be ripe for the centralist state to come into its own, fired with a new nationalism fed on an awareness that the increasing cultural and economic dependence of the region is one of its principal problems. Had circumstances even faintly similar to the present ones occurred, say, half a century ago, a fashionable European ideology would no doubt have been promptly imported by the latest batch of Latin American intellectuals returning home from their grand tour. Today this is no longer possible, partly because the mood is emphatically nationalistic and partly because the prevailing feeling is that the northern hemisphere has precious little guidance to offer: the United States and the Soviet Union are living through critical times themselves and have abandoned much of their ideological fervor in order to adopt pragmatic and short-term solutions. Even those who until recently were willing to grant the benefit of the doubt to some tried old horses—e.g. socialism, capitalism and their variants—are now conscious that their application to Latin America is at least questionable. Indeed, Latin America may for the first time in its history become an exporter of political symbols and ideas. This is suggested by the enthusiastic adoption of Ché Guevara by students in Europe and the United States, while here his political appeal is largely restricted to a genuine admiration for his integrity and heroism.

In the absence of a more elaborate framework within which to fit political action, men tend to fall back on elemental loyalties—tribe, family or, as in Latin America today, straightforward nationalism. Besides being undemanding intellectually, nationalism draws support from all the people, regardless of other interests.

A nationalistic ideology can perhaps get us from a confused present to a more satisfactory future, but the risks cannot be ignored. Nationalism tends to magnify the impact of external factors on domestic situations. Even if it is based on a reasonably civilized understanding of what constitutes the national interest, it courts international friction. In this kind of mood, affecting the major nations of Latin America simultaneously, rearmament, for example, assumes an importance which cannot be overlooked.

At the same time it should be emphasized that the major objective of Latin American nationalism is to reverse the present trend toward cultural and economic dependence on the United States. This, to be fair, is apparently also an objective of enlightened U.S. policy, as shown in numerous official pronouncements calling for a determined effort in Latin America to shoulder a greater part of the burden of its own development. The financial difficulties of the United States may of course make this objective mandatory. At any rate, it must be remembered that independent behavior in nations, as in human beings, cannot easily be confined to some things, excluding others. If the countries of Latin America are to act with greater independence in the planning and implementation of truly national development policies, it should not surprise anybody if they become independent in foreign policy and other fields as well. The military, for example, which until recently have been the most loyal allies of the United States, are now beginning to see the penetration and interference of the great northern power in the same light in which they formerly viewed communism—as an international threat to national sovereignty and integrity. Their indignant reaction to the efforts of the United States to stem their growing purchases of armaments is a significant example of the new attitude.

＊　＊　＊　＊　＊

However important the negative dynamism generated by aggressive independence of the United States, I would suggest that this is not the principal feature of contemporary Latin American nationalism. Rather it is the return to a style of political behavior firmly rooted in an autocthonous centralist tradition. On this tradition is founded the structure of institutions and political habits of Latin Americans; on it, as well, are based the organizational successes of the past decades. Latin Americans are increasingly conscious that in harnessing the momentum of this tradition to the needs of national development they will acquire understanding and mastery of the problems of their nations.

POLITICAL IDEAS AND IDEOLOGIES

Although this novel process of self-discovery is scarcely a few years old it has already offered promising first results in various fields. The original, successful and growing participation of the central government in the Mexican economy; the plans for public multinational corporations which will operate within the sub-regional schemes; the remarkable history of growth and consolidation of the enterprises fathered by the Chilean Development Corporation—all afford evidence of the vitality of this trend. At the same time, the writings of historians, economists and political analysts reflect both a generalized dissatisfaction with foreign imitation and an endeavor to create a new political architecture, using the materials at hand instead of importing them ready-made from elsewhere.

Latin America has been prodigal in the arts and letters—perhaps the world's best contemporary novels have been written during the past decade by Colombians, Peruvians and Argentines—but it has not distinguished itself in the field of political and social ideas. It is not unduly optimistic to think that this is due at least in part to the diligence with which its intelligentsia has in the past looked to the northern hemisphere not only for political answers but for the questions as well. It would be surprising indeed if a reversal of this trend does not prove extremely rewarding.

Traditionally, socialist doctrines have emphasized the principle of equality, and only in the last few decades have they become closely associated with the goal of economic development. In the transitional states, both principles are now commonly advocated but, as the analysis below indicates, several interpretations of socialism can be identified in the political and economic discourse of the leaders of these societies. In addition, there is always the difficult problem of measuring the importance of a doctrine in the formulation of specific policies designed to attain the goals sought by the leaders. Giovanni Arrighi and John Saul briefly examine these issues on the basis of the evidence from African societies.

11. THE THEORY AND PRACTICE
OF AFRICAN SOCIALISM * †

not coping with labour

g i o v a n n i   a r r i g h i
a n d   j o h n   s.   s a u l

— are not emphasizing class organization

It seems relevant at this point to appraise, using rather broad strokes, the theory and practice of African socialism as evidenced to date. In this way the nature of the limitations, both intellectual and contextual, upon socialist experiment in Africa may be clarified. It would, of course, be artificial to separate too categorically considerations as to "theory" and "practice"; an understanding of the latter must serve to illuminate the real texture and function of the former. None the less, many striking ambiguities are readily identifiable on the ideological plane itself, whether this be seen primarily as a determinant of practice or merely as its reflection and rationalisation. The broad outline of the constellation of ideas under discussion, sometimes identified generically as "African Socialism," are by now familiar enough,[1] though they remain difficult to capsulise as we must do here. It should be noted that even the over-arching label of "African Socialism" has been vigorously rejected by some of the continent's more militant practitioners; we must be careful not to schematise away real differences.

Yet there remain certain central themes common to most African writers and speakers on the subject and, more important, some common pattern to the seeming inadequacy of the analysis underlying many of their statements. Professed African socialists are, to be sure, uniformly interested in economic development; they have also sensed that some form of co-ordinated expansion on the agricultural and industrial fronts is required in order to attain that goal. The precise nature of the prob-

* From "Socialism and Economic Development in Tropical Africa" by Giovanni Arrighi and John S. Saul, *The Journal of Modern African Studies*, Vol. VI, No. 2 (August, 1968), pp. 153 (Sec. II)–160. Published by Cambridge University Press. Excerpted by permission of the authors and the publisher.
† G. Arrighi is Lecturer in Economics, and J. S. Saul in Politics, at the University College, Dar es Salaam. An earlier version of this article was presented to the plenary session of the University of East Africa Social Science Conference held at Dar es Salaam in January 1968.
1 See, particularly, J. Mohan, "Varieties of African Socialism," in *The Socialist Register 1966* (London). Also W. H. Friedland and C. G. Rosberg Jr., *African Socialism* (Stanford, 1964); Charles Andrain, "Democracy and Socialism: ideologies of African leaders," in D. Apter (ed.), *Ideology and Discontent* (New York, 1964); and Bernard Charles, "Le Socialisme africaine, mythes et réalités," in *Revue française de science politique* (Paris), xv, 1965, p. 856.

lems of "structural transformation" which are involved is less clearly fixed in their minds, though certain echoes of these concerns are sometimes to be found scattered through their speeches and programmes.

Even socialists, however, have tended to operate in terms of the conventional model of development based upon the expansion of cash crops for the export market, increased industrial capital formation in consumer-goods industries, and the import of foreign—generally private —capital, the requisite amount of infrastructural investment being the responsibility of the state. This is, of course, in essence the ideal type of "perverse growth" in Africa which we have discussed in section 1. Thus the main intellectual limitations, whether they be conscious or unconscious, lie in an inadequate understanding of the process of sustained development and structural transformation, but also, as will become apparent, in an insufficiently subtle and critical picture both of the emerging pattern of African socio-economic stratification (particularly as regards "town–country" relations) and of the realities of the international economy. Small wonder, then, that ideas about "development" and "equality" are themselves not systematically linked, and, in consequence, that "socialist" strategies emerge which leave much to be desired.

In brief, a thoroughly disabused (and disinterested) look at such patterns has rarely been taken by African leaders. This is reflected by the extent to which the general tone of "socialist" thinking in Africa tends to blur these concerns, despite the occasional admissions and qualifications witnessing to rather greater sophistication. Thus, to take one example, Senghor is sometimes alive in his writings to the dangers of a newly privileged, urban-based group of "intellectuals—liberal professionals, functionaries, employers, even workers"—arising to exploit "the peasants, shepherds and artisans." But the point is not pushed nor possible institutional checks hypothesised; rather, he relies largely upon "spiritual values" to avert the danger. Yet excessive self-denial on the part of this "labour aristocracy" (as we have defined it) is certainly not to be expected when so militant a socialist spokesman as Touré himself can note:

In our denunciation of bourgeois tendencies we must not, as do specialists in confusion, accuse of being bourgeois the peasant, the worker or the civil servant who is a convinced democrat and devoted P.D.G. member and who by his personal efforts has been able to build a modern house, purchase a car or acquire honestly anything which contributes to the material well-being of his family. Since the main objective of our revolution is to make it possible for all to attain through work the highest possible degree of prosperity, we cannot blame these people. On the contrary, a man must utilize his energies and faculties for the constant improvement of his living standard.[2]

[2] In *Africa Report* (Washington), May 1963, "Special Issue on African Socialism," pp. 26–27.

Surely this must amount to an overt sanction of the norm of *enrich-issez-vous* for the bureaucratic groups (of party and state), "the new élites of tropical Africa," [3] which have emerged to prominence in the post-independence period. There has really been little grasp, within the doctrine of African socialism, of such a form of inequality and the accompanying possibilities for exploitation by this labour aristocracy. The necessity of bridging the urban–rural gap is rarely given sufficient prominence; the sort of assault on privilege which would free a good proportion of the surplus from urban consumptionism for rural incentives and capital formation is deflected away.

Occasionally certain steps are taken and presented with a logic that seems impeccably to combine the twin concerns of development and equality. Thus an argument postulated upon the social necessity of capital accumulation and the imperative of "hard work" is often used when African governments turn to deal with the trade unions. In most "socialist" countries the latter have been brought to heel, absorbed organisationally into the network of the ruling party. It is argued that they represent a privileged cadre of workers and that their gains are being made at the expense of the country as a whole, of the rural sector in particular. As a step towards general development, they must be disciplined accordingly and redirected from "consumptionist" to "productionist" activities.[4]

Another prime target is the trading community, and again the argument against it is often advanced in terms of the need for both a more egalitarian pattern of distribution and accelerated capital accumulation. The redistribution of excessive profits of local traders and (sometimes) foreign trading houses is demanded, to provide incentive payments for the growers and more finance for productive investment by the state. In addition it is argued that the marketing co-operatives which are further encouraged by such steps in the rural areas represent a collective, and therefore socialist, enterprise which is laudable in its own right. The fact that the trading group to be so displaced is often largely composed of a racial or cultural minority may, of course, ease the acceptance of such policies.

One might be better disposed to accept these latter moves on the terms in which they have been presented by the leaders, were the general line of argument which is used to justify them (that is, the criticism, by presumptive socialists, of inequalities which block development) more consciously and rigorously applied to the society as a whole. Unfortunately this has not been the case: perceived inequalities—what

[3] This is the title of a useful book on related themes edited by Peter Lloyd (London, 1966).
[4] For this distinction see Isaac Deutscher, "Russia," in W. Galenson (ed.), *Comparative Labour Movements* (New York, 1952); and Friedland and Rosberg, op. cit. p. 19.

POLITICAL IDEAS AND IDEOLOGIES

Touré has termed "contradictions"—get very easily swallowed up and blurred analytically within the framework provided by the continent's distinctive "socialist" ideology. Here we refer to that strand of the argument which has been characterised by Peter Worsley as "populism."[5] In Africa this has involved the claim, by almost all leaders, that African societies are, even now, classless. The foundations for pervasive social solidarity are to be found in traditional society and, mediated by a contemporary "attitude of mind," continue to strike against meaningful stratification.

The most outspoken statement of this "model" is to be found in Nyerere's early paper "Ujamaa,"[6] but even so Marxist-tinged a spokesman as Touré has fallen back upon the "communocratic" nature of African society to smooth over, ideologically, certain of the potential class antagonisms he sees in Guinean society. To this Touré adds the argument that such classless uniformity is reinforced by the fact of the whole population's facing, as a body, the neo-colonialist exploiter. Not surprisingly, nationalism provides much of the cement for this populist edifice, being useful also for displacing continuing ethnic or tribal consciousness. Countless quotations could be introduced to demonstrate these general emphases in Africa. Nor, within such a "classless" society, is it surprising that any consideration as to the nature of the social relations of production is seen to be of little fundamental concern to socialist aspirations. Thus Kofi Baako, a man as close as anyone to Nkrumah in Ghana:

In a Nkrumahist-Socialist state, the farmer will not lose his farm; the landlord will not lose his house, but will not be allowed to exploit the tenant; the employer will not be allowed to exploit the worker, nor will the worker be allowed to cheat the employer by idling about; the car owner will still have his car . . . the property or wealth which someone has acquired or earned through hard labour and through honest use of his mental and physical energies [will not] be taken away from him and shared among lazy, unscrupulous, indisciplined but able-bodied citizens.

As Fitch and Oppenheimer observe of such utterances: "Neither landlords nor capitalists will be abolished—they will simply be regulated."[7]

This "populist" strain to African socialism also has important implications for the analysis of the rural sector; moreover, there it is perhaps even more likely to be taken seriously by the ideologues themselves.

[5] Peter Worsley, *The Third World* (London, 1964), ch. 4. For a detailed critique of "populism" see John S. Saul, "On African Populism," in E. Gellner and G. Ionescu (eds.), *Populism* (London, 1968).
[6] This essay is reproduced in J. K. Nyerere, *Freedom and Unity/Uhuru na Umoja* (Dar es Salaam and London, 1966 & 1967), pp. 162–71. It was first published in 1962.
[7] Both Baako's remark and the subsequent comment are to be found in B. Fitch and M. Oppenheimer, *Ghana: end of an illusion* (New York, 1966), p. 112.

Worsley summarises this theme when he writes: "Africa is its peasantry, subsistence producers and cash-crop producers, but independent peasants. This is the basic fact about the social structures of the new African states." We have already seen this to be suspect, given the character of "town-country" relationships in contemporary Africa, but within the rural area itself solidarity is (once again) felt to arise from these facts. Yet, as we have suggested, even the relatively unrevolutionised rural economies of tropical Africa are no longer as undifferentiated as these African leaders like to profess. What is clear, therefore, is that the issue of nascent rural class formation and its implications for development cannot be squarely faced, or effective "long-run" strategies of socialist control and direction developed, within a populist framework of analysis which masks the process of rural change.

Even in the absence of such a searching examination of rural realities, it none the less remains true that the "mobilisation" of the peasantry is regarded as a vital necessity much more vocally in states of "socialist" bent than in others. There, a more generalised release of productive energies is looked to; it is in this context that the strand of "African Socialism" which Friedland had termed "the social obligation to work" becomes most prominent.[8] Socialism is presented as an invocation to effort and, implicitly or explicitly, a certain measure of sacrifice against the promise of some future day is encouraged, in however unspecified a way. Thus *investissement humain* and self-help become a collective exercise in some, often marginal, form of capital accumulation. These projects can be of value in educating people to national consciousness;[9] but, as should be apparent, such emphases may merely encourage the evasion of those more central problems which concern the interaction of traditional and modern sectors and the expansion of surplus productive capacity. All too rarely, for example, is the character of any choice between capitalist and collectivist agricultural accumulation spelt out or related to broader questions of development priorities such as we have posed; policies can therefore quite easily fall between two stools.

Just as the populist strand in African socialism obscures the realities of class formation, so it is important, if somewhat paradoxical, to observe that much of the criticism of "neo-colonialism" in socialist Africa has served to obscure the realities of international capitalism's involvement on the continent. Of necessity, therefore, the range of specific policy options is also artificially narrowed. Even the most vocal of socialists assume the necessity of dealing with "the enemy"; as Jean Lacouture observed in discussing the Dakar Colloquium on African Socialism: "The distinction, always somewhat artificial, between 'revolutionary' and 'reformist' Africa now seems altogether obsolete . . . What is even

8 Friedland and Rosberg, op. cit. p. 16.
9 Cf. K. Grundy, "Mali: the prospects of 'Planned Socialism,'" ibid. p. 192.

more striking is that nobody challenged the necessity of calling upon foreign aid and investment." [10]

But neither did anyone feel too compelled, it would seem, to analyse very systematically the arguments concerning the development potential of such investment by an increasingly monopolistic brand of international capitalism in terms of the choice of techniques and the absorption of labour, the reinvestment of profits, and the generation of internal demand. Policy statements thus oscillate rather erratically betwen the abstract slogans of "neo-colonialism"—a useful instrument with which to forge national unity behind the leaders—and a "forced" acceptance of the "necessity" of encouraging foreign investment in order to obtain skills and capital.

Side-effects tend to drop out of the equation. The application of a long time-horizon might suggest that, despite a time lag, the inflow of unfettered foreign capital must eventually lead to a marked drain of repatriated profits and the like. Therefore an assessment must constantly be made as to its genuine development potential; as suggested, many forms of capital import may be worse than none at all, despite the subsequent existence of plant on the ground and a handful of newly hired indigenous employees. One can, of course, suspect that some of the encouragement given to an increased capital inflow may arise from the élite's concern with short-term balance-of-payments difficulties caused by excessive imports. None the less, for the genuine African socialist, the necessity of *internal capital formation* must be underscored in his arguments and, furthermore, explained clearly to the people.

For, all too often, the promise of a favourable deal to be made by the élite with that most powerful external constellation of technology and economic power which is the western economic system smacks of an attempt to get something for nothing (an unlikely occurrence, but perhaps a useful political case to make to the mass of the population in the short run). Given a clearer perspective, the definition of firmer conditions for such capital as did come in would also become a more pressing imperative than has been the case, however difficult such conditions are to apply in practice. And a vigorous attack upon "balkanisation" and an advocacy of regional groupings, preferably of "like-minded" states, to encourage complementarities and co-ordinated development would become an even more prominent feature.

The relating of an ideology like African socialism to the complex social structure of changing Africa and the identifying of its functions is not an easy task. We have said enough, however, to suggest that more than mere intellectual confusion is at issue. It is true that in colonial and economically under-developed Africa an indigenous dominant class

[10] From *Le Monde* (Paris), 11 December 1962, cited in *Africa Report*, May 1963, p. 18.

with power grounded in the process of production had, by and large, not emerged;[11] the political and bureaucratic groups which did come forward to prominence were therefore defined by a greater "relative social autonomy and plasticity," as Roger Murray has put it.[12] None the less, after independence, when a combination of past education and/or political record and current bureaucratic position came to be the chief determinants of privilege in the new society, it is clear that, in the absence of more rigorous organisation and ideological clarity, a rather narrow vested interest in the system had come to characterise the new élites, "une bourgeoisie plus proche d'un mandarinat," as Dia has called them. Their growing consciousness of a differentiated position vis-à-vis the mass of the population was such that Lloyd, one of the shrewdest observers of this process, could toy with the idea of discarding the "élite" concept and substituting the notion of "class" to describe the position in society of this group.[13]

Thus it is within this sort of context that one must place trends—to an increased centralisation of power, the absorption of quasi-autonomous bodies, and ideological myth-making for popular consumption of the sort we have examined—which are then seen to express a clear institutional and, behind that, a class interest.[14] And within this framework much state intervention, in so far as it seems only marginally related to a generalised socialist development strategy, can in part be explained as the conscious proliferation of jobs for incoming recruits to the dominant group. At the very least, given the nature of the bureaucratic élite, any glib identification, by leaders or observers, of socialism in Africa with étatisme and policies for centralisation of economic control must be viewed with suspicion. In addition, a sustained stand against the blandishments of foreign capitalism, or even a critical scrutiny of its potential contributions, is unlikely from such a group. There is some danger of crude reductionism in such a generalised formulation, but it remains a hypothesis which illuminates a great deal of the empirical evidence at our disposal.

[11] Though the emergence of a small but often outspoken trading class in a country like Ghana, for example, can play an important role in defining the trajectory of socialist experiments.
[12] Roger Murray, "Second Thoughts on Ghana," in New Left Review (London), XLII, March–April 1967, p. 34.
[13] Lloyd, op. cit. introduction.
[14] At the extreme, of course, one has the example of Kenya where the ideology of "socialism" is being used unscrupulously to rationalise the march of the new African élite into all sectors of the economy, public and private. Not all uses of this rationale are so crude, but there is a certain consistency to the African pattern, none the less.

*What constitutes a democratic society or a democratic political
system? With the term almost universally accepted now by the leaders
of all states, it is obvious that the earlier, more limited Western definitions are being severely challenged by those who claim that their quite
different ideas, institutions, and procedures are just as democratic as
those found in Western societies; indeed, the claim is often made that
they are more democratic. In the selection below, Marguerite Fisher
discusses some of the new theories of democracy, forcing the reader to
consider again the core of democratic principles and the admissibility
of Asian concepts of democracy under the rubric of democratic thought.*

12. NEW CONCEPTS OF DEMOCRACY
IN SOUTHERN ASIA[*]

m a r g u e r i t e   j .   f i s h e r

Since the end of the second world war, . . . certain Asian theorists or
leaders, recognizing the incompatibility of Western-style democratic
institutions and traditional Asian cultures, have sought to evolve new
versions of democracy, both in theory and practice. Their objective has
been to construct a new concept of democracy, perhaps unacceptable to
the Western oriented, but nevertheless rooted in Asian cultural patterns
and the realities of Asian life. These new concepts of democracy are
characterized by a number of features in common, including the repudiation of Western-style parliamentary government as too remote and
complicated to be comprehended by the masses of the people. Political
parties, in particular, are condemned as disruptive forces which destroy
the unity needed for national development. The new theories recognize
the fact that the majority of Asians, psychologically as well as physically,
are restricted to the local societal level. Hence attention is focused on
the local or village community and the value of the small group. Social
cohesion, unity and cooperation rather than competition are stressed as
imperative needs. The amelioration of social and economic conditions is

[*] From "New Concepts of Democracy in Southern Asia" by Marguerite J. Fisher,
Western Political Quarterly, Vol. XV, No. 4 (December, 1962), pp. 626–636. By
permission of the University of Utah, copyright owners.

assigned a more important position than "politics." In all these new concepts runs the argument that Asian democratic institutions, to be successful, must have roots in Asian history and tradition.

INDIA

o o o o o

Jayaprakash Narayan

Probably the most significant voice raised in India today on behalf of an Indian rather than Western-style democratic government is that of Jayaprakash Narayan, founder and former leader of the Socialist party. In his youth he was a confirmed Marxist. After participating in Gandhi's civil disobedience movement Jayaprakash Narayan went to the United States, studying at several different universities and supporting himself by working in various odd jobs. On his return to India he helped to organize the Congress Socialist party, the forerunner of the present PSP (Praja Socialist party). He broke with the Communists in 1940 and came increasingly under the influence of Gandhi. During the early years of independence Jayaprakash Narayan was regarded as the likeliest successor to Nehru. In 1954, however, he announced his renunciation of active politics and his resignation as leader of the Praja Socialist party. He declared his intention to devote his life to the *Bhoodan Yagna* [gift-of-land] movement and similar activities outside of regular political channels for the realization of Gandhian ideals of *Sarvodaya* [service to all]. Not the Western alternatives of parliamentary socialism or communism, he decided, but only the principles of Gandhi could effect a sufficient revolution in the lives and values of the Indian masses.

The *Sarvodaya* pattern of society, Jayaprakash Narayan asserted, could never be constructed by legislation from New Delhi. There must be a far more fundamental change, "change at the root." Even though progress had been made by the Indian government in such areas as the community development program, the concept of social organization, he declared, remained the same as that of the atomized society of the West. In 1959 he published his theory of a democratic system for India in a book entitled *A Plea for Reconstruction of Indian Polity*.[1] His purpose in this document, he stated, was to search for "forms of social life, particularly of political life, that would assure the preservation of human values . . . and my approach has been non-partisan and non-sectarian."[2]

[1] Wardha (Bombay State), Sarva Seva Sangh Prakashan.
[2] *Ibid.*, p. ii.

It is questionable, according to Jayaprakash Narayan, "if democrats of all times and climes, social idealists and thinkers, the spirit of man itself, will ever remain satisfied with the current Western definition of democracy. Already . . . all these elements have combined . . . to demand a more satisfying participating democracy. Indeed, it is my firm belief that the extent to which democracy becomes truly participative, to that extent would the onrush of totalitarianism be stemmed and even rolled back." The atomistic and statistical democracy of the West "is based on a negation of the social nature of man and the true nature of human society," conceiving of society as an "inorganic mass of separate grains of individuals." [3]

The evidence "from Cairo to Djakarta indicates that Asian peoples are having second thoughts, and are seeking to find better forms than parliamentary democracy to express and embody their democratic aspirations." [4] The author devotes a whole chapter to the faults of Western parliamentary democracy, listing such points as: governments elected by universal suffrage under the party system are commonly representative of a minority of the voters; present-day mass elections manipulated by the super media of communication "represent far less the electorate than the forces and interests behind the parties and the propaganda machines"; [5] demagogy is inevitable with the need to "catch" votes by any methods; there is an inherent trend toward centralism, a "central state of overwhelming power and resources and the individual voter reduced to abject helplessness" [6] by an ever-increasing autocracy of bureaucracy; the political parties become centralized organizations in which the people have only "fictional" control, while small caucuses of politicians decide all matters of importance; the political parties create dissensions and divisions when unity is the greatest need; and finally, elections create unnecessary passions and excitement, stimulate demagogy, and necessitate fabulous expenditures.

The remedy will never be found in the strong centralized state, the author declares. The concentration of economic power in the hands of a central state, even under democratic conditions, will result in the "thwarting and limiting of political democracy itself." [7] Thus the Western welfare state threatens to enslave man as does totalitarianism. State socialism as found in the Soviet Union offers the worst example of the ruthless power of centralized state bureaucracy, said Jayaprakash Narayan, confessing that he had watched the Soviet experiment "with anguish."

In reconstructing Indian democracy, according to the author, one of

3   Ibid., p. 35.
4   Ibid., p. 36.
5   Ibid., p. 49.
6   Ibid., p. 50.
7   Ibid., p. 9.

the main objectives must be *social integration.* "Man is alone and bored; he is 'organization man,' he is man ordered about and manipulated by forces beyond his ken and control—irrespective of whether it is a 'democracy' or dictatorship." [8] The first necessity is to "put man in touch with man, so that they may live together in meaningful, understandable, controllable relationships. In short, *the problem is to re-create the human community.*" [9] There must be sharing, fellowship, identity of interest, a feeling of unity in the midst of diversity, and voluntary participation by all the people in community affairs. Only then will the "social nature of man and the great humanist ideals of modern civilization find fulfillment." [10]

New forms of Indian democracy must be based on the ancient "social genius of India" and its "organically, self-determining communal life." [11] It is a question of an ancient country finding its lost soul again. Political reconstruction must be founded upon the local democracies of past centuries, "the village councils, the town committees, the trades and artisans' guilds of old." [12] Unless life in India is again organized on the basis of self-determining and mutually coordinating and integrating communities, democracy will "remain distantly removed from the life of the people." [13] Like the author of the *Gandhian Constitution for Free India,* Jayaprakash Narayan devotes considerable space to the historic village *panchayats* on the ground that they are "pivotal not only for the regeneration of Indian polity but for the regeneration of Indian society as a whole." [14]

The author then turns to the subject of appropriate formal structures of government. The highest political institution of the local community is to be the General Assembly, the *Gram Sabha,* in which all adults are members. The Council or *Panchayat* should be chosen by general consensus in the *Sabha.* Each *panchayat* will function through subcommittees charged with different responsibilities. If the people cannot come to a general consensus in the selection of their officials, then the alternative method should be by drawing lots.

Neighboring local or primary communities, in turn, are to be joined together to build a regional community. Each primary community

. . . might be able to provide for a primary school, primary health services, small irrigation works like wells and village banks, and village industries. But a number of primary communities must cooperate together in order to provide for a higher school, an indoor hospital, a power-station and servicing centre,

---

[8]   *Ibid.,* p. 37.
[9]   *Ibid.*
[10] *Ibid.,* p. 38.
[11] *Ibid.,* p. 19.
[12] *Ibid.,* p. 13.
[13] *Ibid.,* p. 23.
[14] *Ibid.,* p. 30.

POLITICAL IDEAS AND IDEOLOGIES

larger industries, larger irrigation works, etc. Thus the regional community comes into existence by an organic process of growth.[15]

The regional community, however, must be an integral community in itself. It is not a superior or higher body that "can control or interfere with the internal administration of the primary communities. *Each in its sphere is equally sovereign.*" [16]

The hierarchical structure erected upon the foundations of the village community, as sketched by Jayaprakash Narayan, is similar to the one outlined by Shriman Narayan Agarwal in the *Gandhian Constitution for Free India.* Above the regional community are larger communities, the district, provincial, and finally the National Community, each with functions and responsibilities appropriate to its area. There is no scope "for political parties to play any role in this process." [17] Such a communitarian society alone can guarantee the ideal participating democracy in which the individual "will be able to save himself from the fate of 'robotism' to which modern civilization has condemned him and find freedom and self-significance as a member of the community." [18]

In the economic area the communitarian society must be so organized that "human needs are satisfied as near home as possible," first in the primary community and then in the higher levels.[19] Each expanding area of community would then be as self-sufficient as possible, and every economic institution would be "integrated with the community to which it territorially belongs." [20] Thus, . . . planning would be facilitated on each level.

✿ ✿ ✿ ✿ ✿

THE PHILIPPINES

As early as 1940 President Manuel Quezon of the Philippines challenged his countrymen to discard one of the "fetishes" of democracy, "the discarded theory that democracy cannot exist without political parties." [21] In a speech delivered by Quezon to the students of the University of the Philippines on July 16, 1940, there was recurring stress on unity, cooperation, and strong national leadership, and denunciation of partisan strife and obstructionism as inimical to true democracy and the economic and social development of the Philippines. Quezon declared:

[15] *Ibid.,* p. 42.
[16] *Ibid.,* p. 43.
[17] *Ibid.,* p. 77.
[18] *Ibid.,* p. 44.
[19] *Ibid.,* p. 56.
[20] *Ibid.,* p. 57.
[21] Address of His Excellency Manuel L. Quezon, President of the Philippines. Manila, Bureau of Printing, 1940.

In the very nature of things the struggle for power between contending political parties creates partisan spirit, and partisan spirit is incompatible with good government. . . . It is party politics that causes inefficiency in government; it is party opposition that causes delay in the execution of needed reforms; it is party spirit that weakens the government and makes it incapable of facing difficult situations. . . . This concept of the need of a majority and minority party is as wrong as saying that, in order that a home may be governed well, it is necessary that there should be a division, that there should be fighting all the time in the family. A nation is like a family, multiplied a thousandfold, and just as it is impossible for a family to be happy or to make progress when there is division among its members . . . so it is impossible for a nation to grow strong and accomplish great ends if the people are always divided, if they are taught to believe that patriotism means division.[22]

Impressed by Manuel Quezon's plea for a different system of democracy, Dr. Ricardo Pascual, head of the Department of Philosophy at the University of the Philippines, devoted his time to an amplification of the theories presented by President Quezon. In a book entitled *Partyless Democracy,* Dr. Pascual advanced a thesis holding that the "next stage in the development of democratic concepts and ideas is inevitably the 'partyless democracy.'"[23] Dr. Pascual begins his argument with a warning that democracy is on trial, not only in the Philippines but in the other new nations of Asia. Much is expected of democracy in the creation of a better way of life for millions of Asian peoples. But the failure to bridge this "wide gap between promise and accomplishment is the source of disgust and reckless swerving to the opposite extreme in the form of reaction."[24] Before popular disillusionment becomes too deep, warns Dr. Pascual, the processes of democratic government must be made more efficient. In this matter the Filipinos must "do their own thinking" and should not blindly copy the great democracies of the West.

Dr. Pascual then proceeds to challenge the Western thesis that political parties are necessary to a liberal political regime. His point of view will encounter strong resistance, he warns, because it runs contrary to the classical line of thought on democracy. He examines various Western arguments for the necessity of the party system and rejects them as inappropriate for the needs and conditions of Filipino society. A scheme of democracy must be constructed, he asserts, in which:

The *opinion* of the *genuine public*, that is, the *genuine public opinion*, is a *compromise opinion* of the *different elements* of a Democracy, not a *triumphant opinion* of the *majority* at the *vanquishment of the minority.* The scheme of Democracy which will carry out this ideal will be one which is not different

---

[22] *Ibid.*
[23] Ricardo R. Pascual, *Partyless Democracy* (Quezon City: University of the Philippines, 1952), p. viii.
[24] *Ibid.*, p. 7.

from the type of organic unity, harmony, and process of a living organism. Biologists tell us that a living organism is the example of composite organization, of mutual participation, of synthetic harmony, of unity in diversity to speak in paradox. But this kind of ideal Democracy . . . is really impractical in the politics of the party system.[25]

Partyless democracy, maintains Dr. Pascual, would be an "organic social polity." In general, the various qualities of a partyless democracy will depend upon the "peculiar necessities of the country in which it is intended to be practiced; but all of them will do away with division, dissension, schism, competition, narrow vested interest, partisanship." [26] In the Western party system, on the other hand, "political parties are still in conflict, in competition, in struggle with one another in much the same way that in the pre-party era the individuals were in conflict, in competition, in struggle with one another. . . . When will Democracy learn to substitute cooperation, organization and mutual help for competition, group struggle, and selfish exploitation?" [27]

Furthermore, contends Dr. Pascual, the greatest need of the Philippines as well as other Asian nations is social justice. "The promotion of the social interest requires cooperation, not division, mutual cooperative mass action, not individual, competitive intrigues, the mustering of all forces toward the production of the social good, not the pitting of individuals against their fellow men. In this sense the partyless system . . . is the means for consummating the ideal of social justice." [28]

But how will partyless democracy work in practice? What structural design and organizational pattern will it assume? Dr. Pascual advocates a legislature based upon functional or occupational representation. First of all, the representatives in the Congress must

. . . come from groups of people but let these groups be determined not by geographical division but by occupations or professions. . . . Let not any geographical division interfere in this occupational grouping. This means that the delegates, let us say, of the farmers, are delegates of all the farmers in the Philippines. In this way we shall *practice unity* among the members of the group of farmers and *not simply dream about it.* This practice shall hold with all occupational groups. Each group shall be bound by the common interest inherent among the members of such group.[29]

The different groups are to be represented in Congress in proportion to their actual members in the nation, but with a stated maximum number of representatives. Whereas proportional representation should be followed in the lower house of Congress, in the Senate each occupational group should have an equal representation. Because the welfare of

25   *Ibid.*, p. 48.
26   *Ibid.*, pp. 119–20.
27   *Ibid.*, pp. 53–54.
28   *Ibid.*, p. 128.
29   *Ibid.*, pp. 167–68.

each occupation is mutually dependent upon the welfare of every other occupation, maintains Dr. Pascual, there would be less reason for competition. The representatives of each group will be elected at large, and only by members of their own group. Thus farmers would not be competing against fishermen because "their candidates are not competing for the same votes." [30] In this system there will be "greater unity among people pursuing the same trade or occupation. . . . The feeling of self-sufficiency within a group which will contribute to the seclusion and aloofness of that group, and hence to the creation of sectionalism, will not be found in each of the occupational groups . . . since each occupation is not independent of others in the scheme of social life." [31] Furthermore, the division of the electorate into occupational groups, according to Dr. Pascual, would encourage and accelerate long-range programs of social legislation, one of the greatest needs of Asian societies. National planning, too, would be facilitated. Under the new system "each occupational group would naturally endeavor to make lasting plans regarding its future." [32]

The author's arguments on behalf of functional representation are reminiscent of those advanced by various European writers of the late nineteenth and early twentieth centuries. But they assume new significance in that they are aimed in Dr. Pascual's book at the solution of problems felt to be characteristic of the new Asian nations.

[30] *Ibid.*, p. 172.
[31] *Ibid.*, p. 176.
[32] *Ibid.*, p. 181.

v. political systems

To the student of politics familiar with the basic stability of political institutions and processes in the American and European states, politics in the developing states is frequently baffling and incomprehensible. So often the political process in these states appears to be one of futility, disorder, and impending—if not actual—chaos. Constitutions are proclaimed, only to be ignored or suspended, civilian governments are overthrown and replaced by military juntas, federations are created and then quickly collapse, individual and collective acts of violence occur—everywhere, it sometimes seems, the developing states are in constant turmoil, unable to resolve the basic problem of establishing stable and effective governments. Yet these events, frequent as they may seem, are the type that capture the headlines; much less frequently noticed are the steady strides taken by some states toward the goals of modernization and effective mass participation in the political process. Less frequently noticed too is the gradual collapse into lethargy and stagnation that overtakes some of the others when they fail to maintain the dynamic forces essential for modernization. A summary of the principal characteristics of developing political systems may suggest the reasons for both the more dramatic cases of instability and disorder and the less publicized cases of slower, more evolutionary changes.

The analysis of developing political systems may usefully begin with a consideration of the political attitudes and values of the populace, which to a large extent determine the stability of political institutions and the efficiency and effectiveness of the decision-making process. In most developing states, the political value system is more highly fragmented than in most European or American states. Traditional values and beliefs remain firmly entrenched and continue to be supported by large numbers of persons, particularly those in rural areas. These persons accept the legitimacy of, and give their primary allegiance to, the tribal and communal leaders who exercise their authority through traditional institutions and processes. In contrast, an often much smaller number of persons adhere to values characteristic of Western political systems: a secular nation-state, political equality, universal suffrage, popularly elected political leaders, an independent judiciary, and an impartial, professional civil service, among others. The political values of a third, and usually increasingly large, group of persons are in a state of transition. Individuals in this group have begun to cast off as unsatisfactory the traditional values of their forefathers, but they have not as yet fully accepted the secular, egalitarian principles underlying Western political beliefs. Their primary loyalties are uncertain and ambivalent. While they may be attracted by the political values the modernizing leaders are attempting to inculcate in their followers, traditional values also exert a strong pull. Their support for the state and its political system is tenuous and qualified, the degree of legitimacy accorded the government fluctuating with its successes and failures.

In many of these states, the development of a broad consensus on political institutions and processes is further impeded by the inability or unwillingness of the different ethnic, tribal, or other major groups to reach agreement. Jealous of their own cultures and patterns of organization, they are often fearful that their own interests are not being adequately protected and promoted. In some cases, this fear has led to secessionist movements and the attempt to establish separate states for the dissident groups. Nigeria, for example, was torn by a long and bloody civil war as the Ibos fought unsuccessfully to establish their own state of Biafra and, as one observer notes, "few of the new nations of Africa lack, as part of their colonial heritage, their potential Biafras." [1] In Asia, East Pakistanis fought a successful civil war in 1971 to establish their own state of Bangladesh.

The developing political systems must also contend with the tensions arising from the changing social and economic conditions in society. Many states are now moving through the initial phases of industrialization, shifting from an almost exclusively agrarian to a more mixed economic base. In contrast to the relatively stable social and economic systems that existed in their traditional societies, the developing states are now confronted with the complex problems resulting from their attempts to modernize rapidly. As new methods of production, channels of communication, and patterns of authority are established, the traditional social fabric is often subjected to intense pressures. Since the governments in the developing states have commonly assumed a direct and active role in promoting modernization, they become the focal point

[1] Geralk L. Caplan, "Barotseland: The Secessionist Challenge to Zambia," *The Journal of Modern African Studies,* VI, No. 3 (November, 1968), p. 343.

of criticism from those individuals and groups adversely affected by the impact of modernization. As many of these governments, including both individual leaders and the institutional framework, have not achieved a high degree of stability and popular support, their capacity to withstand the shocks of social and economic change is limited.

Contributing to the instability of the developing political systems are the significant changes that have been occurring in the composition of political elites and in the bases from which political power is exercised. The political elite in any society consists of both the individual leaders and the groups or classes (from which the individual leaders typically come) who exercise significant influence in political decision-making. While changes in the political elite structure are most apparent in many of the new Asian and African states, alterations in this structure are also evident in many of the Latin American states. In only a few cases, such as Ethiopia and Saudi Arabia, has the traditional elite been able to preserve its dominant position largely intact to the present.

In many developing states, the traditional elite has been largely supplanted at the national level by the "new" elite. Nevertheless, the traditional elite still remains important, particularly at the local and regional levels.[2] This elite is composed mainly of religious leaders, landowners, and hereditary rulers. The relative political power of these groups is declining for a number of reasons. In the case of the religious leaders, the increasing secularization of society is corroding their power. As an increasing number of social issues become disentangled from religious considerations, individuals (particularly in the urban centers) seek the guidance of religious leaders less and less frequently. In the villages and rural areas, however, the religious elite continues to exert its influence in every aspect of the lives of individuals and the community. The principal exceptions to the general decline of religious influence in national politics are found in those Latin American states where the Catholic Church is represented directly in the government, in some of the Middle Eastern and Asian states where Muslim religious leaders exert great authority, and in a few Asian states where Buddhist monks are politically active.

The traditional authority of hereditary chiefs, princes, and local notables has also declined as centralized governments and their bureaucracies have increasingly assumed decision-making power for the society. These traditional leaders have often been vigorously opposed to policies of modernization since the execution of these policies threatens to destroy their traditional base of authority. Despite their opposition, nationalist leaders have frequently had to retain this group of traditional leaders because of the considerable prestige and power they exercise at

[2] Norman N. Miller, "The Political Survival of Traditional Leadership," *The Journal of Modern African Studies,* Vol. VI, No. 2 (August, 1968), pp. 183–98.

the local level. In few states do hereditary chiefs and princes exert significant power directly in the national governments, though their political power at the local and regional levels must often be taken into account in the formulation of national policies. With few exceptions, such as Jordan, Iran, Saudi Arabia, and Ethiopia, monarchies and royal families have been overthrown or their powers severely circumscribed.

The traditional authority of the landed aristocracy is also increasingly being undermined. The principal causes for their decline are the land reform programs that are breaking up the large estates in many states and the increasing industrialization and urbanization that result in the creation of a new urban middle class and new centers of financial power. Again, as with the other types of traditional elites, it is at the local level where the large landowners remain most influential. In some South American and Middle Eastern states, however, the landed aristocracy still holds considerable power at the national level also. This condition is not found in many African and Asian states, since a landed aristocracy was never created; ownership of large estates by aristocratic families was not a common feature of their societies.

The "new" elite that now possesses dominant power at the national level in almost all of the new states in Asia and Africa differs from the traditional elite in its nationalism, secularism, commitment to social and economic reform, and orientation to Western culture and values (though this last point is frequently denied). It is this elite that usually led the nationalist struggle for independence.[3] This elite, composed of both civilian and military leaders, is far less dependent on traditional religious and economic institutions for its political power than on its intellectual and organizational skills. Although its members are not drawn from as definable a group or class as are the traditional elites, most of the "new" elite share a middle or upper-middle class background, possess a Western education, and reside in major urban areas. As is evident, this elite lacks the deeply rooted ties with the tradition-oriented masses that the traditional elites possess. Its relationships with the masses are established primarily through the bureaucracy, the armed forces, political parties, and strong individual personalities who can spark broad, popular support for themselves and their programs. This personal leadership, so prominent in many of the new states, is of course difficult to institutionalize. While a number of leaders have been able to attain a high level of personal popularity, support for the national government and its institutions has often remained markedly low. In states where this "new" modernizing, Westernized elite does not control the national government, as in some of the Latin American and Middle Eastern states, it nevertheless is often increasing its strength as more and more persons join reformist groups and movements.

[3] Edward Shils, "The Intellectuals in the Political Development of the New States," *World Politics*, Vol. XII, No. 3 (April, 1960), pp. 329–354.

The organization and articulation of interests in developing political systems take place through several types of groups. In most developing states, interests organized around traditional loyalties to ethnic, tribal, regional, linguistic, class, and religious groups are important forces. These groups, often highly cohesive in their social organization and in their political outlook and demands, articulate a broad range of social and economic interests considered necessary to protect and advance the welfare of the group. Seldom are these groups formally organized for political action since the traditional ties provide the necessary solidarity for effective identification and communication between the leaders and the members of the group. The comprehensive, integrated demands these groups make on the national political leaders frequently obstruct the formulation and implementation of specific developmental policies.

The political importance of individual associational groups (labor, business, professional, landlord, peasant, and others)—and of these groups collectively—varies significantly from state to state. In a few states, these groups are relatively numerous, well-organized, and politically influential; in most states, however, their importance is greatly overshadowed by the traditional groups and by groups such as the bureaucracy and the armed forces. Nowhere are the peasants very well organized, despite some attempts to establish organizations to represent their interests. The efforts of labor leaders to organize them are obstructed both by the traditional conservatism of the peasants and by their economic dependency on their landlords or money-lenders. Lacking alternative skills and strongly rooted in their communities, peasants are generally unwilling to risk the consequences of organizing in opposition to their landlords' commands. Even where the peasants own their small plots of land individually, they have rarely organized effectively for political action. Largely illiterate, often heavily in debt, and politically unsophisticated, they usually follow the leadership of the traditional rural elite.

Labor unions in a number of states, organized in industries, services, and on plantations, have begun to achieve a voice in the shaping of labor legislation, wage policy, and other programs of interest to them. In many cases, however, the unions have been incorporated into political parties whose programs include other objectives as well.[4] As a result, the specific interests of the unions are often subordinated to the more general objectives of the parties. Business and landlord groups are often not as formally organized for political action as are labor unions. Several reasons account for this fact. In the first place, the number of individuals

[4] Robert N. Kearney, "The Partisan Involvement of Trade Unions in Ceylon," *Asian Survey*, Vol. VIII, No. 7 (July, 1968, pp. 576–588, and Stephen H. Goodman, "Trade Unions and Political Parties: The Case of East Africa," *Economic Development and Cultural Change*, Vol. XVII, No. 3 (April, 1969), pp. 338–344.

is smaller, and informal contacts are often sufficient to decide upon a course of action. Second, the landlords are on the defensive in many states, and the modernizing elite is often intolerant of organized landlord pressure. Third, many of the business enterprises and commercial activities in some states are controlled by aliens—for example, Indians in East Africa, Chinese in Southeast Asia, and American and British in Latin America—who find it expedient to avoid overt political activity in order to preserve their economic opportunities. In some states, since many of the basic industries and the transportation and communications systems are owned and operated by the state, the growth of a large, powerful, private industrial and business elite is largely foreclosed. Despite these limiting factors, business organizations such as chambers of commerce are increasing in number and strength in many states as industrial and business growth takes place.

Professional organizations representing lawyers, teachers, doctors, and military officers, among others, often exert political influence greatly disproportionate to their small memberships. Since the members of these organizations possess many of the technical skills required for modernization, political leaders of the modernizing states frequently look to them for advice and aid in planning the developmental programs. Student organizations are often some of the better organized and more politically active groups in these states. As part of the small but politically significant intelligentsia, students are in many instances leading exponents of change. Their restlessness over current conditions provides an advantageous psychological orientation for political organizers. Though their numbers are relatively small, student bodies are usually concentrated in the capital cities where their demonstrations and other forms of political activity produce the greatest effect.[5]

In the majority of developing countries, particularly in those where associational interest groups are weakest, institutional interest groups— the armed forces, bureaucracies, and in some instances, religious groups —play a predominant role in the articulation of political interests. For both the modernizing elite and the traditional elite (in the oligarchic states), the armed forces and bureaucracies, with their instruments of control and sources of information, constitute principal agencies not only for the maintenance of law and order, but also for the formulation and implementation of social and economic policies. In many of the states, the present centralized, powerful bureaucracies were initially established by the colonial powers which recruited, at least into the lower levels of the civil services, some of the most able and talented persons in the indigenous populations. These Western-trained administrators are

[5] See the surveys of student organizations and activities in "Students and Politics," *Daedalus*, Vol. XCVII, No. 1 (Winter, 1968) and Donald K. Emmerson, ed., *Students and Politics in Developing Nations* (New York: Frederick A. Praeger, Inc., 1968).

now engaged in the comprehensive planning that characterizes most of the developing states. Through their network of departments and agencies, the bureaucracies are also responsible for the administration of many policies and programs: tax collection, transportation and communications, education, land reform, resource surveys, industrial development, and many more.

The armed forces are similarly in a position to exert significant political influence. Many military officers have, like the administrators, received a Western education and are committed to programs of modernization. In addition to their defense functions, the armed forces are commonly engaged in a variety of non-defense and defense-related activities. They are often responsible, for example, for the construction of roads, communications facilities, and irrigation projects. They may also have broad educational responsibilities, teaching basic skills such as reading and writing in addition to specific military skills. As one of the few well-organized, disciplined, and progressive institutions in these states, the armed forces are often indispensable for the successful execution of policies necessary for modernization.[6]

However, the same attributes that make the military forces a most useful agency for modernization also make them a potential—and often actual—threat to civilian control. As has been demonstrated recently and repeatedly in Asia and Africa, the military leadership may become impatient with the pace or direction of policy, or with the alleged inefficiency or corruption of the civilian leadership. The military may then itself assume political control of the government.[7] Usually the military leaders assert that their control is only to be temporary; once the conditions leading to their intervention have been rectified, competent civilian leaders will again be permitted to assume control. Rarely, however, have military leaders been as willing to release their control as they have been to assume it.

The military *coups* so frequently staged in some Latin American states are usually of a different nature and have different purposes than those that occur in Asia and Africa.[8] In general, the struggles for political supremacy reflect either interservice rivalries or personal and factional disputes. The tradition of military leaders in political office is well

---

[6] The nonmilitary functions of military forces have been discussed in a number of works. See, for example, John J. Johnson, ed., *The Role of the Military in Underdeveloped Countries* (Princeton, N. J.: Princeton University Press, 1962), Hugh Hanning, *The Peaceful Uses of Military Forces* (New York: Praeger Publishers, Inc., 1967), and Edward B. Glick, *Peaceful Conflict: The Non-Military Uses of the Military* (Harrisburg, Pa.: Stackpole Press, 1967).

[7] Henry Bienen, ed., *The Military Intervenes* (New York: Russell Sage Foundation, 1968), Claude E. Welch, Jr., ed., *Soldier and State in Africa* (Evanston: Northwestern University Press, 1970), and William Gutteridge, "Why Does an African Army Take Power?" *Africa Report,* Vol. XV, No. 10 (October, 1970), pp. 18–22.

[8] Peter Calvert, "The 'Typical Latin-American Revolution,'" *International Affairs,* Vol. XLIII, No. 1 (January, 1967), pp. 85–95.

established in many Latin American states, and while issues of corruption, dictatorial practices, and violations of constitutional provisions may be involved, personal and service rivalries rather than the general direction of public policy seem to account for more of the *coups* than in Asia and Africa. As part of the traditional aristocracy, the military in Latin America has tended to be a conservative, rather than progressive, political force.

For the very large majority of persons in transitional societies, concern for or involvement in national politics is still minimal. Although elections may infrequently activate the tradition-oriented peasant masses and others of low socioeconomic status, their interest in and understanding of national politics and policies is restricted by their high level of illiteracy, the day-to-day struggle for subsistence, the relative isolation of the villages, and the traditional cultural patterns that restrict the participation of peasants, women, and other groups in deference to the political elites. Few of the devices common to developed societies for the gathering and dissemination of information are available. Newspapers are few and have limited numbers of readers. "Letters to the editor" columns, critical editorials, and public opinion polls that in Western societies provide some indication of support for or opposition to government policies are frequently unknown. Many of the major presses are controlled or dominated by the government, as are the other means of communication, radio, television, telephone, and telegraph. Few official or unofficial advisory committees exist to provide the government with information, and public hearings conducted by government officials are seldom a prominent part of the process of consultation. In short, few organizations or other channels of communication exist to bridge the gap between the modernizing elite and the mass population.

The most important nongovernmental organization—and sometimes this distinction is difficult to maintain—that partially fills this void is the political party. It is difficult, however, to state generalizations concerning the party systems in these states since such wide variations exist in their organizational structure, their specific programs, and the social bases from which they draw their support. In the more traditional authoritarian states such as Ethiopia and Saudi Arabia, organizations with any of the usual characteristics of political parties cannot be said to exist. In these states, the rulers have effectively prevented the organization of political parties; cliques, factions, and personal groups without organizational structures provide the principal links between the rulers and the politically active segments of society. At the other extreme, in a few states well organized political parties exist which aggregate many specific interests and compete for power in a manner familiar to the student of American or European politics. Between these extremes are found a variety of party systems. In some states, such as Pakistan and Thailand, parties may exist in name, but because of military rule they are ineffectual. In a number of other states, particularly in Africa, only one officially designated mass party is permitted to function. Still another type of party system may be found in states such as Mexico where one party has long been dominant, though other parties may enjoy a marginal existence, often at the discretion of the major party.

A broad distinction may be drawn between Latin America, on the one hand, and Asia and Africa, on the other, for purposes of specifying the major characteristics of political parties in these areas. In Latin America, national politics in most states remains the preserve of the upper classes—the "whites"—to the virtual exclusion of the *mestizos*, Indians, and Negroes. Membership in the political parties is thus usually confined to persons of the upper classes. Many of these parties are essentially the personal followings of particularly strong leaders, with relatively little organizational structure or program except that propounded by the leader. Such parties are highly dependent upon the personal political fortunes of the leaders. When a leader is successful, the party prospers and enjoys the spoils of victory; when he is defeated or overthrown, the party has little capacity for survival unless the leader can remain politically active. These personalistic parties have long been a prominent feature of Latin American politics. They have been headed by ruthless military or civilian dictators as well as by paternalistic, benevolent leaders. Increasingly, however, these *caudillo* parties are being challenged by parties that, while still often confined to the upper classes, are more permanently organized and present programs of broad social and economic principles. These parties, such as the Socialist, Communist, and Aprista, are less dependent upon individual leadership than on organizational structure and the popular appeal of their programs.

Political parties in Asia and Africa are distinguishable from those in Latin America in several major respects. They are, of course, usually of more recent origin. They reflect too the impact of the revolutionary movements that have in many cases so recently led to the creation of independent states. In addition, they more frequently possess a more or less elaborate program of modernization, an orientation that tends to shape the organizational structure of these parties along lines other than those that generally characterize Latin American parties.

In the preindependence period, a number of groups, sometimes distinguished with the name party, were in existence. These groups and parties were composed almost exclusively of the Western-oriented minority; they were neither mass organizations nor did they commonly possess and support broad political programs. Depending upon the colonial policies, some groups cooperated with the colonialists while others found it advantageous to oppose them. As feelings of nationalism grew, some of these "parties" broadened their organizational base and became mass movements. While controversies over the timing and direction of the revolution often divided these groups and parties, in general they were able to cooperate in the interests of securing independence. Once independence was achieved, however, the unifying element of the nationalist movement receded, and controversies broke out over the policies to be pursued in the drive for modernization. Although some of the parties that now exist are still primarily the personal followings of the strong leaders, others, such as the Congress Party in India, have achieved a relatively high level of permanent organization.

As noted in the previous chapter, many leaders in the African and Asian states reject the idea of competitive political parties, arguing that they are both divisive when tolerated and unnecessary in fact, since one mass party can and must embody the general will. The tendency toward the establishment of authoritarian, one-party systems is pronounced in these areas.[9] Yet the authoritarianism that is promoted differs from that usually found in Latin America, with the exception of Cuba. Whereas the traditional authoritarianism in Latin America is conservative or even reactionary, seeking to perpetuate the privileges of the upper-class ruling elite, the authoritarianism in Africa and Asia is revolutionary, attempting to build broad support among the masses for the purpose of economic development and social reform. Thus the leaders of most Asian and African parties have attempted to organize and activate the mass populations in their societies for purposes of modernization, though they are frequently thwarted by the elements of traditionalism that still characterize their societies. In most Latin American states, in contrast, the major political parties have not striven for this mass participation. The issues that divide them are principally those of upper-class privileges, including the power of the Catholic Church and the landed aristocracy, rather than those relating to the pace of modernization.

In addition to political parties, one element of most modern states that has found almost universal acceptance in the developing states is that of a written constitution. In addition to provisions establishing the institutions of government and their powers, these constitutions commonly provide an elaborate statement of individual rights and duties and the goals of public policy. The structure of the national government as provided for in most Latin American constitutions follows that of the United States. A presidential system, rather than a parliamentary, has been uniformly adopted, and in a few states, such as Mexico and Argentina, a federal system has been created. In many of the new African and Asian states, the formal governmental institutions were initially patterned after those of the former colonial power. Several reasons account for this development. First, of course, is the fact that the leaders were

---

[9] Martin L. Kilson, "Authoritarian and Single-Party Tendencies in African Politics," *World Politics*, Vol. XV, No. 2 (January, 1963), pp. 262–294, and Thomas Rasmussen, "Political Competition and One-Party Dominance in Zambia," *The Journal of Modern African Studies*, Vol. VII, No. 3 (October, 1969), pp. 407–424.

most familiar with the constitutional framework of the colonial power, many of them having been educated in Europe, in the schools of the colonial power. Second, the colonial administrators often openly and strongly encouraged the new leaders to adopt the colonial power's institutional framework, believing it to be, quite naturally, superior to any other form. An important third reason was that, for the Westernized elite in the former colonies, these institutions represented part of the package of modernization they so ardently desired to attain. To modify substantially the institutional forms and practices appeared to them an admission of having achieved less than full equality with the West.

Formal institutions and processes can be far more readily adopted, however, than can the underlying attitudes, values, and other characteristics of another society that enable institutions to perform in a certain manner. Thus, the formal institutions established at the time of independence quickly broke down in some states and were replaced by others considered more compatible with the characteristics and requirements of the society. In Pakistan, for example, the Constitution of 1956 (which had taken nine years to frame) was abrogated in 1958. President Ayub Khan, justifying this action, asserted that the Pakistani leaders were initially provided with a system "totally unsuited to the temper and climate of the country." Similarly in other states in Africa and Asia, fundamental changes in the constitutional provisions relating to the structure and powers of the national government were effected in the years immediately following independence. In many cases, these changes were directed toward the strengthening of executive leadership, the presidential form of government replacing the parliamentary form that had been initially established.

However modern and efficient the institutional arrangements may appear, decision-making in transitional societies is often slow and inefficient. Leaders intent on achieving rapid changes are burdened with the numerous and complex problems of planning and implementing their revolutionary programs. Lacking adequate aides, and often disinclined to delegate authority, they assume many routine tasks in addition to those of basic planning. Further, traditional practices commonly intermingle with the new, resulting in a political process that often appears irrational and chaotic to foreign observers. In many Asian and African states, for example, the decision-making process is often slowed since unanimous or near-unanimous agreement must be achieved before policies can be announced. Decisions based upon formal votes, in which the members of the minority can be identified, are regarded as less desirable than those based upon unanimous consent. Again, in many Asian bureaucracies, few decisions can be made at the lower levels. Most problems that arise are passed on to high-ranking officials for decisions, since lower echelon bureaucrats are reluctant to make judgments that might be reversed, causing them to "lose face" with their contemporaries.

Recourse to astrology is common in many of these societies before important decisions can be made. In 1964, for example, the Prime Minister of Ceylon delayed the decision to dissolve Parliament and hold new elections until the official astrologers could be consulted for the auspicious date of dissolution.

Whatever the specific format of governmental institutions that characterize a state's political system, the dominant position of the executive is a feature common throughout the developing areas. Rarely do legislatures pose formidable obstacles to the exercise of executive authority or its control of the decision-making process.[10] Indeed, in few states in the world other than in the United States does the legislative body possess a largely independent capacity to participate in the process of enacting legislation. Nor, in most of the developing states, is there a strong tradition of judicial independence capable of disallowing and voiding the acts and decisions of the executive. Not only do the constitutions of most states grant broad powers of authority and control to the executive —including the power, in many countries, to declare a state of emergency and to rule by decree—but there is also a long tradition of executive-bureaucratic domination of the government that is deeply rooted in the values and customs of the societies. The traditional pattern of deference to the ruler, whether traditional or modern, and the expectation that strong leadership will be exercised, even in an arbitrary manner, further reinforce the constitutional prerogatives the executive enjoys. In those cases where only one party is legally permitted, or where one party is clearly dominant in the society, executive power is further enhanced by the controls exercised by and through the party apparatus.

Even with strong executive leadership, however, the probability of soon developing stable political systems in the transitional states is not high, as recent history demonstrates.[11] The dual quests for stability and modernization are frequently incompatible. In the clash of traditional and modern groups and their values, the political systems of the developing states will continue to be subjected to intense pressures. Whether the developing states can successfully resolve their manifold problems must, at present, remain an open question. While the pessimist may point to the chaos and confusion in many states, the gradual progress being recorded in states such as Mexico and Malaysia in resolving their problems must not be ignored.

[10] Legislative functions are discussed in Newell M. Stultz, "Parliament in a Tutelary Democracy: A Recent Case in Kenya," *The Journal of Politics,* Vol. XXXI, No. 1 (February, 1969), pp. 95–118.

[11] James O'Connell, "The Inevitability of Instability," *The Journal of Modern African Studies,* Vol. V, No. 2 (September, 1967), pp. 181–191.

SUGGESTED READINGS

Adu, A. L. *The Civil Service in Commonwealth Africa: Development and Transition.* London: Allen & Unwin, 1969.

Alba, Victor. *Politics and the Labor Movement in Latin America.* Stanford, Calif.: Stanford University Press, 1968.

Alderfer, Harold F. *Local Government in Developing Countries.* New York: McGraw-Hill Book Company, Inc., 1964.

Allott, A. N. *Judicial and Legal Systems in Africa.* London: Butterworths, 1970.

Anderson, James N. E., ed. *Changing Law in Developing Countries.* New York: Frederick A. Praeger, 1963.

Bayley, David H. *Public Liberties in the New States.* Chicago: Rand McNally & Company, 1964.

Bienen, Henry, ed. *The Military Intervenes.* New York: Russell Sage Foundation, 1968.

Braibanti, Ralph, ed. *Political and Administrative Development.* Durham, N.C.: Duke University Press, 1969.

Burger, Angela S. *Opposition in a Dominant-Party System.* Berkeley, Calif.: University of California Press, 1969.

Coleman, James S., and Carl G. Rosberg, Jr., eds. *Political Parties and National Integration in Tropical Africa.* Berkeley, Calif.: University of California Press, 1964.

Eldersveld, Samuel J., V. Jagannadham, and A. P. Barnabas. *The Citizen and the Administrator in a Developing Democracy.* Glenview, Ill.: Scott, Foresman and Company, 1968.

Emmerson, Donald, ed. *Students and Politics in Developing Nations.* New York: Frederick A. Praeger, 1968.

Gutteridge, William F. *The Military in African Politics.* New York: Barnes & Noble, 1969.

————. *Military Institutions and Power in the New States.* New York: Frederick A. Praeger, 1965.

Haddad, George M. *Revolution and Military Rule in the Middle East.* New York: R. Speller, 1965.

Halpern, Manfred. *The Politics of Social Change in the Middle East and North Africa.* Princeton, N. J.: Princeton University Press, 1963.

Heidenheimer, Arnold J., ed. *Political Corruption.* New York: Holt, Rinehart and Winston, 1970.

Horowitz, Irving Louis, ed. *Masses in Latin America.* New York: Oxford University Press, 1970.

Huntington, Samuel P. *Political Order in Changing Societies.* New Haven: Yale University Press, 1968.

Janowitz, Morris. *The Military in the Political Development of New Nations.* Chicago: University of Chicago Press, 1964.

Johnson, Chalmers. *Revolutionary Change.* Boston: Little, Brown and Company, 1966.

Johnson, John J. *The Military and Society in Latin America.* Stanford, Calif.: Stanford University Press, 1964.

————, ed. *The Role of the Military in Underdeveloped Countries*. Princeton, N. J.: Princeton University Press, 1962.

Landsberger, Henry A., ed. *Latin American Peasant Movements*. Ithaca, N. Y.: Cornell University Press, 1969.

LaPalombara, Joseph, ed. *Bureaucracy and Political Development*. Princeton, N. J.: Princeton University Press, 1963.

————, and Myron Weiner, eds. *Political Parties and Political Development*. Princeton, N. J.: Princeton University Press, 1966.

Leach, Edmund, and S. N. Mukherjee. *Elites in South Asia*. Cambridge: Cambridge University Press, 1970.

Lee, John M. *African Armies and Civil Order*. New York: Frederick A. Praeger, 1969.

Lefever, Ernest W. *Spear and Scepter: Army, Police, and Politics in Tropical Africa*. Washington, D. C.: The Brookings Institution, 1970.

Leiden, Carl, and Karl M. Schmitt. *The Politics of Violence: Revolution in the Modern World*. Englewood Cliffs, N. J.: Prentice-Hall, Inc., 1968.

Lieuwen, Edwin. *Generals vs. Presidents: Neomilitarism in Latin America*. New York: Frederick A. Praeger, 1964.

Lipset, Seymour M., and Aldo Solari, eds. *Elites in Latin America*. New York: Oxford University Press, 1967.

Lloyd, P. C., ed. *The New Elites of Tropical Africa*. New York: Oxford University Press, 1966.

Lynd, G. E. *The Politics of African Trade Unionism*. New York: Frederick A. Praeger, 1968.

Maguire, G. Andrew. *Toward "Uhuru" in Tanzania: The Politics of Participation*. New York: Cambridge University Press, 1969.

Millen, Bruce H. *The Political Role of Labor in Developing Countries*. Washington, D. C.: The Brookings Institution, 1963.

Riggs, Fred W. *Administration in Developing Countries: The Theory of Prismatic Society*. Boston: Houghton Mifflin Company, 1964.

Shaplen, Robert. *Time Out of Hand: Revolution and Reaction in Southeast Asia*. London: Andre Deutsch, 1969.

Smith, T. E. *Elections in Developing Countries*. London: Macmillan & Co., Ltd., 1960.

Vega, Luis Mercier. *Guerrillas in Latin America: The Technique of the Counter-State*. New York: Frederick A. Praeger, 1969.

Walter, Eugene V. *Terror and Resistance: A Study of Political Violence*. New York: Oxford University Press, 1969.

Welch, Claude E., Jr., ed. *Soldier and State in Africa*. Evanston, Ill.: Northwestern University Press, 1970.

Woodward, Calvin A. *The Growth of a Party System in Ceylon*. Providence, R. I.: Brown University Press, 1969.

Wriggins, W. Howard. *The Ruler's Imperative*. New York: Columbia University Press, 1969.

A. Political Dynamics

In every society there is great concern for the perpetuation of valued beliefs, institutions, and practices. On the other hand, challenges to the established patterns may arise from a variety of sources, as has already been discussed. In transitional societies new values demand recognition, and new agents of political socialization, particularly the expanding educational systems, are involved in the political indoctrination processes. To explore the role of the schools and values being instilled in the students, David Koff and George Von der Muhll have analyzed the responses of 800 Kenyan and Tanzanian students to a questionnaire, and some of their findings are reported in the following discussion.

13. POLITICAL SOCIALISATION IN KENYA AND TANZANIA— A COMPARATIVE ANALYSIS *

david koff
and george von der muhll

AGENTS OF SOCIALISATION: THE STUDENTS' VIEW

The world of a student in Kenya and Tanzania contains many sources of new perspectives. His teachers ply him with precept and fact; he is asked by political leaders to follow some national credo; his religious leaders advise him on whole ways of life; his parents hope he will avoid their mistakes; and so on. Naturally, not every message, verbal or nonverbal, that is presented to a student will be accepted; many will be rejected, others suspected or ignored. One of the important questions we must therefore ask about the process of political socialisation in East

* From "Political Socialisation in Kenya and Tanzania—A Comparative Analysis" by David Koff and George Von der Muhll, *The Journal of Modern African Studies*, Vol. V, No. 1 (May, 1967), pp. 22–31. Published by Cambridge University Press. Excerpted by permission of the authors and the publisher.

Africa is, What are the sources from which students most willingly accept instruction, advice and guidance? Which institutions or individuals do students perceive to be the primary agents in shaping their own awareness of political and social responsibilities?

As an approach to this question, we focused on the concept of "social trust" as a crucial indicator of the effective influence that different agents of socialisation might have. A student's sense of the trustworthiness of those from whom he might learn is likely to determine how much faith he is willing to place in their words and deeds. A relationship characterised by a high degree of social distrust is probably incompatible with the effective transmission of values and attitudes; it also makes respect and co-operation more difficult.

To look more closely at the feelings of students towards a number of important socialising agents, we asked them to indicate how often they could trust different kinds of people. We presented the question with this introduction:

Some people are almost always fair and honest. It is safe to trust them. There are other people whom it is better not to trust. We must be careful how we deal with them. What about the following people? *In general,* can one trust them?

Each group of people was then introduced with the following phrase: "In general, one can trust . . . ," and four choices were presented: Always, Usually, Not Often, and Never. To simplify Table 2,† we have combined the two positive alternatives and presented their scores as a single measure of social trust.

TABLE 2

Percentage of Students Who Say that Members of Different Groups Can Be Trusted, "Always" or "Usually"

Groups	Kenya Schools		Tanzania Schools	
	Primary [a]	Secondary	Primary	Secondary
Fathers	78	92	85	87
Teachers	80	79	86	77
Religious leaders	74	82	90	84
Government leaders	72	57	89	63

[a] There were some indications that Kenyan primary pupils occasionally reversed the meaning of the choices; this may account for their consistently lower trust scores when compared with Tanzanian pupils.

† [Table 1, in an earlier section, is omitted. Editor's note.]

Towards these four groups, at least, the students in our sample evince a widespread and consistent sense of trust. It is interesting that, on the whole, the degree of trust felt toward teachers and religious leaders is only slightly less than that felt toward parents. And, with the exception of "government leaders," there is no consistent difference between primary and secondary students in their feelings of trust toward the four groups. Other data in our study confirm this tendency on the part of secondary students to be more critical of those in political roles. As secondary students come to view the world generally with a more critical eye, they are not likely to omit their political leaders from its scrutiny, especially in societies where officials are expected to be responsive and responsible to those they govern. Political roles, too, suffer from strains that are less likely to appear in the roles of teacher, priest, or parent: the gap between promise and performance can be much greater for those who depend on and must bid for the support of large groups than for those whose roles are built around individual and personal relationships.

At the same time, it would be misleading to assume that the level of trust that secondary students have in their political leaders is so low as to suggest alienation or hostility. In a study of 256 extra-mural students in Uganda early this year, K. Prewitt found that "politicians" were trusted "always" or "usually" by only 13% of the sample. Parents and teachers had the trust of nearly 90% of the same group.[1] In comparison with these figures, we might conclude that secondary students in Kenya and Tanzania are reluctant to accept all political leaders at face value, but they are certainly ready to grant their trust to many.

The data in Table 2 are most encouraging with regard to the learning environment and the social function of the schools. Teachers who enjoy the trust of a large majority of their students are able to play an effective role as agents of socialisation; indeed, whether consciously or not, teachers set standards and establish goals that others will accept as their own, if only because the examples emanate from people they trust.

We can still inquire, however, into the extent to which the reservoir of social trust that these agents hold with students is effective in promoting the communication of social and political attitudes. Does any one of these highly trusted groups exercise more influence than the others over the political socialisation of students in our sample? We asked students themselves to tell us which agents they thought had taught them the most about being good citizens of their countries. The data in Table 3 spell out clearly the significant status of teachers as perceived agents of socialisation.

Since we cannot attribute the responses in Table 3 to differences in trust for each of the groups, we must assume that both the structure of

[1] K. Prewitt, "Uganda Extra-mural Students and Political Development," unpublished manuscript, 1966.

TABLE 3

Percentage of Students Who Mention Different Agents as Having
Taught Them the Most About Being "Good" Citizens

| | Kenya Schools | | Tanzania Schools | |
Agents Mentioned	Primary	Secondary [a]	Primary	Secondary [a]
Teachers	47	71	35	56
Parents and relatives	27	42	25	47
Politicians and M.P.s				
(Kenya), T.A.N.U. leaders				
(Tanzania)	16	9	29	24
Religious leaders, clergy	2	21	6	16
Other agents; no answer	8	12	5	4

[a] Percentages of secondary responses total more than 100 due to multiple responses. Primary
pupils were allowed one choice, secondary two choices.

the school environment and the explicit transfer of information from
teacher to pupil give teachers an advantage over other possible agents of
socialisation. Another advantage that teachers have is their education;
they may simply know more than most of the other adult figures in the
student's world. On the other hand, the instructional role of parents is
not entirely without substance: only 29% of the Tanzanian secondary
students and 40% of the Kenyans said that they had not learned anything about Tanzania and Kenya, respectively, from their parents.

One important national difference worth noting in Table 3 is that
concerning teachers and political figures: the former are mentioned more
frequently by Kenyans than by Tanzanians as agents of socialisation, the
latter more frequently by Tanzanians than by Kenyans. For Tanzanian
primary pupils, local leaders are seen as more important agents of political socialisation than parents. Taking even the more specific phrasing of
the Tanzanian item into consideration ("T.A.N.U. leaders" as against
"M.P.s and politicians" in Kenya), it is still significant that about a
quarter of the Tanzanian students say they have learned something
about citizenship from people who occupy roles that have come into
existence only in the last generation. In Tanzania, perhaps, local party
leaders are beginning to emerge as "community influentials" whose positions rest as much on the public's appreciation of their qualities as citizens as on their political skills.

Because we allowed secondary students two choices, and primary
only one, we cannot make direct comparisons between them in Table 3.
It would appear, however, that the same agents of socialisation affect
them to more or less the same degree. As long as they are in school,
students are prepared to trust their teachers, and to accept from them

more than just the instruction contained in the syllabus, or required for the examinations.[2] Most of this learning process is probably informal and not directly related to political or social attitudes; it is thus distinguishable from explicit indoctrination or instruction in "civic values," and from the communication of information about the political system itself. This raises a question, then, about the agents of information, the sources of knowledge of the ongoing political and social world. Are the agents of general political socialisation also important for the day-to-day concern of students with facts and opinions about their countries?

We asked students what they thought were the "best ways" to learn about what was happening in their country. Their responses, contained in Table 4, suggest that the primary *sources* of information about current events are the mass media, although it appears that teachers continue to be the leading *agents* involved in the interpretation of the news. It is likely that much of the contact that secondary students have with the mass media occurs within the school context. In many of the schools we visited, libraries contained foreign as well as local newspapers and magazines, and occasionally we found notice boards containing clippings on important events. Most secondary schools have "current events" clubs, for the specific purpose of discussion and debate on contemporary issues. This may help to account for the somewhat greater role allotted to classmates than to parents as sources of information. Further, special radio

TABLE 4

Percentage of Students Mentioning Different Agents as the Best Way to Learn About What Is Happening in the Country

	Kenya Schools		Tanzania Schools	
Agents Mentioned	Primary	Secondary [a]	Primary	Secondary [a]
Radio and newspapers	85	96	60	96
Teachers	9	54	33	48
Parents and relatives	2	3	5	3
Older people in home area	4	3	2	6
Classmates (sec. only)		9		12

[a] Percentage of secondary responses total more than 100 due to multiple responses. Primary pupils were allowed one choice, secondary two choices.

[2] Teachers are also seen as sources of advice on post-school problems. About two-thirds of both secondary samples mentioned their teachers as the best agents for advice on careers; about a quarter attributed the same ability to their parents. At the primary level, 50% of the Kenyans, and 40% of the Tanzanians, chose teachers over parents as the best people they could talk to about their lives after they left school. The teacher's role is thus expected to be mulifaceted; in practice, it may be confined too strictly to formal instruction.

broadcasts are prepared for schools in both Kenya and Tanzania, and again teachers may play an important part in the interpretation of such programmes. The very small proportion of students who mention their parents or older people suggests again that the school is felt to be, and actually functions as, the most important link between the student and the larger society around him.

Our data, then, lend support to the supposition that the school environment, and teachers in particular, play a crucial role in both the implicit and explicit political socialisation of young people. Teachers rank far above any other agents as the models and sources of citizenship values, and they contribute heavily to the student's awareness of his ongoing society. It is interesting that students themselves rank "citizenship training" as the most important purpose that schools can serve. Table 5 contains the ranked indices derived from responses to the question: "These are purposes which schools in Kenya/Tanzania might have. How important are they?"

TABLE 5

Rank Order of Purposes of Schools, by Weighted Indices [a]

| | Secondary Schools | |
Purposes	Kenya	Tanzania
Teach students to be good citizens	869	867
Teach students the skills necessary to get jobs	622	630
Teach students the important things to know for the examinations	579	585
Teach students to be religious (to be good Christians, etc.)	547	428
Teach students about the important African traditions and customs	353	400

[a] Respondents ranked the five purposes in order of importance. The index was constructed by tallying five points each time a problem was ranked first, four points for second, and so on. If all respondents ranked a problem first, it would have 1,000 points, the maximum score; 200 is the minimum.

It is significant that students in both countries rank the diffuse function of "citizenship training" above the specific tasks of teaching skills for jobs and knowledge for examinations. Although these latter two objectives are instrumental to individual mobility and to the economic development of the country, they do not take priority over the contribution that the schools might make to national integration and a politically participant population. . . . It is worth noting that instruction in religious beliefs and in traditions is not considered of great importance. Tanzanians place less weight on religion, and more on tradition, than do their Kenyan counterparts, but both groups are alike in giving them lowest priority.

Schools, then, are seen by students not only as the place where they are actually inducted into the citizen's role, but also as the *proper* environment for this process. For them, teachers and schools seem to replace all other agents of training and arenas of practice in the responsibilities and requirements of being a citizen. This brings us to a further question: What do students have in mind when they speak of "good" citizens? . . .

THE ATTRIBUTES OF THE ``GOOD'' CITIZEN

Most of the students in our study have not yet "come of age" in regard to their roles as citizens; few, if any, have had money or services extracted from them by the state, and most are excluded by their age from voting or participation in the institutions that govern their lives. On the other hand, contact with and obedience to the law, and an active interest in politics, may not be the only, nor even the most important aspects of the citizen's role in the societies we are studying. Although the obligation to obey the law and to take an interest in its creation may fulfil the requirements of "good" citizenship in the classical democratic concept, the relationship between individuals and their governments and societies in East Africa might demand a different concept of the citizen's role.

To obtain a picture of the emphases that students place on a range of attributes that might make up a "good" citizen, we asked them to describe the people they would consider are "the best citizens of Kenya/Tanzania," by choosing three of the seven alternatives shown in Table 6. As the table indicates, our respondents hold ideas about citizenship that are not confined to the classic definition.

Obedience to authority (whether parents and teachers in the case of primary, or law in the case of secondary students) is the most frequently mentioned attribute of the "best" citizen. This attribute is basically a "passive" orientation and is probably one that our respondents share with members of many other societies. Although there is fairly uniform agreement between educational levels and between countries on the importance of obedience, there are greater variations in regard to the next four qualities.

For primary pupils in both countries, education is another principal mark of the good citizen. On the other hand, secondary students, who have already achieved "élite" status within the educational system, appear to turn their attention to the application of their educational skills and only a small percentage consider education in itself to be important to performing the citizen's role. Because they are at the terminal stage of their primary, and perhaps their educational careers, primary students apparently emphasise the importance of the acquisition of education to the successful performance of most adult roles.

TABLE 6
Percentage of Students Mentioning Different Qualities of the "Best" Citizen [a]

Qualities	Kenya Schools		Tanzania Schools	
	Primary	Secondary	Primary	Secondary
Obeys (parents, teachers, laws)	69	64	62	75
Is well-educated, does well at studies	53	18	59	17
Works hard	53	63	24	56
Is interested in government	50	40	54	46
Helps others	41	50	37	15
Knows traditions and customs	14	12	21	17
Is religious	9	12	16	7

[a] Percentages total more than 100 since respondents could give more than one answer.

A willingness to work hard, like the possession of education, is an attribute not usually associated with the performance of the citizen's role. But with the exception of the Tanzanian primary pupils, more than half of our respondents did consider it important. In societies marked by chronic unemployment and underemployment, the man who has a job is expected to work hard at it. The theme of "work" is common in public statements, as is its corollary, that there is "no room for idleness." The good citizen thus becomes the man who does his job, whatever it is, and does it well.

The classic quality of "interest in government" is considered by about half of our respondents to be important to the citizen's role; secondary students feel this in slightly smaller proportions than primary pupils. Interest in government, like willingness to work hard, is an "active" orientation to the citizen's role, although in an individualistic, rather than collective way. Willingness to help others represents a more community-oriented definition of citizenship behaviour, and was chosen by a somewhat larger proportion of Kenyans than Tanzanians. There is no clear-cut pattern here, and the rather surprisingly low proportion of Tanzanian secondary students choosing this alternative may be attributable to their frequent failure to mark three alternatives, rather than to basic attitudinal differences between them and the other three groups.

Both knowledge of traditions and a religious approach to life are clearly of little importance to most of the students in our study, at least as far as their bearing on the citizen's role is concerned. Slightly higher proportions of Tanzanians did consider traditions important, a finding which is consistent with their views as shown in Table 5 above. Knowledge of traditions, like education, represents a means to the achievement of other goals, rather than a definite passive or active orientation. For most primary pupils, traditional knowledge does not seem to be nearly as significant for the citizen's role as modern education, whereas for secondary students neither form of knowledge seems critical.

What impact does exposure to the educational system have on the qualities that are emphasised? Except for education, there are only minor, and not entirely consistent, differences between educational levels. This finding is what we might expect on questions of this type, for the definition of what makes a "good" citizen is, in a sense, a national definition; it represents an ideal to which all members of the society should be able to aspire. In this regard, it is only the quality of education which is automatically beyond the reach of many members of the nations in our study; a man without formal, modern education can still meet the other obligations or qualifications that are contained in Table 6. The primary pupils, then, attribute, perhaps unconsciously, a certain élitist aspect to "good" citizenship; the secondary students in both countries seem agreed upon an open and generally active notion of the citizen's role, with the emphasis distributed between individualistic qualities ("works hard") and collective qualities ("helps others").

In the case of national differences, there are again no consistent patterns. Although we might expect the degree of variation to be greater between secondary than between primary students from the two countries, it is in fact almost the same: the mean variation in percentage between primary pupils for the seven choices is 9%, and between secondary students, 10%. On the other hand, variations between educational levels within each country are more noticeable. While the mean variation between Kenyan primary and secondary students is only 11%, it is 19% for the two Tanzanian groups. There is, then, somewhat less concurrence in emphasis within the Tanzanian system than within the Kenyan. As is evident from Table 6, primary pupils in Tanzania place more weight on education and helping others than do their older colleagues, while the latter group puts more stress on hard work.

The general impression given by Table 6 is one of a diffuse, rather than a specific, notion of citizenship. Five of the seven alternatives received a high proportion of the Kenyan primary choice, while the Kenyan secondary students and Tanzanian primary pupils spread their responses mainly over four alternatives. If a fully stereotyped definition of the "good" citizen existed in either of the two countries, we could expect to find much more evident "peaking" on only three alternatives. As it is, the data suggest that, at both educational levels, students have ideas about the qualities required to perform the citizen's role and that many of these qualities seem of nearly equal importance. The "good" citizen not only takes an interest in government, he also contributes to economic development; not only does he obey the law, he also "helps others." Much of the behaviour that would be associated elsewhere with personal motives is here associated with "citizenship," a concept that ultimately comes to embrace not a purely politically-oriented and idealised relationship between man and his government, but rather a broad and basically realistic set of qualities to which all men may aspire.

As indicated in the selection above, the values of "interest in politics" and "political participation" have become increasingly prominent in the political socialization of all societies. However, the extent to which these values have resulted in the desired behavior patterns of persons in transitional societies is less clear. Few detailed studies have as yet been undertaken of the political behavior of individuals in these societies, but the following study, by Samuel Eldersveld, suggests that the picture is mixed and is likely to remain so for some time. In India, at least, the levels of political understanding and political participation vary widely, and the author questions whether in the face of extensive apathy and ignorance, economic and social planning can be very effective.

14. THE POLITICAL BEHAVIOUR OF THE INDIAN PUBLIC*

samuel j. eldersveld

Scholars of "developing societies", such as India is, constantly emphasize the interrelationship between political, social and economic change. Theoretically, at least, what happens in the sphere of politics is intimately related to social and economic development. Political behaviour sets the limits and provides the political context for social change. It also

* From "The Political Behaviour of the Indian Public" by Samuel J. Eldersveld, *Monthly Public Opinion Survey*, Vol. IX, No. 4 (1964), pp. 3–9. By permission of The Indian Institute of Public Opinion Private Ltd.

helps explain why the social and economic development which takes place occurs in the form and at the time it does. A "development crisis" is presumably, therefore, as political as it is social or economic. This thesis may be argued at length. But certainly no one, not even the most extreme advocates of the irrelevance of politics, would deny that the political culture and behaviour patterns of a society have to be taken into account by the development planners, or that the political actions of the public in a changing society contribute much to the success or failure of the most beautifully conceived economic and social plans.

The surveys which the Indian Institute of Public Opinion has conducted in the past ten years provide a beginning empirical base for the type of analysis suggested above. Unfortunately, most of our research on developing societies is not "developmental". That is, if there is empirical research at all, it consists primarily of research at one point in time. What is needed is sound "historical" or "longitudinal" analysis which permits generalisation about the society at various stages at its development, and which is able to determine to what extent the society is moving towards political or social or economic goals. Such systematic data over time usually cannot be retrieved. In the Indian case, from the middle 1950's on at least, data are available on the political behaviour patterns of the Indian people. . . .

☼ ☼ ☼ ☼ ☼

THE PERVASIVENESS OF POLITICAL INTEREST

In a developing society, such as India, operating as it does on democratic premises, one may argue that political leadership needs an increasingly larger and broadly-based "attentive public" which is informed about public policy, concerned about it, and willing to be at least minimally active in the political arena. Such a public need not be very large at the outset; indeed, it would be unrealistic to expect it to be large. (Even in modernized societies this attentive public does not include even 50% of the public.) But though not large, it should be fairly representative of the social spectrum and its existence as an "interest section" should give the influential political elite both a motivation and opportunity for political communication, as well as provide a meaningful forum for criticism about governmental policy. . . .

There is a basic potential of political interest in the Indian public which appears to have been relatively prevalent already in 1955 and has shown signs of deepening and expanding. **The Institute's data from two of its studies, which approached this problem in an identical manner,** suggest that up to a third of the Indian public is interested in public affairs (See Table 1). In 1961, over 40 per cent of the urban public manifested an interest in politics, compared to 34% of the rural public. **And this percentage was a clear increase in both cases over the level of admitted political interest two years previously, in 1959.** It is also a percentage which, if substantiated by adequate proportions of political knowledge and actual involvement, is not too dissimilar from political interest levels which studies in a country like the United States have documented. In fact, many scholars are willing to take the position that an attentive public of one-third or two-fifths is probably optimal for democratic support and social change in modern political systems.

TABLE 1

Levels of Political Interest

(Do you take an interest in political matters? % "Yes")

Particular Social Groups

			Illiterates		Age Group 21–35		Income Groups Rs. 1—100		350+Rupees	
	Urban	Rural	Urban	Rural	Urban	Rural	Urban	Rural	Urban	Rural
1959 Study	32.1	28.9	6.4	10.2	38.2	33.3	25.2	24.1	65.3	57.7
1961 Study	43.7	33.9	8.1	12.1	46.1	36.5	26.5	25.2	58.6	62.2

One may become somewhat more worried about the level of political interest in particular subsectors of Indian society. **Thus, as Table 1 reveals, the lowest educational and income classes have a relatively low proportion of politically interested citizens. The illiterates are a particular cause for concern, since they represent over 50 per cent of the Indian public. The fact that less than 10 per cent of the illiterates in urban areas say they are interested in politics** is indeed significant, and dysfunctional to the development of political self-consciousness among the Indian people. The rural illiterates are slightly more interested, surprisingly enough. **The same observation is not true, however, for those at the lowest economic levels—fully one-fourth of those making less than 100 rupees a month (less than 22) are interested in politics;** this is true also of those who are in the "blue collar" working class (the skilled and unskilled urban workers, the agricultural labourers, and the unemployed), 22% of whom were politically interested in 1959, compared to 43% of those in the higher "white collar" occupational brackets. **Above all, it is interesting to note that political interest is increasing among almost all of these social groups. (The only exception is the urban** wealthy who professed less interest in 1961.) It seems, then, that the body of potential politically interested citizens is sizable enough, partially inclusive of major social groups, and revealing an accentuation of potential attention rather than a decline in such attention.

TYPES AND CORRELATES OF POLITICAL ACTIVITY

Political activity beyond the mere assertion of interest in politics is, as one would expect, lower. But, if one takes into consideration the particular forms of political participation which are prevalent in the Indian environment, they cannot be considered low (Tables 2 and 3).

TABLE 2

The Channels and Evidences of Political Participation

	Attend public meetings		Join demonstrations		Listening to speeches of Political Leaders and Candidates		Read Newspaper reports about political matters	
	Urban	Rural	Urban	Rural	Urban	Rural	Urban	Rural
1959 Study	20.9%	–	5.5	–	23.6	–	28.9	–
1961 Study	28.8	27.2	10.3	12.3	31.8	28.5	39.7	25.6

TABLE 3

The Political Participation of Selected Social Groups (Urban only)

	Illiterates		Graduates		Lowest Income (Under Rs. 100)		Upper Income (350+Rupees)	
	Attend Meetings	Listen to speeches	Attend Meetings	Listen to speeches	Attend Meetings	Listen to speeches	Attend Meetings	Listen to speeches
1959 Study	3.7	4.5	38.9	44.9	18.8	19.7	34.7	46.9
1961 Study	4.7	5.4	40.8	46.0	20.1	21.7	34.4	42.7

The "occasional" pattern of newspaper reading is probably the most serious problem inhibiting political sophistication in India. . . . With the high degree of illiteracy, this is, of course, understandable. But only 8% were regular daily radio listeners in the total adult population. Despite this problem, Indian adults do engage in other types of political activity—up to 30% attend public meetings and hear political leaders or candidates speak, and close to 10% people took part in political demonstrations or rallies. . . .

It is the low level of participation by the illiterates which again is the disturbing finding. In 1961 these were the findings from the Institute's study of urban and rural illiterates:

% OF WHO HAVE AN INTEREST AND PARTICIPATE

	Urban	Rural
	%	%
Attending public meetings	3.7	8.5
Listen to political leaders and candidates	4.5	7.1
Join demonstrations or rallies	3.3	4.0
Read Newspaper Reports	2.7	1.9
Have an interest in politics	8.1	12.1

Only an extremely small minority of the adult illiterates (who number over 100 million) either have an interest or seem to have the time to take the trouble to implement this latent interest through political interaction with others. It is, perhaps, amazing that in rural areas, where illiterates seem most politically interested, as many as 8.5% do attend public meetings and try to inform themselves about politics. In this connection it is significant to note that in 1961, 59% of the urban illiterates and 68% of the rural illiterates intended to vote in the national elections. We will return to this problem subsequently.

LEVELS OF POLITICAL KNOWLEDGE
AND OPINION CRYSTALLIZATION

When we move beyond mere assertions of political interest and types of political activity and ask how well informed the Indian public is on current political issues, there is a greater cause for concern (Table 4). There is a great wealth of information in the Institute's studies on attitudes towards economic issues. We have taken a few examples from these for illustrative purposes. The "don't know" category of respondents is large—a category which it must be recalled includes both those who are ignorant and those who are ambivalent and have not been able to make up their minds on the question. . . .

On the other hand, opinions of the political leadership elite seem somewhat better structured, although large proportions of the public apparently do not know who the leaders are. **Over 90 per cent of the urban public have opinions about Nehru (and in 1961 only 1% rated**

TABLE 4

Political Information and Knowledge—Urban and Rural

	Don't know which party can best provide cheaper food		Don't know which party can best provide more jobs		Have no opinion		Have no opinion whether there should be a "liberal but non-socialist opposition" party	
					(Urban only)			
	Urban	Rural	Urban	Rural	Nehru	Desai	Urban	Rural
1959 study	42.6	46.1	44.5	—	15.6	61.5	61.7	73.8
1961 study	52.5	54.5	53.2	54.7	9.0	37.9	45.4	73.2

his performance as Prime Minister "bad"). The rural public was less well informed—21.9 per cent having "no opinion". But the other leaders are not as familiar to the public, particularly in rural areas. Lal Bahadur Shastri, now often mentioned as Nehru's successor, in the 1961 study was unknown to 75% of the rural public (41.5% of the urban), compared to 74% and (38%) for Morarji Desai, 70.5% (and 34%) for V. K. Krishna Menon. Yet, there is evidence that the public is becoming more familiar and opinionated about its top leadership, though if anything there is less opinion certainty on the issues of the day.

Some of the findings on critical aspects of governmental policy are indeed alarming in this respect. In the field of foreign policy, 55% of the urban public did not know whether they supported the directions of Indian policy in 1959; from 61% (urban) to 79% (rural) had no opinion about Eisenhower and the United States, virtually the same percentages which emerged when they were asked about Premier Khrushchev and the Soviet Union. When asked whether they thought a military dictatorship for India would be good or bad, 46% (urban) and 65% (rural) had no opinion. In the area of Community Development, on which India's leaders are pinning much of their hope for improving economic and social conditions in the countryside, including agricultural development, from 66% (urban) to 76% (rural) admitted they were not informed about Community Development. And on the critical issues of expanding "the public sector" and restricting "the private sector" of the economy a whole series of questions reveal a basic lack of political knowledge and an incapability to respond to even very general queries. From 50% (urban) to 74% (rural) of the public say they simply "don't know".

These general levels of political ignorance are high enough to raise serious questions as to whether the political capacity of the Indian

POLITICAL SYSTEMS

public, based on adequate knowledge, is in fact "developing" and whether a government which in fact operates on the principle of democratic responsibility, and which also admits that it relies on public support for the implementation of its programmes and plans, can function effectively in its present "style" of political and administrative strategy. It is somewhat ironic that although political interest is present and increasing, and political participation activities are at least at credible levels, the public is not revealing a higher degree of clarity in understanding and responding to the issues of the day. In short, "the don't-know level" of the Indian public, particularly the rural public, is extremely high—*both* for issues and for the successors to Nehru. This level of withdrawal from or unfamiliarity with political reality should be a danger signal to the Indian government.

The degree to which this level of political opinion (ignorance or ambivalence) can be disturbing emerges sharply from an analysis of specific social sectors (Table 5). The "intellectuals" and university graduates are relatively capable of articulating an ópinion, particularly on

TABLE 5

Political Ignorance or Ambivalence by Social Group (1961)

No opinion or undecided upon	Illiterates Urban %	Rural %	Graduates Urban %	Rural %	Low Income (Under Rs. 100) Urban %	Rural %	High Income (Over Rs. 350) Urban %	Rural %
Which party can best provide cheaper food?	85.2	72.6	51.8	44.7	60.7	58.7	44.6	43.3
Would the Congress Party be justified in curtailing the private sector?	95.3	93.9	28.7	44.6	83.6	84.1	35.0	50.0
Would you like to see a liberal but non-socialist party in opposition?	96.0	94.1	20.0	21.5	66.2	81.8	26.7	50.3
Who would you favour as a successor to Nehru?	91.2	91.4	25.7	4.6	66.0	77.2	29.9	55.6

the socialism question, the type of party system preferred, and who should succeed Nehru. They are not unanimous on these questions.

For example, 19.3% of the urban graduates preferred Desai, 21.1% wanted Jai Prakash Narayan, 9.1% preferred Menon and 4.5% Shastri (in 1961). But the great majority of the educated do have opinions. The same is generally true of those in the upper income brackets, with great diversity in opinion present in the findings. But the lowest income group (under Rs. 100 a month) and the illiterates have extremely high rates of political ignorance or indecision on these questions. And the rural illiterates are in some cases better able to express an opinion than is true in urban areas. But, with two-thirds or more of the low income groups having no opinion, and over 30% of the illiterates being uninformed, one wonders whether economic or social planning through India's democratic processes really is reaching and motivating the great mass of the adult public. **The suggestion in these revealing data is clear, and documented by all the studies of the Institute—only a small minority, the educated and well-to-do, are aware and informed of India's political issues and problems and are able to think intelligently about them. While the lower classes may be interested, so far the politics of their developing society has not penetrated to their political consciousness, nor enabled them to respond meaningfully to political controversies— whether these are controversies over what system shall prevail, or the solution of contemporary problems, or what leadership shall be entrusted with the country's future.**

In Western commentaries on politics, the middle classes in a society are often asserted to be the backbone of moderately progressive, stable, democratic regimes. Not surprisingly, then, the apparent absence of middle classes in transitional societies was assumed to constitute a major weakness in the development of stable, democratic political systems. Manfred Halpern, however, argues that a politically significant middle class does indeed exist in the form of the growing salaried middle class. His discussion of the emergence and characteristics of this class in Middle Eastern society and politics contributes to the identification of significant political forces in transitional societies.

15. THE NEW MIDDLE CLASS°

m a n f r e d   h a l p e r n

In our unproductive search for middle classes in underdeveloped areas, the fault has been in our expectations. We have taken too parochial a view of the structure of the middle class. A study of both Western and non-Western historical experience suggests that the British and American middle classes, which have commonly been considered prototypes, were actually special cases. Moreover, with the growing scope and scale of modern enterprises and institutions, the majority of the middle class even in the United States and Great Britain is no longer composed of men whose independence is rooted in their possession of productive private property. Bureaucratic organization has become the characteristic structure of business (or charity or trade unions) no less than of government, and the majority of the middle class is now salaried. They may be managers, administrators, teachers, engineers, journalists, scientists, lawyers, or army officers. A similar salaried middle class constitutes the most active political, social, and economic sector from Morocco to Pakistan.

Leadership in all areas of Middle Eastern life is increasingly being seized by a class of men inspired by non-traditional knowledge, and it is being clustered around a core of salaried civilian and military politicians, organizers, administrators, and experts.[1] In its style of life, however, this new middle class differs from its counterpart in the industrialized states. The Middle East moved into the modern administrative age before it reached the machine age. Its salaried middle class attained

° From Manfred Halpern, *The Politics of Social Change in the Middle East and North Africa* (copyright © 1963 by the Rand Corporation), published by Princeton University Press: Princeton Paperback, 1965, pp. 51–67. Reprinted by permission.

[1] For example, when Tunisia became independent in 1956 under the leadership of the Neo-Destour Party, a party controlled almost entirely by the new middle class, the election for a Constituent Assembly rewarded this class in the following way: To fill 98 seats, the country voted for 18 teachers and professors, 15 lawyers, 11 civil servants, 5 doctors, 4 pharmacists, 2 journalists, 2 commercial employees, 1 engineer, 1 appraiser, 5 workers, 17 farmers, and 17 businessmen and contractors. By contrast, every Middle Eastern parliament prior to 1950, except that of Turkey, contained a majority of landowners and a minority of professional men and industrialists.

power before it attained assurance of status, order, security, or prosperity. In the Middle East, the salaried new middle class therefore uses its power not to defend order and property but to create them—a revolutionary task that is being undertaken so far without any final commitment to any particular system of institutions.

This new salaried class is impelled by a driving interest in ideas, action, and careers. It is not merely interested in ideas: its members are not exclusively intellectuals, and, being new to the realm of modern ideas and eager for action and careers, they may not be intellectuals at all. Neither are they interested only in action that enhances their power: they also share a common commitment to the fashioning of opportunities and institutions that will provide careers open to all who have skills. This involves them in actions quite novel to their society, and hence also distinguishes them from previous politicians. They are not concerned merely with safe careers. They know that, without new ideas and new actions dealing with the backwardness and conflicts of their society, careers will not open or remain secure. The men of this new class are therefore committed ideologically to nationalism and social reform.

Obviously, there is also a part of the new middle class that has neither deep convictions nor understanding. In contrast to the dominant strata of its class, this segment excludes itself from the process of making political choices, and hence does not alter the present analysis. It is also true that some members of the new middle class are interested only in ideas (hence inspire and clarify, or merely stand by), only in action (hence rise spectacularly and fall), or only in safe careers (hence merely serve). Among the last, clerks especially compose the largest yet relatively most passive segment of the new middle class. Our analysis focuses on men interested in ideas, action, and careers because such a description fits the most influential core of this group.

There are also opportunists among them but, by now, of two different kinds which are often confused by those who are taken advantage of. There is the politician who, largely for the sake of satisfying the aspirations of his new middle class constituency and so also staying in power, takes advantage of whatever opportunities may offer, east or west, at home or abroad. There is also the free-floating opportunist—Stendhal's novels describe him very well for a period in French history when values and institutions were similarly in doubt—who represents no one but himself, but represents himself exceedingly well, being loyal only to the art of survival. Some sell their skills as political brokers; some come close to selling their country. In the twentieth century it has become essential, however, to be able to distinguish between those, however perverse they may appear, who are out to gain greater elbowroom for the new middle class they represent and those, however smooth, who also make deals because they can fashion no connections unless they continually sell themselves.

POLITICAL SYSTEMS

In the Middle East, this salaried new middle class assumes a far more important role than the local property-owning middle class. Although the latter is about as numerous as that portion of the new middle class which is actually employed,[2] it has far less power than the salaried group. Neither in capital, organization, nor skills do the merchants and middlemen control anything comparable to that power which can be mustered by the machinery of the state and hence utilized by the new salaried class. In this part of the world, no other institutions can mobilize as much power and capital as those of the state. By controlling the state in such a strategic historical period, this new salaried class has the capabilities to lead the quest for the status, power, and prosperity of middle-class existence by ushering in the machine age.[3]

In the West, a variety of organizational structures and devices—both governmental and private—have gradually made individual entrepreneurship a rare commodity. Stock companies, subsidies, insurance, tariffs, as well as large governmental, business, and union bureaucracies have served, among other things, to reduce individual risk and enlarge institutional predictability. The pressures that make for organization and organization men are much more desperate in the Middle East. In most of the countries of this region, there are few important jobs in the modern sector of the economy available outside the large organizations and institutions that constitute, or are guided by, government. Those who cannot get into them or cannot hold on to them usually count for little, and often cannot make a living. For most there is little hope for safety or prosperity in separate personal endeavors. Indeed, more organization is urgently needed for aggregating separate interests, bargaining among them, and executing a common will.

[2] In this analysis, the term "new middle class" excludes the property owning middle class. However, it includes both those who are now drawing salaries and a far larger group—a "would-be new middle class" which resembles this class in every respect except that it is unemployed. The "would-be" salariat is discussed in greater detail in the next section of this chapter.

✻ ✻ ✻ ✻ ✻

[3] The present work is not the first to notice the emergence of this new class in underdeveloped areas. Professor T. Cuyler Young, drawing in part on his experiences as Political Attaché at the American Embassy in Tehran during 1951–1952, was the first to publish an analysis of the role of the new middle class in the Middle East in "The Social Support of Current Iranian Policy," *Middle East Journal*, Spring 1952, pp. 125–143. Professor John J. Johnson was the first to suggest that in Latin America "the urban middle groups are vitally, if not decisively, important in an area where one still commonly hears and reads that there is no middle class to speak of [and] where, in the view of traditional scholarship, individuals hold the center of the stage." (*Political Change in Latin America: The Emergence of the Middle Sectors*, Stanford, 1958, pp. vii–ix.)

✻ ✻ ✻ ✻ ✻

The intelligentsia, that is, those with knowledge or awareness to see that a social and political revolution is in progress, form the largest and politically most active component of the new middle class. But they are not the only component of this class. Some members of this new class are already middle class in their pattern of consumption but still searching for ideas (hence new in a society once sure of its truths). Others are interested only in ideas about means and not, like the intelligentsia, also about ends, and the concern for truth of the intellectuals does not interest them. The intelligentsia, however, is the predominant force of this class, in part because its knowledge inescapably exposes the weakness or irrelevance of tradition. . . .

        ⚬   ⚬   ⚬   ⚬   ⚬

In the Middle East (as in other rapidly changing, underdeveloped societies) the new intelligentsia acts in behalf of the older ruling classes only until it is strong enough to win control of the government. When this occurs, however, the intelligentsia no longer remains socially unattached but acts in the interests of the new middle class of which it is an integral part. It cannot preserve the privileges of the older ruling classes if it hopes to propel any Middle Eastern country into the modern age. Similarly, it cannot offer the immediate rewards sought by workers and peasants, because its plans for the modernization of the country call for mobilization of the underlying population for new roles and productive sacrifices.

In the Middle East, . . . the new middle class springs largely, though not exclusively, from groups that had not hitherto been important, and hence had more reason and less deadweight to take advantage of new knowledge and skills. . . .

        ⚬   ⚬   ⚬   ⚬   ⚬

Unlike the traditional elite of landowners and trading bourgeoisie or the tradition-bound artisans or peasants, it is . . . . the first class in the Middle East that is wholly the product of the transition to the modern age. Unlike the emergent new generation of peasants and urban workers, it is already powerful and self-conscious enough to undertake the task of remolding society.

The new middle class has been able to act as a separate and independent force because: (1) prior to its seizure of power, it is freer than any other class from traditional bonds and preconceptions, and better equipped to manipulate armies and voluntary organizations as revolutionary political instruments; (2) once it controls the machinery of a modernizing state, it possesses a power base superior to that which any other class in the Middle East can muster on the basis of prestige, property, or physical force; (3) it is numerically one of the largest groups within the modern sector of society; (4) it is, so far, more obviously cohesive, more self-conscious, and better trained than any other class; (5) its political, economic, and social actions, in so far as they come to grips with social change, are decisive in determining the role other classes will play in the future; and (6) it has shown itself capable of marshalling mass support. Wherever the salaried new middle class has become dominant in the Middle East, it has become the chief locus of political and economic power and of social prestige. There are few classes anywhere in the world of which this much can be said.[4]

✿ ✿ ✿ ✿ ✿

. . . An elite in power, whatever the social class from which it springs, faces problems and temptations in the very business of maintaining itself in power which will often distinguish it from those who have the same hopes and interests but not the same responsibilities. Membership in a particular social class is by no means the sole determinant of policy decisions. Differences in political choices among members of the new middle class, however, also reflect differences among the strata of that class and the variant character of its class consciousness.

Such differences are real enough, but they usually become polit-

---

[4] Hence we cannot accept the Marxist idea that the intelligentsia, since it does not start from an economic base of its own, is unable to act in its own interest but must ally itself with one class or another. In areas like the Middle East, Soviet analysts have talked about a "national bourgeoisie," composed of local industrialists, merchants, and bankers, a "lower middle class" which employs little or no outside labor, an "intelligentsia" of students and clerks, even a "military intelligentsia." (See Walter Z. Laqueur, "The 'National Bourgeoisie,' A Soviet Dilemma in the Middle East," *International Affairs,* July 1959, pp. 324–331.) They have failed to perceive, however, the central role of the class which contains such men as Ataturk, Nasser, Kassim, and Bourguiba and which not only leads the nationalist revolution, but is the harbinger and architect of a decisive change in the social structure of the Middle East.

There are fundamental reasons for this failure of recognition. Perceptively, the Marxist philosopher Georg Lukacs has noted: "In such periods of transition, society is not dominated by any system of production. . . . In these circumstances it is, of course, impossible to speak of the operation of any economic laws which would govern the entire society. . . . There is a condition of acute struggle for power or of a latent balance of power . . . : the old law is no longer valid and the new law is not yet generally valid." He adds, "As far as I know, the theory of historical materialism has not yet confronted this problem from an economic perspective." (*Geschichte und Klassenbewusstsein*, Berlin, 1923, pp. 243 and 249.) As far as the present author is aware, this vacuum remains.

ically important only after the new middle class has achieved power. Earlier, all its members normally concentrate on the battle for power, mobility, and status in order to open up the controlling positions in society and administration. Soon after the triumph of the new middle class, however, it becomes apparent that there is simply not room for all of them—that some will be "in" and most will be "out." It also becomes clear that, although they are agreed on the need for the transformation of their society, they are not of the same mind as to what to do with their historical opportunity.[5]

Such differences, however, are never merely political, or merely social, or merely economic. All three realms are entwined as, for example, in one of the most profound of all tensions within the new middle class—between those who are salaried and those who would be like them but are not. Only a minority of the Middle East's new middle class actually holds jobs and draws salaries. The rest either can find no jobs consonant with their skills and values, or else work for status quo regimes which deny this group status and power. It would be quite misleading to exclude the "would-be" new middle class from this middle class. Both components of the middle class possess modern rather than traditional knowledge, and both are eager for a forced march into the modern age. Both are striving for the status, power, order, and prosperity that ought to go with middle-class existence. They resemble each other in every respect except success. This would-be middle class will therefore enlist itself in any movement that promises the kind of education that creates modern skills, the kind of job that opens a career, and the kind of action that gives a mere career individual rewards and social importance.

The inclusion of this group among the new middle class may be unexpected to those who restrict themselves to the classical economic definition of classes. In areas like the Middle East, however, where a modern economy is still to be created, and where control over the state and the forces of social change is more potent than ownership of property, property relations alone cannot serve to define class relations. In the midst of a profound transformation of society, it would also be quite wrong to define a social class statically, in terms of occupation, or employment at a particular moment in time. Each class must be defined in terms of its political, social, and economic role in the process of social change. In the present instance, that means taking account of all who either already perform the role of a member of the salaried middle class or who are bent by revolutionary action, if necessary, to gain a chance to perform this role and no other.

⚬ ⚬ ⚬ ⚬ ⚬

[5] At such a point, the intelligentsia may well split again and speak for different competing factions within the new middle class—another reason why it is not possible to use "intelligentsia" and "new middle class" interchangeably.

Partially overlapping the distinction between the working and job-less sections of the new middle class is the difference between the younger and older members of this class. "Youth" is not a passing phase in this region where half of all the people are under 20 years old, and where population grows so quickly and opportunities so slowly. In this situation men in their forties may still have almost all the naïveté of youth—being untouched by careers, status, and power—yet have none of youth's innocence, for they know what they have missed.

The plight of youth is obvious when the elite is recruited only from traditional classes. This plight is not resolved when the new middle class comes into its own. Initially, it grows worse. Those who have arrived often come to the top in their thirties (Ataturk, Nasser) or their forties (Kassim, Ayub). What they do can have more far-reaching results in the lives of their people than the actions of any preceding government. Yet almost all of them become authoritarians who do not intend to relinquish the reins of power until they die. Nor do members of the leading echelon of administrators and directors in government, business, journalism, schools, etc. mean to depart before the particular head of state to whom they owe their position. The older group of nationalists often learned patience and perseverance in the long struggle for power when a foreign state could always be made to bear the blame for the postponement of success. The younger men now find no target for their frustration except their own ruling elite.

※　※　※　※　※

The sharp and often bitter competition among members of the new middle class, however, does not inhibit the acquisition of a common historical awareness that each of them suffers from the same burden of the past and the same frustrations of the present. In the very fact of their separate individuality lies the essence of their common fate.[6] Coming into being by influx from all social classes—uniting the Western-educated son of a landlord with the army-trained son of a postmaster—the new middle class is the first in Middle Eastern history for whom family connections can no longer help automatically to establish class membership. Also, being itself composed of new men, it is the first which cannot hope to rest on inherited status or existing opportunities. It is the first class for whom communication depends on successful persuasion of

---

6 Some may concentrate on preserving their status, some on enlarging it, others on attaining it. Such competition, however, does not touch their class membership. Separate individuals, to amend only slightly a formulation by Karl Marx (*The German Ideology*, New York, 1938, p. 49), form a class only in so far as they play a common role in relation to social change, and have to carry on a common battle against another class or seek collaboration with it. Otherwise, they may be on hostile terms with each other as competitors.

other individuals; it cannot base itself on the implicit consensus of the past. The new middle class is distinguishable from all other classes in the Middle East by being the first to be composed of separate individuals. It is therefore also the first class for which the choice between democracy, authoritarianism, and totalitarianism is a real and open choice.

In most societies, trade unions constitute one of the best organized and disciplined forces seeking to exert political influence. The relationships of the unions to the centers of political power vary widely, however, for reasons such as the size and strength of the unions relative to other interest groups, the relationship of the unions to political parties, and, in many developing states, the role of the unions in the struggle for independence. In the selection below, some of these variations are examined by John Riddell in the context of African societies and politics.

16. *TRADE UNIONISM IN AFRICA AS A FACTOR IN NATION BUILDING*[*]

j o h n   r i d d e l l

THE GROWTH OF TRADE UNIONS IN AFRICA

. . . [T]rade unionism was a foreign implantation on African soil. It started under the era of colonialism, and although that chapter is now rapidly drawing to a close it has left some imprints which will not easily be effaced. The first trade unions were brought to Africa by European settlers—in South Africa and the Rhodesias—and were naturally patterned on those which they knew in their homelands; in the case of South

* From "Trade Unionism in Africa as a Factor in Nation Building" by John Riddell, *Civilisations*, Vol. XII, No. 1 (1962), pp. 27–40. By permission.

Africa they were sometimes set up even as branches of British unions. French officials did the same in the west and central African colonies, as well as in North Africa, and the organic ties of these unions to the metropolitan French centres remained unchanged virtually to the end of the colonial period.

Later, when the indigenous African workers began to organise towards the end of the twenties, they not unnaturally copied these metropolitan models; in the British territories this tendency received a further impetus when the Secretary of State for the Colonies, Sidney Webb, sent a memorandum to all colonial governors in 1931 urging the introduction of legislation to give a legal basis to trade unions and to provide for their compulsory registration. Labour departments were set up in most British colonies before the outbreak of the second world war, and from 1940 onwards experienced British trade unionists were appointed to advise on the formation of trade unions. In 1937 a French decree granted recognition to trade unions in overseas territories, but membership was so hedged round with restrictions that they were virtually open only to Europeans. Full trade union freedom for the French overseas territories came, in practice as well as in theory, only with the adoption of the Overseas Labour Code in 1952.

❊ ❊ ❊ ❊ ❊

IMPEDIMENTS TO TRADE UNION GROWTH

The legal obstacles to the growth of indigenous trade unions . . . were removed in the French possessions south of the Sahara in 1945, although they persisted in Morocco until 1955, and in the Congo in 1957. In the British territories legal obstacles in the strict sense of the word disappeared well before the first world war, except in South Africa. This does not mean that the trade unions in all African countries have not had serious difficulties of a practical and administrative nature to surmount.

The first and most obvious difficulty is the general economic, social and cultural backwardness of the continent as a whole. So long as subsistence agriculture remains the main economic basis of any country there is clearly little scope for the growth of trade unions in the normally accepted sense of that term; in all African countries, the first unions grew up among public service and transport workers. The absence of a real economic base [1] for a strong trade union movement has not, of course, diminished the appetite of the labour 'élite' to have one; and this

---

[1] The latest available UN statistics (1958) put the total population of Africa at about 195 million, while wage and salary earners may be estimated from I.L.O. and other sources at about 9 million.

is a factor, no less real for being psychological in nature, which cannot be ignored. It has however led to the failure of not a few attempts to build movements from the top, without a solid basis of local cadres capable of at least keeping elementary accounts and records. Administrative provisions, such as compulsory registration and the furnishing of annual returns, while no doubt introduced with the best of motives, have also in some cases acted as a brake on the growth of trade unions in conditions of semi-literacy.

In general however the most serious obstacles to the growth of trade unions in African countries have arisen, not so much from economic, cultural or administrative causes as from political difficulties. While they assumed their most acute and spectacular form in the colonial era, these difficulties have often persisted in a modified form in the newly independent states. The relations of trade unions to governments and political parties, both before and after independence, therefore merit closer examination.

TRADE UNIONS, GOVERNMENTS AND POLITICAL PARTIES

As in all colonial countries, the trade unions of Africa became involved in the struggle for independence at a fairly early stage. While the intellectual 'élite' may have provided the political leadership, it was the unions which furnished the shock troops whenever violent clashes with colonial governments became inevitable. Unlike India, where middle-class intellectuals produced the leadership not only for the nationalist political movement but also for the trade unions (and, in fact, largely continue to do so), where in effect the trade unions were created as a labour front of the nationalist movement, in Africa the unions joined this movement in their own right and indeed sometimes provided the political leadership themselves. There is nothing very remarkable about this; it simply stems from the relative weakness or even complete absence of an indigenous bourgeoisie in most African countries south of the Sahara. Nevertheless, it is a factor which is bound to have, and indeed in some cases has already had, important effects on the political balance of forces after independence.

The situation was somewhat different in North Africa, where the native intelligentsia was far more developed. There the nationalist parties undoubtedly inspired the creation of national trade union movements. Soon after the achievement of independence, however, there took place a polarisation of forces in the Moroccan nationalist party, the Istiqlal, which . . . led to a split in that party and to the formation of a splinter trade union centre; the *Union Marocaine du Travail* now forms the backbone of the opposition party, the *Union Nationale des Forces*

Populaires, which is committed to a policy of radical social reform. One effect of this split on the U.M.T. has been that it has frequently been subject to official interference in the course of its legitimate trade union activities, and has twice had to appeal for the intervention of the International Confederation of Free Trade Unions. In Tunisia, a similar split threatened in 1956 when the *Union Générale Tunisienne du Travail* adopted a programme entailing structural changes in the economy, which clashed with the more pragmatic approach of the Neo-Destour Party. For a time the U.G.T.T. was actually split, but thanks to the statesmanship of President Bourguiba the integrity of the party was maintained. The final outcome was that the former general secretary of the U.G.T.T., Ahmed Ben Salah, joined the government, while the leadership of the labour organisation passed to a man who had sprung from the ranks of the workers, Ahmed Tlili.

It would be extremely rash to attempt any forecast of possible similar developments in the independent Algeria which now seems on the point of emerging after seven years of blood and tears. What can be said for certain is that the *Union Générale des Travailleurs Algériens,* whose members have borne the brunt of the struggle, has a programme of radical social reform very similar to those of the U.M.T. and the U.G.T.T. Whether that programme will in some form or other become government policy, as in Tunisia, or whether it is destined to form the platform of a future opposition, as in Morocco, is a question which only the future can answer.

In French-speaking Africa south of the Sahara the position is far too complex to attempt to describe it here in any detail. The salient fact is that, in face of the highly centralised, presidential types of government which have generally emerged, the trade union movement has so far been too disunited to be able to exert the influence which it might otherwise expect to enjoy. The tragedy is that the grounds of dissension, when not purely personal, have related mostly to ideological and religious differences which have little or no bearing on the economic and social problems facing these countries. It is to be hoped that the continental unity recently achieved at the Dakar conference . . . between free and democratic unions of varying outlook from all parts of Africa may eventually be translated into practice at the national level too. The monolithic unity which apparently characterises the trade unions of Guinea—and of Ghana, too, for that matter—is more illusory than real, having been imposed by the ruling party. Revealing gaps were torn in this façade recently in both countries by widespread strike movements which the national trade union centres were unable to control and which were suppressed only by drastic police measures.

As for the other English-speaking West African countries, the situation in Nigeria is rather similar to that in the French speaking: lack of unity has deprived an otherwise strong movement of much of its potential influence. It is interesting to note that the federal government itself took the initiative in seeking to effect a reconciliation some months ago, but this failed owing to the insistence of the Nigerian Trade Union Congress faction on disaffiliation from international organisations as a prior condition.[2] Sierra Leone is probably unique in West Africa as the only country which has managed to keep a united trade union movement from the outset.

It could be that one of the reasons for the general lack of unity in the movements of both English- and French-speaking West Africa is that independence has been achieved there in the main by peaceful means and that the centrifugal tendencies inherent in any democratic society have consequently had full play. Whatever the reasons, the long-term test of the maturity of the African trade union movement will be its ability to achieve unity on a democratic basis and without recourse to totalitarian methods: a dictum which is equally valid, of course, for some highly developed European countries.

In the British territories of East and Central Africa the trade unions have, as elsewhere, been closely associated with national independence movements from an early stage in their existence. Although in no territory were the unions ever banned as such, many of their leaders and active members fell foul of the authorities, and normal activities were brought to a halt indirectly through the operation of emergency regulations in times of exceptional tension. This was the case in Kenya during the Mau Mau uprising which started in 1952, and in Nyasaland and the Rhodesias in 1959 during the agitation against the Central African Federation, which was, and still is, considered by the African nationalists in those territories as a device for perpetuating colonial rule. Otherwise relations were as amicable as might be expected between governments and trade unions which were eager not only to secure substantial wage rises for their members (many of whom happened to be government employees), but also to take over the functions of government itself at the earliest convenient opportunity. As for the latter ambition the British government from about 1959 onwards did not go out of its way actively to discourage it; on the contrary, it appointed trade union leaders to some of the commissions and conferences set up to formulate recommendations on the terms and timing of self-government and independence.[3] And in the first East African territory to achieve self-

---

[2] How serious this condition was may be judged from the fact that, when it was posed, several N.T.U.C. leaders had just returned from a World Federation of Trade Unions world congress in Moscow.

[3] The late Lawrence Katilungu, then president of the Northern Rhodesian TUC and of its African Mineworkers' Union was a member of the Monckton Commission on the future of Central African Federation; Tom Mboya, general secretary of the Kenya Federation of Labour is a member of the present London constitutional conference on the future of Kenya (March 1962).

government, Tanganyika, the general secretary of the Tanganyika Federation of Labour, Rashidi Kawawa, was appointed minister for local government and housing in 1960, and later deputy prime minister; shortly after the achievement of full independence at the end of last year, he replaced Julius Nyerere as prime minister.

Political parties, as critically important linkages between the masses of society and the centers of political power, have attracted considerable scholarly interest, and a number of typologies and analyses of the problems, advantages, and disadvantages of various parties and party systems have appeared. The fluid nature of many parties and party systems in the transitional societies presents special problems of analysis, but in the case of Latin America, as Robert Alexander notes, the parties are becoming increasingly institutionalized. The characteristics of Latin American parties that the author discusses should be compared with those in Asian and African states, particularly the one-party systems, for a more adequate base from which to evaluate these important instruments of political power; some of the literature on one-party systems is cited in the introductory essay of this chapter.

17. POLITICAL PARTIES IN LATIN AMERICA°

r o b e r t   j.   a l e x a n d e r

THE NATURE OF THE MODERN PARTIES

The kind of political party that has evolved in Latin America since World War I differs fundamentally from the parties of the first century

°   From "The Emergence of Modern Political Parties in Latin America" by Robert J. Alexander in *The Politics of Change in Latin America* edited by Joseph Maier and Richard W. Weatherhead, Frederick A. Praeger, Inc., Publishers, New York, 1964. Selections from pp. 103–122. By permission.

of independence. It is an organization with reasonably well-defined programs and ideologies. The various parties represent the widest spectrum of political philosophy. Often they are organizations representing or seeking to represent the interests of particular groups within the evolving society. It is upon the basis of their ideologies, platforms, and programs, and their appeals to special interest groups, rather than on the grounds of allegiance to a particular political leader, that they recruit their membership.

The new political party in Latin America also has a much more intensive internal life than did the older kind. It has local organizations throughout the country conducting activities of their own most of the year and not merely on the eve of an election or in the morning after a *coup d'état.* They hold periodic membership meetings. They gather for regular local, regional, and national conventions, and they do so even when no election or other change in government is in the offing.

These parties involve relatively large numbers of citizens drawn from various classes. They often carry on organized activities within the ranks of labor unions, professional associations, and other non-political groups. Many support a variety of periodicals and publish pamphlets and even books. Some have organized groups within them to carry on a continuous study of the economic and social problems of their countries— regardless of whether they are, at the moment, in the government or in the opposition. These studies may form the basis for policy and be published. Sometimes, though by no means always, the parties collect dues from their members and issue membership cards or other means of identifying those who belong.

Finally, the new parties are *civilista.* Although they have certainly not completely eschewed political cooperation with groups among the military (including participation in *coups d'état*), such contacts tend to be circumstantial and temporary, and their attention is centered on political action in the civilian field. Generally they seek, at least in principle, to keep the military out of politics.

TYPOLOGY OF PARTIES

There are many possible ways of analyzing the types of organizations that we have included under the heading of "new" or "modern" political parties in Latin America. We shall divide them here into three basic groups, each with its own subgroupings.

There are, first of all, the old traditional parties, which have been able to adapt themselves and their programs to the changing circumstances, the Conservatives and the Liberals.

Secondly, there are the parties of more recent origin following or seeking to follow European models. They include the Radicals, Socialists, Christian Democrats, Fascists, and the Communists and their splinters.

Finally, there are what may be called the indigenous parties of change, which have developed in recent decades. This type may be subdivided into what we shall call the national revolutionary parties and the personalist revolutionary parties.

❖   ❖   ❖   ❖   ❖

THE TRADITIONAL PARTIES

In most of Latin America, the traditional parties of the nineteenth century have ceased to be a major factor in political life or have disappeared altogether. . . .

Only in Honduras, Nicaragua, Colombia, and Uruguay are the traditional parties still the dominant competitors for power, and even in these nations, as we shall see, the Liberals and Conservatives have greatly changed in character. In Panama, Ecuador, Chile, Argentina, and Paraguay, they still have an important role in national politics, but they share the stage with more recent parties.

In countries where the traditional parties have maintained a foothold in the political arena, they have done so at the cost of a radical change in outlook. They have adapted themselves to changing circumstances by appealing to particular interest groups and by modifying their programs and methods of action.

The Conservatives

Where the Conservatives continue to be a factor of importance, they are, in most cases, the party of the large landowning class engaged in a rear-guard struggle to maintain its privileges, or, as the Partido Blanco in Uruguay, the spokesmen of the rural areas against the encroaching power of the cities. Their voting strength in Ecuador and Chile comes largely from the ability of landlords to march their tenants and agricultural workers off to the polls to vote for Conservative Party candidates.

However, even in the Conservative parties, the "winds of change" have not failed to leave things untouched. Generally, the Conservatives are no longer distinguished principally as supporters of the secular power of the Church. . . .

❖   ❖   ❖   ❖   ❖

The Liberals

With the exception of Chile and Nicaragua, the Liberal parties have become the spokesmen for important new segments of the population that have arisen in the wake of the economic and social revolution in Latin America. Thus the Liberal parties of Colombia, Honduras, and Ecuador are the principal political vehicle for the urban workers employed in factories and modern transportation, public utility, and agricultural enterprises. In Colombia and Honduras especially, the influence of the Liberal politicians is extensive within the organized labor movement itself.

✻   ✻   ✻   ✻   ✻

EUROPEAN-PATTERNED PARTIES

Many of the newer-style political parties which during the last two generations have challenged the Conservatives and Liberals were patterned after European models. These include at least one Radical Party roughly similar to the Parti Radical Socialiste of France, various Socialist parties, the Christian Democrats, the Fascists, and the Communists of various shades.

The emergence of European-patterned groups reflects the impact of Old World ideas on Latin America. In not a few cases, immigrants from Europe sought to establish in their new countries the kind of political organizations with which they had been familiar at home. As was perhaps inevitable, most parties took on their own characteristics. At times they moved far from the original European pattern.

The Radicals

The oldest of these European-oriented parties is undoubtedly the Partido Radical of Chile. It was established in the last decades of the nineteenth century as a left-wing offshoot of the Liberals. Like its counterpart in France, the Radical Party of Chile has been the typical expression of the middle class. At first a favorite among artisans and small shopkeepers, it subsequently became the party of the white-collar class, particularly the government bureaucracy.

Like the French Radicals, too, the Chilean party has oscillated violently in political philosophy and orientation. At times proclaiming themselves as socialists, they have at other times participated in Conservative government coalitions. Although they consider themselves to be of the left, they have more truly been the fulcrum of national politics, determining at any given instant whether the left or the right was to have the majority in Congress and even in public opinion.

✿ ✿ ✿ ✿ ✿

The Socialists

The Socialists were among the first political groups on the Latin American scene to advocate a fundamental transformation of their economies and societies. During the 1860's, 1870's, and 1880's, numerous immigrants who had been active in the First International and the first European Socialist parties found their way to America. They established small groups, and some of them sought affiliation with the International. Although most of them remained relatively isolated from the political life of the Latin American countries, a few became nuclei around which Socialist parties were organized.

✿ ✿ ✿ ✿ ✿

Unfortunately, most of the Socialist parties of Latin America have abandoned the camp of Democratic Socialism. In some cases, they have been heavily infiltrated or influenced by the local Communist parties. In most instances, they have adopted xenophobic nationalist positions that have made them violently anti-United States and pro-Soviet. Only the Argentine Social Democratic Party and the Ecuadorean Socialist Party have remained more or less loyal to the ideas they originally espoused.

The Christian Democrats

The Christian Democrats are a relatively new type of party in Latin America. They reflect the emergence of a more socially conscious wing of the Roman Catholic Church, a phenomenon produced largely since World War II. Although the Uruguayan Unión Cívica and the Chilean Falange Nacional antedate the war, all of the others have emerged subsequently.

The Christian Democrats find their philosophical inspiration in the principal papal encyclicals on social problems: *Rerum Novarum, Quadregesimo Anno,* and *Mater et Magistra.* Although their main constituency is found among the middle class, they have in a number of instances successfully sought to gain influence in the organized labor and peasant movements. They are strong advocates of basic social and economic change. The quality of their leadership is generally high. They include among their ranks some of the outstanding intellectuals of the region, particularly those of the younger generation.

The three most important Christian Democratic parties are those of Uruguay, Chile, and Venezuela. . . .

＊　＊　＊　＊　＊

The Latin American Christian Democrats regard themselves as counterparts of the European parties of the same name. They all belong to the Christian Democratic International. In a congress of the International in Santiago de Chile in August, 1961, the Venezuelan and Chilean parties sponsored a successful resolution urging a general alliance between Christian Democrats and other parties of the democratic left in Latin America.

The Fascists

The European totalitarians have had counterparts in Latin America as well. There were Fascist parties in a number of Latin American countries, particularly in the 1930's and 1940's, when fascism was at its apogee internationally. In Brazil and Chile, the Fascists, known respectively as Integralistas and Nacistas, were for some years parties of considerable consequence. They had all the trappings of their European brethren, including uniformed storm troopers and anti-Semitism. With the international defeat of fascism, the Chilean Partido Nacista disappeared, but the Brazilian Integralistas transformed themselves into the Partido de Representação Popular, which in its new form has tried to eschew its Fascist past.

＊　＊　＊　＊　＊

The Communists and Their Splinters

Among the European-patterned parties there are, finally, the Communists. There is now a Communist Party in every Latin American country. Some of them date from the early years of the Comintern, others arose in the 1940's and 1950's. Generally, the Latin American Communist parties follow the pattern of such organizations in other parts of the world. Over the years they have had two basic objectives: to serve the purposes of the Soviet Union and to establish the when and where of possible dictatorships of their own parties. They have followed faithfully the zigs and zags of the international Communist line.

The nature of the Communist appeal has varied from time to time. Generally, they have sought to picture themselves as the only real advocates of social change in Latin America and as the only true defenders of the working class. They have consistently pointed to the Soviet Union and other Communist countries as models that the Latin American nations should follow, first in terms of social revolution and more recently in terms of rapid economic development. In recent decades, they have sought to make the utmost use of nationalism and to turn it especially against the United States.

Until the advent of the Castro regime in Cuba, the Communists in most Latin American countries were little more than nuisance groups. Since 1959, however, they have achieved new importance. Their support of Castro has opened wider fields of contact with other political groups and has removed them from their almost complete isolation of the 1950's. The Castro phenomenon has also made the Communists more willing to use methods of violent insurrection and guerrilla war than they had been during most of their history. Moreover, the Cuban Revolution has sharpened the issue of social and economic revolution in Latin America. Thus, it has created a wider audience for the Communists' propaganda that only their particular totalitarian way would provide the kind of rapid change that the situation demanded.

o   o   o   o   o

THE INDIGENOUS PARTIES OF CHANGE

In addition to the parties that derived their ideological and programmatic inspiration from Europe, there are two groups of parties that have grown out of the changing situation in Latin America itself: the national revolutionary parties and the personalist revolutionary parties.

The National Revolutionary Parties

The single most important group of democratic political parties in Latin America are the national revolutionaries. They have grown out of the particular circumstances of their countries. Because of the similarity of problems in various Latin American nations, however, they have tended to adopt broadly similar ideologies and programs. They include the Acción Democrática of Venezuela, the APRA Party of Peru, the Liberación Nacional of Costa Rica, the Movimiento Nacionalista Revolucionario of Bolivia, the Febrerista Party of Paraguay, the Partido Revolucionario Dominicano, and the Partido Popular Democrático of Puerto Rico. The Partido Revolucionario Institucional of Mexico might also be placed in this category.

These parties present in their platforms a program for the democratic transformation of their particular countries and of Latin America as a whole. They advocate an agrarian reform adapted to the specific needs of their respective nations. They favor extensive social and labor legislation and the development of strong trade union and peasant movements under democratic leadership. They are nationalist without being xenophobic. They seek to bring the key elements of their countries' national economies into the hands of local citizens or the national government. While not rejecting foreign investment, they seek to establish conditions for its entry that will not compromise their national sovereignty. They favor mixed economies, with the government performing the key function of stimulating and directing rapid economic development. Above all, they stand for the firm establishment of political democracy.

In recent years the national revolutionary parties have borne the responsibility of government in Mexico, Bolivia, Venezuela, Puerto Rico, the Dominican Republic, and Costa Rica. To be sure, conditions have varied considerably in each case. In general, however, these nations have been in the vanguard in Latin America because of their insistence on effecting basic social revolution through democratic means. . . .

✻   ✻   ✻   ✻   ✻

All the national revolutionary parties recognize a kinship among themselves. On several occasions they have held international conferences. They have joined with some of the more advanced liberal parties to establish an Institute of Political Education in Costa Rica for the training of second-rank leaders, and they have lent moral support to one another in moments of great crisis.

Personalist Revolutionary Parties

The second category of indigenous parties consists of two organizations, the Partido Peronista of Argentina and the Partido Trabalhista Brasileiro (PTB). These two parties are similar in origin and are likely to evolve in somewhat similar directions in the years immediately ahead.

Both were organized by socially minded dictators, Juan Perón and Getúlio Vargas. In both instances, they were designed as vehicles for organizing working-class support for the dictators and their tenure in power.

Since the disappearance of their founders—Perón is in exile and Vargas committed suicide—the parties have seemingly taken different directions. Yet, there is good reason to believe that they may both end up in the camp of the national revolutionary parties.

○　○　○　○　○

THE DECLINE OF PERSONALISM

This review of the complex network of political parties in Latin America has indicated the key role they play in civic affairs. Among the many effects they have had on the traditional political structure and behavior, one of the most important has been that of diminishing the influence of "personalism" in Latin American politics.

Traditionally, Latin American politics have been viewed only in terms of the conflicting ambitions of rival leaders. During much of the nineteenth and early twentieth centuries, there was considerable justification for such a viewpoint. However, the emergence of political parties of the various types we have noted has been a principal factor in converting politics into something a good deal more complex than a game between personal rivals.

It would be foolish to maintain that leadership is a matter of no importance in the present parties. Particular individuals have played exceedingly important parts in determining the orientation of the older parties and bringing into existence the newer ones. . . . The fact remains, however, that the purpose of these parties is not to advance the fortunes of these men, nor will the parties disappear if they pass from the scene. The parties we have discussed were organized by groups of individuals, not by a single leader, and they were established to advocate and carry out a program.

*In contrast to the relative ease with which opposition parties organize
and operate in many Latin American states, opposition to the dominant parties in Asian and African states often faces difficult problems in
achieving a viable, legitimate political role. Nevertheless, even in those
states where opposition parties are officially outlawed, opposition to the
dominant party continues to erupt and persist. This opposition is often
dealt with harshly, and in the selection below, Edward Shils examines the
arguments frequently advanced by the leaders of the dominant parties of
the various states to justify their attempts to suppress this opposition.*

18. OPPOSITION IN THE NEW STATES
OF ASIA AND AFRICA *

e d w a r d   s h i l s

THE SITUATION OF OPPOSITION PARTIES
IN THE NEW STATES

The new states of Asia and Africa present a variegated picture with
respect to the status and mode of action of their opposition parties.
In only about a third of the new states are opposition parties regarded
as constitutionally legitimate. Israel, Lebanon, Morocco, India, Ceylon,
Sierra Leone, Senegal, Nigeria, Malaysia, Philippines, Sudan, and a few
others allow opposition to exist in a public and institutional form. In
Israel a system of a frequently varying coalition government and open
opposition parties prevails, with full freedom of public discussion. In
Nigeria, the multi-party system with a coalition government and open
opposition parties still functions, although it nearly collapsed earlier this
year because a major, but minority, party in the previous coalition boy-
cotted the federal election—as part of its leader's unsuccessful scheme to
make a *coup d'état.* In India, which has had the most stable and completely civilian government, opposition is free; parties in opposition to
the ruling party are numerous and ineffectual, and for the most part
work within the constitution. Ceylon permits two major parties and a

* From "Opposition in the New States of Asia and Africa" by Edward Shils, *Government and Opposition*, Vol. I, No. 2 (January, 1966), pp. 175–182. Excerpted by
permission of the author and the publisher.

considerable number of lesser parties. Both these South Asian regimes permit full freedom of discussion, although the previously incumbent Ceylonese party had sought to control the press. Pakistan and Sudan, having witnessed the dissolution of parties by military regimes, have now returned to something like party systems. Malaysia, too, maintains one, although it has very recently had to amputate one part of the country to avoid suppression of the locally-based Peoples' Action Party of Singapore. Sierra Leone also maintains a party system which has proceeded without crisis since independence. The Arab Middle Eastern states, the Maghreb states except Morocco, nearly all of the French-speaking African states, Ghana, Tanzania, Uganda, Kenya, Malawi, and Burma, do not have public opposition parties.

None of these new states is immune from oppositional activity. In about half of them, the incumbent governments in the past eight years have had to admit the factual existence of opposition by means of conspiracy, assassination or a successful *coup d'état*. Most of the acts of repression of an illegal opposition allegedly intending to employ violent means have been committed within states already denying both the constitutional legitimacy of opposition and indeed even the existence of any oppositional interests except "reactionary" ones. Opposition has occurred in these states after it has already been legally abolished and its existence implicitly denied.

Among the one-party states, Guinée acknowledged recently that its youth might be tempted to become oppositional. It had already condemned the leaders of its teachers' union for illegal opposition—which it designated as subversion. The most stable of the one-party regimes, Tunisia, has seen one of its major architects in exile and assassinated under obscure circumstances. It has itself contended that it was the object of conspiracy. In Algeria, there has been a *coup d'état* by the military in a harshly repressive one-party state which had already experienced during its brief existence a regional-military rebellion, and the trials of conspirators against the previously ruling government. In the new one-party regime in Tanzania, no opposition is admitted to exist, but the leader of the opposition, Mr Tumbo, is banished from public life. The newly joined members of the government from Zanzibar have encouraged or permitted the resistance of their followers to the desires of the government in Dar-es-Salaam. In Ghana, the government has on several occasions made accusations of subversive intentions, alleged plots to assassinate the President and noted other manifestations of opposition to the rulers of the country. In Togo, President Olympio was assassinated by a group of army officers and non-commissioned officers and politicians recalled from exile to join in the conspiracy. Similar manifestations have occurred in many of the other one-party regimes.

Still, what is notable about the new states is not that opposition exists. That is to be expected. Nor is it surprising that they have not been as successful as the totalitarian states,[1] which some of them admire as embodiments of modernity, in suppressing the emergence from time to time of oppositional interests and sentiments. Their elites have had unwittingly to acknowledge this publicly, on the occasion of their displacement by the forcible action of a previously closed opposition.[2] What is more interesting at this point in our discussion is that in so many states in which the rulers strive for modernity, for progressive and differentiated societies, they should be so intolerant of opposition, and particularly of open opposition in the form of constitutional parties, contending and criticizing in public.

THE ATTITUDE OF DOMINANT PARTIES
TOWARDS OPPOSITION

We must, therefore, seek to answer the question: Under what conditions does the ruling party tolerate the opposition? Or in an alternative formulation: Under what conditions does the ruling party either abolish the legal existence of opposition parties or force them to amalgamate with the ruling party?

As a first approximation, we may say that toleration of opposition exists where one or several of the following factors are present: (i) the ruling party alone or in coalition is obviously safe by a very substantial majority and is confident of its continued safety; (ii) the ruling party has a strong attachment to constitutional government; (iii) the conduct of the opposition is relatively unaggressive; (iv) the opposition is large and difficult to suppress without the probability of strong resistance by arms or by significant public opinion; and (v) the rulers do not regard themselves as the sole bearers of the charisma of nationality.

The ruling party suppresses opposition parties or forces them to coalesce with itself when it feels insecure about the stability of its majority and where the opposition, although weak, is regarded as a danger to the security of the incumbent elite. The assessment of danger to the security of the state is a subjective phenomenon. It is often unconnected with any realistically assessed high probability of a successful effort of the opposition party to displace the ruling party.

Efforts to suppress the public existence of an opposition party have hitherto been successful except where the opposition has a particular

---

1 Not that any totalitarian states have been able for long to avoid manifestations of opposition.

2 Where subversive powers are strong—the army is almost always the only strong subversive power—it is easy for them to overthrow the incumbent party. The institutions of public order in most of the new states are very feeble and cannot successfully cope with strong subversive elements.

territorial or regional base [3] or where it has substantial foreign support (e.g., the difficulties of the central governments in Congo-Leopoldville, Sudan, Iraq, India, and Indonesia in suppressing the territorially based opposition in Katanga and Orient Provinces, in the Southern Sudan, in Kurdistan, Nagaland and Sumatra and the Celebes). The condemned opposition parties have not as parties been able to resist effectively— their leaders have been gaoled or driven out of the country and their party machines have crumbled. They have not been able to call strikes or rally counterpressure when the governing party has wished to take strong action against them.

Despite the almost always evident incapacity of open opposition parties to resist their own destruction—which would lead to the conclusion that they could not by the same token subvert or overcome the incumbent government (even if they wished)—ruling parties in the new states nonetheless incline very often to the suppression of those who oppose them. Indeed if the allegedly subversive opposition parties were strong enough to resist their dissolution, the ruling parties would perhaps be less ready to suppress them.[4]

It seems clear that it is not because the governments have been in real danger from the opposition parties that they have suppressed them. When it suppresses or amalgamates an opposition party the government does not often allege that it is doing so because the opposition actually endangered its position. What it reacts against is an imputed subversive intention—a subversive state of mind—rather than a factual probability of subversion. Prohibition or suppression is a punishment for a wrong state of mind rather than a forestalling of a probable pernicious action.

The argument usually given for the suppression of opposition is that there is no need for an opposition because the ruling party and the people are one. It is also said that because of a shortage of personnel for the exacting tasks of development, it is wasteful for educated persons to be encouraged to spend their time in criticizing when they should be working for the progress of their countries. Another argument is that the criticisms of opposition parties would distract the populace from its concentration on the tasks set by the development programmes. Finally, it is said that the abolition of opposition parties enhances the stability of government and thereby provides the firm framework needed for social and economic development.

---

[3] The survival of the multi-party system in Nigeria is very much a function of the distinctive territorial bases of the various parties.

[4] Conversely, if the opposition parties were as dangerous as their ruling antagonists assert, they probably could succeed in their subversion because the ruling parties and their governments are also very fragile. Their powers of resistance are not very great, judging by the number of successful *coups* undertaken by oppositional elements.

There is not much empirical basis for these arguments. In no country in the world are party and people one, neither in the underdeveloped countries nor in the advanced ones. It is no more than a doctrinaire belief of political elites that they embody completely all the interests of the people whom they rule and that they care for them all equally and completely. But the fact that it is only a belief does not make it less real or less effective. In many cases it probably is a sincerely held belief.

It is certainly true that the new states must economize in the use of scarce educated talent. Very few of the new states have reached the point where they have an unemployable surplus of university graduates and technically trained "cadres." (India is the most outstanding exception.) But the suppression of opposition does not result in the employment of the talents of the opposition. They are very often, as in Ghana, incarcerated or exiled. Even if left at liberty they are seldom given important posts in the government—although in Kenya at least some of the leaders of the Kenya Democratic Union were thus employed when it was amalgamated with the Kenya African National Union. Still, the belief that talents must be conserved and used for the fulfillment of an over-ridingly important goal is a reality, too.

There are no grounds for believing that the inefficacy of so many measures for the improvement of agricultural technique and output, and for the promotion of industrial production in the countries which have permitted open opposition, are attributable to the demoralizing effect of the public criticism of government measures by open opposition parties or a free press. The economic misfortunes of Guinée certainly cannot be assigned to such a cause, because there is no public opposition in Guinée. People do not work harder or more efficiently when they are not allowed to know of criticisms of government policies. States without open opposition do not have higher rates of economic growth than do states which tolerate opposition. Where, as in the case of the Ivory Coast, the economic growth rate of a one-party state is relatively high, it is largely a consequence of foreign aid.

As regards the argument from stability, this, too, has no empirical foundation. The one-party governments—governments which have suppressed their oppositions—are not less unstable than the types of regime they do not wish to resemble. Attempts at *coups d'état* have happened more frequently in one-party regimes than in regimes with open opposition parties (e.g., Mali, Ivory Coast, Togoland, Dahomey, Syria, Iraq).

Since the arguments which are used to justify the suppression of opposition by governing parties seem to be empirically baseless, why are they employed? They are employed in part to give a justification, in terms of a principle involving the common good, to actions which serve the particular advantage of the ruling party. They are invoked because the ruling party is attached to the symbols and roles of power and does not want to be displaced. They are also invoked and applied because they are actually believed.

Why are they believed? The beliefs in question appear to derive from an unarticulated political metaphysic,[5] from a conception of the nation as a metaphysical essence which finds its purest manifestation in those who believe in and give expression to it by the fact of their incumbency in the positions of authoritative responsibility for the custody and propagation of that unitary national essence.[6] The metaphysic of the "national essence" grew into a mind-filling reality in the course of the agitation and negotiations for independence. Those who agitated for the independence of the still scarcely existent nation became possessed by this essence, which they sought to emancipate from the accidents which encumbered it, such as the rule of the ethnically alien, the influence of traditional indigenous authorities, and others who manifested in their political action or in their tribal and communal attachments their non-participation in that essence.

According to this "metaphysic of the nation," one cannot simultaneously be of the nation and yet antagonistic towards its highest and fullest embodiment. Where society is very different from the state, the occupants of the ruling positions in the state regard themselves as the exclusive custodians of what is essential in the society. The empirically existing society, with its tribal divisions, its traditonal leaders, its educated class with divergent loyalties and aspirations, is a bad accident of history, of mistakes by dead and living persons who did not or do not see that their existence is fundamentally anomalous. That is the way in which the rulers conceive of themselves and their competitors.

How could such a conception have arisen? It has two major external intellectual sources: Rousseau and the doctrine of the dictatorship of the proletariat, to both of which many French-speaking African politicians were susceptible in the latter part of the 1940's and more so in the 1950's. Of the four English-speaking African states which have suppressed or amalgamated with their publicly organized opposition, at least one has been markedly influenced by the Leninist idea of the dictatorship of the proletariat, and the others have been somewhat influenced by it. But the doctrinal influences do not explain why the opposition has been suppressed in so many countries which have not been influenced at all by Rousseau and very little by Marxism-Leninism. The dominant political

[5] Professor Arthur Lewis in his forthcoming work, *Politics in West Africa*, writes: "A struggle for independence is highly emotional . . . The men who thrust themselves forward . . . feel that they are Heaven-sent, and that anyone who stands in their way is a traitor to Heaven's cause."

[6] This metaphysic, although of a quite different historical origin, bears a close structural similarity to the historical metaphysics of Marxism–Leninism, which places the Communist Party in an analogous position in the communist countries.

elites have their prejudices and some of them come from and are reinforced by political theories. But by and large, political theory seems a
factor of minor significance—almost an epiphenomenon—entering into a
pattern of thought which is generated from experience, from passion and
the necessities of collective pride, individual dignity and vanity, and
from the colonial situation.

There is an inherent dynamic in the colonial situation of proud
persons with a need for dignity and a resentment against those who deny
it to them. There is a need for self-identification, which enhances dignity.
The nature of this self-identification is influenced by the scope of the
rejected but still obtaining colonial authority, and the ineffable experience of a distinguishing colour. It gains intensity from the self-identification which arises first from an active leading role in the independence
movement and then from the fact of incumbency in the central positions
of authority in the new states. The very thinness of its spread in the rest
of society makes for a more acute consciousness of one's own circle of
confrères as the exclusive bearers of the quality of nationality.

We must not, however, overlook the simple facts of attachment to
power and the prestige and perquisites associated with power, of irrita-
tion at simply being made the focus of criticism, and of touchiness in
response to criticism for shortcomings of which one is more or less aware.
There is also the further unpleasantness of being criticized by persons
who were once one's colleagues, indeed almost brothers. This wounded
and aggressive response to criticism, actual and anticipated, draws additional force from the antagonism felt towards critics from ethnic groups
other than that of the leaders of the dominant party, an antagonism and
rivalry which are prior to the relationship of ruler and critical opponent.[7]

The sense of exclusive custodianship of the national essence which
results in the identification of state, party and society is not equally
pronounced everywhere. There are countries where it has become attenuated by experience and the passing of time and where it has to face a
deeper tradition of constitutional government. In these countries, although ruling politicians become irritated with their critics, they do not
proceed repressively against them because they acknowledge their fundamental right to existence. India is the chief example of a new state
where a longer process of growth of the sense of nationality and a longer

---

[7] Ethnic antagonisms within the broader circles of the elites and counter-elites of
the new states are aggravated by the strain of the ethnic attachments within the self
of those who seek to transcend them in a higher national identity.

It must, however, be pointed out that in spite of the anxieties of the elites of the
ruling parties about the dangers of disintegration because of divergent ethnic attachments, the suppression of open opposition parties in order to avoid such disintegration
has not been justified in the result. The problem of national unity is an urgent one,
but the suppression of parties has not prevented the South Sudanese from revolting.
On the other hand, no state already established and functioning has broken up because of secessionist tendencies among its ethnic minorities.

experience of political activity, as constitutional as was possible under a colonial regime,[8] gradually established a powerfully compelling tradition of respect for the institutions and procedures through which collective decisions are made. Ceylon shows similar features. Pakistan, despite its failures and the military interregnum and despite the rather short history of the sentiment of Pakistani nationality and the grave ecological obstacles to its formation, likewise seems to have benefited to some extent from this prolonged exposure to the culture of constitutionalism.

Sierra Leone and Israel are also the bearers of a well established constitutional culture, and of a longer history of the sense of nationality that is to be found in most of Africa. In Israel, it has been imported with the political culture of the dominant parties. In Sierra Leone, it is part of a relatively well established general culture and also owes much to the exceptional personal qualities of the brothers Margai. In these more tolerant regimes, the image of the nation and the sense of national identity have become sufficiently flexible to coexist with perceived differences which are not held to diminish the reality of the nation. Nationality there does not require uniformity.

Elsewhere in the third world, where opposition parties are permitted to exist as long as they maintain a discreet and modest attitude—as in Morocco and in Senegal—or where they are so strong that to attempt to suppress them would precipitate a crisis more serious than the rulers care to face—as in Nigeria and Lebanon—and in Malaysia until a short time ago—political prudence on the part of sober and artful political leaders seems to be a major factor. Of course, in all these cases there is a mixture of motives.

---

[8] Colonial regimes were not congenial to the growth of a discipline of constitutional or civil politics. In most of the new states a number of parties came into existence only a short time before the granting of independence, when nationalistic enthusiasm was extremely intense.

As studies of Western societies have made plain, political campaigns and elections can take a variety of forms and can serve a number of functions. There are obvious variations in the qualifications required of persons to vote, in the number of political offices to be filled, and the size and type of constituencies, for example. Less obvious than the determination of victors are some of the other functions campaigns and elections may perform, such as those of political indoctrination and a sense of participation. In the selection that follows, the functions of elections in developing states are explored by R. S. Milne.

19. *ELECTIONS IN DEVELOPING COUNTRIES*°

r. s. m i l n e

The number of Nuffield-type studies of elections in developing countries is rapidly growing.[1] But there has been a corresponding lack of discussion of the assumptions underlying the use of elections in these countries.[2] The *forms* of western-type elections change when they are exported. Can it be assumed that the "functions" remain the same?

Experience of what happens to Western institutional and conceptual exports to developing countries suggests that changes may occur before elections are "domesticated" into the indigenous political system.[3] For instance, some aspects of election ritual may be 'non-functional' in the new environment, but may be practised from habit, just because they formerly served useful purposes in elections in developing countries. On the Northeast coast of Malaya the Pan-Malayan Islamic Party owes most of its support to its being identified with Islam and to the activities of religious leaders; yet the party maintains a quite elaborate, and probably partly unnecessary, organization to compete with its more secular rival party, the Alliance. Obviously the environment in developing countries is bound to be different. In some African elections the influence of tribalism is strong, and the support of the chiefs is important.[4] The parties may be relatively weak. In Northern Nigeria the Northern People's Congress is "at present little more than a

° From "Elections in Developing Countries" by R. S. Milne, *Parliamentary Affairs*, Vol. XVIII, No. 1 (Winter, 1964–65), pp. 53–60. By permission.
[1] Notably, to list only some major publications in book form: W. J. M. Mackenzie and Kenneth E. Robinson (eds.), *Five Elections in Africa* (Oxford, 1960); M. Venkatarangaiya, *The General Election in the City of Bombay, 1952* (Bombay, 1953); Jorge R. Coquia, *The Philippine Presidential Election of 1953* (Manila, 1955); R. L. Park and S. V. Kogekar (eds.), *Reports on the Indian General Elections 1951–52* (Bombay, 1956); H. Feith, *The Indonesian Elections of 1955* (Ithaca, N. Y., 1957); I. D. S. Weerawardana, *Ceylon General Election, 1956* (Colombo, 1960); G. Bennet and C. G. Roseberg, *The Kenyatta Election: Kenya 1960–1961* (Oxford, 1961); K. W. J. Post, *The Nigerian Federal Election of 1959* (London, 1963).
[2] But see Mackenzie; Ch. VIII in Mackenzie and Robinson, *op. cit.*; *Free Elections* (London, 1958); "The Export of Electoral Systems", *Political Studies*, Vol. V, No. 3 (1957).
[3] Mackenzie and Robinson, p. 463.
[4] Dennis Austin, "Elections in an African Rural Area', *Africa,* Vol. XXXI, No. 1 (1961), p. 12.

'front' for traditional institutions."[5] Party organization, on the other hand, is often 'elementary',[6] and branch membership, in the sense of paying membership, minute.[7] Electors may not be responsive to appeals couched in terms of national issues. They may have to be approached in terms of local issues[8] or of their trust in the personality of the candidates. Many of the differences may be attributed to the difficulty of 'communication' in such countries, whether resulting from physical obstacles, from illiteracy or from traditional limitations on dealings with members of other tribal, or ethnic, groups. On the highest level the obstacles to effective communication would include the absence of an adequate volume of informed *criticism* of a government's policies. A commentator on the Indian 1957 General Election has pointed to the generally passive, unquestioning and uninformed state of the public, the immunity from critical examination of the Prime Minister's declarations and the absence of political columnists of the calibre of Walter Lippman or James Reston.[9]

These are a few of the obvious general differences between elections in developed and developing countries. Other detailed variations derive from them. For instance, in the 1955 Malayan election, the multi-racial Alliance Party ran some Chinese and Indian candidates, although at that time the overwhelming bulk of the electors were Malays. Their non-Malay candidates were therefore believed to be vulnerable to opposition by a strong Malay candidate. Partly for this reason the Alliance attempted to keep their nominations secret until the last possible moment. Such manoeuvres are in contrast to the practice in many Western countries, where it is believed to be an advantage to choose the candidate early so that he and his name may become familiar to the electors. Differences of this kind are roughly what might be expected when the sequence of operations that constitutes a general election is attempted in a developing country. . . .

＊　＊　＊　＊　＊

It is not easy to say exactly where "free" elections begin or end. In practice there are many degrees of "freedom" in elections. Even in Western countries there may be biases built into the system, such as the tendency in Britain for the Labour Party to need a higher proportion of the vote than the Conservatives in order to win a given number of seats, or the distortions inherent in the United States system because of the

5 Mackenzie and Robinson, p. 478.
6 Austin, p. 14.
7 Post, pp. 134–5, 153. On Indonesia see Feith, *op. cit.*, p. 9.
8 Austin, p. 3.
9 J. R. Roach, "India's 1957 Elections", *Far Eastern Survey*, Vol. XXVI, No. 5 (1957), p. 76.

existence of Presidential electors. There may be *ad hoc* electoral laws introduced to favour particular parties such as the French system of *apparentement* of 1951. Varying degrees of government control of the Press may exist, and also, as in France, great disparities in the amount of radio and television time allowed to government and opposition parties. The financial resources available to various parties may differ widely.[10] Even once the objective conditions under which elections are held have been listed, there is still the *subjective* element in Mackenzie's definition to be considered; in brief, do the electors *consider* that they have a real choice? Perhaps, therefore, we should refrain from calling elections "unfree", unless there is wholesale interference with opposition parties, rampant "stuffing" of ballot boxes or unless an independent judiciary to interpret electoral law and an honest, competent, non-partisan administration to run elections [11] are obviously lacking. Otherwise, perhaps elections should be described merely as "less free" or "more free" than some other elections.[12]

The reasons usually put forward to justify the holding of free elections in Western societies may be summarized as:

1. To make possible peaceful changes of government;

2. To give the ruled a sense of commitment to the decisions made by the government and a sense of participation in their execution. In Western societies a high proportion of the electors will feel a sense of commitment (2) to a government, only if they are convinced that the elections which brought it into power were relatively "free". These generally recognised advantages of free elections in Western societies are similar to those put forward by Professor W. J. M. Mackenzie.[13] They may also be expressed in terms of legitimacy. Changes of government are accepted as legitimate, only if elections are widely regarded as free.

In some developing countries a fairly high and influential proportion of the electors share the western view that it is important that

---

[10] *The Journal of Politics*, Vol. 25, No. 4 (1963), special issue, "Comparative Studies in Political Finance".

[11] Mackenzie, *Free Elections*, p. 14.

[12] Cf. C. G. Field, *Political Theory* (London, 1956), p. 43 on the definition of democracy.

[13] *Political Studies*, pp. 255–6. In *Free Elections*, pp. 13–14 he puts forward two reasons which are substantially the same. See also a review of Bennet and Roseberg, *op. cit.*, by D. J. R. Scott, *Parliamentary Affairs*, Vol. XV, No. 3 (1962), pp. 399–400. Maurice Cowling in *The Nature and Limits of Political Science* (Cambridge, 1963) disagrees with Professor Mackenzie for being normative and for admiring Western-democratic political arrangements too much (pp. 35–7). In fact, in *Free Elections*, Mackenzie immediately makes qualifications about the circumstances under which it is prudent to introduce free elections (p. 14). He is also misquoted by Cowling. Mackenzie's statement that the doctrine of responsibility to an electorate ". . . is the best for ordinary use . . ." (p. 14) is reproduced in Cowling as ". . . is the best for electorate use . . ." (p. 36).

elections could produce a change of government. In the Philippines there has actually been a change of Administration three times since the Second World War, in 1946, 1953 and 1961. In 1949 the elections may not have been free, in the sense that there were claims "that the election results officially proclaimed did not reflect the will of the Filipino electorate as expressed in the ballots".[14] In other countries, such as India and Malaya, a change of government is possible, in principle, at a general election, although a single party has been dominant in each country since independence.

But in elections in some developing countries the emphasis may be on the "commitment" function of elections (2) rather than on the possibility of changes of government (1). Thailand is perhaps an extreme case. Thai elections seem to be one of the ways in which legitimacy is conferred on a government, although *changes* in government take place mainly through *coups*, which are not entirely peaceful. "In the old days the king was made legitimate by the splendid trappings and ceremonial of his court. Under the constitution the ceremonial of election is required for the group in power. The public, in fact, seems not so concerned about the political outcome of elections as that they be held in a seemly clean and orderly manner".[15] To say that in Thailand the nature of political parties and the conduct of elections "distort" the political process is for the observer implicitly to set up norms of what Thai elections "are for".[16]

It has been argued that it is unnecessary for governments in developing countries to attempt to bolster up their legitimacy by going through an election ritual. Government can be equally legitimate, says Cowling,[17] where no election has occurred, or where elections are not part of the normal political process. Perhaps, but this is the argument of a dealer in logical categories rather than of an observer of the process of development. Elections are not a necessary condition of legitimacy in developing countries, but they have been widely used as *one* of a number of devices for acquiring legitimacy. The developing countries, almost without exception, have accepted the western export, "democracy". . . . But, although the developing countries have, by and large, accepted "democracy", they have reserved the right to define it in their own way.[18] Sometimes their definition does not include elections at all, or does not include elections which in form resemble western elections,

[14]   Coquia, p. 3.
[15]   David A. Wilson, "Thailand" in G. McT. Kahin (ed.), *Government and Politics of Southeast Asia* (Ithaca, N. Y., 1959), p. 56.
[16]   Saul Rose, *Politics in Southern Asia* (London, 1963), p. 319.
[17]   *Op. cit.*, p. 37.
[18]   See Hugh Tinker, *Ballot Box and Bayonet: People and Government in Emergent Asian Countries* (Oxford, 1964); Rupert Emerson, "The Erosion of Democracy", *The Journal of Asian Studies*, Vol. 20, No. 1 (1960).

as in Indonesia's "guided democracy" or Pakistan's "basic democracy".[19] Sometimes elections, ostensibly of the western type, are included. But even here the user country determines their exact form and the degree to which they should be "free".

Quite apart from considerations of democracy, in developing countries there may be other reasons for holding (or not holding) elections, whether relatively free or relatively unfree. One of these may be the wish to promote consensus or heightened national consciousness. This would not be an important reason in most western countries, although clearly it is relevant in even well-developed communist countries, such as the U.S.S.R. The view has been advanced that in some African countries orderly elections have in a sense become "the badge of national consciousness, maturity and independence". Election day "has become something of a solemn national occasion. . . ."[20] This link has also been noticed in Malaya. "Through a series of elections at local, state and federal government levels more people are being brought to deal, not only with the problems of democracy, but also at the same time with the issue of nationhood. At each election and in every political party more of the politically conscious are being made to affirm their loyalty to the nation and gradually to identify that nation with the political system which they are learning to manipulate".[21] Clearly, these consequences are regarded as advantageous, primarily because they tend to promote political development. The emphasis is on the educative effect of elections rather than on their actual results in determining who shall rule.

It is possible, however, that, in some countries, instead of *promoting* national consciousness, elections may actually have a *divisive* effect. An account of the 1955 general election in Indonesia claimed that it had the desirable result, *inter alia*, of strengthening all-Indonesian consciousness through the participation of a large number of electors.[22] The absence of any subsequent general election suggests that similar desirable consequences would no longer follow. It has been suggested that violence may occur because of the 'popular public festival' aspect of elections, reminiscent of British elections before the secret ballot was introduced in 1872.[23] Elections may convey too much of an "all-or-nothing" impression to Africans.[24] "A general election . . . is thus a civil war without bloodshed, and its result must be the same as that

---

[19] See especially Tinker, *op. cit.*; Marguerite J. Fisher, "New Concepts of Democracy in Southern Asia", *Western Political Quarterly*, Vol. XV, No. 4 (1962); Michael Brecher, *The New States of Asia* (London, 1963), Chs. 2 and 3.

[20] Mackenzie and Robinson, p. 467.

[21] Wang Gungwu, "Malaya Nationalism", *Royal Central Asian Journal*, July–Oct., 1962, parts 3 and 4 (July–October, 1962), pp. 324–5.

[22] Feith, pp. 89–90.

[23] T. L. Hodgkin, *African Political Parties* (Penguin, 1961), p. 132.

[24] D. J. R. Scott, "Problems of West African Elections", *What are the Problems of Parliamentary Government in West Africa?* (London, 1958), p. 73.

which would have been achieved by such a war." Consequently the question of minority rights becomes irrelevant.[25] If this diagnosis is correct, then elections may actually retard the spread of national consciousness.

Another authority disputes this view that African elections necessarily have such a divisive effect on society. The losing side does not feel it has "lost everything", and traditional society has a great ability to "return to laughter" after a period of conflict.[26] Generalisations on a subject as wide as "African elections" are perhaps risky, at least at this time. However, it would seem that, if little national consciousness already exists in a country, this will probably be reflected, in the way in which the campaign is conducted. . . . In short, unless there is a certain minimum degree of consensus to begin with, elections will not increase the degree of consensus.

The "functions" of elections in developed societies are not so obvious as they were once thought to be.[27] Their "functions" in developing societies are even less obvious. In such countries elections may bear an unexpected relation, or no relation at all, to "democracy". The decision whether or not to hold them may be determined by considerations which are important to the government—for instance, the effect on the promotion of national consciousness, but which have nothing whatever to do with democracy.

[25] Roy Price, "Italy at the Poll", *Parliamentary Affairs*, Vol. IX, No. 3 (1956), p. 77.

[26] Austin, p. 16.

[27] Cf. Graeme Duncan and Steven Lukes, "The New Democracy", *Political Studies*, Vol. XI, No. 2 (1963).

Where power to make important decisions exists, the possibility of corruption also exists. But even if that generalization is accepted, the problems remain of defining political corruption, measuring its extent, and determining its consequences. Several interesting attempts to probe the levels and implications of corruption in transitional societies have been undertaken, and a selection of them has been compiled by Arnold Heidenheimer in Political Corruption. *In the excerpt below, drawn from a full-length study of corruption, the authors briefly survey several types of corruption and some of its consequences.*

20. CORRUPTION IN DEVELOPING COUNTRIES*

r o n a l d   w r a i t h
a n d   e d g a r   s i m p k i n s

Throughout the fabric of public life in newly independent States runs the scarlet thread of bribery and corruption. This is admitted by everybody; very little can ever be proved about it.

The reaction of the educated citizens of these countries to this state of affairs is that of any other people; they are angry, ashamed, indifferent, cynical according to their different temperaments. What distinguishes them from people who live in a more fortunate atmosphere is that circumstances force even the angry and ashamed into a resigned apathy. Those who have tried to live as moral men in an amoral society have generally given way sooner or later under agonizing pressures; the pressure of legitimate ambition which can only be achieved by illegitimate means; the pressure from families, insatiable for help; the slow, insidious pressures of a society in which material success is adulated (even by the standards of the twentieth century), and where moreover material failure is ruthlessly mocked; the pressure of increasing defeatism, on realizing that public opinion stigmatizes the transgressor so lightly, and that so little seems to be gained from trying to swim against the tide. This is the general picture. Within it, some go on trying, a few with rare persistence; corporately they achieve little, since most of them are teachers or civil servants, firmly enmeshed in the system which they want to destroy, and silenced by the terms of their official employment.

°   °   °   °   °

It is frustrating to try to write, one's phrases wrapped in a cocoon of ambiguity, about something which everybody knows, which no one dares openly to acknowledge, which can rarely be proved and which may lead to serious trouble if one is in the least incautious. Perhaps that is why studies of contemporary corruption are rare.

What can be said about corruption among the mandarins, and in the high places, can amount to no more than a few careful generalizations. Of corruption among the common or less gifted citizens one may

°   From Ronald Wraith and Edgar Simpkins, *Corruption in Developing Countries* (London: George Allen and Unwin Ltd., 1963), pp. 11–31. By permission.

write a little more freely. It is only of municipal corruption that one is able to write at large, free from the shadow of the law of libel; to write also with some precision, since the field especially in Nigeria has been admirably documented by successive Commissions of Inquiry, whose published works, now assuming a considerable bulk, are among the livelier contributions to contemporary Nigerian literature. It is a pity they are not better known.

Some years ago Dr Nkrumah shocked many Christians by permitting the base of his statue outside the Law Courts in Accra to be inscribed with the words—carved imperishably out of granite—'Seek ye first the Kingdom of Politics and all else shall be added unto you'. It is clear from subsequent events that this was hardly an over-estimate so far as some of his own supporters were concerned, and the Osageyfo himself was courageous enough in 1961 to compel his own Ministers to declare their business assets and commercial interests, and to do a full-time job for a full-time salary. This is no final solution, since people cannot be compelled to be honest, and a man of influence in public life has many opportunities to circumvent the letter of the law, through relatives, agents and foreign bank accounts. But the Osageyfo's gesture gave hope to many Africans.

✧ ✧ ✧ ✧ ✧

The writer has been told in more than one West African country, however, that corruption among top people must be seen with an understanding eye. It is not necessarily concerned with personal enrichment, or at least only in moderation. The root of the matter is that political parties need money, and the small subscription from the average man is not available. The large subscription from the man of influence must therefore take its place, and the accession of certain large sums to the party funds represents something not reprehensible, but notably self-sacrificial, on the part of those who are the channels of this communication. An unofficial percentage on a contract (and there are some big contracts), the compulsory purchase of land at an unorthodox price, a little wise direction in the development of real estate—these must not be too hastily condemned. It may well be.

It is unfortunate that Ministers, among whom are men of ability and integrity, should almost gratuitously have made themselves a butt, defined by the Oxford Dictionary as 'an object of teasing or ridicule', by possessing motor cars of embarrassing size and living in houses which are commonly said to have cost the taxpayer well over £30,000. Anyone who happens to travel in a car of extravagant aspect is now liable to have the word 'Meenister' shouted after him by the local urchins. . . . West Africa is sadly afflicted by the love of ostentation, and thousands of men on the middle and lower rungs are crippled financially because of it. Ministerial ostentation can perhaps be excused on the grounds of dignity of office, or more straightforwardly because Ministers can afford it; but it is an unfortunate example, and gives rise to cynicism.

How much is true and how much is false about corruption in high places nobody outside a small circle can ever know for certain. What *is* certain, and can be said without circumlocution, is that to wander through the corridors of power in these countries is to wander through a whispering-gallery of gossip, in which the fact of corruption at the highest levels is taken utterly for granted, and the only interest lies in capping the latest story with one that is even more startling.

There is of course an illicit glamour about alleged ministerial corruption which causes it to be talked about more perhaps than it deserves. It is certainly unfair to those Ministers who are free of it that they should be linked in the generic word 'ministerial' with those who are not.

It is indeed always unfair to speak of people in categories instead of as individuals. In the writer's experience the civil services in West Africa can, as a corporate whole and at the time of writing, be proud of their general integrity; on the other hand there is little doubt that the depredations of some civil servants are considerable. Those who deal direct with the public and are in a position to bestow benefits on individuals, or to influence their bestowal, are of course more vulnerable than the rest, and the known fact that some such men have avoided or declined promotion to higher salaried grades tells its own story.

✿   ✿   ✿   ✿   ✿

The problem has been openly and officially recognized in Ghana and Nigeria by the appointment of Advisory Commissions on the suppression of corruption in the public service, and more than one Government maintains an Anti-Corruption Officer on its normal strength.

✿

The economic effects of all this on a country may not be very considerable. The sum total of illicit gains is no doubt small in relation to the revenue, and there is no evidence from more developed countries where large-scale corruption is common that corruption and inefficiency are necessarily correlated. The taxpayer is of course being robbed, either directly in cash or indirectly by unsuitable appointments being made on his behalf. But by far the more serious loss is the loss of self-respect and the growth of frustration and cynicism. It is above all a moral problem, immeasurable and imponderable. And politicians and civil servants who are guilty are more guilty only in degree than the mass of people whom they represent and are supposed to serve.

❖

For while some of the corruption of which one hears in high places has at least a robust and buccaneering flavour, the corruption which one experiences oneself, or learns of at first hand through the tribulations of African dependants, is depressingly mean and squalid; and it is all-pervasive.

It is distressing that people who in the life of family, clan or tribe are generous with one another to the point of destitution should in the world of cash services, and among strangers, become so mean that the simplest service is extorted, quite illicitly, for a 'dash' or rake-off.

It is incongruous that in the merciful professions of nursing and medicine the out-patient must find his twopence for admission, at the head of the queue, to his rightful place; that in the most ignominious of human emergencies the bed-pan can only be secured for a penny; that the pound note is looked for under the pillow of the consulting room of the Government doctor.

To put a man in the way of a job at £5 a month ought, one would have supposed, to be a simple human kindness among people so under-privileged that to have a job at all is to be an aristocrat. To spoil it by the demand of a rake-off of several shillings a week for a year seems grasping and callous.

❖   ❖   ❖   ❖   ❖

One turns to corruption in local government with a mixture of relief and dismay—relief because the actual facts have been more precisely investigated, and can be quoted; dismay because as matters stand at the time of writing local government in the southern Regions of Nigeria [1] has reached the point of being a conspiracy against the public, so riddled is it with bribery, nepotism, politics and corruption.

For many years the critics have been pointing to the folly of the colonial administration in forcing a veneer of British local government on West African territories, supposing in their blindness that a plant which has only been known to flourish in the temperate, misty and kindly atmosphere of England and Wales could be transplanted to the harsh, exotic climate of the African tropics. They happen to have been wrong in their facts, because the colonial administration, from the Colo-

---

[1] The North is less well documented.

nial Office to the District Officer, has done its best to restrain West African governments from adopting *in toto* a system that they knew could never work; the pressure for its adoption came from within West Africa, and was based on the suspicion that differentiation meant discrimination, that modification meant the second best. . . .

The adoption of British local government, with ultimate power in the hands of elected councillors, but shorn of the restraints of British convention, compromise and mutual respect between elected representative and paid officials has amounted to an open invitation to corruption, an invitation eagerly if incredulously accepted.

The only supposition on which the English kind of local government can rest is that elected councillors are people who for one reason or another wish to serve the community. It may be due to the inherent goodness of their natures alone, or this may be fused in varying degrees with the love of power, the satisfaction of public regard, or an inability to mind their own business; but whatever the motive it could hardly be financial. In West Africa the position is otherwise. A government, presumably in its right senses, proposed to confer on councillors, with minimal constraints, the right to allocate market stalls, to control paid appointments and to award contracts. Even if the bribe required to get on the council in the first place were increased many times over, it would still become a sound investment. . . .

It may seem strange to an English councillor that the allocation of market stalls should be of such importance to serious men, but among market-minded people in West Africa the possession of a stall in a big market means a comfortable income, of a strategically placed stall comparative wealth, and the control of a number of stalls for illicit subletting an enviable unearned competence. . . .

The tendency of councillors to allocate stalls to themselves, their wives, their relations, and then to the highest bidder can only be described as pronounced.

If a man has spent a month, as the author of the Aba Report did, in investigating such a highly specialized racket, he may presumably lose a little of the calm and detachment proper to an administrative officer. At any rate his language was more forthright than that of some of his colleagues working in the same general field, though with their wider opportunities and more varied interests. He was moved to say in his conclusions that he could

'only gasp at the entirely shameless conduct of the councillors and the executive staff. No moral principle and no prick of conscience appears to have entered their minds at any stage. . . . I find that all the councillors must be held jointly responsible for their decisions and actions. Not one has resigned in protest, and not one has asked that his name be recorded as voting against the scandalous allocations of . . . The Chairman of the Council is principally noteworthy for his sanctimonious announcements, deliberately calculated to deceive the public. This makes his deeds even more intolerable . . . My impression of Mr . . . , as a witness and as Chairman of the Markets Committee, is that he is without scruple.'

Although the language is slightly exceptional, the facts, regrettably, are not. There is even a silver lining to his Report, as he postulates the possibility of an honest council:

'Unfortunately, a policy that, in the hands of an honest council, operates satisfactorily and with justice may become an instrument of evil and oppression in the hands of a venal council. One needs two policies: one for the honest council and one for the corrupt council. Regrettably however it is not possible to devise any policy which can wholly defeat the depredations of a dishonest council. At some stage, when it comes to allocating market stalls, it is essential to separate the sheep from the goats if genuine traders only are to be allocated stalls. That means interviews and that in turn means opportunities for corruption.'

Others working in the sphere of local government find it difficult to grasp the concept of an honest council, since such a thing has never come their way; they have grown up with the racket and they assume— who can blame them?—that that is what local government means.

     ✧   ✧   ✧   ✧   ✧

A more sinister trend is the tendency of councillors not only to demand bribes for securing employment but for retaining it—what is known in more conventional gangster circles as protection money. The fact that influential councillors have been to council employees 'in the night' [2] and said that if they do not produce a given sum within a given time they will be sacked, has long been known to students of local government, who are grateful to Mr Nicholson in his Report on Ibadan for bringing it into the light of day. A considerable section of this Report (p. 20 onwards) is devoted to the almost incredible case of councillors who, to the Commissioner's satisfaction, blandly informed four 'revenue collectors' at the same car park that failure to pay £10 each would result in their dismissal. It is an interesting reflection that the councillors had no doubt that people who collected money on car parks, although presumably earning a bare living wage, would be in a position to pay this money. . . .

     ✧   ✧   ✧   ✧   ✧

---

[2] A phrase widely used in Nigeria to cover a shady transaction; it does not necessarily mean that the deed was done after the hours of darkness, though these are favoured, but indicates rather a state of mind.

The word corruption, as usually employed, means the illicit gain of money or employment, and that is the principal sense in which it is discussed in these pages. A reference to corruption in local government would however be incomplete without some mention of political jobbery, which is corruption of another kind.

Local councils in Africa have tended to become extensions of national or regional political parties; they may be said to combine in one body what in Britain would be found in the local authority, concerned with the administration of services, and the local constituency organizations of the political parties, concerned with winning the next election. This has resulted in some painful situations; dismissal of council staff who were not politically acceptable; the appointment of party men with minimal qualifications for the job, or sometimes less; and the suppression of conscience.

In the higher reaches of the Lagos Town Council Mr Storey felt compelled to write as follows:

'Looked at from whatever angle you will, the incident (of the appointment of the Town Clerk) is calculated political jobbery without a single redeeming feature. It shows a callous disregard for the principles of honest local government, and is a matter of which the Democratic Party in the Lagos Town Council may even now feel ashamed. I condemn it without reserve.'

An election is traditionally the *locus classicus* of bribery and corruption, and it is impossible that Nigeria should escape the general infection. On the other hand one does not contemplate the conduct of an election in Nigeria with any great sense of outrage; it is the grotesque rather than the venal that weighs upon the spirit.

At the approach of an election considerable numbers of people lose their heads, and even leaders of ability and standing revert to a tender mental age. Wild and intemperate accusations fill the air. All sense of shame evaporates. The conduct of a campaign is, to put it mildly, uninhibited. This pandemonium, however, is caused by a few people and by the newspapers. Small stage armies of party agents, supporters and hangers-on, concerned more to draw attention, *fortissimo,* to the huge delinquencies of their opponents than to disseminate a creed, roam the streets and tear along the main roads, filling them with sound and fury. The newspapers, who must sell to an unsophisticated public (the lesser ones being themselves barely literate) treat all this as if it were an adult activity. It signifies, in fact, very little.

It has an occasional ugly side, since from time to time the police will find an electioneering van with weapons of a murderous kind. Their investigations generally reveal small parties of thugs on the loose, disowned by their parties, execrated by the mass of the people, and even they themselves whipped up not so much by a lust for blood as by an obsessional conviction that their opponents are doing the same thing; they are beastly, but in the total picture unimportant.

To see the picture in perspective, one has only to consider election day itself, when the melodramatic curtain-raiser is over and the general public takes the stage for the play itself. Almost invariably, election day is calm, level-headed, mature. The ordinary man and woman, unaffected by the vapourings that have gone before, behaves like a textbook citizen. It is a pity that the parties do not rise to the level of the people.

The serious thing from the point of view of national self-respect is the unquestioned assumption that opponents will cheat, and the inordinate effort that goes into the prevention of remote and improbable types of fraud. That fraud takes place, and that some of it is of a wildly improbable kind, is not to be denied; but that it has any significant effect on the results of an election is equally improbable.

In the fevered imaginations of party organizers their opponents plan to insert ink, glue or nitric acid into their ballot boxes,[3] to tear off their names and symbols from them, to forge ballot papers (in which they overestimate their technical proficiency), to bring in lorry loads of illicit voters, to bribe polling officers.

In cold fact, very few specific allocations are ever made, and most of these dissolve into a mist at the touch of the precise, searching question.

◊ ◊ ◊ ◊ ◊

But—and it cannot be too often repeated—all this activity, often degrading, sometimes farcical, is largely carried on by a few people whose professional business it is to do so, and in whom the electorate is not interested. It does not fairly represent the temper of the people, who are on the whole very sensible about elections.

It may be that the most venal aspect of elections, and the most harmful to the national interest, is that about which no vestige of proof can be offered—the purchase of candidatures and seats by bribery. It is rare that anyone who bribes or is bribed reaches the point of saying so, and the chances of ever discovering the facts about this matter are remote.

On the fringe of the problem, light relief is occasionally afforded by the hopeless independent candidate, who invests his deposit in the full intention of withdrawing at the last moment, as some regulations allow, and accepting a consideration from the rival who is in most fear of his vote being split. Occasionally also there are engaging arguments as to whether a 'feast' or any other form of the customary, almost obligatory,

---

[3] Each candidate has his own, with his name and the symbol of his party pasted on it.

African hospitality constitutes 'treating', a cold and inappropriate word for an alien concept.

But the central and troubling question of what proportion of the candidates bribe, how they do it and how much they spend are unanswerable. There are not lacking those who claim to know; but when it comes to the point they will not say. It is clear that a high degree of corruption in government and administration makes candidature a sound and profitable investment, and it is assumed by all that the investment is widely made.

B. Political Leaders, Institutions, and Processes

"Of writing constitutions there is no end" is a phrase that seems appropriate for many developing states. With their old and now highly esteemed constitution, Americans in particular are apt to be puzzled by the frequency with which new constitutions are written and abandoned in many states, usually forgetting the restructuring of their own political system during its formative years and the many formal and informal amendments that have been made to the United States constitution. In the selection below, J. Lloyd Mecham examines the substance and purpose of constitutions in Latin America and finds both to be in some respects significantly different from those in North America and Europe.

21. LATIN AMERICAN CONSTITUTIONS: NOMINAL AND REAL*

j. lloyd mecham

If the drafting of democratic constitutions serves as preparation for practice in the art of popular government then, indeed, Latin Americans

* From "Latin American Constitutions: Nominal and Real" by J. Lloyd Mecham, *The Journal of Politics*, Vol. XXI, No. 2 (May, 1959), pp. 258–272. By permission of the publisher and the author.

are well prepared. Since gaining independence the twenty republics have essayed a grand total of 186[1] *magna cartae*, or an average of 9.3 each. A breakdown per country reveals the following: Argentina 4; Bolivia 14; Brazil 5; Chile 7; Colombia 6; Costa Rica 7; Cuba 2; Dominican Republic 22; Ecuador 16; El Salvador 10; Guatemala 5; Haiti 18; Honduras 10; Mexico 5; Nicaragua 8; Panama 3; Paraguay 4; Peru 12; Uruguay 4; and Venezuela 24. Today thirteen of the Latin American republics are governed by constitutions adopted since 1940, and only two antedate World War I.[2] There seems to be no end to constitution making.

This points up an anomaly: on the one hand apparent devotion to constitutionalism as a cure for national problems, and on the other, lack of respect for constitutional mandates. Nowhere are constitutions more elaborate and less observed. Politically, Latin Americans seem to be unqualified optimists, for the long succession of constitutional failures has never dampened hopes that the perfect constitution—a cure-all for national ills—will be discovered eventually.

THE NOMINAL CONSTITUTION

Since it is the objective of the present inquiry to show how widely government in operation departs from constitutional mandate, we first note the constitutional norm, *i.e.*, a composite or average constitution of the Latin American republics.

The Composite Constitution

This constitution is a lengthy instrument of about 35 pages, in contrast to 13 pages for the Constitution of the United States. . . .[3]

The composite constitution contains no preamble. It sets about forthrightly to declare that the nation is sovereign, independent, and unitary or federal as the case may be; that the government is republican, democratic, and representative; that sovereignty is vested in the people who express their will by suffrage which is obligatory and secret for all

[1] There is no agreement concerning the total number of Latin American constitutions. This is because many amended or revised constitutions were promulgated as new instruments. "It has been the habit of new political regimes to adopt new constitutions rather than to run the risk of loss of prestige by operating under the instrument identified with an opposing and defeated party." William W. Pierson and Federico G. Gil, *Governments of Latin America* (New York, 1957), p. 160.

[2] Argentina (1853) and Colombia (1886); both extensively revised.

[3] Using Russell H. Fitzgibbon (ed.), *The Constitutions of the Americas* (Chicago, 1948), as a basis for comparison. Since issue of this collection new constitutions have been adopted in the following countries: Costa Rica (1949), El Salvador (1950), Nicaragua (1951), Uruguay (1952), and Venezuela (1953).

citizens, male and female, over 20 years of age.[4] No literacy or property tests are required. This is universal suffrage in its most liberal sense.

The guarantees of individual liberty, the familiar rights of man, are spelled out in great detail. These include: the freedoms of speech, press, assembly, and petition; equality before the law; *habeas corpus;* no unreasonable searches or seizures; due process; no retroactive penalties; and no capital punishment. Religious freedom is guaranteed, and all cults receive the equal protection of the state.[5] The minute enumeration of the inalienable rights of the individual is inspired by a desire to erect a constitutional barrier to tyranny.

The effectiveness of this barrier is weakened, however, by provisions for the suspension of the individual guarantees in times of stress. This device is called "declaration of state of siege," a temporary annulment, by presidential decree, of all constitutional guarantees and privileges. This important presidential power is restricted only by the formality of securing congressional approval before the act if the Congress is in session, and after the act when that body is convened. The easy suspension of the constitutional guarantees is evidence of the fact that they are considerably less than absolute.[6]

One of the most detailed and lengthy sections of the constitution deals with "social rights and duties," a recent addition to Latin American constitutional law. Conforming to contemporary conceptions of social justice, social rights and duties are enumerated *in extenso* under the subheads: labor, family, education, and the economic order.

✿ ✿ ✿ ✿ ✿

The supreme powers of government are divided for their exercise, by application of the principle of the separation of powers, into the legislative, the executive, and the judicial. Two or more of these powers shall never be united in one person or group of persons, for by counterbalancing and checking each other they will prevent the establishment of a tyranny.[7]

The legislative power is vested in a Congress composed of two houses, a Chamber of Deputies and a Senate. Both deputies and senators are chosen by direct popular vote, for terms of four and six years

[4] In some of the states the minimum age is eighteen years, if married.

[5] For the status of religion in the respective states, see J. Lloyd Mecham, *Church and State in Latin America* (Chapel Hill, N. C., 1934).

[6] See Segundo V. Linares Quintana, *La denaturalización del estado de sitio como instrumento de subversión institucional* (Buenos Aires, 1946). See also Harold E. Davis (ed.), *Government and Politics in Latin America* (New York, 1958), pp. 280–282.

[7] On the application of the classic separation of powers see Óscar Morales Elizando, *El principio de la división de poderes* (Mexico, 1945).

respectively. . . . In general both houses of the national legislature possess the same powers and perform the same functions. They are equal partners in the legislative process. Although each chamber possesses certain special powers these are of no particular consequence.

✻ ✻ ✻ ✻ ✻

The executive power is exercised by the president with a council of ministers. The president is chosen by direct vote of the people (even in the federal states), serves for a term of four years, and is not eligible for re-election until after one term intervenes. There is no provision for a vice-president because this heir apparent might become the magnet for conspiracies against the constituted government.[8]

The powers of the Latin American president are relatively greater than those of the president of the United States, for, in addition to the customary executive grants, he is authorized to directly initiate legislation in the national Congress, expel foreigners on his own authority, suspend the constitutional guarantees, and in federal states impose his will on state administrations by exercise of the power of intervention. His decree-making power is so broad as to be quasi-legislative in character; indeed, the constitution authorizes the Congress to delegate, in emergencies, extraordinary legislative powers to the president. Constitutional checks on dictatorship are thus cancelled out by contrary constitutional delegations.[9] The end result is that dictatorships are possible within the terms, if not the spirit, of the Constitution.

The composite constitution provides that the president shall be assisted by ministers of state, the superior chiefs of their respective departments. . . .

The judicial system, independent and coordinate, is composed of a hierarchy of courts; [10] a supreme court, appellate courts, and inferior courts or courts of first instance. . . . The justices are appointed and serve for limited terms. The Latin American countries base their legal system on the Roman Law and so do not make use of trial by jury. United States influence is discovered however, in the constitutional provision conferring on the supreme court the power to declare laws unconstitutional.

[8] Of the twenty republics only eight (Argentina, Bolivia, Brazil, Cuba, Ecuador, Honduras, Panama and El Salvador) have retained the vice-presidency.
[9] See Oswaldo E. Mirando Arenas, *El jefe de estado en las constituciones Americanas* (Santiago, Chile, 1944), and Karl Loewenstein, "The Presidency Outside the United States," *Journal of Politics*, XI (August, 1949), 447–496.
[10] See Helen L. Clagett, *The Administration of Justice in Latin America* (New York, 1952), pp. 21–41.

In addition to the regular courts there are a number of special courts, notably the administrative tribunals and the electoral tribunals. . . .

In its organization of local government the composite constitution for the unitary state provides a highly centralized system as in France. The nation is divided, principally for administrative purposes, into departments, and each department has a governor appointed by the president, and directly responsible to the minister of interior. There is no departmental assembly. Insofar as self government exists on the local level it is found in the municipalities which have their own elected mayors and councils.[11] It should be recognized however, that neither mayor nor councilman actually has much to do. The various national ministries, particularly the *gobierno* or ministry of the interior which controls the police, absorb most of the local jurisdiction. Local self-government functions under highly restrictive limitations both in law and custom.[12] Within the respective states of the federal unions the organization of local government conforms rather closely to that of the unitary nations.

Reflective of the prominence which the military assumes in the political life of the Latin American nations, a separate constitutional chapter is devoted to "the armed forces." In addition to national defense the military are assigned the role of "guaranteeing the constitutional powers." This provides a basis for political intervention despite the injunction that the armed forces are "essentially obedient and not deliberative." This is another of the numerous but ineffective constitutional word-barriers to the rule of force.

The constitution is easily amended. The proposed amendment must receive a two-thirds vote in two consecutive legislative sessions. The executive cannot object. This is meaningless, however, since the amendment would have little chance of adoption if the president opposed. There is no popular ratification of constitutional amendments; indeed, the original constitution itself was not popularly ratified.

THE OPERATIVE CONSTITUTION

The foregoing, in broad outline, is the composite "paper" constitution of the Latin American republics, together with certain distinctive variations. It is now in order to describe that constitution as actually operative. With the exception of Uruguay, and the doubtful addition of

[11] For municipal democracy see Carlos Mouchet, "Municipal Government," Davis, *op. cit.*, pp. 389–390.
[12] Austin F. Macdonald, *Government of the Argentine Republic* (New York, 1942), pp. 398–402.

Costa Rica, Chile and Mexico, democratic government does not exist in Latin America.[13] A majority of the countries are either undisguised personalistic dictatorships or pseudo-democracies. In either case the proud constitutional assertions that these are popular, representative, democratic states, and that all governmental authority derives from the people in whom sovereignty resides, are mere verbiage, or at best declarations of ideal aspirations.

Divergences in Actual Practice

Universal suffrage, provided by more than half of the constitutions, is actually exercised by only a fraction of those qualified, even in countries where voting is supposed to be compulsory.[14] These few votes must then run the gamut of the "official count." It is a well-known fact that a requisite more important than honest voting is the honest poll of the votes. Since governments in power are usually in control of the voting and the tabulating of the vote, it is a commonplace that Latin American administrations never lose elections. On the rare occasions when this happens, as in Cuba in 1944 when Batista "allowed" the election of Dr. Grau San Martin, the shock of the unusual event reverberated throughout Latin America.[15]

What shall we say about the observance of those fundamental guarantees of individual liberty: the freedoms of speech, press, assembly and conscience? What of the guarantees of domicile and all of the components of what we know as due process of law? Since from the earliest days of their independence, Latin Americans have been so profoundly engrossed in the constitutionalizing of an ever expanding enumeration of civil liberties, it seems that they should, by this time, have attained a status of sanctity and respect. This however is not the case.[16] The guarantees are respected only at governmental convenience and by sufferance. The constitutions generously supply the executives with the means to be employed in emergencies, to suspend the guarantees. This device, known as "state of siege," is abused by overuse for it is the

[13] See Russell H. Fitzgibbon, "A Statistical Evaluation of Latin American Democracy," *The Western Political Quarterly*, IX (September, 1956), 607–619.

[14] For electoral practices see Frank R. Brandenburg, "Political Parties and Elections," in Davis, *op. cit.*, pp. 216–218.

[15] Since 1945 opposition parties have won presidential elections in Brazil, Chile, Ecuador and Peru. This may indicate a wholesome democratic trend. For description of electoral trickery see William S. Stokes, *Honduras: An Area Study in Government* (Madison, Wis., 1950), pp. 231–264.

[16] "Rights are null, declarations are mere words, if means are not provided to make them effective; these means are the penal code, responsibility of authorities, inflexible punishment of all attack on the conceived rights. This and nothing else constitutes the guarantees." Justo Arosemena, *Estudios constitucionales sobre los gobiernos de la América Latina* (Paris, 1888), II, 303.

customary resort to overwhelm opposition and entrench dictatorship.[17] It is ironical that democratic constitutions bestow so lavishly on the executive the means to destroy the feeble manifestations of democracy. With respect to the status of the individual guarantees, therefore, much depends on the attitude of the president.

A principle of the "paper constitution" which is transformed beyond recognition in the operating constitution is the separation of the powers. Theoretically the three powers—executive, legislative and judicial—are separate, coordinate, and equal. Numerous safeguards, many of which are found in our own constitutions, are provided to prevent wanton exercise of authority by any one of these powers. Because of the well-founded belief that it is the executive which will be most prone to irresponsibility and be acquisitive of power, the most numerous constitutional limitations are those imposed on the presidents. Despite all this, and responsive to the strongman tradition in Latin governments, the executive overshadows the other two powers. Latin American governments are emphatically of the strong presidential type.

That the president is the dominant power in the government is never doubted. His supremacy derives from his dual position as constitutional chief-executive and as extra-constitutional *caudillo*, chief or boss. From the earliest days of their independence Latin Americans have shown a strong disposition for *caudillos*, preferably for those with a military background, for the magnetic attraction of the man on horseback can always be expected to reinforce the lure of demagogues.[18] The *caudillo* embodies the program of his political partisans; he is the platform of his pseudo-party. This is what is called *personalismo* in Latin American politics, which means placing emphasis on individuals rather than on public policies. The *caudillo* because of his hold on the popular imagination, but more significantly because of his control of the army, meets with docile acceptance. Neither the disguised dictatorship, nor the pseudo-democracy is a government of laws, all are governments of men. One of the least effective of the constitutional checks on ambitious presidents is the no-reelection provision. *Caudillismo* and *personalismo* have transformed the constitutional office of the presidency beyond recognition.

In consequence of the dominance of the executive it is hardly necessary to indicate the position of the congress and the courts. Both are subordinate to the executive. . . .

Freedom and equality of the courts is also a fiction, for the judiciary, like the legislature, is subordinate to the executive, numerous constitutional provisions to bulwark the power and independence of the courts to the contrary notwithstanding. . . .

[17] Hector R. Baudón, *Estado de sitio* (Buenos Aires, 1939).
[18] Charles E. Chapman, "The Age of the Caudillos: A Chapter in Hispanic American History," *Hispanic American Historical Review*, XII (August, 1932), 281–300.

It is not necessarily because the presidents have ways of getting rid of objectionable judges which accounts for their surrender of independence; rather it is because of a long standing tradition of Spanish origin that there must be no interference by the judiciary with the policies of the chief executive. The old principle that the king can do no wrong is observed by the deference paid by the courts to the wishes of the president. . . .

✿   ✿   ✿   ✿   ✿

Equally as fictitious as Latin American federalism is the constitutional mandate that the army does not deliberate, *i.e.*, intervene in politics. Any practical discussion of Latin American politics which omits reference to the political role of the army would be sadly unrealistic, for the most significant feature of Latin American politics has always been the predominance of the military authority over the civil. It is an old story dating from the independence period when the possession of governmental authority became the prize of contesting arms. None of the countries has escaped the blight of military political intervention, and today the military are in control, openly or disguised, in most of the nations of Latin America.

The very nature and purpose of the army invites political activity, for it is designed more to preserve internal order and support the regime than to defend the frontiers against foreign invaders. Several of the constitutions impose on the army the responsibility of guaranteeing the fulfillment of the constitution and the laws. The militarists do not shirk this obligation for they regard themselves as the most competent, unselfish, and patriotic interpreters of the national interest. . . .

Violence Institutionalized

One of the most patent facts of Latin American government, and certainly the best-known to Anglo-Americans, is recurring *revolution*. The term is a misnomer, for it usually refers to nothing more than a *coup d'état* or a *cuartelazo* (barrack revolt), the classic "substitution of bullets for ballots," the ousting of the "ins" by the "outs," or perhaps the enforcement of the principle of "alternability of public office." These are not popular movements, for relatively few people participate, outside the military. The rabble, of course, assembles in the main plaza to acclaim impartially each succeeding *caudillo*.[19]

Since the great revolution for independence early in the nineteenth

[19] William S. Stokes, "Violence as a Power Factor in Latin American Politics," *The Western Political Quarterly*, V (September, 1952), 445–468.

century there have been few authentic revolutions in Latin America, that is if we restrict the term to those deep-seated popular movements aimed at fundamental change in the political, social, and economic orders. Only a limited number of the demonstrations of force so common to the political scene are worthy of designation as revolutions; this, notwithstanding the crying need in most of the countries for a thorough revamping. What Latin America needs, paradoxically, is not less but more revolutions. Fundamental revolution may be the specific for the cure of chronic pseudo-revolution.

Although some of the most illustrious leaders of the developing states such as Nasser, Sukarno, and Nkrumah have been toppled from power by death or political opposition, the peculiar qualities of charismatic leaders continue to fascinate students of politics. By definition, charismatic leaders possess a dramatic flair for words and actions that can inspire their followers to give them their full support, at least for a time. The strengths and weaknesses of such leaders with respect to the difficult problems of development are analyzed in the next selection.

22. THE RISE AND ROLE OF CHARISMATIC LEADERS*

a n n   r u t h   w i l l n e r
a n d   d o r o t h y   w i l l n e r

Max Weber adapted the term *charisma* [1] from the vocabulary of early Christianity to denote one of three types of authority in his now classic classification of authority on the basis of claims to legitimacy. He distinguished among (1) traditional authority, whose claim is based on "an

* From "The Rise and Role of Charismatic Leaders" by Ann Ruth Willner and Dorothy Willner, *New Nations: The Problem of Political Development, The Annals*, Vol. 358 (March, 1965), pp. 78–88. By permission of the publisher and the authors.
[1] The term is of Greek origin, meaning "gift," and was originally identified as a "gift of grace" or a divinely inspired calling to service, office or leadership.

established belief in the sanctity of immemorial traditions," (2) rational or legal authority, grounded on the belief in the legality of rules and in the right of those holding authoritative positions by virtue of those rules to issue commands, and (3) charismatic or personal authority, resting on "devotion to the specific sanctity, heroism, or exemplary character of an individual person, and of the normative pattern or order revealed by him." [2]

Of these types—and it must be emphasized that they are "ideal types" or abstractions—charismatic authority, according to Weber, differs from the other two in being unstable, even if recurrent, and tending to be transformed into one of the other two types.[3] While elements of charismatic authority may be present in all forms of leadership,[4] the predominantly charismatic leader is distinguished from other leaders by his capacity to inspire and sustain loyalty and devotion to him personally, apart from his office or status. He is regarded as possessing supernatural or extraordinary powers given to few to have. Whether in military prowess, religious zeal, therapeutic skill, heroism, or in some other dimension, he looms "larger than life." He is imbued with a sense of mission, felt as divinely inspired, which he communicates to his followers. He lives not as other men. Nor does he lead in expected ways by recognized rules. He breaks precedents and creates new ones and so is revolutionary. He seems to flourish in times of disturbance and distress.[5]

❄ ❄ ❄ ❄ ❄

NEW STATES AND THE EMERGENCE
OF CHARISMATIC LEADERSHIP

❄ ❄ ❄ ❄ ❄

Charismatic leadership seems to flourish today particularly in the newer states that were formerly under colonial rule. Their very attain-

[2] Max Weber, *The Theory of Social and Economic Organization*, ed. by Talcott Parsons (New York: Oxford University Press, 1947), p. 328.
[3] This notion of transformation or "routinization" has led to criticism that Weber uses the concept of charisma ambiguously, that is, on the one hand as a characteristic of certain classes of people in certain situations, on the other as a more general quality that can be transmitted to and identified with institutions such as the family and the office; see *Ibid.*, p. 75 and Carl J. Friedrich, "Political Leadership and the Problem of Charismatic Power," *The Journal of Politics*, 23 (February 1961), p. 13. Such criticism overlooks the possibility that during the course of charismatic leadership, a transfer can be effected of aspects of the belief induced by the leader toward another object, especially if designated by him.
[4] Authority is here defined as the sanctioned basis for the exercise of a leadership role, whereas leadership refers to the individual seen as capable of exercising the role for the situation in which direction is called for.
[5] Weber, *op. cit.*, pp. 358–362; also H. H. Gerth and C. Wright Mills, *From Max Weber: Essays in Sociology* (New York: Oxford University Press, 1946), pp. 245–250.

ment of independence generally signified that the old order had broken down and the supports that sustained it had disappeared or were rapidly being weakened. We might more correctly distinguish two "old" orders in postcolonial countries: (1) the precolonial traditional system, many of whose elements survived during colonial rule and (2) the colonial system, a close approximation of Weber's rational-legal type, which was superimposed upon but did not completely efface the traditional system. Particularly under the "indirect rule" type of colonial regime, much of traditional belief and observance, political as well as socioeconomic, existed beneath the order imported from and imposed by the metropolitan country and in the more rural areas side-by-side with it.

The basis of traditional authority, however, was eroded by colonialism and indigenous nationalism, and the basis of legal authority was undermined by indigenous nationalism. Traditional authority, whether exercised through kingship and dominant caste, chieftainship and special lineage, or whichever of the many and varied institutions found in the many traditional societies, had been part of and based upon indigenous patterns of social organization, land tenure, economic activity, and other elements of a relatively integrated social system. Traditional social systems tended to disintegrate or be transformed under the impact of institutions imposed by the colonial power. Concomitantly, traditional prescriptions and procedures for the selection of rulers, for the control of conflict and the settlement of disputes, and for the maintenance of what had been considered appropriate relations between rulers and ruled were modified and in varying degrees displaced by colonial systems of authority. Even where colonial administrations supported or tolerated some maintenance of traditional authority, this was restricted to traditional contexts.

The attitude that traditional authority systems were inadequate to cope with the urban and industrial institutions introduced into colonies by Europeans was transmitted to and absorbed by the native elites educated in accordance with European standards and values and recruited into the colonial bureaucracies and business organizations. Nationalist intellectuals among the native elites also came to deprecate their own traditions, seeing them as weaknesses which had made colonialism possible and which were used by their colonial rulers to keep them in subjection.

✣　✣　✣　✣　✣

In retrospect, it is clear why one of the major difficulties faced by leaders of successful national independence movements as they sought to establish their own governmental systems was the lack of respect for impersonal legal authority based on rational norms. For in successfully having discredited the colonial rulers and their works, they also unwittingly discredited the rule of law introduced by the colonial powers. However, the certainty of the traditional order had already been shattered during the colonial period. Thus there were no longer clear-cut and generally acceptable norms for the legitimacy of authority and the mode of its exercise. Their absence created the need for leadership that could serve as a bridge between the discredited past and the uncertain future. A climate of uncertainty and unpredictability is therefore a breeding ground for the emergence of charismatic leadership.

SOURCES AND VALIDATION OF CHARISMA

Having indicated the conditions propitious for the emergence of charismatic leadership, we now describe how it comes into existence and what sustains it. . . .

The process, broadly stated, is one of interaction between the leader and his followers. In the course of this interaction the leader transmits, and the followers accept, his presentation of himself as their predestined leader, his definitions of their world as it is and as it ought to be, and his conviction of his mission and their duty to reshape it. In actuality, the process is more complicated, involving several groups of followers and several stages of validation. There is the small group of the "elect" or "disciples," the initial elite whom the leader first inspires or who throw up from among themselves one who can inspire others. There is the public at large which, in turn, can be divided into those of predominantly traditional orientation and those oriented toward a newer order. In the societies with which we are concerned, further divisions may exist along ethnic, tribal, religious, regional, and linguistic lines. The point to be made is that the nationally significant charismatic leader can command the loyalty of all or most of these groups.

To understand how he can do so, it seems advisable to distinguish two levels on which his appeal is communicated and responded to. The first level is that of special grievance and special interest of each group; its significance is probably greatest during the stage in which the charismatic leader mobilizes the population in opposition to a prevailing order and in assertion of the possibility of a new order. In the situations of transition with which we deal, this stage is that of opposition to the rule of a colonial power.

Changes during the colonial period resulted in losses and uncertainties for many groups in the colonized population. Traditional agrarian land rights were interfered with, and unfamiliar forms of taxation were imposed on peasants. The monetary gains of those pushed or pulled out of their traditional agricultural, pastoral, or handicrafts occupations to become plantation and industrial workers may have been more than offset by the problems of adapting to unfamiliar environments. Traditional merchants and traders often lost out to the competition of imported manufactures. Traditional ruling groups may have given outward obedience to colonial overlords who allowed them to retain their titles and some vestiges of their past powers, but often resented their loss of real power. Those who gained from the new opportunities generated by the colonial system—and there were many—chafed at the limits placed upon their continued advancement. Native embryonic capitalists could not easily compete on equal terms with European businesses backed by the facilities of the metropolitan country. Native officials of the governmental and business bureaucracies often felt themselves unfairly excluded from the high-level posts. The intellectuals, especially those who were trained at European universities, became bitter at the disparity between the expectations aroused by their education and the blocks that appeared in the way of maximizing this education. For all of these groups, the colonial system was or could be made to appear the cause of their grievance.

While the attraction exercised by the charismatic leader can, in part, be attributed to his ability to focus and channel diverse grievances and interests in a common appeal, unifying a segmented population in pursuit of a common goal, this explanation is insufficient to account for the acceptance of a given leader. Nor does it tell us how a leader maintains charisma in the conditions of uncertainty and fractionalization following the attainment of the goal of independence.

To turn to a deeper level, we suggest that the charisma of a leader is bound up with and, indeed, may even depend upon his becoming assimilated, in the thought and feelings of a populace, to its sacred figures, divine beings, or heroes. Their actions and the context of these actions, recounted in myth, express the fundamental values of a culture, including its basic categories for organizing experience and trying to resolve basic cultural and human dilemmas.

☼   ☼   ☼   ☼   ☼

We wish to suggest that recent events in a people's politics, particularly those marking a major transition or extraordinary occurrence in public life, can become endowed with the quality of myth if they fit or can be fitted into the pattern of a traditional myth or body of myths. Furthermore, insofar as myths can be regarded as charters for action, validating ritual and moral acts,[6] or, indeed, any culturally prescribed behavior, the assimilation of a historical event to the pattern of traditional myth or of a given individual to a mythic figure endows the event or individual with the aura or sanction of the myth itself.

[6] Bronislaw Malinowski, "Myth in Primitive Psychology," *Magic, Science and Religion* (Boston: Beacon Press, 1948), pp. 96–108.

The charismatic leader, we suggest, is able to communicate to his followers a sense of continuity between himself and his mission and their legendary heroes and their missions. Since "a myth remains the same as long as it is felt as such," [7] he and his claims are legitimated by his ability to draw on himself the mantle of myth. How a particular leader does this can be considered his strategy of "cultural management," [8] in part conscious and deliberate, in part probably unconscious and intuitive.

The particular strategies of individual charismatic leaders are a subject for empirical investigation.[9] Elements of such strategies might be broken down into such categories as: rhetoric employed in speeches, including rhythm; [10] use of simile and metaphor and allusions [10] to myth and history; use of gesture and movement; employment of ritual and ceremony; manner of dealing with felt doubt and opposition; and mode of handling crises. While this list can be refined and extended, it suggests some of the categories in terms of which the charismatic appeal of leaders can be analyzed.

It should be stressed that the elements of behavior indicated by such categories vary from culture to culture. This, of course, would be true of the behavior of any leader, charismatic or not, who seeks to mobilize popular support. Specific to the charismatic leader, according to our theory, is the role of myth in validating his authority. His appeal, therefore, can best be understood by reference to the body of myth in a given culture that his strategy taps and manipulates, and the actions and values associated with and sanctioned by these myths.[11] In brief, the charismatic leader is charismatic because, in the breakdown of other means of legitimizing authority, he is able to evoke and associate with himself the sacred symbols of his culture.

✧   ✧   ✧   ✧   ✧

[7] Claude Lévi-Strauss, "The Structural Study of Myth," *The Journal of American Folklore*, Vol. 68 (October–December 1955), p. 435.

[8] See Lloyd A. Fallers, "Ideology and Culture in Uganda Nationalism," *American Anthropology*, Vol. 63 (August 1961), pp. 677–678 and McKim Marriott, "Cultural Policy in New States," in *Old Society and New States* (New York, 1963), p. 29.

[9] We deliberately refrain from giving concrete examples of strategies here; for, as is suggested below, to make meaningful the illustration of even a single strategy of a single leader would require an elaboration of the myths and values of his culture which lack of space prohibits.

[10] For example, it might be worth examining the frequency of Biblical allusions in the speeches of FDR, such as the reference in his first inaugural address to driving the money-changers out of the temple, and the extent to which his rhetoric paralleled the cadences of the St. James Bible. Similarly, it would be interesting to compare the rhythmic patterns of the speeches of Nkrumah and other African leaders with the predominant drum and dance rhythms of their societies.

[11] See Malinowski, *op. cit.*

We do not, however, suggest or wish to imply that a charismatic leader either achieves power or retains it on the basis of charisma alone. Charismatic appeal provides the source of and legitimates his authority. Other supports may be needed and are frequently employed to gain and maintain power, especially when charismatic appeal begins to decline.[12]

CHARISMATIC LEADERSHIP AND THE DILEMMAS OF DEVELOPMENT

As we have earlier indicated, the mission of the charismatic leader in the societies with which we deal is twofold, incorporating two distinct, although somewhat overlapping,[13] stages. The first is the destruction of the old order; the second, which might be termed "political development," is the building of the promised new and better order.

Political development, whether considered as a goal or as a process, can be viewed in the context of new countries as encompassing two distinct goals or processes. One is that of achieving and maintaining an autonomous and viable state or political community that can be recognized as such by, and participate with, other states in the international political community. The second is that of gaining and maintaining central government capacity to manage technological modernization and cope with its socioeconomic concomitants.[14]

These goals or processes are not necessarily synonymous or complementary, as is often assumed. While they may be interrelated and interdependent in some respects, they can be antipathetic and incompatible in others. What appear to be rational policies pursued in support of one goal may only serve to inhibit or prevent the attainment of the other.

Many new countries cannot begin either form of development at the point where their predecessors left off. In the first place, they start with less internal cohesion than existed in the same territories under colonial

---

[12]   As David Apter points out in *Ghana in Transition* (New York: Atheneum, 1963), pp. 328–29, charisma can decline in favor of secular authority or, as he found in Ghana, as a result of conflict with traditional authority.
[13]   These stages may overlap in several ways. The formation of a political unit that can gain external recognition can take place while the struggle against the old order continues. For some leaders, such as those of Indonesia and the United Arab Republic, the old order is not extinct, despite political independence, as long as former rulers retain ownership or control of important segments of the new country's economy
[14]   We use technological modernization rather than a more inclusive concept of modernization, not only because technological advance is the core of other forms, but because there are universally accepted and non-ethnocentric criteria to define and measure technological change. This leaves open the types of social, economic, and cultural systems which are or can be compatible with the development of a modern technology.

control or during nationalist mobilization against it. The very tactics of nationalist mobilization confront the new governments with new sets of expectations and conditions, limiting the alternatives open to it.

As recent Asian and African history has demonstrated, the preindependence solidarity forged in the common struggle of diverse groups against their common ruler does not long survive the departure of that ruler. The vision of a single nation submerged under colonial control fades before the reality of competitive subsocieties, each of which tends to view independence as a mandate to reassert its traditional heritage and strengthen its claims against those of other groups.

No longer can the conflicting interests and ambitions of different ethnic groups and, cross-cutting these, the different economic segments of the population be merged in the single overriding goal of freedom. Now they are couched in the concrete terms of more land and lower taxes for peasants, higher wages for workers, subsidies for small businessmen, boosts in status and salary for bureaucrats, or whatever particular benefits people had sought or been led to expect as the immediate and inevitable fruits of successful anticolonialism.

Moreover, nationalist leaders were committed to representative government, whether through personal conviction or because explicit adherence to democracy in its Western institutional forms was the implicit condition of American support for their cause. Soon new parliaments, parties, unions, and associations provide new forums to articulate expectations and arouse new aspirations.[15] Rival contenders for ethnic, regional, and national roles of intermediate political leadership press upon the central government the rival claims of those they lead.

But the already hard-pressed new governments have less capacity to provide even the expected services than had their colonial counterparts. This is not merely a matter of limited financial resources or unanticipated needs to rehabilitate refugees and reconstruct installations destroyed by military action. The replacement of skilled administrators and technicians by less trained or unskilled ones, especially where nationalist zeal and political reliability are the major criteria of appointment,[16] means that preindependence norms of governmental performance are difficult to restore, much less improve upon to meet the new aspirations. In this respect, India perhaps suffered least and the Congo most.

[15]   In place of the conventional concept of *demand*, we prefer to distinguish between *expectation* and *aspiration* which are differently derived and have different potential for violence when frustrated. Expectations constitute claims made on the basis of prevailing norms whose satisfaction is felt as owed by right; aspirations are hopes of future gains not previously enjoyed which are seen as desirable but not necessarily due one. Whereas unrealized aspirations result in disappointment, frustrated expectations produce an often intolerable sense of deprivation.

[16]   The provision of government jobs to the disciples and their followers may be seen as booty distribution, noted by Weber as one of the means of support of charismatic leaders.

At almost any stage of planning policies and programs or implementing them, dilemmas multiply and internal conflict increases. Basic dilemmas over how to allocate scarce resources as between long-run investment goals and short-run consumption requirements and between projects stimulating industrial growth and those needed to maintain levels of employment [17] are further complicated by struggles over the distribution of the available pie.[18] Satisfaction of one set of claims, even in terms of national developmental goals rather than particularistic ones, produces, at minimum, accusations of favoritism leveled against the central government and counter-claims from those feeling themselves disadvantaged. At maximum, it produces large-scale violence and even overt insurrection.

The charismatic leader can conceivably use his appeal to integrate the state and to create strong central government institutions to modernize the society, that is, to further development in both senses of the term as defined earlier. But the extent to which he can focus simultaneously on both will depend on the particular conditions and resistances in his society.[19] In circumstances of acute subgroup competition, many national modernization goals weaken or tend to be shelved. Of necessity, the leader concentrates his charisma on holding together a potentially fragmenting country. Priority is given to maintaining and unifying the state or gaining some semblance of solidarity whatever the cost.

In a society fissioned by parochial identifications and particularistic goals, the charismatic leader may be the single symbol of unity surmounting the diversity and the primary means of creating consensus on objectives. To the many who need some tangible referent for a loyalty still somewhat beyond their comprehension, he is the visible embodiment of the nation come into being. And to those confused by the loosening of familiar ties and the profusion of new groups and activities claiming their attention, he provides the reassurance that links them with the old and sanctions the new.

✻   ✻   ✻   ✻   ✻

[17] For fuller treatment of this and preceding points, see B. F. Hoselitz and A. R. Willner, "Economic Development, Political Strategies, and American Aid," in M. A. Kaplan, *The Revolution in World Politics* (New York: John Wiley & Sons, 1963), pp. 357–71.

[18] Even the implementation of a universal goal, such as education, can provoke dissent and conflict. The advantages of a single language of instruction that will also serve as a unifying force has often been countered by demands for education in the local languages. The very groups who have requested vernacular schools, after gaining their objectives, may often exhibit resentment when their members do not easily have access to posts and occupations that demand fluency in the dominant national language.

[19] This has been far more possible in India, Israel, and the United Arab Republic than in Indonesia or Ghana.

The charismatic leader can be seen as a double-visaged Janus, projecting himself on the one hand as the omniscient repository of ancient wisdom and on the other as the new man of the people, not only leading them toward, but sharing with them, the trials of revolutionary renewal.[20] . . .

Of major significance in the creation of a national identity can be the use by the charismatic leader of the international stage. Part of the sense of self derives from the measurement of self against others and much of the feeling of strength comes from the awareness of one's impact on others. The presence and prominence of their leaders in distant capitals and exerting obvious influence on international conferences, spelled out to their peoples through all the media of mass communication, give the latter a sense of national identity and pride.

There is another way in which charismatic leaders tend to have an impact on the international stage which often annoys and outrages the leaders and peoples of more established countries. This is the constant raising of such issues as cryptocolonialism, "disguised" imperialism, and perceived foreign "interference." These may strike outside observers as unwarranted and dangerous shadow battles. But they, too, serve the function of maintaining internal cohesion. . . .

While charismatic leadership may contribute in many ways to the consolidation of the state, its exercise may also delay the kind of institutionalization and continuity of authority needed for concrete tasks of development. The charismatic leader may become trapped by his own symbols and substitute symbolic action as ends instead of means. Viewing himself as the indispensable prop of his country's existence and the only one in whose hands its destiny can be trusted, he may treat constructive criticism as treason. Those surrounding him may do little more than echo him and vie for his favor while awaiting his demise and hoping for the mantle to descend on themselves. Charismatic leadership does not provide for orderly succession. In its absence the crisis of succession may undo much that was built up and conserved.

[20] This double-projection is frequent in the speeches of Sukarno and can also be found in some of Nasser's statements.

Military governments today control about half the developing states. However, they do not constitute a closely knit group with common "military" features. Rather, like their civilian counterparts, they differ significantly in their structures, processes, and policies. The differences between Thailand and Burma that John Badgley discusses below are indicative of the variations military regimes in Latin America, Africa, and Asia display in their attempts to cope with the problems confronting their societies.

23. TWO STYLES OF MILITARY RULE: THAILAND AND BURMA *

j o h n   h.   b a d g l e y

The diverse policies of Burmese and Thai governments obscure the similarities between these two countries. To contrast their political styles highlights these similar features and also reveals a general political change that applies also to much of Asia. That trend is towards the politization of military leaders and their creation of political parties to sustain their power base. Civilian experts and civil organizations increasingly serve these military governments and thereby tend to bolster their legitimacy.

It is two decades since the European powers commenced their withdrawal from Southeast Asia. Considerable political experimentation followed as leaders of these states adjusted their freshly won sovereignty to fit their weakened condition. Democracy burst on the region like a river in spate. Without exception every central government employed elections to legitimize itself. Then (but for the Philippines, Malaysia and Singapore) military juntas moved to seize power from impotent legislatures. Liberals saw military totalitarianism sweeping Asia, conservatives viewed the nationalization practices as statism that crushed private initiative.

Although the problems of administration are real enough, this type of judgement is not realistic for it obscures more fundamental problems. Such evaluation is founded on a procrustean Western bed of assumptions

* From "Two Styles of Military Rule: Thailand and Burma" by John H. Badgley, *Government and Opposition*, Vol. IV, No. 1 (Winter, 1969), pp. 100–113. Excerpted by permission of the author and the publisher.

about politics. The form and style of politics familiar to most political scientists *assumes* a locus of political authority congruent with the state. Political institutions *are assumed* to be linked to the state. Political leaders *are expected* to represent policies relevant to the state. But where the state is a new political form, as in South East Asia, time must pass before its meaning, purpose and relationship to the people becomes clear. Now time has passed and some things are clear, at any rate clearer than in 1948 when Burma and Thailand were both struggling to launch democratic political processes. This article will comment on one aspect of their political processes, the manner of conducting politics in both states; in so doing the overwhelming importance of time and place again emerges as determinant of style and form.

POLITICAL STYLE

The shared characteristics of Burma and Thailand are apparent but often forgotten. Most commentators see Thailand clinging to its American ally and adopting American ways, while Burma seems to be floating along on an isolationist sea. In fact both states are predominantly peasant societies of cultivators who farm their own small holdings on the riverine plains. The culture of both peoples is derived from the Mon-Khmer; their Theravada Buddhism, music, art forms, written scripts, normative traditions and even dress and eating habits originally came from ancient India while the Thai and Burmans, as well as their hill people, are migrants from central and western China. The ecology of both lowland peoples is almost identical, with a monsoon climate and alluvial soil offering a comfortable subsistence life for villagers. Their civilizations have matured along parallel paths despite the hostility that marked their relationship in pre-colonial times.

The British occupation of Burma severed that relationship. From 1885 to 1942 the Burmese experienced a completely different rule from the Thai, who retained their monarchy. English ways, and Indian Civil Service administration, penetrated rural Burma, particularly among minorities, so deeply that U Nu and the first generation of post-independence nationalist leaders governed as though their country really shared the nation-state democratic heritage of the United Kingdom. Gradually the nativistic culture of peasant society seeped up, primarily through the military, and in 1962 a group of officers seized power who shared with many rural leaders a compulsion to exorcise colonial influences and return to "pure Burmeseness." The purity so many Burmese evoked in fact meant that Burman communal values would dominate the political process and sweep foreigners and minority leaders from influence. Not only Indians and Chinese, but Eurasians, Shans, Kachins and Karens lost high positions as the Burmanization process ran its course in the 1960s.

While colonialization and decolonialization account for much of what has happened in Burmese public life over the past century, Thai leaders have cautiously proceeded towards modernization. Without a colonial presence to eschew, the Thai in straightforward fashion have developed a unique political style reflecting their culture. Politics is administered in the same fashion as economics, religion and education. The political structure has changed slowly. The current monarchial dynasty, the Chakri, gained power late in the 18th century and, despite one assassination, the king has retained authority as head of state. Since Sukothai days, in the 14th century, the aristocracy has provided both military and civilian leaders to administer the kingdom. After the 1932 coup both aristocracy and crown played diminished but still significant roles while the civil service and military—which began modernizing late in the 19th century—have produced most cabinet ministers and premiers. Since 1932 eight constitutions have been promulgated, the most recent on 20 June 1968, while political powers rests within an oligarchy that has nicely merged the military with the Chinese entrepreneur elite and the civilian administrators through the great business boards that manage Thai economic life.

In Thailand today political style is shaped by a power relationship which evolved in the 1940s and 1950s under Premier (General) Pibun Songgram, then Premier (General) Sarit Thanarat, and now continues with the leading position shared by Premier (General) Thanom Kittikachorn and Interior Minister (General) Praphas Charusatien. That relationship is based on a patronage system. Under this system Thailand has enjoyed rapid economic development, over 5 per cent annually in the past decade. Forty years ago Burma and Thailand had the same national income, twenty years ago they had the same size population; today Thailand's national product is nearly triple that of Burma ($4.6 billion to $1.7 billion), the rate of growth is over three times greater, and the population is six million larger. Bangkok, the same size as Rangoon before the second world war, is now three times larger and consumes electric power, petrol, taxes and manufactured imports at a far higher rate than Rangoon. Forty thousand American troops stationed in Thailand accentuate the rapid pace of westernization. Economic growth is rooted not only in tourism but in diversified crops, intensified rice production, mining, new manufacturing, dams, building and road construction. Human resources are also increasing rapidly. Thailand has 32 teacher training colleges, eight universities and nearly three million children in school. This substantial infra-structure has progressed enough to sustain the power base of the oligarchy; at the same time it has produced a liberal opposition sufficiently vocal and strong to force an occasional return to constitutional government.

But what is called patronage in the West is labelled as corruption in Thailand, perhaps because it is so blatant. Premiers Pibun and Sarit, as well as the current Minister of the Interior made personal fortunes while in office, although a large portion of Sarit's holdings were seized by the government after his death. Several hundred ranking military and police officers have done very well financially as board members of the major Thai businesses which are mainly capitalized by resident Chinese.[1] Perhaps a dozen are members of three or more boards, while all key generals and cabinet ministers are executives of at least one major business. The custom seems to be essential to provide enough emoluments for high officials to meet the expenses of their office, for their salaries are very low; yet the custom is so institutionalized that the opposition, be it liberal or communist, is inclined to view the entire governing establishment as corrupt.

These inequities are frequently noted in the press, and educated Thai generally feel free to discuss them. Yet the question is often raised as to corruption's political significance. Some argue that it saps the loyalty of civil servants and police. The status of the police in the provinces is accordingly low because many believe they demand extortion for protection. In the poorer regions of the country ·the government traditionally offered no services, thus the image that is popularized is one of a political leadership that earns profits rather than working for better education and welfare.

Since 1963 two major government programmes have operated among the ten million north-east Thai, primarily in six provinces on or near the Laotian border, with a view to earning rural loyalty through good works. The civilian Accelerated Rural Development Programme and the army's Mobile Development Units (with about $50 million in American aid annually) have opened much of the area through a huge road construction programme. Initially it was administered with little thought to political mobilization of the villagers. Then, as the communist Thai Patriotic Front accelerated its campaign of cadre training and terror, the government responded with intensive propaganda, via USIS, visiting teams of Thai medical and agricultural technicians, greater credit for agro-business, and the commitment of several brigades of troops for counter-insurgency operations. Within the past year similar programmes have opened in the northern provinces and along the Malay border to counter heightened insurgency there. However there remains the most serious problem the government faces, the conventional assumption that it is corrupt and uninterested in the public welfare, except when faced with insurrection.

In Burma, since the Revolutionary Council seized power in 1962,

[1] F. W. Riggs, *Thailand; the Modernization of a Bureaucratic Polity*, Honolulu, East-West Center Press, 1966.

the style of politics has been quite unlike Thailand's, although the military have also controlled the political process and the economy. There are no rich men in Burma. The entire economy has been nationalized. Military officers and civilians who attempt to enrich themselves breach the trust of the Revolutionary Council and are peremptorily fired or jailed.

Ostensibly the harsh policy was aimed at "economic insurgents" or those who attempted to compromise the socialist philosophy of government. Actually, Chinese and Indian merchants bore the burden of the nationalization process that dispossessed entrepreneurs and turned most business over to twenty-two State Corporations. In extracting Rangoon's wealth from its merchants, the socialist colonels have nearly turned it into a country town—Rangoon has few neon lights, automobiles, practically no tourists and a vast number of night bazaar peddlers. The several hundred military officers who assumed responsibility for the economy had no experience in business or banking and within a few years the distribution of goods and the operation of public services had so declined that a black market sector sprang up, "State Corporation 23." Rice exports declined annually and foreign exchange reserves dropped steadily after 1965.

Failures in economic policy have affected the political process but have yet to modify the style of rule. The press carries some complaints and insurgent activity has increased over the past three years. Minorities and the underground communist parties have gained arms and new members from the disaffected and the Chinese communists: particularly since the spring of 1967 when Red Guard militancy first affected the Burmese communists. But the political style of Burma's only official party, the Burma Socialist Programme Party, *Lanzin,* is unchanged as the radical socialists press their ideology upon the bureaucracy and educators. At the outset, opposition—whether from politicians, monks, technicians, officers, journalists or educators—was not brooked, and thousands were imprisoned. Gradually most political prisoners were freed, but the Lanzin remains the only legitimate party. Its Political Science Academy continues to operate as the re-education centre for the civil service, military and teachers as well as the fountainhead of official ideology.

The state is as authoritarian as if it were under a harsh colonial regime. There is slight tolerance for divergent political opinion and independent minds are imprisoned, literally as well as figuratively, by secret police widely believed to have penetrated every organization. The closed society is imposed upon the Burmese by a minority of the military leadership dedicated to a rapid revolution, who find precedents for this style of rule in Burma among historic military leaders and kings.

The current policies can be partially explained by a long repressed rage at colonial occupation and a compulsion to excoriate those groups and institutions favoured by colonialism. Another motive is the threat, since independence, of communal fragmentation and the disintegration of the state. The possibility that cold war tensions would exacerbate relations between the minorities and the Burmans was omnipresent in the minds of top leaders. The only issue Burma took to the United Nations was that of Nationalist Chinese aid to local KMT and Shan insurgent forces in Kengtung. Thai and Formosan aid has continued to flow to Shan and KMT insurgents, and expatriate Karen, Burman and Kachin leaders operate out of Thailand. Since July 1967 the People's Republic of China has promised aid to the Kachin Independence Army, the Karen National Unity Party as well as the White Flag Communist Party of Burma. So there is justification for the government's fear that their state might be crushed by foreign intervention if severe restrictions are not imposed.

One must look more deeply into Burmese history than this, however, to find an even more compelling reason for contemporary policies. The Burmans were never an outward-looking trading people. Their path to the Bay of Bengal and the Indian Ocean was blocked by the Mons and Arakanese. Their kingdoms were in the dry zone of Burma, not the delta, and they always depended upon foreigners for their sea trade. Burmese did and do travel overland, to Laos, Yunnan, Manipur, Assam and Siam for trade, and their armies went along the same routes. But the Burmans remained landlocked while the Thai founded their greatest kingdoms in the lower reaches of the Chao Praya and later sent ships up the China coast and fished the Gulf of Siam. Out of Burma's isolation evolved a set of attitudes towards foreigners, and a view of the world that persisted among villagers through the British occupation. A people does not forego a thousand year heritage in a few decades. Probably more that any other reason it is that heritage that keeps Burma inward looking and suspicious of foreign involvements.

POLITICAL FORMS

This comment on the similarities and differences in the political styles of Burmese and Thai provides the substance for an analysis of their political forms. Political institutions do not operate as a system isolated from culture, economy, geography. Two recent studies of Burmese village behaviour testify to the influence of folk culture and ecology upon all institutions below the town level,[2] while another an-

[2] Manning Nash, *The Golden Road to Modernity; Village Life in Contemporary Burma,* New York, Wiley, 1965; and Melford Spiro, *Burmese Supernaturalism; a Study in the Explanation and Reduction of Suffering,* New York, 1967.

alysis of Buddhist influence upon centrist politics helps to explain Burma's unique "revolutionary" policies.[3] My own study of town and district politics reinforces the general conclusion pressed upon the student of Burmese politics by these analyses, namely that the western democratic political institutions left in Burma by the British were irrelevant to most Burmese outside Rangoon.[4] Much of post-war politics can be explained by the tension between those who viewed the state with an essentially western eye, and those who found the authority of the state to be alien and who are bent upon grafting indigenous values and institutions on to the state to make it more familiar. U Nu, for example, felt compelled to make Buddhism into a state religion, and to adopt the Buddhist calendar as the official reckoning for the year and for festivals. Lunar festivals and holidays, plus a five or six day week (depending on the moon's position) became official, giving Burma more state holidays than any country in the world. More recently, Ne Win attempted to fuse the traditional folk festival—the *pwe*—into a state political institution, the peasant seminar: giant assemblies of headmen are called together to hear the top leaders and view "national" entertainment.

These examples illustrate the efforts to combine the modern function of state-building with traditional institutions. The blend seems incongruous if one is uninitiated into Burmese ways; yet they are all efforts aimed at penetrating the peasant communities so that communal identity might be replaced by a national identity. In fact, the reverse process seems to have happened; communalism is as rampant as in the first years of independence when Karen, Burman and Shan insurgents went underground. Communal parties were outlawed in 1962 and the Lanzin (Socialist Programme Party) has attempted to recruit political activists from minority areas. The goal appears to be engagement is secular rather than sectarian politics, for many of the minorities are Christian, Muslim, or belong to other Buddhist sects than the two major sects (*Thuddhamma* and *Shwekyin*) that dominate religious life among Burmans.

The Lanzin party has drawn its most active leadership from former "Red Socialist" politicians who formed the Burma Workers and People's Party early in the 1950s. Rural members from the old People's Volunteer Organization, the People's Progressive Party, and a range of tiny parties that blossomed late in the 1950s have helped to swell "candidate" membership (the main category of party membership) to something over 180,000. The former dominant party, the Anti-Fascist People's Freedom League was dissolved when its major leaders U Kyaw Nyein and U Ba Swe were imprisoned in 1963, and U Nu's following collapsed with his

---

[3] M. Sarkisyanz, *Buddhist Backgrounds of the Burmese Revolution.* The Hague, 1965.
[4] J. H. Badgley, *Burman Politics,* forthcoming, 1969.

confinement. The core cadre of the Lanzin, however, is drawn from the military, for every district party committee has a military member detached from regular duty. The Secretary-General of the Party, Brigadier San Yu, is also Chief of Stáff and Defence Minister. Other colonels determine the curriculum in the Political Science Academy and play a dominant role in the conduct of party affairs. Such old Marxist stalwarts as U Ba Nyein and Thein Pe Myint have played leading roles in formulating economic and education policy. But they are clearly responsible to the key military leaders within the Revolutionary Council, a dozen colonels and brigadiers who guide policy in the great corporations.

The structure of party and government closely overlaps at the centre, in the district and town, and even at the village level. The critical organization through which the political and governing functions fuse is the Security and Administrative Council. The pyramid of power follows the old British pattern of administrative councils beginning at the township level, to include the important headmen, and to be responsible for the security and administration of their territory and people. The municipal, district, division and central authorities operate in a chain of command that theoretically provides an efficient mechanism for decision-making. Actually the Burmese peasant seems to feel little more identification with the SAC groups than with the colonial councils, and probably for the reason, that they both represent the state which is an alien and bothersome institution to village communities accustomed to being self-sufficient and belligerent towards officialdom. The central motive is very reasonable, no government in Burma has offered more advantages than disadvantages to the peasant. The demands—from the villagers' vantage-point—have been greater than the rewards, whether under the monarchy, colonial administration or sovereign statehood.

In Thailand the political structure also closely parallels the administrative structure. The lowest-level civil servant operates in the municipality and *amphur*, which is comparable to the Burmese municipality and township (except for the more restricted definition of municipality in Burma). Beneath the amphur are some 4,475 commune (*tambon*) councils which include key headmen who receive a small stipend for minor administrative tasks, but most villages have no resident officials. Nor is there normally any resident politician within villages. As the amphur office is located in small towns, so the locus of power for the amphur also tends to be situated there. Traders, school teachers, important monks, police and technical personnel constitute this group, apart from the village community itself. Above the amphur is the province (*Changwad*) headquarters, the next highest level of authority. Thailand has 71 such bodies; and it is in the provincial governor's office that the greatest rural influence rests.[5] Though in past elections political

5 Riggs, *op. cit.*

parties have operated in municipalities and at the province level, and they are being reorganized to contest national elections in 1969, the governor (a career civil servant) is normally the most powerful person in the province. He is responsible for all government activities, including the police, courts, taxation, sanitation, road and school operation, and communications. This office (like that of ambassador in the foreign service) is a career within the Ministry of Interior and illustrates the centralized nature of the power structure in Thailand. Rarely does an elected provincial leader have the power to compete with the governor, who controls a substantial budget; only the wealthier town physicians or businessmen can usually aspire to influence close to that of the governor.

The new Thai constitution stipulates elections early in 1969 for the lower house, while the upper legislative body is entirely appointed. The Government Party was formed this year from the highest levels of the bureaucracy including Thanat Khoman, the Foreign Minister, Serm Vinicchayakul, Finance Minister, and five key generals including police General Prasert Ruchuavongse as Secretary General of the Party. The Democratic Party (*Prachatipat*) will constitute the major opposition and has a nucleus of leaders drawn from the old Khuang Aphaiwongse faction that governed in the late 1940s and early 1950s. Seni Pramoj and Yai Switchata, both important politicians from those days, assumed the mantle of Khuang's leadership following his death. Lesser parties, which may win a few seats, include the Independent Party (*Prachachon*) led by Liang Chaiyakarn, an independent north-easterner and leader of the moderately leftist People's Party which was disbanded in 1957; the Socialist Front (*Setthakon*) led by Nai Thep Chotinuchit, a more radical socialist; and a Young Men's Party led by Dr Phaithun Khruakaew with support from politically active faculty members at Chulalongkorn, Thammasat, and Khesetsart Universities.[6] Smaller factional parties have sprung up, even including a Moscow-oriented Communist Party led by Prasert Sabsunthorn. Of course the strongest leftist organization, the Thai Patriotic Front, is underground, conducting guerrilla warfare in the north-east and along the Malayan border. Louis Lomax in his book *Thailand: The War That Is, the War That Will Be,* makes much of two young Mao-oriented Communists, Rassamee and Yod Pathisawata, who lead the insurrection in Nakornpanom province, but the chance of their arousing the countryside against Bangkok is slender indeed, particularly since 1966 when the government finally took seriously the problem of political mobilization. The constitution is an additional response to that threat and although elected government will probably not change the style of rule, it reflects a cumulative response to demands for liberal changes.

One aspect of governance that is remarkably similar in Burma and

---

[6] Bangkok *Post,* June and July issues daily carried information about the new parties.

Thailand is the integrity of the higher courts. In both countries there is considerable suppression of civil rights outside the courts, but once a case is entered the law usually prevails. Both Chief Justices, Dr Maung Maung in Burma, and Sunya Thammasat in Thailand, are insulated from political or economic pressures and their integrity and capacity for independent adjudication is widely recognized. Both are active Buddhist laymen and are considered to be among their respective countries' most prominent intellectuals. The legal profession is important in both countries and it provided most politicians before the military regimes began to rule by decree. Legal codes accumulated through the years continue to function both for political cases, and "economic crimes" in Burma which are tried by new People's Courts, but even these cases are ultimately reviewed by the high court and most have been dismissed.

CIVIL-MILITARY RELATIONS

Comparison of the relations between the military and civilians in selected functional sectors reveals the fashion in which political authority is exercised under two markedly different ideologies within similar *milieux*. These sectors, for the purposes of this discussion, include agriculture, the armed forces, the civil service, business, education and religion. In both states cultivators usually own some land although it is not uncommon also to share crop with absentee owners. The life style of most Thai and Burmese is closely identified with the cycle of planting and harvest, therefore government leaders can induce change only with great difficulty for it means disturbing the entire culture. Agricultural officials in both countries have been cautious in pressing for modernization, and depend largely on model farms, land clearing operations, and co-operative credit programmes to induce change. In recent years the military in both countries have entered into agricultural development with a lust for immediate change. A number of top-ranking officers in Thailand (most notably Marshal Sarit) with prior knowledge of new roads, purchased large parallel tracts of land and invested heavily in development of new commercial crops, particularly maize and tapioca. Others, through their links with the business boards, liberalized imports of farm equipment and (with local Chinese merchants) credit for tractor rentals and mechanized farming on several million acres. Much of this modern farming is practised on freshly cleared land and attracts the more mobile and enterprising younger farmers. The social as well as economic impact of the military leaders, as private investors in agriculture has been considerable.

In Burma, the military under Ne Win have also been very active in formulating agriculture policy. Experiments with new loan programmes, seed standardization, tractor use, chemical fertilization and resettlement have been tried and have largely failed, assuming success to be measured by increased production and export. Soldiers and officers serving in the districts aid in the harvest and planting; but the distance between military and villagers appears not to be bridged by such practices.[7] Two of the greatest problems in Burmese rice production, milling and storage, have not been met because of the nationalization programme. This dispossessed the larger mill owners, usually Chinese, and left their operation under the control of inexperienced officers. Many mills have broken down, or operate poorly because of worn parts that cannot be replaced because of the restriction on imports. The military has improved storage facilities but without better milling the grain in the husk rots in a year.

This superficial comparison of agricultural policy and military involvement illustrates the pragmatic practice in Thailand and the dogmatic quality of military-civil relations in Burma. Radical socialist thought combined with anti-Chinese and Indian sentiment dominate the policy making process in Burma and have prevented the government from capitalizing on the talent of the private sector. In Thailand, the military leadership married themselves into the Chinese economic system and profited personally and nationally in the process. The corruption that followed has been a source of political instability but it seems thus far to be contained within limits acceptable to the public. Meanwhile, economic progress, particularly in the agriculture sector, has been remarkable.

The business communities in the two countries have experienced a very different relationship with the military, although in both cases the corporate structure has been brought under military influence. The Burmese military, by viewing entrepreneurship as a tool of colonialism and capitalism, brought the business community to heel; the top Thai military, by joining in the business process, profited enormously in the early years and laid the base for close co-operation between the three million Chinese, who dominate Thai commercial and manufacturing life, and the military who are drawn entirely from the Thai community.

The civil service and military in both countries have experienced tensions as defence budgets have risen and civil programmes have been curtailed. But in Burma the relationship has been most strained due to the hostility nationalist leaders felt towards the bureaucrats who were reared in the British tradition. When he seized the premiership in 1962, Ne Win called in the entire senior level of civil servants and berated them for unpatriotic sentiments and "bureaucratic" habits. The army

[7] The *Guardian*. The government-owned newspaper reprints letters to the editor which reveal critical views not expressed in articles or editorials. Issues from May to August 1967 devoted considerable coverage to the rice crisis and the peasant-government relations.

officers who took over the higher positions soon learned the difficulties experienced by bureaucrats in attempting to carry out new policies. There has followed a gradual rapprochement between the civil and military administrators. The Thai bureaucrats, because of their uninterrupted service, and an aristocratic attitude, held in common with the military, have not suffered as severe a communications gap. The relationship is symbolized by the uniform that Thai civil officials wear and the hierarchical structure of each government agency: it has a military cast. Most of the Thai educated elite encourage at least one son to enter the military while others enter the civil service and private business. This interlocking family structure enhances communication and reinforces the elite structure of the government, be it civil or military.

The military role in education has been much greater in Burma since the 1962 coup. The universities were reorganized as institutes, and officers assumed trusteeship responsibilities. Colonel Ha Han became Minister of Education, and exercised great influence on the nationalization of private education and the Burmanization of education among the minorities. The mission schools, over a four year period, were absorbed by the state and a common pattern of primary, secondary and vocational education now prevails. Five new colleges were opened—tending to decentralize higher education in the districts—but the status of Rangoon University remains superior to the outlying institutions. The military academy has prospered, some contend that it now offers the best higher education in Burma. Conversely, the quality of higher education (particularly in the social sciences and humanities) has declined, reflecting its low esteem within the Revolutionary Council as compared to their strong commitment to technical and natural science education. Dr Nyi Nyi, a geologist with socialist views, was appointed Secretary of the Ministry of Education and vigorously pursued the programme of the military.

In Thailand, the Ministry of Education is also very strong, as it directly employs all the teachers. However, in 1965 General Praphas transferred responsibility for teacher appointments to the Ministry of the Interior, allegedly fearing that they might become too liberal. The resentment that followed this move has not died, despite the fact that real control remains in the Ministry of Education. Praphas is also Rector of Thailand's most prestigious university, Chulalongkorn, but shows little interest in normal university affairs. There is considerable freedom of speech by students and faculty and some very liberal professors lecture in the military and police academies. Private education is very important in Thailand: as it still is in Burma through a kind of black market teacher tutorial system. A few Bangkok private schools funnel most of the elite into the universities, a role the mission schools once played in Burma.

Religious affairs, and the Buddhist clergy, have represented major obstacles to the secularized generals and colonels in both countries who would like to see their respective states progress. The general conservative nature of religion is particularly manifest in Burma, where monks have worked actively against the Ne Win regime, and where villagers retain their belief in occult practices. Rationalization of state-building processes are anathema to peasants with primary links within their local community. In Thailand the problem is less apparent for the clergy is better educated. There are two Buddhist universities, and the religious system had an uninterrupted century of modernization under the Chakri monarchs. Under the British there was a withering away of the supreme authority (*thathanabaing*) of the Burmese *sangha,* thus impairing its capacity to internalize new ideas. By contrast, the Thai monarchy played a crucial role in cleansing the order of occult and animistic practices. Uneducated village monks still retain many of the old beliefs, as do villagers; but compared to Burma, the system is more receptive to change. The military has simply ignored the religious issue in Thailand, apart from observance of festivals and ritual by commanders.

In these vital sectors of the society then—agriculture, business, civil service, education and religion—the relations between civilians and the military in both countries is a function of their ideology. Whereas the Thai generals value free enterprise and a vital private sector in which they can participate, the Burmese colonels value public control and personal direction of institutions that affect the public welfare. Yet both regimes are alike in depending upon military force to retain power; force that has been called into play within the past decade in both states.

Do military governments stimulate or inhibit social and economic development? This question, to which Eric Nordlinger addresses himself in the selection below, is of obvious interest both because of the number of military governments in the developing states and because of the apparent strengths of the military forces to accomplish the goals of their highest officers, given the disciplined troops and other resources they command. The forcefulness with which military officers justify their coups in terms of eliminating the chaos, inefficiency, and corruption of their civilian predecessors, and the need to get on with the modernization of society all suggest that the military is a progressive force. But such statements, of course, must be weighed against the evidence of military regimes in action, and this is what Nordlinger attempts to do.

24. SOLDIERS IN MUFTI:
THE IMPACT OF MILITARY RULE
UPON ECONOMIC AND SOCIAL CHANGE
IN THE NON-WESTERN STATES * †

e r i c a. n o r d l i n g e r

When military officers are either sitting in the governmental saddle or have one foot securely in the stirrup, is it likely that such military controlled governments will pursue policies of socio-economic change and reform? What are the officer-politicians' motivations in reacting to the possibilities of such modernizing changes? Under what conditions are their motivations likely to vary? This essay attempts to answer these questions with regard to the contemporary non-western states. . . .

* * * * *

I. THE STATE OF THE LITERATURE

A number of respected political scientists have already offered a substantial answer to our central question. According to this perhaps prevailing interpretation, the likely consequences of military rule are economic growth, the modernization of economic and social structures, and a more equitable distribution of scarce economic values and opportunities. As sponsors of these types of change, soldiers in mufti are depicted as progressive forces, whose politicization is to be commended if not recommended, rather than being condemned as an usurpation of civilian authority. A number of factors are said to have shaped the officers'

* Excerpts from "Soldiers in Mufti: The Impact of Military Rule Upon Economic and Social Change in the Non-Western States" by Eric A. Nordlinger, *The American Political Science Review*, Vol. LXIV, No. 4 (December, 1970), pp. 1131–1138. By permission of the publisher and the author.

† The research and writing of this article was generously supported by the Center for International Affairs, Harvard University, and the National Science Foundation (grant number 01-GS-2098). For their much appreciated suggestions and criticisms I am indebted to Amos Perlmutter, Gary Orran, John D. Powell, Donald Hindley, George A. Kelly, and James F. Guyot.

progressive motivations in carrying out the *coup* and in governing the country in the post-*coup* period.

Lucian Pye has suggested that the continuing modernization of the military's organization and weaponry has instilled in the officers the belief that their society ought also to be modernized. "Above all else the revolution in military technology has caused the army leaders of the newly emergent countries to be extremely sensitive to the extent to which their countries are economically and technologically underdeveloped. Called upon to perform roles basic to advanced societies, the more politically conscious officers can hardly avoid being aware of the need for substantial changes in their own societies." [1] Similarly, with respect to the Middle East and North Africa, Manfred Halpern has written: "the more the army was modernized, the more its composition, organization, spirit, capabilities, and purpose constituted a radical criticism of the existing political system." [2] With reference to Latin America, John J. Johnson has pointed to a related consequence of military modernization: the officers' technical-managerial orientation is said to have made it easier for them to accept the shift in political power from the land-holding elite to the new "urban alliances." [3]

The officers' social backgrounds are also thought to be relevant. Edward A. Shils has noted that in non-western societies officers tend to be recruited from lower middle class families of traders, craftsmen and small farmers, and that these men are painfully aware of the distance separating them from the wealthy and powerful. When these officers do achieve political influence they are not sympathetic to big businessmen and conservative politicians, and thus by implication, they are favorably disposed toward the redistribution of wealth.[4] With respect to Latin America, Johnson has claimed that the increasing recruitment of officers with lower middle class and working class backgrounds means that "the armed forces may be expected to be more inclined than formerly to gravitate toward positions identified with popular aspirations and to work with the representatives of the popular elements." Furthermore, as officer recruitment penetrates to lower social strata, "the industrial-commercial bourgeoisie in Latin America will be surrendering control of the

---

[1] Lucian W. Pye, "Armies in the Process of Political Modernization," in John J. Johnson (ed.), *The Role of the Military in Underdeveloped Countries* (Princeton, 1962), p. 78; also see pp. 80–82.

[2] Manfred Halpern, *The Politics of Social Change in the Middle East and North Africa* (Princeton, 1963), p. 258. Similarly, see Morroc Berger, *The Arab World Today* (New York, 1962), pp. 389–390, and P. J. Vatikiotis, *The Egyptian Army in Politics* (Bloomington, 1961), esp. pp. 211, 233.

[3] John J. Johnson, *The Military and Society in Latin America* (Stanford, 1964), p. 237.

[4] Edward A. Shils, "The Military in the Political Development of the New States," in Johnson (ed.), *op. cit.*, p. 17. But cf. p. 31 for the soldiers' distrust of anti-traditional modernizers.

armed forces, which are maintained by their taxes, to groups more radical than themselves." [5]

In referring to the officer corps of Southeast Asia, Guy Pauker states that they "are not the product of social classes with feudal traditions." Rather, their participation in the struggles for national independence and modernization, has produced an officer corps that is unlikely to become "the natural allies of feudal or other vested interests. Their natural propensities are progressive." [6] Then there is Halpern's contention that in the Middle East and North Africa, the officers showed "an acute awareness of the chronic ills of their countries," having joined the military in order to escape from the economic frustrations of civilian life compounded by the established elites' failure to encourage economic growth.[7]

This last comment of Halpern's is only one part of his powerfully stated argument in which officer-politicians act as effective agents of socio-economic change because of their close connection with "the new middle class." The defining feature of this new middle class is its salaried position, in contrast with the propertied and land-owning middle class. It is made up of teachers, administrators, scientists, lawyers, engineers, white collar workers and military officers. This class is said to be committed to the refashioning of society; it is only through social reforms that careers will be opened and secured for people like themselves who constitute a meritocracy rather than an established class. The new middle class is sufficiently self-conscious and powerful to "undertake the remolding of society," in large part because it has enlisted the military in this effort. "The army has become the instrument of the new middle class." And in adhering to this alliance the army has been transformed "from an instrument of repression in its own interests or that of kings into the vanguard of nationalism and social reform." [8]

Since this essay is an attempt to establish the plausibility of an alternative interpretation of the consequences of military rule I should like to make two points quite clear at the outset. First, I am not going to take up the question of whether the particular reasons these writers offered for their conclusion that the military in politics are agents of economic change are valid or invalid. In passing, I would say that they

[5] Johnson, op. cit., pp. 152, 250. Also see Lyle N. McAlister, "The Military," in John J. Johnson (ed.), Continuity and Change in Latin America (Stanford, 1964), pp 145–160.

[6] Guy J. Pauker, "Southeast Asia as a Problem Area in the Next Decade," World Politics, 11 (April 1959), pp. 339–340.

[7] Manfred Halpern, "Middle Eastern Armies and the New Middle Class," in Johnson (ed.), The Role of the Military . . . , p. 295.

[8] Manfred Halpern, Social Change . . . , pp. 52–54, 253, 258 and passim. See the criticisms levelled at Halpern's thesis in Amos Perlmutter, "Egypt and the Myth of the New Middle Class: A Comparative Analysis," Comparative Studies in Society and History, 10 (October 1967). The ensuing debate between Perlmutter and Halpern is found in ibid., 11 (January 1969) and 12 (January 1970).

have presented remarkably little evidence for their arguments, while failing to analyze—as opposed to simply stating—the supposed connections between the officers' technical orientations and social backgrounds and their hypothesized modernizing activities and motivations.[9] Even if they are correct in thinking that the officers' technical orientations and anti-conservative social backgrounds do predispose them to carry out programs of economic and social change, other factors have been ignored which have a sufficiently powerful effect upon the officers' motivations to overshadow their possible modernizing predispositions.[10] And where the military do sponsor certain types of economic change they do so for reasons which are quite different from those that have been suggested. Secondly, a number of political scientists, among them Shils, Pye, and Halpern, believe that a country's military establishment is likely to have important modernizing impacts over and above those already alluded to. Hans Daalder presents the following list of such consequences: military considerations have dictated the building of roads, communications networks and heavy industries, which have "benefited social and economic life generally;" the skills learned within the military may be applied to civilian pursuits after the officers and men leave the service; and the rational basis of military organization has a spillover effect upon organizational patterns throughout the society.[11] My reaction to this list of happy

[9] Although he is only referring to Latin America, Schmitter's comments are even more applicable to those continents in which military intervention is not quite the hallmark it has become in Latin America. Studies of military intervention in Latin America have "surprisingly . . . focused exclusively on (its) *causes* . . . and have neglected almost entirely (its) *consequences*. They leave us with the generals (or colonels as the case may be) battering down the gates to the presidential palace . . . and tell us very little about what these triumphant groups do with their newly acquired power." The officer-politicians become the "objects rather than the subjects of analysis." The literature abounds with speculations and scattered observations regarding the consequences of military intervention, but they "are rarely accompanied by evidence." Relying upon cross-national and longitudinal aggregate data, Schmitter systematically analyzes the impact of Latin America's officer-politicians upon governmental outputs and economic outcomes, although he does not attempt to explain the officers' political behavior. For the most part his findings dovetail with the aggregate analysis reported below. Philippe C. Schmitter, "Military Intervention, Political Competitiveness and Public Policy in Latin America: 1950–1967," mimeographed, 1970, Center for International Affairs, Harvard University, pp. 1, 7.
[10] Morris Janowitz also suggests that the officers' technical education and their opposition to religiously defined traditions *inclines* them to act as modernizers. However, he does not argue that these predispositions are sufficiently pervasive and powerful to overcome other factors, which would allow him to say that soldiers in mufti generally act as modernizers. See *The Military in the Political Development of New Nations* (Chicago, 1964), pp. 28, 44, 67.
[11] Hans Daalder, *The Role of the Military in the Emerging Countries* (The Hague, 1962), pp. 18–20. For similar claims, including socialization into national as opposed to parochial attitudes, see Janowitz, *op. cit.*, pp. 81–82; M. J. V. Bell, "The Military in the New States of Africa," in Jacques Van Doorn (ed.), *Armed Forces and Society* (The Hague, 1968), pp. 263–264; Lyle N. McAlister, *op. cit.*, pp. 136–144; Johnson, *op. cit.*, p. 258.

outcomes is simply this: the military may or may not be making these contributions, but whether they do or do not is almost completely unrelated to their acquisition of *political* power. The validity of Daalder's generalizations is at best marginally affected by the presence or absence of military officers in decision-making circles. Which is to say that these generalizations are beyond this essay's confines.

Returning to the questions with which I began this paper, my answers to them can now be set out. At the level of descriptive generalization, when military officers occupy the highest seats of government, or when they have a good measure of control over the civilian incumbents, the officer-politicians are commonly unconcerned with the realization of economic change and reform, and where there are civilian organizations and strata pressing for such changes the officers purposefully oppose them. This statement must, however, be immediately modified by adding that within a particular social and political context (when there is hardly a middle class to speak of, and when workers and peasants have not been politically mobilized), soldiers in mufti sometimes allow or even encourage economic modernization. At the level of explanation, I would point to two motivations that go a long way toward accounting for the officer-politicians' conservative tendencies in protecting or failing to alter the economic and social *status quo*. These are the officers' determined pursuance of their corporate interests in combination with their deeply inculcated military values that assign overriding importance to the preservation of a particular type of political stability, and the officers' attachments to their middle class interests and identities. This interpretation does not include the claim that regimes featuring a politicized military are necessarily less successful in bringing about modernizing changes than are regimes of a purely civilian variety. I am only suggesting that, except under certain conditions, soldiers in mufti are not agents of modernization as has been commonly asserted, concomitantly offering some explanations for this descriptive generalization. And even if it turns out that civilian politicians fare no better as modernizing agents than officer-politicians, the motivations and values underlying the activities of the latter are commonly quite different from those of the former.

II. THE OFFICERS' CORPORATE INTERESTS AND MILITARY VALUES

Dankwart Rustow offered an incontrovertible generalization when he wrote: "In the mid-twentieth century, any serious claimant to power, regardless of his antecedents, associations, or intentions, will justify his claim by professing profound concern for national independence, for popular aspirations, for social justice and for economic development." [12]

[12] Dankwart A. Rustow, *A World of Nations: Problems of Political Modernization* (Washington, D.C., 1967), pp. 16–17.

In the words of another writer, "At the hour of the political triumph, all army officers in the postwar Middle East have claimed to be card-bearing reformers." [13] However, when the military are a more or less autonomous state within a state, without a constituency to which they are responsible or an executive to which they are subordinate, they are unlikely to be motivated by the goals of popular responsiveness, social and economic reforms, or economic development. The officers' corporate interests and military values go a long way in accounting for their disinclination to match their original *pronunciamientos* with governmental decisions.

In discussing the various factors which dispose the armed forces to intervene, S. E. Finer attributes a good deal of importance to the officers' corporate self-interest. "The military is jealous of its corporate status and privileges," which, in its most aggressive form, "can lead to the military demand to be the ultimate judge on all matters affecting the armed forces. . . . these certainly include foreign policy, and invariably include domestic economic policy and may well include all the factors making for morale, i.e., education and the mass media of communication. . ." [14] While I certainly agree with this point, I would like to expand upon it by suggesting how this corporate self-interest is more encompassing than implied by Finer's statement and his supporting examples, concomitantly showing how it hinders economic and social change.

When we add the enormous political power frequently enjoyed by the military to their corporate interests, it comes as no surprise to find that the armed forces have sometimes been characterized as the country's most powerful "trade union." And as is true of most unions, the military act to maintain or increase their wealth and prerogatives even when these values conflict with the aspirations and interests of larger segments within the society. In countries suffering from economic scarcity, and in the absence of internal or external threats, funds devoted to military expenditures hinder the rate of economic growth, and limit the size of progressive social service, health and welfare programs. What is more to the point here is the existence of a relationship between size of these economically and socially unproductive military expenditures and the military's political strength. In Latin America, with a sizeable proportion of governmental expenditures already being devoted to the armed forces, these expenditures were increased whenever a military government came to power.[15] In those Latin American countries with a politically non-involved military the mean level of defense expenditures as a proportion of central government expenditures is 9.3 per cent; in countries with an officer corps that has intermittently entered the polit-

[13] J. C. Hurewitz, *Middle East Politics: The Military Dimension* (New York, 1969), p. 117.
[14] S. E. Finer, *The Man on Horseback: The Role of the Military in Politics* (New York, 1962), p. 47 and *passim.*
[15] Edwin Lieuwen, *Arms and Politics in Latin America* (New York, 1961), pp. 147–148.

ical arena the percentage is 14.1; while the figure reaches 18.5 per cent in countries dominated by the military circa 1960. This last group of Latin American countries also evidenced a 14.0 percent average annual increase in defense spending circa 1960 to 1965, this figure dropping to 3.3 per cent where the military were intermittent political actors and 2.8 percent where they were politically non-involved.[16] In their exceptionally reliable compilation of aggregate data for 74 non-western, non-communist countries to which the United States has extended some foreign aid, Adelman and Morris classify these countries according to the "political strength of the military." [17] Relying upon the World Handbook of Social and Political Indicators for the proportion of these countries' GNPs spent on defense (circa 1960),[18] we find that in those countries in which the military had occupied governmental office during at least part of the 1957–62 period (N = 18), the average percentage of GNP spent on defense is 3.6. This proportion is slightly lower (3.4 per cent) among those countries in which the military did not serve as governmental incumbents, but did exert a good deal of influence upon the civilians (N = 20). Among those countries in which the military's activities remained circumscribed within their instrumental role (N = 36), the percentage drops to 1.9. Thus the proportion of GNP devoted to defense is almost twice as large in countries overtly ruled by the military as it is in countries with a non-politicized officer corps, indicating that soldiers in mufti actively pursue their corporate interests and that they do so in a way that detracts from economic and social change.

There is good reason for the officers to view the lower classes as a real or potential threat to their corporate interests, and as such, they are not about to sanction economic programs that will benefit the disadvantaged strata. I would point to three possible factors that lead the military to perceive a politically active peasantry and urban working class as a threat to the military establishment: as an additional contender for political power within a zero-sum political arena, mass political mobilization will decrease the political strength of the military, and thus the ability to pursue its corporate interests; the lower classes are likely to attack the military establishment itself when the officers have previously opposed them in their bid for an effective political role and a larger

[16] Schmitter, *op. cit.*, p. 25. In terms of defense expenditures as a percentage of GNP (1960), the ordering is somewhat reversed, with the "intermittent" regimes averaging 2.7 per cent, and only 2.1 per cent of GNP being spent in military-dominated regimes. (The figure is 1.2 per cent where the military are completely out of politics.) Schmitter accounts for this pattern by noting that the civilian elites attempted to buy off the military as they moved in and out of politics. (p. 51)
[17] Irma Adelman and Cynthia Morris, *Society, Politics and Economic Development* (Baltimore, 1967), pp. 74–76. See below, p. 1138 for an explication of this three-fold division.
[18] Bruce M. Russett, *et al.*, *World Handbook of Social and Political Indicators* (New Haven, 1964), pp. 79–80.

slice of the economic pie; and the lower classes will try to reduce superfluous military expenditures in order to channel precious economic resources into the modernization process. Insofar as the officers are aware of the close connection between economic modernization and political mobilization, they have an additional reason for preserving the economic status quo. These possibilities take on some illustrative flesh by briefly noting two Latin American examples.

The Guatemalan Army leadership sponsored a strongly reform oriented *coup* in 1944, only to act against the very benefactors of that *coup* in 1954 and 1963. Lieuwen accounts for this reversal when he writes that

the present Army leadership has turned its back on the revolution it made in 1944. It got its fingers badly burned by involvement in the upsetting process of fundamental social change and reform. The revolutionary program, the civilian leadership, the workers and peasants, not to mention the Communists, all turned out to be threats to the very existence of the armed forces. Having eliminated these threats in 1954, (the officers) took every precaution to guard against their resurrection only a decade later. For not only do they now oppose social reform in principle, but they feel they must now protect themselves against the revenge that would surely be forthcoming if Arévado and the labor-left should return to power. Thus, institutional self-preservation was a prime motive for the March, 1963, *coup*.[19]

The officers of the Dominican Republic were similarly inspired in the September, 1963 *coup* that removed Juan Bosch from office. The officers reacted against Bosch's expensive development and welfare proposals which were bound to get the lion's share of the governmental budget —an interpretation supported by the fact that it was the Air Force, with its costly equipment and whose request for $6 million of new aircraft had just been rejected by Bosch, that sparked the *coup*. In addition, the military leaders became alarmed at Bosch's encouragement of the urban and rural workers' organizational efforts, insofar as their new found power would ultimately represent a counterpoise to the military.[20] Although these two examples refer to the motivations underlying military intervention in Guatemala and the Dominican Republic, we may safely assume that if these interpretations of the *coups* are valid, the subsequent military governments would hardly be disposed to act as agents of socioeconomic change.

There are, of course, instances in which a military government or a civilian government largely under the military's influence does bring about economic change and reform. But even in this minority of cases the officers' corporate interests decrease the extensiveness of such efforts.

[19]   Edwin Lieuwen, *Generals vs. Presidents: Neo-Militarism in Latin America* (New York, 1964), pp. 42–43.
[20]   *Ibid.*, pp. 60–61.

The officer-politicians may permit the government to carry out developmental and reform programs, but only if the military's corporate interests are first satisfied, the costs of the latter thereby detracting from the extensiveness of the former. For example, the Venezuelan armed forces allowed President Betancourt to serve out his entire constitutional term of office (the first time this had occurred in the country's military-dominated history) despite the implementation of agrarian reforms and a progressive tax law which redistributed both liquid and landed wealth. However, Betancourt was only able to move in these directions after he endorsed a more than liberal defense budget, even permitting the purchase of jet aircraft for the military's mythical defensive role, and a generous allotment of fringe benefits and promotions. In addition, the officers were presumably reassured that the cost of the development programs would not reduce these perquisites in the future because of the enormous oil revenues accruing to the government.[21] There is one type of economic change that officer-politicians have sometimes endorsed, *because* it enhances their corporate interests. The military often place a high value upon industrialization, both for its symbolic indication of military might and its presumed guarantee of national self-sufficiency in the event of an improbable war. Yet industrialization is not always an especially successful strategy of economic development,[22] and given the identification of industrialization with the military's corporate interests, the officer-politicians' determined pursuit of the latter is likely to produce an over-emphasis upon industrialization. The industrializing impetus would then exacerbate the country's economic problems, as in some Latin American countries where the military rulers' "drive for economic independence often led to overhasty industrialization programs." [23] At a minimum, industrializing efforts detract from the oftentimes more desired and desirable objectives of increased agricultural productivity, land reform, educational expansion and the provision of social and medical services which are unrelated to the military's corporate interests. The military's corporate interests may positively incline them toward economic modernization, but rarely toward economic and social reform, for the latter almost never coincide with even the broadest of corporate interests.

[21]   *Ibid.*, 86–91; Philip B. Taylor, Jr., *The Venezuelan Golpe de Estado of 1958: The Fall of Marcos Perez Jimenez* (Washington, D.C., 1968), pp. 48–52, 67–71.

[22]   For the persuasive argument that "The postwar dogma, so widespread among the less developed countries, that modern economic growth is dependent wholly on industrialization has done much harm," see Theodore Schultz, *Economic Growth and Agriculture* (New York, 1968), p. 21 and *passim,* where it is also suggested that the agricultural sector of most non-Western countries might contribute most to economic growth.

[23]   Lieuwen, *Arms and Politics . . . , op cit.,* pp. 146–47. Also see Jae Souk Sohn, "Political Dominance and Political Failure: The Role of the Military in the Republic of Korea," in Henry Bienen (ed.), *The Military Intervenes* (New York, 1968), pp. 114–116.

I would underline the tenacity with which the officers pursue their corporate interests by pointing out that these are inextricably bound up with their self-image as the selfless and dedicated guardians of the nation's interests. The military's corporate interests are largely defined, legitimized and rationalized by their close identification with the nation's interests. The officers are thereby able to justify their actions to others and to themselves by identifying with the nation rather than with any of its constituent parts; opposition to their actions are viewed as expressions of partial and selfish interests. This close identification between their own and the nation's interests is so deeply inculcated that the officer-politicians readily come to believe in the necessity and legitimacy of their actions, no matter how self-interested and abusive they may appear to an outside observer. Moreover, this equation of the two interests cannot be questioned. To do so might very well entail the enfeeblement of the military establishment; for its *esprit de corps* is founded upon service, duty, and responsibility to the nation. Any challenges on this score cannot arise, or if they do, they must be rationalized away or defeated. In short, those corporate interests which block socio-economic change and popular responsiveness are strengthened and legitimized by their inextricable association with the nation's interests.

A second aspect of the military establishment that hinders economic change are those near-universal military values—the normative attachments to order, dignity and hierarchy—with which most officers are strongly imbued, out of which emerges an overwhelming concern for political stability, and thus a keen sensitivity to any divergence from the status quo that contains the potential for unwieldy change. Given the brittleness of most non-western governments, we would expect these military values to have an especially pronounced impact upon the officer-politicians' activities; where governmental institutions are weak the officers have good reason for thinking that practically any type of socio-economic change could reduce the level of stability. However, it is one thing to place an extremely high value upon stability in the context of a fissiparous politics, it is quite another when stability is merely intended to replace a cacophonous politics. Consequently, even in those small number of instances in which a politicized military is interested in change and reform, when it becomes apparent that a small cost might have to be paid in terms of some political instability, their military values leave them little time for hesitation. Even in the estimate of John J. Johnson, who is certainly not as critical of the Latin American military as is Edwin Lieuwen, officer-politicians in Latin America might be willing to sanction land reform, but only if the cost to them is not too high and so long as it can proceed in an orderly manner.[24]

Not only does this normative and cognitive map of the political

[24] Johnson, *op. cit.*, p. 147.

world dictate a conservative reaction to the possibilities of change, the officer-politicians are wedded to a particular form of political stability— what may be described as the creation of an apolitical calm—that further reduces any possible modernizing predispositions. The goal is political stability, "but it is the stability of a vacuum, a state undisturbed by the erratic movements of partisan bodies." [25] Politics as regulated conflict, competition and compromise is transformed into the apolitical politics of consensus, acquiescence and government by fiat. For example, the attempt to create an apolitical stability in Burma during Ne-Win's military dictatorship is manifested in the establishment of a national "political" movement with the give-away name of the National Solidarity Association. According to Zolberg, military rulers in tropical Africa

conceive of national unity as "oneness," defined negatively by the absence of social conflict stemming from regionalism, primordial loyalties such as ethnicity or religious affiliations. In all countries, "ethnic particularism" has been condemned and its manifestations through voluntary associations prohibited. The goal seems to be the achievement of homogeneity by political fiat, as if the rulers genuinely believed that the absence of conflict somehow *produces* national integration.[26]

The tendency of newly established military governments in tropical Africa to arrest and deport even those politicians who had opposed the previous civilian regime and favored military intervention, and their abrogation of bargaining efforts on the part of occupational groups, may also be interpreted as manifestations of their particular conception of political stability.[27] This vision of political stability hinders social and economic change insofar as such changes are a product of governmental responsiveness to articulated and forcefully promoted demands; repressing these demands largely rules out their fulfillment.

Although I am attributing a good deal of importance to these two broad aspects of the military, they do vary in their explanatory power. Soldiers in mufti do not pursue their corporate interests in as determined a fashion where the military establishment is a small one. Where the armed forces number less than 2,000 men we would not expect the "weight" of such a small establishment to have as pronounced an impact upon the emergence of a broadly defined and intensely pursued corporate interest as in the case of a larger military establishment. Nor

---

[25] M. D. Feld, "Professionalism, Nationalism, and the Alienation of the Military," in Doorn (ed.), *op. cit.*, p. 68.
[26] Aristide R. Zolberg, "Military Intervention in the New States of Tropical Africa," in Bienen (ed.), *op. cit.*, p. 87. Zolberg goes on to say that the military rulers "think much like their predecessors in the one-party states." However, the impression that I derive from his essay, combined with some knowledge of African single-party states, is that the military do place greater emphasis upon governmental suppression of actual and potential conflict groups.
[27] *Ibid.*, pp. 89–90.

would we expect military values to be as pervasively and deeply inculcated where the armed forces have only been recently created, without a long tradition to give shape and support to these values and without an extensive period within which these values may be instilled and internalized. Where either one or both of these conditions prevail a politicized military will still detract from the possibility of socio-economic change, but their negative impact will be significantly softened. In geographical terms, these two mitigating conditions most frequently obtain in the tropical African countries. Almost half of these 33 countries supported a military establishment of less than 2,000 men as of 1966, and only 6 had a sizeable force numbering more than 10,000 men.[28] And it is in Africa that we find more than two dozen countries that have only recently gained their independence, and thus their military establishments are practically brand new.

[28] David Wood, *The Armed Forces of African States*, Adelphi Paper no. 27 (London, 1966); André Martel, "Les Armées africaines," in Leo Hamon (ed), *Le Role Extra-Militaire de L'Armée dans le Tiers Monde* (Paris, 1966).

It has already been observed that constitutional provisions with respect to the major political institutions and processes in transitional societies have often undergone rapid and extensive changes. The colonial heritage has proven to be far less significant, it seems, in terms of formal political institutions than in such aspects as trade relationships, where the patterns established during and immediately after the colonial period have often endured. In the article that follows, Newell Stultz examines the residue of British influence on the political structures and processes of their former African colonies and the types of changes that have occurred since independence was achieved.

25. PARLIAMENTS IN
FORMER BRITISH BLACK AFRICA *

newell m. stultz

Between March 1957 and October 1966, Great Britain conferred sovereignty upon twelve of her possessions in sub-Saharan Africa.[1] The forms of government existing among these states at their independence varied in important respects. In each, however, there had been established a national legislature whose institutional structure and constitutional functions were patterned on, or adapted from, those of the British Parliament. Since their independence, a number of these countries have altered certain of the structural features of their legislatures. Furthermore, in all of these new states distinctive patterns of parliamentary performance have evolved. What, if any, structural and performance characteristics are now common to parliaments in former British Black Africa? [2]

This paper suggests eleven such characteristics. The first four items identify structural features and rest upon a review of national constitutions. The remaining items describe parliamentary performance. Here the basic sources are published commentaries upon the activities of individual parliaments.[3] But these commentaries cover only six countries:

* From "Parliaments in Former British Black Africa" by Newell M. Stultz, *The Journal of Developing Areas*, Vol. II, No. 4 (July, 1968), pp. 479–493. By permission of the publisher and the author.

[1] The twelve, in order of their gaining independence, were: Ghana, Nigeria, Sierra Leone, Tanganyika, Uganda, Zanzibar, Kenya, Malawi, Zambia, Gambia, Botswana, and Lesotho. In 1964 Zanzibar and Tanganyika joined to form Tanzania.
[2] Constitutional government was replaced by military rule in Nigeria and Ghana in 1966 and in Sierra Leone in 1967. References made to these countries are for the period up to the commencement of military government.
[3] D. G. Austin, "The Ghana Parliament's First Year," *Parliamentary Affairs*, XI (Summer 1958), 350–60; J. M. Lee, "Parliament in Republican Ghana," *Parliamentary Affairs*, XVI (Autumn 1963), 376–95; Jon Kraus, "Ghana's New 'Corporate Parliament,'" *Africa Report*, X (August 1965), 6–11; G. F. Engholm, "The Westminster Model in Uganda," *International Journal*, XVIII (Autumn 1963), 468–87; B. S. Sharma, "Parliamentary Government in Uganda," *International Studies*, VII (January 1966), 448–56; William Tordoff, "Parliament in Tanzania," *Journal of Commonwealth Political Studies*, III (July 1965), 85–103; Anirundha Gupta, "The Zambian National Assembly: Study of an African Legislature," *Parliamentary Affairs*, XIX (Winter 1965–66), 48–56; John P. Mackintosh, "The Nigerian Federal Parliament," *Public Law* (Autumn 1963), 333–61; J. H. Proctor, "The Role of the Senate in the Kenya Political System," *Parliamentary Affairs*, XVIII (Autumn 1965), 389–415; and Cherry Gertzel, "Parliament in Independent Kenya," *Parliamentary Affairs*, XIX (Autumn 1966), 486–504.

Ghana, Kenya, Nigeria, Tanzania, Uganda, and Zambia. Moreover, these reports were prepared at different times by different authors who had, inevitably, somewhat different interests. In matters of parliamentary performance, then, we can not yet generalize for all or even most parliaments in former British Black Africa. Instead, items 5-11 identify only recurring patterns of behavior among those several parliaments for which secondary evidence is now available.

1. *Unicameralism.* Single-house national legislatures prevail. Only four countries have had bicameral parliaments: Nigeria, Kenya, Botswana, and Lesotho. Kenya abolished its upper house in 1967 and now conforms to the general pattern. Bicameralism, where it exists, is a recent phenomenon, a product of constitutional negotiations during the terminal stage of the colonial period.[4]

The role of second chambers has been to protect tribal and parochial interests. This specialized and limited function can be seen in both the composition and powers of these bodies.[5] In fact, the absence of a second chamber in most countries is one indication that most African leaders at the national level oppose the institutionalization of tribal interests and believe in strong, unitary government.

2. *Popular election of legislators.* Popular election from single-member constituencies is the prevailing mode of recruitment to parliamentary office. Excluding second chambers, 92 percent of all MP's in office at independence had been elected in this way.[6] The remainder, 95 members distributed among nine parliaments, had secured office variously: through direct executive appointment, 15; "special election" by elected members of the legislature, 25; election by whites voting communally, 13; election by chiefs, 4; indirect election by lesser bodies, 33; or by ex officio appointment, 5. This latter figure does not include the attorney-general who now sits ex officio but without a vote in the parliaments of five countries.[7] The National Assembly of Zanzibar had the smallest proportion of popularly elected MP's, just 74 percent.

Since independence, five countries have altered the composition of their legislatures. In Kenya the number of elected members in the lower house was increased in 1967, at the time the Senate was abolished, in

[4] In Nigeria, for example, the Senate, the upper house of the Nigerian Federal Parliament, came into being less than one year before that country gained independence in 1960. A bicameral legislature had, however, functioned in the Northern Region of Nigeria from 1946 and in the Western Region from 1951.

[5] For example, the Senate in Lesotho, composed of twenty-two chiefs plus eleven other persons nominated by the paramount chief, has no power to veto ordinary legislation. Its assent is required, however, to constitutional amendments protecting the position of the paramount chief, of chieftainship in general, and of land tenure, among other matters.

[6] Figures for both Zanzibar and Tanganyika are included. A universal adult franchise for Africans was approximated everywhere except Northern Nigeria, where a universal manhood suffrage prevailed.

[7] The five are Uganda, Kenya, Gambia, Botswana, and Nigeria.

order to accommodate the former senators. This constituted no change in the principle of representation. Change in principle has been introduced in four countries and appears to manifest two desires. One is to eliminate special forms of representation that can not be controlled by the executive. In 1966 reserved seats for whites were abolished in Malawi, as they will be in Zambia also at the first dissolution of parliament. In Uganda the right of the regional assembly in Buganda (the Lukiko) to elect Buganda's representatives in the National Assembly was taken away in 1966; hereafter, MP's from Buganda will be elected directly.

The second desire, in the words of the constitution of Zambia, is "to enhance the representative character of the Assembly." The method adopted has been the appointment of MP's by the executive. At independence, Gambia, Tanganyika, Zambia, and Zanzibar provided for nominees of the executive in the assembly. In addition, Kenya, Uganda, and Botswana provided for the election of a number of MP's by the regularly elected members of the legislature. Because of government majorities in these assemblies, these "specially elected" members were, in fact, indirect appointees of the executive.[8] Uganda has now abolished the institution of "specially elected" members, but in 1967 the president of Uganda was empowered to appoint up to one-third of the eighty-two members of the National Assembly. The right of the executive to nominate MP's was introduced in Ghana in 1965, in Malawi in 1966, and was extended in Tanzania in 1965.[9]

Thus in seven parliaments (eight if we include Ghana) there are some MP's who owe their positions to direct or indirect executive appointment rather than to popular election. The number of such members is commonly not more than 15 percent of all members, but it is considerably higher in Tanzania, Uganda, and formerly in Ghana, i.e., in three of the five countries that changed the composition of their legis-

---

[8] Chanan Singh notes that the idea behind the prescribed mechanism for the election of "specially elected" members in Kenya was to prevent a party capturing all such seats. But, Singh continues, the constitutional draftsmen forgot that a majority party could arrange its voting strength just so it could indeed capture all seats. Singh, "The Republican Constitution of Kenya: Historical Background and Analysis," *International and Comparative Law Quarterly*, XIV (July 1965), 935.

[9] In Ghana the manner of executive appointment was circuitous. In 1965 the National Assembly in Ghana was increased in size from 114 to 198 members. In principle, the basis of representation remained as before: Members were popularly elected from single-member constituencies. But Ghana was now a legal one-party state, and the penalties for individual political opposition were severe. In consequence, only candidates of the ruling party entered for the election, and on election day all were returned unopposed without a vote having been cast. These candidates had been selected by the party executive, which in Ghana was much the same as the national executive. Ninety-six of these candidates were holdovers from the former Assembly. The remainder, however, had been selected to give representation to a broad range of associational and institutional groups. See Kraus, "Ghana's New 'Corporate Parliament,'" *Africa Report* (August 1965), p. 8.

latures after independence. The net result of all these changes has been to reduce to 80 percent the proportion of all MP's dependent upon popular election to office.

The presence of MP's directly or indirectly appointed by the executive in most parliaments is an interesting departure from the Westminster parliamentary model and deserves further comment. In part, the appointment of MP's is a carry-over of the earlier practice common during the colonial period whereby the governor nominated members to sit on the legislative council. In the contemporary period, however, there are three benefits of a system allowing for the appointment of MP's by the executive. It makes it possible for the executive to bring persons with special talents into the assembly; it allows the executive to bolster, if necessary, its legislative majority; and it makes it possible for the executive to guarantee legislative representation for certain groups in the population, e.g., women, whites, workers, farmers, trade unionists, etc. This last point is perhaps of greatest importance. G. F. Engholm has written that "candidates to Uganda's National Assembly have been drawn from the numerically very small professional elite. Agricultural interests are poorly represented measured against the industry's economic contribution." [10] Little data on the occupations of MP's in Africa exists. Such data as has been compiled supports the view, however, that except for such groups as teachers, civil servants, and businessmen, important occupational categories, particularly farmers, are under-represented in most African parliaments.[11] It is doubtful that *any* popularly elected assembly will closely represent the distribution of occupations (or the distribution of any demographic variable) within the electorate. The integrative needs of African politics, however, as well as the desires of some African leaders for national political cohesion, are great.

3. *Presidentialism.* Except for Zambia and Botswana, which gained independence as republics, all the states at their independence were constitutional monarchies with an executive patterned on the Westminster parliamentary model. Executive authority was nominally vested in a constitutional monarch who, except in the case of Lesotho, was Queen Elizabeth II; [12] but political power rested with a prime minister and his cabinet who were responsible to a popularly (or substantially so) elected assembly.

This constitutional form has been retained only in Lesotho and Gambia, and it existed in Sierra Leone until the military takeover in

[10] Engholm, "The Westminster Model in Uganda," *International Journal* (Autumn 1963), p. 478.
[11] See, for example, Mackintosh, "The Nigerian Federal Parliament," *Public Law* (Autumn 1963), pp. 336–37, and Guy Hunter, *The New Societies of Tropical Africa* (New York: Praeger, 1964), p. 285.
[12] In Lesotho the head of state is the paramount chief of the Mosotho, presently King Moshoeshoe II.

1967.[13] Elsewhere some variant of a presidential executive has now been adopted. The changes in Nigeria and Kenya were comparatively minor. With the ending of the monarchy in Nigeria in 1963, the duties that had been exercised by the governor-general—but only those—devolved upon the new post of president.[14] In other respects, the political structure of Nigeria remained as before. In Kenya in 1964 both the posts of governor-general and prime minister were abolished, and their duties and powers were combined in the newly created office of president. The president of Kenya, who is both head of state and head of government, is thus responsible to the National Assembly for the exercise of his office. Constitutional arrangements similar to those of Kenya after 1964 were found in Botswana at independence.

In the four remaining countries—Malawi, Tanzania, Ghana, and Uganda—the presidential form of government adopted after independence broke two principles of the Westminster parliamentary model.[15] As in Kenya and Botswana, the functions of ceremonial head of state and political head of government were joined in a single office. More important, the executive (i.e., president) in these countries no longer needed the continuing support of a simple majority in the assembly; the constitutional powers of parliament were accordingly lessened. The executive in Zambia already possessed this character at independence in 1963.

Political deadlock between the executive and the legislature is thus constitutionally possible in four countries, as it was also in Ghana at the time of Nkrumah's overthrow. In an era of dominant mass parties and charismatic political leadership in Africa, such conflict would seem unlikely; nevertheless, these countries have introduced certain constitutional safeguards against this possibility. Except for Tanzania, where the president is elected directly by the people independent of the election of assembly members, the mechanism for the selection of the president was designed to insure political harmony between the president and the assembly, at least at the outset of the fixed presidential term. In Uganda MP's select the president, as was to be the case in Ghana for presidents succeeding Nkrumah.[16] In Malawi the president is elected

13 In November 1965, a proposal that Gambia become a republic failed by 728 votes to gain the necessary two-thirds vote in a national referendum. Creation of a republic was an issue in the Sierra Leone election of March 1967 which precipitated the military takeover in that country.
14 The president of Nigeria was elected to a fixed five-year term by an electoral college consisting of both houses of the Federal Parliament.
15 Uganda became a republic in 1963 with an executive substantially similar to the Nigerian executive after 1963. This arrangement lasted until 1966, when the character of the Uganda executive was changed again to its present form. This is discussed below.
16 Kwame Nkrumah was named the first president of the Republic of Ghana in the constitution of 1960.

by the people, but MP's play a role in his nomination.[17] In Zambia the president is also elected by the people, but presidential elections are tied to the election of MP's in such a way as to make it likely, although not certain, that a newly elected president will have the support of a majority in the National Assembly.[18] If, however, conflict does occur despite these mechanisms, the president in all four countries (and formerly in Ghana) may dissolve parliament, although he is not required to do so.[19] In fact, a president might wish not to dissolve parliament, for if he does, he must in all cases himself stand for reelection.

4. *Constitutional supremacy.* At their independence all the new states of former British Black Africa had written constitutions defining the organs, functions, and limits of government. In no country could parliament by simple majority vote amend any and all provisions of the constitution. In this sense, the constitution, to the extent that it was protected from amendment by ordinary legislation, represented a body of fundamental law. Parliament was not supreme.

Since independence new constitutions have been adopted in several countries, while in certain others the independence constitutions have been revised in important respects. Everywhere, however, the principle of the supremacy of the constitution has been retained, except, of course, in those countries where constitutional government has been overthrown by the military.

"The status of the constitution as supreme law," S. A. de Smith has written, "is determined by the procedure prescribed for its amendment. Those provisions which are thought to be especially important will be protected from alteration by legislation passed in the ordinary manner and form." [20] Such provisions are commonly said to be "en-

[17] In Malawi only one candidate may be nominated for the presidency. The electorate, therefore, votes "yes" or "no." In the event a majority vote "no," no election occurs, a second candidate is nominated, and the electorate votes again, and so on until a nominated candidate is supported by a majority of those voting. The candidate is nominated by an electoral college consisting of officials of the ruling party, district council officers, MP's, and chiefs. Similar arrangements govern the nomination and election of the president of Tanzania.

[18] Before the election each candidate for election as an MP must declare a preference for one of the announced candidates for president. On election day the voter votes concurrently for MP and for president. The candidate for president receiving the greatest number of popular votes throughout the country is elected. A system only slightly different than this is found in Kenya, Botswana, Uganda, and formerly in Ghana. As in Zambia, candidates for election to parliament declare their preference for one of the announced candidates for president, but on election day the voter votes only for MP. A candidate for president is elected if a majority of those elected to parliament had previously declared their support for him.

[19] With the following exception: If the president of Zambia vetoes a bill and the National Assembly again passes it with a two-thirds majority, the president must sign the bill within twenty-one days or dissolve parliament.

[20] S. E. de Smith, *The New Commonwealth and Its Constitution* (London: Stevens, 1964), p. 110.

trenched." The matters covered by entrenched provisions vary from country to country depending upon local circumstances, although generally the states under consideration have entrenched constitutional provisions dealing with individual rights, the basis of responsible and representative government, the independence of the judiciary, the standing of traditional authorities, and the procedure for the amendment of the constitution, among other matters. Five countries have entrenched their entire constitutions: Gambia, Zambia, Malawi, Kenya, and Tanzania.

Three methods of constitutional entrenchment are found:

(a) The simplest and most common is the requirement that bills proposing a constitutional amendment be passed by parliament with a special majority. In nine countries this is a two-thirds majority.[21] To this requirement is sometimes added a mandatory period of delay. In Sierra Leone, for example, two two-thirds votes were required with a general election intervening.

(b) A second method requires that an amendment to the constitution be approved by a body other than the legislature. Ghana has provided the only example. Under the Ghanaian constitution of 1960 power to "repeal or alter" seventeen of its fifty-five articles was "reserved to the people," that is, required the approval of a simple majority at a public referendum.

(c) A third method combines in some measure (a) the requirement that a constitutional amendment be passed by parliament, usually by a special majority, and (b) the requirement that the amendment be accepted by some other body, or bodies, usually the electorate voting in a public referendum. This is the most elaborate method of constitutional entrenchment, and in the six countries where it has existed, it has been used to protect only those provisions of the constitution that are deemed particularly sensitive. In Nigeria, however, this included some 100 of 166 sections of the constitution.[22]

5. *Impotence of second chambers.* Writing in 1965 on the role of the Senate in the politics of Kenya, J. H. Proctor termed the legislative contribution of the upper house "of slight value," its control over the executive "insignificant," its influence on public opinion "negligible," and its protection of the constitution "irresolute." [23] Similarly, John Mackintosh found the Senate in Nigeria to be a "negligible body." [24] In both countries the senate appears to have been virtually ignored by both the executive and the public.

[21] In Kenya a 65 percent majority is now required.
[22] Richard L. Sklar and C. S. Whitaker, Jr., "The Federal Republic of Nigeria," in *National Unity and Regionalism in Eight African States,* ed. G. M. Carter (Ithaca, N. Y.: Cornell University Press, 1966), p. 62.
[23] Proctor, "The Role of the Senate in the Kenya Political System," *Parliamentary Affairs* (Autumn 1965), p. 414.
[24] Mackintosh, "The Nigerian Federal Parliament," p. 359.

The impotence of the senate in both Kenya and Nigeria was to some extent intended. In the enactment of ordinary legislation neither body had more than the power of delay, on the pattern of the House of Lords. Proctor asserts, however, that after sixteen months the Senate in Kenya "had not even exercised its assigned powers in such a way as to realize fully the purposes intended by those who urged its creation." [25] That this should have been so seems due to the absence of political notables in the Kenya Senate and the fact of a safe and docile government majority. According to Mackintosh, senators in Nigeria who were elected by the regional assemblies were likewise "all loyal party men." [26] Information is lacking, but there seems little reason to expect that the upper house will be more effective in either Lesotho or Botswana, the only countries, it will be recalled, that now have a second chamber.

6. *Absence or ineffectiveness of a formal parliamentary opposition.* The institution of the parliamentary opposition has been a common casualty of African independence. Except for Tanganyika and Malawi, a parliamentary opposition existed in each state at its independence. In 1964 opposition parties were formally outlawed in Ghana, a practice subsequently copied in Tanzania and Malawi. Elsewhere, oppositions have commonly experienced a marked decline in both numbers and influence. In Kenya, for example, the opposition now includes only eight MP's in the National Assembly of 170 members. A sizable opposition is now found only in Lesotho, but one existed in Sierra Leone also at the time of the 1967 military coup. Small size alone would seem to prevent most parliamentary oppositions from adequately providing alternative programs and personnel to those of the government.

Available commentaries suggest that, on the whole, oppositions have performed poorly; their criticisms of the executive have usually been ill-informed, uncoordinated, and limited to specific questions rather than general policy. I observed this myself in the National Assembly in Kenya in 1966. Mackintosh has observed that in Nigeria the opposition "never tried to organize a concerted barrage of questions on any given topic or aimed at any specific Minister." [27] (Further confirmation of this conclusion appears under item 9 below.)

In fairness, it must be added that the performance of the opposition has frequently been burdened by the failure of the executive to respect its role; indeed, many African political leaders appear to regard merely the existence of an opposition as a danger to their regimes. Anirundha Gupta has written that a "major aim" of the executive in Zambia would seem to be "to discredit the ANC [opposition] and thus to get rid of

[25] Proctor, "The Role of the Senate in the Kenya Political System," p. 413.
[26] Mackintosh, "The Nigerian Federal Parliament," p. 356.
[27] *Ibid.*, p. 342.

it as soon as possible." [28] Mackintosh has asserted that had the Nigerian opposition exploited more systematically the "extremely limited" opportunities open to it, the only result would have been new restrictions imposed by the government.[29] In 1964 Prime Minister Obote of Uganda rejected the need for a parliamentary opposition, calling it a "capitalist notion." [30]

7. *Independence of government backbenchers.* Government backbenchers, in their capacity as private members, have frequently assumed responsibility for airing public grievances and criticizing official policy. In 1966 Cherry Gertzel wrote that "the most significant fact about the Kenya Parliament as it entered its third session was that the [then one-party] House of Representatives had become a public forum where the representatives of the people fully exercise their right to debate critically the actions of the Government." [31] William Tordoff has pointed out that in Tanzania backbenchers "attach considerable importance to their right to question ministers," [32] while in Uganda, according to Engholm, "in the era of independence, an M.P. feels he must assert himself and justify his position to his constituents." [33]

The independence of government backbenchers seldom extends to recorded formal divisions which, indeed, are rare, although in June 1964 government backbenchers in Kenya supported the opposition at a division to defeat the government on a question pertaining to East African federation. Backbench independence, however, is much in evidence at question time. Engholm states that in the National Assembly in Uganda, "it is now *de rigueur* to jump to one's feet and try to embarrass the minister . . . regardless of party affiliation." [34]

The extent to which government backbenchers do assert themselves appears to vary from country to country. Tordoff found that, except during the period allowed for questions, Tanzanian backbenchers made limited use of opportunities for expressing their feelings, while Gupta has described government backbenchers in Zambia as being "more or less passive," even if they are "interested to see that certain points are raised by the Opposition so as to get information." [35] In general, it appears that the independence of government backbenchers will be greater when

[28] Gupta, "The Zambian National Assembly," *Parliamentary Affairs* (Winter 1965–66), p. 52.

[29] Mackintosh, "The Nigerian Federal Parliament," p. 344.

[30] Donald Rothchild and Michael Rogin, "Uganda," in *National Unity and Regionalism,* ed. Carter, p. 399.

[31] Gertzel, "Parliament in Independent Kenya," *Parliamentary Affairs* (Autumn 1966), p. 490.

[32] Tordoff, "Parliament in Tanzania," *Journal of Commonwealth Studies* (July 1965), p. 90.

[33] Engholm, "The Westminster Model in Uganda," p. 480.

[34] *Ibid.,* p. 485.

[35] Gupta, "The Zambian National Assembly," p. 54.

there is no formal parliamentary opposition, when backbenchers do not participate in the decisions that precede the preparation of parliamentary business, and when party organization at the constituency level is weak.

8. *Absence of lobbying.* Lucian Pye has written that the non-Western political process operates largely without the benefit of political "brokers" and explicitly organized interest groups.[36] This appears characteristic of the legislative process in the six countries of former British Black Africa for which we have information. Negative evidence is most obvious; still, discussing the first year of the Ghana parliament, D. G. Austin maintained that, "except for political parties, there are virtually no nationally organized societies capable of informing, persuading, moving its members and the general public for or against a particular act of government policy." [37] Similarly, Engholm has identified the "virtual absence of pressure groups" in Uganda.[38] But even were interest groups to exist, one would suppose they would not seek to influence parliament, but would rather focus their attentions on the executive and the bureaucracy. J. M. Lee, writing also of Ghana, contended that because of executive dominance of the legislature, it would be pointless to lobby parliament. "No one," Lee stated, "who wished to promote change would think of approaching individual M.P.s in their capacity as legislators." [39]

9. *Parochialism of demands and inexpertness of debate.* Debate in parliament for the most part is discussion carried on between members of the cabinet and assistant ministers of subcabinet rank on the one hand, and ordinary MP's on the other. The latter may be members of the opposition if one exist or, as we have seen, the government's own backbenchers. Ministers and assistant ministers have at their disposal the resources of the bureaucracy, but the ordinary MP lacks these. In the absence of external and independent sources of opinion and information such as might be provided by lobbyists, the ordinary MP in the countries for which we have data seems most often obliged, in Austin's words on Ghana, "to exercise his own judgment, supported by whatever meagre supply of facts he can discover for himself." [40] Engholm has noted similarly that the politician in Uganda "cannot be a broker of ideas; he is forced back on his own intellectual resources." [41] These are usually limited. Few MP's have specialized training, and the research libraries

[36] Lucian W. Pye, "The Non-Western Political Process," *Journal of Politics,* XX (August 1958), 485.
[37] Austin, "The Ghana Parliament's First Year," *Parliamentary Affairs* (Summer 1958), p. 355.
[38] Engholm, "The Westminster Model in Uganda," p. 479.
[39] Lee, "Parliament in Republican Ghana," *Parliamentary Affairs* (Autumn 1963), p. 382.
[40] Austin, "The Ghana Parliament's First Year," p. 356.
[41] Engholm, "The Westminster Model in Uganda," p. 479.

that are found in each parliament are inadequate and little used. Ordinary MP's necessarily must draw heavily upon their own personal knowledge and experience. As a result, demands articulated by these members are most often specific in content, unaggregated, and rooted in the local circumstances of the member's constituency. The ordinary MP performs in the role of delegate; that is, he is a person, in the words of Apter and Lystad, usually without special talents who is completely responsive to the demands of his public constituency.[42] Mackintosh has observed that the Nigerian "electorate regards representation largely as a matter of sending an emissary to put their immediate needs before the government,"[43] and Gupta writes that in Zambia MP's view it as "of utmost importance" that they bring "to the notice of the Government specific problems and grievances of their constituencies."[44] These demands may be fully aired, but broad questions of public policy are seldom adequately debated in parliament.

Parliamentary debate of national issues is thus usually inexpert and of low standard. Gertzel has noted that MP's in Kenya frequently reveal "their general lack of information on a wide variety of subjects," particularly on details of financial policy.[45] And Engholm writes that in Uganda "members display little inclination to concern themselves with the minutiae of Acts, or indeed the significance of what is left out," in part because few possess legal training. "If the subject matter is at all technical," Engholm continues, "there may be no debate at all."[46] One consequence of inexpert consideration of proposed legislation is that bills are enacted speedily. Tordoff has noted that in February 1964, nineteen bills were passed by the Tanganyika National Assembly on the same day they were introduced.[47]

Greater use of standing committees of parliament might make for more expert consideration of legislation because MP's assigned to these committees would likely be encouraged to develop expertise in particular subject areas. This would be even more probable were these committees to have staff assistance. The standing orders of each parliament provide for the creation of standing and select committees, but thus far committees have been little used. Everywhere the "committee stage" is nearly always taken by a committee-of-the-whole. Engholm notes that

42   David E. Apter and Robert A. Lystad, "Bureaucracy, Party, and Constitutional Democracy: An Examination of Political Role Systems in Ghana," in *Transition in Africa: Studies in Political Adaptation*, ed. G. M. Carter and W. O. Brown (Boston, Mass.: Boston University Press, 1958), p. 29.
43   Mackintosh, "The Nigerian Federal Parliament," p. 354.
44   Gupta, "The Zambian National Assembly," p. 53 footnote.
45   Gertzel, "Parliament in Independent Kenya," p. 492.
46   Engholm, "The Westminster Model in Uganda," pp. 474, 483.
47   Tordoff, "Parliament in Tanzania," pp. 91–92.

at this point in the legislative process in Uganda, "lack of familiarity with legal jargon reduces almost the entire Chamber to silence."[48]

10. *Executive dominance.* Writing of the National Assembly in Kenya, Gertzel states that backbench criticism "has not forced the Government to make any major changes in its legislative programme."[49] Likewise, Mackintosh asserts that the control exercised by the House of Representatives in Nigeria over the executive up to 1963 was "negligible."[50] In fact, executive dominance of the assembly is a recurring theme in all the published writings cited at the beginning on parliaments in Ghana, Nigeria, Kenya, Uganda, Zambia, and Tanzania. In their legislative function, parliaments in these countries have been executive rubber stamps. No important piece of legislation desired by the executive has been refused; indeed, such legislation has been enacted not infrequently with unseemly haste. Moreover, legislative initiative has rested almost entirely with the executive. There have been very few examples of private members' bills introduced in parliament, and no such bill has been enacted. Finally, conciliar control over the personnel of the executive has been virtually nonexistent. Each of these countries has experienced cabinet crises; but while these have been reflected in parliament, none has resulted from the assertion of the authority of the assembly over the executive. Indeed, in Tanzania, Uganda, and Zambia the executive is not responsible constitutionally to a simple majority in the legislature, as has been mentioned. This is also true in Malawi, and was formerly true in Ghana.

Executive dominance of the legislature is clearly the result of many factors: the national political standing of those in top cabinet positions resulting from their leadership during the struggle for independence, the ineffectiveness of the parliamentary opposition, the gulf in expert knowledge between the cabinet and ordinary parliamentarians, and the allocation of constitutional authority, among others. Except for the first, all these factors have already been indicated. In addition, there are two other less apparent determinants of executive dominance that should be mentioned. One is the brevity of parliamentary sessions. Nowhere has the assembly sat for more than one hundred days in a year, and annual sessions of two months or less are common. The National Assembly in Tanzania sat for only twenty-six days in 1964. For this reason alone, Tordoff concluded, MP's were "quite unable to keep current events under review."[51]

The second reason is that the appointment of MP's to cabinet posi-

---

48 Engholm, "The Westminster Model in Uganda," p. 484.
49 Gertzel, "Parliament in Independent Kenya," p. 499.
50 Mackintosh, "The Nigerian Federal Parliament," p. 352.
51 Tordoff, "Parliament in Tanzania," p. 89.

tions has served to neutralize the assembly in most states. Except for the Nigerian Federal House of Representatives, which had 312 members, most assemblies have small memberships. Seven parliaments, for example, have fewer than one hundred members. It has thus been possible to employ a significant proportion of the assembly in cabinet positions, reducing the number of backbenchers upon whose support the government is in principle dependent. For example, in the middle of 1966 fifty ministers and assistant ministers constituted 39 percent of the membership of the House of Representatives in Kenya.[52] The government required the support of only fifteen backbenchers to remain in office, or less than one-fifth of all backbenchers. Under these circumstances, legislators in Kenya could scarcely hope to control the executive.

11. *Functional ambiguity.* Here, while speaking generally, we again limit ourselves to those six parliaments in former British Black Africa whose activities have been described at length in the writings of specialist-observers. Among these institutions it seems clear that a decision-making role in politics has been virtually nonexistent.[53] There has been somewhat greater performance of the demand-making function. In each case, although to varying degrees, the institution has seemed to serve as a political safety valve, allowing for the ventilation of political grievances. Still, there is reason to doubt the adequacy of legislative demand-making. As has been noted, certain groups are often not represented in the assembly, and ordinary MP's are frequently poorly informed on broad questions of national policy. Thus while specific and parochial demands have been articulated in these assemblies, it seems possible to assert that these institutions have not provided their executives with adequate means, in the words of Pye, "for calculating the relative distribution of attitudes and values throughout the society." [54]

What, then, is the value of parliament to these countries? Mackintosh has written that the Federal Parliament in Nigeria provided "salaries and prestige for a number of men of the second rank in political importance, while giving Ministers an extra opportunity to . . . keep an eye on their supporters." [55] It seems likely that this is a universal parliamentary function. It might be termed the patronage function of parliament.

The supposition is that it is worthwhile to support second-rank poli-

[52] The comparable figures for Tanzania and Uganda in 1964 were 37 percent and 30 percent respectively.

[53] It must be allowed, however, that in the event of a crisis of political succession, parliament in a number of countries could, in Lee's words, "acquire a brief moment of glory" (p. 392), i.e., parliament could perform an essential function of political recruitment.

[54] Pye, "The Non-Western Political Process," *Journal of Politics* (August 1958), p. 482.

[55] Mackintosh, "The Nigerian Federal Parliament," p. 360.

ticians, that legislators apart from their legislative roles can perform valuable political services. In 1963 Lee noted that in Ghana MP's were regarded by the president to be "more important in their 'out-of-school' activities." The purpose of these activities was, in the words of Nkrumah, to broaden "the front or support for the leadership." [56] Other African leaders have similarly defined the work of parliamentarians to include the education and mobilization of public opinion behind the government. In 1960, for example, Julius Nyerere, then chief minister of Tanganyika, directed MP's to explain official policies to their constituents.[57]

The performance by MP's of the support-building role commonly assigned them appears, however, to have been disappointing. In 1958 Austin wrote that MP's in Ghana were taking their duties seriously, regularly visiting their constituencies on party campaigns to explain new legislation.[58] But by 1962 President Nkrumah felt it necessary to accuse MP's publicly of becoming "a new class of self-seekers and careerists," [59] and after June 1965, MP's in Ghana received no salary for performing their parliamentary duties. They were expected to hold full-time jobs to support themselves. Jon Kraus observed that the necessity of holding a job would inevitably diminish the extent of close contact between the MP and his constituents.[60] Tordoff asserts that since 1965 the Tanzanian government has apparently attached little importance to the work of MP's in their constituencies, while Engholm has doubted that MP's in Uganda "can translate the sophisticated categories of explanation utilized by government into vernacular languages." [61] My own view in Kenya in 1966 was that MP's were ineffectual in building support for the regime among their constituents. Indeed, few appeared to find it necessary to try.

At the least, parliament does offer an additional platform from which the government can publicly articulate its policies. There is, however, some question about the extent of the audience for parliamentary debates. Gupta believes that in Zambia there has existed "great public interest" in the proceedings of the National Assembly and that these have provided "an opportunity to the people to know as to what goes on in the higher echelon of national administration." [62] In contrast, Engholm suspects that what occurs in the Ugandan National Assembly is "remote" from public opinion and information, and in a similar vein Mackintosh wrote in 1963 that victories in debate in the Nigerian parliament ap-

---

[56] Lee, "Parliament in Republican Ghana," p. 385.
[57] Tordoff, "Parliament in Tanzania," pp. 97–98.
[58] Austin, "The Ghana Parliament's First Year," p. 360.
[59] Lee, "Parliament in Republican Ghana," p. 387.
[60] Kraus, "Ghana's New 'Corporate Parliament,'" p. 10.
[61] Engholm, "The Westminster Model in Uganda," p. 476; Tordoff, "Parliament in Tanzania," pp. 98–99.
[62] Gupta, "The Zambian National Assembly," p. 53.

peared to "count for little." [63] In 1958 Austin believed it was necessary in Ghana to "sell the idea of Parliament" to the public.[64]

Writing in 1963, Lee observed:

It is one of the principal ironies of the transplantation of the Westminster model from Britain to Ghana that it has produced almost a complete reversal from the "decorative" and "efficient" institutions of government to which Bagehot referred. The President of Ghana has inherited . . . a position which corresponds very closely to the Prerogative of the English Crown . . . , and yet remains the "efficient" part . . . . The National Assembly of Ghana, in contrast, might well be regarded as the "decorative" part.[65]

It seems possible to extend Lee's characterization to other countries for which we now have data: Parliament is primarily a decoration of the state. But decorations in politics are symbols and herein lies the most general value of parliament, for symbols confer meaning. Two specific meanings are implied in the existence of parliament. One is national political equality. After all, an assembly of some form is found in nearly every sovereign state, irrespective of its political character. A national legislature would appear to be a necessary accouterment of independence. The second meaning is popular government. No other institution seems capable of symbolizing these values as well as does parliament, especially in Africa, where the struggle against colonialism, i.e., for popular government and national independence, commonly focused on the powers and composition of the legislative council. It may be asked for whom parliament is a symbol—the electorate, the national elite, foreign diplomats? The answer to this question is not clear, although it appears to be a general supposition that parliament is a popular symbol. "It would be psychologically difficult," Lee has written, "to replace a parliament of M.P.s by a congress of party secretaries in Ghana because such an action would be contrary to the constitutional mythology of the nation's origin." [66] In 1965 in Tanzania the Presidential Commission on the Establishment of a Democratic One Party State rejected a similar proposal, holding "it as a basic principle that the supreme law-making body in the State should be directly elected by universal suffrage." [67] Despite its considerable expense,[68] the institution of parliament seems likely to endure, if only for reason of its presumed symbolic content. Even in Ghana, Nigeria, and Sierra Leone, where parliament has been

---

[63] Engholm, "The Westminster Model in Uganda," p. 476; Mackintosh, "The Nigerian Federal Parliament," p. 347.
[64] Austin, "The Ghana Parliament's First Year," p. 360.
[65] Lee, "Parliament in Republican Ghana," p. 389.
[66] Ibid.
[67] Africa Report, X (October 1965), 22.
[68] In Kenya, for example, the cost of maintaining the National Assembly in 1965–66, while less than 1 percent of the annual budget, was greater than the cost of maintaining any one of six ministries.

abolished, the military governors have construed this as but a temporary suspension. In Africa, as elsewhere, a national political life without a parliament is unthinkable.

Conclusions. Among the six states whose parliaments we have been able to consider in some detail, the institution appears to matter little. Parliament neither structures the political process nor adds materially to the content of political decisions. Nor does it affect the distribution of political power. But if parliament in these states does not shape politics, it is itself shaped by politics. Parliament does appear to register, or mirror, many of the dominant political characteristics of its environment. It thus may be important analytically.

At the most general level, two contradictory characteristics of national political life in these African states stand out. One is the commitment of politicians in these countries to *popular government.* This can be seen in the elimination of second chambers, the predilection for presidential forms, the intention that parliament act as an agent for political socialization and popular mobilization, the place of public referenda in the constitutional amendment process, and the retention of a one-man, one-vote franchise, even while allowing the appointment of MP's by the executive to increase the "representativeness" of the assembly. The second feature is the *isolation and concentration of decision-making power.* This is shown in the absence of lobbyists in the legislative process, the inexpertness of parliamentary debate, the ineffectiveness of oppositions, the fact of the dominance of parliament by the executive, and the independence of government backbenchers. The last named would appear to be a consequence of the isolation of decision-makers rather than its manifestation, a product of the contradiction between populist ideology and the reality of elitist rule. The future of politics in the countries we have considered will doubtless be much influenced by the working out of this contradiction. Evidence of this process certainly will be mirrored in the actions and compositions of the several parliaments.

One of the principal purposes of political institutions and processes is, of course, the formulation of public policy. In every society, many forces impinge upon the processes of policy-making, and a number of these forces in the developing states have already been identified. Over time, some general characteristics of policy-making in the developing states have emerged, and in the selection below, the author identifies and discusses some of them and their effect upon the allocation of resources, particularly with respect to social and economic development.

26. PUBLIC-POLICY-MAKING IN AVANT-GARDE DEVELOPMENT STATES*†

y e h e z k e l   d r o r

CHARACTERISTICS AND DOMAIN
OF VALIDITY OF THE PURE TYPE
"AVANT-GARDE DEVELOPMENT
STATE" CONSTRUCT

Development states vary considerably in their level of technology, man-power resources, history, ideology, financial means, social structure and political regimes; therefore every generalization on "development states" in general has many exceptions. In order partly to overcome this difficulty, we shall direct our remarks at a "pure" development-state-type to be called "avant-garde development state". The main character-istics of this composite construct of one type of development states include: a very low level of technological development; strong tribal or communal structure which is in the process of breaking up; a mass leader with a small political elite aspiring to achieve radical social-economic transformation within a short time and having a strong grip on the masses, both through charisma and force; nearly no middle class; a long history of colonial rule terminated recently after a period of mil-itant nationalism; and a large scope of public-policy-making, including economic activities. This composite picture fits well most of the Central and West African and some of the Southeast Asian new states. It also fits to a significant degree many North African and Middle Eastern states and applies in the main to Communist China. Most of the characteristics do not fit some development states which either do not yet engage in radical directed social change (such as Liberia and Ethiopia) or which are already well developed in some respects (such as India, Israel,

* From "Public-Policy-Making in Avant-Garde Development States" by Yehezkel Dror, Civilisations, Vol. XIII, No. 4 (1963), pp. 395–405. By permission.
† This article was written while the author was a Fellow at the Center for Ad-vanced Study in the Behavioral Sciences.

Puerto Rico and the United Arab Republic [Egypt]); but even in respect to these, some of the characteristics do apply. Therefore the characteristics of public-policy-making to be presented fit fully some of the development states—namely those approaching the avant-garde pure type—and fit in part most other development states.

MAIN CHARACTERISTICS OF PUBLIC-POLICY-MAKING IN AVANT-GARDE DEVELOPMENT STATES

Having completed the necessary preliminary steps, we can now take on our main task, namely presentation of the main characteristics of public-policy-making in avant-garde development states. Relying on the conceptual framework presented above, we shall proceed by discussing first some general findings, then findings on input, output, structure and process respectively.

1. General Findings

(1). Both the actual quality and the maximum feasible quality of public-policy-making in the development states are much lower than those in modern states. The maximum feasible level is lower because of the dearth of resources which—even if fully utilized—are insufficient for high quality public-policy-making. The real level of public-policy-making is even lower because of a variety of factors which prevent full utilization of available resources, to be detailed in the following findings. While, therefore, the actual level of public-policy-making could be increased with available resources, it is unavoidable that for a considerable time—and even assuming the best of conditions—the overall quality of public-policy-making in the development countries will be significantly lower than that in the modern countries. This remains true, though to a lesser degree, even if large public-policy-making resources are transferred from the latter to the first.

(2). Contemporary public-policy-making systems as a whole, and most of their aspects and components in particular, are in all countries the result of historic evolution tempered by conscious renovations. These renovations were in most cases either improvisations directed at imminent crises, or/and reforms following radical changes in the political and value environment. All in all, systematic efforts to direct human intelligence at improving public-policy-making systems have been limited in scope and effect, though growing in importance and of significant aggregative impact in the modern countries. In the avant-garde development states, historic evolution and personal accidents are relatively even more important, conscious, systematic and rational reforms necessarily being as yet a very minor force in shaping the public-policy-making system.

(3). The basic strategy of public-policy-making in the avant-garde development states is one of maximax (that is, directed at achieving the maximum of positive results with relative disregard of possible negative consequences) with a low security-level. In other words, achievement of the desired goals requiring a sharp break with the past. Very little experience in accelerated and directed large-scale social change being available, incremental change cannot be utilized and "muddling through" (in the sense of cautious and marginal action through slow trial-and-error) is of no avail.[1] The only possible strategy of public-policy-making fitting the goals and conditions of avant-garde development states is one of far-reaching change involving high risks.[2] The real danger implied in such a strategy is much reduced because of the assured survival (see finding 13 below) which makes a maximax strategy in development countries much less dangerous than in modern and more risk-sensitive states.

(4). Public-policy-making in the avant-garde development countries penetrates both less and more into social activities than in the modern countries. It penetrates more in respect to the selected issues with which it deals, because of the radical change aimed at and the near monopoly of public-policy-making as a method for dealing with social problems (which results both from the absence of private policy-making and the pro-central-public-policy-making basic ideology). It penetrates less, because public-policy-making concentrates on some clusters of problems—mainly those involving economic development—mono-focal objectives and scarcity of resources making necessary abandonment of many spheres of social activity to non-directed change. This often leads to unbalanced development which creates new acute social problems, which earlier or later will become foci for public-policy-making.[3]

---

[1]   On this problem, see Charles E. Lindblom, "The Science of 'Muddling Through' ", *Public Administration Review*, Vol. 19 (1959), pp. 79 ff. and Yehezkel Dror, "Muddling Through—'Science' or Inertia?" (forthcoming).

[2]   The fact that most of the relevant experience in extensive "social engineering" is concentrated in the USSR and that their experts are more predisposed to radical action, presents a serious challenge for Western Democracy in the struggle over the future political orientation of the avant-garde development states. Much care must be taken not to transfer philosophic approaches and solutions based on totally different conditions to the development states. In this respect, experts coming from democratic countries which did engage in large-scale directed social change—such as The Netherlands and Israel—may have a significant advantage.

[3]   This may sometimes be an important advantage, decreasing the burden on public-policy-making and encouraging strenuous efforts. See Albert O. Hirschman, *The Strategy of Economic Development* (New Haven: Yale University Press), 1958, and Albert O. Hirschman and Charles E. Lindblom, "Economic Development, Research and Development, Policy Making: Some Convergent Views", *Behavioral Science*, Vol. 7 (1962), pp. 211 ff.

(5). Value-priorities and, to some extent, operational goals, are relatively more developed because of the clear predominance given to technological and economic development. A number of inconsistent values remain—such as raising the educational level of the masses ("primary education for all") vs. education directed at preparing manpower for economic development.[4] Basically, many values accepted in modern states are regarded as expendable, thus enabling concentration of resources on fewer goals and facilitating public-policy-making.

(6). A basic paradox of public-policy-making in nearly all avant-garde development countries is the intense predisposition toward radical social change on one hand and strong conservatism in regard to the basic design of public-policy-making itself on the other hand. In some respects, it seems to be easier to uproot whole tribes and change patterns of social action going back many generations than to change personal patterns of work and reorganize small circles of collaborators so as to increase the quality of public-policy-making.

(7). The value-ecology within which the public-policy-making system operates and which conditions its basic characteristics is not conducive to optimality. Especially disturbing is the absence of a basic pro-rational orientation deeply rooted in culture, as found in Western societies. Also the after-effects of the traumatic experience of becoming an independent nation have a tendency to lead either to highly emotional patterns of activity and/or to apathy, both being barriers to the optimistic matter-of-fact approach required for optimum public-policy-making.

2. Findings on Input

(8). The total resources available in development societies are very limited. Especially scarce are qualified manpower and data, which are the most important resources for public-policy-making. Considerable resources are required for basic collections of data and surveys of the physical and social ecology which are taken for granted in modern countries. Even though there is a strong tendency for the better-qualified manpower to go into the public-policy-making occupations, the absolute scarcity of available qualified manpower results in lack of suitable personnel and reliance on under-qualified persons in many important policy-making positions.

(9). The resources-input into public-policy-making is determined in a rather haphazard manner. Increasing attention is paid to resources-allocation to substantive operations and various techniques, such as performance budgeting, are sometimes introduced for that purpose. But public-policy-making as such is often regarded as a sort of "overhead costs" or "administrative expenses", with the concomitant tendency to

[4] I am indebted to Frederick Harbison and Charles Myers for this illustration.

try and save money by cutting these expenses. This tendency is reinforced by the absence of measurable or obvious output-changes, which make input items into public-policy-making a favorite target for so-called "efficiency drives". On the other hand, the forces of inertia often prevent any really penetrating reform in the established patterns of resources allocation.

(10). More specifically, public-policy-making lacks especially the following inputs: resources for research; resources for comprehensive information-collecting, storing and retrieval; resources for thinking-units; and resources for policy-training.

(11). In regard to manpower input, it is possible to distinguish between two main relevant occupations: politics and civil service. The degree of differentiation and turnover between these two policy-making occupations varies between different avant-garde development countries, the tendency being towards some fusing of the two. Recruitment to both occupations is characterized by the dearth of qualified manpower and the priority enjoyed by persons who were active in the independence-movement. Little conscious activity to train reserves of policy-making cadres takes place.[5]

(12). A unique resources-source is foreign aid, in the context of public-policy-making—mainly foreign experts. Foreign experts, supplied partly by the various international agencies under the auspices of the Technical Assistance Board of the United Nations and partly through bilateral and multi-lateral agreements, present an unprecedented effort at import of public-policy-making resources. Their overall contribution to the improvement of public-policy-making in the avant-garde development countries is impressive but limited. Foreign experts are more difficult to utilize in public-policy-making than in more technical activities because of the higher political sensitivity of many policy-issues and because many foreign experts are quite ignorant of the relevant socio-political background. Also, no amount of foreign experts can compensate for lack of data on one hand and lack of rational patterns of behavior on the other. Therefore, while foreign experts have very beneficial short- and long-range effects on public-policy-making, they cannot fully compensate for the lack of local qualified manpower resources and the absence of rational values and behavior patterns.

3. Findings on Output

(13). One of the most interesting features of public-policy-making in all development countries are the relationships between the maximum

---

[5] For a series of relevant papers, see INCIDI, *Staff Problems in Tropical and Subtropical Countries* (Bruxelles: International Institute of Differing Civilizations), 1961.

feasible and real output-results on one hand [and] the objective survival level and minimum aspiration level on the other. The basic findings to be noted are that however low the actual quality of public-policy-making, the objective survival level is nearly always achieved (the exception being problems of possible external aggression); and that even if the maximum feasible level of public-policy-making were achieved, it would fall far below the level of minimum aspiration, not to speak of the much higher aspiration level of "satisfactory achievement".

The explanation of these findings is quite simple: The basic social structure of the development countries is still autonomous from public-policy-making and would survive even if all (non-local) public-policy-making were to break down. A complex modern society would not survive any real breakdown in public-policy-making, in the simplest meaning of nearly all the population dying unless a very complex network of services, depending *inter alia* on quite high-quality public-policy-making, is maintained. The less complex development societies are not as sensitive and are well able to survive the worst public-policies or even a total breakdown of the public-policy-making system.[6] On the other side of the picture, in most modern societies the gap between actual policy-results and the medium aspiration level is not very high; in the avant-garde development states the aspiration level has been imported by the elite from modern countries and is quickly becoming diffused in the population. This aspiration level—while not defined in detail—includes a standard of living and levels of economic activity patterned on the highest developed Western societies, to be achieved in "the near future"—and this is simply impossible, even with optimal public-policy-making and tremendous assistance from the modern states. This large gap between what is wanted and often promised and what is possible, constitutes a most serious source of tension which may well lead to social explosions once the expectations are clearly frustrated. Substitution of more realistic levels of aspiration for the utopian ones is, therefore, a basic long-range requirement for preserving environmental conditions for high-quality public-policy-making and for the highest feasible rate of actual socio-economic progress.

(14). Despite the predisposition to plan, overall desired output determination for public-policy-making is non-existent because of the concentration of public-policy-making on limited issue-clusters (see finding 4 above). Even in regard to limited projects, realistic target-setting is found only in the relatively more developed development-countries,

---

[6] Therefore, they are less sensitive to nuclear warfare. Assuming that radioactivity would not wipe out all life, but that all central directory and regulatory activities would be disrupted, most of the population in modern countries would die because of lack of food, water, energy and medical services. Nothing comparable would happen in the development countries, where most of the population still lives in self-sufficient local units.

such as India. In most of the avant-garde development states both the necessary knowledge and action-patterns are absent, realistic planning being more often imposed from abroad as a condition for financial assistance than being practiced on local initiative.

4. Findings in Regard to Structure

(15). The public-policy-making structure is much simpler than in the modern states. Individual and small-group decisions play a relatively greater role than organizational processes and the aggregation-functions are less complex and easier to observe. Private individuals and legislatures have much less influence on public-policy-making, being more passive material for manipulation and channels for recruitment of support respectively than active contributors to public-policy-making. Private intellectuals are nearly non-contributing to public-policy-making, being either non-existent or influence-less and politically apathetic. Interest-groups are active, but are smaller in number and more integrated; they operate more in the manner of cliques than as autonomous social units. Leaders have a predominant influence, being aided by small cadres of followers.

(16). Most of the occupants of the central public-policy-making roles have a predisposition to improvisation and extra-rational decision-making, which is a carry-over from the pre-independence period. During the pre-independence period, the politicians of the independence movement operated mainly through improvisation, one of the main required skills being an ability to improvise in the face of quickly changing circumstances in which every small opportunity had to be taken advantage of without delay. The main qualifications for success were highly developed political acumen and charisma, there being little scope for rational long-range policy-making. These patterns of behavior were tremendously reinforced through the successful achievement of independence; therefore, when the pre-independence leaders took over the new policy-making positions they brought with them strongly ingrained behavior-patterns which are not congruent with those required for optimal public-policy-making in a development state. Some outstanding politicians did change their patterns of behavior but most of them neither feel the need nor are able to do so.[7] It may therefore take some time until natural and non-natural turnover of leaders bring to the main policy-

[7] In some development countries the pre-independence type of leader is still essential for building up a unitary nation, a task for which extra-rational and even mystic modes of operation may be optimal. Under such conditions, the quality of public-policy-making as such cannot as yet serve as a relevant criterion, other tasks being more important. In these cases, the problems of incongruency between actual and needed patterns of behavior by the senior political stratum are delayed but not avoided.

making positions persons whose action-patterns fit the requirement of optimum public-policy-making.

(17). The consequences of the last observations are strongly reinforced by the weaknesses of the higher civil service. With a few exceptions, most of the senior positions had been occupied during the pre-independence period by foreigners. When independence was achieved, these positions were taken over in most countries by persons who were often highly intelligent and devoted, but never had the opportunity to acquire the knowledge and patterns-of-work needed for public-policy-making under development conditions. The insufficiency in the contribution of the government bureaucracy to public-policy-making is further aggravated by an overload with new problems and programmes. Also, in some of the development countries the new indigenous civil service absorbed the patterns of social behavior of the former senior class of expatriates, which do not fit the new conditions and which seriously impair contact between the civil servants and the new political leaders and/or the masses. The cumulative result is that in most development countries the senior civil service necessarily contributes much less to public-policy-making-optimality than their counterparts in the modern countries, thus compounding the non-optimal action-patterns of the politicians instead of compensating for them.

5. Findings in Regard to Process

(18). Extrarational processes play a tremendous role in public-policy-making. In some avant-garde development countries intuition is explicitly regarded as superior to knowledge, a phenomenon associated with some kind of *Führer* ideology. In most cases, rationalization (in the psychological sense) to justify public policy is extensively relied upon.

(19). As a result of the already mentioned facts, most of the elements needed for high-quality public-policy-making are little developed. Especially weak are the rational elements, most of which are in an embryonic stage. The extra-rational elements are relatively better developed, but also not very much so.

SOME IMPLICATIONS

The actual state of affairs in respect to public-policy-making in avant-garde development states must be compared with both their aspirations and their often expressed intention to base activities on the best available knowledge. The gap between actual public-policy-making and optimal, knowledge based, public-policy-making is very large indeed. In part this is unavoidable; in part this gap can be bridged, but only with the help of vigorous action, whole-hearted devotion and determination similar in intensity—but not in direction and method—to those which enabled these countries to achieve independence. At the same time, considering the critical role of public-policy-making for the achievement of their goals and the large gap between reality and minimum aspiration level, improvement of public-policy-making is one of the most urgent and promising challenges faced by the avant-garde development states.

With governments increasingly involved in the search for answers to economic and social problems, bureaucracies everywhere have grown and assumed more authority. In transitional states, bureaucracies are often relatively more powerful than their counterparts in more developed states, but they also possess some characteristics that diminish their full potential. In the next selection, S. N. Eisenstadt explores some of the strengths and weaknesses of bureaucracies in the exercise of political influence and in the administration of public policy in the developing states.

27. PROBLEMS OF EMERGING BUREAUCRACIES IN DEVELOPING AREAS AND NEW STATES*

s. n. eisenstadt

I

In all developing countries, bureaucracies very rapidly tend to develop and extend their scope. As the post-colonial new states attained inde-

* From "Problems of Emerging Bureaucracies in Developing Areas and New States" by S. N. Eisenstadt. Reprinted from: *Industrialization and Society*, by F. Hoselitz and W. E. Moore, eds., (Unesco/Mouton, 1963), with the permission of Unesco. Selections from pp. 159–171.

pendence, and as some of the older states (e.g., Latin America or the Middle East) surged toward modernization and expanded the range of state activities, they took over many organs of public administration remaining from the former period; the scope of their activities greatly expanded, and new organs were created. Each became a very important part of the political framework in these countries. Since, in most of these countries, the government plays a great role in economic development, the bureaucracies also began to engage significantly in the activities of the economic sphere. The bureaucracy's activities could then have great influence on the direction and tempo of the country's economic development.

✿   ✿   ✿   ✿   ✿

I I

One of the striking facts about the bureaucracies of the developing areas is that, in most of these areas there exist not one but usually two or three, bureaucracies—or, at least, different layers of bureaucratic organization and structure. First, there is what may be called the "pre-modern" or "pre-development" layer, which had developed before the attainment of independence or the introduction of modernization. The second stratum has, as a rule, developed since World War II. It was engendered by the dual impacts of the attainment of independence and of modernization and of establishing new social, political, and economic goals.

In the post-colonial new states, the "old" colonial civil service still survives in remaining personnel, organizational structure, and tradition. The structure and organization of the old civil service provided the basic framework for the extension and development of bureaucratic administration after the attainment of independence.

Within these societies, the initial emergence of bureaucracies had been rooted in the need of the colonial powers for various resources and for the maintenance of law and order. The bureaucracy was based on over-all political control by the metropolitan powers; the administration participated minimally in the indigenous political and social life of the community. This necessarily limited its activities, confining them to the basic administrative services It also dictated some of the bureaucracy's structural characteristics, such as the high degree of centralization, the great adherence to legal precepts and rules, and the relatively small internal differentiation. Thus the pre-independence bureaucracies helped establish the framework of modern, universalistic legal and administrative practices and organizations. On the other hand, they were highly apolitical. They did not meddle in politics, and they kept up the ideal of a politically neutral civil service. They were also apolitical in that they never really participated in the indigenous political life of the countries in which they served. Their very limited goals were prescribed by the colonial powers, who were not responsible to the political groups and opinions of the countries which they ruled. . . . It is significant that the scope and impact of the activities of the colonial civil service were much greater in countries, such as India, in which "direct rule" was applied, than in countries governed according to precepts of "indirect rule," where the native population was left more or less alone to manage its own affairs, especially on the local level.

The second main layer of the bureaucracies in the new states consists of those departments and echelons which were developed after the attainment of independence. Here a new civil service—"new" in personnel, goals, departments, and activities—evolved. This stratum had to be staffed with new recruits—frequently with inadequately trained recruits whose chief claim to or qualification for office was their former participation in the nationalistic political movements. These new bureaucratic organs have had new types of goals, like economic development, social betterment, educational advancement, or community development.

Unlike members of the "colonial" civil service, most of the recruits to the new have usually had a clear and articulated political orientation and sense of political responsibility. They have very often perceived themselves as representatives of their respective movements, parties, or sectors. Moreover, they frequently have seen themselves as fulfilling chiefly political functions—either as implementing political goals, or as representing, articulating and regulating the political interests and activities of different groups and social strata.

The relations between the older bureaucracy and the new echelons have not always been easy. In the first period after independence, particularly, the nationalist leaders' prevailing attitude toward the remnants of the older colonial services was distrust. In some cases, this led to the almost complete destruction of the older structure. In most instances, however, some sort of *modus vivendi* has been evolved between the older and newer echelon. One or the other is usually predominant; but necessarily the implementation of new social, political, and economic goals has been strongly emphasized, and the involvement in the political process has been much greater than before.

An even more explicitly politically oriented type of bureaucracy has tended to emerge in most of the new states. This type consists of the different "party" bureaucracies which grew out of the leading nationalistic movements which became dominant parties—e.g., the Congress in India, the PCP in Ghana or the Neo-Destour in Tunisia. These party bureaucracies have been oriented more to the political manipulation of groups of population and to the provision of political support and loyalty to the new regime than to the upholding of universalistic legal norms, the development of public services, or the creation of new public administrative services. In personnel or over-all political supervision, the party bureaucracy has often been very similar to the new echelons of the governmental bureaucracy, and has sometimes also been closely related to it, especially through the activities of prime ministers and cabinet ministers. However, the basic patterns of activities and orientations of the members of the party bureaucracy have frequently differed to a very great extent from those of the governmental bureaucracy, and have sometimes clashed.[1]

III

The bureaucracies in developing countries which have not been under colonial rule exhibit a somewhat different, although not entirely dissimilar, pattern. Within each there existed, first, a traditional bureaucracy—whether "royal" (as in the Middle Eastern countries) or "oligarchical-republican" (as in most Latin American countries). These bureaucracies usually dominated the political scene until the end of World War II. Within them, some traditional elements were mixed with more modern ones. Frequently, the modern elements were copied from some European country—for example, the French pattern had strong influence in most Latin American countries.

These administrations were usually concerned with supporting the interests of the ruling oligarchies, and with implementing rather limited social and economic objectives. Whatever tendency to modernization they may have exhibited—e.g., in the fields of military affairs or education —their major political aim was to restrict modernization to those minimal spheres in which it was necessary to maintain the viability of the then existing system.

With increasing modernization, with the growing impact of internal democratization, and with the development of new social, political, and economic goals, these bureaucracies had to extend the scope of their activities and to recruit new personnel. However, the older pattern usually continued to leave its imprint on the new echelons and departments, in administrative training, organization, and to some extent also in social and political orientation.[2] . . .

[1] See D. Apter and R. A. Lystad, "Bureaucracy, Party and Constitutional Democracy," in G. M. Carter and W. O. Brown (eds.), *Transition in Africa* (Boston, 1958).
[2] See the papers by G. Blanksten and D. Rustow in G. A. Almond and J. S. Coleman (eds.), *The Politics of the Developing Areas* (Princeton, N. J., 1960). See also the papers by W. R. Sharp (on Egypt), A. Lepawsky (on Bolivia), F. Heady (on the Philippines), and J. N. More (on Thailand), in W. J. Siffin (ed.), *Toward the Comparative Study of Public Administration* (Bloomington, Ind., 1957).

In most of these older countries, the party bureaucracies were usually less important than in the new states. . . .

Both within the formerly colonial societies and in the states with longer traditions of independence, another distinct type of new bureaucratic organization has also emerged—the big economic or business corporation. Within the older countries, these corporations are usually more concentrated in the private sector; in the new states, more in the public or mixed sectors. In all these societies, however, the corporations play an important role in the economic and political life of the country.

I V

We see thus that, in each emerging country, the pattern of development of bureaucracies has been very mixed and heterogeneous. Each part of the bureaucracy developed under somewhat different conditions and in response to different types of needs and pressures. It was only after the attainment of independence, and/or the development of goals and programs of modernization, that these parts were brought together into a common framework and confronted with the need to find some *modus vivendi* in order to deal with the new tasks which they faced.

Perhaps the most important general problem which faced all the bureaucracies was the necessity to adapt themselves to the goals, new spheres of activity, and new social needs that arose from the growing differentiation and diversification of the social structures, the extension of the scope of social and political participation of many groups in the society, and the development of new social and political goals. In trying to adapt themselves, the emerging bureaucracies developed several characteristics which were greatly influenced by their heterogeneous origins and by the conditions in which they found themselves.

✽ ✽ ✽ ✽ ✽

The first and most important development in the social and political orientations of these bureaucracies is their high involvement in the political process in their respective countries. This is manifested in several ways.

In many of these countries, for example, the bureaucracy becomes not only the administrative arm of an executive, supervised by the legislature; it also constitutes itself as an effective executive or a component thereof, and plays a basic part in establishing, determining, and implementing political goals and major policy directives. In many nations, the bureaucracy may be the main or the only body which, apart from the head of the executive, is capable of formulating clear political and administrative goals and objectives.

The second major aspect of the bureaucracy's involvement in the political process is grounded in the fact that it tends to evolve as one of the principal instruments of political regulation—one of the main channels of political struggle in which and through which different interests are regulated and "aggregated"—and it tends to be very important, even predominant, in this facet of the political process. In some cases, e.g., in some Latin American countries, the bureaucracy also becomes a powerful pressure and interest group in its own right, strongly allied to other oligarchical groups.

Thus, in all these countries, the bureaucracy may tend to fulfill different types of political functions and—like parties, legislatures, and executives—become a center of various kinds of political activity. Although, through such activities, it may establish some of the basic frameworks of modern politics, it may also minimize the extent of differentiation of divers types of political roles and activities. In the latter case, it would greatly impede the development of autonomous and differentiated political activities, organizations, and orientations.

The second basic characteristic of the social orientations of emergent bureaucracies is that they are also major instruments of social change and of political socialization in their respective countries.

These bureaucratic organizations are (at least initially) based on universalistic and functionally specific definitions of the role of the official and the role of the client. The majority of the population of these countries, however, have a different orientation. In social life, their traditional orientations and structures, such as the extended family, are predominant. In these societies, most of a person's role relations are set within traditional groups; and rights and duties are defined in terms of personal relationships. Previous experience with bureaucratic organizations was restricted, and was rarely of any great significance.

Thus, the contacts of the public with governmental organizations provided a framework for a wider process of political socialization. The public's accommodation to the new political structure became, to a considerable extent, dependent upon its successful learning in these situations of contact. This has very often forced the bureaucracies to go beyond their proper specialized roles and to assume various roles of social and political leadership and tutelage—without which they could not have effected the necessary changes in the behavior of the population at large. This need to foster change often extended the scope of the activities of bureaucrats beyond their specific goals, and made them reach also into the realm of family, kinship, and community life of wide strata of the population.

✿   ✿   ✿   ✿   ✿

V

All these forces—the cultural orientations prevalent in these societies, the political and economic processes and pressures—necessarily have their repercussion on the structure of the bureaucracies and on their ability to implement major political and social goals and to provide continuous services to the population.

Among the most important of such structural problems, the following have often been noted: [3] (a) the low density of administrative structure, i.e., the relatively small ratio of officials to population and tasks; (b) the lack of fully qualified and adequate personnel; (c) the small extent of diversification of functions, and consequent overlapping between different organizations; (d) inadequate communication between different echelons and departments; and (e) overcentralization, poor co-ordination, and lack of autonomy and initiative of the linestaff.

Riggs has aptly summarized some of these problems, especially as they apply to older independent countries:

Obstacles to identification of personal with program goals are especially conspicuous in the way the work load and responsibilities of different officials are allocated, that is, in "organization and management." These often make it impossible for anyone to carry out a constructive project without waiting for the concurrence of many others, whereby many people have the power to block action. One result is often to elevate the level of settlement of even minor disputes to ministerial, cabinet, and chief executive levels. Top administrators become embroiled in continual interagency conflicts while subordinates piddle away their energies waiting for requisite approvals. Moreover, because many persons far from the scene of action become involved in decision making, questions are often referred to persons with only remote interest in them, it becomes difficult to assign responsibility for action, and final decisions hinge on the outcome of power struggles among individuals only indirectly concerned.[4]

In some countries, elaborate ministerial secretariats, staffed by generalists, who rotate frequently between headquarters and district assignments, have been placed in the line of communication and command between ministers and executive or administrative departments and divisions. Invariably, great delay ensues while secretariat officials review more and more of the work nominally assigned to and originating in the departments. We may quote the words of a distinguished former civil servant in India about the result:

The head of the department is deprived of all initiative and instead of being allowed to attend to and make progress with his own work, has to spend a

---

[3] See, for instance, J. L. Quermonne, "La sous-administration et les politiques d'équipement administratif," Revue française de science politique, IX, No. 3 (Septembre, 1959), 629–67.

[4] F. W. Riggs, "Public Administration—A Neglected Factor in Economic Development," Annals of the American Academy of Political and Social Science (May, 1956), pp. 70–81.

great deal of time submitting unnecessary reports, explaining the position in individual matters to the Ministry and getting its orders on points which lie well within his own sphere of authority.

Because of overcentralization and lack of delegation, those close to the goals of action cannot easily cooperate with their colleagues in other agencies whose work directly affects the success of their own efforts. Characteristically, to overcome this stagnation, new agencies are often set up in the hope that, outside the bog of established structures, action may be possible. But the new agencies simply add to the intra-bureaucratic conflict and competition, increasing the burden on the top of the hierarchy to impose coordination.[5]

The relative importance of these problems naturally varies in different countries. In the post-colonial countries, the most critical problems seem to be lack of adequate staff, overcentralization, and too little diversification. In the independent countries, the most vital problems are the excessive control, rigidity, and lack of initiative of the officials, and their regarding their offices as sinecures. However, there is much overlapping between these different structural aspects. And beyond all these, there always hovers the double specter of corruption and growing inefficiency of the bureaucracy.

[5]   A. D. Gorwala, *Report on Public Administration* (New Delhi, 1951), p. 39. See also Paul H. Appleby, *Public Administration in India; Report of a Survey* (New Delhi, 1953), Sec. II, especially p. 21.

vi. problems in nation-building

A broad array of complex social and political problems, many of which have already been identified, confront the developing states. Some of these problems involve the fundamental questions concerning the unit that is to constitute the state, the state's social and political institutions, and the system of law upon which political authority is to rest. Another group of problems concerns the basic policies to be pursued for the solution of major issues. Priorities must be set and decisions reached on the general allocation of scarce resources for purposes of modernization and development, for example. A third group consists of problems of a more specific nature. Decisions must be made on a variety of issues, such as the allocation of funds for specific projects, the location of roads, schools, and industry, the provisions for fire and police protection, public housing, health, and sanitation, and all the other routine problems confronting any state. Of course, no clear distinctions can be drawn between these several groups of problems; a problem that may deeply divide one society may be of quite secondary importance in another, and problems that at one time appear to be of major significance for a society may later seem to be of much less importance. Nevertheless, a broad distinction can be drawn between the problems that concern the very existence of a state and those that involve policy decisions on a wide range of social and economic questions.

In any society, most problems other than those involving the basic issues of human survival are "created" in the sense that existing conditions are regarded as unsatisfactory and alternatives are perceived to exist. In the developing states, many problems have been created by the gradual exposure of persons to different social, economic, and political values and institutions through various types of contact with the outside world. In many states, however, the masses (particularly in the rural areas) only dimly perceive the prospects for, or advantages of, change, though this condition is being altered, in some instances very rapidly. The limited physical and intellectual world in which the masses generally still live has conditioned them to accept life as inevitably harsh and often cruel. This attitude itself constitutes a major obstacle for the modernizing elite, who identify many more conditions in society as problems capable of resolution than do the masses. On the other hand, once the desire for change is stimulated, policies must be developed, taking into account the consequences of different alternative solutions to the problems that have been identified.

As the previous chapter has indicated, many of the transitional states have not as yet been able to develop stable political institutions and processes. Until a broader consensus is developed on the basic framework of the state and its principal institutions, efficient, effective decision-making is impeded. The development of such consensus is itself obstructed, however, by the ineffectiveness of the decision-making process in many states in resolving the increasing number of problems that have been identified as capable of political solution. Conversely, the demonstrated effectiveness of political institutions in achieving popular solutions usually tends to promote support for the institutions, processes, and individual leaders.

Among the most basic political problems confronting any state are those of defining the geographical limits of the state and the relationships of the constituent parts to the whole. In some of the developing states, great difficulty has been encountered in establishing the geographical basis for statehood. The Federation of Malaysia, for example, created in 1963, was fractured by the withdrawal of one of its constituent states, Singapore, in 1965. Similarly, in the Middle East, Egypt's unification with Syria in 1958, establishing the United Arab Republic, collapsed in 1961 when Syria reasserted its independence. In sub-Saharan Africa, several unsuccessful attempts have been made to create viable federations. The Mali Federation, initially agreed upon by Senegal, Soudan, and Upper Volta in 1959, was disrupted within one month by the withdrawal of Upper Volta and collapsed completely in 1960. The Central African Federation, established by the British in 1953 for its colonies of Northern and Southern Rhodesia and Nyasaland, disintegrated in 1963 when Nyasaland, renamed Malawi, became a fully independent state and withdrew from the Federation. Northern Rhodesia, taking the name Zambia, achieved its independence in 1964, while Southern Rhodesia proclaimed its independence as Rhodesia in 1965, despite the vigorous opposition of the British Government. Undoubtedly the greatest disappointment to most observers of the developing states was the disruption in 1967 of the Nigerian Federation, created at the time independence was granted by the British in 1960. A notable exception to this list of failures to organize new states was the creation in 1964 of Tanzania out of the formerly independent states of Zanzibar and Tanganyika.

In several other states, dissident minorities have sought, unsuccessfully so far, to establish their own independent states or autonomous regions. The Karens, along with several other groups in Burma, have demanded their own states, as have the Kurds in Iraq, who have occasionally resorted to armed conflict to support their claims to independence. A long period of conflict and the eventual dispatch of military forces under United Nations authority in 1960 resulted from the attempt of Katanga, one of the principal provinces of the newly established Republic of the Congo, to assert its independence. Ethnic and other regional groups have from time to time voiced their demands for independence in other states in Asia and Africa, as in Thailand and India, sometimes taking up arms against the central government in support of their demands.

The specific issues that have encouraged efforts to merge several independent states, and those that have contributed to the disintegration of states and the demands for independence, have varied from case to case. Economic advantages and ethnic or racial ties are usually the motivating forces for mergers, as in the case of the Mali Federation. The threat of possible discrimination, the right of self-determination, and the economic advantages of independence, on the other hand, are the principal justifications cited by those groups and their leaders who seek to create new, independent states. In the case of Pakistan, for example, independence from India was demanded on the grounds that the Muslim population would be discriminated against by the dominant Hindu population. Katanga sought its independence primarily because it did not wish its advanced economy to be burdened by the backward conditions existing in the other provinces of the Republic of the Congo.

In addition to the problem some states have had in establishing a legal identity, boundary disputes have also disrupted attempts to create stable, geographically defined nation-states. In Latin America, the boundaries of most states have remained fixed for some time, though Paraguay and Bolivia engaged in a bitter war from 1932 to 1935 over the Chaco territory, and Argentina and Chile have a long-standing controversy over parts of their long common border. In Asia and Africa, boundary disputes are more common, in part because of the imprecise boundaries drawn by the colonial powers, and in part because of traditional rivalries and the refusal to recognize boundaries agreed upon by earlier governments. Recent examples of boundary disputes, in some cases leading to hostilities, include China's controversy with India, Malaysia's disputes with Indonesia and the Philippines, Pakistan and India's long rivalry over Kashmir, and the controversies between the

PROBLEMS IN NATION-BUILDING

several Arab states, and between them and Israel. Most of the developing states have had difficulties, at some time in their history, in fixing firm boundaries, and border disputes remain an important source of contention between states in many areas.

For many of the developing states, a much more urgent problem than that of boundaries is the problem of establishing a stable political system. A number of these states, as noted earlier, have either discarded the constitutions adopted at the time independence was achieved, or they have modified in important details the institutional arrangements of their governments. In many cases, e.g. Burma, Pakistan, Indonesia, Nigeria, and a number of Latin American states, the overthrow of the civilian government by the military destroyed the previous constitutional framework of government and initiated the search for new institutional arrangements. The need for stronger, more efficient and effective political authority has been the usual justification for replacing one form of government with another. The urgent problems of nation-building and social and economic development require, many leaders assert, the vigorous leadership that only the armed forces can supply. Even where the military has not assumed direct control, it frequently is a principal agency through which the developmental programs are executed.

Aside from, but intimately related to, the problems of creating a stable, geographically defined state and its political system, none of the problems facing the governments of the developing states is more basic than that of the lack of national unity and identity on the part of many groups and individuals in society. This problem is particularly acute in many of the new states in Asia and Africa, but it is found in almost all of the other developing states as well. Traditional loyalties to ethnic, regional, linguistic, tribal, and religious groups frequently take precedence over national loyalties. In those states that attained their independence only after a protracted struggle, these groups often cooperated against the colonial power, but the primary identification of most individuals remained with their own groups. These traditional loyalties not only threaten the continued existence of some states, as evidenced above in the demands for separate states or autonomy within the state, but they also undermine the stability of governments and thwart the implementation of national policies. To encourage a sense of national identity and purpose, the governments of the developing states employ a variety of techniques and policies.[1] In some cases, force has been necessary to prevent secessionist movements from succeeding. The resort to force to preserve national unity is, of course, by itself an unsatisfactory solution since it often increases the solidarity and isolation of the dissident

---

[1] Several contrasting policies designed to mobilize rural societies are discussed in Douglas E. Ashford, "The Politics of Rural Mobilisation in North Africa," *The Journal of Modern African Studies,* Vol. VII, No. 2 (July, 1969), pp. 187–202.

group. Persuasion, rather than coercion, is more conducive to the development of national loyalties and the stability of the state and its government.

Many of the policies designed to encourage nationalism have, in addition, their own intrinsic or practical justification. The establishment of an educational system, for example, is supported as essential for the development of individual dignity and intellectual growth as well as for the development of those skills necessary for a modern economy. At the same time, however, these policies may also, at least in their more immediate consequences, result in increased tensions and strains within the society. An increasing educational level may, using our example, stimulate demands for more rapid changes than can be successfully executed, or it may lead to a greater awareness of the differences among the several groups in society, each seeking to protect its unique characteristics. Thus, in devising and coordinating policies that will promote national unity and development, account must be taken of the possible adverse effects of these policies in the transitional period before their full advantages can be realized.

Despite the possibility of adverse consequences, leaders of the modernizing states place great emphasis upon the development of a comprehensive educational system not only because an increasingly literate and skilled population is necessary for economic development, but also because national unity will be strengthened. The assumption is that as achievements are registered in raising the standard of living and in creating a more interdependent economy, national unity will increase. Yet, in planning and executing their educational policies (and this applies in other policy areas as well), the leaders are obstructed by a combination of psychological and material factors. The funds that can be allocated to educational programs are, of course, limited. The general shortage of qualified teachers is intensified in the rural areas, since many teachers are reluctant to accept the low pay and often poor working conditions in these areas, preferring the more favorable urban environments. In addition, the leaders' emphasis on technical training in higher education runs counter to the traditional preference of students for education in law and the humanities; technical training is commonly regarded as inferior education and socially unacceptable.

The attempt to establish an official language for the state, to be used as the medium for instruction in the schools as well as in business and governmental transactions, has sharply divided a number of states. While there is general recognition of the utility of a single language in promoting national unity and the economic and social development of the states, there is often little agreement on which language to choose. Some of the Westernized elite prefer to retain the language of the former colonial power. Some of them have used this language so long that they are far more competent in it than in any of the indigenous languages in their states. Further, they prefer the Western language on grounds that it facilitates trade and other relationships with Western states on whom they must rely for aid, both in financial matters and in the supply of technical skills. Other leaders and groups, however, demand the use of an indigenous language, asserting that the use of one of their languages will protect and promote their cultures and establish their identities apart from the former colonial powers. The choice of a single indigenous language, however, poses its own difficulties. The decision in favor of any language is often vigorously contested by those groups whose language and culture are to be accorded a secondary position. The conflict over an official language in India and several other states has, at times, become so intense that the basic structure of the state has been threatened. In India, lingual states have had to be recognized to preserve the national state. This solution is opposed, however, by many leaders in other states who regard a single language as essential to unity and progress.

Industrial expansion, with its corollary development of transportation and communication networks, is also regarded as a means to promote both the unity and the welfare of society. Although general support for programs of industrialization is common, the leaders must again overcome many obstacles in addition to those concerning the financing of new industries. The traditional values and habits relating to work, savings, and investment are frequently not conducive to rapid expansion of industrial production. Further, hostile reactions have often arisen from groups who believe that their welfare is being threatened by the industrial policies of their national leaders. The specific location of industries is frequently vigorously contested. While the location of government-sponsored industries and developmental projects, such as dams and irrigation works, is also a politically involved issue in more developed states, the economic and political implications of such decisions in the developing states are more acute because of the relatively greater role of the government in economic development programs, the relatively greater impact of individual industries on the economy of an area, and the existing higher level of social fragmentation.

In addition to the economic and social policies designed to promote the unification of the state, leaders also attempt to evoke an emotional response to the nation-state. They seek to develop a sense of pride in the accomplishments of the state, stressing that these were possible only as a result of the unified efforts of the people. Those common elements (such as religion) of the various groups in the state are emphasized, while the divisive factors are ignored as far as possible. Single mass political parties, as has been indicated, are another means used to promote unity, as are the ideologies articulated by the leaders. Thus, through ideas as well as material advances, attempts are being made to advance the level of consensus among the disparate groups in society.

Even in the relatively well-integrated states, a number of problems demand the attention of the governments. Rapidly growing populations, command attention. One of the most urgent of these in many states is the high rate of population growth with all its corollary problems of food, housing, jobs, education, and other public services. Latin America is the area currently experiencing the highest average annual growth rate with a figure of 2.9 per cent, reaching a level of 3.4 per cent in Middle Latin America. The average growth rate for all of Africa is 2.4 per cent, though in Northern Africa alone it is 2.9 per cent. In Asia as a single region the figure is 2.0 per cent, but in the sub-region of South Asia it is 2.5 per cent. The states with the highest growth rates thus face the prospect that their populations will double in less than twenty years if the present rates are maintained, a prospect that causes some consternation but, so far, has resulted in few effective policies. For the present, the "green revolution" has increased food production sufficiently rapidly to undermine the widespread fears of massive starvation being expressed a few years ago, but millions of persons are undernourished and death by starvation is by no means unknown.

Attempts to reduce the growth rate in those states in which it has become a serious problem frequently encounter much opposition. Some leaders profess to see any attempts to restrain the growth of their states' populations as insidious and devious forms of colonialism pressed by the developed states for their own selfish interests. More importantly, large families are prized in many cultures for both social prestige and economic security. Since few governments as yet have extensive old-age assistance or medical care programs, families must rely on their own resources for support in cases of illness and unemployment. The birth control programs that have been proposed and instituted have met with more active and passive opposition than success. Some persons refuse to support or participate in such programs on religious grounds while others find specific birth control devices objectionable for a variety of reasons. The result is that the traditional fertility rates have been largely maintained while death rates, particularly infant mortality rates, have declined sharply, resulting in the population explosion and an enormous number of youths in these societies.

The rapid growth in the number of young persons coming into the work force has resulted in severe pressures to expand job opportunities. As agricultural methods improve through increasing mechanization, fewer agricultural workers can be absorbed in the agricultural sector of the economy, the largest one in these societies. At the same time, the industrial sector, while often expanding, is usually not creating enough jobs to meet the demand. In Mexico, for example, it is estimated that 400,000 persons are being added to the work force every year, but industry is able to create only 180,000 new jobs annually; in Indonesia, a million persons enter the labor market each year to compete for the 150,000 new jobs created yearly.[2] Compounding the problem of providing sufficient industrial jobs is the fact that many of the new industries being established are not very labor intensive. The result is that in many societies, unemployment and underemployment are serious problems, in some cases affecting half the total work force.[3]

With such limited agricultural employment opportunities available, many persons have moved to the urban areas, there to compete for the scarce industrial and service jobs. Cities have grown rapidly, many of them at rates of 5 to 8 per cent annually, thereby doubling their populations every ten to fifteen years. Slums are also growing rapidly, and it is estimated that "between now and 1980 the urban population of Latin America will increase from 130 million to 216 million, with more than 100 million living in shantytowns."[4] The provision of basic services in the urban centers has been difficult for a number of reasons. One reason is that the tax base of the cities has usually grown far less rapidly than have the demands for services, since the movement of large numbers of persons into the cities has preceded the expansion of business and industry. In addition, the population turnover in the cities tends to be high as many persons move from city to city seeking jobs or else return to the rural areas. Housing is often in desperately short supply as is pure water, electricity, and telephone service, and municipal corruption often reaches high levels as individuals compete for these scarce goods. There is little evidence at present that the complex problems of the urban areas are being solved. Perhaps the most surprising fact is that the urban residents have remained so passive in the face of the conditions they confront in their daily lives.[5]

The changing conditions—and the aspirations for even more extensive changes—in the social, economic, and political systems of the developing states have thus created difficult problems for their political leaders. Heavy demands are placed upon them to devise policies that will enable their societies to progress in an orderly fashion to the goals to which they aspire. As yet, it is too early to estimate the chances for success for most states; what is certain is that a profound social, economic, and political revolution is reshaping the societies that until recently were of little concern to the major powers of the world.

[2] See the "World Economic Surveys" published early each year in *The New York Times.*
[3] Gavin W. Jones, "Underutilisation of Manpower and Demographic Trends in Latin America," *International Labour Review,* Vol. XCVIII, No. 5 (November, 1968), pp. 451–69, and David A. Morse, "Unemployment in Developing Countries," *Political Science Quarterly,* Vol. LXXXV, No. 1 (March, 1970), pp. 1–16.
[4] William L. Flinn and Alvaro Camocho, "The Correlates of Voter Participation in a Shantytown Barrio in Bogota, Colombia," *Inter-American Economic Affairs,* Vol. XXII, No. 4 (Spring, 1969), p. 47.
[5] Joan Nelson, "The Urban Poor: Disruption or Political Integration in Third World Cities?" *World Politics,* Vol. XXII, No. 3 (April, 1970), pp. 393–414.

SUGGESTED READINGS

Abernethy, David B. *The Political Dilemma of Popular Education: An African Case.* Stanford, Calif.: Stanford University Press, 1969.

Adams, Don, and Robert M. Bjork. *Education in Developing Areas.* New York: David McKay Company, 1969.

Alexander, Robert J. *Organized Labor in Latin America.* New York: The Free Press, 1965.

Andreski, Stanislav. *The African Predicament: A Study in the Pathology of Modernization.* New York: Atherton Press, 1968.

Beling, Willard A. *Modernization and African Labor.* New York: Frederick A. Praeger, 1965.

Beyer, Glenn H., ed. *The Urban Explosion in Latin America.* Ithaca, N. Y.: Cornell University Press, 1967.

Binder, Leonard. *Religion and Politics in Pakistan.* Berkeley, Calif.: University of California Press, 1961.

Braibanti, Ralph, and Joseph J. Spengler, eds. *Tradition, Values, and Socio-Economic Development.* Durham, N. C.: Duke University Press, 1961.

Breese, Gerald, ed. *The City in Newly Developing Countries.* Englewood Cliffs, N. J.: Prentice-Hall, Inc., 1969.

Carter, Gwendolen M., ed. *National Unity and Regionalism in Eight African States.* Ithaca, N. Y.: Cornell University Press, 1966.

Chandrashekhar, S., ed. *Asia's Population Problems.* New York: Frederick A. Praeger, 1967.

Coleman, James S., ed. *Education and Political Development.* Princeton, N. J.: Princeton University Press, 1965.

Cowan, L. Gray, James O'Connell, and David G. Scanlon, eds. *Education and Nation-Building in Africa.* New York: Frederick A. Praeger, 1965.

Crozier, Brian. *The Morning After: A Study of Independence.* New York: Oxford University Press, 1963.

Curle, Adam. *Educational Problems of Developing Societies.* New York: Frederick A. Praeger, 1969.

Deutsch, Karl W., and William J. Foltz, eds. *Nation-Building.* New York: Atherton Press, 1963.

Dotson, Floyd, and Lillian O. Dotson. *The Indian Minority of Zambia, Rhodesia, and Malawi.* New Haven: Yale University Press, 1968.

Fishman, Joshua A., Charles A. Ferguson, and Jyotirindra das Gupta. *Language Problems of Developing Nations.* New York: John Wiley & Sons, Inc., 1968.

Froehlich, Walter, ed. *Land Tenure, Industrialization and Social Stability.* Milwaukee, Wisc.: The Marquette University Press, 1961.

Geertz, Clifford, ed. *Old Societies and New States.* New York. The Free Press of Glencoe, 1963.

Hance, William A. *Population, Migration, and Urbanization in Africa.* New York: Columbia University Press, 1970.

Herbert, John D., and Alfred P. Van Huyck, eds. *Urban Planning in the Developing Countries.* Frederick A. Praeger, 1968.

Hoselitz, Bert F., and Wilbert E. Moore, eds. *Industrialization and Society.* Paris: UNESCO, 1963.

Lambert, Jacques. *Latin America: Social Structures and Political Institutions.* Tr. by Helen Katel. Berkeley, Calif.: University of California Press, 1968.

Liddle, R. William. *Ethnicity, Party and National Integration: An Indonesian Case Study.* New Haven: Yale University Press, 1970.

Livingstone, Arthur. *Social Policy in Developing Countries.* London: Routledge & Keegan Paul, 1969.

Mason, Philip. *Patterns of Dominance.* New York: Oxford University Press, 1970.

Miner, Horace, ed. *The City in Modern Africa.* New York: Frederick A. Praeger, 1967.

Montgomery, John D., and William J. Siffin, eds. *Approaches to Development: Politics, Administration and Change.* New York: McGraw-Hill Book Company, 1966.

Mukherjee, Kartick C. *Underdevelopment, Educational Policy and Planning.* London: Asia Publishing House, 1967.

Nayar, Baldev R. *Minority Politics in the Punjab.* Princeton, N. J.: Princeton University Press, 1966.

Pike, Frederick B. *The Conflict Between Church and State in Latin America.* New York: Alfred A. Knopf, 1964.

Schramm, Wilbur. *Mass Media and National Development.* Stanford, Calif.: Stanford University Press, 1964.

Sinai, I. R. *The Challenge of Modernization.* New York: W. W. Norton & Company, Inc., 1964.

van den Berghe, Pierre L., ed. *Africa: Social Problems of Change and Conflict.* San Francisco: Chandler Publishing Company, 1965.

Weiner, Myron, ed. *Modernization.* New York: Basic Books, Inc., 1966.

"Where do we start?" That question has undoubtedly been asked countless times by the leaders of the developing states as they confront the problems of building their nations. Before they can go very far in solving the difficult specific problems of development, however, several fundamental issues relating to the composition of the state and its political structures must first be settled. That these issues have not been resolved in many of the new states in particular is evident in the continuing threats of secession and the frequent overhauling of political structures and institutions. In the selection below, Arnold Rivkin examines some aspects of these basic questions of nation-building.

28. THE POLITICS OF NATION-BUILDING: PROBLEMS AND PRECONDITIONS°

a r n o l d   r i v k i n

The problems of nation-building are so formidable that, out of cynicism or realism, many political leaders in the new and emerging states have taken refuge in the unreality of the doctrine of supranationalism. Out of this flight into unreality has come the principal political problem confronting would-be nation-builders—definition of the physical proportions, the geographic configuration, the legal limits of the unit within which the nation is to be built. The supranationalist phenomenon has appeared in the aftermath of World War II as Pan-Africanism in Africa, Pan-Arabism in the Middle East, and the export variety of Chinese communism in Asia and Castroism in Latin America. All would override territorial boundaries and build regional or continental nations. Somehow, by some undefined mystique or magic their protagonists appear to believe, the problems of finding and building national identities for the newly independent peoples of the world would disappear in the new messianic-like movements searching for regional-wide or continental-wide personalities. This at any rate is the dynamic of supranationalism in the underdeveloped areas of the world today.

Related but separable is the second principal political problem of today's nation-builders—the structure of the state within which to build the nation once the geographic limits are defined. In the conflicts raging around the structure of the state in such widely-dispersed areas as the new state of the Congo in the heart of Africa and the somewhat less new state of Burma in Southeast Asia, this problem has frequently been oversimplified as one between strong centralized unitary states and weak decentralized federal states. Thus Prime Minister Lumumba risked his political role, and paid with his life, in his campaign to translate the ill-defined unitary structure of the state envisaged in the *Loi Fondamentale* of the Congo into a centralized reality; and Prime Minister U Nu found himself under arrest . . . for his seeming failure to resist ardently enough the pressures of various national groups in the Burmese union seeking to find expression in a federal structure.

° From "The Politics of Nation-Building: Problems and Preconditions" by Arnold Rivkin, *Journal of International Affairs*, Vol. XVI, No. 2 (1962), pp. 131–143. Reprinted by permission.

Related to the problems of defining the national unit and building a state structure within which to develop the nation is the third principal political problem of the nation-builders—the approach and techniques to be employed in constituting the nation, in investing disparate groups within the state with a consciousness and sense of national identity, in making Nigerians out of Yorubas, Ibos and Hausas, in forging a national consensus.

Under the three headings—the concept of the national unit, state-structure and methodology—are subsumed, in our opinion, the problems of the politics of nation-building. . . .

THE CONCEPT OF THE NATIONAL UNIT

Mamadou Dia, Prime Minister of Senegal, in his book, *The African Nations and World Solidarity*, confronted the political problem of the concept of the national unit. He recognized the reality of the territorial limits which the new states have inherited from the colonial period, but in his anxiety to escape from the reality—the artificially contrived but nevertheless vested boundary lines of the new states—he propounded a theory of African national units ("nations") transcending the territorial limits of legal boundaries of the new states.[1] This led him to champion the founding of the Federation of Mali.

In an epilogue to his book, a sadder but wiser Mamadou Dia, writing about the abortive attempt to constitute the Federation of Mali, confessed that his "theories on the formation of the African nation and . . . theses on the process of setting up of large economic complexes" were in fact wrong. In his words:

Taking our ideal for a reality, we thought we had only to condemn territorialism and its natural product, micronationalism, to overcome them and assure the success of our chimerical undertaking. . . . We are faced with micronationalisms that need be tamed, micronations that will have to be organized. Thus it is necessary for us to start with these micronationalisms and micronations, which are the realities of this strange twentieth-century African universe. Then we can build modestly, gradually, the bases of a great African nationalism and the foundations of a great African nation.[2]

○   ○   ○   ○   ○

What then are the elements of the Mali lesson? In essence the dissolution of the Federation of Mali within a little over a year of its

---

[1] See Mamadou Dia, *The African Nations and World Solidarity* (New York: Praeger, 1961), p. 7 ff.

[2] *Ibid.*, p. 138, 140 and 143.

birth, if one includes the longest period of its existence in the pre-independence period, poses the question of the necessary preconditions for establishing the geographic parameters within which a nation may successfully be built. First and foremost, the Mali experience raises the issue of timing. Does grouping together territorial units which have not yet (and this is true without exception in Africa) forged a national consciousness, found a national consensus and evolved a national identity aid or hinder the task of nation-building? The union of Senegalese and Soudanese at their respective stages of development in the Federation of Mali before either had developed cohesiveness as national units or widespread modern economies merely served to compound the difficulties of welding together disparate ethnic, tribal, cultural, linguistic, religious, political and economic groups into a national unit. The Mali experience suggests that, at a minimum, a certain degree of political development and economic growth is desirable and probably indispensable if territorial units are to be merged successfully and a nation built within enlarged national frameworks. Otherwise, as in the Mali case, the conflict for control of power at the center will divert energy from the basic tasks of nation-building; political consensus and building of the economy, the life blood of nation-building in the component parts, are likely to be neglected and retrogression probably will set in. Both Senegal and the Soudan (which has retained the name Mali) suffered, and will continue to, as a result of the bitterness engendered by the ill-fated attempt at political union. The rail link between the Senegalese capital of Dakar, Mali's only outlet to the sea, and Bamako, the capital of the new state of Mali has been cut, to the mutual disadvantage of both states.

Second, the Mali case also puts in issue the possibility of two essentially one-party states successfully uniting without, as a precondition, one or the other of the monolithic and exclusive parties agreeing to subordinate its identity to the other. Neither the Senegalese section of the *Parti de la Fedération Africaine* nor the *Union Soudanaise* could tolerate the political incursions of the other in its theretofore exclusive domain. And yet an inevitable consequence of a union of territorial units would seem to be a free flow not only of manpower and capital across territorial lines and within the united area but also of political ideas and their proponents, *i.e.*, political party spokesmen. . . .

❊   ❊   ❊   ❊   ❊

THE STRUCTURE OF THE STATE

Behavioral scientists notwithstanding, next in importance to the political issue revolving around the size and shape of the basic nation-state is the political question of the structure of the state within which the multiple efforts are to be made to compose into national units disparate groups, including the so-called "detribalized" Africans who have given up or been deprived of the security deriving from the relatively static system of the subsistence sector. Even the charismatic leader needs a framework within which to operate, and his success in leading into nationhood his state and its transitional society, somewhere on the scale between traditionalism and modernity, depends to a significant degree on the suitability of the state structure circumscribing his efforts. For example, the late Prime Minister of the Congo, Patrice Lumumba, was foredoomed to failure as a nation-builder. Once the artificial constraint of the colonial power was removed, only a gradualist approach reflected in a federal structure was likely to lead to building a single Congolese nation. Lumumba's concept of a unitary state, which he read into the *Loi Fondamentale*, required building in one thrust a Congolese nationality in a huge area with no tradition of unity and justified the use of violence and terror to accomplish this purpose.

Even the Federation of Nigeria, with a background of at least ten years of careful preparation for independence and with much stronger ties binding together its three very different regions than the Congo had linking its six very different provinces, owes much of its performance to a state structure which affords the national leadership time to develop the concept of Nigerian nationality. Obviously, the appropriate structure does not insure adequate performance, but it does afford the opportunity for it. A unitary structure in Nigeria would probably have prevented the emergence of a single state, and if by some chance the state had emerged as a unitary one, it might well have ended in a series of secession bids by one or another of the groups not in power.

✿　✿　✿　✿　✿

THE POLITICAL SYSTEM

The questions of dispersion of political power and recognition of cultural differences lead naturally to the third major political issue confronting the nation-builders. In political terms, what system of government should be employed? Should it be, to oversimplify, a system which views national unity as identical with uniformity and hence accepts as inevitable, and even as desirable, the achievement of unity through exhortation, organization, coercion and compulsion? Or should it be a system which seeks unity amidst diversity and seeks to evolve plural loyalties which at various levels will be compatible—to the nation-state, to the region or tribal grouping, to religious institutions and so forth?

For many of the African leaders one-party authoritarian systems are the answer—the way to forge national unity, to build a nation-state, to create a nationality. Perhaps most eloquent on this score is President Sékou Touré of Guinea. First, he posed the issue of nation-building this way:

Is it necessary to repeat that the people of Guinea has not been mobilized to satisfy the needs of such and such an individual, but that each individual has been mobilized to satisfy the needs of the people of Guinea? [3]

Then he proceeded to answer it with these observations:

Each one must consider himself as a "part," an element indissociable from a "whole" and subject to the laws and exigencies of this "whole." [4]

And again:

Our fundamental principles are simple; we recognize valuable only that which serves the cause of the people, and which accelerates the pace of the history of the nation. This discipline to which we freely submit and this orientation which constitutes the main task of a vanguard democratic party, this is indeed dictatorship. . . . As far as we are concerned . . . in giving preeminence to the people, in letting it participate directly in all the important decisions that can bind the nation, we expressly want this dictatorship to be popular and democratic.[5]

For other African leaders—perhaps fewer in number than the authoritarian-minded but often cast in significant roles, such as the leadership of Nigeria—the task of nation-building and the political approach to it are seen in vastly different terms than those of Sékou Touré. Prime Minister Sir Abubakar Tafawa Balewa of Nigeria formulated the problem in these words:

The . . . point concerns the problem of national unity. No problem is more urgent and none more difficult of solution. . . . It is true that Nigeria was the creation of the British, but it is no longer a mere geographical expression. The various peoples in the geographical area called Nigeria have lived together for almost a century and have developed common sentiments and a feeling of belonging together. It would be a great pity if nothing was done to forge a secure link which would, for all times, band all these peoples together as members of one nation.[6]

The Prime Minister then prescribed what must be and is in fact being tried in Nigeria:

The leaders of the various political parties and various other associations must place loyalty to Nigeria above other loyalties. If the leaders are willing to

---

[3] Sékou Touré, *Toward Full Re-Africanisation* (Paris: Présence Africaine, 1959), p. 53.

[4] *Ibid.*

[5] *Ibid.*, p. 55.

[6] Sir Abubakar Tafawa Balewa in the Foreword to the book by Chief H. O. Davies, *Nigeria: The Prospects for Democracy* (London: Weidenfeld and Nicholson, 1961), p. xi.

foster national unity, the common man will respond. . . . [After the 1959 General Elections] . . . the NPC [Northern People's Congress] and the NCNC [National Council of Nigeria and the Cameroons] agreed to form a coalition government because both parties believed that the only way to preserve the unity of the country was for the two parties to enter into coalition. . . . The present arrangement is the only one which in the circumstances can ensure the continued growth of parliamentary government in Nigeria. . . . The prospects for the survival of parliamentary democracy in Nigeria are favorable; however, this goal can only be attained if we address ourselves to the task of nation building with honesty, tolerance and devotion.[7]

These two dramatically opposed approaches to nation-building are at the ends of the African spectrum. The intermediate shadings are to be found in different countries. Interestingly enough, Guinea and Nigeria are also at opposite ends of the spectrum on Pan-Africanism and nationalism in one state, and on the issue of unitary and federal structures—a circumstance which suggests something more than coincidence. We can only suggest the hypothesis here[8] that there is at least a meaningful correlation, and perhaps even a causal interrelationship, between the views of African states on Pan-Africanism, the structure of the state and the political system chosen.

¤   ¤   ¤   ¤   ¤

BEYOND AFRICA

Nation-building is in process across the broad expanse of Asia and beyond it in most of Latin America. In vastly different circumstances, the underdeveloped states of these two continents are confronted by common political problems and by the common need to establish the necessary preconditions if their nation-building efforts are to be successful.

Because of the many significant differences between Africa and the other two continents—in population density, availability of food, social structure and class system, land ownership, traditional culture and religion, and many other factors—their responses to the political problems they all share are likely to vary considerably. And in any event, the psychology of nationalism in the many different states in the three continents will probably lead to different results in the individual states. Nevertheless, the underlying unities imposed by the similarity of problems to be faced and preconditions to be established by the new states and the re-awakening old states wherever they may be in pursuit of the

---

[7] *Ibid.*, p. xii.
[8] To be examined in the author's forthcoming study, tentatively entitled *The African Presence in World Affairs.*

goal of nation-building are likely to impart discernible lines of development which will allow for comparative study.

A quick look . . . would seem to confirm that the same trio of difficult political problems—determination of the concept of the nation, state structure and political system—confronts the nation-builders of all these continents.

Although political instability is an obvious characteristic of many transitional states, its causes are less apparent and the means to eliminate the causes even less well understood. But as a first step, the identification of the causes is essential, and in the selection below, Kenneth Johnson postulates some basic causes of instability in Latin America. While a somewhat different array of causes may be identified in Asian and African states, the difficulty of breaking the interlocking and self-reinforcing circle of causes suggests that political instability in transitional states will plague their search for development for years to come.

29. CAUSAL FACTORS IN LATIN AMERICAN POLITICAL INSTABILITY *

k e n n e t h   f.   j o h n s o n

THE INSTABILITY SYSTEM

Political instability occurs when the governing institutions of organized society are ineffective in gratifying popular wants and expectations. In that sense, governments are "maximizers," to use David Apter's term, sending out streams of satisfactions.[1] Failure of governments to gratify

* From "Causal Factors in Latin American Political Instability" by Kenneth F. Johnson, *Western Political Quarterly*, Vol. XVII, No. 3 (September, 1964), pp. 435–441. By permission of the University of Utah, copyright owners.
[1] David E. Apter, "A Comparative Method for the Study of Politics," *American Journal of Sociology*, 64 (1958), 225.

popular wants leads to political alienation in varying degrees of intensity. Alienation, in turn, is not a fixed quality but varies according to a number of causal factors. Political alienation may be defined as a deeply felt resentment toward social and governing institutions which is so intense as to be manifested in happenings which contribute to political instability. Political instability, accordingly, is defined as a state of conflict between governments and (competing) power groups which is characterized by overt acts of violence, by support for extreme political radicalism, or by apathy in the face of movements which are committed to extreme, radical, or violent dislocations of the status quo.[2] Thus, political alienation is seen as a widely shared attitude-potential and instability is viewed as those phenomena proceeding therefrom.

✿ ✿ ✿ ✿ ✿

Causal factors in Latin American political instability may be viewed as actors in a circular or self-reinforcing system. Their cumulative effect is a barrier to the drives of Latin American nations toward economic development and political stability. As a result of low socioeconomic development, maldistribution of wealth reaches critical levels; frustration of mobility expectations is widespread and produces popular and elite alienation, disaffection, and outright aggression toward the state.

Political instability in Latin America results from the circular interaction of three general categories of factors: (1) entrepreneurial deficiencies (includes passive and flight capital, social values and cultural influences, religious institutions, illiteracy); (2) high degrees of role substitutability among politically relevant performance entities; and (3) accelerated urbanization and overpopulation.

Entrepreneurial Deficiencies

As a human dynamic, entrepreneurship is defined as "the function of perceiving and effectuating new combinations of factors of production in order to take advantage of existing or anticipated market situations."[3] The commercial entrepreneur deals in ideas, supported by capital from credit or familial sources, in such a way as to realize a marginal profit. Governmental entrepreneurship relates largely to leadership expertise at problem-solving through public policy and administration. Both entre-

[2] Apathy on the part of politically relevant populations is considered a reinforcement factor in the sense of tacit endorsement through inaction.
[3] Charles Wolf and Sidney Sufrin, *Capital Formation and Foreign Investment in Underdeveloped Areas* (Syracuse: Syracuse University Press, 1958), p. 21—derived from Joseph Schumpeter, "Economic Theory and Entrepreneurial History," in *Change and the Entrepreneur* (Cambridge: Harvard University Press, 1949), pp. 23–24.

preneurial forms require available active capital for effective functioning. The relative absence of entrepreneurship accounts for much of Latin America's backwardness and contributes to political instability.

Chronic to all underdeveloped countries is illiteracy, a tremendous entrepreneurial deficiency. . . .

Social attitudes and values act to inhibit entrepreneurial growth in Latin America. Throughout the area, there is a general lack of individual preparedness to take big financial risks in order to capture lucrative gains. Although many Latin Americans are willing to invest in stocks, bonds, mutual funds, and securities, the majority of investors prefer something safer such as land or independently issued credit at high rates of interest. One frequently hears stories of private money caches both great and small. According to informal reports, one would expect fairly impressive sums to appear if all of these passive investors were to declare their resources.

Because a genuinely competitive and collaborative spirit is lacking, Latin Americans are suspicious of impersonal institutions which control and allocate capital. Investors prefer to keep their funds out of banks and government-sponsored lending institutions where they might otherwise be available for entrepreneurial use as development capital. Reluctance to mobilize capital for entrepreneurship accompanies failure to achieve volume marketing conditions through increased unit output. According to testimony and empirical observation in Colombia and Mexico, there seems to be an ingrained notion that it is better to sell a few items at a high price than to improve one's total income through promotion of volume sales at a reduced price.[4]

Another entrepreneurial deficiency lies in the problem of excessive centralization of decision-making where allocation of credit for commercial development is concerned. In Mexico, for instance, major credit decisions are regularly made at the "home office" level which normally means the capital city.[5] Moreover, thousands of decisions of relatively small consequence also require central validation. Interviews in both Mexico and Colombia revealed the belief among businessmen that provincial locations are definitely less favored than central ones where credit dispensation is concerned. . . .

Still a further barrier to effective entrepreneurship is found in Latin American religious institutions. Drawing on the works of Tawney and Weber, the general proposition may be made that the Roman Catholic ethic, being preoccupied with achieving and preserving grace in the

---

[4] In Bogotá, for instance, the author learned that there are hundreds of dwellings remaining vacant much of the year because proprietors favor a high and prestigeful rental price even though a lower one might bring more tenants and an improved total income for the landlord.

[5] Paul Lamartine Yates, *El desarrollo regional de México* (México: Banco de México: segunda edición, 1962), p. 205.

sight of God, discourages the vigorous competitive spirit needed for accomplishment within an entrepreneurial value hierarchy.[6] Besides Roman Catholicism, anthropologists have noted in certain Indian societies value systems which discourage capital formation for other than ceremonial purposes. Eric Wolf found that the Maya Indians of Mexico and Guatemala accumulate capital for annual religious displays which wipe out family savings.[7] Specifically Wolf says of the Maya, "he is not a capitalist nor free of restrictions; his economic goal is not capital accumulation but subsistence and participation in the religio-political system of his community." [8]

Ultimately, in the deep recesses of Latin American culture, one comes to the inescapable conclusion that collusion rather than collaboration is the dominant characteristic of human enterprise. . . . The absence of a truly collaborative spirit is an enormous entrepreneurial deficiency which Latin America cannot easily overcome.

Entrepreneurial deficiencies constitute a market imperfection which allows capital to flow into passive rather than active forms. The process is circular and affects the public and private sectors of the economy jointly. Exploitive tributary taxation and corrupt fiscal allocation by governments discourage private investment and capital formation. Public fiscal dishonesty inspires nonpayment of taxes and wastes much of whatever funds are collected. Accumulated capital is hoarded or invested in ritual and prestige items or in usurious investments with proceeds concealed from taxation or exported abroad. Public treasuries are thus impoverished and public services remain at low levels. Controlling value systems sustain corrupt public officials and inhibit adoption of policies aimed at socioeconomic betterment. Low entrepreneurial growth means that Latin American economies cannot absorb rapid population increase without hardship. Frustration of mobility expectations is therefore widespread and dictates to political alienation and instability.

Role Substitutability Among Politically Relevant Performance Entities

Gabriel Almond's definition of a pre-industrial political system emphasized the relative ease with which performance entities could usurp

---

[6] R. H. Tawney, *Religion and the Rise of Capitalism* (New York: Harcourt Brace, 1926). Tawney speaks of barriers to entrepreneurship in the sense of ideology rather than specifically in terms of capital formation. In contrasting Roman Catholic and Calvinist-Puritan views toward commercial enterprise he says that Puritanism "insisted, in short, that money-making if not free from spiritual dangers . . . could be, and ought to be, carried on for the greater glory of God." P. 199.

[7] Eric R. Wolf, *Sons of the Shaking Earth* (Chicago: University of Chicago Press, 1959), p. 216.

[8] *Ibid.*, p. 224.

each other's natural role. This condition has been endemic to Latin America and is a major causal factor in political instability. George Blanksten notes that in some Latin American countries the army performs a number of unspecialized and undifferentiated functions ranging from administering public education to conducting elections.[9] With increasing functional differentiation in the private economy, Blanksten sees the possibility of a trend toward "more specialized functions of political institutions . . . and basic alterations in the commitments of governing elites."[10] Whereas in Colombia, Peru, and Ecuador the Church is landowner, public educator, and political practitioner as well as a religious institution, "with the march of the developmental process it is likely that the last of these functions will tend to become the exclusive, specialized and differentiated role of the Church."[11]

The prevailing lack of role specialization and interdependence among performance entities in Latin America is a continuing invitation to armies and government bureaucracies to usurp each other in a power grab. Likewise, the failure of Latin American universities to become specialized seats of learning has relegated student groups to extreme and radical political roles. The same may be said for trade unions which, in countries such as Bolivia, Venezuela, and Argentina, constitute veritable "parties" in themselves and are frequently embroiled in extreme acts which contribute to political instability.

The apparent ease with which performance entities have usurped each other in Latin America may be partly explained in terms of the relative absence of social pluralism within that political culture. Involving as it does a multiplicity of overlapping group memberships, social pluralism has a decidedly moderating effect upon political behavior. One's performance in a given membership context is certain to have implications for other memberships as well. Social pluralism is one of the hallmarks of Latin America's incipient middle class which has been viewed by Charles Wagley as moderately conservative.[12] According to John J. Johnson, the Latin American middle sectors are "harmonizers" which avoid the dangers inherent in strictly negative and absolute postulates.[13]

Because of the relative lack of social pluralism in Latin America, performance entities become psychologically compartmentalized and politically semi-autonomous. Vocational roles tend to circumscribe social

[9] George I. Blanksten, "The Aspiration for Economic Development," *Annals*, 334 (March 1961), 17.
[10] *Ibid.*, p. 19.
[11] *Ibid.*, p. 17.
[12] Charles Wagley, "The Brazilian Revolution: Social Changes Since 1930," in *Social Change in Latin America Today*, ed. Lymon Bryson (New York: Harper, 1960), pp. 221–22.
[13] John J. Johnson, "The Political Role of the Latin American Middle Sectors," *Annals*, 334 (March 1961), 25.

PROBLEMS IN NATION-BUILDING

attitudes and political attachments. Armies, bureaucracies, legislatures, are found each with its own highly subjective *élan vital,* an aggressive expansionist force marked by the all-consuming lust for control and easily infused with a moral purpose to justify intrusion upon other roles. For many Latin Americans, a career in the army or government bureaucracy is life's only road to socioeconomic mobility. . . .

Urbanization and Overpopulation

During the past several decades, urbanization in Latin America has taken on proportions of acute social change.[14] Rural-to-urban migratory patterns complicate efforts to promote urban economic growth and to stimulate new agrarian entrepreneurship. Displaced peasants seek welfare and opportunity in great cities. Frustration of their expectations produces alienation and, thus, urbanization exacerbates existing symptoms of political instability.

The following causes of Latin America's accelerated urbanization may be listed at this point: (1) urban industrialization and the promise of a better life lures unemployed groups from the country; (2) exploitation of rural workers by *latifundistas* forces exodus as does material impoverishment of *minifundistas;* [15] (3) terror and violence perpetuated by bandit groups especially in Colombia, Venezuela, and Peru make rural life unbearable; [16] (4) certain legal structures promote social and economic development of a capital or central city at the expense of the rest of the country as in the case of Haiti; [17] (5) many peasants are motivated to leave their farms because of exploitation by the bureaucracy of an agrarian reform program as in the case of Mexico; [18] and (6) in at least one country, Colombia, there is specific evidence that service in the military brings many young peasants into the city who are unwilling to return to an agrarian life upon completion of their duty.[19] These motivational factors for rural-to-urban migration have meaning for the majority of Latin American nations. Urbanization has brought increased demands upon governments and socioeconomic systems for accommodation of the

---

[14]   This contention is based on the author's "Urbanization and Political Change in Latin America" (Ph.D. dissertation, Ann Arbor, University Microfilms Inc., 1963).
[15]   See Robert Carlyle Beyer, "Land Distribution and Tenure in Colombia," *Journal of Inter-American Studies,* 3 (April 1961), 281–91, *passim.*
[16]   See Roberto Pineda Giraldo, *El impacto de la violencia en el Tolima: El caso de El Líbano* (Bogotá: Universidad Nacional de Colombia, 1960).
[17]   Achille Aristide treats this problem in *Problemes Haitiens* (Port-au-Prince: Imprimierie de L'Etat, 1958).
[18]   See Rodrigo García Treviño, *Precios Salarios Mordidas* (México: Editorial América, 1953).
[19]   Kenneth F. Johnson and Fernando Gallo C., "Encuesta para un grupo de infantes de marina" (Cartagena: Facultad de Economia de la Universidad de Cartagena, 1962, unpublished sample survey).

expanding work force. Because of the entrepreneurial deficiencies discussed earlier, popular expectations for achievement and mobility are frustrated which leads to political alienation and instability.

A concomitant of urbanization has been overpopulation in both urban and rural areas. Though government programs of disease control have sharply reduced infant mortality throughout Latin America, urbanization has not produced a significant decline in over-all fertility rates.[20] While rural populations have continued to grow, rural food production has not always kept pace with urban needs. This keeps food prices high and militates against the already depressed and alienated social sectors. Migrants to the cities find that large families are no longer the asset they were in the country as family incomes are dissipated by nonproducing members who continue to consume. With children under fifteen years making up approximately 40 per cent of Latin America's total population, the need to provide for these dependents heavily burdens the head of a household. He is at a major disadvantage in seeking to improve his level of living through accumulation of capital for investment or for family emergency.[21]

As Latin American overpopulation continues, pressure mounts upon the already inadequate rural land forcing more and more persons into the great cities where entrepreneurial deficiencies make it doubtful that their wants will be gratified. Growing popular frustration and alienation are manifest in popular support for aggressive radical movements which voice mistrust of government and hatred for the dominant classes.[22] At this point, opportunities for usurpation of governing roles may be seized upon by armies, bureaucracies, or other power groupings and political instability moves across the continuum from latent to overt.

[20]   Pertinent here are a series of studies done by Harold L. Geisert and Carr B. Lavell which were published by George Washington University Press in 1959 and 1960: cf. Geisert, *Population Problems in Mexico and Central America,* and *The Caribbean: Population and Resources;* and Lavell, *Population Growth and Development of South America.* On the topic of birth control, see J. Stycos, Curt Back, Reuben Hill, "Contraception and Catholicism in Puerto Rico," *Milbank Memorial Fund Quarterly,* 34 (April 1956), 150–59.

[21]   Geisert, "Population Problems . . . ," *loc. cit.*

[22]   This theme is prominent in Oscar Lewis' study of the slums in Mexico City: *The Children of Sanchez: Autobiography of a Mexican Family* (New York: Random House, 1961), p. xxvii.

During the past few years much attention has been focused on the world's population explosion and the problems of overpopulation. Far less consideration, however, has been given to the problems of states having small populations, even when in relative terms they are densely populated. Since there are a number of small states, the failure of many of them to prosper may well contribute to unrest and instability in the international arena, and consequently their problems merit attention. In the selection below, Donald Keesing examines the problems of national development.

30. SMALL POPULATION AS A POLITICAL HANDICAP TO NATIONAL DEVELOPMENT * †

donald b. keesing

This paper advances some hypotheses on the connection between a country's size and its development which, if true, mean that the internal political effects of a small population exacerbate and compound economic difficulties, especially under twentieth-century conditions. The effects postulated here are discussed under three headings: (1) the conflict between "nationalism" and sound economic policy; (2) the difficulty of motivating leadership and "class traitor" behavior needed for development; and (3) the effects of small numbers of people in each social and political role.

The current importance of the problem is suggested by the fact that there are now over fifty poor countries with populations under five million, about half of them with less than two million. Another twenty developing countries have from five to fifteen million people. Most countries with less than five million people are found in Africa (twenty-seven) and in the Americas (fifteen).

* From "Small Population as a Political Handicap to National Development" by Donald B. Keesing. Reprinted with permission from the *Political Science Quarterly* 84 (March 1969), 50–60.
† The valuable suggestions of Richard R. Fagen, associate professor of political science, Stanford University, have improved the paper, but he is exonerated from responsibility for the results.

No attempt is made to test scientifically the hypotheses put forward here. I admit that an objective test would be difficult, for two reasons. First, multiple political and economic influences interweave to cause the development problems of small countries, creating a serious identification problem. Second, small countries are statistically distinct from larger ones in other important respects besides their populations. For example, countries with small populations typically enjoy greater natural resources per inhabitant than more populous countries as a result of being sparsely settled, or else they are tropical islands or virtual islands with special possibilities for tourism and orientation toward the sea. Such differences make it hazardous to interpret, for instance, the observed tendencies for small populations to be associated, at a given income level, with smaller per capita industrial output.[1]

Of extra importance to their politics, small countries have distinct modal patterns of culture and history. Most are former French possessions in tropical Africa, former British coastal colonies, or one-time Spanish possessions in America. Only twelve less-developed countries with populations under five million (in 1964) have been nominally independent for over a hundred years. They could hardly be considered a random sample in any sense; ten are in Spanish America. But they do suggest, viewed as a group, that small developing countries frequently (though not always) generate unfortunate politics and do not undergo rapid social and economic change over the long run, compared to more populous poor countries. The twelve countries are Bolivia, Costa Rica, the Dominican Republic, Ecuador, El Salvador, Guatemala, Honduras, Nicaragua, Paraguay, Uruguay, Haiti, and Liberia.[2]

We still know too little about the economic handicaps of smallness. We can safely say, however, that a small country experiences at least the following disadvantages:

(1) High costs in the many "social overhead" and public sector activities that involve increasing returns (economies of scale), a problem that is especially acute when the population is spread thinly.

---

[1] See, for example, Hollis B. Chenery, "Patterns of Industrial Growth," *American Economic Review*, L (1960), 624–54, and Donald B. Keesing, "Population and Industrial Development: Some Evidence from Trade Patterns," *American Economic Review*, LVIII (1968), 448–55.

[2] Of the ten small Spanish American countries listed first, only Costa Rica and Uruguay have had any large share of liberal governments; and only they are roughly equal to the Spanish American average in income. One indicator of industrialization is per capita energy consumption in metric tons of coal equivalent. In 1964 the Spanish American average stood at 919 tons, while of seven larger Spanish-speaking countries in America, Colombia in last place had a per capita energy consumption of 494 metric tons. Among the small countries mentioned, equivalent figures were 830 for Uruguay, 268 for Costa Rica, and 105 to 231 for the other eight Spanish American countries (based on United Nations *Statistical Yearbook, 1965* [New York, 1966], tables 142 and 19). Panama, independent over sixty years, stood at 907. Such statistical differences can be interpreted in many ways, and might have an economic basis, but they do suggest systematic contrasts in development.

(2) High costs in manufacturing industries involving economies of scale, in which sales must be largely limited to the home market. These include bulk processing industries and some assembly-line operations in which transport costs are substantial.

(3) A general lack of competition from within, for lack of sufficient numbers of modern enterprises, resulting typically in sluggish monopolistic behavior unless competitive pressure is brought to bear from outside.

(4) Insofar as the country is intellectually isolated, a tendency toward poor standards of performance, low productivity, and stagnant technology, relative to the prevailing per capita level of education and training, due to insufficient interaction and consequent meager stimulus from exchange of ideas among trained people.

(5) To the extent that the country is physically small, a narrower range of natural resources than in a large country.

(6) The serious disadvantage of being surrounded by other nations' tariff and migration barriers, quantitative import restrictions, and other discriminatory measures. These barriers restrict prospective exports and other international transactions, and turn the terms of trade against the country.

In combination, these circumstances mean, first, that a small country can expect to achieve less per capita output than a large country from given per capita resources, including natural resources, capital, education, and the like. Second, a small country is far more dependent than a large country on international transactions, in order to compensate for its disadvantages listed above. Third, throughout development, an appropriate policy balance for a small country must be extremely "outward-looking," encouraging international exchanges of ideas, competition with foreign enterprises, borrowing of technology, and a high degree of international specialization, so that reasonable economies of scale can be achieved and local resource deficits can be overcome through trade. This in turn means that protection or subsidies must be applied very selectively; redundant protection is an invitation to inefficiency, whereas in a large country internal competition tends to correct such policy errors.

Another very obvious difficulty, more political than economic, is the political-military weakness of any small country and its vulnerability to interference and manipulation by the larger powers, with little opportunity to reciprocate in kind. This may be, in its own right, a crucial obstacle to development, if the great powers stand actively opposed to the types of internal policies and leadership that are essential for successful development. I am not emphasizing this aspect of the problem, which has been widely recognized and discussed, but foreign intervention can easily aggravate the internal political difficulties described here.

I

The emotional feelings for one's country, commonly known as nationalism, that are so much a part of recent world history offer, I hypothesize, serious obstacle to constructing and maintaining appropriate development policies, especially in small countries. Nationalism, after all, is an integrating force on the national level, but a devisive force at the international level.[3]

The positive aspects of nationalism are restricted and the negative ones enlarged when nations are small. Integrating a nation of two or three million people does not achieve much economically, whereas turning fifty or a hundred million people into a single economy already represents a major step forward. When the small country is also economically backward, with no more than a hundred or two hundred dollars' per capita income, the home market is incredibly small and utterly inadequate to support efficient development from within.

Nationalism has its emotional side that cannot be easily curbed or curtailed by practical considerations. Thus, in addition to the barriers thrown up by other countries, and the inhibitory effect on international transactions inherent in independence because of the latent threat of autonomous legal actions, a small country is moved by nationalism to add its own maze of obstacles to the barriers that cordon off its economy and society. In a large country, this effect would not be so serious—economies of scale, competition, exchanges of ideas, pressures for technological improvement could still be generated, up to a point, from within. But in a small country the results are apt to be plainly disastrous, a perpetuation of high costs, stagnation, and backwardness. Given such added obstacles, we can anticipate any number of vicious circles. New exports become more difficult to achieve, foreign investment resources cannot be attracted except at a frightful price in concessions, balance of payments problems encouraged ubiquitous and spiralling protection,

[3] Largely for this reason, no doubt, specialists in development tend to divide along predictable lines in their attitudes to "nationalism." This is only secondarily because integration is more unambiguously desirable in economics than in politics, and because the word "nationalism" means somewhat different things to different people. Professionals whose work makes them most aware of the inner conflicts and fragmentation typical of backward countries—specialists in the internal politics of development, economic planners, sociologists, country specialists—generally welcome the integrating effects. Other professionals' training encourages them to take national integration almost for granted, but to see all too keenly the costs of division at the international level. This group includes most economists and specialists in international relations. These people tend to regard nationalism as an almost unmitigated disaster, an irrational impulse for which mankind pays a staggering price. Clearly both viewpoints can be reconciled, to some extent, by recognition of the double-edged nature of nationalism.

poverty holds down public expenditures that could promote development, multiplying controls encourage corruption and inefficiency, and an unpromising economic climate helps to drive educated people abroad. The spirit of nationalism itself may act as a powerful inhibitor to recognition of achievements abroad that are worth borrowing.

To put the matter less pessimistically, an intelligently led government, bent on promoting development, must walk a tightrope in its policies, and it cannot afford to imitate completely the policies of large countries which are the best known examples of past development. In the creative and difficult task of forging appropriate outward-looking policies, popular nationalism is an enemy, a source of constant pressures toward error. This is also true, to some extent, in a larger country, since the economy is never large enough to look entirely inward, and since the nation's size leads to advocacy of ambitious but mistaken projects that a small country would not be able to consider. But, on balance, the conflicts between nationalism and sound economic policy would appear more acute in a small country. At least, this is my first hypothesis.

II

My second major argument starts with the observation that development, in a small as in a large nation, depends on able and intelligent political leadership, above all, on an appropriate and vigorous use of public fiscal resources and other instruments of public social and economic policy. This is all the more apparent in countries that have remained backward into the twentieth century, since the spontaneous and private forces leading toward development are obviously weak and unreliable in these countries.

The problem starts with the fact that appropriate leadership requires not only high-quality people, who presumably are potentially present even in a small population, but also motivation. And it is, I submit, a much less inspiring historic task to help build a nation of one, two, or five million people, who started the twentieth century very backward, than to have contributed some decades ago to the building of, say, Germany, Russia, or Japan.

In fact, it can be so much less inspiring that development is likely to founder for lack of an appropriately motivated leadership. And unfortunately, the ideologies that are most successful in inspiring people in small, backward countries to sacrifices for the sake of history are linked to autarkic policies that would be sheer economic disaster for these countries.

It is important to observe that promoting development requires some extremely difficult decisions, involving personal sacrifices, hard work, un-popularity, and even (in an almost general case) "class traitor" behavior. Political power offers temptations—how many leaders of small countries have become wealthy and found comfort in high living, and at what costs to their nations? The disproportionate frequency with which this burden falls on small countries is a reflection of the difficulties in moti-vating the leadership to higher goals.

Development is always a long process, and the payoff takes more than a lifetime; one must act for future generations. Moreover, for a small country, even in proportion to its size, sound development policy, as I have suggested, calls for restraint in the uses of central power. A country of two million will never require a huge and glorious bureau-cracy, nor ubiquitous controls or planning; these would tend to ruin its ability to take advantage of the international transactions on which its development depends. What is generally needed is a small, efficient, carefully balanced administrative operation that, to be successful, must be almost inconspicuous. For this, the country's ablest leaders must be asked to sacrifice all the empires, glories, and comforts that they could hope to win at home or abroad by actions that would *not* contribute to their country's development. This is a tall order.

One aspect of the problem worth elaborating is the "class traitor" dimension. Many backward countries are dominated socially, eco-nomically, and politically by landed and commercial aristocracies and their wealthy brethren who have moved into modern sector industries and public service.[4] Such landholder and commercial families, with their immense economic advantages and superior educations, tend to supply the leaders who assume the new positions of political and economic power.

Yet to promote development, political leadership must place the nation as a whole ahead of the privileged classes. First, development requires a systematic destruction of social class and caste privileges in order to promote social, geographical, and occupational mobility. Pre-viously disadvantaged groups must even be given special favorable treat-ment to try to offset their cultural and educational backwardness in order to speed the day when they can contribute positively to the society and economy. Burdens such as debt servitude must be eliminated. Second, development requires effective taxation to support heavy public expenditures. The largest share of this burden must be placed squarely on the well-to-do and property-owning classes. Third, favoritism and

[4] This is by no means fortuitous, since the surplus from the land, the labor that can be fed from this surplus, and the control of commerce were the commanding heights of any traditional agricultural economy. Whoever controlled those heights became a dominant elite. Under Western military and ideological pressures, widely varying arrangements for control of those heights have been converted into property arrange-ments.

public support of entrenched profitable positions in the modern sector must be avoided. The government must foster competition at home and from abroad, discourage inefficiency, prevent excess profits, and seek to minimize corruption, indolence, waste, and inefficiency in the public as well as in the private sector. Fourth, traditional land tenure systems must generally be attacked and reformed, particularly absentee landlordism and ancient practices such as sharecropping and the *hacienda* system, designed to extract a constant surplus from the land with a minimum of effort on the part of the owners. I would not myself generally recommend dividing land among the cultivators, at least as an economic measure; promoting large modern commercial farms usually makes more sense. But any land reform is bound to be resisted by a traditional elite. Fifth, the vested interests that must necessarily be hurt are sure to include various foreign enterprises, whose powerful governments are capable of many kinds of intervention. Clearly, a political leadership that tries to implement the requisite changes faces formidable opposition.

Since the leadership is almost certain to be drawn from the privileged classes, it must deliberately choose to put nation above class and accept the opprobrium of acting as "class traitors." It seems to me that almost every currently-advanced country has been led to its present eminence, in part, by just such "class traitors." But, surely, behavior along these lines, like foregoing comfort and wealth, is far easier to motivate when leaders are helping to build a great and powerful country.[5]

My second hypothesis, then, is that development is less frequently and less vigorously promoted by leaders in small countries, because competing incentives weaken their motivations.

III

My third hypothesis is that politics, and above all the politics of social change, are different in a small compared to a large country, in such a way that it is much easier for a small group of people to impose their power and unprogressive policies indefinitely on a small country. Pressures similar to those that would lead to progressive policies, political upheavals, or even social revolution in a large country can be much

[5] In many countries in Africa and Southeast Asia, the landholder elite problem is not present in the form just sketched. Quite a number of lightly-populated, largely tribal, peasant societies were taken over by administratively advanced colonial powers such as Britain, France, and the Netherlands, who chose to extract the surplus from the land to support their administrations through modern systems of direct and indirect taxes. Here, leaders who have seized the administrative machinery have inherited power in the wake of the colonial regiment. But even in these cases there are surely strong competing loyalties, to themselves, their families and friends, their tribes, and the army or civil service to which they belong, that conflict regularly with the requirements of development.

more easily resisted, though ease of political communication may be a positive asset if the right sort of leadership and policies can be found.

The essence of this argument is that numbers of political actors make a big difference. With hundreds of thousands or millions of educated adult citizens, each trying to influence policy, largely in progressive directions, ideas and currents of opinion develop a momentum that ultimately influences even the most cynical, reactionary, or dictatorial of governments. The number of possible personal contacts and cross-influences grows geometrically with the number of actors, to the point where politically active groups must be treated, even in repression, by categories or in some more or less randomized fashion. Under the circumstances, the milder forms of political action and cross-influence flourish in virtual immunity—political jokes, for example—while there exists a considerable statistical likelihood of getting away with more serious maneuverings. The probability of some of these efforts connecting and bearing fruit is also higher.

A related aspect is that even when the politically active classes are proportionally small, if they are numerically fairly large, there can be a feeling of something more than a group of individuals, that is, a mass or bandwagon effect, almost impossible to achieve in a much smaller country, at least when it is plagued by severe contrasts in incomes, education, and socio-political status.

Another political difference, as a corollary to the previous hypothesis, is that the opposition and other intermediate actors, as well as the leadership itself, are more moved by the historical and cosmic importance of their actions, and are thus more likely to take something broader than a selfish view.

In some contrast, in a small country with a very low educational and economic level, the number of important potential political actors is only in the thousands, the people with real wealth perhaps only in the hundreds. It is not impossible for a political leader to establish a personal relationship with nearly everyone who represents a potential key actor, or at least to extend police surveillance and persuasive measures to everyone likely to prove influential. If serious opposition appears among the lower classes, violence can be applied on a considerable scale with relatively little fanfare or notoriety, compared to the results of proportionally equivalent measures in a much larger country.

Of course, it would be absurd to say that a dictator cannot "get away with" a great deal, even in a large country. Especially in wartime and other times of crisis, all sorts of horrors have been perpetrated. But I submit that such actions are taken at greater risk, and with more concessions to pressures for progress (including development), than in a small country. Even when one tyrant gets away with socially undesirable policies, changes are forced upon his successors. In large countries, at least in modern times, the constellation of policies and political forces is always changing from generation to generation, and the results almost always include a succession of serious efforts at reform. Not even imperial China or Rome remained static for long in this regard; and the pressures for change have become incomparably greater in the last century or two, in backward countries faced with the fact of their backwardness.

IV

Let me emphasize that the tendencies suggested, even if they do in fact exist, are only statistical likelihoods, and do not automatically apply to any particular small country. Examples to the contrary are not hard to find. Several countries have become impressively advanced despite their small populations.[6] Others that are still poor are making admirable political and economic headway—Lebanon, Singapore, and Jamaica, for example.

I would also be the first to agree that the hypotheses put forward require careful research, to try to shed some really scientific light on them. Until this is done, they cannot be regarded as proven. Yet it seems to me that scale phenomena on the level of countries are among the most complex of the puzzles confronting the social sciences; and it will be years before we will be able to tackle such matters scientifically with any degree of assurance. Meanwhile, the special difficulties of small countries offer pressing practical problems. Under the circumstances, it is desirable to try to leap ahead and anticipate the eventual results of cumulative scientific method.

Too often specialists in the study and practice of development have ignored inherent political tendencies. Politics are a key to development. If there are scale effects in politics, such as I postulate here, this could be a matter of great practical importance.

---

[6] Norway, Denmark, Finland, New Zealand, and Israel still have less than five million people. Until recently the same was true of Switzerland.

In contrast to the previous selection, the next one is concerned with the population problem as it is more commonly defined. Although the causes for the rapid increase in population are well known, there is much disagreement both on the extent of the problem and on the policies to be pursued to deal with it. In the following case study, John Clarke examines a situation typical of many developing states, a situation in which strong traditional values inhibit and undermine the weak and vacillating government policies intended to stem the rate of population increase to economically and socially manageable limits.

31. POPULATION POLICIES AND DYNAMICS IN TUNISIA *

j o h n i. c l a r k e

The achievement of independence by many African countries since mid-century has generally increased the influence of political policies and boundaries upon population distribution and dynamics. Governments are taking a strong line with respect to alien (especially colonist) groups within their territories and are jealously guarding their sovereignty. In addition, most governments are making determined and successful efforts to lower mortality, with the result that natural increase has risen rapidly.

The small Muslim country of Tunisia, with about 4,700,000 people (1968 estimate) living on 48,195 square miles, clearly exhibits all these traits. Moreover, faced with a higher population density than most North African and Middle Eastern countries—a reflection in particular of long traditions of sedentary and city life, the profound impact of French rule (1881–1956), and the restricted size of its desert and semidesert areas, and in spite of its modest endowment of natural resources—Tunisia has taken the unusual and bold step, for a Muslim country, of introducing a family planning program in order to reduce fertility and natural increase and thus maintain its standard of living.

* Excerpts from "Population Policies and Dynamics in Tunisia" by John I. Clarke, *The Journal of Developing Areas*, Vol. IV, No. 4 (October, 1969), pp. 45–58. Tables have been omitted. By permission of the publisher and the author.

PROBLEMS IN NATION-BUILDING

Unfortunately, this much publicized program has had much less striking demographic results than other government measures, and the present increase in the rate of population growth is contrary to the government's hopes and expectations. This article will examine the demographic effects of the Tunisian government's actions, and will seek to explain why its population forecasts have proved inaccurate, with potentially damaging consequences to the success of the development program.

Population Data. It is never easy for the government of a developing country to have a precise knowledge of the rate and volume of its population growth. Decennial censuses are costly and often inaccurate; vital registration of births, marriages, and deaths is incomplete; and statistics of international migration are insufficiently detailed to calculate accurately the balance of immigration and emigration. These problems are demonstrable in Tunisia, although it has a longer series of demographic data than most Middle Eastern countries.[1] The first two censuses in 1886 and 1891 applied only to the French population. In 1896 and quinquennially thereafter, censuses enumerated the whole European population, but were not extended to the Tunisian population until 1921. However, the censuses of 1921, 1926, 1931, and 1936 are not very reliable because tax lists were sometimes used instead of family or household questionnaires. The only modern censuses are those of 1946, 1956, and 1966, but they throw considerable light on the last decade of the French protectorate and the first decade since independence.

Vital registration dates from 1886 for Europeans and from 1908 for Tunisians, but little accurate data are available for the Tunisian population before 1957, except for the city of Tunis. In general, registration of births is much more complete than that of deaths, although registration of female births is less frequent than that of males, and there is a dearth of information on births according to nationality, age of mother, etc. Similarly, there is little information on deaths by age group. Fortunately, registration of marriages and other types of registration have improved greatly in recent years.[2]

Population Growth. At the last census in 1966, the total population enumerated was 4,533,351, well above twice the 1921 total. Indeed, the Tunisian Muslim population, always the vast majority, has grown at a faster rate than the population as a whole and nearly doubled between 1936 and 1966. In contrast, three other broad elements of the population —Europeans, Tunisian Jews, and foreign Muslims—all increased gradually until various times in the 1940s or 1950s, when there were numerous departures from the country. . . . These departures of foreigners

[1] Mahmoud Seklani, "Les sources et les données fondamentales de la démographie tunisienne," *Revue Tunisienne de Sciences Sociales,* no. 5 (1966): 7–51.
[2] The results of a sample survey of 23,000 households held in 1968 will provide invaluable indications of vital rates throughout Tunisia.

and Tunisian Jews meant that during the intercensal period (1956–66) the total population increase was only 1.5 percent per annum. This gives a false picture of reality, however, as the Tunisian Muslim population increased annually by 2.3 percent during this period and is at the moment increasing much more rapidly.

International Migrations. Before the rapidity of population growth is examined, it is important to consider the substantial volume of emigration from Tunisia. Since independence, Tunisia has experienced a net annual out-migration ranging from 20,000 to 50,000, and the cumulative net out-migration between 1956 and 1966 exceeded 350,000, a large figure in relation to a fairly small total population. It is difficult, however, to calculate either the precise rates of departure or the numbers of foreigners present in the country. Published figures of the entry and exit of persons of different nationalities are complicated by the many foreign tourists, Europeans working in technical or cultural cooperation or for European companies, and those foreigners who come and go annually because they have property or money in Tunisia.[3] Moreover, no accurate record is available of the number of foreign residents, for the number registered at the various embassies is not a true indication.

✳   ✳   ✳   ✳   ✳

Rate of Increase. One important effect of the emigration of the various foreign elements and Tunisian Jews is that the Tunisian population is more homogeneous than at any other time in this century. Consequently, the interplay of fertility and mortality of the Tunisian Muslim population will determine almost entirely the rate of population growth in future years. In these circumstances the government's attitudes toward public health and family planning are of great significance. Unfortunately, the Tunisian government has made inaccurate assumptions as to the relative movements of fertility and mortality.

In the *Perspective Décennale de Développement* (*1962–1971*), prepared to enable Tunisia to embark upon a period of planned economic development, it was assumed that the actual rate of growth of the Muslim population was 2.2 percent per annum. This was certainly a conservative estimate, for the natural increase for 1962 was probably nearer 2.5 percent. However, more serious is the fact that the *Perspective Décennale* was based upon the hypothesis that there would be a pro gressive decline of the population growth rate during the ten-year period; it assumed an average annual increase rate of 1.9 percent between 1961 and 1966 and only 1.7 percent between 1966 and 1971. On this basis the total Tunisian Muslim population would increase from 3.9 million

---

[3]   It is a legal offense to remove Tunisian dinars from the country.

in 1961 to 4.7 million in 1971, an average annual rate of 1.8 percent. It was expected that improved social and economic conditions and rising per capita incomes would effect this considerable reduction in natural increase.

It is already apparent that the *Perspective Décennale* was unduly optimistic about a decline in the rate of population growth. In assuming that fertility would decline more rapidly than mortality, it was arguing that Tunisian experience would run contrary to that of all other developing countries. In fact, Tunisia is at the moment a typical example of the many developing countries whose demographic growth is mostly determined by rapid mortality decline accompanied by little change in fertility patterns. Instead of declining, natural increase has augmented annually, so that by 1966 it was approaching 3.0 percent per annum.

The present population growth largely confirms projections based on constant fertility made by Seklani in 1960 and by the Service Tunisien des Statistiques in 1964. . . .[4] Seklani assumed that the annual increase of the Tunisian population would be 2.5 percent between 1956 and 1961, 2.8 percent between 1961 and 1966, and 3.0 percent between 1966 and 1971. Both projections envisage a much higher population for 1971 than forecast in the *Perspective Décennale*.

It is impossible to calculate the present rate of natural increase from published registration data, because although birth registration gives fairly reliable birth rates, incomplete death registration provides death rates which are well below reality. . . . The differences between the numbers of births and deaths registered each year, 130,000 to 160,000, are therefore exaggerated.

Declining Mortality. In a detailed study of mortality in Tunisia, Seklani calculates that between 1946 and 1965 the crude death rate declined from 26.0 per thousand to 15.0. . . .[5] He points out that in 1946 mortality conditions in Tunisia were comparable with those of Sweden in 1820, France in 1850, and Spain in 1910; by 1956 they were comparable with Sweden in 1872, France in 1895 and Spain in 1930; and by 1966 they were probably similar to those of France in 1930. The general decline in mortality is closely linked with the considerable decrease in morbidity. The first phase in the development of medicine and public hygiene in Tunisia, which drew to a close in the late 1950s, saw a massive reduction in a number of endemic or epidemic infectious diseases, such as smallpox, typhus, typhoid fever, and malaria. A second phase

[4] Mahmoud Seklani, "La population de la Tunisie: Situation actuelle et évolution probable jusqu'en 1986," *Population* 16 (1961): 473–503, and Secrétariat d'Etat au Plan et aux Finances, *La Population de la Tunisie* (Tunis, May 1964).
[5] Mahmoud Seklani, *La Mortalité et le Coût de la Santé Publique en Tunisie*, 2 vols. (Tunis: Centre d'Etudes et de Recherches Economiques et Sociales, 1967 and 1968).

which began in the late 1940s has been primarily concerned with social maladies such as tuberculosis and infant mortality. The latter has declined spectacularly from about 220 per thousand in 1946 to about 100 per thousand in 1960, and this is rapidly broadening the base of the population pyramid (fig. 1).

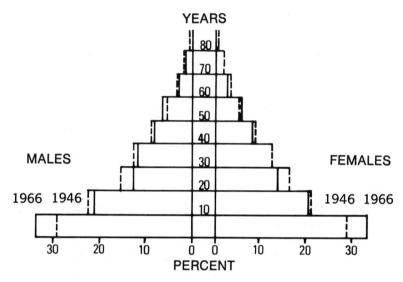

Fig. 1. The changing age-structure of Tunisia, 1946-66. Note the broadening of the base of the population pyramid.

In consequence, the average expectation of life at birth has risen from 37 years in 1946 to 55–56 in 1966. Seklani postulates that by 1970–71 the crude death rate will be as low as 13 per thousand and the average expectation of life of a Tunisian 60–62 years. This is still well below expectancy levels of European countries and of the former European population of Tunisia (66.5 years expectancy in 1956), but the difference is diminishing, partly because of the youthful age structure of the Tunisian population. However, an appreciable rise in standards of living is necessary before the gap can be closed.

Mortality decline mainly results from improved medical and public health facilities. Before the First World War Tunisia had only two or three main hospitals, concentrated in Tunis; by 1965 there were sixteen with a scattered distribution, and 33 hospital beds per 10,000 inhabitants. In 1966 there were 666 doctors, one for every 6,800 inhabitants, a fairly high level for a developing country. As medicine has been socialized and made more available to the Tunisian population, the number of sick persons treated has constantly risen. Tunisians now feel much freer to visit hospitals, and this is posing great difficulties to the hospital system, thus affecting its efficiency. The cost of this progress is increasing and will continue to do so; Seklani has demonstrated that the part of the national budget allocated to public health doubled between 1946 and 1966, and the expenditure per inhabitant rose four times.[6] Its effect was to reduce mortality by approximately 40 percent and to increase the average life expectancy by about 33 percent. Admittedly, these are inadequate indexes of the improved health of the nation, but they are indicative of a radical change in mortality conditions.

As expected, mortality tends to be lower in the capital than in the country as a whole, but the difference is not great, partly because the distribution of medical facilities is not as uneven as in many developing countries and partly because housing in some *bidonvilles* of Tunis is appalling.[7] Bchir notes that the infant mortality rate of Tunis is higher than in wealthy suburbs like Carthage, healthy hill towns like Zaghouan, and towns with more socially homogeneous populations like Sousse.[8]

High Fertility. In contrast with the remarkable decline in mortality in Tunisia, fertility has remained largely uncontrolled and therefore high. Islam, the backbone of society, stresses the advantages of large families, which are a source of pride and honor. Moreover, many parents believe that a large family provides an insurance against old age, there being more chance that one son will make good—President Bourguiba himself was the youngest of eight children. Until recently, celibacy was rare and disapproved, and sterility was a common motive for the repudiation of a wife and for remarriage. The superiority of the male sex, affirmed by the Koran, tended to reduce women to excessive childbearing, seclusion, and drudgery. Traditionally a high proportion of women in the reproductive age group were married, and women married young: in 1960, 51.2 percent of all women married for the first time were under 20 years old, compared with only 5.2 percent of males.[9]

The average size of the completed Tunisian family in 1956 was about 5.6 children. Seklani calculated a general fertility rate of 191 per thousand for 1960, a gross reproduction rate of 3.32 and a net reproduction rate of 2.37; that is to say, a woman reaching the end of her reproductive period would have an average 2.37 girls.[10] He also found

6 Ibid., 2:15.
7 A number of studies have been devoted to the suburbs and *bidonvilles* of Tunis, including: Jean B. Dardel and Charles Klibi, "Un faubourg clandestin de Tunis: Le Djebel Lahmar," *Cahiers de Tunisie*, no. 10 (1955): 211–25; Paul Sebag, "Le bidonville de Borgel," *Cahiers de Tunisie*, nos. 23–24 (1958): 267–309, his "Le faubourg de Sidi Fathallah," *Cahiers de Tunisie*, nos. 29–30 (1960): 75–136, and his *Un Faubourg de Tunis: Saïda Manoubia* (Paris: Presses Universitaires de France, 1960); and Jacques Taieb, "Une banlieue de Tunis: L'Ariana," *Cahiers de Tunisie*, no. 32 (1960): 33–76.
8 M. Bchir, "Données récentes sur la structure de la mortalité infantile en Tunisie: Résultats d'enquêtes," *Revue Tunisienne de Sciences Sociales*, no. 10 (1967): 43–72.
9 Seklani, "Les sources et les données fondamentales . . . ," p. 32.
10 Ibid., pp. 28–29.

little variation in fertility according to the socioeconomic category of the father, and that any differential fertility was probably linked more with the age at marriage of the mother and with the duration of the marriage than with social class.[11]

Since 1956 the fertility situation has changed. In the period 1955–59 the average birth rate was 39.8 per thousand, in 1960–64 it was 44.2, and now it is about 45–46 per thousand. By 1966 the average family size was probably 5.8 children (the census results are awaited), and there are indications of stronger differential fertility according to socioeconomic class. This rise in fertility is despite the reduction in the proportion of women aged 15–49 from 49.3 percent of all females in 1946, to 46.2 percent in 1956, and to 43.1 percent in 1966; and it is one result of the recent reduction in morbidity and mortality, increasing the chances of survival of young adult couples and their children. This is particularly evident in Tunis, whose population has lower mortality and a higher proportion of young adults than most other regions of Tunisia; its crude birth rate is over 50 per thousand.

Female Status and Family Planning. The sustained high fertility in Tunisia is in spite of the Bourguiba government's success in raising the status of women. Remarkable social advances were made soon after independence by the introduction in August 1956 of the Personal Status Code, which replaced Koranic law with a single legal system for all Tunisians. Polygyny was prohibited, divorce modified, and the minimum age of marriage postponed to 17 for women and 20 for men. Women were given the vote, and the veil was condemned as a "dust rag." Increased education and employment of women also helped in the process of modernizing Tunisian womanhood; the number of girls attending primary school rose from 64,549 in 1956–57 to 277,553 in 1966–67, which represented more than half of all girls of primary school age. In 1966–67 there were also 8,046 girls taking intermediate and professional education and 18,829 receiving secondary education. In addition, there has been a substantial increase in the number of women employed in industry, commerce, and administration. Indeed, by 1966 they amounted to one-fifth of the total nonagricultural labor force.

After legislation to raise the status of Tunisian women, more direct measures were taken to influence family size. The traditional pronatalist regime, supported by the French, was modified. In 1960 a decree limited family allowances to four children only, and in the following year the import and sale of contraceptives was permitted. In 1962, the government, aware that economic development was being impeded by population growth, began consultations with the Ford Foundation with a view to implementing a family planning program as a means of check-

[11]   Mahmoud Seklani, "La famille tunisienne au seuil de la contraception: Etat actuel et transition possible," *Revue Tunisienne de Sciences Sociales*, no. 11 (1967): 53–54.

ing the rate of population growth. With technical assistance from the Population Council (of New York) and a grant from the Ford Foundation, Tunisia became in 1964 the first African or Arab country to undertake a national family planning program.[12] The president, the government, the Destourian Socialist party, and lately the medical profession, gave support and publicity to the program; moreover, surveys indicated that a high proportion of Tunisian couples wanted family planning information and services although few knew how to limit family size.[13] By 1968 it was hoped that 120,000 women would be using intrauterine contraception, which would reduce the birth rate by 8–10 percent. In addition, a 1965 law legalized abortion for women aged 30 or more with five or more living children. Sterilization is also permissible by law, and many female sterilizations are performed.

The family planning program has not progressed nearly as rapidly as its organizers would have wished. In the four years between June 1964 and May 1968 only 42,460 first insertions of intrauterine devices (IUDs) had been made, about one-third of the original aim. . . . Obviously there were many rejections, and by 30 May 1968 only about 34,000 women, or 3.6 percent of the total number of women aged 15–49, were "protected" by any form of contraception.[14] Women aged 30 or more with large numbers of children represent a high proportion of those receiving intrauterine contraception.[15] There is also evidence to suggest that two-thirds of the women receiving free family planning services are wives of workers, *journaliers,* or unemployed men.[16] However, wealthier Tunisians probably obtain contraceptives privately through pharmacies.

One major reason for the program's limited success has been female disillusionment over IUDs, especially after coercion had been exercised in some rural areas to make women accept family planning. Such coercion provoked resentment, which in any case is also felt by many men. It was inevitable that a modern family planning program would run into difficulties in a Muslim country like Tunisia, but the difficulties were increased by President Bourguiba's change of heart on the desirability of family planning. In a televised speech on 12 August 1966 he cast grave

---

[12] See George Brown and Amor Daly, "The Tunisian Family Planning Programme," in *The Population of Tropical Africa,* ed. John C. Caldwell and Chukuka Okonjo (London: Longmans, 1968), pp. 419–23, and Amor Daly, "Tunisia," in *Family Planning and Population Programs,* ed. Bernard Berelson et al. (Chicago: University of Chicago Press, 1966), pp. 151–61.
[13] Jean Morsa, "The Tunisia Survey: A Preliminary Analysis," in *Family Planning,* ed. Berelson, pp. 581–93.
[14] Jacques Vallin, "The Number of Tunisian Women 'Protected' Against Pregnancy as of 30 May 1968" (Tunis: Population Council, 1968), cyclostyled note.
[15] Jacques Vallin, "Contraception intra-utérine selon trois variables démographiques en Tunisie (Juillet 1966–Décembre 1967)" (Tunis: Population Council, 1968), cyclostyled paper.
[16] Seklani, *La Mortalité,* 1:64.

doubts on the need for family planning. He stated that "the results of the census have shown that the rate of population increase is relatively slight, around 2.2 or 2.3 percent." He went on to say that it was a national duty for every Tunisian of marriageable age to found a family, and that "every family should be satisfied with four children," a figure which was sufficient to regenerate the population and enable it "to grow at a reasonable rate." "Rather than induce people with large families to limit their birth rate, the practice of family planning should lead young people from the age of twenty-five to set up homes and help rejuvenate the population." He also admonished celibates, who were shirking their social responsibilities. This change in attitude may have been due to a misinterpretation of the rate of population increase; the rate of 2.2 to 2.3 percent was obtained by comparing the 1956 and 1966 totals, and is well below the current natural increase rate. Other reasons may include apprehension either over the moral behavior of some young Tunisians or over the smallness of the total population in relation to other Arab countries. Whatever the reasons, the speech greatly affected the family planning program. Publicity for it nearly dried up, and the administrative services lost much of their raison d'être.

The program survived, however, and a new one was launched in January 1968, largely financed by the Ford Foundation and USAID, with a new office and administration, mobile medical and educational teams, improved visual aids, and less emphasis on IUDs. There is now a much greater demand for contraceptive pills, and it is hoped that they will cause less reaction than IUDs. This new program may be able to achieve a wider spread of family planning. At least, most people in Tunisia are now aware of the availability of family planning services, which are by no means confined to the cities. In the long term, legislation concerning age at marriage and increased education will probably have great influence upon fertility, but their effects are not immediate like family planning.

Vallin has recently calculated that if fertility in Tunisia remains unchanged until 1975, the Tunisian population will rise to 5,890,000.[17] If each year 1.5 percent of women aged 15–49 accept IUDs, the birth rate would decline to 43.9 per thousand in 1974 and by January 1975 the population would be 5,790,000. Such is the result, a fairly small one, if the present family planning program is successful. Only with much greater effort in family planning, such as was originally intended with 7 percent of women aged 15–49 accepting IUDs each year, would the birth rate be reduced to 34.6 per thousand by 1974. Even then the population would be 5,525,000 by January 1975. With such prospects, the recent half-heartedness over family planning may have serious eco-

17 Jacques Vallin, "Planning familial et perspective de population en Tunisie, 1966–1975," *Revue Tunisienne de Sciences Sociales*, no. 12 (1968): 71–88.

nomic repercussions. Mortality declines annually, but as yet Tunisia does not have the social motivation to be able to effect a comparable reduction in fertility.

The situation is going to become more difficult through progressive broadening at the base of the population pyramid (fig 1). In 1966, 46.3 percent of the population were aged under 15, compared with 42.1 percent in 1956 and 41.3 percent in 1946. It is worth noting that in the Ten-Year Plan it was forecast that only 39.8 percent would be aged under 15 by 1966, and 37.0 percent by 1971. This degree of error for a short-term forecast is enormous. Moreover, in 1966 over one-third (33.7 percent) were under 10 years and well over one-half (54.7 percent) under 20 years. This increase in the proportion of young persons is in spite of a persistent decline in the proportion of women in the reproductive age groups.[18] Obviously, the increased survival of children will mean a great rise in the number of potential parents during the 1970s; unless the size of families diminishes, Tunisia can expect spiraling population growth.

Although the social legislation to raise the status of Tunisian women and the family planning program to reduce the average size of families were major innovations in the Arab world, their demographic effects are still small. As yet they do not offer a good example to other Arab countries.

[18] Tunisia is one of many Arab countries where the number of males enumerated exceeds the number of females; in 1966 there were 959 females for 1,000 males. This sex ratio arises partly from underenumeration of females, partly from relatively high female infant and child mortality, and partly from the youthfulness of the population (in many advanced countries male mortality is much higher than female mortality among the older age groups).

Although many Westerners, particularly Americans, may make unwarranted assumptions about the benefits of education, especially mass education, the leaders of many transitional states have made it clear that they are determined to raise the educational levels of their societies as rapidly as possible as one important means to the general modernization of their societies. Since the education of a society is not just an end in itself, however, the educational policies have to be related to the other goals of society, and this is not an easy task anywhere. Adam Curle, in the study below, examines some of the particular problems the developing states confront in devising an educational system that adequately takes into account the conditions and goals of society.

32. SOME ASPECTS OF EDUCATIONAL PLANNING IN UNDERDEVELOPED AREAS*

a d a m   c u r l e

. . . In the last fifteen years an unprecedentedly large amount of aid has flowed from the rich to the poor countries; but viewed as a whole, the results have been disappointing: the "take off," as Rostow [1] calls it, has been achieved by very few of the underdeveloped nations. The character of this help has been largely based on the assumption that the chief lack of the underdeveloped countries was capital, and the technical personnel required to form capital. This assumption is now being vigorously challenged by many economists, who maintain that underdevelopment is not merely an economic but also a social phenomenon. Galbraith [2] in particular makes this point vigorously, stressing that a literate population and a highly educated elite are just as important for development as the inflow of capital. He goes on to list three other items relating to the social system as being of equal importance. These are social justice, an efficient administration, and clear understanding of what development entails.

EDUCATION AND THE SOCIAL STRUCTURE

The significance of education in particular is now generally maintained, as was demonstrated by the recent conference of the OECD on *Economic Growth and Investment in Education* (Washington, October 1961). Some economists have attempted to quantify the contribution of education to economic expansion. Schultz,[3] for example, maintains that

---

* From "Some Aspects of Educational Planning in Underdeveloped Areas" by Adam Curle, *Harvard Educational Review*, Vol. XXXII, No. 3 (Summer 1962), pp. 293–300. By permission of the *Harvard Educational Review* and the author.

[1] W. W. Rostow, *The Stages of Economic Growth: a non-communist manifesto* (Cambridge, England: Cambridge University Press, 1960).

[2] J. K. Galbraith, "A Positive Approach to Foreign Aid," *Foreign Affairs*, Vol. XXXIX, No. 3 (April 1961).

[3] Theodore W. Schultz, "Capital Formation by Education," *Journal of Political Economy*, Vol. LXVIII, No. 6 (1960), pp. 571–583, and his other writings. H. M. Phillips gives even greater weight to education in "Education as a Basic Factor in Economic Development," *Final Report* of Conference of African States on the Development of Education in Africa (Addis Ababa, May 1961; Paris: UNESCO, 1961).

less than a third of the increase in the national income of countries can be explained by quantitative increases in factor inputs. The residual has not been accurately broken down, but the most important factors appear to be the improvement of the human material through better health and training, and through the development of science and technology.

Encouraging though such developments may be, it is perhaps limiting that many people who are concerned about speeding the educational growth of underdeveloped countries think in rather narrow terms of increasing the supply of skilled manpower. If we stop to consider the social context responsible for the previous failure to produce this manpower, we see that the problem is wider than this. Underdeveloped societies are underdeveloped because they are not geared to the types of activity which development entails, and one of these is education in the general sense of the word. Many of these societies espouse systems of belief which are antipathetic to the flexible, empirical spirit necessary to technical achievement. Their social systems are often of a sort which would impede the growth of large commercial or industrial undertakings, or of individual capital accumulation. Large proportions of their populations, being chronically malnourished or diseased, are physically incapable of taxing technological work or agricultural innovation even if they were emotionally oriented and intellectually prepared for it. The enormous poverty of the majority of people in the underdeveloped world forms an almost unbreakable vicious circle with sickness, disease—and underproduction. The perimeter of this circle is very often reinforced by either political considerations, or the non-egalitarian character of the society, or both.

It is common knowledge that the ruling classes of many nations have been reluctant to spend much money on the education of those who might then compete with or supplant them. The differences between these classes and their poorer compatriots reflect and are similar in principle to the differences between nations.[4] Even without explicit government policy, the enormous gulf between rich and poor, powerful and impotent, well educated and illiterate is incredibly difficult to bridge. Underdeveloped societies tend to be highly stratified in terms of race, religion, tribe, region, class, or caste. In consequence the path of advancement for any one born in the lowest strata is hard and steep. He has to cross obstacles in the shape of indifferent schooling, of his own physical difficulties—malnourishment and chronic disease—and of social inertia. Eventually he has the final problem of establishing himself in a world in which there is no ready-made place for him.

For all these reasons, only a fraction of the potential talent of the underdeveloped countries is put to productive use, and it is very largely

---

[4] This is neatly illustrated in "Problems of Regional Development and Industrial Location in Europe," *Economic Survey of Europe in 1954* (Geneva, 1955).

for this reason that they remain underdeveloped. The problem is one which education is qualified to tackle, at least in part, so long as it is borne in mind that we are not thinking simply of producing the people, but also of changing the society; or rather of producing the people who will change the social structure as they contribute to the economy. Naturally these things always go together, but the emphasis we lay on one or other aspect of the development continuum affects our priorities.

One of the main things lacking in the underdeveloped countries is a middle class. In the traditional land-based economy there is little to stimulate the entrepreneur, while the growth of the technical, professional, and administrative class has been so slow, because of the inadequate educational system, that its members have tended to align themselves with the existing power groups. Thus the small emergent middle class, instead of establishing its own standards of competence, of professional integrity, and of appointment in terms of ability and training, has often striven to become as exclusive as the old elite, emulating rather than rivaling it. This proclivity is reinforced and illustrated by the difficulty of filling the intermediate posts, which is almost as serious an impediment to development as the complete lack of trained persons. Compare, for example, the figures for doctors and less highly trained medical personnel in the United Kingdom and in India.

The reasons for the inversion of the British pattern are complex, but one implication is that hierarchy matters even to the "new class" and that it frequently sets up barriers as strong as those through which its members have themselves broken. The high prestige of the top grade occasioning the lack of intermediate personnel is one cause of slow professional growth; it also leads to inefficiency and waste, as when a doctor spends half of his time as his own laboratory technician.

This is not to say that education is doing a bad job, but that to have its full social effect, it must have a sufficient volume. If the middle class is to be influential enough to break through resistances against effective economic behavior, to establish high standards of efficiency in administration, industry, and business, and gradually to draw together the extremes of the population, then it must be sufficiently large.

TABLE 1 [5]

Type of personnel	Per number of persons	
	India	United Kingdom
1 doctor	0,300	1,000
1 nurse	43,000	300
1 health visitor	400,000	4,710
1 midwife	60,000	618

[5] Government of India, Planning Commission, *The First Five Year Plan* (New Delhi, 1952), p. 490.

PROBLEMS IN NATION-BUILDING

In the old days when the British Colonial Office was planning a slow socio-educational evolution for Africa, it was assumed that the middle class would grow gradually over a period of decades. But political pressures and the urgency of reaching what Sax calls the Demographic Transition [6] give us very much less time. The African countries, among others, feel the urgency most keenly, and ambitious plans of educational expansion are being everywhere developed. From the point of view of the arguments I am putting forward, this is excellent, but when we get down to the details there are vast difficulties.

ECONOMIC CONSIDERATIONS

First there is the problem of how much a country can spend on education, and I will not attempt to answer this, except to say that the answer will to some extent depend on the apportionment of resources between activities which have a more and a less rapid impact on the economy. . . .

. . . There can be little doubt that the most immediate short-term returns can be obtained from investment in adult education. On-the-job training in metal, engineering, and building trades, agricultural extension, apprenticeship schemes, and all the educational activities which go with community development will obtain results in weeks or months, whereas schemes involving formal education may take ten years or more to mature.

There is another extremely important side to this. A poor country's capacity to absorb trained personnel is not great. For one thing, the jobs are few; for another, the wage expectation of the small number of educated persons is relatively much higher than in a richer country. In Ghana, for example, a primary school teacher is paid four times more relative to the national average income than one in the U.S.A. Therefore the poor countries can afford proportionally fewer trained people than the rich ones, although their need is so much greater. Here is one of the many vicious circles of underdevelopment. If primary education is expanded as rapidly as political pressure and national pride demand, the result—as in many West African countries—is the unemployed primary school graduate. In the Philippines and India [7] the academic level at

---

[6] Karl Sax, *Standing Room Only: The World's Exploding Population* (Boston: Beacon Press, 1955). This is "the transition from a high-birth-rate, high-death-rate culture (with low living standards) to a low-birth-rate, low-death-rate culture (with relatively high living standards)," p. 4.

[7] It is calculated that there are 50,000 unemployed graduates in India. In the Philippines there are 250,000 college and university students, most of whom are working for qualifications which are both academically worthless and useless for obtaining employment.

which unemployment occurs is higher, but the principle is similar. There are no jobs at a level which young people consider proper for themselves, and so, having wasted their country's money on their education, they proceed to waste their family's resources on their maintenance. Given time, the number of available jobs will go up, or the aspiration of the school leaver go down, but again we have not got this kind of time and we cannot afford this kind of waste.

The speediest way in which an underdeveloped country's absorptive capacity can be increased is through its main industry of agriculture. This appallingly neglected field could absorb, as extension workers, community development workers, assistant agriculture officers, and the like, millions of young men and women who at present scorn it as a form of activity representing the backwardness they are attempting to escape from, and who see very slender rewards to be gained from it. (It takes 75 per cent of the working population of Asia to produce an inadequate 2,500 original calories per head per day for the inhabitants of the continent. In the U.S.A. 15 per cent of the working population produce 10,000 original calories per head per day. These figures illustrate the size and the urgency of the problem.) But if suitable training for different levels of scholastic attainment were devised and adequate possibilities of promotion established, the people might well be attracted to types of work which have an immediate impact on the economy, rather than to the normal favorite avocations of clerk or school teacher.

If agriculture can do most to absorb skilled and semi-skilled labor, industry comes second and can do more to increase a nation's wealth. However, the poorer a country is, the less it can sustain those factors which tend to strengthen the labor force and to increase production. Two of these factors, the amount of vocational training and the membership of labor unions, tend to vary proportionately with national wealth, as is shown by the following figures for underdeveloped areas.

TABLE 2 [8]

Group of countries	Percentage of secondary school population (age 12–19) in vocational training, according to national per capita income			
	up to $100	$100–250	$250–500	$500–750
Africa	3.5	25.3	— [*]	—
Asia	2.4	14.6	20.9	48.8
Latin America	47.1	41.4	36.5	61.0

[*] Only the Republic of South Africa comes within this group.

An entirely untrained and unadapted labor force drifting between agricultural under-employment and the alien life of the factory town is

[8] Derived from Norton Ginsburg, *Atlas of Economic Development* (Chicago: Chicago University Press, 1961), and from UNESCO, *Basic Facts and Figures* (1960).

PROBLEMS IN NATION-BUILDING

cheap and easily obtained labor in which management is not inclined to invest. Nor is it attractive to install new plant calling for skilled handling. So industry lacks efficiency and the labor force lacks the steady

TABLE 3 [9]

Per capita gross national product		Percentage of population in labor unions
Up to $100	(21 countries)	0.82
$100–$250	(20 countries)	2.59
Over $250	(15 countries)	6.42

Note: .The average for the lowest income group has been almost doubled by the figure for Bolivia of which 7.7 per cent of the population belongs to labor unions.

employment which would make it efficient. But these workers, by the very fact that they have shaken loose from the traditional life and sought industrial employment, are part of the nucleus of the new class which will transform society. Anything spent on their appropriate training or on efforts to organize them will have both a short-term productive and a long-term social effect.

A STRATEGY FOR EDUCATIONAL
EXPANSION

If I seem to have strayed away from the field of education proper, it is because I wanted to stress that we have to use the term widely in relation to the underdeveloped countries. I also wish to show why educational planning and especially planning of the long-term investment in schools, universities, and technical colleges, has to be related in the widest sense to all other aspects of social and economic planning. A country's capacity to absorb persons of different educational levels and abilities; the factors which can be brought to affect this capacity; the relationship between the educational, social, and economic factors in productivity—all these and many other things have to be borne in mind when planning the rate of expansion of an educational system and the priorities to be assigned within that system to its several parts.

Nevertheless, despite the fact that every country presents its own problems, it is possible to suggest some of the broad lines of the strategy of educational expansion. Firstly, common sense would advocate an absolute maximum ratio of growth for primary education of 10 per cent per annum. But common sense is unlikely in this case, as in many others, to prevail against political expediency. We are forced to the next best

[9] Derived from Ginsburg, *op. cit.*, and Gabriel A. Almond and James S. Coleman, eds., *The Politics of Developing Areas* (Princeton, New Jersey: Princeton University Press, 1960).

thing, which is a series of measures designed to reduce the damage to standards caused by over-rapid expansion. This means emphasis on teacher training (including upgrading of existing teachers) and on such methods as will enable teachers both to deal with more children and help bad teachers to teach better. The growth of secondary education is far more significant to economic development, and it is on this that resources should be concentrated. Universities are, of course, also of great importance, but their expense is enormous and in any case the greatest shortage is of persons educated up to secondary level (particularly where there has been a considerable component of vocational or technical training).

The great problem is to determine the rate of growth. . . . This is an almost universal dilemma: a country needs a considerable number of trained and educated persons to build up and consolidate its development, but until it is developed it has not the resources to educate the people.

What can be done, however, is to place heavy emphasis initially upon such activities as will without great cost bring about rapid improvements in the economy. Such activities would be training rather than education in the broadest sense; vocational rather than general. They would be directed towards key sectors of the economy. Agriculture and industry have already been mentioned in this connection: training for management is also extremely important. A further principle would be to make full use of existing potentialities, of the people already employed. Both public and private employers would be encouraged to provide in-service training to upgrade their staff.

To concentrate heavily upon this form of technological training is, of course, only a short-term expedient designed to strengthen the economy and to increase the absorptive capacity so that, in the next phase, the weight can be gradually transferred to the formal system of education. From this will come men and women who not only possess the necessary skills, but an outlook sufficiently broad to contend with the extreme problems of a society undergoing rapid change.

*Of all the problems facing the developing states, few seem as in-
tractable as those arising from the continuously rapid growth of urban
centers. Although the urban poor have been surprisingly docile, considering their problems, the further rapid growth of urban areas will
undoubtedly accelerate the levels of tension in many states. Some dimensions of the problems of rapid urbanization are considered below by
Philip Hauser.*

33. THE SOCIAL, ECONOMIC, AND TECHNOLOGICAL PROBLEMS OF RAPID URBANIZATION*

philip m. hauser

Urban problems and the problems of rapid urbanization are quite different in the economically advanced and the economically underdeveloped
areas of the world respectively. In the economically advanced nations,
urbanization is both an antecedent and a consequence of high levels of
living. It both makes possible and is a manifestation of great increases in
division of labor and specialization, in technology, in skill, and in productivity. In the economically underdeveloped areas, it does not usually
have these properties. There, large concentrations of urban population
are only to a minor degree symbols of man's mastery over nature—they
represent more the transfer of underemployment and poverty from an
overpopulated rural countryside to an urban setting. In consequence,
the social, economic, and technological problems of rapid urbanization
must be considered separately for the underdeveloped and the developed areas of the globe respectively.

ECONOMIC PROBLEMS

The economic antecedents of urbanization in the economically more
advanced areas differ greatly from those of the less advanced areas.

° From "The Social, Economic, and Technological Problems of Rapid Urbaniza-
tion" by Philip M. Hauser. Reprinted from: *Industrialization and Society*, by F.
Hoselitz and W. E. Moore, eds., (Mouton/Unesco, 1963), with the permission of
Unesco. Selections from pp. 201–211.

Although much remains to be learned, the emergence of the urban agglomeration has been reasonably well traced for Western civilization. . . . In the West, urbanization is both an antecedent and consequence of rapid industrialization. There are no highly developed economies in the world in which large cities and a high degree of industrialization are not present.

Urbanization in the economically underdeveloped areas of the world is the product of very different forces. The "primate" cities in South and South-East Asia are less the result of indigenous economic development than they are the product of economic development oriented essentially to one or more foreign countries. They developed as links between the colonial and mother country. Today, they usually still have an external orientation, serving as a link between the local elite and the outside world, rather than as an economic outpost of the national economy.[1] Urbanization in Latin America is characterized by the hypertrophy of capital cities. These, reflecting unique aspects of Latin American history, are concentrated on the seaboard, or in the mountain districts in the tropics.[2] In Latin America—as in Asia and Africa—prior to World War II, economic and urban development was largely directed toward external markets in the framework of patterns established under colonial administration. Moreover, the process of urbanization in the underdeveloped areas has been accelerated by the low land-population ratio arising from excessive population growth in relation to agriculture resources; by the disruption and disorganization produced by the last war, which forced refugee populations to choke already swelled populations in cities; by the lure of urban existence, to which large parts of the peasant population were exposed as the result of military service and other wartime dislocations; and by various other forces which pushed population to the city instead of attracting it by economic opportunity of the type experienced in the West.[3]

Thus, the underdeveloped areas of the world are "over-urbanized," in that larger proportions of their population live in urban places than their degree of economic development justifies. In the underdeveloped nations, a much smaller proportion of the labor force is engaged in non-agricultural occupations than was the case in the West at comparable levels of urbanization.[4] Furthermore, during the postwar

[1] Philip M. Hauser (ed.), *Urbanization in Asia and the Far East* (Calcutta, 1957), pp. 86 ff; Mark Jefferson, "The Law of the Primate City," *Geographical Review* (April, 1939); Norton S. Ginsburg, "The Great City in Southeast Asia," *American Journal of Sociology* (special issue on "World Urbanism"), LX, No. 5 (March, 1955), 455–62.
[2] UNESCO, *Report by the Director-General on The Joint UN/UNESCO Seminar on Urbanization in Latin America* (Paris, 1960), p. 6.
[3] Hauser, *Urbanization*, pp. 33 ff; UNESCO, *Report by the Director-General*, p. 15.
[4] Kingsley Davis, "Urbanization and the Development of Pre-Industrial Areas," *Economic Development and Cultural Change*, III, No. 1 (October, 1954).

period, the rate of urbanization in the underdeveloped areas has continued proceeding more rapidly than the rate of economic development.

To say that the underdeveloped areas of the world are over-urbanized is to pose the major economic problem with which they are confronted, namely, that they do not at the present time have an adequate economic base to support present urban populations by the standards of the Western world. They must find a way of achieving higher levels of economic development to support their present, let alone their prospective, urban population. Continued rapid rates of urbanization are, therefore, likely to aggravate, rather than alleviate, present urban poverty and distress. In general, the outlook for the remainder of this century is a dismal one indeed. It is very doubtful that, over this span of time, the underdeveloped nations can attain economic development of adequate dimensions to meet Western standards of living for their present and future city dwellers.[5] The fundamental economic objective of the underdeveloped areas is that of increasing productivity; and the many difficulties they meet in their efforts to attain this objective are likely to be exacerbated rather than ameliorated by present and prospective rapid rates of urban growth.[6]

This general problem may be analyzed into a number of components.[7] Virtually all of the underdeveloped nations have ambitious programs for economic development. The cores of these programs generally consist of plans to increase industrialization. At the present levels of productivity and limited savings, a central problem is that of allocating resources for development between the agricultural and industrial sectors of the economy. If the criterion of maximizing product per head be accepted as the objective of economic development programs, then it is possible, at least in the short run, that the advancement of the agricultural sectors of the economy may be more productive than efforts to induce industrialization. The achievement of adequate balance between agricultural and industrial development is a major difficulty which confronts almost all of the economically underdeveloped nations.

Another issue involves the allocation of scarce investment resources between "social investment" and "productive investment." This problem, although it exists both in the urban and rural sectors, assumes its

---

[5] Philip M. Hauser, "Demographic Dimensions of World Politics," *Science,* CXXXI, No. 3414, 16–43.

[6] United Nations, *Determinants,* chap. xv; United Nations, *Report on the World Social Situation* (New York, 1957), chaps. ii, vii, viii, ix; Joseph J. Spengler, "Population and World Economic Development," *Science,* CXXXI, No. 3412, 20.

[7] Discussion of economic problems is drawn largely from Hauser, *Urbanization,* chaps. i, ii, vi, vii, UNESCO, *Report by the Director-General;* and *United Nations Seminar on Regional Planning* (New York, 1958). These publications summarize the UN/UNESCO Seminar considerations of economic problems associated with urbanization.

most acute form in the cities. Cities in the underdeveloped areas are characterized by inadequate infrastructure development, precluding the usual amenities of urban existence found in Western cities. The temptation to devote scarce savings to social purposes—e.g., piped water, sewerage, better housing, etc.—is great, particularly in view of the expectations which have accompanied political independence and the opportunity for self-determination. Yet social investment of this type, badly needed as it may be, is possible only at the expense of decreased productive investment—investment in power plants and factories, or in tractors and fertilizers, designed to increase productivity.

Another difficult problem posed by the continued accelerated rates of urbanization in the underdeveloped areas is that of the location of industry. At the present time, numerous small commercial towns serving agricultural areas are widely dispersed, largely in accordance with the location of agricultural activity and the density of agricultural population. Larger towns are superimposed on the widespread distributional pattern of the smaller commercial centers. They are usually near transport nodal points—river and road junctions and, more recently, railroad junctions. These centers, and the seaports, are the "break-of-bulk" points; their essential function is the transshipment and distribution of goods between land and water and within the interior. Such cities have increasingly become convenient points of location for processing and light manufacturing industry. In most underdeveloped areas, the growth of towns and cities and industrialization, apart from primate and capital cities, has gone little beyond this point.

Efforts to increase industrialization, and to deal with the many pressing problems of swelling urban populations, are forcing decisions about the location of economic development projects. In the economically more advanced nations, the locations, as well as the size and function of urban places, were largely the products of the play of market forces. In the economically underdeveloped areas, these decisions are usually centrally administered. They involve considerations of raw materials, power sources, availability of labor, the location of consumer markets, national policy concerning centralization or decentralization of industry, regional development, and general national economic development. In centralized decision-making about the location of new industry, there are dangers of serious dis-economies.

Decentralization is necessary because the "great city" tends to be "parasitic," in that it usually retards the development of other cities in the nation, and may contribute relatively little to the development of its own hinterland because it is oriented primarily to the contribution of services abroad or to the indigenous or remaining Western elite inhabiting it. On the other hand, the decision to decentralize industry may produce dis-economies by ignoring the productive factors already available in the larger urban agglomerations. The larger cities in the underdeveloped areas represent already available labor supply, markets, and a wide variety of public services which may be utilized for industrial and business development. To duplicate such agglomerations of population in efforts to decentralize may well be redundant and wasteful.

Underdeveloped areas with rapidly growing urban populations face another difficulty in making policy with respect to employment opportunities. To provide work for hordes of unemployed and underemployed immigrants to urban centers, there is a tendency to emphasize labor-intensive techniques. If carried too far, this tendency may adversely affect the growth of the nation's net aggregate product by retarding labor-saving technological developments. In general, policy determination presumably must aim toward obtaining balance in industrial development between employment opportunities, in the short run, and technological advance to insure maximum product per head, in the longer run.

Low productivity and poverty are distinguishing traits in both rural and urban areas in underdeveloped nations. Because internal migratory flow from agricultural to urban centers is a major factor in the present and prospective increase in urban populations, programs designed to keep rural people in agricultural areas may be important in any effort to deal with urban, as well as national, economic development problems. Programs that raised the level of living of rural populations would undoubtedly moderate the excessive flow of migrants from rural to urban areas. In a number of underdeveloped nations, outmoded land tenure systems contribute to rural proverty. Agrarian reform resulting in higher productivity, giving the agricultural population a stake in the land and an opportunity to raise its level of living, may well be an important means of alleviating urban problems by helping to reduce the flow of city-bound migrants. Similarly, the establishment of cottage industries and small industries in rural areas may keep their population from emigrating.

Western cities have undergone development and transformation with changing industrial technology. Economically underdeveloped areas today have the choice of adopting twentieth- or nineteenth-century types of industrial equipment. The extent of actual choice depends, of course, on the availability of electric, as contrasted with steam, power; on cost factors for older, as against more modern, equipment; and on the emphasis placed on labor-intensive rather than automated equipment. The adoption of twentieth-century industrial technology would undoubtedly create patterns of urban development quite different from those which characterized the West during the nineteenth. Moreover, the problem of maintaining balance in economic development is also at stake in the decisions made with respect to the types of technology adopted in different sectors of the industrial economy.

Urbanization has an impact on income, levels of living, savings, and capital formation that requires brief mention, even though most of what can be said is necessarily speculative. Urban residents in the under-developed areas, in spite of underemployment and low productivity, are generally engaged in nonagricultural activities which provide them with a relatively higher money level of income and expenditure than is achieved in rural areas. While it is a moot point whether urban real income is higher than rural real income in such areas, the higher urban money income is undoubtedly one of the factors attracting populations to cities.

The transition from the rural to the urban economy involves a shift, of course, from a subsistence to a monetary economy in which mobiliza-tion of savings can be facilitated. Urbanization produces alteration in consumption patterns, in which the proportion of consumer expenditures for food tends to decrease below the rural level; while expenditures on amusement, education, transport, services, footwear, rent, and taxes tend to rise. . . .

Finally, in the underdeveloped nations another crucial decision is necessary: the interventions of government and of market forces respec-tively, in dealing with the economic problems of the nation as a whole, as well as with the specific industrial and urban developments, must be determined. For a number of reasons, historical and contemporary, cen-tral decision-making and management of economic affairs inevitably must play a more important role in the economically underdeveloped nations than they did in the history of the economically advanced na-tions. If the mix of central planning and government interventionism is increased, it may be expected that patterns of economic, as well as urban, development are likely to follow different routes than they did in the West. Some types of problems engendered by Western industrializa-tion and urbanization may be avoided or ameliorated; but it is also possible that new and critical kinds of problems will be encountered, and that the dangers of serious dis-economies will be increased. The interplay of forces most conducive to efficient and balanced economic development and orderly urbanization is far from being fully under-stood. . . .

❖   ❖   ❖   ❖   ❖

PHYSICAL PROBLEMS

The most visible consequence of overurbanization and rapid rates of urban growth is the decadence of the urban environment in underde-veloped areas.[8] The physical city is characterized by a large proportion

---

[8] The materials on "physical problems" are drawn largely from Hauser, *Urban-ization*, chaps. i, ii, xi; UNESCO, *Report by the Director-General*; and Philip M. Hauser (ed.), *Urbanization in Latin America* (UNESCO, 1961).

of shanty towns and tenement slums; inadequate urban services, including housing, water supply, sewerage, utilities, and transport; uncontrolled land use; excessive population densities; deficient educational and recreational facilities; and inefficient commercial and marketing services. Rapid urbanization in the underdeveloped areas is accompanied by not only a defective but, also, by a deteriorating urban environment. It is estimated that, in Latin America alone, some four or five million families live in urban shanty towns and slums. The miserable physical conditions of cities create great pressure for "social" instead of "productive" investments. However, many of the public housing and physical improvement programs which have been undertaken in such areas have necessarily tended to benefit families with moderate incomes rather than to meet the needs of the lowest-income families—the residents of the shanty towns and slums.

Of course, the underdeveloped nations are very aware of the need for city and regional, as well as national, planning. But the city planner in the underdeveloped country is confronted with insuperable difficulties. These stem largely from low income levels; from rapid population growth, including hordes of immigrants from rural areas who are ill-adapted to urban living; from inadequate urban infrastructure development—all in all, from a bewildering array of needs, each of which seems to have first priority.

Although urban agglomerations of the size of Western cities are to be found, the physical amenities associated with such in the West have not yet developed—at least, not for the mass population. The amenities of urban existence are available only to very small fractions of the total urban population. It is in the impact on the already inadequate urban physical plant that the rapid rate of urbanization produces some of its more serious consequences.

○　○　○　○　○

SOCIAL PROBLEMS

The city represents not only a new form of economic organization and a changed physical environment. It also is a profoundly modified social order affecting man's conduct and thought. Urbanization produces the city as a physical and economic artifact, and also produces "urbanism as a way of life." [9] The size, density, and heterogeneity of population—aspects of "social morphology"—affect the nature, intensity,

[9] Louis Wirth, "Urbanism as a Way of Life." The framework materials in the introductory part of "social problems" are drawn from the general sociological literature, and particularly from the works of the men to whom reference is made in the text.

and frequency of contact, and, therefore, influence the nature of the process of socialization and human nature itself. The city is a type of mutation in culture that has far-reaching effects on social structure and process and on social institutions, including the structure and function of government. The transition from pre-urban to urban living necessarily involves frictions, which are manifested in social and personal problems. Rapid urbanization exacerbates these frictions.

. . . The chief effects of urban living on the personal level are, probably, discernible in the changed nature of interpersonal relations and in the relative flexibility of personal patterns of behavior. On the cultural and social level, they are to be found in the changed nature of the forces making for cohesion, in the changed genesis and function of social institutions, and in the changed structure and role of government.

On the personal level, contacts in the urban setting become secondary, segmental, and utilitarian, rather than primary, integral, and sentimental as in the traditional social order. Personality tends to change from a relatively rigid structure molded by the traditional social heritage to more fluid flexible patterns, arising from the necessity to exercise choice and from rationalism in behavior, as the hold of tradition loosens and new urban problems emerge. On the social level, cohesion in the urban social order becomes a function of interdependence engendered by increased specialization and division of labor; it is no longer the product of the constraint of convention in a relatively homogeneous and closed traditional order. Social institutions in the urban setting become "enacted" rather than "crescive" as older functions become attenuated or disappear and new instrumentalities arise to cope with unprecedented situations and problems. Even the basic social institutions—the family and the church—are subjected to forces which modify their structure, their role, and their hold on the behavior of the person.

In the urban setting, the role of government is one of increasing interventionism as organizational complexity and interdependence increase. In the West, the transition from a feudal to an industrialized and urbanized order has been characterized by the emergence of complex formal organization—bureaucracy—not only in government, but also in business, labor, voluntary associations, and virtually all organized aspects of the mass society.

o   o   o   o   o

. . . The acute as well as chronic aspects of social problems that result from rapid urbanization are, perhaps, most discernible in the adjustment of in-migrants to urban living. The rural in-migrant to the city is typically from a relatively homogeneous origin. In the city, he is confronted with a bewildering and almost incomprehensible vastness and heterogeneity. He usually lives for some time with his fellow villagers or relatives and only gradually becomes accommodated to city life. He must adapt to new and unfamiliar ways of making a living; a money economy; regular working hours; the absence of warm family living; large numbers of impersonal contacts with other human beings; new forms of recreation; and a quite different physical setting, often involving new kinds of housing, sanitation, traffic congestion, and noise. One of the greatest adjustment problems centers around the transition from a subsistence to a monetary economy, and dependence on a job for subsistence.

Furthermore, the in-migrant often finds his area of first settlement is the shanty town, in which the decadence of the underdeveloped urban environment is manifest in its most extreme form. Consequently, superimposed on problems of adjustment there may be severe problems of health and nutrition, and of extreme poverty and squalor in living conditions. In such a setting, the in-migrant frequently displays personal disorganization as the subjective aspect of social disorganization. It is in the in-migrant family that the greatest incidences of personal and social pathology are found—delinquency, crime, prostitution, mental illness, alcoholism, drug addiction, etc.

Another element contributes to the social problems and is source of severe problems for the economy as well. This is the fact that rural in-migrant workers often lack rudimentary skills for industrial work, possess high rates of illiteracy, and are otherwise ill-prepared for city living. Throughout the underdeveloped countries, the need to increase literacy and to provide minimum vocational training for urban employment is acute. In fact, the provision of adequate educational and vocational training, both to the in-migrant and to the more permanent inhabitant of urban places, is among the most critical social problems which confront the underdeveloped areas.

Rapid urbanization is accompanied by increasing tempos of cultural, social, and personal change. A number of scholars have maintained that underdeveloped areas with non-Western cultures possess ideologies and value systems that tend to resist change in general and, therefore, changes of the type induced by urbanization. A rapid rate of urbanization, as contrasted with a slow one, conceivably increases the frictions of transition from non-Western to urban (and presumably Western) value systems. It is, of course, disputable whether Western values identified with urbanism as a way of life are an antecedent or a consequence of industrialization and urbanization; and whether they are the only values consonant with urban living. Conceivably, the difference between non-Western outlooks produces different kinds of "urban mentality" and interpersonal and social relations in the urban setting. Whatever the answer to this question may be, it *is* true that rapid urbanization increases the tensions and frictions of adjustment in value systems from pre-urban ways of life.

vii. economic development

Few problems in the transitional states are regarded as more urgent than the problem of economic development. A widespread belief persists among most leaders of these states—as well as among those in the West who support foreign aid programs—that if substantial, long-term progress can be achieved in economic growth, many other problems confronting their societies will be far more readily resolved. But the problem of achieving substantial economic development is extremely complex, and despite a few significant exceptions, most of the developing states have not yet succeeded in generating and maintaining a high, continuous growth rate. The reasons are not solely economic, however; they also involve some of the social, political, and psychological characteristics of these societies. In this chapter, some of the more important internal aspects of economic development are considered, while the next chapter will examine several dimensions of the international arena that affect the economies of these societies.

There are many reasons that account for the high priority accorded economic development. One basic reason is, of course, that of eliminating the extreme forms of poverty found in many of these states. Large numbers of persons still suffer from inadequate food, clothing, and shelter, with premature death often the result. The extensive famines in India and China during the past decade were only a more acute form of a common problem. Humanitarian considerations require that the bare essentials of life be provided, either through increasing domestic production or through expanding exports that will earn the foreign exchange necessary for the importation of food supplies and other essential commodities. To meet the basic needs of their rapidly growing populations, particularly in the urban areas, states must increase the level of agricultural and industrial production.

There is also another form of poverty with which the leaders must contend. This form of poverty is more psychological and subjective than absolute. It springs from a recognition of the gap that separates the poor from the rich, whether internally within a society, or externally among the states in the international community. In a world in which egalitarian political and economic ideas are becoming increasingly accepted, the continuation of gross disparities in standards of living leads to bitterness and frustration. Leaders in many new states held out the hope to their followers that once political independence was achieved and the oppressive economic conditions of colonialism were removed, a rapid development of the economy would ensue, bringing material benefits to all. Demands that these promises be fulfilled have led to intense pressures on these leaders to raise the standard of living. The prospect of a better life is increasingly stirring the masses to political action in their desire for a standard of living more commensurate with that of a privileged few.

A further reason for seeking economic development is to relieve the present heavy dependence on the export of one product, a situation found in many developing states. Since the export of this product, usually a raw material or food product, is often subject to extreme and sudden price fluctuations on the world market, the income from its sale is highly unstable. This instability of income, in turn, makes sound planning and financing of domestic programs difficult to achieve. By developing their other resources, these states hope to diversify their exports and attain a higher and more stable income. Simultaneously, the development of their other resources will also provide a more adequate base for the development of domestic industries. Such industries will enable these states to supply many of their domestic needs that must at present be imported.

Economic development is also sought for reasons that are more specifically social and political than economic. For example, many leaders view economic development as a means of promoting social and political unity among the diverse groups within their states. By creating a more complex, interdependent economy, regional, cultural, and economic groups are brought together in the common cause of economic progress. The transportation and communication networks that are created as part of the developmental schemes help to link regions and groups together not only physically but also psychologically. National pride is stimulated by the accomplishment of economic growth, particularly in the industrialized sector. Such growth, in turn, permits an expansion of educational facilities and other welfare programs, all of which, it is hoped, will further serve to unify the society.

Another objective served by economic development is the promotion of greater economic and social equality by narrowing the division between rich and poor within society. Industrialization results in the creation of a middle class of technicians, engineers, and managers, and a working class of skilled and unskilled laborers, all of whose incomes are higher than those of the rural masses. Programs of land reform are also usually included in the plans for economic development. These reforms are expected to result in increased income for the peasants and farmers. Together, agrarian reform and industrial development are viewed as a means to reduce the sharp differences in income that characterize the traditional agrarian economy.

Further, the self-interest of the political elite in promoting economic development cannot be overlooked. The modernizing elite may undertake industrialization as a means of restricting and diminishing the power of the recalcitrant, traditional, landed aristocracy and other traditional elites. Neither the industrialists nor the workers can be controlled economically or politically by the traditional elites as can the rural masses. Gradually, economic and political power is being transferred to the more forward looking middle and working classes whose geographical base is in the urban areas, not the countryside. Thus, industrialization develops increasingly powerful allies for the modernizing political elite in their struggle to reshape society. Through industrialization the economic and political power of the usually highly conservative, traditional elites can be diminished.

Even the more conservative political elites may feel constrained to promote economic development to maintain their positions. Failure to alleviate the poverty and suffering of the masses or refusal to acknowledge the demands for more rapid economic growth may result in an increase of the appeal and power of more radical groups such as the communists, military leaders, and professional and intellectual elites.

In addition to domestic considerations, leaders may promote economic development to enable them to play a more prominent role in international politics. A strong economy with a substantial industrial capacity is regarded as essential if power and influence are to be exerted in the international community. This assumption leads to a strong emphasis on the development of heavy rather than light industry or agricultural development. With heavy industry, modern, well-equipped military forces can be maintained and an independent foreign policy pursued, as in the case of Communist China.

A mixture of these motives is usually advanced by those leaders who are attempting to advance the level of economic development in their states. The goal of economic development is more easily stated, however, than realized. In plotting the strategy for economic development, these leaders must resolve a number of complex problems.

First, the decision to seek economic growth has to be balanced with other national objectives. While a high rate of growth is commonly desired, it is not the only goal that the leaders of the developing states are pursuing. The maximum theoretical growth rate is often sacrificed, for example, to maintain a large military force. Resources that might otherwise be allocated for agricultural or industrial development are often diverted for support of the military establishment. Frequently the military budget accounts for as much as fifty per cent of the total governmental expenditures. Similarly, resources are often diverted for expenditures designed to promote national unity. Transportation systems that must be heavily subsidized are nevertheless justified as a means of increasing interregional cooperation. Other appropriations have been made, as in Indonesia, for example, to construct huge stadiums in which national and international games and other events can be staged. Such expenditures on national showplaces, while often not economically profitable, are believed to contribute to feelings of national pride and unity. Again, the maximum growth rate is sometimes restricted by the determination of the modernizing elite to achieve greater income equality. Tax structures have been designed to favor low income groups at the expense of the wealthy even though the latter's ability and incentive to invest in economically productive enterprises are thereby reduced. Policies of this type have been employed in Cuba, the United Arab Republic, and Indonesia, among many others.

In designing their programs for economic development, the leaders of the developing states have had to determine the appropriate roles for the public and private sectors of the economy. As has already been indicated, many leaders are prejudiced against capitalism as the dominant economic philosophy because of its alleged economic inefficiency and the promotion of social injustices. The pattern of public and private ownership varies greatly from state to state, however, and even some of those who most vigorously espouse socialist principles have been forced to rely fairly heavily on private enterprise for increasing production. While the private sector is severely limited in states such as Communist China, much greater emphasis is placed on it in the Latin American states. In between these extremes are a number of socialist economies, such as that in India, in which the state owns many of the principal industries, but in which private enterprise plays a significant role as well. In almost all developing states, great emphasis is placed on central planning, both for the public sector and for controlling and guiding private investment.

The complex problems of financing the programs of industrial expansion and agricultural development continually confront the planners. Domestic investment capital is, of course, extremely limited in most of these states, and even the amount that is nominally available may be difficult to direct into investment. In many of the more conservative states, as in Latin America, the wealthy segment of the population is almost untaxed. Even in states where income and inheritance taxes are sharply progressive, inefficient collection systems and corruption frequently combine to reduce to a very low level the taxes actually collected. While many modernizing leaders regard high taxes on the poor masses as socially and politically undesirable, the masses in most states nevertheless bear the major share of the tax burden, paid largely through a variety of consumer taxes.

Private investment is often difficult to stimulate. Those persons who possess great wealth generally prefer either to invest in land (usually with little intention of reforming the traditional, semifeudal agrarian system) or to invest abroad, either in industry or banking. Merchants have traditionally sought high profits on a small turnover of goods and are often suspicious of mass production techniques and merchandizing methods that assume small profits on a high turnover. The instability of governments and the uncertainties surrounding future economic conditions are further obstacles to private investment.

In addition to taxes as a source for investment capital, some states have established monopolies in certain sectors of the economy, such as utilities and some exports. The excess income over operating costs can then be reinvested either in the same segment of the economy or in other areas. In other states, royalties on the resources extracted by foreign companies provide substantial capital, as in the case of oil royalties paid to several Middle East governments by American and European oil companies. Loans from international lending agencies such as the Export-Import Bank, the International Bank for Reconstruction and Development, and the Inter-American Development Bank of the Organization of American States,[1] as well as loans and grants provided by the United States and other countries, have injected billions of dollars into the economies of the developing states for developmental purposes. Although this aid is often criticized as being too little, many of the developing states have not as yet been able to use efficiently and effectively the aid already extended. The internal problems of these states, such as the shortage of trained personnel, unstable governments, and a reluctance on the part of some leaders to undertake internal reforms of tax systems or agrarian reform programs, have all impeded the expansion of capital from external sources.

The financing of expansion programs is complicated by the great pressures on the economic planners to permit an immediate increase in the standard of living. In view of the low standard of living, the decision to restrict current consumption in favor of investment—and thus to achieve a higher rate of growth in the future—is difficult to make and maintain. In most states, an uneasy compromise has been achieved that attempts to increase the standard of living rapidly while at the same time expand investments.

As a result of these factors, inflation has been a serious problem for most of these states. Many governments have undertaken massive pro-

[1] The organization and functions of regional banks are discussed in Manmohan Singh, "Regional Development Banks," *International Conciliation,* No. 576 (January, 1970).

grams of expansion, the cost of which cannot be covered by the taxes collected. Large deficits have been incurred which have been covered by loans from central banks and foreign lending institutions. Since large amounts of money are poured into the economy as the development programs (such as industrialization) are executed, competition for the limited supply of goods has rapidly driven prices upward. Although wages have also been increased, they usually tend to lag seriously behind the increase in prices of all commodities. Thus the industrial workers, who depend upon their wages for subsistence, are in effect subsidizing the economic developmental programs in their societies. In some cases, inflation has exceeded 100 per cent a year, and price rises of 25 to 50 per cent are not unusual in many developing states. Although limited inflation may enable governments to expand their development programs, excessive inflation has disrupted sound planning and has forced some states to reduce drastically the scale of some schemes.

The planning for economic development is usually highly centralized in an official government planning board or commission. Even in states that do not subscribe to socialist principles, conditions have forced the governments to assume active leadership if systematic economic development is to be achieved. The planning boards usually have great responsibility and authority; they, along with the political leaders, make all major decisions relating to the type of development program to be pursued, its financing, and its general execution. Since the planning boards wield considerable power, they become deeply involved in the political bargaining process. A variety of interests attempt to influence their decisions both on major issues, such as land reform and foreign investments, and on the more specific issues, such as the precise location of industrial plants. The breadth and complexity of the problems they have to consider frequently impose severe strains on their limited manpower resources with the result that the plans developed are sometimes quite unrealistic in terms of the societies' actual capacities for development.[2]

The severe shortage of skilled personnel and the lack of stable, efficient political and administrative institutions enormously complicate the task of economic development. In some cases, the acute shortage of skilled native personnel has been intensified as a result of nationalistic policies that have forced out many or all of the bureaucrats of the former colonial state. In Indonesia, for example, the intense hostility toward the Dutch eventuated in the withdrawal of almost all Europeans soon after independence was achieved. While the forced withdrawal was justified by the Indonesian leaders on grounds of national pride and the fear of

[2] For an interesting discussion of the problems of planning, see R. Cranford Pratt, "The Administration of Economic Planning in a Newly Independent State: The Tanzanian Experience, 1963–1966," *The Journal of Commonwealth Political Studies*, Vol. V, No. 1 (March, 1967), pp. 38–59.

further economic exploitation, the impact of their removal was immediately noticeable in the sharp decline in agricultural and industrial production. To replace the departed colonial bureaucrats, some states have eagerly sought the aid of other outside experts and advisers. Although technically competent, such advisers are sometimes inadequately attuned to the subtleties of the social and political structures of the states whose economies they are attempting to aid. Through programs such as the Peace Corps and scholarship programs to train students in the United States and other countries, efforts are being made to supply the developing states with a core of skilled technicians and administrators.

For programs of economic development to succeed, deeply rooted traditional values, attitudes, habits, and political and economic institutions often have to be modified or replaced. In rural areas, the patterns of life based upon subsistence farming are often quite resistant to change. Many agrarian development plans have floundered because of the failure accurately to assess the response of the rural inhabitants to changes that, to the urban bureaucrat, represent such obvious improvements. New types of grains have been rejected, for example, because they did not provide the desired taste even though they were more nutritious and produced higher yields. Programs for agrarian reform are usually vigorously opposed by the large landowners whose standard of living and traditional authority are threatened by these programs. Traditional business attitudes too, as indicated above, have not been conducive to economic development, nor have the attitudes of many workers toward their jobs. Only gradually, for example, is the long afternoon break in the Latin American's workday being eliminated. In many societies, the industrial work force is unstable, given the propensity of workers to return to their native villages as soon as possible. Under these circumstances, the development of a skilled labor force is difficult to achieve.

While a few states such as Mexico, Turkey, and the Philippines are making substantial progress in economic development, for many others the outlook is highly uncertain. Indeed, for some states the prospects of orderly development are simply bleak. As two advisers to the Iranian government have written concerning that state's program of land reform, it may be that "the situation can be so miserable and reforms so overdue that planned development is impossible."[3] If progress is often slow internally, the prospect of closing the gap between the poor and rich states in the world seems even more difficult to attain. A simple illustration indicates why this is so. If two economies, one of which provides a gross national product per capita income of $2,000 and the other of $200,

[3] P. Bjorn Olsen and P. Norregaard Rasmussen, "An Attempt at Planning in a Traditional State: Iran," *Planning Economic Development*, ed. Everett E. Hagen (Homewood, Illinois: Richard D. Irwin, Inc., 1963).

each grow at an annual rate of 2 per cent, at the end of a year the former will have increased to $2,040 while the latter to only $204. Thus the initial difference in per capita income of $1,800 will have grown to $1,836 at the end of one year. To maintain the initial difference of $1,800, the less developed state would have to grow at an annual rate of 20 per cent, or 10 times as fast, a figure that is unlikely to be maintained by many states over a period of years.[4] Yet since we are dealing with a problem that is in large part psychological, the inability to narrow the gap in absolute terms is undoubtedly of less importance to persons in the underdeveloped states than is the realization of immediate benefits resulting from substantial and sustained internal economic growth. However, even a modest increase in the per capita income is difficult to attain in many of these states in the face of their increasing populations. In our example, a population increase of 2 per cent would eliminate any increase in the per capita income. To attain an increase of 2 per cent in the per capita income simultaneously with an increase of 2 per cent in the population would, of course, require an annual economic growth rate of 4 per cent. Such a growth rate, while not necessarily unrealistic, would nevertheless provide only a very gradual increase in the standard of living and would not begin to close the gap between the rich and the poor nations.

The economic progress the developing states are able to make will continue to be a principal factor affecting the stability of their political institutions as well as the stability of the international community. Failure to meet the rising expectations for a higher standard of living is likely to produce frustrations and tensions that can have only a most disruptive effect upon the development of a more peaceful world.

[4]   Hla Myint, *The Economics of the Developing Countries,* (New York: Frederick A. Praeger, Inc., Publishers, 1965), p. 18. Even Japan, a state that has had great success in controlling its population increase while undergoing rapid economic expansion, achieved an average annual growth rate of only 13 per cent from 1965–69, slipping to 11 per cent in 1970.

SUGGESTED READINGS

Agarwala, A. N., and S. P. Singh, eds. *Accelerating Investment in Developing Economies.* New York: Oxford University Press, 1969.

Bangs, Robert B. *Financing Economic Development: Fiscal Policy for Emerging Countries.* Chicago: University of Chicago Press, 1968.

Baranson, Jack. *Industrial Technology for Developing Economies.* New York: Frederick A. Praeger, 1969.

Benveniste, Guy, and Warren F. Ilchman, eds. *Agents of Change: Professionals in Developing Countries.* New York: Frederick A. Praeger, 1969.

Brown, Lester R. *Seeds of Change: The Green Revolution and Development in the 1970's.* New York: Frederick A. Praeger, 1970.

De Gregori, Thomas R., and Oriol Pi-Sunyer. *Economic Development: The Cultural Context.* New York: John Wiley & Sons, 1969.

Ewing, A. F. *Industry in Africa.* London: Oxford University Press, 1968.

Galenson, Walter, ed. *Labor in Developing Economies.* Berkeley, Calif.: University of California Press, 1962.

Hagen, Everett E. *The Economics of Development.* Homewood, Ill.: R. D. Irwin, 1968.

Hambidge, Gove. *Dynamics of Development.* New York: Frederick A. Praeger, 1964.

Hapgood, David, ed. *The Role of Popular Participation in Development.* Cambridge: MIT Press, 1969.

Harbison, Frederick, and Charles A. Myers. *Education, Manpower and Economic Growth.* New York: The McGraw-Hill Book Co., 1963.

Hetzler, Stanley A. *Technological Growth and Social Change: Achieving Modernization.* London: Routledge & Kegan Paul, 1969.

Honey, John C. *Planning and the Private Sector: The Experience in Developing Countries.* New York: The Dunellen Company, Inc., 1970.

Maddison, Angus. *Economic Progress and Policy in Developing Countries.* London: George Allen and Unwin, Ltd., 1970.

Mellor, John W. *The Economics of Agricultural Development.* Ithaca, N. Y.: Cornell University Press, 1966.

Millikan, Max F., and David Hapgood. *No Easy Harvest.* Boston: Little, Brown and Company, 1967.

Myint, Hla. *The Economics of the Developing Countries.* New York: Frederick A. Praeger, 1965.

Ness, Gayl D., ed. *The Sociology of Economic Development.* New York: Harper & Row, Publishers, 1970.

Onslow, Cranley, ed. *Asian Economic Development.* New York: Frederick A. Praeger, 1965.

Rostow, Walt W. *The Stages of Economic Growth: A Non-Communist Manifesto.* Cambridge: Cambridge University Press, 1960.

Smith, T. Lynn, ed. *Agrarian Reform in Latin America.* New York: Alfred A. Knopf, 1965.

Warriner, Doreen. *Land Reform in Principle and Practice.* New York: Oxford University Press, 1969.

Wharton, Clifton R., ed. *Subsistence Agriculture and Economic Development.* Chicago: Aldine Publishing Company, 1969.

Wietz, Raanan, ed. *Rural Planning in Developing Countries.* Cleveland: The Press of Western Reserve University, 1966.

An enormous effort has been made over the past several decades to define the necessary strategies less developed states should pursue to achieve economic development. Nevertheless, the proper strategies remain elusive for, as the authors of the selection below note, there is often an element of incompatibility among the goals desired. Accordingly, success in striking a satisfactory balance between those goals is difficult to achieve. Still, priorities must be established if available resources are to be used effectively, and the authors discuss some of the attendant problems of planning for development.

34.   PRIORITIES IN ECONOMIC DEVELOPMENT °

b i l s e l   a l i s b a h
a n d   a l b e r t   b e r r y

Economic development is a shorthand expression for certain goals which represent the hope for a better way of life. The active pursuit of these goals by underdeveloped nations reflects a decision to influence the allocation of scarce resources and a willingness to alter existing institutions. The determination of the goals, of the institutional framework and of the allocation of resources all call for priority decisions. The goals are ideally an expression of society's preferences, though in practice they are what leaders correctly or incorrectly perceive them to be. . . .

Most underdeveloped countries would cite as their major goals a rapid growth of per capita income, a low level of unemployment and some degree of income equalization. But there is often a lack of awareness, both inside and outside these countries, of the possible degree of incompatibility among the objectives. Such countries are usually faced by high rates of unemployment caused by the shortage of the complementary factors, capital and entrepreneurship. This leads to a conflict between growth and full employment in situations where a choice must

°   From "Priorities in Economic Development" by Bilsel Alisbah and Albert Berry, *Journal of International Affairs*, Vol. XVI, No. 2 (1962), pp. 172–182. Reprinted by permission.

be made between a mechanized method of production and a less efficient labor-intensive one. . . . Income equalization, by reducing high incomes, also conflicts with growth in countries where such incomes provide a large portion of total investment. In these cases, if all incomes are at about the same level—necessarily low—savings may be very small. A dilemma thus arises: a country can have inequality of incomes now, with the resultant investment leading to higher future incomes, or it can have more equality of incomes now, low investment and less hope of higher incomes in the future. . . .

The second group of decisions, those concerned with possible institutional changes, are the subject of an important current debate. Some hold that land reform [1] and tax reform [2] are in many cases such crucial preconditions of growth that other efforts are wasted until these problems are solved. (This view has recently been widely publicized in connection with Alliance for Progress aid to South American countries; certain officials hold that the aid should be withheld until there is more evidence of serious intent to undertake the desired reforms.) Certainly some form of a reasonably stable government, a banking system and a revenue system will be essential. But the real question is one of degree. It can be persuasively argued that none of the now developed countries had achieved anything approaching an ideal taxation or banking system until the process of development was far along in its course.

. . . Today this function [of allocating resources] is performed largely through the rapidly mushrooming planning boards. Economic planning is, of course, far from homogeneous. It varies with respect to the importance assigned to it, its sophistication, the detail in which it is carried out and the relative size of the public sector. But the basic problem facing all the planners is the same: to assign priorities in such a way that resources will be allocated in the best possible manner.

This would be a conceptually easy task if the economist could measure the total contribution to national income of every possible investment. He would then select the ones which yielded the highest returns per dollar, and would allocate his resources among these in such a way that the last dollar's worth of resources in each use yielded equal returns. The best allocation of resources among different sectors would follow automatically without the need for any additional considerations.

[1] Land reform is often defined more in social than in economic terms; it usually refers to the breaking up of large estates so that the peasants will own the land which they cultivate. Sometimes this increases agricultural output by increasing the incentive to produce, but if the estates were well managed before the breakup, output may decrease. Even if this is true, however, there may be a net economic gain if ex-landholders invest their funds in industry.

[2] A major problem of taxation in underdeveloped countries is the political difficulty of imposing high taxes on the rich; this group usually has an influence far out of proportion to its size. Many other weaknesses are common as well, such as inefficiency and corruption in the gathering of taxes, the use of poor kinds of taxes, *etc.*

In underdeveloped countries, unfortunately, the estimation of a project's contribution to national income is especially difficult. Economists commonly divide this contribution into the direct effects and the indirect effects. The former refer to the value of goods and services produced less the value of raw materials used in production; this is equal to the sum of incomes generated by the project (*i.e.* wages, rent, profits, *etc.*). The latter simply include any other effects on national income. If, for example, an innovating entrepreneur sets up the country's first modern textile plant, the total effect on national income may surpass the direct effect since others may copy its technology and thereby increase their own productivity. Again, the establishment of a canning plant may lead to an increase in the incomes of local fruit growers (indirect effect) by cutting the wastage which is common in underdeveloped areas with their poor storage facilities; thus the increase in national income will be greater than the total rewards to the employees and owners of the canning plant.

Direct effects, while not particularly difficult to determine when the enterprise is operating, may be hard to predict beforehand, especially in a rapidly changing economy where in many cases a project may be the first of its kind. Indirect effects are always hard to estimate. . . .

✧   ✧   ✧   ✧   ✧

Along with . . . broad ideas concerning the appropriate balance (or imbalance) of growth, the planner will think in terms of "sectoral principles and generalizations." These revolve around two questions: what should be done and who should do it? The first deals with the most desirable allocation of resources among sectors, the most important of which are agriculture, industry, education and mining.[3] The second is basically concerned with determining the proper extent of the government's role.[4]

In the latter connection the balanced growth doctrine has important implications. Its requirements of sizable and more or less simultaneous

[3] An alternative to this sectoral approach runs in terms of "bottleneck factors." In recent years writers have successively stressed a lack of natural resources, a lack of capital and a lack of high level manpower as being, in some sense, the "crucial missing link." At one point it was often implied that a country could be developed merely by pumping in enough capital. Currently this view is not popular and surprisingly low estimates of a country's ability to absorb capital are common. In any case, this general approach to the matter leads one to think of the priority problem less in terms of "which sector should a country develop fastest" and more in terms of "which factor should it try to get more of."

[4] By the "government's role" we mean, as well as the operation of industries, any other methods used to influence the pattern of outputs and prices in the economy. We are primarily concerned with those economic reasons for this role which are especially characteristic of underdeveloped countries.

investments in all industries call for a "big push." This, in turn, requires the government to play a major role to insure the proper timing of investments and to see that the necessary funds are forthcoming. The government will have to indulge in heavy taxation or in forced saving by inflation (*i.e.* printing money and spending it), since the private sector cannot be expected to provide an adequate volume of savings voluntarily.

Certain other situations, peculiar to underdeveloped countries, also imply the need for government operation or intervention. Most underdeveloped countries still lack the infrastructure needed for development (roads, railroads, bridges, public facilities, *etc.*), and the fulfillment of this need is primarily a function of the government. Furthermore, the lack of entrepreneurial talent and experience, coupled with the desire to avoid risk-taking, means that many projects with a good chance of success will not be undertaken by the private sector. The public entrepreneur, who unlike his private counterpart is not risking his own capital, will be more likely to attempt such projects. Even where private entrepreneurial talent is not particularly scarce, investment is often channeled in directions which are not socially productive, *e.g.* the purchase of real estate or land, speculation on rising prices or the purchase of foreign bonds.[5] These investments, unfortunately, are usually less risky than truly productive ones, and hence highly attractive to the investor. An additional problem is the danger of monopoly power when a few new plants are set up to satisfy a fairly small market for some industrial product. Competition from imports will often be ruled out on "balance of payments" or "infant industry" grounds, enabling the lucky firms to relax and even stagnate to some degree while maintaining their profits by high prices. A final element in enlarging the government's sphere of activity is that international capital now largely takes the form of public loans and grants rather than private investment.

Although the above arguments imply the need for government operation, such operation on too large a scale has its own disadvantages. Some private entrepreneurial skills may be wasted because the government cannot attract them. Furthermore, some voluntary saving, which would have been induced by opportunities for private investment, will not occur. Saving will largely have to take the form of taxation, which is difficult and inefficient in most underdeveloped countries, and inflationary finance, which causes well-known disturbances and problems.[6]

[5] These investments are socially undesirable as compared, for example, with investment in factories, which increase the country's productive capacity. The purchase of land or real estate is merely a transfer of existing wealth, not a creation of new wealth.

[6] These considerations do not necessarily suggest that the government's role as a whole should be curtailed; they may alternatively imply wider use of other types of intervention besides government operation, *e.g.* subsidies, controls of various sorts, *etc.*

Viewing the public-private question as a whole, however, it seems clear that for some time to come governments should play an increasing role in developing economies. This statement remains valid to a considerable extent even if we cannot assume that administrators are as honest or efficient as their counterparts in developed countries, since much of what the government does would not be touched otherwise.

We turn now from broad considerations of growth as a whole to questions of inter-sectoral resource allocation. Probably the most widely discussed priority issue of this sort is "agriculture vs. industry." Many economists charge that underdeveloped countries consistently under-estimate the importance of agriculture and consequently trip over this sector while chasing the dream of industrialization. Although the two sectors are often assumed to be in serious competition for scarce re-sources, we will argue that they can be, in fact, quite complementary. The only satisfactory course for most developing countries is the twofold one of industrializing *and* increasing agricultural output.

In dealing with the proper relationship of agriculture to industry it is very important to distinguish between the long and the short run. In the long run the relative contribution of industry to national income will definitely grow, since as incomes rise a greater percentage is always spent on industrial products. In all developed countries the ratios of industrial to agricultural output and of industrial to agricultural workers are higher than in underdeveloped countries. This holds true even for Denmark and New Zealand—the two most agriculturally oriented of the wealthy nations—both of which have less than 20% of their populations in agriculture. The real issue, therefore, is the priorities to be assigned in the next few years, *i.e.* the path to be pursued in moving toward a fairly definite long run position.

In some cases, where rural overpopulation is very serious and there are few unexplored avenues for increasing agricultural output, heavy emphasis on industrialization is a sheer necessity. In less extreme cases a relative increase in the industrial sector may remain desirable on other grounds.[7] It usually leads to greater total savings and investment by increasing the incomes of entrepreneurs, the major savers in underde-veloped countries. And the industrial sector, which is often coterminous

---

[7] A number of unsound arguments for industrialization coexist with the valid ones. One of the most interesting and completely fallacious is the contention that, since the value of an industrial worker's daily output is greater than that of the farmer, national income could be raised by transferring workers to industry. This argument fails to consider the costs of the expensive machinery with which the typical indus-trial laborer works and to which his high productivity must be largely attributed. It may be that one more worker adds very little to the total output. In an extreme case other factors such as capital and entrepreneurship may be fixed in quantity with the maximum amount of labor already employed. In this case there would be nothing for the newcomers to do except to cheer on those already employed—at best a somewhat doubtful method of increasing production.

with the "money economy," is easier to tax than the agricultural sector, where the limited use of money makes attempts to determine incomes and transactions very difficult. Finally, industrialization makes people more receptive to change and progress by tearing them away from their traditions and instilling in them the "monetary incentive."

. . . [E]mphasis on agriculture, where marked increases in production are possible, has very important advantages of its own. Until industrial ventures become able international competitors, agricultural exports will, despite the disadvantages of severe price fluctuations, be a major means of payment for the various imports needed in development. An agricultural expansion will also ease the inflationary pressures caused, in a developing economy, by people's tendency to spend most of the increases in their incomes on food. Finally, since the agricultural sector is such a large portion of the economy, its general prosperity and buying power are very important to all the other sectors.

More arguments can be presented on either side, and it may appear that little can be said by way of generalization. The crucial point, however, is that in many cases agricultural output can be spurred by methods requiring relatively little capital or high level manpower, the factors especially necessary in industry. . . .

☼　☼　☼　☼　☼

We pointed out earlier that the importance of the industrial sector as a whole is virtually certain to grow over the long run as development proceeds. The optimal long run relation among specific industries is much harder to estimate because of the difficulty of predicting changing tastes, new inventions (nylon, for example, ruined the silk industry in Japan) and the discovery of new resources. One does not even know the latent industrial talents of the population itself. Unpredictable behavior by other countries further complicates the situation; a country which has a comparative advantage in steel production may not wish to specialize too much along this line if it feels power and prestige motives will lead other countries to build their own steel plants. Because of these difficulties, errors in the direction of specialization are a constant threat. Although the cost of such errors is somewhat mitigated in a growing economy, where excess capacity tends to come into use over time, the extreme scarcity of resources clearly calls for great care in their allocation.

One facet of the inter-industry allocation problem is the "heavy vs. light" issue. Despite economists' advice that developing countries, due to the scarcity of their capital, should specialize in light industry and acquire the products of heavy industry through trade, these countries continue to be lured by such symbols of industrialization as the steel plant. There seems, however, little cause to worry that they will quickly become exporters of heavy industrial products; advances in this direction have been rather modest so far. And such modest advances may be of considerable value, since in setting up heavy industry a country must import. foreign technology and use rationalized procedures, some elements of which, hopefully, will spread to other parts of the economy.

Underdeveloped countries which are large and well endowed with iron ore and mineral fuels, or which feel that imports of industrial products are too uncertain to be relied on, may be quite justified in stressing heavy industry. Countries less well endowed must weigh carefully certain disadvantages of doing so. The most serious of these, probably, is that since heavy industry has a low labor-capital ratio, the greater the relative emphasis on it, the higher unemployment is likely to be. Light industry has the further advantage that it can more often be established in towns or villages. This means not only that the costs of transferring people to the cities can be avoided but also that the seasonal underemployment in agriculture—so typical of underdeveloped countries—can be reduced by having villagers work in industry for part of the year. Furthermore, since the typical firm in light industry is relatively small, the entrepreneurial function will be spread wider and valuable experience obtained. In view of the usual shortage of entrepreneurial ability,[8] this idea may appear implausible; the point, however, is that people not presently engaged in enterprise are more likely to make the jump if production is done on a small scale. Taking the "heavy vs. light" issue as a whole, it must be conceded that conditions vary too much from country to country for any valid generalizations to be made.

Finally, education, that sector of the economy which produces knowledge, has come increasingly to the forefront of allocation discussions. Decisions concerning the emphasis to be placed on education as a whole, and on the various levels and types of it, are perhaps the most difficult in the field of development. The problems of measurement here are gigantic. Even for the direct effects of different levels of education on an individual's income, it is extremely difficult to arrive at an accurate estimate. Analyses of these matters are just now beginning in developed countries; in underdeveloped areas most of the current discussion consists of educated guesses.

One view, which we tend to share, is that, in the short run it will be best to stress technical as opposed to general literary education. Considerable evidence shows that the latter is quickly forgotten when the student returns to the farm. In many cases it will be economically wise to postpone mass elementary education as well, since it may conflict

---

[8] The unproductive bargaining skills of the middleman, which are so abundant in many underdeveloped countries, should not be mistaken for entrepreneurship. The time spent haggling in bazaars, while it may enrich the individual concerned, certainly makes no contribution to national income.

sharply with the training of the technicians and engineers who are so important in development. We emphasize, however, that we are viewing this issue only from an economic point of view, and that in this case, perhaps more than in any other, one can expect the noneconomic considerations to be paramount.

In the previous selection it was noted that one problem that must be resolved in establishing priorities involves the issue of agriculture versus industrial development. After an initial emphasis on industrialization, many leaders and observers began to reconsider the arguments in favor of agricultural development. The arguments of each are, of course, important to consider since much of the future prosperity of the individual transitional states hinges on the correct choice being made now. In the analysis that follows, Ian Livingstone states and examines the arguments for each type of choice.

35. AGRICULTURE VERSUS INDUSTRY
IN ECONOMIC DEVELOPMENT * †

i a n   l i v i n g s t o n e

TWO ARGUMENTS IN SUPPORT OF AGRICULTURE

(a) *The Interdependence of Agriculture and Industry*

A rich agricultural sector clearly facilitates industrial development. The income earned in the sector provides the purchasing power necessary for

* From "Agriculture Versus Industry in Economic Development" by Ian Livingstone, *The Journal of Modern African Studies*, Vol. VI, No. 3 (October, 1968), pp. 330–341. Published by Cambridge University Press. Excerpted by permission of the author and the publisher.
† Director of the Economic Research Bureau, The University College, Dar es Salaam, and from 1965 to 1968 Reader in Economics, Makerere University College, Kampala.

the setting up of the minimum viable sizes of industrial plant. High agricultural productivity, by satisfying food requirements more easily, can permit the release of labour for work in industry. Food is supplied cheaply to industrial workers, the "terms of trade" between agricultural and industrial products thus being favourable to the development of the industrial sector. The supply of savings and of tax revenue from a rich agricultural sector can be used to promote general development, and so on.

From this point it is often argued that there should therefore be a "balanced growth" of industry and agriculture. But what specifically does such "balance" mean? In policy terms it can only refer to the distribution of development effort in terms of the finance and administrative resources available. It cannot mean that such resources should be divided fifty-fifty between the two sectors, since there is no *a priori* reason why one should arrive at any such precise figure. But a choice must be made: the interdependence of the two sectors does not alter the fact that, with limited resources for distribution, more for one means less for the other, though not as much less as in the absence of the favourable effects of interdependence. Clearly the distribution should be determined by the relative rates of return "at the margin" (to additional resources applied) calculated so as to include the repercussions of each sector on the other.

(b) The Predominant Position of Agriculture

It is frequently pointed out that because agriculture forms a large part of G.D.P. in the poorer countries a high over-all rate of growth in the economy will be difficult to obtain without a reasonable rate of growth in agriculture. This is of course a statement of need, rather than of possibility. Even as such it would not be valid if the rate of return to industrial investment were independent of the volume of industrial expansion in any period of time.

In fact, the amount of new industrial development which can feasibly be undertaken in a *given* period *is* likely to depend upon the "external economies" (advantages provided by *other* industries or developments) arising from the previous period. And the amount will be limited by the supply of entrepreneurs, the growth of administrative capacity within government departments and agencies, and the development of general and technical education in the country. This means that, as a statement of need only, there is an element of truth in the argument for agriculture based on its predominant position. Now, however, it is necessary to examine in turn the arguments put forward to justify tilting the balance towards industrialisation, and to see how far each is valid.

AGRICULTURE VERSUS INDUSTRY

ARGUMENTS FOR INDUSTRIALISATION

(a) Industrialisation to Absorb Excess Labour

Those favouring industrialisation often do so in the belief that the marginal rate of return in agriculture is low. There are two reasons why this is commonly thought to be the case, reasons which are related, but which it is important to distinguish. The first is that, due to social and institutional obstacles, agriculture is "notoriously sluggish or stagnant." [1] Part of the reason for this is very often the land tenure system, which results in small plots and often fails to guarantee security of tenure to the individual. This factor is generally aggravated in regions subject to population pressure. Apart from this, the entire social fabric of life in the rural areas may be inimical to economic development, and it may be held that the only way to break through traditionalism is to place people in an entirely new environment.

Analytically separate from the effects of social organisation is the operation of the law of diminishing returns; that is, of land shortage due to population pressure. Excess population does dictate a policy of industrialisation based on the export of manufactured goods, as Lewis has recommended for the West Indies.[2] But it is important to point out that population pressure sufficient to cause land shortage currently exists only in localised areas in Africa. There is a danger here of generalising from the Asian model of the overpopulated, under-developed economy. It is true, of course, that Africa exhibits high rates of population increase, which will certainly frustrate efforts to raise standards of living if real income cannot somehow be increased at a much faster rate.

Apart from reducing returns in agriculture, population pressure may also result in "free" labour being available to industry. The existence of disguised unemployed labour, apart from providing an opportunity for industrialisation, is said to *require* industry to be set up for its absorption.

Very strong evidence exists to show, however, that in practice manufacturing industry does *not* absorb workers at a very rapid rate. Thus wage employment in Uganda has been fairly constant over the last decade despite expansion of the manufacturing sector; [3] and the same phenomenon is observable elsewhere in Africa. Even in Puerto Rico, one of the recent success stories of industrialisation policy, the position

[1] T. Balogh, "Agriculture and Economic Development," in *The Economics of Poverty* (London, 1966).
[2] W. A. Lewis, "The Industrialisation of the British West Indies," in *Caribbean Economic Review* (Kingston, Jamaica), II, 1, May 1950.
[3] See J. Knight, "The Determination of Wages and Salaries in Uganda," in *Bulletin of the Oxford Institute of Economics and Statistics* (Oxford), xxix, 3, 1967.

is similar.[4] Minimum wage policies have contributed to this, as well as trade union and political pressures, which have tended to raise money wages in the towns compared to the rural areas. The main factor, however, is the necessity for fairly rigid proportions between capital and labour in manufacturing. This is even more the case with large-scale industry, which is particularly advocated for Africa by Ewing and which he himself admits "is not a significant employment creator."

For the *rapid* absorption of excess labour, agricultural development would seem to be necessary, where land shortage does not rule this out. Not only is agriculture highly labour-intensive, but it possesses *flexible* production functions, i.e. it permits variations in input combinations to suit the circumstances. Development plans frequently advocate the choice of techniques of low capital-intensity; but it is probably the case that the only way to reduce substantially the aggregate capital/output ratio for a country is to alter the economic structure, particularly in favour of agriculture, rather than to alter techniques within each type of production. Here we should admit, however, that in calculating capital/output ratios in agriculture account should also be taken of "social overhead capital" (services such as water supplies, communications, power, etc.) for which the demands of agriculture, as we note again below, may be much greater than industry. It is worth pointing out, nevertheless, that the favouring of industry, from the employment-absorption point of view, does clash with the favouring of techniques of low capital-intensity in the face of dear capital.

A special application of the labour-absorption argument is the case made for the protection of industry in developing countries, based on the fact that, even though positive money wages have to be paid to industrial workers, the "shadow price" or social opportunity cost of employing their labour may be zero. In these circumstances, the whole of the product of unemployed labour newly absorbed in a protected industry represents a net social gain, which can offset the loss to the consumers who have to pay higher prices for domestically produced goods. As has been pointed out by Dudley Seers, this argument is not for a temporary tariff, as under the "infant industry" criterion, but for a permanent one.[5] Nor is it one which should stimulate retaliation. The argument could of course apply equally well to the protection of an agricultural product, such as Kenya maize, which might result in much greater absorption of "free" labour.

---

[4] See L. G. Reynolds, "Wages and Employment in a Labour Surplus Economy," in *American Economic Review* (Cambridge, Mass.), XLV, 3, 1965.

[5] D. Seers, "The Role of Industry in Development: some fallacies," in *The Journal of Modern African Studies*, I, 4, December 1963.

(b) Low Rates of Return in Agriculture

If we turn to the question of rates of return, is it in fact the case that returns in agriculture are inevitably low and the scope for improvement narrow? Even in food production, where one might expect the least scope for change, B. F. Johnston and others have noted that very rapid increases in productivity in Japan's rice production were achieved without massive reorganisation, by the introduction of new strains; [6] and similar increases have been noted elsewhere in Asia, most recently in Ceylon. The following example indicates the possible magnitude of the effects of such innovations in Africa:

A striking example has been reported by the plant breeder at the Kakemega experimental farm in Kenya. A synthetic hybrid corn grown on African farms, with careful supervision of seedbed preparation, fertiliser application, and other operations, gave yields of 140 bushels of maize to the acre, of the order of eight times as high as typical yields in the area.[7]

While Africa is generally unfortunate as far as irrigation possibilities and water supplies are concerned, where they do exist the scope for agricultural transformation may be considerable. There are also many other agricultural schemes, such as tea outgrowers' schemes, where the injection of capital is less important than the provision of organisation, supervision, and marketing and processing facilities. There is also evidence that scope exists for the introduction or expansion of new crops and activities such as cattle rearing, at least in East Africa, with which the author is most familiar. The expansion of African agriculture in Kenya under the Swynnerton Plan illustrates the possibilities, even if opportunities vary greatly in different part of Africa; thus in 1956 African farmers received £5.86 million in gross revenue from cash crops, and in 1964 £14 million.[8]

The "Big-Push" Argument for Industrialisation

It may be, moreover—despite Bauer's arguments to the contrary [9]—that in many instances agricultural development is kept back by the

[6] B. F. Johnston and J. W. Mellor, "Agriculture in Economic Development," in *American Economic Review* (Wisconsin), September 1961, p. 571.
[7] B. F. Johnston and S. Neilson, "Agriculture and Structural Transformation in a Developing Economy," in *Economic Development and Cultural Change* (Chicago), XIV, 3, 1966.
[8] I. Livingstone and H. W. Ord, *An Introduction to East African Economics* (London, 1968), table 36.
[9] P. T. Bauer, "The Vicious Circle of Poverty," in *Weltwirtschaftliches Archiv* (Hamburg), 1965.

existence of indivisible factors, which preclude small-scale development, thus requiring a "big-push" approach in agriculture, rather than in industry, for which this policy is commonly suggested. In the first place transport and communications, which present a major indivisible factor in Rosenstein-Rodan's original big-push theory,[10] are at least as crucial in agriculture as in industry. Transport is probably the most critical constraint in Africa, within the category of social capital, and the extension of feeder roads may bring high returns through expanded agriculture. Remember we are talking here about *new* transport facilities: the main lines of communication which are already established in Africa serve the existing pockets of industry fairly well, since industry does concentrate itself geographically.

But the really great indivisibility may exist in the effort to transform attitudes. An all-out political and economic campaign for a "bootstrap operation" in agriculture may, by getting at the mass of the population, be successful in setting rolling a boulder which could rapidly gain momentum. The Swynnerton Plan mentioned above suggests that a distinct change in development tempo can result from concentrated efforts combining wide publicity, increased extension work, and the supply of funds. The political enthusiasm of newly independent states carries great, if not yet well-tested, potential in Africa.

(d) Increasing Returns and External Economies

Industrialisation is also advocated on the grounds of increasing returns: that is to say, because industry offers scope for constantly increasing specialisation and division of labour, and the application of machinery, as well as providing greater opportunity for innovation and the introduction of new technology. In contrast, agriculture is said to offer, if not decreasing returns, at least only the constant returns obtained by bringing more land into cultivation with more or less given methods of production.

Closely related to increasing returns is the concept of external economies. In assessing the value of any investment project it is not the private profitability which is relevant, but the social marginal product— including the total benefits obtained, even by other projects, from the development of this one. If we think in terms of a dynamic sequence, with one project acting as a "growing point" and generating, through external economies, a chain of further projects, the direct and indirect returns to that project may be very high.

Ewing argues specifically in favour of large-scale industry for Africa

10 P. N. Rosenstein-Rodan, "Notes on the Theory of the Big-Push," in H. Ellis (ed.), *Economic Development for Latin America* (London, 1961).

on this basis. The grounds are, firstly, that "the income elasticities of demand for the products of larger-scale industries are high"; secondly, that "Growing points are necessary, industries which themselves stimulate the growth of other industries as users of their products—a role beyond the scope of most small- and medium-scale industries;" and, finally, that "It would be disastrous . . . to give priority to the creation of new jobs rather than the search for economic efficiency and higher productivity."

We may note first that this productivity argument conflicts with Ewing's own use of the labour-absorption argument, which is itself based on the efficiency of using the "free" factor of production. Moreover, the significance of high productivity in a capitalistic enterprise is reduced if the capital is foreign-owned.

In relation to "growing points," however, Ewing seems to make use of two categories of external economies: (a) the opportunities provided by an industry in supplying products which can form the basis of further industry or in providing a market for the products of other industries—what one may call direct forward and backward linkages—and (b) opportunities provided in "centres where the concentration of population, transport, and commercial facilities offers the external economies normally associated with areas where industrialisation has already started." Only the former category, however, seems to demand large-scale industry, and the latter may well be a much more practical source of external economies at this stage in the development of Africa.

A similar point may be made if we consider whether industry as a whole, as compared to agriculture, is likely to have this property of generating external economies. The answer may well depend on the *stage* of industrial development reached. In the early stages of such development, as in Africa today, such links are probably not of great significance. It may be that general factors, such as the effects on the investment climate in the country, or on the development of the labour force, are more important than specific links through the sale of products to other firms or the purchase of inputs from them. At this stage new industries are likely to be at the expense of imports, in which case what may be most vital would be, first, the size of the market and, secondly, the supply of finance, private and public. Since a substantial rise in agricultural incomes would improve both, it is not at all certain that industry would generate far greater pecuniary external economies than agriculture.

(e) The Marginal Reinvestment Quotient

A special kind of external economy may operate through the effects of investment on the subsequent rate of saving. Galenson and Leibenstein have argued that investment criteria should favour projects with a high "marginal reinvestment quotient." [11] Projects using a high proportion of capital to output will increase the share of profits and, since a higher proportion of profits than of wages are reinvested, this will increase the rate of saving in the economy and thus the rate of capital accumulation. The application of this criterion to the choice between agriculture and industry provides an extreme illustration. The development of agriculture is likely to produce greater equality of income than industry, and thus a lower rate of saving.

Galenson and Leibenstein need to assume, however, that the desired distribution of income cannot be achieved by more direct means. It could be argued, on the other hand, that the peasant farmer can be fairly easily taxed in Africa; and that, if the proceeds could be ploughed back into social capital such as roads, irrigation and water projects, marketing and processing facilities, the response might be considerable and the returns good. Moreover, as stated earlier, if the industrial concerns are largely foreign-owned and the capital is internationally mobile, reinvestment will be far from automatic and may be determined more by the supply of local opportunities than by the supply of funds.

(f) Modern Technology and Social Trends

We need not spend time on the popular fallacy (sometimes shared by governments) that the "modernity" of industry, its use of more complex technology, makes it necessary for a country to develop industrially.[12] Similar thinking has produced skyscrapers in Africa and uneconomic national airlines. The misconception that, although there is

---

[11] W. Galenson and H. Leibenstein, "Investment Criteria, Productivity, and Economic Development," in *Quarterly Journal of Economics* (Cambridge, Mass.), LXIX, 1955.

[12] The fallacy that "industry is more modern" is the counterpart of the one that "food and agriculture come first," that developing countries should first satisfy their primary needs, especially food, before considering other forms of production. Nicholls, in "The Place of Agriculture in Economic Development," in C. K. Eicher and L. W. Witt, *Agriculture in Economic Development* (New York, 1967), has been charged with "propagating the physiocratic doctrine that food comes first." A more obvious example is in an article by G. Papi, "The Place of Agriculture in Balanced Growth," in E. A. G. Robinson (ed.), *Problems in Economic Development* (London, 1965). He states that: "Before anything else, the living conditions of the people must be improved and barring exceptional cases, economic development should therefore begin with raising the production of foodstuffs, agricultural raw materials, clothing and housing, and should then lead to producing industrial equipment requiring low capital investment . . . The problem had best be considered in the setting not of one single country or one single zone, but of the world economy. If we take it for granted that in the initial phase of development first priority belongs to the production of the goods for the . . . satisfaction of the population's primary needs . . ." Apart from the fact that it is not helpful to assume that the world has just started, one need only point out

a correlation between the size of industrial output and the level of income, the former is the "cause" of the latter, is not much more helpful.

But the "modern industry" argument may be valid to the extent that manufacturing "contributes to an intellectual environment which is less tradition-bound", and is "more favourable to the creation of an entrepreneurial class, the expansion of new skills, technical innovations, and falling birth rates." [13] Yet it has by no means been proved that manufacturing does do this, particularly in the *short* run. We have already noted that industrial development does not rapidly increase employment: its development as an enclave with limited links with the surrounding economy reduces its effectiveness in propagating change, even though rural–urban migration may considerably increase the diffusion of skills and ideas.

However, agricultural development will affect many more people. Historically, the introduction of cash crops has increased commercial-mindedness on a wide scale; and there is evidence in many countries that indigenous entrepreneurs have frequently moved from agriculture into trade, or into small-scale industry, rather than starting from scratch.[14] This is particularly so, perhaps, because the supply of finance is critical in the early development of enterprises. Wage employment may generate new skills, but does not on the whole provide finance for new entrepreneurs.

(g) The Terms of Trade of Primary Products

Ewing's case is based especially on the thesis of Raoul Prebisch "that the underdeveloped countries depend for their export earnings on a relatively limited range of primary products, the prices of which are falling in relation to the prices of manufactured goods which they must import." [15] The detailed argument is that, whereas increasing productivity in the industrial countries should have been reducing prices of manufactured goods steadily over time, to the benefit of the developing countries purchasing them, in fact trade-union pressure, especially,

---

that agricultural cash crops are mostly produced for export, not domestic markets, while existing imports of manufactured goods indicate that domestic demand is not merely for "basic" items.

[13] Balogh, op. cit p 59.

[14] For examples of this as wide apart as Turkey and Kenya, see A. P. Alexander, "Industrial Entrepreneurship in Turkey: origins and growth," in *Economic Development and Cultural Change*, July 1960; and P. Mbithi, "Famine Crises and Innovations: physical and social factors affecting new crop adoptions in the marginal farming areas of Eastern Kenya," Rural Development Research Paper no. 52, Makerere University College, 1967.

[15] A. F. Ewing, "Industrialisation and the U.N. Economic Commission for Africa," in *The Journal of Modern African Studies* (Cambridge), II, 3, October 1964.

has prevented this fall, so that the benefits of increasing productivity have accrued instead to the rich countries.[16]

C. Kindleberger has criticised the theoretical basis of the Prebisch argument, saying that the only effect on prices of manufactured products would have to operate through imperfections of the product, not the factor, markets.[17] This is incorrect: a high-priced input, in this case labour, can raise product prices even in a competitive situation. The monopolistic position of labour in the richer countries has been subject to attack from the exports of countries exploiting the advantage of cheap labour: but it is only the success of the former in maintaining high wages that has afforded them this opportunity.

The question is therefore whether the Prebisch hypothesis has sufficient empirical basis. P. T. Ellsworth has argued that, for some periods only, the evidence is corroborative.[18] Other well-known evidence exists, on the other hand, that the share of wages in the national income in the U.K., for example, has been roughly constant for long periods. It is worth noting that, if labour merely succeeded in maintaining its share of income, it would appropriate only a constant share of increases in productivity, the remainder being passed on to consumers (including those in the developing countries) in the form of lower prices of manufactured goods.

We should not minimise the danger, particularly in the *long* run, of a deterioration in the terms of trade. Nevertheless (1) individual primary product prices have behaved, and will behave, in very different ways, and the position for individual countries in the short term may not be at all bleak; and (2) opportunities in individual countries, particularly for expanding the *volume* of output in old or new lines, may be sufficient to more than offset the depressing effect of stable prices. Even leaving out of account a high rate of time preference, development priorities must emphasise the short-run possibilities, and ensure that they are fully exploited, since short-run success improves long-run prospects.

(h) Export Instability and Diversification

Apart from the long-term trend in primary-product prices, their short-term instability has provided an argument for industrialisation, as a means of diversifying the economy. A. Macbean, applying regres-

---

[16] See R. Prebisch, *The Economic Development of Latin America and its Principal Problems* (Economic Commission for Latin America, 1950), and "Commercial Policy in the Underdeveloped Countries," in *American Economic Review, Papers and Proceedings* (1959).

[17] C. Kindleberger, *The Terms of Trade* (New York, 1956), ch. 10.

[18] P. T. Ellsworth, "The Terms of Trade between Primary Producing and Industrial Countries," in *Inter-American Economic Affairs* (Washington), X, 1956.

sion analysis to data from various countries, has recently exploded a number of myths in this area. He doubts, first, whether the developing countries have suffered from export instability very much more than advanced countries and, secondly, whether such instability has had much effect on development.[19]

Part of the explanation for the low correlation coefficients he obtains, however, is that he takes in his sample a very large number of underdeveloped countries, whose characteristics are far from homogeneous. Countries with relatively small foreign trade sectors, like India, are included beside others exhibiting a marked dependence on trade. Combining non-homogeneous groups will drastically reduce the correlation coefficient, which, calculated for separate groups, may in some cases be high. To some extent his findings corroborate the wise dictum that generalisations regarding the whole range of poor countries are dangerous. It could still be that for a large group of countries the export-instability argument carries weight. Ewing's conclusion, however, that "diversification of exports in the developing countries . . . means rapid industrialisation" need not follow, if scope exists for diversification within agriculture. This will vary with the particular situation in each country.

(i) Income Effects

Moreover, the development of industry may be less effective in stabilising the incomes of the mass of the people, who live in the rural areas, compared to the addition of a new crop. Additional industry may directly increase the incomes of a comparatively small part of the population and have only restricted multiplier effects on incomes elsewhere.

This is related to the effects on the distribution of income, which may be even more important at low levels of income than elsewhere. Due to the trade-union and other pressures already mentioned, the development of industry typically produces a marked contrast between urban and rural areas in the poor countries, which fiscal policy is unlikely to be effective in correcting. In the most socialist countries of Africa, such as Tanzania, incomes policy is given great weight.

Movement to the towns is, moreover, costly, not only in terms of housing requirements and the higher standards of living demanded by townsmen, but also in terms of the social costs associated with the creation of slums, the encouragement of crime, and the like. The "costs of development" frequently referred to are in fact largely costs of urbanisation.

[19] A. Macbean, *Export Instability and Economic Development,* (London, 1966).

ECONOMIC DEVELOPMENT

(*j*) *Industrialisation via Import Substitution*

Noting the importance of imports in relation to gross domestic product in Africa, Ewing points out, correctly, that there is still scope for massive import substitution in Africa. Imports are certainly an important guide both to the volume and the direction of new manufacturing potential. It is important to note, however, that transport facilities may considerably limit the size of the market, especially since the transport and marketing systems in Africa are strongly export-import orientated. Thus, in Eastern Africa, industries in Uganda or Kenya would have serious difficulties in supplying, say, Somalia or Zambia. This particularly affects Ewing's arguments in favour of large-scale industry dependent on a wide market. He also mentions Africa's special problems of large geographical area, scattered population, low incomes per head, and small national markets. While these disadvantages can be reduced by policies of regional integration, which he advocates, this nevertheless represents a major obstacle which has to be surmounted. Regional integration is not likely to be easily achieved in Africa—and Ewing cannot offer more promising experience elsewhere.

Both the inadequacy of internal transport systems and the necessity of working towards regional integration do, moreover, bring in the time factor; they reduce the pace of industrialisation which is likely to be achieved. This pace will also be limited by the supply of entrepreneurship—since the industrial corporation requires entrepreneurship of an entirely different nature from that which Africa has been able to tap in peasant farming—and by the availability of finance. It is these constraints, indeed, to which critics of the big-push strategy refer.

The above should not be taken as an attempt to play down industrialisation as an ultimate goal, nor to minimise the immediate scope for the expansion of industry. What is fundamental, however, is the time dimension—what *pace* of industrialisation can realistically be achieved, and what share of the limited development effort should be appropriated to it. Ewing's position is quite clear:

there must also be emphasis on the creation of small- and medium-scale industries for domestic markets, and also on modernisation of the rural sector: subsistence agriculture, handicraft production, and so forth [notice that he does not mention export crops] . . . Yet the overriding importance of large-scale industry remains, if incomes are to grow: if, in fact, real economic development is to take place.[20]

Though regional economic integration to permit larger-scale industries is of vital importance to Africa, there are limits to what can be

[20] Ewing, op. cit. pp. 355–6.

achieved in the short or medium term, though prospects in East Africa are better than elsewhere. Ewing would appear distinctly to overstate the case, and simultaneously to underestimate both the factors limiting the pace of industrialisation and the scope for rapid increase in agricultural proceeds. The main feature of African agriculture is probably its diversity: export markets are not all bleak; the scope for diversification within agriculture varies, and so do the possibilities for agricultural transformation.

A major issue in the economic development of most transitional societies is the issue of agrarian reform. However, the reform that is needed varies greatly, for in some societies the problem is one of combining too-small individually owned plots of land, while in others it is that of dividing up large estates into smaller individually owned units. In either case, a number of social and political factors have to be taken into account in addition to the economic ones if strategies for reform are to succeed. In the following excerpt, some dimensions of agrarian reform in Asia are discussed, and some successful and some unsuccessful policies of reform described.

36. *AGRARIAN REFORM IN ASIA* [*]

w o l f   l a d e j i n s k y

It is no longer news that land reform is a critical issue throughout Asia, the Near East and Latin America. We are not surprised to see the Shah of Iran going about the country sponsoring a drastic redistribution of private holdings. . . . President Macapagal in the Philippines, President Betancourt in Venezuela and Prime Minister Nehru in India have

[*] From "Agrarian Reform in Asia" by Wolf Ladejinsky, *Foreign Affairs*, Vol. XLII, No. 3 (April, 1964), pp. 445–460. Excerpted by special permission from *Foreign Affairs*, April 1964. Copyright by the Council on Foreign Relations, Inc., New York.

similarly been using "agrarian reform" in their search for answers to some of their countries' instabilities.

. . . [T]he problems . . . are fundamentally the same: How relieve the plight of cultivators working mostly for a pittance? How revive stagnating agricultural economies? How root the peasant securely and beneficially on the land he cultivates? The one important departure from the conditions of a bygone age is that the stated problems have the closest bearing on the overall economic development of Asia, as indeed elsewhere.

II

The answer to these questions constitutes what is broadly known as "agrarian reform." The term can mean various things to various people within the free world, let alone as between the Communist and non-Communist worlds. As exemplified by Soviet Russia and Communist China, agrarian reform is simple enough: it is a means to political power, based on a promise to the peasant of the one thing he wants most—ownership of the landlord's land—in exchange for his political support. Once the Communists are in power, all the land is confiscated, peasants become farm hands on collectives, communes and state farms, and harsh production and delivery quotas complete the rude awakening from an exhilarating but all-too-brief experience of freeholding.

In non-Communist Asia, agrarian reform is not without political motivation. The emphasis, however, is not on consolidating the power of the state *over* the peasantry but on increasing the state's well-being. The need for drastic changes stems from such questions as who owns or doesn't own the land, how it is used, who gets what out of the land, the productivity of the land, the rate of economic development, and, of course, social status and political power. These are not unique in any one part of Asia; all cut across cultural and national boundaries and together they represent the Achilles' heel of the Asian socioeconomic structure.

The mere enumeration of the issues points to the fact that no single panacea can deal with them effectively; even redistribution of the land will not do it unless it is accompanied by the necessary means to work and improve the land. The economic opportunity and psychological incentives which come with the possession of land or security of tenure must go hand in hand with a host of other developmental measures. For this reason, agrarian reform in the sense considered here encompasses all or most of the following elements: distribution of land among the landless and favorable financial arrangements for tenant land-purchases; security of tenure and fair rents; better methods of cultivation through technical assistance, adequate credit, co-operative marketing facilities, etc. Agrarian reform is a combination of a great many things, and not all of them are of equal importance. Important though the other ingredients are, unless those who work the land own it, or are at least secure on the land as tenants, all the rest is likely to be writ in water. And this is the most difficult step to achieve. It is relatively easy to use science to increase production, but only if the cultivator's relationship to the land and the state's treatment of him and of agriculture create incentives to invest, to improve the land and to raise productivity. Too many of Asia's cultivators are still waiting to find that incentive.

◦ ◦ ◦ ◦ ◦

Directly related to this problem is the fact that four-fifths of Asia's vast population are peasants; millions of them are on too little land, and hordes of others are crowding onto the same land. Inadequate tools, archaic methods of cultivation and institutional arrangements over which the peasant has no control underscore his plight and explain his resentment.

Newspaper headlines in Asia are snatched by the glittering economic development plans with their emphasis on industrialization as the cure-all. Yet agriculture, not industry, is the pivot of economic life there. The ambitious postwar schemes for industrialization throughout Asia no longer are mere blueprints, but so far they have made only a small dent in the continent's traditional character. The factory is bringing material advancement to some groups, but surely not to a degree, even in the foreseeable future, to obscure the fact that the heart of the problem of Asia still lies in the countryside. It is on the farm that solutions must be sought and found, if the empty rice bowls are to be filled, if something is to be added to the half-empty ones and if the economic development of the various countries is to proceed by their own efforts.

III

When looking at rural Asia today, nearly two decades after the start of the reform movement, we see that the old order in the countryside has been under attack—vigorously in some countries, much less so, and with results to match, in many more. The reforms have certain things in common, and not only with regard to the condition of the peasantry. Their purpose is the same whatever the wording of an official pronouncement. President Macapagal of the Philippines spoke for all of them when, in signing the recent Agrarian Land Reform Code, he observed: "Let this signing be recorded in our annals as an Act of Emancipation of the toiling farmer from his slavery to debt, poverty and misery and of his dignification as a human being and as a citizen. By this Act of Emancipation a new revolution is on." After a series of land reform failures in the Philippines over a quarter of a century, whether this is so remains to be seen, but it does mirror the ultimate hope often voiced by all Asian countries when this thorny subject is approached. To bring it about, the Philippine Code relies on two general features common to all attempted reforms in Asia: security of tenure and the creation of peasant proprietorships.

On issues of substance, however, the reforms speak in a variety of voices, which more often than not are a far cry from the exalted pronouncements made on the supposedly historic occasions. They reflect inevitably the political climate in the country concerned. This determines the will or lack of will to proceed with the task; the kind of specifics with which the general measures are or are not endowed; the care or lack of care with which the enabling legislation is formulated; the preparation or lack of preparation of the pertinent technical and administrative services; the presence or absence of technical agricultural services with their bearing upon success or failure; and, finally and most importantly, the drive or lack of drive behind the enforcement of the provisions of the law. For these reasons, the results of the reform movement in Asia are anything but uniform. They run the full gamut, from Japan and Taiwan where fulfillment in the widest sense has been achieved; to Korea where much land has actually been redistributed but with results far from satisfactory; to South Viet Nam where land reform has been carried out in its essentials, but engulfed by a civil war before it came to fruition. Then there are the Philippines, Nepal, Pakistan and Indonesia—all knowledgeable in writing reform laws, some of them at variance with their fervent preambles—where the record to date ranges between poor performance and non-performance. Finally, there is India, significant and encouraging for what it has attained in unprecedentedly difficult and bewildering conditions, and just as significant and discouraging for what it has failed to attain, and for the reasons why.

The picture, clearly, is mixed, and in order to assess it a number of questions must be raised. The primary one is: Why have some reforms succeeded, others fallen short of their goals, and still others failed to get off the ground?

Just as Soviet Russia was the progenitor of the Communist type of reform, Japan and Taiwan are the progenitors of non-Communist reforms in Asia. Japan, the leader, and Taiwan, the follower and innovator, provided between them all the pertinent elements of leadership, content and implementation which made for a successful reform.

In Taiwan as in Japan, reforms were not designed to satisfy the claims of both contending parties: the tenant was to gain at the expense of the landlord. Without going into details, we may cite a few main provisions to demonstrate the emphasis on the ideological underpinnings and the lack of vacillation about the real intent of the measures. Security of tenure is one of the cases in point. The sharp reduction of rents in Taiwan was an important move; but more important were the provisions that, for all practical purposes, the tenants could remain on the leased land undisturbed even after the expiration of a contract. This virtually insured the enforcement of rental provisions. Less carefully worded stipulations might have undermined this part of the reform program, as has been the case in India, not to mention others.

Provisions for security of tenure in overcrowded Asian villages, where tenants compete fiercely for the privilege of cultivating somebody else's land, are notoriously difficult to enforce; yet in Taiwan a land redistribution program for the benefit of tenants who cultivated 40 percent of the land became much more feasible as a result of such provisions. . . .

The idea that the reforms were meant to benefit the tenants is also apparent in the principal provisions about land redistribution and the creation of peasant proprietorships among tenants. Absentee landlords had to sell all of their land at fixed government prices; resident landlords were compelled to sell their land in excess of the permissible ceiling. Neither Japan nor Taiwan aimed to do away with tenancy as an institution; but with determination to enlarge the area of individual, private ownership, the low ceiling made it possible to extract a great deal of surplus land for redistribution. The result is that whereas before the reform 54 percent of Japan's land was owner-operated, after the reform the figure had risen to 92 percent; the respective figures for Taiwan are 60 and 85 percent.

What matters is not only at what level the ceiling is set, but also that it not be evaded. The problem of West Pakistan, to cite but one case, is not merely that the ceiling of 500 irrigated acres and 1,000 unirrigated acres is altogether too high where two-thirds of the owners average five acres each; it is also the exceptions and subdivisions of large holdings among members of a family which were made on the eve of the reform and which have combined to divest the ceiling and, by the same token, the entire land distribution program of any meaning. It is not surprising, therefore, that even if West Pakistan had implemented this part of the reform, only an estimated 7.5 percent of the country's 2,000,000 tenants might have obtained land. And Pakistan is no exception. In Japan and Taiwan, on the other hand, the acreage that could be retained by a landlord was fixed retroactively, both on the basis of the household as a unit and on the basis of land owned by that household.

With a low ceiling, no evasions and effective implementation, the majority of the tenants become peasant-proprietors.

A crucial feature of any reform not intended to result in out-and-out confiscation is price and method of payment. Whatever the differences displayed in Asia in formulating and implementing a program, there is a consensus on one point: the price fixed must be considerably below the market price. Land-purchase under a reform is not an ordinary real estate transaction where seller, broker and buyer meet in a free market. If it were, and if tenants were able to pay the "going price," there would be no need for a reform. The price fixed by a government is an arbitrary one, the degree of its arbitrariness depending upon how a reformer answers this question: "For whose benefit is the reform designed?"

The question of how to pay for the land is of paramount importance for government, landlord and tenant. No matter what the price, experience in Asia has shown that a government cannot pay in cash, in one lump sum. Here Taiwan provides a lesson worth pondering. In content, Taiwan's reform is in many respects similar to that of Japan, but in method of paying it is not. In Japan, what appeared to be a reasonable price when first fixed was later on swallowed up by a galloping inflation, virtually confiscating the landlord's land. To avoid this possibility, Taiwan tied the price of land to payments in two principal products of the land and to shares of stock in government-owned industrial undertakings. In practice this meant that 70 percent of the value of the land was in the form of commodity bonds, payable in 20 semi-annual installments over a period of ten years, and 30 percent was paid outright in stocks.

This novel method has worked well for all parties involved. . . .

o o o o o

. . . [W]ith the exception of important bright spots here and there in India, only very few . . . gains can be found in other Asian countries which have gone to the trouble of writing reform laws, but largely limited and vague in content and with just as limited intent to translate them into action. The writing of reform laws—and some nations have done it more than once—may be good practice in preparation for the day when the execution of such laws becomes unavoidable. But as of the moment, it may be said in general that the high hopes reposed in agrarian reform during the immediate postwar years have not materialized in action. Before suggesting why this is so, we will find instructive a brief review of India's vast experience in the course of 15 years of reform activities.

I V

It is safe to say that all the disabilities which peasant and land can suffer are to be found in many of the 600,000 villages of India. An observer will find many striking and promising manifestations of a resurgent agriculture; but these are still only tiny islands in the vastness of the debilitating conditions noted elsewhere. The result is that the yields of basic food crops are too low in relation to the potential of the land and existing food needs, and particularly in view of the grim fact that between 1961 and 1976 the Indian agriculture will have to provide food for nearly 190,000,000 additional people. To remedy the situation, the Indian Government after independence set itself to ease the lot of the peasantry by a drastic overhaul of the land system, the complexity of which almost defies description. This would-be agrarian revolution was to have been attained through the familiar pattern already described, and through the elimination of the "zamindari" system, a peculiarly Indian problem.

The zamindari system was a by-product of the early British rule under which a zamindar or intermediary was given the right to collect land taxes and undertook to pay the British administration a fixed revenue. In return, he was not only permitted to keep a portion of the revenue but was also recognized as the proprietor of the revenue-bearing land. In time the system covered more than 40 percent of the cultivated land of India, and it created, too, some of the worst abuses that can be perpetrated upon a peasantry, including a long chain of non-cultivating sublessees all getting a share of the highly inflated rent from the same piece of land and the same cultivator. As one student of the problem put it, "His landlords form a Jacob's ladder in which each rung is occupied not by an angel but a tenure holder, and the topmost by the proprietor." This ladder the Indian Government set out to do away with as almost the first order of agrarian reform.

Despite opposition and administrative problems, the zamindari tenures have been virtually abolished. . . . Why this measure succeeded is not difficult to answer. The zamindari system, with its absurdities and injustices, was the weakest enemy to attack, because it was imposed by a foreign power which handed out property rights to which neither the British nor most of the recipients had any claim. Thus abolition of the system became one of the symbols of freedom from the British rule, and it is not surprising that the abolitionists largely succeeded in eliminating it.

Getting rid of this system did not put an end to tenancy in India.

ECONOMIC DEVELOPMENT

Even in the ex-zamindari areas the "home-farms" of the former middle-man continued to be operated by tenants, and not all the subtenants were eliminated. But above all there was the multitude of tenants—not to mention the millions of agricultural wage laborers—cultivating at least a fourth of the country's arable land in "ryotwari" areas (as distinguished from the former zamindari areas) where owner-proprietorship predominated. The Government of India decided to provide tenants with security of tenure and reduction of rents, and to confer landownership upon the tenants through the familiar ceiling device and officially fixed land prices. Under the guidance and continuous prodding of the Planning Commission, the States have enacted a voluminous body of legislation presumably designed to meet these goals.

Both from the point of view of the content of the legislation and the enforcement of it these reforms are in serious difficulties. . . .

Administrative problems are a formidable obstacle to implementation of the reforms. On the other hand, judging by the experience of the largest and most populated state of India, Uttar Pradesh, this is not an insurmountable difficulty—if there is the will to overcome it. More to the point is the faulty content in many legislative enactments. In India, the most glaring manifestation of this is the seemingly reasonable but ill-defined right of the landlord to resume tenanted land for what is euphemistically called "personal cultivation." As the writer saw in widely separated parts of the country, this has led to mass evictions of tenants; to "voluntary surrenders" of land by tenants in order to salvage some relationship to the land, even if it be as a hired hand; to augmentation of the ranks of agricultural workers; and, inevitably, to the failure of the new rent regulations.

The ceiling provisions did not fare well at all. While the tenancy reforms can claim achievements in a few states, the same cannot be said about ceilings as a means of acquiring ownership. . . . For the moment, the question of how much land might have been available for redistribution is academic; of India's 80,000,000 acres or more of tenanted land very little is available for redistribution. In anticipation of ceiling provisions, the landlords divided up the land among members of their families so as to make certain that holdings were *under* the ceiling; for the legislative provisions, unlike those in Japan and Taiwan, did not contain the teeth to preclude such transfers. More recent amendments designed to annul such transfers have had, so far, little effect on the evasions committed.

Needless to say, such developments do not produce the incentives which lead to better living conditions, investments in land, improvement of land and a rise in agricultural productivity. Yet these were the goals of the tenancy reforms—the goals that Mr. Nehru so aptly summed up in the phrase, "placing the peasant in the center of the piece."

v

From the experience of Japan and Taiwan and from that of India one may learn why so few reforms in Asia have succeeded and so many have not. Neither success nor failure can be attributed primarily to the presence or absence of experts or to a special reform mystique. The usefulness of facts, figures and preparatory work no one can deny; but reforms cannot be "researched" or "studied" into existence. Of far greater importance is the acceptance of the reform idea, to begin with, in such a manner that technical problems are not an excuse for inaction but something to be resolved. There is no country in Asia, however underdeveloped, which does not know how to write a reform law, or what its implications might be. They have written them, and many have not been carried out—precisely because the political decision-makers understood their implications and their inevitable repercussions.

The politicians make or unmake agrarian reforms. It is they who provide the impetus or lack of impetus, who decide between reform and "reform." They alone can create a condition "when the economic sails are filled with political wind." [1] There is no gainsaying the fact that the economic environment, population pressure on the land, and customary relationships sanctioned by a long history of social and religious traditions exert great influence on what happens to legislation designed to break old institutional molds. But this does not invalidate the main premise—that the content and implementation of agrarian reform are a reflection of a particular political balance of forces in a country. This premise assumes even greater significance in Asia because the peasants themselves, while discontented, have not developed a movement, whether in the form of tenant-unions like those of Japan before the reforms, or peasant political parties like those of East Europe after the First World War. For a time, the Communists in Hyderabad, Tanjore and Kerala exploited the peasant grievances for their own ends; the Communist Huks in Central Luzon played a similar role. For the most part, however, the peasants behaved as if any change in their condition depended upon somebody else. By their apathy they have disproved the reasonable assumption that in an agricultural country a government must have peasant support. The fact is that national and state legislatures in Asia do not represent the interests of the peasantry; if they did, reform might have taken on a different character altogether. The reality is that even where voting is free, the peasantry in Asia is not yet voting its own interests. Except in Japan, the peasants do not yet know that

[1] Doreen Warriner, "Land Reform and Development in the Middle East." London: Royal Institute of International Affairs, 1957, p. 9.

they can be bearers *and* recipients of political gifts; the idea that "we support those who support us" has yet to take root. More important, then, is the role of the articulate and politically powerful pro-reform groups.

VI

In Japan and in Taiwan both the forces which were indigenous and those which were created as a result of the war favored a drastic agrarian reform and a redistribution of income and social and political power. In the case of Japan, the defeat by the United States and the American influence as an occupying power were crucial in the timing of the reform but were of only limited importance in giving it a radical character. Other factors were also the memories of peasant rebellions; the numerous, if unsuccessful, prewar reform measures; the strong tenant-unions; the windfall of the Communist opposition to the "MacArthur reform"; the emergence of large groups of Japanese who were disillusioned with the old oligarchy; and an eager and active pro-reform leadership in the Ministry of Agriculture which drafted the enabling legislation. This "political wind" found expression in the firm proposition that "those who cultivate the soil of Japan shall enjoy the fruits of their labor." This meant clearly defined provisions, a minimum of half-measures and a minimum of loopholes. Similarly on the enforcement side, the reformers recognized not only that the cultivators had to be made aware of the essence of the main provisions, but that they—and only they—had to be the true implementors of the reform if it were to succeed. This attitude led to the creation of a practical enforcement agency, the local land commissions—so far shunned by all other countries engaged in reform save Taiwan.

The situation in Taiwan on the eve of the reforms was not the same as in Japan, but here, too, special circumstances—primarily non-economic or sociological—created the setting for action. The final decision rested with the politicians or, more specifically, with a political and military leader. The Communist victory on the mainland and the subsequent prevalent belief among the Nationalist politicians that the Communists won because of the promise of land to the tillers played a crucial role in creating the favorable climate. Certain elements in the Nationalist ideology worked to the same end, especially when the beleaguered government realized it needed greater social stability as a means to military security. But none of these factors might have sufficed were it not for the fact that General Chen-Cheng, then Governor of Taiwan and an influential member of the Nationalist Party, had resolved that rural Taiwan was to undergo a thorough change. . . .

To return to India: while the need for reform there is surely as great as in any country in Asia, the difficulties in the way are incomparably greater. Among them are the sheer size of the subcontinent; the administrative decentralization, with each state a law unto itself; the paucity of good land records; the fact that a third of the tenanted land belongs to owners with five acres or less; the fierce competition for any tillable plot of land on almost any terms; the lack of peasant initiative and his inability to comprehend the complex laws; the poor prospects for alternative occupations despite the country's progress of industrialization; and the millions more people added annually to the already overcrowded land.

All these are sufficient to give one pause before rendering any hasty judgment about the tortuous and far from successful path of Indian reforms (other, that is, than the elimination of the zamindari). And yet the handicaps, especially the technical handicaps, do not quite explain why so much of the intent of the reforms is still unrealized. There are States in India which have demonstrated that, given strong leadership, many of the problems can be overcome. What is significant is that most of the handicaps, including the principal one—poor enforcement or non-enforcement—are not always causes but in a large measure consequences of attitudes displayed by state politicians and legislatures. This anti-reform sentiment has proved to be a crucial element in thwarting India's expectations.

By extension, and with variations, the same is true of most Asian countries. . . .

Clearly, the key to successful reform in Asia is the degree to which the controlling political forces of a country are willing to support reform and their readiness to use *all* instruments of government to attain their goals. Those against whom the reforms are directed will not divest themselves of their property and of political and economic power simply because a government wrote out a decree. Besides, despite the threat of Communism, the great fears generated by the French Revolution or by the Bolshevik Revolution in 1917 are not immediately in evidence in Asia. The conclusion is inescapable: if the peasantry is to get what is promised, peaceful and democratically managed reforms are not going to fill the bill. Government coercion, whether practiced or clearly threatened, is virtually unavoidable.

Are the obstacles to development really so severe as they usually seem to be? Many analyses have concluded that the combination of traditional cultures, limited resources, population pressures, and the other characteristics of transitional societies makes it almost impossible for developmental schemes to succeed. In the following selection, this conclusion and the assumptions on which it rests are challenged by a noted observer of development, Albert Hirschman.

37. OBSTACLES TO DEVELOPMENT: A CLASSIFICATION AND A QUASI-VANISHING ACT *†

a l b e r t o. h i r s c h m a n

One could think of several ways of classifying obstacles: natural (lack of resources) and man-made (lack of law and order, lack of capital), objective (lack of resources or of capital) and subjective (lack of entrepreneurship and risk-taking, lack of a desire for change, contempt for material success), internal (all the factors so far named) and external (exploitation by a foreign power), etc.

I find it useful, however, to adopt a classification which is grounded in the concept of "obstacle" itself and which, in the process, questions its solidity from the outset. It is a principal contention of this note that the concept is far from solid, that it is not possible to identify either a finite number of "reliable" obstacles to development or a hierarchy among these obstacles which would permit us to arrange them neatly into boxes marked "basic," "important," "secondary," etc.

* Reprinted from "Obstacles to Development: A Classification and a Quasi-Vanishing Act" by Albert O. Hirschman, *Economic Development and Cultural Change*, Vol. XIII, No. 4 (July, 1965), by permission of The University of Chicago Press and the author. Copyright 1965 by The University of Chicago. Selections from pp. 385–393.
† This article was written as a contribution to a symposium on obstacles to economic development organized by Professor François Perroux. It will be published in French by the Institut d'Etude du Développement Economique et Social in a forthcoming volume of the series *Etudes Tiers-Monde*. The author is indebted to Terence K. Hopkins and Immanuel Wallerstein for helpful comments.

The traditional method of identifying an obstacle to development points immediately to the conceptual weakness we have in mind. The method consists in looking up the history of one or several economically advanced countries, noting certain situations that were present at about the time when development was brought actively under way in one or several of these countries (a temperate climate, a population belonging to the white race, "primitive" accumulation of capital, coal deposits, law and order, widespread literacy, a group of Schumpeterian entrepreneurs, a fairly efficient and honest civil service, agrarian reform, the Protestant Ethic, etc., etc.), and then construing the *absence* of any of these situations as an obstacle to development. This procedure could lead one to conclude that the more countries develop, the more difficult does it appear for the remainder to do the same, for each successfully developing country does so under a set of special conditions, thus lengthening the list of obstacles (i.e., the absence of these conditions) which have to be "overcome."

Fortunately, this conclusion is as implausible as it is dismal. The usual way of escaping from it is by the successive substitution of a newly discovered *fundamental* obstacle for those that held sway before the latest theoretical or historical insight. In this paper we shall proceed in a more empirical vein and attempt to classify obstacles in the order of their greater or smaller *reliability* as obstacles, on the basis of what evidence we have been able to collect.

Suppose some specific situation or condition can be shown to have been essential for the development of country X at time t; in other words, the absence of this condition performed as an insuperable barrier to the development of X. Now it is possible that the development experience of other countries confirms that of X; on the other hand, one can think of the following ways in which the barrier or obstacle would fail to perform as such in other countries:

(1) The obstacle does not constitute an *absolute* barrier in the case of country Y; certain forward moves are available to this country, and the obstacle, while still exerting a negative influence on development, can be dealt with, perhaps more easily, at a later time.

(2) The alleged obstacle, in view of another set of circumstances, turns out not to be an obstacle at all and therefore does not need to be removed, either now or later.

(3) The alleged obstacle, in view of yet other circumstances, turns into a positive advantage and asset for development.

In justifying each of these possibilities—and, in the process, discovering several other variants—we shall invert the order in which they have been cited and thus start with the most extreme case.

I. AMBIVALENCE: ALLEGED OBSTACLES THAT TURN INTO ASSETS

How difficult it is to classify certain concrete situations as unequivocally hostile or favorable to economic development is well illustrated by the institution of the *extended* or *joint family*. Several Western economists belonging to quite different schools of thought have taken the position that the extended family dilutes individual incentives and that its demise and replacement by the nuclear family is required for dynamic development to occur.[1] This is, of course, a highly ethnocentric argument. Westerners who hold this view find it difficult to imagine that any one would want to exert himself if the fruits of his labors accrue largely to what they consider as distant relatives; implicit in the idea that the extended family is a bar to economic progress is therefore the judgment that no one in his right mind can really care for the welfare of his third cousin.

But suppose "they" do? In that case the argument against the extended family not only falls to the ground, but one can immediately perceive of several advantages in an arrangement in which the basic economic decision-making unit is not the nuclear family, but a wider grouping. For one, the special relationship existing among the members permits them to undertake new tasks requiring cooperation without prior mastery of such complications as hiring labor and keeping accounts.[2] Furthermore, the members may pool their resources not only for consumption, but equally for investment purposes; and thus it may be possible for them to finance business ventures as well as advanced education for the more gifted among them.[3]

Can we save the proposition for the rather special situation where the extended family still exists as a formal behavior code but can no longer command the full loyalty of the individual member of the society and is perhaps actively resented by him? In that case the strictures of our economists would seem to apply fully. Yet, such is the variety of possible situations that even here we must tread with care. For example, the very desire to withhold extra earnings from one's family may deflect the more enterprising members of the family from a bureaucratic career (where earnings are fixed and a matter of public knowledge) into a

[1] P. T. Bauer and B. S. Yamey, *The Economics of Under-Developed Countries* (Chicago, 1957), p. 66; and Benjamin Higgins, *Economic Development* (New York, 1959), p. 256.

[2] C. S. Belshaw, *In Search of Wealth: A Study of the Emergence of Commercial Operations in the Melanesian Society of South-Eastern Papua* (Vancouver, 1955), Chs. 5 and 7.

[3] Peter Marris, *Family and Social Change in an African City* (London, 1961), p. 138. The importance of kinship ties in the early spread of banking and mercantile enterprise in the West is of course well established.

business career (where earnings are uncertain and can be concealed).[4] Moreover, if there is any time lag between the newly won affluence of the individual and the famous moving-in of all the relatives to share in his newly won riches, then the institution of the extended family combined with the desire to escape from it provides a stimulus to ever new spurts of temporarily relative-exempt entrepreneurial activity.[5] Hence, even if the sharing implicit in the extended family system is resented, the obligation to share may act like those taxes that stimulate individuals to greater effort at securing non-taxable gains (and at tax evasion).

Our point is strengthened by the observation that, just as the extended family cannot be held to stunt growth under all circumstances, so the nuclear family will not always promote development. If the economic operator perceives no possibility of common interest, action, or gain with anyone outside his immediate blood relatives, then economic advance is likely to be severely hamstrung, as I have explained elsewhere and as has been documented by several empirical studies.[6]

A more general remark is in order at this point. We have said that an obstacle to development may usually be defined as the absence of a condition that was found to be present in a country which subsequently developed. But in many cases the question that ought to have been asked is *how much* of this condition was present. Too much may be just as deleterious as too little. It is too much rather than too little individualism and entrepreneurship and too little willingness to work with discipline in a hierarchical organization that plagues much of Southeast Asia and also other underdeveloped lands.[7] Too much law and order may be as stifling as too little is disruptive. Let us arrange the possible states of society along a horizontal scale with two such extremes at opposite ends. Suppose we measure the chances for development along the vertical scale. In most cases, these chances will seriously drop off at *both* ends of the scale, but they may well be tolerably good during a wide stretch in the middle. In other words, societies that are *all* individualistic entrepreneurship or that are *all* hierarchical discipline will both be hard put to develop, but in the real world we are likely to encounter predominantly individualistic and predominantly hierarchical societies

---

[4] *Ibid.*, p. 139.

[5] "The fact that, under the customary rules of inheritance, individual property was always in process of conversion to family property provided individuals with a great incentive to acquire additional lands, over which they had, for some time at least, unlimited control." Polly Hill, *The Migrant Cocoa-Farmers of Southern Ghana* (Cambridge, 1963), p. 16.

[6] A. O. Hirschman, *The Strategy of Economic Development* (New Haven, 1958), pp. 14–20; Edward C. Banfield, *The Moral Basis of a Backward Society* (Glencoe, Ill., 1958); Clifford Geertz, *Peddlers and Princes* (Chicago, 1963), pp. 42–47, 73 ff., 122 ff.

[7] "Malaya probably suffers from an excess of enterprise, since this is a factor which tends to disintegrate existing business." T. H. Silcock, *The Economy of Malaya* (Singapore, 1956), p. 44.

that contain some, perhaps well hidden, ingredients of discipline and of entrepreneurship, respectively; hence, they may both be capable of development, even though the paths on which they will set out toward this goal are likely to be very different.

II. ALLEGED OBSTACLES WHOSE ELIMINATION TURNS OUT TO BE UNNECESSARY

We turn now to a somewhat less paradoxical type of situation: the presumed obstacle no longer changes colors and becomes a blessing in disguise; its existence simply leads to the charting of a hitherto unfamiliar path to economic progress, and the resulting, economically more advanced society exhibits a profile that is "different" because of the survival of certain institutions, attitudes, etc., which were originally thought to be incompatible with development. These situations can be difficult to distinguish clearly from the preceding ones, for if the presumed obstacle has at all survived, then one can frequently show that it is not only tolerated, but actually lends strength to the new state of affairs. Nevertheless, there is a difference, at least initially, between an obstacle that is being turned or neutralized and one that turns out not to be an obstacle at all, but a factor that promotes and propels development.

The confusion on this score is due to the somewhat shapeless notion of "challenge." Any difficulty or obstacle can be transmuted by a sort of semantic hocus pocus into a challenge which evokes a response. But these Toynbeean terms are not helpful, for they dissolve the concepts of difficulty and obstacle altogether, instead of permitting the differentiated analysis we are aiming at here. To recall an example from our preceding section, it is incorrect to say that the existence of the extended family is a "challenge" to developers; it is rather a real troublemaker in some respects and some situations and a valuable asset in others, as we have shown. The notion of challenge is similarly ineffectual in the case, now under consideration, of obstacles which have no positive dimension, but which do not preclude development via some "alternate route" (alternate to the removal of the obstacle). Let us take a country which lacks an important natural resource such as coal or whose history has not permitted any sizeable "primitive accumulation of capital"; when such countries substitute hydroelectric energy for coal, or bank credit and state finance for private equity capital,[8] they are not "responding" to a "challenge." They are merely encountering a different way of achieving growth which, of course, they might never have discovered had they been more "normally" endowed. "Believe me," says the Marquise de Merteuil in Laclos' *Les Liaisons Dangereuses*, "one

[8] Alexander Gerschenkron, *Economic Backwardness in Historical Perspective* (Cambridge, Mass., 1962), Chs. 1 and 2.

rarely acquires the qualities he can do without." Yet, to acquire these very qualities is less a matter of responding to a challenge than of discovering one's comparative advantage. In doing so a country may not even have been aware of the fact that the lack of a certain natural resource, institution, or attitudinal endowment constituted a special difficulty, an obstacle, or much less, a "challenge."

If a country lacks one of the conventional "prerequisites," it can overcome this lack in two distinct ways. One consists in inventing its own substitute for the prerequisite; as just mentioned, Gerschenkron has given us an exceptionally rich and convincing account of such substitution processes for the Marxian prerequisite of primitive accumulation of capital. The other possibility is that the purported "prerequisite" turns out to be not only substitutable, but outright dispensable; nothing in particular needs to take its place, and we are simply proven wrong in our belief that a certain resource, institution, or attitude needed to be created or eradicated for development to be possible. In other words, the requirements of development turn out to be more tolerant of cultural and institutional variety than we thought on the basis of our limited prior experience. . . .

✿   ✿   ✿   ✿   ✿

III. OBSTACLES WHOSE ELIMINATION IS POSTPONABLE

We are now ready for those obstacles which we come closest to recognizing as such, those that refuse to turn mysteriously into assets or to be accommodated in an unexpected fashion within an economically progressive society. They stubbornly remain factors detrimental to development which ought to be eliminated. In many cases, however—and this is the point to the present section—the priority which this task commands can be shown to be less rigidly defined than had been thought.

I am returning here to a theme which I have set forth at length in my previous writings. I have drawn attention to "inverted" or "disorderly" or "cart-before-the-horse" sequences that are apt to occur in the process of economic and social development; and I have argued that, under certain circumstances, these sequences could be "efficient" in the sense of making possible the achievement of stated goals of economic expansion within a briefer time period or at a smaller social cost than would be possible if the more orderly sequence were adhered to.[9]

[9] See, e.g., *The Strategy of Economic Development, op. cit.*, pp. 80–81, 93–94, 154–55; *Journeys Toward Progress: Studies of Economic Policy-Making in Latin America* (New York, 1963), p. 260.

The implication of this approach for the notion of barrier and obstacle is evident. While it grants that insufficient electric power, inadequate education, or the absence of agrarian reform are serious defects, it is suspicious of theories that erect the elimination of such defects into *prerequisites* for *any* forward movement; in addition to the head-on assault on these defects, it will evaluate, look for, and scrutinize ways in which the economy can be moved forward elsewhere and how thereby additional pressure can be brought to bear on the acknowledged obstacles. If they are truly hindrances, then any forward move that can be instigated in spite of them is going to make it even more imperative than before to get rid of them; if, on the other hand, this additional pressure is not generated, then perhaps these obstacles are not to be taken quite so seriously, and they belong, at least in part, in our second category (assumed obstacles that, as it turns out, can be accommodated into an economically progressive society).

¤   ¤   ¤   ¤   ¤

As the search for the conditions of economic development has been unremittingly pursued by social scientists over the past years, increasing attention has been given to the role of attitudes, beliefs, and basic personality characteristics favorable to the emergence of innovation, entrepreneurship, and the like. While these theories, with their expeditions into psychology and psychiatry, are frequently fascinating, the message they leave behind is almost as dismal as that of the very first theories of development which attributed a decisive role to such unalterable factors as race, climate, and natural resources. Rooted, as they are purported to be, in childhood experiences and transmitted unfailingly from one generation to the next, the deplored attitudes or personality structure appear to be similarly refractory to any but the most radical treatment.

¤   ¤   ¤   ¤   ¤

Fortunately, while the behavioral scientists have become depth psychologists, the psychologists have come up with the discovery that attitudinal change can be a *consequence* of behavioral change, rather than its precondition! From a variety of approaches exploring this nexus, I shall single out the *Theory of Cognitive Dissonance*, which was originated in 1957 by Leon Festinger in a book bearing that title. Since then the theory has been widely investigated, tested, and discussed; much of the empirical evidence which has been gathered, together with a chapter on the applicability of the theory to problems of social change, can be found in a volume by Jack W. Brehm and the late Arthur R. Cohen, *Explorations in Cognitive Dissonance* (New York, 1962).[10]

Briefly and in non-technical language, the theory states that a person who, for some reason, commits himself to act in a manner contrary to his beliefs, or to what he believes to be his beliefs, is in a state of dissonance. Such a state is unpleasant, and the person will attempt to reduce dissonance. Since the "discrepant behavior" has already taken place and cannot be undone, while the belief can be changed, reduction of dissonance can be achieved principally by changing one's beliefs in the direction of greater harmony with the action.

The theory thus predicts significant shifts in attitude consequent upon commitment to discrepant behavior, and its predictions have been verified empirically. . . .

. . . A . . . fruitful field of application of the theory may be the process of attitude change which is required in the course of economic development. The following quotations from the Brehm-Cohen volume are suggestive:

> The theory is different in its essential nature than most other theoretical models in psychology. Where the major concern in other theories has been largely with the guidance of behavior—that is, with what leads to a given behavior or commitment—dissonance theory deals, at least in part, with the *consequences* of a given behavior or commitment (p. 299).
>
> Dissonance theory attempts to understand the conditions under which behavioral commitments produce cognitive and attitudinal realignments in persons (p. 271).

In other words, dissonance theory deals with the possibility of replacing the "orderly" sequence, where attitude change is conceived as the prerequisite to behavioral change, by a "disorderly" one, where modern attitudes are acquired *ex-post*, as a consequence of the dissonance aroused by "modern" type of behavior which happens to be engaged in by people with non-modern attitudes. One question will, of course, be asked, namely: how can a commitment to "modern" behavior be obtained from people whose values and attitudes preclude in principle such behavior? Actually, however, this is not much of a problem among *late coming* societies surrounded by modernity and by opportunities to transgress into or try out modern behavior; at one time or another, it is likely that the latecomer will stumble more or less absent-mindedly into such behavior as pursuit of individual profit, entrepreneurial risk-taking, promotion according to merit, long-term planning, holding of demo-

---

[10] It should be pointed out that the theory is by no means universally accepted. For a highly critical appraisal, see N. P. Chapanis and A. Chapanis, "Cognitive Dissonance: Five Years Later," *Psychological Bulletin* (January 1964), 1–22.

cratic elections, etc.; dissonance will thus arise and will then gradually lead to those changes in attitude and basic beliefs which were thought to be prerequisites to the just-mentioned modes of behavior. The art of promoting development may therefore consist primarily in multiplying the opportunities to engage in these dissonance-arousing actions and in inducing an initial commitment to them.[11]

One observation will conclude this section. A country which achieves economic advance and modernization through the process just described, i.e., where behavioral change paces attitudinal change, is likely to exhibit a personality rather different from the country whose elite right at the outset of the development journey is imbued with the Protestant Ethic and saturated with achievement motivation. Because, in the case of the former country these motivations are being laboriously acquired *ex-post* and en route, its path will be more halting and circuitous and its typical personality may well be subject to particularly strong tension between traditional and modern values.[12] While a country can well develop without being endowed at the outset with all the "right" values and attitudes, its development profile and experience cannot but bear the marks of the order and manner in which it accomplishes its various tasks.

CONCLUSION

This is the end of our exercise in classification. It goes without saying that its purpose was not to destroy entirely the notion of barrier, obstacle, or prerequisite. In the first place, the classification was not meant to be exhaustive, and there may well exist a residual category of obstacles which by no stretch of the imagination can be considered as assets, which

[11] If one were to extend the above-mentioned "refinement" of the theory to the development context, one would conclude that the conditioning of foreign aid on internal reform can do positive harm at the stage when an underdeveloped country is about to commit itself to new types of "modern" or reform actions; to reward such perhaps partly dissonant behavior would lead to less cumulative change than if the behavior could not be dismissed by the actors as something they did just to get hold of the aid funds. In this way, the theory throws some light on the difficulties of using aid as a means of promoting internal reform which have beset the Alliance for Progress since its inception. Besides many other constructive uses, foreign aid may be helpful in promoting reform and will serve as a reinforcing agent when it is conceived and presented as a means of reducing the cost of a reform to which the policy-makers in the recipient country are already firmly committed; but it is cast in a self-defeating role if it is proffered as a *quid pro quo* for the reform commitment itself.

[12] In *Journeys Toward Progress, op. cit.*, pp. 235 ff., I have drawn a related difference by distinguishing between societies which, in the process of tackling their problems, let motivation to solve problems outrun their understanding, and those that do not usually tackle problems unless the means to solve them are close at hand. Here also the two styles of problem-solving are shown to result in sharply differing development experiences.

cannot be accommodated or neutralized, and whose removal must be accomplished before any other forward step can be usefully attempted. Secondly, if certain alleged obstacles turn out to be blessings in disguise, quite a few factors, hitherto considered as wholly favorable to development, are likely to function in some situations as *curses* in disguise.

Finally, and most important, while our exercise points to many ways in which obstacles can be made into assets or lived with or turned, it says nothing about the *ability to perceive these possibilities* on the part of the policy-makers in developing countries. If this ability is strictly limited, as is often the case, then this very limitation emerges as a super-obstacle, which commands and conditions the existence and seriousness of the more conventional obstacles. And it can now be told that the survey here presented was really aimed at loosening the grip of this central difficulty.

viii. international relations

Despite their limited industrial and military capacities, the developing states have had a profound impact on international affairs since the end of World War II. Not only have there been the organizational consequences for the world community resulting from the emergence of new states that have more than doubled the number of actors; much more basic have been the new directions in international politics stemming from the demands and aspirations of the developing states. No longer is the course of world history determined solely by the decisions of a few European and American powers, with the nations of Asia and Africa the pawns in the struggle for supremacy. Instead, the new states in these areas, as well as the older ones in Latin America, are vigorously participating in the decisions of the international community.

The principal goals that shape the foreign policies of the developing states are also those of the more advanced states: (1) the maintenance of political independence, (2) protection against aggression, (3) advantageous political, economic, and cultural relations with other states, (4) the respect of other states, and (5) the ability to influence the foreign policies of other states. The differing perceptions of these goals by the developing states and the more advanced ones arise from their different histories, internal conditions, and relative capacity to exert power and influence in the world community.

For many developing states, the effects of—and reaction to—the recently concluded period of colonialism are fundamental factors influencing their relations with other states. During the period of colonialism, trade patterns developed that are not easily modified. Ambiguous political relationships reflect the often bitter controversy leading to independence, the search for new allies, and the consequences of two major divisions in the world: the one economic, separating the rich from the poor states, and the other political, dividing the world along ideological lines. In addition, the foreign policies of the developing states are, of course, affected by their internal economic and political characteristics: an underdeveloped economy, a fragmented social structure, limited intellectual resources, and, in many cases, unstable political institutions and processes.

Since the developing states were dominated politically and economically by the major powers for so long, it is not surprising to find great emphasis on the development of policies that properly reflect the newly secured freedom to decide their own destinies. Leaders often appear obsessed with the need to demonstrate their independence. Many feel compelled constantly to remind the major powers that they no longer rule the world but must now treat the developing states as equals. The fear of new forms of political and economic imperialism is often reflected in the statements of these leaders. Warnings are issued to the major powers not to interfere in the internal affairs of the developing states, and in speeches to their followers, exhortations to watchfulness against this interference are frequently voiced. At the same time, there is usually a recognition of the benefits to be derived from the maintenance of close relations with both the former colonial powers and the other major nations. The result of these mixed feelings is, frequently, a rather schizophrenic attitude toward the major powers. On the one hand, there is widespread admiration for the economic and technological accomplishments of the advanced states. On the other hand, however, there is a feeling that these accomplishments were in large part the result of colonial policies that exploited the underdeveloped world, and that the major powers are not above future attempts to dominate the developing societies.

Since many of the developing states are small in size and population and all of them are, by definition, relatively weak in economic and military power, they all confront some major obstacles in promoting their interests in the international arena. Few of them, for example, need or could afford to maintain a large number of consulates and embassies, but without the basic services such agencies provide, it is often difficult to stimulate interest in possible trade or other relations between the states. Further, although cooperative ventures of various types, such as common markets, are widely endorsed in principle, the vigorous expressions of nationalism and the still tender roots of independence often make it difficult to aggregate the interests and power of the developing states in joint endeavors.

Within the several organs of the United Nations, however, the developing states have found one set of forums through which to advance their interests and objectives. The admission of many new states into the United Nations—the number of African states, for example, leaped from 4 in 1955 to 41 in 1968—has led to a profound reordering of priorities by the various agencies as the developing states, now constituting a majority, have vigorously used their voting power to reorient the direction of policy making.[1] Not only were the Security Council and the Economic and Social Council enlarged in 1965 as a result of intense pressures by the newly admitted states, but the dominant issues before the agencies have become significantly different from those of the pre-1960 period. In recent General Assembly sessions, the principal issues have been those of decolonization, economic aid, and human rights, all of which have been vigorously pressed by the developing states, particularly those in Asia and Africa. By 1967 it was rare to hear any defense of Western colonialism in the halls of the United Nations and now, having secured a general moral condemnation of colonialism, the African and Asian states have been attempting to persuade the United Nations to impose effective sanctions against such recalcitrant racist states as Rhodesia and the Union of South Africa.[2]

The budgets of United Nations agencies similarly reflect the concerns of the developing states. With their voting majority, the developing states have been able to expand the budgets of agencies engaged in development-related activities; for example, the budget of the World Health Organization increased by over 200 per cent between 1960 and 1967. Over 80 per cent of the personnel and funds of United Nations agencies are now involved in development-related projects. Because the budgets are derived from assessed contributions from the member states on the basis of ability to pay, it is the more developed states that are, consequently, underwriting the enlarged United Nations programs as demanded by the developing states. Thus, the 82 poorest states that collectively contribute only 5.67 per cent of the assessed United Nations budget (of these, 54 are assessed at the minimum rate of .04 per cent) have repeatedly used their numerical voting majority to force the developed states to participate in the cost of social and economic development as undertaken by the United Nations agencies in the developing states.[3]

The developing states have also forced the United Nations to become concerned with the problems of trade that confront them. When the 27 states, including the major trading countries of the world, signed the General Agreement on Tariff and Trade (GATT) in 1947, little attention was given to the problems confronting the developing states. Even though the parties to GATT became increasingly concerned with those

[1] David A. Kay, "The Politics of Decolonization: The New Nations and the United Nations Political Process," *International Organization*, Vol. XXI, No. 4 (Autumn, 1967), pp. 786–811.

[2] David A. Kay, "The Impact of African States on the United Nations," *International Organization*, Vol. XXIII, No. 1 (Winter, 1969), pp. 20–47.

[3] Walter M. Kotschnig, "The United Nations as an Instrument of Economic and Social Development," *International Organization*, Vol. XXII, No. 1 (Winter, 1968), pp. 16–43.

problems over the years, the developing states have regarded progress on a number of important issues, such as the reduction of tariffs, as slow and uncertain. Consequently, many of them have turned to the United Nations to undertake a concerted attack on the barriers to trade that inhibit the economic growth of the developing states.

In December, 1961, the United Nations General Assembly designated the 1960s as the Decade of Development and noted the importance of trade for the developing countries. The first United Nations Conference on Trade and Development (UNCTAD) was held in 1964 and examined a number of problems, after which it decided to initiate a number of fact-finding studies on trade and development. But when the second UNCTAD conference convened early in 1968, virtually all of the most difficult problems remained unsolved, including the problems of tariffs, agricultural commodity agreements, the use of synthetics to replace natural products, price stabilization, etc.[4] Some observers in the developing states have been led to conclude that the existing trade relations between the developed and the less developed states are more than a major cause of the poverty of the latter states, as "the U.N. General Assembly emphasis on trade *under the existing international division of labour* is not only misplaced but may be regarded as a calculated strategy by the capitalist countries to mislead the developing countries."[5] What is clear is that while in absolute terms the exports of the developing states have risen by 67 per cent from 1959 to 1968, their share of total world exports has declined from 27 per cent in 1953 to 19.3 per cent in 1968.

Another very disturbing fact to the leaders of the developing states is that while the rich states get richer, the flow of aid from them to the poor states has leveled off and, indeed, as measured in terms of a percentage of the national income of the developed states has actually declined. Thus, the net flow of financial resources to the developing states from the United States, for example, fell from .65 per cent of gross national product in 1961 to .35 per cent in 1969, while that of France declined from 1.41 per cent to .69 per cent during the same interval. While many billions of dollars and other currencies have been made available to the developing states through grants and loans by the United States, Great Britain, France, and the Soviet Union, with smaller amounts from other European and non-European states such as Communist China and

[4] Sidney Wells, "The Developing Countries, GATT and UNCTAD," *International Affairs*, Vol. XLV, No. 1 (January, 1969), pp. 64–79, and Reginald H. Green, "U.N.C.T.A.D. and After: Anatomy of a Failure," *The Journal of Modern African Studies*, Vol. V, No. 2 (September, 1967), pp. 243–267.
[5] J. F. Rweyemamu, "International Trade and the Developing Countries," *The Journal of Modern African Studies*, Vol. VII, No. 2 (July, 1969), p. 211. For a reply to this position, see Leslie Stein, "Developing Countries and International Trade—An Alternative View," *The Journal of Modern African Studies*, Vol. VIII, No. 4 (December, 1970), pp. 605–616.

Australia, the developing states face a chronic shortage of capital and severe competition exists for that aid which is available. With doubts increasingly being voiced in the developed countries about current foreign aid programs, and with the United States, the principal donor, engaged in an expensive foreign war in Vietnam and faced with costly domestic problems, there seems little likelihood that the demands by the developing states for expanded aid will be heeded.

The developing states have not limited their search for the elusive solutions to their problems to the United Nations and to the donors of foreign aid, however. They have also been exploring the opportunities of promoting economic development through regional cooperation. For example, in 1961, the United States and the Latin American states joined together in a highly publicized Alliance for Progress, a program of social reform and economic development that over a ten-year period was to provide the Latin American states with twenty billion dollars of developmental funds. The Alliance soon began to lose its verve, however, and its long-term impact seems likely to be minimal. Not involving direct United States participation is the Latin American Free Trade Area, established in 1960 with the signing of the Treaty of Montevideo. Patterned after the European Common Market, the Latin American Free Trade Association now includes Argentina, Brazil, Chile, Uruguay, Paraguay, Peru, Mexico, Colombia, Ecuador, Bolivia, and Venezuela. The Treaty provides for a twelve-year time span within which to complete the establishment of a duty-free trade zone among the signatory states, though no provision is made for a common protective barrier against the outside world. However, substantial difficulties have been encountered in reaching agreements on tariff reductions, and the Association has been only partially successful in attaining its goals. The five Central American states established their own Central American Common Market in 1962 which provides for both a reduction of trade barriers among themselves and a common tariff wall to the outside world. Within this Common Market, trade quadrupled in five years, but the political hostility between Honduras and El Salvador—an aftermath of the brief war between the two countries in 1969—as well as difficulties encountered in achieving economic cooperation among the members led to the virtual withdrawal of Honduras from the group early in 1971, and the future expansion of the Common Market is uncertain.

At present, trade among the Latin American states is still relatively limited, mainly because they are still principally producers of raw materials, with only a limited industrial capacity to provide the manufactured goods they need. The attempts to create common markets reflect not only the advantages believed to exist in expanding the markets for the new industries in the area, however, but also the growing threat to the exports of the Latin American states to the European Common

Market countries. Since the former colonies of France in Africa (and if Britain joins the Common Market, presumably their former colonies) enjoy preferential treatment in the European Common Market, the Latin American states will have increasing difficulty in competing with the African exports of the same products. The Latin American common markets are also designed to decrease dependence on American manufactured goods by protecting and encouraging the growth of domestic industries. At the same time, however, the United States remains a major trading partner of most Latin American states. Fears continue to be expressed by many Latin Americans about the economic power of the United States over their economies. These fears are based on the power of the United States to determine to a large degree the export prices of their commodities and the economic and political consequences of the high level of North American investments in Latin American industries.

In Asia and Africa as well, attempts have been made to organize and advance regional interests through cooperative ventures. The East African Community has been one of the more successful organizations. Composed of Kenya, Uganda, and Tanzania, with Zambia, Ethiopia, Somalia, and Burundi seeking membership, the Community has undertaken a variety of projects designed to promote the economic development of the region. The railway systems of the member states have been improved, harbor facilities expanded, telecommunications networks extended, and agricultural research enlarged. But the Community has confronted increasing difficulties arising out of conflicts among its members, which threaten its stability and progress. Asian regional organizations have been much less prominent and, unlike the situation in other developing areas, most of them have been products of outside persuasion and leadership.[6] While a few organizations, such as the Association of Southeast Asian Nations which includes Thailand, the Philippines, Malaysia, Singapore, and Indonesia, have been created by the Asian states themselves, the individualism of the Asian states and the lack of strong intra-regional cultural bonds have inhibited the growth of regional organizations to the extent that they exist elsewhere. Although the twenty-two participant states in the Colombo Plan, first negotiated in 1950 and extended in 1965 through 1971, have had some success in working together for economic development, as through the exchange of experts and the training of students, no comprehensive plan for economic cooperation has as yet been devised.

In addition to plans for economic integration within the several areas of the developing world, the idea of political integration has also been explored and some tentative first steps have been taken toward regional political organization. The idea of eventual political unification of the Latin American states has existed ever since independence was achieved

[6] Maruyama Shizuo, "Asian Regionalism," *Japan Quarterly*, Vol. XV, No. 1 (January–March, 1968), pp. 53–61.

early in the nineteenth century. Although the realization of this objective seems remote, the Latin American states have established—in some cases with the participation of the United States—several regional institutions that enable joint action to be undertaken. The Pan-American Union, created late in the nineteenth century, and the Organization of American States, established in 1948, are the most inclusive organizations, designed to promote understanding and action on common problems. However, many Latin Americans regard these organizations to be of limited utility for purposes of regional cooperation. The feeling is widespread that the United States dominates these organizations to its own advantage, with little regard for the revolutionary changes occurring in Latin America. A mutual defense pact, the Treaty of Rio, signed in 1947, provides for joint consideration of military threats to the hemisphere.

The Pan-African and Pan-Arab movements that have been activated differ from the Pan-American movement as well as from each other. Even within the Pan-African movement several variations can be identified. In one form, of little importance today, the term is used to denote the attempts to unite Negroes throughout the world in a struggle to destroy the derogatory image of Africans and Negroes. In another, more important version, the term is used to indicate those attempts to organize the states and peoples of sub-Saharan Africa. In still another form, one which has been given concrete expression in the Organization of African Unity, the term designates the movement to organize the African continent, including the northern, Mediterranean states.

The promotion of unification movements among the African people, whether on the basis of the Negro groups alone or on a continental basis, has a long history. Even before independence was achieved, a number of conferences had been held in which ideas concerning unification were discussed, despite the fact that in the precolonial period there had never been widespread unity among the people on the continent. Initially, the objectives of the Negro leaders, many of whom lived in Europe and the United States, were the termination of racial discrimination by the European colonial powers, economic advancement for the Negro populations, and eventually political independence for the African societies. Once independence was achieved after World War II, the problem of unifying a large number of diverse states arose. Although the racial appeal of Pan-Africanism has had a strong emotional attraction, a number of factors have inhibited the emergence of a United States of Africa, the goal of some leaders (in particular Kwame Nkrumah, the former president of Ghana). The checkerboard division of Africa by the European powers, especially in West Africa, and the development of complex networks of economic, social, and political relationships between the colonial powers and their possessions have left the African states with relatively few substantive links with each other except for those of race.

The individual economies are not particularly interdependent; they are more often competitive for world markets and are still quite closely linked with the former colonial powers. Competition for scarce development capital, urgently needed throughout all of Africa, also divides the states. Further, as noted earlier, the states that are relatively well developed have been reluctant to unite with less developed ones. In addition, strong leaders of individual states, capable of cooperation as equals, are not readily induced to yield their power and assume subordinate roles in a larger community. Finally, the nationalism within each state has inhibited unifying movements. Despite the emotional identification of Africans of all states with each other on the basis of race, the emotional attachment of politically conscious Africans to their individual states is strong and, it seems, often growing stronger. The longer unifying movements are delayed and individual governments successfully meet the minimum requirements of their people, the less likely political unity of a continental, or subcontinental, scope will occur.

Nevertheless, cooperative movements providing for less than full political unification have been initiated. The outstanding achievement has been the creation of the Organization of African Unity, established in 1963. This Organization brought together within one body several more limited organizations that had previously existed. The OAU has been instrumental in channeling the vigorous opposition of the African states to the Union of South Africa and to Portugal, which has no intention of granting independence to its African colonies. In addition, a wide variety of common problems have been considered by the Organization's several organs and commissions. In the economic field, limited economic cooperation has been achieved among fourteen signatories to the Charter establishing the Afro-Malagasy Organization of Economic Cooperation, first established in 1961 and reorganized in 1964. Although proposals for an African common market have been advanced, no agreement has been achieved on its establishment. Several limited customs unions have been created, though without notable success.

Less successful than the recent attempts to organize the African states have been the longer efforts to institutionalize the Pan-Arab or Pan-Islamic movements. Although the memory of Arab unity before the era of European domination exerts a strong appeal, deep divisions among the Arab leaders have prevented the Arab League, founded in 1945, from being an effective organization for promoting either common policies (even in opposition to Israel) or the creation of a united Arab state. The Pan-Islamic movement is even less organized, though the Islamic religion supplies a loose unifying element throughout much of the Middle East and Asia.

Although broad Asian cooperation has been supported by a number of leaders, the relatively greater national self-identity of the individual

Asian states and several bitter disputes among them have not encouraged Pan-Asian unity movements. Before World War II, several conferences of Asian leaders were held, as among African leaders, to demand independence for the Asian states and to promote regional cooperation. Anticolonialism has been the principal issue on which agreement can be attained, however. Further cooperation is inhibited by a number of factors. A deep ideological division separates the communist states, led by Communist China, from the noncommunist nations. Religious and other issues, such as control of Kashmir, divide India and Pakistan, and boundary disputes continue between India and China. Sukarno's opposition to Malaysia led to military clashes, although relations between Indonesia and Malaysia improved after Sukarno lost his control of policy. Asian leaders are also divided over the United States involvement in Vietnam. In addition, while many leaders regard the economic strength of Japan as a threat to the economic development of their states, they have not been able to establish common policies to meet the Japanese challenge. These factors, among others, effectively override the emotional identification of Asians as a unified group.

The most significant effort to develop cooperation among the Asian states occurred at the Bandung Conference in 1955, attended by representatives of twenty-nine Asian and African states. However, the deep divisions among the delegates were clearly evident. Little agreement could be reached among the three groups of states—the pro-Western, the communist, and the neutralist—except on issues of independence for the European colonies and the desirability of peace. A "second Bandung" conference was scheduled to be held in Algeria in 1965, but it failed to materialize because of the bitter controversies among the Asian and African leaders. No permanent organizational structures were created at the Bandung Conference to provide a medium for continual consultation or the development of common political policy, nor has any other organization been established.

At the Bandung Conference and at major meetings in Belgrade in 1961 and in Cairo in 1964, and at lesser conferences since then, attempts have been made to chart a course of action for the developing states that would avoid permanent alignments with either of the great major power blocs while simultaneously enabling them to influence the policies of both. During the 1950s and on into the 1960s, much effort was expended trying to define the doctrine of nonalignment and to make it operational. However, the nonaligned states were divided on the interpretation of nonalignment. Some believed that the nonaligned states should create an organized third force, but others argued that any organization destroyed the concept and utility of nonalignment. With the decline of the Cold War and with the political demise of some of the most vigorous and articulate advocates of nonalignment, more attention began to be given to practical, pragmatic means of solving problems, with less emphasis on the ideological dimensions of international politics.[7]

For states not directly involved or immediately threatened, the international wars in Asia and in the Middle East and the civil wars in sub-Saharan Africa and elsewhere seem remote, with few if any security, military, or economic consequences. The combination of internal problems, limited military forces, weak economic positions, and fear of long-range military alignments with the major powers have led most developing states to confine their involvement in major international political disputes to the verbal level or, at most, symbolic material aid for one side or the other. Thus, while the United States finds little support among the developing states in its attempt to win a military victory in Vietnam, Laos and Cambodia, few of the developing states have given more than verbal support to the North Vietnamese.

The transition from colonial status to full and effective participation in the international community has proven to be difficult and is by no means yet completed. As the gap between the rich and powerful states and the poor and weak states continues to grow, the problem of creating a strong, well-ordered international community will become increasingly exacerbated. Whether a world increasingly persuaded by the ideas of equality, participation, and prosperity can survive the growing disparity of states will constitute one of the most profound and difficult questions of the last quarter of the twentieth century.

[7] Several interpretations of nonalignment can be found in *Nonalignment in Foreign Affairs, The Annals,* Vol. 362 (November, 1965).

SUGGESTED READINGS

Ball, M. Margaret. *The OAS in Transition.* Durham, N. C.: Duke University Press, 1969.

Bhagwati, Jagdish. *Trade, Tariffs, and Growth: Essays in International Economics.* Cambridge, Mass.: M.I.T. Press, 1969.

Červenka, Zdanek. *The Organization of African Unity and its Charter.* 2d ed. New York: Frederick A. Praeger, 1969.

Cochrane, James D. *The Politics of Regional Integration: The Central American Case.* The Hague: Martinus Nijhoff, 1969.

Gardner, Richard N., and Max F. Millikan, eds. "The Global Partnership: International Agencies and Economic Development," *International Organization,* Vol. XXII, No. 1 (Winter, 1968).

Hilton, Ronald, ed. *The Movement Toward Latin American Unity.* New York: Frederick A. Praeger, 1969.

Hinton, Harold C. *Communist China in World Politics.* Boston: Houghton Mifflin Company, 1966.

Hovet, Thomas. *Africa in the United Nations.* Evanston, Ill.: Northwestern University Press, 1963.

Jackson, Sir Robert, ed. *A Study of the Capacity of the United Nations Development System.* Geneva: United Nations Publications DP/5, 1969.

Jansen, G. H. *Nonalignment and the Afro-Asian States.* New York: Frederick A. Praeger, 1966.

Kahin, George McT. *The Asian-African Conference, Bandung, Indonesia, April 1955.* Ithaca, N. Y.: Cornell University Press, 1956.

Kahnert, F., *et al. Economic Integration Among Developing Countries.* Paris: Development Centre of the Organization for Economic Co-operation and Development, 1969.

Kay, David A. *The New Nations in the United Nations, 1960–1967.* New York: Columbia University Press, 1970.

Lall, Arthur. *The UN and the Middle East Crisis, 1967.* New York: Columbia University Press, 1968.

Legum, Colin, ed. *The First U. N. Development Decade and Its Lessons for the 1970's.* New York: Frederick A. Praeger, 1970.

————. *Pan-Africanism.* Rev. ed. New York: Frederick A. Praeger, 1965.

Levinson, Jerome and Juan de Onis. *The Alliance that Lost Its Way: A Critical Report on the Alliance for Progress.* Chicago: Quadrangle Books, Inc., 1970.

London, Kurt, ed. *New Nations in a Divided World.* New York: Frederick A. Praeger, 1963.

Lyon, Peter. *War and Peace in South-East Asia.* London: Oxford University Press, 1969.

MacBean, Alasdair I. *Export Instability and Economic Development.* Cambridge: Harvard University Press, 1966.

Macdonald, Robert W. *The League of Arab States: A Study in the Dynamics of Regional Organization.* Princeton, N. J.: Princeton University Press, 1965.

Maizels, Alfred. *Exports and Economic Growth of Developing Countries.* New York: Cambridge University Press, 1968.

Martin, Laurence W., ed. *Neutralism and Nonalignment.* New York: Frederick A. Praeger, 1962.

McKay, Vernon, ed. *African Diplomacy.* New York: Frederick A. Praeger, 1966.

Mecham, J. Lloyd. *A Survey of United States–Latin American Relations.* Boston: Houghton Mifflin Company, 1965.

Nielson, Waldemar A. *The Great Powers & Africa.* New York: Frederick A. Praeger, 1969.

Pearson, Lester B., *et al. Partners in Development: Report of the Commission on International Development.* New York: Frederick A. Praeger, 1969.

Phillips, Hiram S. *Guide for Development: Institution-Building and Reform.* New York: Frederick A. Praeger, 1969.

Robson, Peter. *Economic Integration in Africa.* London: Allen & Unwin, 1968.

Safran, Nadav. *From War to War: The Arab-Israeli Confrontation, 1948–1967.* New York: Pegasus, 1969.

Schoenbrun, David. *Vietnam; How We Got In, How to Get Out.* New York: Atheneum, 1968.

Sen, Sudhir. *United Nations in Economic Development: Need for a New Strategy.* Dobbs Ferry, N. Y.: Oceana Publications, Inc., 1969.

Welch, Claude E., Jr. *Dream of Unity: Pan-Africanism and Political Unification in West Africa.* Ithaca, N. Y.: Cornell University Press, 1966.

Zagoria, Donald S. *Vietnam Triangle: Moscow, Peking, Hanoi.* New York: Pegasus, 1967.

Some of the difficulties transitional states encounter in playing the traditional roles of sovereign states in the international community have already been noted. In the following discussion, the relations between two large but economically underdeveloped areas are analyzed in more detail; as the study indicates, the common bond of poverty has not yet resulted in strong political or economic coherence or interaction.

38. SOUTHEAST ASIAN RELATIONS WITH AFRICA °†

fred r. von der mehden

The "normal" view of international relations envisions some sort of contact between and among states, including diplomatic relations involving an exchange of ambassadors, formal agreements, trade and other forms of international interaction. In the case of Southeast Asian relations with Africa, such contacts have been both sporadic and meager, and this in spite of constant references to Afro-Asian friendship, exchanges of students and missions, efforts by Africans and Asians to establish closer contacts and even the existence of periodicals solely interested in Afro-Asian problems. To be more precise about the current level of contact between Africa and the nine states of Southeast Asia it is necessary to analyze four factors, (1) regular diplomatic exchanges, (2) relations in formal international organizations, (3) Afro-Asian conferences, and (4) trade relations.

African-Southeast Asian Diplomatic Relations: Formal diplomatic exchanges between states in the two areas have been sparse and seemingly haphazard. There are comparatively few Southeast Asian embassies in Africa and even fewer African embassies in Southeast Asia, the

°   From "Southeast Asian Relations with Africa" by Fred R. von der Mehden, *Asian Survey*, Vol. V, No. 7 (July, 1965), pp. 341–349. By permission.
†   This is a revision of a paper originally prepared for presentation before the Asian-African Relations panel at the 17th Annual Meeting of the Association for Asian Studies, San Francisco, April 2–4, 1965.

tendency being for states south of the Sahara not to exchange embassies with smaller non-African powers. Only the United Arab Republic has exchanged embassies with a majority of the Southeast Asian states— Burma, Cambodia, Indonesia, Thailand, the Philippines and recently North Vietnam. Relations between Egypt and several Southeast Asian states have been of comparatively long duration. For example, in 1951 Indonesia was prepared to recognize King Farouk as king of both Egypt and the Sudan, and the Philippines opened an embassy in Cairo as early as 1957. However, outside of the North African region, there are only eight embassies from Southeast Asia and no obvious pattern has emerged among them. Indonesia has an embassy in Guinea, North Vietnam in Mali and Guinea, South Vietnam in Niger and Senegal, Thailand and the Philippines have diplomatic relations with Nigeria, Thailand with Ethiopia, and consulates have been established in the Union of South Africa by both Thailand and the Philippines. Burma, Cambodia, Laos and Malaysia have no embassies in Africa south of the Sahara.

To the extent that there is any pattern among these, Thailand and the Philippines have relations with more pro-Western powers and North Vietnam and Indonesia with the more "neutralist" states of Africa south of the Sahara. Nor have formal treaties of defense or friendship normally been formed between countries in the two regions, an exception being an Indonesian treaty of friendship with Egypt, established in the early '50's. There are no regional collective defense agreements involving both areas. This lack of formal exchanges is probably due to a combination of insufficient funds for embassies and the small amount of commercial and other business carried out between the two areas.

DIPLOMATIC RELATIONS BETWEEN AFRICA AND SOUTHEAST ASIA—1964

Embassies of Southeast Asian States in Africa

African state	Burma	Cambodia	Indonesia	NVN	Phil	Malaysia	SVN	Thai
UAR	X	X	X		X	X	X	X
Guinea			X	X				
Nigeria					X			X
Niger							X	
Senegal								
Sudan			X					
Mali				X				X
Ethiopia								
Union S. Africa					Con			Con

Africa and Southeast Asia in the U.N.: The one arena where constant contact does take place is within the United Nations, where there has been diplomatic interplay between countries of Southeast Asia and

Africa from the first years of the organization. However, except for a short period in the mid '50's the numbers and influence of the delegations from the two regions have not been equal. Up to 1955 the African states played only a small role in the Afro-Asian caucus, with the dominant members actually being Arab and South Asian. As of 1950, there were but four African states in the U.N. (Ethiopia, Liberia, Egypt and South Africa) and four Southeast Asian (Burma, Indonesia, Philippines and Thailand) out of a total of fifteen members from Afro-Asia. At this time the Afro-Asian caucus as a caucus had only recently been organized (in fact, the Afro-Asian group really took form as late as the Korean War crisis). The height of Southeast Asian membership in this period was in 1955 when it totaled six to the five delegations from Africa (Libya was by then a member, and two years later Malaya was voted in). During this first decade the Afro-Asian members did meet on common problems from time to time and voted in a generally cohesive pattern on questions such as Algeria, Tunisia and efforts at independence by various other colonial peoples (South African treatment of its non-white population, Indonesian independence, the West Iranian question and problems of self-determination in general). However, during the first years of Afro-Asian caucusing there was not a high degree of agreement within the caucus on other issues, and the caucus did not find itself with the majority of the General Assembly on a good many measures (next to the Soviet Bloc, the Afro-Asian Caucus voted least with the majority of the United Nations in the General Assembly).[1]

The second decade of the United Nations has seen a similar pattern of voting on colonial issues but in an entirely different atmosphere. With the withdrawal of Indonesia from the U.N., the Southeast Asian delegations have been reduced to six and have been swallowed by the over thirty-five African delegations in the Afro-Asian caucus. The present caucus thus has approximately 60% African members and about 10% Southeast Asian. Lest these figures provide an inaccurate perception of the role of Southeast Asia in the caucus, it should be pointed out that experience and merit have provided Southeast Asian delegations with a louder voice than the size of its membership alone would normally allow. Although it is difficult to assess the relative effectiveness of specific delegations within the U.N., it is interesting to note the number of

---

[1] For materials on U.N. voting, Thomas Hovet, Jr., *Africa in the U.N.* (Northwestern Univ. Press, 1963). In reviewing this material, ten General Assembly votes on questions relating to Africa and Asian problems (Indians in South Africa, Indonesia-Dutch relations, West Irian, Suez, Congo, etc.) were checked. These votes showed that Thailand and the Philippines did not always vote with the African states and other Southeast Asian states on African issues and that in the early years of their U.N. membership, Laos and Cambodia had a tendency to vote with France against the Africans. On such questions as the Congo, both areas were split. For a good analysis of such questions, see Somaan Farajallah, *Le Groupe Afro-Asiatique Dans Le Cadre Des Nations Unies* (Geneva: Librairie Droz, 1963).

high positions to which Southeast Asians have been elected and the recent election of countries from that region to the Security Council. However, the over-all impact of increased African representation in the General Assembly has been a decrease in the voice of the Southeast Asian states. As well, the expansion of the Afro-Asian caucus to some 58 members has made it almost unmanageable and with the resignation of Indonesia there is no strong spokesman from the Southeast Asian region within the caucus.

Within the U.N. there has been a mutual interest expressed in the regional problems of the respective areas. African delegates spoke, but did not always vote unanimously, on Southeast Asian issues such as the West Irian and Malaysian issues. At the same time Southeast Asian states have spoken in support of the independence of the former French North African colonies and have entered the debate on the Congo. Southeast Asian governments have also sent troops to Africa on U.N. peace-keeping missions in the Congo and Gaza strip.[2] However, no special relationship appears to have emerged between Southeast Asia and the new African states other than one based on the fact that they are all "underdeveloped states" with certain common problems.

Afro-Asian Meetings: A somewhat similar pattern has emerged with regard to Afro-Asian conferences held over the past two decades. Initial meetings were composed almost entirely of representatives of Asian states and the African delegations were often ill-prepared, at times only observers and generally outside of the mainstream of political influence. The first Asian Relations Conference, an "unofficial" meeting of 28 Asian states, was held in New Delhi in 1947 and had but one African delegate, Egypt. The meeting dealt almost entirely with Asian questions although many of these had a wider significance. The New Delhi conference on Indonesia held in 1949 was again dominated by the South-Southeast Asian representatives and had but two African delegations, Egypt and Ethiopia. At the first Asian Socialist Conference held in Rangoon in 1953, only Egypt sent an official delegation (there were eight Asian delegations including three Southeast Asian) although observers were sent from organizations in Algeria, Tunisia, Kenya and Uganda. The small degree of interaction in this early period is best shown by the first truly Afro-Asian conference in Bandung in 1955. Attending the conference were 29 countries, only five African (Ethiopia, Sudan, Egypt, Libya and what was then called the Gold Coast). Only two countries represented "black Africa" and they remained relatively silent. Although Nasser of Egypt did play a role (not as large as he

---

[2] In the Gaza affair, Burma, Indonesia and the Philippines offered aid to the UNEF and Indonesian forces served until September 1957. In the Congo operation Malaya sent 1,518 officers and men, Burma a contingent of 9 and Indonesia 1,152. D. W. Bowett, *U.N. Forces* (New York: Praeger, 1964).

hoped or has since) the African delegation was so ineffective that not one of its members was on the sub-committee on colonialism (which led the Ethiopian delegation to raise objections, but unsuccessfully). Even the Egyptian resolution on French North Africa was attacked as too mild. The final communique of the conference, while taking up South Africa and French North Africa, was largely silent on other questions relating to that continent.

At Bandung several Southeast Asian states were very active, Indonesia being the host country and along with Burma one of the five proposers of the conference. Indonesia, Burma, Cambodia, Thailand and the Philippines all actively participated in discussions and special meetings at Bandung, although there was disagreement among the Southeast Asian representatives on major issues before the conference. Spokesmen from Thailand, the Philippines, Laos and, to a lesser extent, Cambodia were more suspicious of the intentions of the Communists in general and China in particular than were Burma and Indonesia. The Philippines, Thailand and Cambodia were among the early leaders attacking Communist as well as Western colonialism. To the extent that splits developed at Bandung, these states plus Laos generally lined up with the "pro-Western" camp while Burma and Indonesia were to be found among the "neutralists."

The years since the Afro-Asian conference at Bandung have not seen the hoped-for development of Afro-Asian relations as such. Instead, conferences have tended to go in two directions, a concentration on their own problems among African members resulting in the formation of organizations composed of only African states and, secondly, the calling of conferences of a wider geographic significance and narrower ideological content. Thus the Africans have become involved in discussions within the organization for African unity and splinter groups such as the Brazzaville, Monrovia and Casablanca groupings. With regard to Afro-Asian meetings, the past several years have seen the inauguration of neutralist and other conferences of Afro-Asians and Latin Americans or of countries from respective regions whose policy was oriented along specific ideological lines. The Cairo Afro-Asian economic conference did have primarily Afro-Asian states and the Southeast Asians at that time, 1958, did have a strong voice. However, the conference of Chiefs of State of Non-Aligned Governments held in Belgrade in 1961 was composed of states somewhat ideologically oriented in terms of neutralism and included Latin American states. It should also be noted that at this time the Africans began to show their strength and there were 13 African states and only 3 Southeast Asian among the 25 delegations. The only Southeast Asians to take active roles in the conference were President Sukarno of Indonesia and, to a lesser extent, U Nu of Burma. The Conference of Economic Development held in Cairo in 1962 was composed of 31 delegations, including 13 African and but 4 Southeast Asians, and also included Latin American members. The initiative for this conference, unlike some earlier ones, did not come from Asia but from Presidents Nasser and Tito. Other ideologically oriented conferences took place at Conakry and Moshi, Tanganyika, where the Afro-Asian Peoples Solidarity Conferences were held. These meetings were composed of official or non-official delegations from "leftist" organizations and states; only Indonesia and North Vietnam of the Southeast Asian states attended as active participants. Even the tenth anniversary of the first Asian-African Conference at Bandung this year displayed this continuing tendency for meetings along ideological lines as a number of the more "pro-Western" states sent their regrets or sent lesser officials as delegates. The decline of Afro-Asian meetings (perhaps due to the over-use of official conferences of developing nations) was illustrated at the anniversary meeting by the general lack of heads of state among the delegates and the paucity of publicity given the meeting throughout the world (with exceptions such as Indonesia). Over all, recent conferences have shown something of an about-face from the first years when the African states were on the outside and power was in the hands of Arab and Asian states. Exclusively Afro-Asian meetings appear to be on their way out.

At present, with the exception of Indonesia and to an extent North Vietnam, the Southeast Asian states have not been highly influential in Afro-Asian meetings. In fact, other states often do not participate in the multitude of official and unofficial conferences. The Indonesians have made a major effort to make up for the silence of their neighbors. Central to the Indonesian ideology is anti-imperialism and the unity of the oppressed Afro-Asian states, and the government of Indonesia has been anxious to place itself as the leader of the developing nations, and particularly of the neutralist bloc. In activating this policy Indonesia has participated in Afro-Asian meetings more often than any other Southeast Asian state and has played host to a variety of international conferences. She has hosted in the past few years special professional conferences such as the Afro-Asian Journalists, sports extravaganzas such as the Asian Games, and more recently the Ganefo Games (Games of the "New Emerging Forces"), and international political and social conferences such as the Bandung meeting of Asian-African states and Afro-Asian Islamic Conference, both held in 1965. Within the meetings, Indonesia's general line has been strongly anti-Western colonial and anti-capitalist combined with generally laudatory remarks for various facets of her own political philosophy. Recently, Indonesia has also attempted to gain support for specific policy lines such as her anti-Malaysia campaign.

Trade Relations: The final area to be considered is that of interregional trade. Here again interaction has not been great. Trade did increase between the two regions from 1956 to 1962 but has never been large. Using United Nations figures for trade between Southeast Asia and Africa and the Middle East (this is the best we have for several countries) exports to Africa and the Middle East in 1956 averaged 13.7 million U.S. dollars a quarter, while imports stand at 27.4 million. By 1962 the respective figures were 23.6 million and 28.9 million. Over these years the total of imports and exports amounted to less than 2½% of the trade of the respective regions. Of the Southeast Asian states, what is now Malaysia was the major trader with Africa, followed by Thailand and Burma. Trade was infinitesimal or non-existent between Africa and the Middle East and Brunei, Cambodia, Laos and Vietnam. Selectively using the three years between 1956 and 1962 there were no exports from Laos and Brunei and only in 1956 were there exports from Cambodia to the African and Middle Eastern regions. The story of imports was much the same.

¤   ¤   ¤   ¤   ¤

In sum, we can state that trade was very small in amount between both continents and that political relations have had little to do with trade balances. Whereas over half the trade is with the white-dominated governments of southern Africa, no Southeast Asian country has an embassy in those states and only Thailand and the Philippines have honorary consuls in the Union of South Africa. Elsewhere there is no particular correlation between diplomatic relations and trade activities.

In conclusion, in no particular area has any special international relationship grown between Africa and Southeast Asia. Nor have there been extensive efforts in recent years to intensify relations, with the exception of Indonesia. The only forum for continuing policy exchanges remains the United Nations. Even there the very size of the Afro-Asian caucus makes some types of contact difficult. Aside from Indonesia, relations between Africa and Southeast Asia remain sparse, sporadic and unspectacular.

From the perspective of the older and more developed states, the audacity of the younger and less prosperous ones in claiming attention for their problems and consideration for their solutions to complex world issues has often been disconcerting and irritating. On the other hand, the developing states have become increasingly disillusioned both by the complexity of the problems and the unwillingness of the major powers to accept the solutions they have proposed. In the following selection, Linda B. Miller discusses some of the characteristics of the international community as it has evolved under the impact of the new states.

39. THE NEW STATES AND THE INTERNATIONAL SOCIETY *

l i n d a   b.   m i l l e r

I

Although it has become fashionable to assert that the international system is "changing," it is obvious that the direction of change and the elements of change are ambiguous. As the decolonization era draws to a close, it is necessary to consider the salient developments in the relationships of the new states with each other and with the superpowers, as they affect these states' interests. Clearly, the expectations of the new states toward international organizations, as foreign-policy instruments for the satisfaction of demands, are shaped by these two sets of relationships.

The African and Asian territories that gained independence in the years after 1957 had no tradition of international relations with each other or with Latin American states except via the European countries. Not surprisingly, a lamentable lack of preparation for self-rule was frequently revealed after independence (the Congo is but a convenient example), upon the departure of European administrators and the collapse of European institutions. Of course, some countries, notably India

* Excerpts from "The New States and the International Society" by Linda B. Miller, *Protagonists, Power, and the Third World: Essays on the Changing International System, The Annals*, Vol. 386 (November, 1969), pp. 103–110. By permission of the publisher and the author.

and Pakistan, displayed considerable adaptive skill in shaping parts of the European heritage to their political needs. Despite differing colonial experiences or stresses of decolonization, most new states entered an international system already marked by heterogeneity and ideological conflict as weak, poorly integrated units. Understandably, the "developing areas" appeared to offer fertile ground for the extension of American-Russian economic and political rivalries, so long as direct military confrontations could be avoided. While nuclear weapons had rendered traditional interstate wars "unacceptable," they permitted the transfer of conflict to lesser levels of violence. Africa, Asia, Latin America, and the Middle East appeared to be suitable geographical loci for such conflicts; there the stakes seemed to justify the use of a wide range of economic and propaganda techniques and selected uses of national nonnuclear forces.

Evolving Relationships

From the standpoint of the new states, the policy priorities of the superpowers have had both positive and negative effects. The rigidity of Soviet and American diplomacy, expressed in the Dulles and Khrushchev efforts to woo the leaders of the newly independent states, confronted their leaders with tempting but difficult choices. Unfortunately, they had failed to establish viable relationships with each other across continental or regional lines, or, in many cases, to transform *de jure* independence from the European metropoles into a *de facto* status. Therefore, a distinctive note of intragroup tension was introduced into the relationships of the new states with each other, as they sought to respond to the Soviet Union and the United States both as individual states and as a collective "camp." Unwilling to commit themselves to the fortunes of either superpower, yet desirous of gaining advantages from one or both, many of the new states' leaders sought to play off the two in their bilateral relations, or in multilateral settings where their combined strength could be brought to bear. In such circumstances, international institutions assumed an important role in the calculations of the leaders of the new states, who hoped to compensate for their economic and diplomatic weaknesses.

Especially in the year 1957–1960, the apparent "logic" of the international milieu helped to generate high expectations, as the new states first approached the United Nations and the regional organizations. For the Latin American leaders, whose "colonial" experience contrasted with that of their African or Asian counterparts, the United Nations offered a link to other countries whose history of economic underdevelopment and political subordination seemed similar. For the Africans and Asians, membership in the United Nations could legitimize their independence. Moreover, the institutional framework of these organizations, as opposed to such temporary structures as the Bandung or the All-African Peoples Conferences, could be used to dramatize the need for protection from "external threats," especially "neocolonialism." A strident style seemed well suited to express the *leitmotif* of "redistribution"—whether of natural resources, of wealth, or of technological information. Similarly, their demands for racial justice, the protection of human rights, or an end to "discriminatory" legal codes and commercial practices could be couched in flamboyant terms. As long as the international organizations enabled new states to stress the glaring discrepancies between rich and poor, white and nonwhite, "secure" and "insecure," or "new" and "old" states, it appeared that the organizations would serve as vital forums for developing countries threatened by isolation and inexperience and seeking visibility, acceptance, status, and dignity.

Emerging Dissatisfactions

It is therefore necessary to ask why the prevailing moods of frustration and disillusionment which seem to characterize the attitudes of new states toward the international society in general and international organizations in particular have flourished? It can be argued that the expectations of the new states for radical change in international affairs have generated widespread disappointment, because these hopes were excessive and unrealistic. Yet, shifts in political configurations that leaders of the new states have been unable to prevent or to exploit are, perhaps, as important. A number of shifts that have called into question the enthusiasms of the earlier 1960's should be noted. Within the group of new states, complete independence for all African and Asian territories could not be attained before postcolonial tensions arrived to plague their leaders. Additional expectations were stimulated as the first-generation leadership sought to consolidate the shaky gains of independence. These tensions, often expressed in internal conflicts,[1] have generally revealed a lack of national consciousness and an array of loyalties to tribes or entities other than the state.

The plethora of postcolonial internal conflicts placed more complex demands on the political councils of the United Nations and later the Organization for African Unity (OAU)—and to a lesser extent, the more "hegemonic" Organization of American States (OAS)—as these organizations have been expected to condemn "internal" threats in the form of separatist or secessionist movements or to replace the metropoles as sup-

---

[1] See Linda B. Miller, *World Order and Local Disorder: The United Nations and Internal Conflicts* (Princeton, N.J.: Princeton University Press, 1967).

pliers of military assistance in the event of challenges to the central authorities. Because the international organizations have been asked to intervene diplomatically or militarily, and, at the same time, to regulate the interventionary behavior of other actors in internal conflicts, their inadequacies have been clarified. Without review procedures and the physical resources or political support that would make such activities possible, the international organizations have, at worst, reinforced tacit "spheres of influence." With few exceptions, they have, at best, encouraged member-states' self-restraint by adoption of innocuous resolutions. When the international organizations have become committed to particular outcomes in the variety of intrastate or interstate conflicts in the modernizing areas, their capacities to affect events in subsequent controversies have been circumscribed.

Increasing Cleavages

As these conflicts have preoccupied leaders of the new states within and beyond the councils of international organizations, the apparent uniformity of demands placed on the more advanced states has not masked the evolution of splits within the group of new states. In the United Nations, the limits of cooperation between the Latin American states and the Africans and Asians have emerged with greater clarity.[2] In addition, the separate concerns of Asian and African states have become apparent as the Africans have sought to use their numerical superiority in bargaining contexts where voting is pre-eminent—if necessary, against the Asians. A further note of unpredictability has been introduced into these relationships with the elaboration of theories of intervention that may be used to justify attempts to manipulate the internal affairs of other countries. Egypt's rationale for its intervention in Yemen or Algeria's defense of anti-Israel actions exemplify this tendency.[3] The absence of a hierarchy of legitimacy to guide the actions of "third-world" policy-makers vis-à-vis each other stands in striking contrast to the norms often adduced to guide their actions vis-à-vis Rhodesia, South Africa, or Portugal. As a result, the regional organizations identified with the modernizing "subsystems" have fared poorly as instruments of peaceful change (with the possible exception of the OAU's role in helping to settle African border disputes).[4]

[2] For useful examples, see David Kay, "The Politics of Decolonization: The New Nations and the United Nations Political Process," *International Organization* 21 (Autumn 1967), pp. 786–811.
[3] Some interesting differences between African and Arab conceptions of permissible norms of "interference" in other states are assessed in I. William Zartman, "Intervention Among Developing States," *Journal of International Affairs*, vol. 22, no. 2 (1968), pp. 188–197.
[4] See Linda B. Miller, "Regional Organization and the Regulation of Internal Conflict," *World Politics* 19 (July 1967), pp. 582–600.

Fluctuations in the leadership of the new states augment other frustrations. Although the poses of "self-assertion" employed to conceal serious cleavages in domestic polities have by no means disappeared from the international scene with the downfall of Nkrumah and Sukarno, their fate has proved instructive for aspiring leaders who would pursue ephemeral international prestige at the expense of social problems at home. The cost of such neglect now exceeds the routine charges of corruption or bureaucratic bungling.[5] The rash of military coups that toppled numerous African leaders in 1965–1966 thus included among their casualities the grandiose designs for pan-African "unity" that would transcend either the artificial boundaries bequeathed by the colonial powers or the suspicions engendered by rival transnational movements. Intracontinental and interregional competitiveness have become prominent features of subsystemic relations in Africa, Asia, the Middle East, and Latin America in response to the tendencies toward fragmentation in the group of new states.

Shifting Priorities

In recent years, the North-South focus in international organizations has often overshadowed, but has not completely replaced, the East-West confrontation. During this period, the policies of the superpowers toward the developing countries have undergone alterations as their encounters with the vagaries of "third world" politics have multiplied. Although both American and Russian policy-makers appear to have discarded crude and unsatisfying attempts to "buy friends," their more sophisticated approaches have not always proved successful. For the United States, the massive military effort in Vietnam first exacerbated relations with a host of smaller countries, and later resulted in a retrenchment of foreign-aid programs. The Soviet Union, having abandoned attempts to penetrate zones of United States influence with the techniques that precipitated the Cuban missile crisis, has concentrated its greatest efforts, in recent years, in the Middle East. Is it unrealistic to assume that the aftermath of the "Six Day War" found Russian leaders shaken by some of the same disappointments previously experienced by the Americans in Vietnam? A comparable inability to control events or to co-ordinate the actions of "clients" has distinguished both American and Soviet policies in circumstances of maximum commitment to third-world regimes. As the United States and the Soviet Union have sought to reinforce their par-

[5] Some interesting propositions about the functions of corruption in the politics of development are advanced in J. S. Nye, Jr., "Corruption and Political Development: A Cost-Benefit Analysis," *American Political Science Review* 61 (June 1967), pp. 417–427.

tially collaborative relationship, through such mechanisms as the non-proliferation treaty, their limited-adversary relationship in modernizing areas, and elsewhere, has assured the prevalence of denials over gains.[6]

The fluidity of the contemporary international environment militates against stable patterns of relations among the new states or between them and the superpowers. As the gulf between the developed and the developing states continues to widen, neglect, rather than unregulated intervention, is emerging as the most critical problem in the relations of the advanced and developing states. The changes in the international political milieu that divide the early years of independence from the end of the 1960's present new opportunities both for new states and for those who retain a prime interest in "defining the rules of interstate politics."[7] Despite the failure of international organizations to assure rapid economic development on a regional, or other, basis, their performance of a "harmonizing" role is not excluded if the new states express their demands in more temperate tones. A cynical rejection of these institutions, or an unwillingness to appreciate the limitations of divergent institutions in responding to the differing requirements of threats to peace or social modernization, could preclude even this modest role in the 1970's.

II

The quality of debate in the General Assembly and other international bodies lends credence to an incident related to an American political scientist by a United Nations delegate:

A representative of a new country happened to sit beside me, and always asked what the subject was on which the committee was going to vote. I was very helpful, and explained the questions to him, but he always voted opposite from me. And, in fact, he occasionally voted against his own interests and the interests of the Afro-Asian group. Once, in conversation, he asked, "Do you know how I am voting?" I replied that I thought he was voting the opposite way from me. He said no, that he merely looked at Portugal and South Africa to see how they were voting, and voted the opposite way.[8]

Although this deceptively straightforward approach may have served the interests of many new states adequately in the 1960's, it is difficult to foresee its continued usefulness in the more complicated issues that may

[6] A subtle analysis of the reasons for the prevalence of denials over gains in contemporary world politics is offered in Stanley Hoffmann, *Gulliver's Troubles: Or the Setting of American Foreign Policy* (New York: McGraw Hill, for the Council on Foreign Relations, 1968), Part 1.

[7] Ciro Elliot Zoppo, "Nuclear Technology, Multipolarity, and International Stability," *World Politics* 18 (July 1966), p. 589.

[8] Quoted in Robert O. Keohane, "Political Influence in the General Assembly," *International Conciliation*, no. 557 (March 1966), p. 27.

crowd the agendas of both regional and global institutions in the 1970's. Undoubtedly, some new states will continue to frame their demands within the narrow confines of anticolonialism; yet, their influence in the United Nations and in other forums will diminish if they fail to become well informed on other issues or to master the details of the issues that affect their interests most directly.

Indeed, what could be termed "the information gap" has already aroused the concern of observers and participants in United Nations "development" activities:

The forced pace at which the economic sector in the United Nations has been transformed in recent years has left little time for contemplation or analysis in depth of the results achieved. There has been an unprecedented proliferation of meetings, conferences, working parties, and seminars. The stamina of those most directly involved as delegates, experts, and advisers has been tested almost beyond endurance as they rush from conference to conference, from caucus to caucus. The stacks of documentation mount steadily and few persons, if any, are conversant with all that is published. Even major countries, such as the United States, are finding it increasingly difficult to provide the manpower and expertise necessary to keep on top of all the new developments, to formulate policy, and to adequately brief their delegations. Many of the smaller countries are clearly unable to maintain informed positions on the myriad issues with which the United Nations confronts them. This fact in itself encourages rash action, often taken without benefit of formal instructions or informed judgment. It also increases an uncritical reliance by countries on the group to which they belong and look for guidance.[9]

Rising Demands

The tendency toward an uncritical reliance on the group to which the majority of new states belong has been fostered in the United Nations in an era when voting majorities have been regarded as the most effective weapons in the new states' diplomatic arsenal. It is by no means certain that voting majorities will continue to enjoy an exalted status as the chief technique of expressing consensus in international organizations, especially after the entrance of ministates into the United Nations. Therefore, the ability of the new states' representatives to master other aspects of parliamentary diplomacy and to cultivate a favorable image in the eyes of other delegations should become more relevant. The new states may well experience additional difficulties in achieving satisfactory responses to their demands in the 1970's, in part because their capacity to play off Soviet and American policy-makers to advantage has declined.

[9] Walter M. Kotschnig, "The United Nations as an Instrument of Economic and Social Development," *International Organization* 22 (Winter 1968), p. 37.

Equally consequential is a growing resentment on the part of the advanced states at the attempts of new states to use international entities to impose "obligations" on the developed states. The efforts to "legislate" within the councils of international organizations express the new states' desire to link the fields of international peace and security and economic and social development. The new states' rejection of *ad hoc* procedures in both spheres reveals a lack of confidence on the part of many of their leaders in the developed states' willingness to correct inequities.

The accomplishments of the new states in linking the two spheres and in using international organizations as legislative bodies are uneven. Both efforts attest to the obvious fact that the demands of the new states for some visible signs of change are not satisfied by simply keeping issues before the councils of regional or general international organizations. In the international peace and security issues, the sanctionist approach to Rhodesia, after a circuitous policy of United Nations investigation, debate, and resolution, is illustrative.[10] Even in circumstances of policy-agreement, the African states, alone or with other new states, continue to lack sufficient power to "impose" a settlement on Portugal, South Africa, or Rhodesia. The pattern of settlement in previous cases indicates a bilateral framework for eventual solutions rather than a multilateral or regional one. But there are benefits in United Nations or OAU presentations that stress violations of human rights and the compatibility of regional and global concerns. Because the new states' leaders know that the possibilities of mandatory actions in such politically delicate situations are minimal, their advocacy of strong interventionary positions carries with it few responsibilities. Although there may be little reason for expecting consistent Western compliance with sanctions against countries like Rhodesia, Portugal, or South Africa, the process of escalating pressure against such regimes has in itself gained support as a surrogate for more direct forms of revision. Of course, there are very definite limits to the effectiveness of such an approach. It has scant application in conflicts involving the superpowers, for example, Vietnam, and it could, in time, provoke additional frustrations if it appears to yield too few effective measures against regimes that the new states have discredited.

Accelerating Pressures

Increasingly, the new states' impatience with an unfavorable status quo finds its most powerful expression in the economic and social

---

[10] See J. Leo Cefkin, "The Rhodesian Question at the United Nations," *International Organization* 22 (Summer 1968), pp. 649–669. See also Kay, "The Politics of Decolonization," pp. 800–811.

sphere. Inasmuch as most international organizations devoted to these questions have their own "development strategies," [11] they have become vital targets for the new states, who resent both proportional voting dominated by the interests of developed states and mechanisms that merely stress short-term assistance for temporary balance-of-payments problems. Because the developing countries want more goods and more aid, with fewer conditions and less control,[12] the International Monetary Fund (IMF) and similar institutions are less satisfactory to them than the United Nations Conference on Trade and Development (UNCTAD), whose short history is replete with examples of the new states' eagerness to "legislate," to give binding force to recommendations deemed in their interest. Many new states' leaders insist that the Final Act of UNCTAD [13] contains principles that commit the developed countries to certain courses of action on the international plane, despite the fact that these same developed states had previously opposed and voted against them in the first United Nations Conference on Trade and Development—and in later meetings of the General Assembly and of the Economic and Social Council of the United Nations (ECOSOC).[14]

As Walter Kotschnig observes:

The wording of resolutions is fought over as if a new constitution were being written. . . . The "majority" seems to care little that such "obligations" often relate to matters within the domestic jurisdiction of all Members.[15]

Not only could this attitude provoke constitutional crises, but it encourages the disaffection of the developed states who would prefer to use existing organizations before embarking on new endeavors or "special funds" with provisions for "taxing" them. The UNCTAD "takeover pattern," [16] so consequential in establishing group lines that cut across differences among developing countries, and in encouraging an enlargement of General Assembly and ECOSOC bodies, as well as the composition of ECOSOC itself, has given the developing countries automatic

[11] Stephen D. Krasner, "The International Monetary Fund and the Third World," *International Organization* 21 (Summer 1968), p. 670.
[12] *Ibid.*, pp. 670–688.
[13] U.N., *Proceedings of the United Nations Conference on Trade and Development, Geneva, 23 March–16 June 1964*, Vol. I: *Final Act and Report*, United Nations Publication Sales No: 64.II.-B.II, UN Document E/CONF. 46/141, Vol. I (New York: United Nations, 1964).
[14] Kotschnig, "The United Nations as an Instrument of Economic . . . ," p. 30.
[15] *Ibid.*, p. 29. Nevertheless, it would be unfair to suggest that leaders of the new states are not aware of difficulties in the planning and administration of United Nations and other developmental activities, difficulties often lumped together under the rubric of "co-ordination." In fact, as Kotschnig notes, some leaders of the new states have recommended a complete overhaul of existing institutional structures and an avoidance of repetitive programs with the inevitable problems of underfunding. Yet, this awareness need not necessarily lead to a less legislative approach to existing developmental organizations on the part of the new states.
[16] *Ibid.*, p. 31.

majorities and extensive representation in numerous secretariats. Although it is not clear that UNCTAD, with its legislative thrust, will dominate the development activities of the entire United Nations system in the 1970's, an important gain for the new states will be registered if it should. But the success of legislative techniques must be measured by the compliance of other states with specific resolutions, not only by the tactical behavior of various groups in the bargaining processes of international organizations. Judgment should be reserved until an assessment can be rendered of compliance with UNCTAD's principles over a larger span of time.

Although one of the attributes traditionally ascribed to a sovereign state is the right to determine its own affairs free from intervention by other states, the increasing interaction and interdependence of states make this principle more and more difficult to define and apply in practice. In addition, the principle itself is being challenged by some leaders as they attempt to cope with the contemporary problems of nation-building. In the essay below, I. William Zartman examines the modifications of the traditional principle of non-intervention that has been taking place in the African and Arab regions.

40.   INTERVENTION AMONG DEVELOPING
STATES *

i. william zartman

Observers often have a tendency to confirm normative judgments with empirical observations. This is as true for "intervention" as for other political phenomena. It is often maintained, for example, that a state's interference in another's affairs is not only wrong but unnatural or aber-

* Copyright by the Board of Editors of the *Journal of International Affairs*, reprinted from Volume XXII, Number 2, pages 188–197, 1968. Permission to reprint is acknowledged to the Journal and to the author.

rant. Yet these are two very different judgments that should be kept apart. The distinction between the normative and the empirical must be made in any study of intervention, and an examination of intervention among developing states may give some indication of the manner in which the distinction can be made. Here it will be argued that interventions among developing states are normal, even typical, although *not* inevitable. It will also be argued that they can be considered wrong or not, depending on goal assumptions that have nothing to do with normality.

REGIONAL AND IDEOLOGICAL JUSTIFICATIONS FOR INTERVENTION

"Intervention" implies that a sovereign unit has been violated.[1] However, there are many ways in which the inviolability of the sovereign state can be challenged. It has often been noted, for example, that crises of identity and ideology and dilemmas of independence and unity are endemic to developing states, and that such crises and dilemmas are sufficient to explain the widespread incidence of guerrilla warfare, terrorism, subversion, conspiracy, and propaganda in developing areas such as Africa and the Middle East.[2] "In an era of informal penetration," Andrew Scott has noted, "the attack on the legitimacy of the government in the target country frequently denies the very principle of legitimacy on which the government is based or reinterprets it in a significantly different way. . . . Treason is thus presented as a higher loyalty."[3]

If the concept, "We are all Africans," or the notion of an Arab nation has any meaning, it is that African and Arab politics are the affairs of Africans and Arabs, and are only broken down into component state politics for procedural reasons. "We place the Arabs' high interest before us and cooperate with all who believe in this interest," said ex-King

[1] Relevant general background on penetrability is found in John H. Herz, *International Politics in the Atomic Age* (New York: Columbia U.P., 1959) and "The Rise and Demise of the Territorial State," reprinted from *World Politics* in James N. Rosenau, ed., *International Politics and Foreign Policy* (New York: Free Press, 1961), pp. 80–86; and Rosenau, "Pre-Theories and Theories of Foreign Policy," in R. Barry Farrell, ed., *Approaches to Comparative and International Politics* (Evanston: Northwestern U.P., 1966), pp. 27–92.

[2] These categories are taken from the discussion of intervention in I. William Zartman, *International Relations in the New Africa* (Englewood Cliffs: Prentice-Hall, 1966), p. 88. Although such categories can be helpful, there is no way of making them rigorous or exclusive. By the same token, although escalation is a useful concept in connection with these categories, there is no evidence of any automatic process since the choice of the next step, while taken within a particular context, is a free policy choice. On escalation and related policy choices in Africa, see I. William Zartman, "The Foreign and Military Politics of Boundary Problems," in Carl G. Widstrand, ed., *Boundary Problems in Africa* (Uppsala: The Scandinavian Institute of African Studies, pending).

[3] Andrew M. Scott, *The Revolution in State-Craft* (New York: Random House, 1956), pp. 169–170.

INTERNATIONAL RELATIONS

Saud in early 1967 on his arrival in Cairo.[4] In this way, an Arab who happens to be born in Syria, or an African born in Guinea, can take part in Jordanian or Camerounian politics with no more presumption of illegitimacy than that assumed by Robert Kennedy in running for the Senate in New York, or by Michel Debré in running for the National Assembly from Réunion. There is likely to be some opposition criticism of carpet-bagging, but not enough feeling of illegitimate interference in sovereign state politics to cause rejection.

A hierarchy of symbols and loyalties may be assembled about an extended national or racial entity in order to legitimize component states when they follow policies, proclaim attitudes, and allocate values consistent with the larger unit. "There are real Africans and there are those who are not," said Ahmed Ben Bella in March 1965 about the Congo. "Sooner or later the others will come, for there is no other way." [5] If there is a true African or true Arab way of thinking or acting, and it is endowed with higher legitimacy, then that way is more important than the naturalization papers of the agent.[6]

As Ben Bella's quotation indicates, it is not only identification with a region, race, or extended nation that authorizes intervention, but also the justification of ideological universalism or inevitability. One can fight or work for a global cause, as do missionaries and members of Lincoln Brigades, but an ideological cause can also be limited to a region, race, or extended nation, such as that which serves as focus for pan-Africans and pan-Arabs. Leaders such as Ahmed Shuqairy, Antun Saadeh, Michel Aflaq, Abdulaye Diallo, Doudou Gueye, and Peter Koinange, were not merely immigrants attracted into the politics of another subdivision of the same extended nation; rather, operating from a national base and inspired by a dual motivation of region and revolution, they worked to influence the politics of surrounding states (including their native states). Revolutionary or ideological universalism is important as an additional justification for interference because it authorizes far more intense types of intervention than mere regional identification. A man who believes himself compelled to promote or defend some higher value without which life is not worth living feels justified in using violent, rather than merely political means of intervention.

[4]   Middle East News Agency, 1 January 1967.
[5]   Radio Paris, 15 March 1965.
[6]   In the Middle East the "anti-Arabist" term, shu'ubiya, carries an older and stronger negative connotation than, for example, "nationalism," as used by Europeanists. See Hisham Sharabi, Nationalism and Revolution in the Arab World (New York: Van Nostrand, 1966), pp. 96, 100; and George H. Gardner and Sami A. Hanna, "The Ethnic Factor in International Relations: A Study of Arab Resistance to 'Internationalization' as seen in the "Urubah-Shu'ubiy yah Controversy," paper presented to the Sixth World Congress of Sociology, Evian, September 1966.

Such nonconventional moral justification has been frequently noted—and its validity debated—in regard to individual action, but it becomes more complex when state actions are involved. An individual can shift his loyalty to a broader geographic context without acting contradictorily, but when a state confuses its identity with that of the extended nation to which it belongs, the opposition can easily cry "imperialism" or "domination." Since unequal power relations are a reality in both individual and collective life, what matters is not whether imperialism or domination is in fact "good" or "bad," but that its justification is vulnerable when expressed only in geopolitical terms. Thus, when Nasser's regime intervened in neighboring states' affairs the action was attacked as "Egyptian domination" or "Ghanaian subversion," even though it was defended as Arab or African "solidarity" and "unity."

Thus, the need to explain state intervention in terms stronger than the mere confusion of geographic identities leads to the use of ideological justifications. The state becomes a base for a broader political movement of extended national dimensions; the ideological movement takes over territorial units of the extended nation and comes to the aid of its believers in other such units for the supposed good of the believers, units, and the entire expanded nation.[7] Mohammed Hasanayn Haykal has explained that "Cairo is . . . the natural and logical place for any meeting of Arab revolutionary forces [because] 1. Cairo is the home of the most advanced revolutionary experience. . . . 2. . . . the most capable Arab country serving its own principles outside its borders. . . . 3. Consequently Cairo is willingly or unwillingly a party in the political and social struggle inside every Arab country."[8] Ideo-political legitimization is thus added to geopolitical legitimization; both "Egyptian" and "domination" are supposedly swept away under the appeal of "Arab revolution," just as "Ghanaian subversion" becomes unrecognizable in the context of "African socialism."

As long as revolutionaries feel justified in banding together across state lines their opponents can justify similar actions as defensive counter-intervention. Such counterjustification is inherent in the process of intervention: active revolutionaries as well as beleaguered conservatives claim that they are merely responding in kind. The revolutionaries justify their action as a continuing answer to the past domination of colonialism or the reassertion of imperialism. Since the revolutionary or regionalist intervener accepts only one attitude as legitimate for the movement or for the extended nation, he cannot admit that the opposing

---

[7] For a detailed discussion of African unity, which appears to involve a confusion between a social movement and a state role couched in revolutionary terms, see Immanuel Wallerstein, *Africa: The Politics of Unity* (New York: Random House, 1967).
[8] *Al-Ahram*, 19 August 1966.

attitude is also a legitimate expression of indigenous needs and interests. It must be, he will argue, the result of foreign influence, i.e. of prior but extraregional intervention.

The defensive justification of intervention is further reinforced by the concepts of ideological inevitability and regional popularity; if the revolution is inevitable and the extended nation is in the hearts of the people, then defeats and delays are *prima facie* evidence for a powerful outside hand that stays the natural course of history. If foreign intervention has already taken place, how can the response in kind be unjustified?

STATE AND REVOLUTION

The dual nature of "state and revolution" is a frequent phenomenon in the developing world. It is a natural outgrowth of the colonial period in Africa, where the organizational unit of interest and identification—the party—antedated the territorial and popular units—the country and the nation. The party set out to capture a country and create a nation, but it did not derive from the antecedents of country and nation and was—or many of its members were—often quite flexible in their attachment to any territorial or popular base. Furthermore, the party's job was to destroy a fixed governmental order—colonial rule—and the organizational unit it sought to supplant was itself international in nature.

All of these characteristics easily led successful nationalists to a confusion of roles. The successful leaders were in charge of the governmental machinery of a new state, but they were also part of an international political movement and were themselves a cause of some neighbor's independence. It was natural to consider the new state a geographic base for the spread of an ideology, and what was suddenly called "intervention" was viewed as only a continuation of the same solidarity as before, often with the same allies. The fact that some other newly independent states in Africa seemed less clearly independent than the revolutionary base was double justification for this revolutionary role: current solidarity was merely part of the same struggle as before, and any intervention that occurred came from the neocolonialists and imperialists outside the continent.

Viewing intervention as merely a continuation of the struggle for independence also helps explain its decline in Africa. For when the generation of militant nationalists passes away, and new leaders whose past experience does not hinder them from perceiving a new situation have come to power, the continuity is interrupted.[9] The independence movement had its effect (at least throughout most of the continent) and has moved on: no wave of history washes the same shores over and over

[9] This sort of conclusion could be fruitfully tested by opinion surveys. Victor Le-Vine's excellent *Political Leadership in Africa* (Stanford: The Hoover Institution, 1967) gives tangential results on this particular question.

again. Furthermore, the relative failure of intervention as a means of changing regimes, and the inability of interventionist regimes to maintain themselves in power, lead the organizational unit to settle down in its territorial base and cultivate its own popular garden—in other words, to turn to state and nation-building.

The same terms can be used to account for the dual nature of "state and revolution" in the Arab world, although the emphasis is different. Here the extended nation existed as the unit of interest and identification before it achieved a fixed and sovereign territorial form or was organized through a party or government. The territorial divisions of colonial rulers, maintained in the form of independent states, were not able totally to restructure popular loyalties. Since loyalties remained divided, rivalries within the extended nation and among its states were quickly translated into "state-nationalist" vs. "extended-nationalist" terms by competing parties and governments.[10] With the addition of ideological differences, the intensity of the earlier competition forced the new debate to align on the ideo-political dimension. Thus, the reality of the Arab nation (even though it also contains lesser component nations), with all the implications of legitimization of actions and division of loyalties that reality conveys, makes any Arab state less than sovereign, and any Arab party or government forced either to intervene in its neighbors' affairs or to defend itself against its neighbors' intervention.

The different bases of intervention in Africa and the Arab world suggests that the phenomenon of intervention will continue for a longer time among the Arab states than among the African. Arab interference in other Arab states' affairs has been quite successful, if effectiveness in changing others' regimes and permanence of the intervening regimes are used as yardsticks. Intervention pays in the Middle East; it does not in Africa. Part of the success of the Arab states' intervention is doubtless due to the fact that it rests on greater legitimizing reality. There is an Arab nation, but there is no African (or even West African or East African) nation.[11] The *geo-political* referent can be used to anchor the *ideo-political* justification. For these reasons alone, intervention is likely to continue in the Arab world.

There are some dilemmas of "state and revolution" that render dynamic this ambiguous, dual nature.[12] The contradictions are well expressed by Haykal:

---

[10] Doudou Thiam, *The Foreign Policy of African States* (New York: Praeger, 1965), speaks of "micro-" and "macro-nationalism," pp. 5–21.
[11] This point appears to be the basic weakness of the theme of Ali Mazrui, *Towards a Pax Africana* (Chicago: Chicago U.P., 1967). Unable to speak of a single African nation, Mazrui is caught between proposing and analyzing the phenomenon in other terms, such as "racial sovereignty" and "continental jurisdiction," see esp. pp. 38–40, 112–24.
[12] It also offers increased options for action in foreign policy; see Scott, *op. cit.*, pp. 162, 168.

As a state, Egypt deals with all Arab governments, whatever their forms or systems. . . . As a revolution, Egypt should only deal with people. This does not imply interference on our part in the affairs of others, since the fundamental premise of our struggle is that the Arab people are a single nation. If Egypt as a state recognizes frontiers in her dealings with governments, Egypt as a revolution should never hesitate or halt at frontiers, but should carry her message across to them. . . . We have no right to separate ourselves from the struggle of other citizens of our nation. . . . We should also be prepared for a break in official relations with any Arab country ruled by reaction if it should seek to pressure us into suspending our legitimate appeal for freedom, socialism, and the unity of all people of the Arab nation.[13]

A more stable relationship among states could be achieved if all focused their identities, turned their ideologies inward, and gave up intervention. Or stability could be attained if the forces of revolution fulfilled their promises, conquered, reformed, united the extended nation, and eliminated foreign intervention by making all affairs internal.

Yet in the developing world the coincidence of interest and identity on either of these two planes (revolution and state) has not been fully attained. Instead, the revolutionary state with a regionalist calling continues to act in its dual capacity, more or less successfully sorting out the demands of its national interests on one hand and its pan-regional interests on the other. This dilemma was Nkrumah's undoing, for he depleted his state base without effectively spreading the revolution to neighboring regimes; for his pains, he won himself external enemies and internal bankruptcy.[14] Nasser has been much more successful; although he too has not been willing or able to incorporate and hold converted regimes, he has always been able to retreat to a solid domestic base when rebuffed abroad, and after a period of domestic concentration, he has always been invited to extend his aid to belligerent allies in other Arab states. Neither of these two is alone of course; they are merely examples. If Saudi Arabia and Ivory Coast lack the revolutionary legitimization, they can justify their interventions as defensive state-action.

ANTI-INTERVENTIONIST NORMS

States on the defensive, however, can also be expected to seize upon this role instability and try to force interventionist regimes to act only as states and not as revolutions. The most effective way of doing this is by turning the coin of legitimization against the very intervention it was

[13] *Al-Ahram,* 29 December 1962, as quoted by Malcolm Kerr, *The Arab Cold War* (New York: Oxford U.P., 2nd ed., 1967). See also the U.A.R. National Charter of July 1962, quoted in part by Sharabi, *op. cit.,* esp. pp. 134–35.
[14] For a unique study of the process, see W. Scott Thompson, *The Foreign Policy of Ghana* (Princeton: Princeton U.P., pending).

invoked to justify, or, in other words, to establish anti-interventionist norms. African states have followed a concerted campaign in this direction. Moderate states came together in the Brazzaville and then the Monrovia Group in 1961 in order to meet the threat of intervention from radical states against Mauritania and Congo, but also against Niger, Ivory Coast, Senegal, Cameroun, etc. Nnamdi Azikiwe told the Lagos Conference in 1962:

There is one basic difference of an ideological nature between the two groups, which should attract the serious attention of all who sincerely advocate African unity. It is the conspicuous absence of specific declarations on the part of the Casablanca states of their inflexible belief in the fundamental principles enunciated at Monrovia regarding the inalienable right of African states, as presently constituted, to legal equality, irrespective of their area and population; the right of African states to self-determination; the right of African states to safety from interference in their internal affairs through subversive activities engineered by supposed friendly states; the right of African states to be secure in the inviolability of their territories from external aggression.[15]

The breakdown of the Casablanca Group on the eve of the all-African summit at Addis Ababa in 1963 allowed the Brazzaville-Monrovia theses to dominate the new OAU (Organization of African Unity), and the assassination of Olympio at the beginning of the year—the result, many wrongly suspected, of a Ghanaian plot—was a timely example of the need for anti-interventionist norms. When Ghana did not cease supporting Freedom Fighters despite these all-African injunctions to do so, the Entente states and the Brazzaville Group, threatened by Ghanaian intervention, forced an end to Ghana's interventionist policies as a condition for holding the 1965 OAU heads of state meeting in Accra. Less than six months later Nkrumah's regime fell from within. The end of Ghanaian intervention did not mean the disappearance of all intervention from the African scene, for Ghana was by no means the only practitioner. It was only the most flamboyant; the list of other states guilty of intervention varies according to the number of practices labeled intervention. The OAU norms have been reinforced by numerous bilateral pledges and agreements since 1963, with the result that normative restraints have indeed been created.[16]

The Arab League has been less effective as a forum for such norms.

---

[15] Nnamdi Azikiwe, "Let Us Build a New Africa," Nigerian Consulate General Press Release, 3/62, p. 6, to the Lagos Conference of January 1962; also quoted in Claude S. Phillips Jr., *The Development of Nigerian Foreign Policy* (Chicago: Northwestern U.P., 1964) p. 93.

[16] A further dilemma is present for Africa: there, the other side of the intervention coin—African solutions for African problems—is strongly stressed, for the same reasons as can be used to justify intervention. Where collective security is championed but intervention is frowned on, ambiguity is high and action low, as the OAU role in the Nigerian crisis shows.

Jordan, walking out of the League Council sessions of March 1967 under attack from Shuqairy, called it a "framework without a concept." [17] No anti-interventionist resolutions have been passed, beyond Article 8 of the League Charter, nor are any likely to be adopted as long as Egypt (UAR) maintains a dominant position in the organization and in the region. The practice of intervention among Arab states may rise and fall over time and draw individual or coordinated criticisms from its targets, and regimes may foreswear it in times of "unity of ranks" (when the external enemy threatens). But when the enemy is internal to the Arab nation and it is time for "unity of purpose"—a moment that is subjectively, not objectively defined—intervention is a predictably available policy.

CONCLUSIONS

In the preceding review of attitudes in the Arab and African worlds an attempt has been made to explain intraregional intervention as an inherent adjunct of nation-building, regionalism, and revolution. African and Arab regional systems are setting up and continually re-evaluating their norms of interaction, much as Europe did during the period of dynastic relations and the Western Hemisphere has done through its attention to "inter-American law." [18] Such norms may be established implicitly in favor of or explicitly against intervention, depending on the values that dominate the region and the effect of experiences in the recent past.

The argument can be summarized as a theorem: the more that ideopolitical identification is attached to geopolitical symbols, the greater the justification for—hence the occurrence of—intervention. Or, from another point of view: The more the sole or predominate legitimacy of the nation-state is challenged or subordinated by other legitimizing symbols, the greater the justification for—and hence the occurrence of—intervention.

Western observers may deplore the violation of units that are sovereign and inviolable by Western standards.[19] They may also prefer these

---

[17]   Amman radio, 15 March 1967.
[18]   See C. Neale Ronning, *Law and Politics in Inter-American Diplomacy* (New York: Wiley, 1963), esp. pp. 63–84. Castroism has not only introduced a new practice, but also attempted to shake the norms. See also, for European systems, "direction" or "ethos" as discussed by Richard Rosecrance, *Action and Reaction in World Politics* (Boston: Little, Brown, 1963). For a discussion of norms on a broader level, see Peit-Hein Houben, "Principles of International Law Concerning Friendly Relations and Cooperation Among States," *American Journal of International Law,* Vol. DXI, 3:703–36, esp. 717–18 (July 1967).
[19]   "Even today the sense of Arab unity cuts across boundaries. During 1958 and when every one of the five Arab states we are discussing was involved in political disputes with at least one other, none questioned the 'right' of any Arab government to appeal across frontiers to the people presumably loyal to any other. Whatever

standards of inviolability for sentimental or very practical reasons, such as the inherent instability of split allegiances in a system. But they must take into account the fact that symbol and value hierarchies may be very different in other systems in the process of formation, and that the very act of imposing Western values can be termed "intervention." (Indeed, one of the reasons for deploring endemic intraregional intervention is that extraregional precedents—colonialism and imperialism—are inevitably cited, and extraregional allies frequently sought, thereby escalating the intervention process.) Western observers should also remember that if Western legal standards have pretensions of absolutism, the theorems of intervention represent a continuum and suggest that some tendency to justify intervention exists in any interstate system of values. Peter Calvocoressi has perceptively noted, "It is not at all clear whether the United States is a territorial state on the old European pattern or a political organ dedicated like the U.S.S.R. to an idea . . . [T]he heirs of the American revolution like to see themselves as the continuing protagonists of a revolution born of the Enlightenment, a movement to be contrasted with the later and less estimable revolution of which the Russians are the champions. Hence a picture of the West as a revolutionary force of a different kind, a polity in motion and dispensing living ideas." [20]

harsh words were exchanged between Iraq and Egypt, for example, neither one questioned the 'right' of the other to compete for the loyalty of Syria even after it had joined Egypt in the United Arab Republic. It was only the Western Powers, the Soviet Union, and the United Nations which spoke in these terms," Monroe Berger, *The Arab World Today* (New York: Doubleday, 1962), p. 267.

[20] Peter Calvocoressi, *World Order and the New States* (New York: Praeger, 1962), pp. 107–08. See, for further discussion, Vernon Aspaturian, "Revolutionary Change and the Strategy of the Status Quo," in Lawrence Martin, ed., *Neutralism and Nonalignment* (New York: Praeger, 1962), pp. 165–95.

During the past decade or so, a rather serious malaise has infected a number of international and regional organizations. The hopes that these prestigious organizations could deal effectively with the complex problems of the world have declined, and a transitional period seems to have set in while leaders attempt to find new types of organizations to cope with the old and new problems of a changing world. In the following selection, Jerome Slater discusses the causes for the decline of the Organization of American States and the grounds for its possible resurgence or supplementation by other regional organizations.

41.   THE DECLINE OF THE OAS * †

j e r o m e   s l a t e r

It seems clear that the Organization of American States (oas) has entered a period of disarray and political decline. The signs are everywhere present: the bitterness in Latin America over the unilateral United
States intervention in the Dominican Republic and the failure of the oas
to constrain effectively Washington's actions there, the refusal of the
organization to adopt internal structural reforms long considered desirable, and the unwillingness of the majority of the member states to
allow an inter-American role in problems of political change in Latin
America.

In retrospect, curiously enough, the period of the greatest political
vitality for the inter-American system seems to have been the 1940s and
1950s. Curiously, because during this period the organization was rent
with most of the same conflicts that exist in heightened form today, and
oas participants and observers alike hardly thought they were living
through a golden era of inter-American co-operation. Yet, despite the
decline of the goodwill that had characterized the days of the Good
Neighbor policy, despite the bitter disappointment at the failure of the
United States to provide substantial economic assistance to Latin America, and despite the heavy-handed diplomacy of John Foster Dulles,
the organization somehow succeeded in playing a significant role in the
management and control of interstate political conflict in the hemisphere.[1] It succeeded in settling or at least damping down a number
of small-scale, but potentially explosive conflicts in the Central American
and Caribbean area. Backed by the strong support of the United States,
with all that such support implied in the way of heavy political, economic, and even military pressures, the organization typically was able to

---

*   From "The Decline of the OAS" by Jerome Slater, *International Journal*, Vol.
XXIV, No. 3 (Summer, 1969), pp. 497–506. By permission of the publisher and the
author.

†   Associate Professor of Political Science, State University of New York at Buffalo;
author of *The OAS and United States Foreign Policy* (1967) and *Intervention and
Negotiation: The United States and the Dominican Revolution* (1970).

1   For a detailed discussion of these activities, see especially my monograph *A Re-
valuation of Collective Security*, Mershon Center for Education in National Security
Pamphlet No. 1 (Cleveland, 1965) and my book, *The OAS and United States
Foreign Policy* (Cleveland, 1967).

interpose itself in conflicts in a variety of ways—gathering facts by on-the-spot investigations, separating belligerents through the establishment of OAS patrols, facilitating consultation between contestants or directly mediating disputes, and sometimes even spelling out and imposing settlements.

Despite all the political differences within the hemisphere, then, a number of factors had converged to make it possible for the OAS to act. For one thing, the "western hemisphere idea"—the notion that the hemispheric states shared a common history, philosophy, and destiny that distinguished them from the rest of the world—had not yet lost all its force as an integrative mechanism. In operation, the idea provided the rationale for the attempted insulation of the hemisphere from European political influences. During the 1930s and early 1940s, with the development of the Nazi threat to Western civilization, this traditional hemispheric goal had taken on added meaning. As a result, during World War II there was a considerable degree of ad hoc inter-American political and military collaboration, and in the immediate postwar years there was nearly unanimous agreement on the need to create much more effective and institutionalized mechanisms.

The postwar consensus was also a reflection of two new factors: changes in United States policy and the development of the cold war. In the past, Latin American distrust of the United States had precluded the creation of an effective hemispheric organization with strong political functions, for it was feared that such an organization would serve only to institutionalize and legitimate United States domination of the hemisphere. Roosevelt's Good Neighbor policy, however, resting as it did on strict non-intervention in Latin American internal affairs, had so quieted these fears that they were now outweighed, particularly among the many conservative and oligarchical Latin American governments, by the spectre of a worldwide communist challenge. Besides, it was hoped that the formal adherence of the United States to a permanent inter-American system might increase the constraints on Washington and make more unlikely a return to the interventionist policies of the early twentieth century. The outbreak of the postwar crisis in Europe settled all remaining doubts and provided the final impetus to the drive for greater inter-American co-operation that culminated in the signing of the Rio Treaty in 1947 and the OAS Charter in 1948.

Later, even after Latin American fears of the USSR began to fade and disenchantment with the United States again set in, common interests remained. With the revolutionary and populist currents that were to erupt in Latin America in the 1960s still mostly below the surface or successfully repressed, most of the hemispheric governments—certainly including that of the United States—wanted little more from the inter-American system than the preservation of peace and the maintenance of the political status quo. And that the organization was able to do fairly well. Most of the conflicts that broke out among the Caribbean states in the late 1940s and again in the late 1950s stemmed from attempts of exile groups, based in and supported by friendly countries, to overturn existing governments in their homelands. Thus, the effect of organizational action was not only to dampen and contain interstate conflict but also to insulate the Caribbean dictatorships from pressures for change.

By the 1960s, however, this limited convergence of interests had largely broken down. With fear of a dangerous common enemy no longer providing external pressure for co-operation, the impact of the western hemisphere idea on operational policy had markedly diminished. Moreover, as the United States increasingly sought to use the OAS as an anticommunist alliance to mobilize the hemispheric states on behalf of its cold war policies, the value of the organization to the Latin Americans sharply declined—one of the primary functions of the system in Latin American eyes was to insulate the hemisphere from rather than involve it in world conflict. Similarly, the emergence of anticommunism as the overriding concern of American hemispheric policy undermined the ability of the inter-American system to constrain American unilateralism. Beginning with the Guatemalan crisis in 1954, continuing through the Bay of Pigs affair, and culminating in the Dominican intervention, the United States made it clear that it considered the exigencies of the cold war, as defined exclusively by itself, to override its multilateral commitments, no matter how explicit and solemnly formalized. Thus, Latin American concern with American domination of the hemisphere once again became paramount.

Finally, rising Latin American ideological conflict and nationalism have further weakened the bonds of the inter-American system. Ideological conflict has undercut the peacekeeping system, for Cuban dedication to the spread of revolution and, conversely, the determination of the status quo or counter-revolutionary states to prevent radical change have overriden commitments to the norms of non-intervention and the maintenance of international peace. Nationalism, at least in its current emotional and exaggerated state, has dealt yet another blow to international co-operation, which of necessity involves a certain subordination of sovereignty to the collective will. Moreover, in the inter-American setting nationalism is particularly devastating to multilateralism, for it usually takes the form of anti-Americanism, and the instrument for collaboration is frequently seen as a mere extension of Washington's will.

Let us turn now to more specific evidence of fragmentation and debilitation in the inter-American system.

There has apparently been a sharp increase in the disenchantment of Latin America with the oas as a result of the failure of the organization to prevent, or even to condemn verbally, the United States intervention in the Dominican Republic. The reputation of the organization throughout the hemisphere seems to be at an all-time low.[2] Another recent manifestation of the oas decline was the refusal of the organization, in three hemispheric conferences in 1965–7, to implement a number of structural reforms widely considered to be both necessary and politically realistic. The political capabilities and defined scope of action of the oas have always been quite limited, reflecting the unwillingness of the Latin American states to dilute their "sovereignty" any more than is absolutely essential, the general distrust of the United States, and the fear of dictatorial and/or conservative régimes of a strong organization that might be capable of applying pressures for domestic change. None the less, before the Dominican crisis there seemed to be considerable agreement throughout the hemisphere on the desirability of revising and strengthening the organization in several important ways.

First, there was strong support for giving the oas Council a greater role in the peaceful settlement of hemispheric disputes that had not yet broken out into armed hostilities but which had that potential if not de-fused by international action. Under its existing statutes, the council could deal with political questions only through the mechanism of the Rio Treaty. Invoking that treaty was considered to be a very serious matter, however, for it implied that an act of "aggression" had taken place and suggested the possibility that sanctions would be imposed on the disturber of the peace. Given this interpretation, Rio Treaty action over minor territorial or jurisdictional disputes was usually politically impossible. To fill this gap in organizational political authority and to provide a more flexible mechanism for quiet mediation, the proposed changes authorized the council to suggest methods for the solution of any hemispheric political problem at the request of any member state.

Secondly, there was an apparent convergence of views on the desirability of authorizing the secretary-general to play a role in peaceful settlement procedures. Unlike the United Nations secretary-general, the oas office had not developed an important political capacity, and there was general agreement that the organization should at least partially remedy this situation. The new roles envisaged were quite modest: the secretary would be authorized to bring to the attention of the council any matter that in his view might threaten the peace of the hemisphere, and he could help mediate such disputes when specifically authorized to do so by the council.

Other more controversial reforms were in the air, although no con-

[2] This theme is developed in my article "The Limits of Legitimization in International Organizations: The OAS and the Dominican Crisis," *International Organization*, XXXIII (winter 1969), 48–72.

sensus for them had been attained. Proposals by Ecuador and Bolivia (which had unsatisfied territorial claims against, respectively, Peru and Chile) would in effect have made the council into a compulsory arbitration board, authorizing it not merely to mediate conflicts but to dictate the terms of settlement by threatening to apply sanctions against recalcitrant states. Proposals by Costa Rica and Venezuela would require mandatory diplomatic and economic sanctions (including exclusion from the inter-American system, collective non-recognition, and the denial of economic assistance) against régimes coming into power as a result of coups d'état against democratically elected governments. Finally, some states, led by the United States, were calling for the creation of a permanent inter-American peace force, to serve as the military arm of the organization in future collective actions.

Whatever consensus had existed for even the most modest of these proposals abruptly disappeared in the wake of the American intervention in the Dominican revolution. Suddenly, the overriding concern of most Latin American states became the traditional one of *minimizing* the political role of the OAS, not expanding it. In the ensuing three charter-reform conferences—at Rio de Janeiro in the autumn of 1965, Panama in the spring of 1966, and Buenos Aires in early 1967—the position of the majority progressively hardened. It is an open question whether the council was actually strengthened more than it was weakened. On the one hand, its peaceful settlement role was modestly expanded, for it was given the authority to play a conciliatory role in non-violent hemispheric disputes so long as *all* the contending parties agreed.[3] While this meant, of course, that a state standing to lose by international action could veto a council role, the expansion of the council's formal jurisdiction represented a step forward from the existing situation. (Although the rejection of more far-reaching proposals was in part a reflection of the hostility of states satisfied with their existing borders to the possible reopening of old disputes, it was also clearly a function of the larger reaction against adding major new powers to an organization that rarely seemed to differ with Washington.)

On the other hand, in some ways the role of the council was diminished. The most important of these is a new provision that the foreign ministers must meet annually instead of in emergency situations only. Thus, in the future many even fairly routine matters that until now have been handled by the council will probably be dealt with at higher levels. The change in procedures reflected the growing suspicion that council delegates, many of whom double as ambassadors to the United States, are

---

[3] The Ecuadoran proposal authorizing a council role at the request of *any* of the parties was defeated by a vote of six in favour, nine opposed, and five abstaining. (Document 113, Minutes of the 15th Plenary Session, Panama Conference on Amendments to the Charter, 1966).

more likely to defer to Washington's views than are the foreign ministers.

The strong opposition to any expanded political role for the organization was also reflected in the fate of the other proposed revisions. Hostility to the United States plan for a permanent inter-American military force was so great that it was dropped before the conferences even began. The much more modest suggestions for an increase in the authority of the secretary-general also had to be dropped; indeed the only action taken in this area was a *reduction* in the secretary's term from ten to five years. In an even more significant cutback, the Panama conference terminated the temporary authority granted to the Peace Committee in 1959 [4] that later had helped lay the basis for the OAS's post-Trujillo role in the Dominican Republic; [5] just for good measure it was also specified that no future amendment to the statutes of the Peace Committee could restore that authority. Finally, the Costa Rican proposal for sanctions against *golpistas* was whittled down to a meaningless provision for hemispheric "consultation" after the overthrow of elected governments. (Since then, hemispheric consultations after the Brazilian and Peruvian military power seizures have led to no action whatever.)

The decline of the OAS as an important mechanism for the resolution of hemispheric conflicts has been confirmed by the organization's inability to affect, or even deal with, the several South American border disputes (Argentina-Chile, Ecuador-Peru, Bolivia-Chile) that have recently heated up, occasionally even to the point of small-scale military skirmishes. More significantly, the organization has been unable to develop a meaningful role in the process of political change in Latin America. To be sure, this is nothing new, for since its inception the OAS has been deliberately excluded from the internal politics of the hemispheric states (except for its role in the Dominican Republic, a product of some very special circumstances); thus, although the organization in the 1950s periodically reaffirmed its commitment to democracy and social change, it did practically nothing about it. None the less, in the 1960s this gap in organizational action is more serious, for the increased political instability that will almost certainly accompany the process of urbanization and industrialization in Latin America may simply make the OAS irrelevant to the major problems of the hemisphere.

Some qualifications are in order. There are some indications that the organization is not yet moribund. For one thing, the election of Galo Lasso Plaza to succeed José Mora as secretary-general was an encouraging sign, for it was hardly likely that a man of Plaza's experience and stature would have accepted the position without strong private assur-

---

[4] To "study the relationship between violations of human rights or the nonexercise of representative democracy, on the one hand, and the political tensions that affect the peace of the hemisphere, on the other."

[5] See chapter 5 of Slater, *The OAS and United States Foreign Policy.*

ances that the office would not be relegated to an administrative clerk-ship. For another, the Human Rights Commission has been able to continue and even to expand a little its modest work. Despite its clear "interference" in the internal affairs of some hemispheric states, the com-mission's prestige is now apparently great enough to preclude attacks on it by even the repressive states. In the last few years, the commission has reported on human rights violations in the Dominican Republic, Haiti, Cuba, Paraguay, Ecuador, Guatemala, Nicaragua, and Honduras, and, according to commission members, has often succeeded in obtaining remedial action.

A third indicator of the system's continued viability has been the unwillingness of the Latin American majority to turn in wholesale fashion to the United Nations or other extra-hemispheric actors to offset the power of the United States.[6] To be sure, there no longer is automatic Latin American support for the old United States tactic of using the OAS as a shield to fend off any United Nations role in hemispheric affairs (e.g., Guatemala, 1954), and as a result the United States was forced to acquiesce in a nominal United Nations role in the Dominican crisis. None the less, even in the Dominican affair there was no Latin American disposition to work *primarily* through the world body rather than the OAS, and after the first wave of anger at the unilateral American inter-vention, the traditional inclination to close ranks and solve hemispheric problems within the family reasserted itself to a surprising degree.

Finally, despite the recent Latin American refusal to institutionalize important new political capabilities in the OAS, the door to an ad hoc political role is far from closed. Whatever the reluctance to resort to the Rio Treaty, its vague authorization of collective action in the event of any "fact or situation that might endanger the peace of America" con-tinues to provide the juridical vehicle for multilateral action when the majority is so disposed. It is safe to predict that in the foreseeable future organizational political capabilities will not be significantly increased or decreased, with the action of the system reflecting, as in the past, the balance of political forces in each case.

Pursuing this train of thought, one can imagine several kinds of situations in which the OAS might play a major political role, even in the face of the general trend toward minimal organizational action. Para-doxically enough, some of the very forces that have thus far contributed to the decline of the organization could, in certain circumstances, lead to strong collective action. For example, as Latin American political in-stability, ideological conflict, and even civil warfare intensify, there are

<hr />

[6] See the essay by Michael O'Leary in Robert Gregg, ed., *International Organization in the Western Hemisphere* (Syracuse, 1968). For other discussions of the recent re-lation of the OAS to the United Nations see Ronald Yalem, *Regionalism and World Order* (Washington, 1965) and Bryce Wood and Minerva Morales, "Latin America and the United Nations," in Norman J. Padelford and Leland M. Goodrich, eds., *The United Nations in the Balance* (New York, 1965).

likely to be occasions in which domestic political conflict will become so violent or will spill over into interstate conflict at such a level that the organization will be forced to intervene. The tragic Haitian situation already contains all the seeds for that kind of crisis. It is widely feared in both State Department and oas circles that upon the passing of the Duvalier régime, whether through the death of the Haitian dictator or an internal uprising, the thin fabric of Haitian society will dissolve into bloody chaos. Under such circumstances a major oas intervention would be far from out of the question, particularly if humanitarian considerations should be reinforced by a Dominican threat to intervene unilaterally or a Cuban attempt to foster a Castroite revolution. Indeed, current contingency planning in Washington envisages the possibility of a long period of oas trusteeship over Haiti, for the abysmal poverty of the country and the absence of established and reliable political institutions and leadership may leave no other responsible choice.

Similarly, a continuation of United States anticommunist or counterrevolutionary activism in the Caribbean could precipitate reluctant oas action, much as unilateral American intervention quickly forced the oas to involve itself in the Dominican crisis. Like the Cuban missile crisis before it, the Dominican affair suggests an interesting hypothesis that is only superficially ironic: the more likely the United States is to act unilaterally if necessary, the more likely it is that in fact the oas will act. The logic is persuasive enough—in crisis situations defined by the United States as vital to its national interests, the only way the Latin Americans can exercise leverage over Washington's policies is through at least partial co-operation with it.

There are several general directions in which the Organization of American States could now go. One possibility that has considerable support in Latin America as well as some in the United States (e.g., Senator Fulbright) would be a gradual loosening of inter-American ties in favour of all-Latin American groupings. There are some signs that this is already happening, as the Latins increasingly are caucusing together to develop common policies—especially in economic matters—vis-à-vis the United States. Still, as with other such movements in the past, it is doubtful that in the last analysis this trend will go very far, for even the most anti-American governments recognize that it is hardly sensible for them to jettison gratuitously their major forum for collective influence over United States economic and political policies. It is far more likely that, for the present, the organization will simply continue its recent emphasis on economic and other widely accepted non-political tasks. Later, if the United States should abandon its efforts to use the oas as an anticommunist alliance and the current wave of nationalistic militarism in Latin America should subside, it is not impossible that the organization could once again emerge as a central institution for common political tasks.

Should regional economic integration be a basic tactic in the overall strategy for economic development? The economic arguments in favor of this tactic are well-known and the practical advantages seem to have been demonstrated by the success of the European Common Market. But the developing states are not, of course, in the same position as the members of the European Common Market, and the supposed advantages of economic unity may not apply, or they may apply in a different manner, to some members of regional organizations in the developing areas. In the selection that follows, the experiences and problems of two regional associations in Latin America are examined for evidence to support or refute the proposition that regional economic integration is an advantageous step toward economic development.

42. INTEGRATION AND DEVELOPMENT * †

miguel s. wionczek

> The process of economic integration in Latin America will perhaps take three decades; it is, however, a relatively short period when compared with one and one-half centuries of economic disintegration. . . .
> From a statement made in early 1969 by Galo Plaza, Secretary-General of the OAS.

I

Ten years have passed since the governments participating in the meeting of the United Nations Economic Commission for Latin America (ECLA) in Panama City reached an agreement in principle concerning

* Excerpted from "Integration and Development" by Miguel S. Wionczek, *International Journal*, Vol. XXIV, No. 3 (Summer, 1969), pp. 449–461. By permission of the publisher and the author.
† Adviser with the Center for Latin American Monetary Studies (Mexico City) and the co-editor of the *Journal of Common Market Studies* (Oxford, England); author of *Mexican Nationalism and Foreign Investment*, and *Latin American Integration and U. S. Economic Policy*; editor of *Economic Cooperation in Latin America, Africa and Asia—a Handbook of Documents* (1969). The views expressed in this essay are solely those of the author.

the establishment of a regional free trade association (LAFTA) which would embrace the whole area except Central America. Five small Central American countries also established their own common market (CACM) a decade ago. Two years have passed since the hemispheric conference, held at Punta del Este, Uruguay, and attended by all Latin American heads of state and the then President of the United States, Lyndon B. Johnson, committed itself to setting up, by 1985, a Latin American common market through the "gradual convergence" of LAFTA and CACM. Little has been heard lately about the Punta del Este project and the news from Latin America reaching the outside world strongly suggests that not only LAFTA but also CACM, the most successful economic integration experiment in the southern hemisphere, face considerable difficulties.

Two schools of thought concerning economic integration are prevalent in Latin America. The first, composed of many long-time supporters of regional co-operation, proclaims that both LAFTA and CACM are passing through a series of serious crises which endanger their futures. The second, led by spokesmen for the LAFTA and CACM secretariats and other Latin American institutions, like the Inter-American Development Bank, which are deeply involved in integration efforts, suggests that the present difficulties of the two schemes are only "crises of growth" that will eventually be overcome if only because integration is vital to the economic development of the region. The picture is further complicated if one also takes into account the opinions of high officials in some Latin American republics who continue to express support for the principle of economic integration but qualify their support by stating that domestic interests and objectives must have clear priority over regional growth and co-operative goals.

These conflicting opinions lead one to wonder where in fact Latin America is going a decade after the first experiments with regional integration were launched in an atmosphere of great expectation. The available factual evidence suggests that unfortunately Latin America is going in many directions at the same time or rather that it is drifting without any clear direction in response to the mounting pressures of unsolved internal and external problems. Consequently, it is extremely difficult to predict where the region will find itself not just by 1985, when according to the Punta del Este agreement a Latin American common market was to be established, but even by 1973, the date when LAFTA is supposed to be a full-fledged free trade zone. This uncertainty in respect to the short and middle future has its roots in the fact that both Latin America as a region and most Latin American republics individually found it impossible to undertake or were enjoined from implementing long overdue economic, social, and political reforms in the years since World War II. Unable to resolve the problems inherited from the past,

INTERNATIONAL RELATIONS

Latin America is thus poorly equipped to deal with those which are emerging in a world now characterized by technological revolution, rising expectations, and demographic explosion.

It is not that Latin America did not witness economic growth in the past two decades. The region's gross national product has increased about three times in real terms since 1945 and an impressive degree of industrialization was achieved by the large and middle-sized republics. But the area's population doubled in the same period and growth did not translate itself into development. In socio-political terms Latin-America in the late 1960s is probably the most tradition-minded and conservative part of the world. As a leading Chilean political scientist put it recently: "In spite of its reputation for frequent and violent political upheaval perhaps the principal contemporary problem of Latin America is excessive stability. There exists in the region a resilient traditional structure of institutions, hierarchical arrangements, and attitudes which conditions every aspect of political behaviour and which survived centuries of colonial government, movements for independence, foreign wars and invasions, domestic revolutions, and a confusingly large number of lesser palace revolts. More recently it has not only successfully resisted the impact of technological innovation and industrialization, but appears to have been strengthened by it."[1] This social and political stagnation breeds an apparent inability to approach external and domestic economic difficulties in a modern and rational way. It is also largely responsible for the present deep crises in the ambitious attempts at regional integration.

II

It must be remembered that the idea of economic co-operation was born during the 1950s in the minds of a particular coalition of Latin American technocrats and reformist politicians. Experts recruited from the region by ECLA, led by Raúl Prebisch, then the commission's executive secretary, looked upon economic integration as a potentially powerful development factor in two senses. It would stimulate the abandonment of a traditionalist export trade and help modernize the Latin American economies by forcing them to specialize within the framework of an expanded and protected regional market. While accepting ECLA's general development theses, some individual political figures saw in economic integration an important political vehicle that would permit them to redress somewhat the lack of balance in hemispheric relations. By the mid-'fifties the economic growth in most of Latin America, induced largely by World War II and sustained by the international commodity

[1]   Claudio Véliz in his introduction to *Obstacles to Change in Latin America* (London-New York-Toronto, 1965), p. 1.

boom during the Korean conflict, petered out; at the same time the chief member of the inter-American system, the United States, continued to pay little attention to the development problems of the region.

Beset by foreign trade problems and lacking external assistance Latin Americans found the idea of regional co-operation attractive. Between 1958 and 1960 the Central Americans established their common market. At the same time, in a parallel but geographically broader movement, the majority of the South American republics and Mexico opted for a free trade zone scheme that in the 'seventies—it was hoped—would evolve into a common market covering the whole subcontinent. Drawing upon the example of Western Europe both schemes put an accent upon trade liberalization as a vehicle for regional division of labour. The Central American arrangement provided for the creation of a common market by 1966 for all but a few commodities. The Latin American free trade zone was to be set up by 1972, through annual product-by-product tariff negotiations.

The Central American regional co-operation scheme provided not only for commercial but also for financial, monetary, fiscal, and industrial co-operation. In the early 1960s an impressive array of institutions supporting the common market emerged in the area, among them a regional development agency (the Central American Integration Bank), a monetary council, a clearing house, and an industrial research institute. While these agencies work with relative efficiency, co-ordination of major economic policies, particularly in respect to the siting of new industries and the common treatment of foreign investment, has proved very difficult. The inability to reach agreements in the key field of industrialization, partly because of an absence of national economic planning mechanisms in Central America, proved in the late 1960s to be the major source of CACM's difficulties.

The LAFTA agreement (known as the Montevideo Treaty) was less specific in respect to non-commercial co-operation mechanisms. However, it did commit the participating countries—whose initial number of seven increased to eleven by 1968—"to facilitate increasing economic integration and complementary economies" by making "every effort to reconcile their import and export régimes, as well as the treatment they accord to capital, goods, and services from outside the Area." Furthermore, the Montevideo Treaty envisaged "progressively closer coordination of the corresponding industrialization policies" through agreements "among representatives of the economic sectors concerned." Very little, however, has been achieved in these fields during the first eight years of LAFTA. No regional agreement about the co-ordination of foreign trade and industrialization policies has been reached and none is in sight. Neither was it found possible to agree upon a common treatment for private foreign capital. Only a few agreements designed to make industrial developments complementary, by specialization of production in individual industrial branches with concomitant freeing of trade for their output, have been signed. Only one of them (covering chemicals and signed in 1968) deals with an important industry. While some degree of co-operation was achieved in respect to the multilateral clearing of regional trade balances and maritime transport, these agreements had very little impact upon the expansion of intra-LAFTA trade and no effect whatsoever upon the acceleration of regional economic growth.

The achievements of CACM and LAFTA have been measured to date mainly by the growth of trade within their respective areas. Consequently, by 1968 it appeared that the Central American Common Market was an unqualified success whereas the Latin American free trade zone was making only slow and hesitant progress. In fact, trade within Central America responded to the establishment of a common market with amazing dynamism. Regional trade flows, measured in terms of imports, increased from US$37 million to $215 million between 1961 and 1967, or by about 35 per cent a year. They continued growing rapidly in 1968. About two-thirds of intra-Central American trade consists of manufactures, mainly consumer goods, pointing to a significant diversification of zonal commerce and the apparent impact of the common market upon the region's production structure.

LAFTA trade achievements are much less impressive. The signing of the Montevideo Treaty was followed by five years of a relatively rapid intra-regional trade expansion, partly in response to early progress in tariff negotiations. By 1966 intra-LAFTA export trade (excluding Bolivia and Venezuela who joined the scheme in 1967) exceeded US$700 million (10 per cent of the member countries' total export trade) as compared with $300 million (6 percent) in 1960. The regional trade of some newcomers—Mexico, Peru, and Ecuador—grew very rapidly from the low levels registered at the end of the 1950s. The bulk of commercial exchange continued to be concentrated in the three southern republics—Argentina, Brazil, and Chile—which had a long tradition of reciprocal trade and still account today for over two-thirds of intra-LAFTA trade. In spite of the impressive number of tariff reductions (exceeding 11,000 by the end of 1968), very little was achieved in respect to regional trade diversification in products. In 1967 the foodstuffs and other primary products traditionally exchanged by South American republics still represented something like 70 per cent of intra-LAFTA trade. But the biggest setback to LAFTA was that regional trade ceased to expand in 1967 and 1968. According to preliminary statistics, it has stood at $700 million for the last two years although LAFTA trade with the rest of the world has continued to register healthy growth rates.

From the statistics it might seem that while the rapid setting up of a common market in Central America proved an efficient way of accelerating trade and growth within that small area, the trade liberalization measures of the Montevideo Treaty were too weak to produce a similar effect within LAFTA. But it is not only LAFTA which is languishing these days; the CACM also faces serious difficulties. One is led to suspect that although regional trade liberalization programmes may be necessary to stimulate economic growth they do not by themselves guarantee much to the underdeveloped participants in such schemes.

III

A closer look into the CACM's experiences suggests that the positive impact of common market arrangements of a traditional type upon the economies of its underdeveloped member countries has been over-publicized. In the absence of joint or even national long-term development policies, particularly of an industrial and fiscal type, the establishment of a common market brought relatively little real growth to Central America, all the impressive figures on intra-area trade notwithstanding. Some independent sources estimate that only 1 per cent of the annual 7 per cent average growth rate in the GNP came through common-market–induced activities. The setting up of a regional trade barrier that was somewhat higher than the previous tariffs of the individual countries did not lead to serious industrialization but rather to the rapid expansion of all types of "final-touch" industries in the integrated area. Many consumer goods imported in finished form before 1960 are now imported in parts or at intermediate stages in production. After undergoing final processing (bottling or packing only in a few extreme cases) they circulate in the region as "Central American" manufactures.

The high regional protection offered to finished goods, the low tariffs extended to raw materials and intermediate products, the race of CACM member countries for "new industries" together with the oligopolistic structure of the market led to an impressive expansion of intra-regional trade in "manufactures" at a considerable economic and social cost to the area. Among the economic costs of this particular type of regional integration are a rapidly growing bill for imports from third countries, a decline in fiscal revenues, the high prices of new regional "manufactures," and the exorbitant profits accruing mainly to foreign manufacturing investors who moved *en masse* into CACM, once aware of the profitability of the new ventures. To make matters worse, the haphazard industrialization that followed the emergence of CACM led to political complications by accentuating differences in intra-regional development levels. Most of the new "final-touch" industries settled in the more advanced countries—Guatemala and El Salvador—which became the principal exporters of manufactures to the area. Since the liberalization of agricultural trade proved more difficult, the least developed members—Honduras and Nicaragua—found themselves in an uncomfortable situation. They became markets for expensive manufactures from the rest of the region while being unable to increase their intra-regional exports of traditional agricultural commodities.

As long as the over-all balance-of-payments position of Central America was satisfactory relatively few complaints about the growing imbalance in regional development were heard. But in 1967 the area found itself facing a major payments problem *vis-à-vis* the outside world. The rapidly growing import bill was due both to CACM industrialization and to the high level of luxury imports resulting from the unequal income distribution in the area. Subsequently, the CACM ran into heavy criticism from its less developed members. The unequal distribution of benefits accruing from integration became the key issue and Honduras and Nicaragua began to press for special concessions from the rest. The conflict became exacerbated when the attempts to deal with the regional balance-of-payments difficulties through tariff surcharges on most imports from third countries and an equalized consumption tax on a large list of luxury commodities of regional origin met with opposition from Costa Rica. In early 1969 Nicaragua, which had accumulated a sizable commercial deficit within the region and was unable to export agricultural goods to neighbouring countries introduced—without warning and in clear contravention of the CACM treaty—levies on regional imports. It lifted them only after the other members ratified the pending regional protocols. The most important of these was a protocol for the equalization of fiscal incentives, its absence in the original treaty having permitted the race to attract foreign industrial investment.

While the Nicaragua crisis has been solved, it appears that CACM will never be the same again. The long-simmering conflict between the three more developed members and the two poorer ones will continue to feed nationalist attitudes in individual countries, and tremendous negotiating skill will be needed to keep CACM intact. Moreover, while the issue of equal benefits for all member countries may be resolved, another one continues to overshadow the area. Both the Central American left and many local conservatives insist with growing vehemence that whatever gains from CACM may accrue to the region, foreign industrial investors are the principal beneficiaries of the common market arrangement. Given the force of nationalism in the underdeveloped countries, such a frame of mind can hardly be considered conducive to the future orderly progress of the Central American economic integration scheme, especially considering that ten years after the setting up of the common market the area is socially and politically as backward as before.

I V

Within LAFTA, the disenchantment began even before intra-regional trade stopped growing in 1967. A number of attempts to accelerate the implementation of the non-trade commitments of the Montevideo Treaty were made, starting in 1964, by the main proponents of regional integration, including President Eduardo Frei of Chile, Raúl Prebisch, and the president of the Inter-American Development Bank, Felipe Herrera. These initiatives led to the establishment of LAFTA's Council of Ministers and indirectly to the conference of American presidents at Punta del Este. But after two meetings in 1966 and 1967, the Council of Ministers ran out of ideas, while the Punta del Este declaration calling for the establishment of a Latin American common market was quietly shelved. External and regional political difficulties proved stronger than the superficial idea of Latin American solidarity.

While there are many reasons for LAFTA's disappointing performance and the apparent lack of enthusiasm for a common market, some of them are particularly important. One is the ambitious geographical scope of LAFTA. In the name of a Latin American community of interests, economies of all sizes and at all levels of development were put under one roof. The highly publicized declarations of regional solidarity notwithstanding, the events of the last few years proved that each of the three groups of LAFTA (the industrial "giants"—Argentina, Brazil, and Mexico; the middle group led by Chile, Colombia, and Venezuela; and the most backward republics—Bolivia, Ecuador, and Paraguay) faces specific problems which hardly lend themselves to joint action. All. the major conflicts that arose in LAFTA involved the economic relations among these three groups. The poor members and the middle group insist that they are getting little if anything from the regional free trade scheme and in fact are running the risk of becoming markets for the industrial surplus of the "big three." And while Argentina, Brazil, and Mexico are obviously interested in markets in neighbouring countries, their dependence on exports to the rest of LAFTA is not great enough to force them to grant the unilateral commercial and other concessions for which the less fortunate republics have persistently asked. Recently Argentina made it clear that its interest in LAFTA and any future regional common market is limited strictly by considerations of domestic economic development. While Brazil abstains from making public statements, its position is basically similar. Only Mexico shows some sympathy for the smaller countries' plight but Mexico alone can hardly determine LAFTA's future.

While the differences in economic development levels within the LAFTA family may be the main reason for its disappointing performance, a second obstacle has its roots in the flaws in the ECLA doctrine that served as the rationale for the establishment of a Latin American free trade zone in 1960. ECLA claimed, though the reality of the 1960s has disproved it, that the Latin American countries must integrate because the import-substitution process on a national level had run its course by the mid-'fifties. But the post-LAFTA experiences of the "big three" and of some of the middle countries have shown that the national industrialization programmes can continue in Latin America for a considerable time without an increase in the level of protection. In response to the differentiation of domestic demand for industrial inputs and final goods, new manufacturing establishments continue to appear in Argentina, Brazil, and Mexico ten years after ECLA's declaration that this type of industrial growth was running into a blind alley. Eventually, perhaps within a decade, these large republics may run into the difficulties predicted by ECLA but as long as they are not too severe and the nationalist ideology remains strong, none of the three countries sees a manifest necessity to support LAFTA fully.

The possibilities of continuing such inward-directed industrialization in the middle group of countries are somewhat more limited. This may explain in part their interest in an Andean subregional common market, a project which has been under negotiation since 1966 with little apparent success. But the strong objections to that scheme expressed in Peru and Venezuela prove that the large segments of the private sector in these two republics believe that national industrialization programmes are still feasible in most places regardless of market size, natural resources endowment, and the availability of modern technology. Industrial entrepreneurs in Venezuela are particularly vocal in this respect, predicting a major national disaster in the case of the opening of Venezuelan borders to the "cheap labour" products of neighbouring countries. There is little reason why industrial interests in Venezuela should think otherwise. After all they are reaping very handsome profits behind high protective barriers. And in traditional and conservative Latin America, profits and national interest are easily equated.

Paradoxically, the third major obstacle to regional co-operation arises from the improvement in the international commodity trade picture, registered in recent years under the impact of the economic boom conditions in the advanced countries. Contrary to the pessimistic ECLA predictions, the external demand for Latin America's traditional commodities improved considerably in the 1960s. Although the rate of expansion of the region's exports stayed behind that of trade among industrial countries, the results were better than expected. Between 1963 and 1968 Latin America's merchandise sales increased by 25 per cent from US$9,200 million to $11,400 million. If Venezuela's oil exports which behaved sluggishly over the period are excluded, the five-year increase in export revenue of the region amounted to 30 per cent. The improvement of the export picture made internal industrialization efforts much more attractive politically than the alternative, a negotiation of regional industrial co-operation schemes which might have affected certain interest groups in individual countries. As at other times and in other places, once the atmosphere of impending crisis began to dissipate, long-term problems were conveniently forgotten.

The preference shown in the capital exporting countries for the practices of tied public loans and of private suppliers' credits in lieu of untied foreign aid only strengthened the propensity of Latin American countries to think in terms of national inward-directed development and industrialization. Whatever their external payments situation might have been, in the 1960s, Latin American republics were swamped with offers of external credit for individual industrial projects involving the import of capital goods. These offers were readily taken up. As a consequence, the duplication and overlapping previously characteristic of primary activities in the region was extended to the industrial sectors. With new high-cost foreign-financed self-contained industrial plants springing up even in the most backward countries economic integration became more rather than less difficult of attainment during the present decade.

The absence of co-ordinated aid policies toward Latin America among the donor countries and the United States' lack of interest in supporting LAFTA politically and financially brought about another important obstacle to integration.[2] Through its aid agencies the United States gave financial support to the Central American Common Market from the very start. The CACM members agreed in turn to accept the "proper" rules of the game by abstaining from any interference with free market forces and foreign investment. Moreover, the possibility of a political challenge to the United States from the Central American integration scheme was virtually nil while the acceleration of that area's growth was attractive to the United States as a possible means to lessen the socio-political tensions in a strategically important part of Latin America.

The United States attitude to LAFTA was considerably more ambivalent, however. In the 1950s the United States gave no support to Latin American integration efforts if only because the initiatives came from an ideologically suspect ECLA. With the emergence of the Alliance for Progress in 1960, the United States position began to fluctuate between a "hands-off policy" and "neutral benevolence." Only in 1965 did the United States begin to express qualified support for Latin American integration. In the winter of 1966–67 prior to the conference of American heads of state, President Johnson offered aid for the readjustment of the econo-

---

[2] For details, see Miguel S. Wionczek, "Latin American Integration and United States Policies," in Robert W. Gregg, ed., *International Organization in the Western Hemisphere* (Syracuse, N. Y., 1968).

mies that might be affected in the process of the gradual establishment of a regional common market. But the United States Congress refused to support the executive's offer, and in any case the amount of aid offered was considered by most Latin Americans to be ridiculously low.

This aid, informally promised, has never materialized. The United States claims that the Latin American lack of interest in the implementation of the Punta del Este agreement made any external financial help superfluous. The Latin American countries, in turn, put forth the view that they would perhaps be ready to take the Punta del Este common market proposals more seriously if only the United States had not backed out of its promises. Obviously, this is merely verbal shadow-boxing. Both the United States and Latin America put other matters far ahead of broad and serious regional economic integration and both are fairly satisfied with traditional bilateral methods of hemispheric aid distribution. Given the attitudes prevalent in the United States Congress, the executive can hardly ask for additional funds for integration. Moreover, in a period of declining aid, the maintenance of bilateralism is not unattractive to the countries receiving aid. Each hopes that it will somehow get more than others because of its "special" relation with the powerful donor. Besides, since the earmarking of certain funds for integration might affect the amount of bilateral aid available, no Latin American country is willing to press for financial assistance for integration. Thus, traditional aid distribution patterns continue, while both Latin America and the United States find themselves in the comfortable position of being able to blame the other side for the failure of the agreements arrived at by the heads of state in 1967.

The final major obstacle to LAFTA's efficient functioning and to its evolution toward a regional common market arises from the latent conflict between Latin American societies and foreign private investment, particularly the giant multinational corporations. In many Latin American quarters fears are expressed that because of their managerial and technological power these corporations would reap the major benefits from integration and in the process destroy many weak domestic industries. In principle, these problems might be taken care of by regional harmonization of policies toward foreign private capital and by special financial and technical assistance on a regional scale to the domestic industries. In practice, the harmonization of such policies seems a forbidding task. Less developed LAFTA members claim that the introduction of equal regional treatment for foreign investment would result in its concentration in the few large countries. The latter, in turn, insist that offering the poorer republics the right of more liberal treatment for foreign capital on the top of unilateral regional trade concessions would result in the swamping of Latin America with manufactures assembled by foreign firms in the less developed republics. Unable to resolve this particular regional dilemma, LAFTA members continue to maintain highly varied national foreign investment policies geared mainly to individual industrialization needs. Thus, on the regional level a curious argument emerges. While each country talks about the dangers of foreign domination of the free trade zone or a future common market, only foreign investment located outside one's own national territory is considered a threat. And since local foreign-owned enterprises become somehow the extension of national economic power, negotiating battles are fought to give them access to the neighbouring markets. Under such conditions the elaboration of a regional foreign investment policy is more than a forbidding task. It appears an impossible exercise.

The "Cold War" that developed between the superpowers after World War II took several forms and had a number of side effects, but one of the most paradoxical forms with the most pernicious side effects was the arming of many developing states. It was paradoxical because the spreading of military weapons added such a minute increment to the destructive power of either superpower, while it greatly increased the opportunities for mischievous conduct by the newly armed states and the possibility of localized conflict eventually involving the great powers. In the following selection, Stephen Gibert examines the scope of military aid programs and notes briefly the positions taken by the recipient states on some issues in the United Nations in comparison with those of their benefactors.

43. SOVIET-AMERICAN MILITARY AID COMPETITION IN THE THIRD WORLD * †

s t e p h e n   p.   g i b e r t

PRIORITY REGIONS IN SOVIET AND AMERICAN MILITARY AID PROGRAMS

Both the Soviet Union and the United States have concentrated a large part of their military aid in those countries which are proven allies or "satellites." Significant amounts of Soviet aid have gone to East European countries, North Korea, and, in earlier years, Communist China. Currently an undetermined but undoubtedly substantial amount of aid is being furnished to North Viet Nam. The United States formerly directed the bulk of its military aid to its West European allies and Japan. More recently, the principal recipients have been South Korea, China (Taiwan) and South Viet Nam. Any comparisons of the rival American and Soviet arms aid programs must begin, therefore, by emphasizing that the observations are limited to the less developed, relatively uncommitted countries of Asia, the Middle East, Africa and Latin America. It is in these "nonaligned" or "Third World" countries that the military aid programs of the two superpowers are in competition.

Since the objective here is to analyze military aid diplomacy in the Third World, countries completely identified with either the Soviet bloc or the United States have been omitted. These include North Korea, Mongolia, North Viet Nam, South Korea, South Viet Nam and Nationalist China. Had such countries been included, of course, the aid totals would have been larger than those presented in this article.

Table 1 lists fifty-four Third World countries that received American

* Excerpts from "Soviet-American Military Aid Competition in the Third World" by Stephen P. Gibert, Orbis, Vol. XIII (Winter, 1970), pp. 1118–1124, 1130–1133, and Tables V and VI, pp. 1134 and 1135. Reprinted from ORBIS, a quarterly journal of world affairs, published by the Foreign Policy Research Institute, Philadelphia, Pa. By permission of the journal and the author and, for the tables, of Johns Hopkins Press. Table 4 and footnote 1 in the original article have been omitted.
† This article is based on a chapter in Wynfred Joshua and Stephen P. Gibert, Arms for the Third World: Soviet Military Aid Diplomacy (Baltimore: The Johns Hopkins Press, 1969). Used with permission.

TABLE 1
Estimated United States Military Aid to Third
World Countries: FY 1956–FY 1967
(in millions of U.S. dollars)

Country	Amount	Country	Amount	Country	Amount
Afghanistan	$ 3.2	Guinea	$ 1.0	Morocco	$ 26.7
Argentina	23.5	Haiti	3.2	Nicaragua	8.4
Bolivia	15.8	Honduras	5.0	Niger	0.1
Brazil	160.8	India	200.0	Nigeria	1.0
Burma	35.0	Indonesia	59.8	Pakistan	750.0
Cambodia	87.1	Iran	627.6	Panama	2.3
Cameroon	0.2	Iraq	41.3	Paraguay	5.1
Chile	67.2	Israel	52.0	Peru	63.8
Colombia	57.9	Ivory Coast	0.1	Philippines	262.5
Congo-Kinshasa	16.1	Jamaica	0.8	Saudi Arabia	33.0
Costa Rica	1.7	Jordan	48.0	Senegal	2.6
Cuba	7.5	Laos	150.0	Sudan	0.7
Dahomey	0.1	Lebanon	8.8	Thailand	600.0
Dominican Republic	14.1	Liberia	4.9	Tunisia	16.3
Ecuador	29.0	Libya	12.4	Turkey	1,735.5
El Salvador	4.7	Malaysia	0.4	Upper Volta	0.1
Ethiopia	95.8	Mali	2.8	Uruguay	33.8
Guatemala	10.8	Mexico	1.5	Venezuela	6.4

Source: Compiled from U.S. Department of Defense, Military Assistance Facts (Washington: March 1968), pp. 14–15. Figures for countries whose aid totals could not be adapted from this document were derived from articles in the press, principally from the New York Times.

military aid during the period 1956 through 1967. Large recipients included Brazil, India, Iran, Laos, Pakistan, the Philippines and Turkey. Currently Thailand is the Third World country receiving the largest share of U.S. military aid allocations. Its total aid is still slightly less than that of Iran and Pakistan, however, and much less than that of Turkey, the largest Third World recipient.[2]

During approximately the same period of time, the Soviet bloc [3]

[2] The current emphasis on "forward defense countries" in U.S. military aid allocations will raise Thailand's total even higher. Of $500 million requested for FY 1969, $365 million was allocated to countries "which, because of their geographical proximity to the USSR and Communist China, are exposed to the direct threat of Communist aggression." See U.S. Department of Defense, *Military Assistance Facts* (Washington: March 1968), p. 7.

[3] The terms "Soviet aid" and "Soviet-bloc aid" are used interchangeably. All Soviet-bloc aid except for a small fraction has been aid from the USSR itself; only Czechoslovakia among the bloc countries has contributed a measurable amount of military aid. "Soviet bloc" refers to the USSR and the members of the Warsaw Pact. The use of the term is merely a convenience; it does not imply monolithic unity among the Warsaw Pact nations. Military aid by Communist China is not included in Table 2.

aided twenty-four Third World nations. Major recipients of Soviet arms were the United Arab Republic, Indonesia, India and Cuba. Currently (1969) few if any weapons are being provided to Cuba and Indonesia, but India and the UAR continue to receive substantial Soviet military aid. Cairo in particular relies heavily on Moscow's willingness to provide both weapons and training for Egypt's military forces. Table 2 lists Third World nations that have received Soviet military assistance, with estimates of the amounts of aid converted to American dollars.

TABLE 2

Estimated Soviet-bloc Military Aid to
Third World Countries: 1955 Through 1967
(in millions of U.S. dollars)

		Estimated Military Aid
Afghanistan		$ 260
Algeria		200
Cambodia	between 5 and	10
Congo-Brazzaville		1
Cuba		750
Cyprus		28
Ghana	between 10 and	15
Guinea	at least	6
India	between 600 and	700
Indonesia		1,200
Iran		100
Iraq	at least	500
Laos	between 3 and	5
Mali	at least	3
Morocco		20
Nigeria	between 10 and	15
Pakistan	between 5 and	10
Somali		35
Sudan		N.A.
Syria	at least	300
Tanzania	between 5 and	10
UAR		1,500
Uganda		N.A.
Yemen		100
Total up to:		$5,768

Sources: U.S. Department of State, Communist Governments and Developing Nations: Aid and Trade in 1967, Research Memorandum RSE-120 (Washington: August 14, 1968); Joshua and Gibert, op. cit., pp. 23, 45, 73, 102. Soviet-bloc military aid to the Middle East countries (Algeria, Iraq, Morocco, Syria, UAR and Yemen) provided after the June 1967 war is not included.

Table 3 illustrates the regional emphases in the American and Soviet programs. Again disregarding Soviet aid to other communist countries, and examining allocations only to the relatively uncommitted states of Asia, the Middle East, Africa and Latin America, it is clear that Soviet assistance has been directed principally toward the Middle East and South and Southeast Asia. In Latin America, only Cuba has received Soviet military aid. In Africa, on the other hand, the small amount of Soviet aid has been disbursed among nine countries.

TABLE 3

Comparison of Regional Priorities in Soviet and
United States Military Aid

(in millions of U.S. dollars)

Region	Estimated Total Aid		Percentage of Total Program		Number of Recipients	
	USSR	U.S.	USSR	U.S.	USSR	U.S.
Middle East	$2,748	$2,602	48	48	8	10
South/Southeast Asia	2,185	2,148	38	40	6	10
Latin America	750	523	13	10	1	21
Africa	85	126	1	2	9	13
Totals	$5,768	$5,399	100	100	24	54

We find some interesting similarities and contrasts between the Soviet and American military aid programs. In terms of amounts of military aid allocated, the regions are ranked in the same order for the two superpowers. For both countries, the Middle East has been the area of most importance, whereas Africa has received the least amount of military aid. The fact that the Middle East and South and Southeast Asia have received more than 80 per cent of the total U. S. and Soviet allocations suggests the importance the superpowers accord to these regions in their competition for influence in the Third World.

A second comparison of the two programs indicates the relative concentration of Soviet efforts, in contrast to the dispersion of American aid. Although the total amounts involved are nearly the same for each donor for the twelve-year period, the Soviet Union has concentrated its $5,768 million in only twenty four recipient countries, averaging approximately $240 million per recipient. The United States, on the other hand, has spread its $5,399 million among fifty-four recipients, with an average of approximately $100 million per recipient. These figures suggest that the Soviet government targets its aid with objectives in mind which differ basically from the goals pursued by the United States. The USSR chooses recipients that may be expected to agree with Soviet policies or to maintain friendly relationships with the Soviet Union. United States aid goes not only to countries allied with or sympathetic to American goals and aims, but also to countries tending to oppose U. S. policies. The United States expects that such countries receiving American aid will at least preserve their own independence and thus contribute to a stable, noncommunist world.

Logically, it can be assumed that large amounts of aid will give the donor country greater influence in the recipient country than a small amount of aid. If this is true, it would appear that Soviet aid is designed to secure for the Soviet Union a position of significant influence in a limited number of recipient countries, while American aid appears designed to maintain at least a minimum aid relationship with a large number of countries. Of course such a conclusion is tentative in that analysis of the competing aid programs must take into account qualitative as well as quantitative factors. But it is evident that the USSR and the United States tend to pursue somewhat different aid strategies.

To some extent, the relative dispersion of American military aid and the relative concentration of Soviet military aid are affected by the special position occupied by Latin America in the foreign policies of the two donors. Where Latin America is concerned, the United States appears determined to maintain its preeminent influence, and the Soviet Union seems to accept this status. It has been frequently argued that Soviet foreign policy may be distinguished from Czarist Russian diplomacy in that the former is unlimited in scope and worldwide in its interests and ambitions, whereas Czarist aims centered on areas of the world geographically adjacent to Russia. Michael Karpovich supports this point of view. He argues that "pre-revolutionary Russian imperialism was essentially no different from the imperialism of the other great powers," but the foreign policy of the Soviet Union is radically different: it is global in scope, "seeking to achieve a number of aggressive aims simultaneously in various corners of the earth. This alone sharply distinguishes Soviet policy from the policy of the Tsars, who, as a rule, pursued limited aims. . . ." [4] However, while Soviet ideology proclaims a worldwide policy of spreading communism, Moscow's military aid program indicates that Soviet policy, like that of imperial Russia, still emphasizes regions adjacent to the USSR and is still cautious about moving into distant areas such as Latin America. In this light Soviet aid for Cuba is an exception to the general conduct of Soviet foreign policy, for in aiding Cuba Moscow sought to extend its influence thousands of miles from the Russian homeland.

American aid to Latin America during the period 1956 to 1967 has

[4] Michael Karpovich, "Russian Imperialism or Communist Aggression?," in Robert Goldwin, editor, Readings in Russian Foreign Policy (New York: Oxford University Press, 1959), pp. 659–660.

totaled only $523 million. Yet every Latin American country received at some time or another during those years at least token aid from the United States. This contrasts with other regions of the world where American aid has been much more selective. The inclusion of all Latin American countries in the U. S. military assistance program goes far to explain the relative dispersion of U. S. efforts. Were Latin America excluded, the U. S. program spread would resemble that of the USSR more closely. It also points up the importance accorded by the United States to maintaining good relations with the countries of the Western Hemisphere, especially since there is no "rational" need to arm them.

Africa, like Latin America, appears to be a low-priority region in Soviet military aid diplomacy. To some degree the small amounts contributed to Black Africa by the United States and the Soviet Union, less than 2 per cent of their total combined allocations, are due to the inability of relatively backward societies to absorb large amounts of military aid. The generally small armed forces of the African countries lack sufficient training to utilize sophisticated and costly weapons systems. The token aid also reflects geographical remoteness from both donors and its inability to affect drastically the military security of the superpowers. The USSR has extended a total of $85 million to nine African countries; the United States has contributed approximately $126 million to thirteen African recipients. Both Washington and Moscow appear to accept a situation in Africa where neither is predominant and where competition is muted and hence cheap in terms of military aid.

The competition between the United States and the Soviet Union is most intense in the critical regions of the Middle East and South and Southeast Asia. To those two regions the bulk of each donor's military aid flows, and as the superpowers vie for influence and prestige there is the serious risk that their military aid policies will contribute to escalating local conflicts into a clash between them. In South and Southeast Asia the presence of Communist China, hostile to both the United States and the Soviet Union, complicates an already dangerous rivalry. Nevertheless, both superpowers continue to accord high priority to the Middle East and South and Southeast Asia. Eighty-eight per cent of the American military aid commitment to the less developed world has gone to these areas, as has 86 per cent of the total Soviet military aid program.

* * * * *

FOREIGN POLICY ORIENTATIONS
OF MILITARY AID RECIPIENTS

Both the United States and the Soviet Union have declared that their military aid programs are intended to support their foreign policy objectives in Third World countries.[5] To measure their success, an analysis of roll-call voting in the United Nations by Third World recipients of American and Soviet military aid has been undertaken with the purpose of comparing recipient positions on important roll-call votes with the positions taken by the superpowers. This approach rests on the belief that a government's voting record on questions before the United Nations is as objective a measurement of its international political position as can be devised.[6]

The test was applied to voting in the United Nations by Third World countries during the period 1958 to 1964 and considered two categories of issues voted upon: political and security issues affecting nations generally; and trusteeship and colonial questions of particular interest to Third World governments.[7]

Table 5 lists all Third World nations which received military aid valued at one million dollars or more during the 1958–1964 period. It then compares the "scores of agreement"[8] between aid donors and aid recipients. It will be observed that, except for Cyprus, the ten countries aided exclusively by the USSR agreed with the Soviet Union most of the time. Algeria, with an agreement score of eighty-one, was the nation most in agreement with the USSR on political and security issues.

[5] See, for example, U. S. Department of Defense, *Military Assistance and Foreign Military Sales Facts* (Washington: May 1967), p. 7; T. Bulba, "International Significance of the Development of Communism in the USSR," *Kommunist Vooruzhennykh Sil* (*Communist of the Armed Forces*), December 1964, p. 37; and unsigned editorial, "Fifty Years of the Great October Socialist Revolution; Thesis of the Central Committee, CPSU," in *ibid.*, July 1967, pp. 37, 41.

[6] Obviously measuring the degree of identification on UN roll calls between aid donors and aid recipients is only one method of estimating the military aid-foreign policy nexus. The test implies correlation only, not causality, since it cannot be ascertained whether aid recipients agreed with aid donors because they received aid, or received aid because they agreed with donor policies.

[7] Roll calls selected were from both committee and plenary sessions of the General Assembly. They had to meet at least one of the following criteria: (a) the division on the roll call was such that 20 per cent or more of the voting governments were opposed to the majority position; and (b) the Soviet Union and the United States voted differently on the issue. These criteria were designed to ensure that only "politically significant" roll calls were included in the sample, and to screen out those on which there was little or no disagreement. The distinction between "political and security" rolls calls and those on questions concerning non-self-governing territories and trusteeships, hereafter referred to as "colonial" roll calls, is that of the UN Secretariat, as reported in the annual volumes of the *Yearbook of the United Nations*.

[8] The "scores of agreement" presented in Table V are a measure of the percentage of times nations agreed with the Soviet Union or the United States on the 102 roll calls examined. The method employed assigns weight to abstention votes as against positive and negative positions. It also allows for the fact that not all governments voted on all 102 roll calls, since several were not UN members throughout the entire period and since there were occasional absences. The formula used to compute the scores of agreement is that devised by Arend Lijphart, "An Analysis of Bloc Voting in the General Assembly: A Critique and a Proposal," *American Political Science Review*, December 1963, pp. 909–910.

SOVIET-AMERICAN MILITARY AID COMPETITION

Except for Laos, the nine countries aided by both the Soviet Union and the United States agreed more often with Moscow than with Washington.[9] While it was to be expected that governments aided exclusively by Moscow would have high agreement scores with the Soviet Union, it is surprising that nearly all mutually-aided nations had higher scores of agreement with the Soviets than with the United States.

Considering the thirty-five nations aided exclusively by the United States, it was found that twenty-eight had higher scores of agreement with Washington than with Moscow. Six, on the other hand, agreed with the Soviets more than with the Americans despite the fact that the

TABLE 5

Scores of Agreement Between Aid Donors and Aid Recipients on Political and Security Roll Calls in the United Nations: 1958–1964 *

| Aid Recipient | Aid Donor | Percentage Agreement with | | Aid Recipient | Aid Donor | Percentage Agreement with | |
		USSR	U.S.			USSR	U.S.
Algeria	USSR	81	19	Dominican Republic	U.S.	21	83
Cyprus	USSR	41	62	Ecuador.	U.S.	24	77
Ghana	USSR	62	40	El Salvador	U.S.	23	81
Guinea	USSR	80	22	Ethiopia	U.S.	57	46
Somali	USSR	57	48	Guatemala	U.S.	20	83
Sudan	USSR	64	37	Haiti	U.S.	27	74
Syria	USSR	73	27	Honduras	U.S.	16	86
Tanzania	USSR	75	25	Iran	U.S.	34	72
UAR	USSR	72	30	Israel	U.S.	19	81
Yemen	USSR	71	30	Jordan	U.S.	51	51
Afghanistan	USSR-U.S.	71	34	Lebanon	U.S.	54	47
Cambodia	USSR-U.S.	59	44	Liberia	U.S.	35	68
Cuba	USSR-U.S.	69	32	Libya	U.S.	59	42
India	USSR-U.S.	62	43	Mexico	U.S.	37	66
Indonesia	USSR-U.S.	68	35	Nicaragua	U.S.	9	92
Iraq	USSR-U.S.	71	30	Pakistan	U.S.	35	68
Laos	USSR-U.S.	28	74	Panama	U.S.	24	78
Mali	USSR-U.S.	80	28	Paraguay	U.S.	15	87
Morocco	USSR-U.S.	75	26	Peru	U.S.	17	84
Argentina	U.S.	17	84	Philippines	U.S.	25	77
Bolivia	U.S.	27	74	Saudi Arabia	U.S.	64	38
Brazil	U.S.	25	78	Senegal	U.S.	39	61
Burma	U.S.	64	41	Thailand	U.S.	23	87
Chile	U.S.	23	81	Tunisia	U.S.	54	48
Colombia	U.S.	17	84	Turkey	U.S.	18	88
Congo-Kinshasa	U.S.	40	60	Uruguay	U.S.	19	84
Costa Rica	U.S.	18	83	Venezuela	U.S.	25	77

* Includes all Third World nations which received military aid valued at one million dollars or more from either the Soviet Union or the United States during the 1958–1964 period. The Aid Donor column lists the source or sources of aid. Scores of agreement may total more than 100 per cent since the USSR and the United States were not in total disagreement on all roll calls. Aid relationships after 1964 are not included.

9   The fact that Cyprus has not supported Soviet policy in the United Nations, despite receiving military aid, may be explained because Cyprus did not become an aid recipient until 1964. The Laos case was also exceptional in that some Soviet aid went to the neutralist incumbent Laotian government, some to the combined neutralist-Pathet Lao forces, and some to the Laotian communist guerrillas.

INTERNATIONAL RELATIONS

United States was the exclusive military aid donor. Jordan was precisely neutral in its voting.

The results indicate a strong relationship between military aid policy and attitudes, as expressed in UN voting, on political and security issues. The Soviet government has tended to be "rewarded" by military aid recipients to a somewhat greater degree than has the United States. Foreign policy attitudes definitely correlate with receipt of military aid.

But while Cold War problems may be of paramount importance to the Soviet Union and the United States, Third World nations perhaps are more intensely concerned with the colonialism issue than with matters of international political security. With few exceptions, Third World countries are former colonies of European powers, and they tend to view the issue of colonialism and national self-determination emotionally. Just as the Cold War has split the United Nations, so has the conglomerate of problems labeled "colonial" questions. In recognition of the impor-

TABLE 6

Scores of Agreement Between Aid Donors and Aid Recipients on "Colonial" Roll Calls in the United Nations: 1958–1964 *

Aid Recipient	Aid Donor	Percentage Agreement with		Aid Recipient	Aid Donor	Percentage Agreement with	
		USSR	U.S.			USSR	U.S.
Algeria	USSR	100	0	Dominican Republic	U.S.	61	50
Cyprus	USSR	88	25	Ecuador	U.S.	68	50
Ghana	USSR	93	21	El Salvador	U.S.	50	50
Guinea	USSR	97	23	Ethiopia	U.S.	87	29
Somali	USSR	100	0	Guatemala	U.S.	67	38
Sudan	USSR	93	18	Haiti	U.S.	74	26
Syria	USSR	93	7	Honduras	U.S.	50	63
Tanzania	USSR	100	0	Iran	U.S.	85	25
UAR	USSR	95	15	Israel	U.S.	63	37
Yemen	USSR	91	22	Jordan	U.S.	91	22
Afghanistan	USSR-U.S.	98	17	Lebanon	U.S.	91	22
Cambodia	USSR-U.S.	81	20	Liberia	U.S.	88	26
Cuba	USSR-U.S.	90	26	Libya	U.S.	95	19
India	USSR-U.S.	91	24	Mexico	U.S.	76	38
Indonesia	USSR-U.S.	95	16	Nicaragua	U.S.	20	80
Iraq	USSR-U.S.	95	19	Pakistan	U.S.	83	31
Laos	USSR-U.S.	61	60	Panama	U.S.	65	40
Mali	USSR-U.S.	100	22	Paraguay	U.S.	64	36
Morocco	USSR-U.S.	95	19	Peru	U.S.	47	59
Argentina	U.S.	67	38	Philippines	U.S.	88	26
Bolivia	U.S.	66	56	Saudi Arabia	U.S.	96	32
Brazil	U.S.	55	50	Senegal	U.S.	91	9
Burma	U.S.	95	20	Thailand	U.S.	72	43
Chile	U.S.	68	48	Tunisia	U.S.	92	18
Colombia	U.S.	55	45	Turkey	U.S.	25	85
Congo-Kinshasa	U.S.	89	11	Uruguay	U.S.	74	32
Costa Rica	U.S.	68	53	Venezuela	U.S.	76	38

* Includes all Third World nations which received military aid valued at one million dollars or more from either the Soviet Union or the United States during the 1958–1964 period. The Aid Donor column lists the source or sources of aid. Scores of agreement may total more than 100 per cent since the USSR and the United States were not in total disagreement on all roll calls. Aid relationships after 1964 are not included.

tance of these issues, Table 6 presents the scores of agreement with the Soviet Union and the United States of Third World military aid recipients on colonial roll calls in the UN. Following the same procedures as with the political and security roll calls, twenty-one "important" votes on colonial issues from 1958 to 1964 were selected for analysis.

All ten nations that received military aid exclusively from the Soviet bloc had high scores of agreement with the Soviet Union on colonial votes. The aid recipients mutually assisted by Moscow and Washington also showed strong agreement with the USSR. Laos, the one Soviet recipient which was not in majority agreement with the Soviet Union on political and security questions, had a relatively low agreement score on colonial roll calls as well.

However, the thirty-five nations receiving aid solely from the United States did not show high scores of agreement with Washington. While only six of the thirty-five failed to agree with American positions on political and security questions, most of the thirty-five disagreed sharply with the United States on colonial issues. Three Latin American nations and Turkey, the Third World beneficiary of the largest amount of U. S. military aid, were the only states in substantial agreement with the United States.

Comparing the findings in Tables 5 and 6, it is clear that the USSR has succeeded in identifying itself with the positions of the less developed countries on colonial questions, but not to the same degree on roll calls involving political and security issues. In the case of the United States, the opposite holds true. U. S. positions on political and security questions generally coincided with those taken by Third World countries relying on U. S. aid. There was, however, virtually no identity in the positions of the United States and Third World countries on colonial issues. While political attitudes may be swayed by military aid diplomacy, the issue of colonialism is so intensely felt as to override other considerations. Aid recipients may modify their positions on international security questions to conform to those of the donors of aid; they do not do so on colonial problems. For both superpowers military aid appears to be a significant but not a decisive factor in affecting the foreign policy orientations of aid recipients.[10]

10 For a discussion of variables other than military aid which correlate with voting positions in the United Nations, see Bruce M. Russett, *Trends in World Politics* (New York: Macmillan, 1965), Chapter 6. Also see Henry Teune and Sig Synnestvedt, "Measuring International Alignment," in Julian Friedman, Christopher Bladen and Steven Rosen, editors, *Alliance in International Politics* (Boston: Allyn and Bacon, 1970). The authors found that the four most reliable indicators of international alignment were military commitments, votes in the UN, diplomatic recognition patterns, and exchanges of diplomatic visits.

APPENDIX*

* Data compiled from United Nations publications, including the *Compendium of Social Statistics 1967, Statistical Yearbook 1969,* and *Demographic Yearbook 1969.*

State	Former colony of	Date of independence	Area sq. miles	Population	Population density per sq. mile	Per cent rate of annual population growth	Life expectancy at birth by sex	
							M	F
LATIN AMERICA								
Argentina	Spain	1816	1,072,067	23,983,000	22.4	1.5	63.1	68.9
Barbados	Great Britain	1966	166	254,000	1,503.1			
Bolivia	Spain	1825	424,163	4,804,000	11.3	2.6	49.7	49.7
Brazil	Portugal	1822	3,286,470	90,840,000	27.6	3.0	39.3	45.5
Chile	Spain	1818	286,397	9,566,000	33.4	2.4	49.8	53.4
Colombia	Spain	1824	439,512	20,463,000	46.6	3.2	44.1	45.9
Costa Rica	Spain	1848	19,652	1,695,000	86.3	3.4	54.6	57.0
Cuba	Spain	1898	44,218	8,250,000	186.6	2.2		
Dominican Republic	Spain	1865	18,703	4,174,000	223.2	3.6	57.1	58.6
Ecuador	Spain	1830	105,684	5,890,000	55.7	3.4		
El Salvador	Spain	1821	8,260	3,390,000	410.4	3.7	56.6	60.4
Guatemala	Spain	1839	42,042	5,014,000	119.3	3.1	43.8	43.5
Guyana	Great Britain	1966	83,000	742,000	8.9	3.1		
Haiti	France	1804	10,714	4,768,000	445.0	2.0	32.6	
Honduras	Spain	1838	43,277	2,495,000	57.7	3.4		
Jamaica	Great Britain	1962	4,411	1,959,000	444.1	2.4	62.6	66.6
Mexico	Spain	1821	761,600	48,933,000	64.3	3.5	55.1	57.9
Nicaragua	Spain	1838	57,143	1,915,000	33.5	3.7		
Panama	Spain	1903	28,753	1,417,000	49.3	3.3	57.6	60.9
Paraguay	Spain	1811	157,047	2,303,000	14.7	3.2		
Peru	Spain	1821–1824	496,222	13,172,000	26.5	3.1		
Trinidad and Tobago	Great Britain	1962	1,980	1,040,000	525.3	2.0	62.1	66.3
Uruguay	Spain	1825	72,172	2,852,000	39.5	1.2		
Venezuela	Spain	1821	352,142	10,035,000	28.5	3.5		
SUB-SAHARAN AFRICA								
Botswana	British Protectorate	1966	231,804	629,000	2.7	3.0		
Burundi	Belgian Man.-Trust	1962	10,747	3,475,000	323.4	2.0		
Cameroon	French Man.-Trust	1960	183,376	5,680,000	31.0	2.1		
Central African Republic	France	1960	241,313	1,518,000	6.3	2.5	33.0	36.0
Chad	France	1960	534,363	3,510,000	6.6	1.5	30	
Congo (Brazzaville)	France	1960	134,749	880,000	6.5	1.3		
Congo (Leopoldville)	Belgium	1960	905,063	17,100,000	18.9	2.2	37.6	40.0
Dahomey	France	1960	44,696	2,640,000	59.1	2.9		
Ethiopia			457,142	24,769,000	54.2	2.1		
Gabon	France	1960	102,317	665,000	6.5	1.0	25.0	45.0

Number of persons per doctor	Per cent illiterate	Newspapers per 1,000 persons	Radio receivers in thousands	Per cent urban population	Gross domestic product per capita	Per cent growth rate of gross domestic product per capita	Power consumption in kilograms per capita
670	8.6	128	9,000	52.7	$600	1.3	1,411
2,350	8.9	115	57	40.3	423		524
3,160	67.9	23		35.0	158	2.8	205
2,290	39.3	36		45.1	291	1.1	450
2,100	16.4	118		68.2	518	2.3	1,151
2,470	37.7	53	2,210	38.0	301	1.5	576
1,200	15.7	60		34.5	422		346
1,180		88					1,026
1,680	35.5		155	30.3	261	−0.7	205
5,290	32.7		801	36.0	214	1.0	261
	51.0		398	38.5	261		200
3,690	70.6			34.0	297	2.2	240
2,630					283	−1.5	899
14,000	89.5		80	12.2	86	0.8	32
5,400	55.0		140	23.2	248	2.0	217
2,020	18.1	71	425	23.4	466	2.7	1,010
1,810	34.6	116	10,932	50.7	553	3.0	1,064
2,560	50.4	49	105	40.9	359	4.5	349
3,090	26.7	81		41.5	585	4.8	1,303
1,850	25.7			35.4	215	1.3	141
1,560	39.4	47		47.4	268	2.9	633
3,820	26.2		169	17.5	749		4,222
850	9.7		1,075	82.2	584	−0.3	788
1,210	34.2		1,680	67.4	977	1.4	2,543
20,880			6		94		
56,320					46		7
33,950					126		83
33,650	.6		40	22.3	106		36
73,330	.4		50		68		17
11,640	1.3			22.3	161	2.7	204
31,250					69		85
20,090			60		69		30
68,520					59	3.0	22
5,860			50	17.8	406		439

State	Former colony of	Date of independence	Area sq. miles	Population	Population density per sq. mile	Per cent rate of annual population growth	Life expectancy at birth by sex M	F
Gambia	Great Britain	1965	3,997	485,000	121.3	2.1	43	
Ghana	Great Britain	1960	92,100	8,600,000	93.4	2.7	38	
Guinea	France	1958	94,926	3,890,000	41.0	2.5	38	
Ivory Coast	France	1960	124,502	4,195,000	33.7	2.3	35	
Kenya	Great Britain	1963	224,960	10,506,000	46.7	2.9	40–45	
Lesotho	Great Britain	1966	11,720	930,000	79.4	2.8		
Liberia	U.S. Supported		43,000	1,150,000	26.8	1.9		
Malagasy	France	1960	230,035	6,643,000	28.9			
Malawi	British Protectorate	1966	45,747	4,398,000	96.1			
Mali	France	1960	464,874	4,881,000	10.5	1.9	27	
Mauritania	France	1960	419,229	1,140,000	2.7	2.0		
Niger	France	1960	489,206	3,909,000	8.0	2.7	37	
Nigeria	Great Britain	1960	356,669	63,870,000	179.1	2.4		
Rhodesia	Great Britain	1965	150,332	5,090,000	33.9	3.2	50	
Rwanda	Belgian Man.-Trust	1962	10,169	3,500,000	344.2	3.0		
Senegal	France	1960	76,124	3,780,000	49.7	2.2	37	
Sierra Leone	Great Britain	1961	27,925	2,512,000	90.0	1.5		
Somalia	Italy- Great Britain	1960	246,201	2,730,000	11.1	2.7		
Tanzania	Great Britain	1961–1963	362,844	12,926,000	35.6	2.5	35–40	
Togo	French Man.-Trust	1960	21,853	1,815,000	83.1	2.5	31.6	38.5
Uganda	Great Britain	1962	93,981	9,500,000	101.1			
Union of South Africa	Great Britain	1910	472,359	19,618,000	41.5	2.4	44.8	47.8
Upper Volta	France	1960	106,000	5,280,000	49.8	2.0	32.1	31.1
Zambia	Great Britain	1964	290,584	4,208,000	14.5	2.1	40	
MIDDLE EAST								
Afghanistan			250,966	16,516,000	65.8	2.1		
Algeria	France	1962	919,591	13,349,000	14.5	3.0	35	
Iran			636,363	27,892,000	43.8	3.0		
Iraq	British Mandate	1932	167,568	8,840,000	52.8	2.4		
Israel	British Mandate	1948	7,992	2,822,000	353.1	2.9	70.2	72.9
Jordan	British Mandate	1946	37,297	2,160,000	57.9	3.2		
Kuwait	British Protectorate	1961	6,178	570,000	92.3			
Lebanon	French Mandate	1941	4,015	2,645,000	658.8	2.5		
Libya	Italy	1951	679,358	1,869,000	2.8	3.7		
Malta	Great Britain	1964	122	323,000	2,647.5	−0.3		
Morocco	France	1956	174,471	15,050,000	86.3	2.9	49.6	
Saudi Arabia			872,722	7,200,000	8.3	1.6		
Southern Yemen	British Protectorate	1967	111,074	1,220,000	11.0	2.2		
Sudan	British Control	1956	967,491	15,186,000	15.7	2.8		

Number of persons per doctor	Per cent illiterate	Newspapers per 1,000 persons	Radio receivers in thousands	Per cent urban population	Gross domestic product per capita	Per cent growth rate of gross domestic product per capita	Power consumption in kilograms per capita
22,000	87.6		60	8.8	83		40
			700	23.1	219		128
20,610			85	8.3	96		98
19,080		3	67		231		167
12,820		9	500	7.8	118		144
25,820					$ 78		284
	91.1		152		272		
49,250	93.5		100		52	—1.4	40
		.5	50	11.2	76		21
30,000				6.7	111		60
64,740	99.1	.4	75		83		14
44,230	88.5	7		16.0	75	2.2	29
7,570				18.1	189	3.1	550
76,200					39		9
18,760	94.4		265	22.7	197		147
16,440					145	4.2	61
30,000			40		65		27
18,240			138	15.3	67	1.4	53
27,100			35	9.7	118		42
11,600	74.9		509	4.8	80	2.0	61
1,900	68.5		2,700	46.7	622	3.8	2,721
			80		44		10
21,820	58.6		55	19.6	260	5.0	553
22,140		7	248		73		27
8,950	93.8	14	650	30.7	200	5.6	415
3,880	87.2		2,500	31.4	299	4.7	478
4,760	85.5			44.1	285	3.3	644
410	15.8		774		1,311	4.3	2,014
4,040	67.6	12	250	43.9	243		279
810		52			4,719		11,906
1,390			550		163		687
3,160	78.3	20	76		1,227		501
680							
12,120	86.2	14	826	29.3	190	0.4	181
13,000					487		510
2,140					194		428
30,720	88.0			8.3	100	—1.0	89

State	Former colony of	Date of independence	Area sq. miles	Population	Population density per sq. mile	Per cent rate of annual population growth	Life expectancy at birth by sex M	F
Syria	French Mandate		71,228	5,866,000	82.4	2.8		
Tunisia	France	1956	59,952	5,027,000	83.9			
Turkey			301,380	34,375,000	114.1	2.5	46.0	50.4
United Arab Rep. (Egypt)	British Protectorate	1922	386,100	32,501,000	84.2	2.5	51.6	53.8
Yemen			75,290	5,000,000	66.4			
ASIA								
Burma	Great Britain	1948	261,789	26,980,000	103.1	2.2	40.8	43.8
Cambodia	France	1954	66,607	6,701,000	100.6	2.2	44.2	43.3
Ceylon	Great Britain	1948	25,332	12,240,000	483.2	2.4	60.3	59.4
China (Mainland)			3,691,502	740,000,000	200.5	1.4		
China (Taiwan)			13,952	13,800,000	989.1	2.8	61.3	65.6
India	Great Britain	1947	1,261,416	536,984,000	425.7	2.5	41.9	40.5
Indonesia	Netherlands	1949	575,893	116,000,000	201.4	2.5		
Laos	France	1954	91,428	2,893,000	31.6	2.4		
Maldive Islands	Great Britain	1965	115	108,000	939.1	2.2		
Malaysia	Great Britain	1963	128,207	8,487,000	66.2	3.4	55.8	58.2
North Korea			46,814	13,300,000	284.1	2.5		
North Vietnam	France	1954	60,156	21,340,000	354.8	3.1		
Pakistan	Great Britain	1947	365,529	111,830,000	305.9	2.1	53.7	48.8
Philippines	Spain-U.S.	1946	115,707	37,158,000	321.1	3.5	48.8	53.4
Singapore	Great Britain	1963	224	2,017,000	9,004.5	2.1		
South Korea			38,452	31,139,000	809.8	2.5	51.1	53.7
South Vietnam	France	1954	65,948	17,867,000	270.9	2.6		
Thailand			198,455	34,738,000	175.0	3.1	48.7	51.9
Western Samoa	New Zealand Man.-Trust	1962	1,097	141,000	128.5	2.7		

Number of persons per doctor	Per cent illiterate	Newspapers per 1,000 persons	Radio receivers in thousands	Per cent urban population	Gross domestic product per capita	Per cent growth rate of gross domestic product per capita	Power consumption in kilograms per capita
5,110	70.5			36.9	223	2.3	434
8,990	86.6		450	35.6	201	1.6	235
2,860	61.9		2,933	34.4	338	3.2	450
2,380	80.5			37.8	161	2.2	298
					44		13
11,900	30.1	9	388	10.4	70	1.3	57
18,760	42.3	11	1,000	10.5	127	2.0	47
5,820	32.3	44	400	14.9	140	1.4	114
		19					
2,470	46.1	64	1,402		267	7.1	816
5,780	72.2		9,275	18.0	77	0.3	184
34,820	57.1		1,500	14.9	93	−0.2	99
20,000		3			59		29
49,000							
		75	423	28.0	280		422
			2,258				
6,200	81.2	18	1,150	13.1	130	3.4	96
1,330	28.1	27	639	29.9	282	1.1	248
1,790	50.2			63.1	672		686
2,710	29.4	75		28.0	173	5.6	555
37,430			1,506		152	2.7	325
8,820	32.3		2,766	18.2	150	4.3	198
2,240